Patricia A. Steers

# ABOUT THE AUTHOR

EDWARD STEERS, JR., is a highly esteemed scholar of the Lincoln assassination. He is the author of several books on the subject, including: *Blood on the Moon: The Assassination of Abraham Lincoln* (University Press of Kentucky, 2001), *The Trial: The Assassination of President Lincoln and the Trial of the Conspirators* (University Press of Kentucky, 2003), and co-editor of *The Lincoln Assassination: The Evidence* (University of Illinois Press, 2009) and *The Lincoln Assassination Conspirators: Their Confinement and Execution, as Recorded in the Letterbook of John Frederick Hartranft* (Louisiana State University Press, 2009). Steers is a retired research scientist and former deputy science director with the National Institutes of Health. He lives in Berkeley Springs, West Virginia, with his wife, Pat.

# ALSO BY EDWARD STEERS, JR.

*The Escape and Capture of John Wilkes Booth*
*Lincoln: A Pictorial History*
*The Quotable Lincoln*
*His Name Is Still Mudd*
*Blood on the Moon*
*Don't You Know There's a War On?*
*Lincoln Legends*

# The Lincoln
# ASSASSINATION
# Encyclopedia

## EDWARD STEERS, JR.

*With a Foreword by James L. Swanson*

HARPER ● PERENNIAL

NEW YORK • LONDON • TORONTO • SYDNEY • NEW DELHI • AUCKLAND

HARPER ● PERENNIAL

HarperCollins books may be purchased for educational, business, or sales promotional use. For information please write: Special Markets Department, HarperCollins Publishers, 10 East 53rd Street, New York, NY 10022.

FIRST EDITION

Designed by Justin Dodd

Library of Congress Cataloging-in-Publication Data is available upon request.

ISBN 978-0-06-178775-1

10 11 12 13 14    OV/RRD    10 9 8 7 6 5 4 3 2 1

*This work is dedicated to my wife, Pat, who makes it all worthwhile. Funny how life just falls into place somehow.*

# CONTENTS

Foreword by James L. Swanson      ix

Introduction      xi

Assassination Chronology, 1860–1865      xxv

*The Lincoln Assassination Encyclopedia*      1

Acknowledgments      595

# FOREWORD
## BY JAMES L. SWANSON

The assassination of President Abraham Lincoln on April 14, 1865, was one of the most dramatic and haunting passages in American history. While Lincoln and John Wilkes Booth will be remembered forever for their starring roles, a cast of hundreds played essential supporting parts in determining exactly how events unfolded. These include doctors, conspirators, detectives, stage actors, generals, spies, and former slaves, among many more who were swept up by the tragedy. Indeed, most of the people and places that made the events of April 1865 so compelling have been lost to popular memory. Their names live only in the thousands of obscure documents, books, and transcripts that now lie scattered beyond the reach of Google, buried in libraries and private collections across the country.

Lincoln enthusiasts and students of his assassination have long awaited the publication of Edward Steers, Jr.'s, *Lincoln Assassination Encyclopedia*. Here, at last, is the definitive resource on the subject, written by the foremost expert on the conspiracy and murder. Never before has an author gathered all the characters, places, events, and miscellaneous facts in a single work. Moreover, rarely has a scholar so skillfully executed a reference project of any kind. I can quite easily say that this is an indispensible book I wish I had in my hands when I researched and wrote *Manhunt: The 12-Day Chase for Lincoln's Killer*. It will become a valuable companion to readers of *Manhunt,* or any book about Lincoln or Booth.

Through Steers's clear prose and judicious cross references, one can easily understand how any of the many minor players fit into the bigger picture. It is fascinating to explore the book, for each entry, no matter how small, leads to another and another, gradually illuminating the entire drama. Steers even addresses the numerous colorful myths, hoaxes, and controversies that have emerged over time—see his "Booth mummy" entry, for instance. Further, the *Encyclopedia*'s comprehensive introduction and useful timeline provide a firm footing from which any reader can begin an exploration of the events. Without Edward Steers's invaluable one-stop source for everything and anything pertaining to the assassination, one might have to search for hours through dozens of books, many of them rare and difficult to find. In addition to its scholarly contributions, it will become clear to anyone who dips into its pages that *The Lincoln Assassination Encyclopedia* is a splendid read—an expertly guided adventure through one of history's richest and saddest chapters. Anyone interested in the life and death of our greatest president must have this book.

# INTRODUCTION

On the evening of April 14, 1865, Abraham Lincoln decided to take a respite from the pressing duties of the presidency and visit Ford's Theatre to see a rollicking comedy titled *Our American Cousin*. Although fighting was still taking place, nearly everyone knew it was only a matter of days before the bloodiest conflict in American history would finally come to an end. Among the few who continued to cling to the hope of Confederate independence was John Wilkes Booth, an actor of star quality whose love of the Confederacy led him to give up his illustrious career on the American stage for a far greater role, the assassin of Abraham Lincoln.

On May 28, 1864, Booth gave his last paid performance and embarked on a mission to capture the president and present him to the authorities in Richmond, Virginia, as a bargaining chip in the exchange of Confederate prisoners of war.[*] With the evacuation of Richmond on April 2, followed by the surrender of Robert E. Lee's Army of Northern Virginia on April 9, Booth came to the conclusion that, "our cause being almost lost, something decisive & great must be done."[†]

On learning that President Lincoln and General Ulysses S. Grant would attend Ford's Theatre on the evening of April 14, Booth met with three members of his team to go over his "decisive & great" plan to save the Confederacy. Meeting at a boardinghouse located two blocks from the theater, Booth assigned Lewis Thornton Powell the task of murdering Secretary of State William H. Seward, and to George Andrew Atzerodt the job of murdering Vice President Andrew Johnson. He would leave the murder of President Lincoln to his own hand, thus ensuring that the honor for ridding the nation of a terrible tyrant would fall on his shoulders alone.

[*] Samuel Bland Arnold, *Memoirs of a Lincoln Conspirator*, ed. Michael W. Kauffman (Bowie, Md.: Heritage, 1995), 42.

[†] Quotation from Booth's diary. For an excellent discussion of Booth's diary, see William Hanchett, "Booth's Diary," *Journal of the Illinois State Historical Society* 72, no. 1 (February 1979), 39–56.

While Booth left two lengthy letters explaining why the president did not deserve to live and should be killed, he did not explain what he hoped to accomplish by killing the president, vice president, and secretary of state. We can only guess at his reasoning from the writings he left. By decapitating the Federal government, Booth hoped to create chaos within it and thereby allow the beleaguered Confederacy time to gather her scattered troops into a cohesive fighting unit and turn them against Grant and the North, thereby forcing a negotiated peace. Booth's objective was unrealistic, but to some in the rapidly sinking Confederacy, it provided the only hope left for gaining independence.

Shortly after nine o'clock on the evening of Friday, April 14, Booth walked his horse up the alley leading to the rear door of the theater. Opening the door, Booth quietly called for Edman Spangler to come outside to hold his horse. Spangler, a longtime friend of Booth's, protested, telling Booth he had to shift scenes between acts. Booth told Spangler he would only be a few minutes and quietly slipped into the backstage area, leaving Spangler holding the horse's reins. Spangler turned the reins over to Peanut John, a helper of sorts around the theater whose main job was guarding the stage door from unauthorized use during performances. Peanut John took the reins and stretched out on a bench near the rear door to rest. He knew Mr. Booth was an important man and that he best do as he was told.

Entering the backstage area, Booth lifted a trapdoor that led to a dugout cellar beneath the stage. Passing under the stage to the opposite side, he ascended a second set of stairs and emerged through a second trapdoor. Booth was able to move from one side of the stage area to the other without being noticed or interfering with the play. He then exited through the stage door into a narrow passageway that opened onto Tenth Street and the front entrance to the theater. Because of his knowledge of the theater, Booth was able to leave his horse safely behind the theater while he entered through the front door, into the theater lobby. Booth made his way up the stairs that led from the lobby to the balcony known as the Dress Circle. Making his way across the rear of the Dress Circle, he approached the door leading to the presidential box.

Only one person stood between Booth and the door: Charles Forbes, the president's valet and messenger. Forbes had accompanied the president and his party to the theater. After the president had entered the theater, Forbes had followed behind, climbing the stairs to the Dress Circle, where he took a seat at the end of the row placing him closest to the outer door of the presidential box. Forbes was not a policeman and had no duties involving the president's personal safety.

Booth paused for several seconds as he stood next to Forbes. He took a small card from his vest pocket and handed it to Forbes. Forbes glanced at the card and waved Booth into the box.* Booth opened the door and stepped inside. He found himself standing in a narrow vestibule outside two boxes, 7 and 8. Earlier in the day, the partition separating the two boxes had been removed, creating a single, larger box. Once inside the outer vestibule, Booth closed the door, and picking up a piece of wood taken from one of the orchestra's spare music stands, wedged it between the door and a notch cut into the wall by Booth earlier in the day. The door secure, Booth cautiously approached the door leading into the box. Stepping inside, he raised the small derringer, aimed at the back of the president's head, and squeezed the trigger. The muzzle, two feet from the back of the president's head, exploded with a loud noise sending a small ball of lead smashing into the base of

The moment of assassination

---

* Ben Perley Poore, *The Conspiracy Trial for the Murder of the President*, 3 vols. (1865; reprint, New York: Arno, 1972), vol. 1, 194–95.

Lincoln's skull. The president went limp, his head bent forward with his chin resting on his chest.

Realizing someone had been shot in the president's box, a young army surgeon by the name of Charles Leale rushed from his seat in the Dress Circle and entered the box once the wedge had been removed. Examining the comatose president, Leale concluded that the wound was mortal and the president had little time to live. Attended by Leale and several others, Lincoln was carried across the street to the house of a tailor named Petersen, where he was taken to a rear bedroom rented by a young soldier working as a clerk in the Quartermaster's Department.

When it was realized that Lincoln was too tall to fit comfortably in the bed, his body was placed diagonally across the bed. After he was stripped of his clothing, hot water bottles were placed against his cold legs and a large mustard plaster prepared for his chest.

For the next nine hours, Lincoln remained unconscious, unable to respond to the doctors tending him or to his distraught wife's pleadings to say a word, letting her know he was alive and aware of his surroundings. At twenty-two minutes past seven o'clock on Saturday morning, Lincoln died. Reverend Phineas Gurley, pastor of the New York Avenue Presbyterian Church, where the Lincoln family rented a pew and enrolled their children in Sunday school, offered a prayer. When he finished those present offered an "Amen," while Secretary of War Edwin M. Stanton, with tears rolling down his cheeks, uttered the words, "Now he belongs to the angels," only to have history later remember them as "Now he belongs to the ages." In either case, they were fitting words.

The president's body lay in bed for another hour and a half while Stanton assembled several members of the cabinet for a special emergency meeting.[*] He ordered the door to the room where Lincoln's body lay locked and posted a guard to make certain no one entered without his express permission.[†] For the next several hours Stanton assumed control of the government. It was a time for someone with a strong hand to take charge of what was in danger of becoming a chaotic situation. No one knew how wide the conspiracy was and whether more murders were soon to follow.

---

[*] Howard K. Beale, ed., *Diary of Gideon Welles*, 3 vols. (New York: Norton, 1960), vol. 2, 288. Present were Stanton, Welles, Usher, Dennison, and Speed. Absent were McCullough and Seward.

[†] Maunsell B. Field, *Memories of Many Men and of Some Women* (New York: Harper & Brothers, 1875), 326.

When the meeting ended, a contingent of soldiers from the Veteran Reserve Corps carefully wrapped the naked body of the president in an American flag and placed him in a plain pine box sent to the Petersen house.*

Leaving the Petersen house, the hearse along with its escort walked the several blocks to the White House. Arriving at the White House, the body was taken to the guest room in the West Wing on the second floor. Here the body was placed on a table that had been set up especially for the autopsy. It was 11:00 A.M. Army Surgeons Joseph Janvier Woodward and Edward Curtis performed the autopsy. Curtis later described the scene: "as I was lifting the [brain] from the cavity of the skull, suddenly the bullet dropped out through my fingers and fell, breaking the solemn silence of the room with its clatter, into an empty basin that was standing beneath. There it lay upon the white china, a little black mass no bigger than the end of my finger . . . the cause of such mighty changes in the world's history as we may perhaps never realize."†

The autopsy completed, Dr. Charles D. Brown, of the Washington undertaking firm of Brown & Alexander, cleaned and then embalmed the body, placing a fine, white cloth over it when finished. Later that afternoon Stanton personally supervised the dressing of the body. He used the same Brooks Brothers suit worn by Lincoln at his second inauguration ceremony. The suit Lincoln had worn to the theater would be returned to Mary Lincoln, who would give it to Alphonso Donn, the White House doorkeeper, who was a loving friend to young Tad Lincoln, the president's youngest son. The suit would later be donated to the National Park Service and displayed in the museum at Ford's Theatre.

At the same time that Booth entered the presidential box at Ford's Theatre a second attack was taking place at the home of Secretary of State William H. Seward a few blocks west of the theater. Fortunately, Seward's attacker failed in his attempt to murder the secretary, leaving him in a pool of blood on the floor of his bedroom. Seward was convalescing from a serious carriage accident of several days earlier.

---

* Mose Sanford, letter to John Beatty, April 17, 1865, collection of Randall Truett. Mose Sanford writes: "General Rucker came immediately to our Shop and had a Common pine box made to bring him from 10th St to the White House in."

† Edward Curtis, quoted in Dorothy Meserve Kunhardt and Philip B. Kunhardt, Jr., *Twenty Days* (New York: Harper & Row, 1965), 95.

Lewis Thornton Powell, his attacker, fled from the scene of the attempted murder leaving five people wounded in his wake. A few blocks to the south of the Seward home, George Atzerodt entered the Kirkwood House hotel. Booth had assigned Atzerodt the task of killing Vice President Andrew Johnson. Atzerodt ordered a drink from the barkeep and, swallowing it down, waited for his courage to rise up. It never did, and he turned and fled the hotel only to wander about the city, aimlessly looking for some place to rest.

Within an hour of the attacks, a massive manhunt was begun involving several civilian and military law enforcement agencies. Civil agencies included the District of Columbia Metropolitan Police. The military response involved members of several separate provost marshal groups as well as the National Detective Police (NDP), a special agency operating within the War Department under Stanton. In addition, numerous local jurisdictions throughout the region joined in the manhunt for the president's killers.

Shortly after midnight, several of the investigative groups concluded that a wider conspiracy was at work. How wide was not known and the dragnet began sweeping up suspects with little regard for individual rights. Within a few days hundreds of people were in custody under suspicion of being involved in some way with Booth's plot.

The war had seen the necessity of unusual powers being exerted by the president. In 1861, Lincoln suspended the writ of habeas corpus, the first president to do so. At first, the suspension was limited to narrow areas where the enemy was thought to be actively working to defeat the Federal government. The suspension soon spread over a wider area, eventually covering the entire country within Union control. Strong-arm tactics had to be adopted if the war was to be successfully prosecuted and reunion take place. With Lincoln's assassination, there was little regard for the civil liberties of anyone thought to be involved. The perpetrators of the horrible murder needed to be caught and brought to justice.

By late Monday night, only seventy-two hours after Lincoln was shot, the authorities had in custody five of the eventual ten conspirators believed involved with Booth. Six days later another conspirator, George Atzerodt, was arrested, and by the tenth day, a seventh, Dr. Samuel A. Mudd, was in custody. On the twelfth day, Booth and David Herold were captured. Only John Surratt remained at large, his whereabouts unknown. John Surratt was in Canada where members of the Confederate underground and Catholic priesthood were caring for him. Surratt would make his way to Europe, ending up at the Vatican, where he was discovered two years later. After a daring escape, he was finally captured in Alexandria, Egypt, in 1867 and returned to the United States, where he was tried before a civilian court. He was set free when the jury could not come to a unanimous agreement.

America's greatest criminal manhunt lasted less than two weeks, during which time hundreds of people were being swept up in the government's dragnet and thrown into prison, including those unlucky enough to be needed as witnesses in support of the government's case against the conspirators. In some instances it was difficult to tell the accused from the witnesses, given the conditions under which both were incarcerated. The government held certain witnesses in Old Capitol Prison as a matter of routine to ensure their availability when needed to testify. Unless held, there was no guarantee that these witnesses would appear when called by the prosecution.

Mary Surratt and her co-defendants were not as fortunate as her son John, who was tried in civil court. She and the seven remaining defendants would be tried before a military tribunal. On May 1, President Andrew Johnson issued an executive order establishing a military tribunal consisting of nine "competent military officers." They were also combat veterans who distinguished themselves at various times during the war. The nine men were Major General David Hunter (president), Major General Lew Wallace, Brevet Major General August Kautz, Brigadier General Albion Howe, Brigadier General Robert Foster, Brevet Brigadier General Cyrus B. Comstock, Brigadier General Thomas Harris, Brevet Colonel Horace Porter, and

Lieutenant Colonel David Clendenin. Within twenty-four hours of their appointment, Comstock and Porter were relieved as judges and replaced by Brevet Brigadier General James Ekin and Brevet Colonel Charles Tomkins. The tribunal was directed by the president to establish its own set of rules on how to proceed, giving it power well beyond that of any civil court.

In this same executive order, Johnson appointed John Frederick Hartranft as special provost marshal and military governor of the military prison at the U.S. arsenal in Washington. It became Hartranft's responsibility to supervise every aspect of the prisoners' daily lives, from making sure they were fed and clean to ensuring that no one communicated with them except on the written orders of Stanton.

The use of a military tribunal was not without precedent. During the four years of the Civil War, more than 4,200 tribunals had been held involving more than thirteen thousand defendants, the majority of them civilians.[*] Congress passed legislation on several occasions between 1862 and 1864 authorizing the use of military tribunals, but it referred only to military personnel subject to the Articles of War.[†] It did, however, include individuals described as spies and enemy belligerents acting within military lines. It was this latter category that Attorney General James Speed seized on in his opinion in support of a military tribunal.

President Johnson asked Speed for an official opinion on whether the accused should or could be tried by military tribunal. Speed's lengthy opinion can be reduced to two points: 1) The offenses the accused were charged with were offenses against the laws of war, as spelled out in General Order No. 100; and 2) the defendants were "enemy belligerents" who served as "secret, but active participants [spies] in the recent hostilities."[‡] According to Speed, it was the military who must decide whether the accused were participants in the hostilities. If they were active participants, it was the duty of the military to take them prisoner and deal with them as the laws of war directed. Speed cast a net about the accused, placing them in an exclusionary category that denied them a trial in the civil courts.

Speed acknowledged that the civil courts in the District of Columbia were func-

---

[*] Mark E. Neely, Jr., *The Fate of Liberty* (New York: Oxford University Press, 1991), 23, 168.

[†] Louis Fisher, *Military Tribunals and Presidential Power. American Revolution to the War on Terrorism* (Lawrence: University Press of Kansas, 2005), 50–51.

[‡] James Speed, "Opinion on the Constitutional Power of the Military to Try and Execute the Assassins of the President," in Edward Steers, Jr., ed., *The Trial* (Lexington: University Press of Kentucky, 2003), 403–9.

tioning, but he dismissed their right to jurisdiction. He wrote: "The civil courts have no more right to prevent the military, [to try the accused] in time of war than they have a right to interfere with or prevent a battle."* To Speed, the issue was straightforward: the commander in chief of the nation had been murdered by enemy agents within a military zone that had been subjected to invasion by hostile forces at a time when martial law existed throughout the District of Columbia.

On May 10 the defendants were brought into the courtroom and asked if they had any objection to any member of the tribunal. None objected. The charges and specifications were then read to them, and the defendants were asked to plead even though not all eight had attorneys to represent them. All eight answered "not guilty." The tribunal adjourned to allow the defendants that had not secured attorneys time to do so. By May 12, all eight defendants had secured counsel. Samuel Mudd would be represented by Frederick Stone and Thomas Ewing, Jr. Mary Surratt would be represented by Frederick Aiken and John W. Clampitt. Stone would also represent David Herold while Ewing would represent Samuel B. Arnold and Edman Spangler. William E. Doster would represent Lewis Powell and George Atzerodt. Michael O'Laughlen was represented by Doster. Mary Surratt asked the court to approve Reverdy Johnson, a U.S. senator from Maryland as her third attorney.

One of the trial judges, Thomas Harris, opposed Reverdy Johnson, claiming that he had previously shown that he did not recognize the moral obligation of the "loyalty oath." Johnson had sent a letter to the Baltimore newspaper stating that the requirement that a citizen of Maryland must take a loyalty oath before being allowed to vote on the new state constitution was illegal. Johnson stated there was no constitutional requirement for such an oath and therefore a citizen could take the oath without regard to obeying it if this was the only way a citizen could vote. Johnson, of course, was correct in his constitutional claim and after several minutes of discussion, Harris withdrew his objection and Johnson was recognized. The incident left a bitter taste in Johnson's mouth, and he absented himself from appearing in the courtroom. He did, however, show up to give the final summation on Mary Surratt's behalf.

The trial was held in the women's block of the old Federal prison at Washington

---

* Ibid.

Arsenal, now Fort Lesley J. McNair as well as the site of the Army War College. Testimony began on May 12 and lasted until June 29. In all, 366 witnesses were called to testify. They were nearly evenly divided between prosecution and defense.[*]

President Johnson's executive order of May 1 designated Judge Advocate General (army) Joseph Holt to conduct the trial on behalf of the government along with Assistant Judge Advocate John A. Bingham and Assistant Judge Advocate Colonel Henry L. Burnett. The attorneys for the defense and prosecution were all good attorneys and conducted themselves well despite the unfamiliarity of law as it applies to military tribunals.

For the first several days of the trial the government attempted to provide evidence linking several leaders of the Confederate government, and their agents in Canada, to the conspiracy to murder Lincoln. Several witnesses were called to show that Confederate president Jefferson Davis's agents planned a series of actions that violated the laws of war, including burning northern cities, poisoning water supplies, mounting raids on shipping, and worst of all, attempting to spread smallpox and yellow fever in northern cities. The prosecution claimed that if Davis sanctioned such heinous acts in violation of the laws of war, it was easy to assume he ordered the assassination of Abraham Lincoln.

Several witnesses testified to seeing Booth in Canada consorting with Davis's secret service agents. Some claimed they heard Jacob Thompson, the leader of the covert operation, talking to Booth about Lincoln's assassination. By tying Booth to Davis through his agents in Canada, it was a simple matter to tie the eight prisoners in the dock to Booth. It later turned out that three of the prosecution's key witnesses perjured themselves, through no fault of Holt or his associates.[†] Holt was duped. Even though considerable doubt had been cast over the prosecution's witnesses, Holt held firmly to his belief that the plan to murder Lincoln originated in Richmond. After his attempt to tie the Confederate leadership to Lincoln's assassination, Holt turned his attention to the eight defendants in the dock.

The tribunal officers deliberated on June 30 and found all eight defendants guilty. David Herold, Mary Surratt, Lewis Powell, and George Atzerodt were sentenced to death and were hanged on July 7. Samuel Mudd, Samuel Arnold, and Michael

---

[*] Edward Steers, Jr., *Blood on the Moon* (Lexington: University Press of Kentucky, 2001), 217.

[†] Steers, ed., *The Trial*, xxxii.

O'Laughlen were sentenced to life in prison and Edman Spangler was sentenced to six years at hard labor.

While the government seemed perfectly satisfied it had in its custody the cast of characters that had planned and carried out the plot to murder the president, vice president, secretary of state, and General Grant, there were numerous others that had a hand in Booth's plot and, after the assassination, helped Booth and Herold in their attempt to escape. Bits and pieces of evidence were interspersed among the reams of paper evidence the government had amassed in building its case. With more time and greater diligence, the government could have identified others who had played a role. Several of these people were in custody in Old Capitol Prison or its annex at some point during the trial. Players such as Samuel Cox, Thomas Jones, Elizabeth Quesenberry, William Bryant, Franklin Robey, Willie Jett, and Thomas Harbin all slipped through the government's net and lived out their lives unmolested. Evidence existed in the government's files that would have made its case against Mary Surratt and Samuel Mudd even stronger than it was, leaving little doubt in most people's minds of their collaboration with Booth, or at the very least, knowledge of his plot.* When Lewis Powell made the statement "You have not got the one-half of them,"† he was referring to people like Harbin, Cox, and Jones—three men who would have been convicted and who might well have been hanged had the government pursued the evidence against them that was sitting in its files.

With time, events of the assassination faded, and the country was satisfied justice had been served. The perpetrators had been found guilty and punished. What the government had contended was a general conspiracy reaching all the way to Richmond soon became a simple conspiracy in which a lone, mad actor had taken revenge on the president who saved the Union and freed the slaves.

In 1937, the story of Lincoln's murder took a sharp turn with charges of murderous treason. Otto Eisenschiml, a chemist turned historian, published a seriously flawed book titled *Why Was Lincoln Murdered?*‡ Eisenschiml skillfully manipulated the data from the War Department files to lead his readers to the conclusion that Secretary of War Edwin M. Stanton was behind Lincoln's assassination. Eisenschiml's erroneous claims captured the imagination of the public, who seemed enthralled by the idea of a cover-up of a greater conspiracy involving high levels of government. Over time, historians destroyed Eisenschiml's thesis,§ only to see it reemerge as the same corpse dressed in a different suit. The alleged treason now spread to high-ranking politicians and successful financiers whose motive was greed. In this scenario Lincoln stood in the way of certain people who were about to make hundreds of thousands of dollars trading cotton. The only solution was to remove Lincoln from office by any means necessary.

---

* Edward Steers, Jr., *His Name Is Still Mudd* (Gettysburg, Pa.: Thomas, 1997). Laurie Verge, "Mary Elizabeth Surratt," in Steers, Jr., ed., *The Trial*, lii–lix.

† Testimony of Thomas T. Eckert, *Judiciary House Committee, House of Representatives: The Impeachment Committee Investigation* (Washington, D.C.: Government Printing Office, 1867), 673–75.

‡ Otto Eisenschiml, *Why Was Lincoln Murdered?* (Boston: Little, Brown, 1937).

§ William Hanchett, *The Lincoln Murder Conspiracies* (Urbana: University of Illinois Press, 1983), chapter 6.

All of these stories, and they are just stories, are based on fabricated evidence, and in some cases, on authentic evidence deliberately misrepresented. No amount of scholarly research, it seems, can dissuade the general public, encouraged by the print and television media, from believing false conspiracies. The only solution is diligent research allowing the evidence to lead us wherever it takes us rather than to where we want it to take us.

# EDITORIAL NOTE

*The Lincoln Assassination Encyclopedia* includes all of the known persons, places, events, myths, hoaxes, and legends that touch on the assassination. In choosing the subject matter for inclusion a simple criterion was used: the subject must be related in some way to the assassination of Abraham Lincoln. That criterion also applies to biographical material. The biography of an individual is in most cases limited to the information about that person pertaining to the assassination and does not include general biographical information, except in a few cases where background material is felt necessary to give an appropriate understanding of the person's role.

"Sources" at the end of each entry gives the reader the author's suggested best source for further reading on the particular subject, and is in most cases the specific source of the data. Many subjects are cross-referenced at the end of an entry with the words "See also." Hopefully, this results in a fuller understanding. For instance, "Booth's Diary" is cross-referenced with "Missing Pages."

# ABBREVIATIONS

NARA, National Archives and Records Administration;
RG 94, Record Group 94 (Records of Adjutant General's Office);
RG 153, Record Group 153 (Records of the Bureau of Military Justice, later the Office of the Judge Advocate General);
M-599, Microcopy 599 (Investigation and Trial Papers Relating to the Assassination of President Lincoln);

M-619, Microcopy 619 (Commission on Reward for Apprehension of Lincoln Assassins and Others).

Poore, *Conspiracy Trial*, Ben Perley Poore, ed., *The Conspiracy Trial for the Murder of the President*, 3 vols. (1865; reprint, New York: Arno, 1972).

Pitman, *Trial*, Benn Pitman, *The Assassination of President Lincoln and the Trial of the Conspirators* (New York: Moore, Wilstach & Baldwin, 1865).

# ASSASSINATION CHRONOLOGY

## 1860

### NOVEMBER 8

Abraham Lincoln elected president with 39 percent of the popular vote and 59 percent of the electoral vote.

### DECEMBER

John Wilkes Booth drafts lengthy speech showing his support for the South, and vilifying Lincoln and the Republican Party.

## 1861

### FEBRUARY 23

Plot to assassinate president-elect Lincoln is foiled when he slips through Baltimore nine hours ahead of schedule. This is the first of several plots to capture or assassinate Lincoln.

### MARCH 4

Abraham Lincoln inaugurated sixteenth president of the United States. Seven southern states have already seceded from the Union (South Carolina, Mississippi, Florida, Alabama, Georgia, Louisiana, and Texas).

## April 12

At 4:30 A.M. Fort Sumter in Charleston Harbor, in South Carolina, is fired upon, beginning the Civil War.

## April 17

Virginia is the eighth and most important of the southern states to secede.

## May 6

Arkansas becomes the ninth state to secede followed by the tenth state, Tennessee.

## May 20

North Carolina becomes the eleventh and final southern state to secede, completing the formation of the Confederacy.

# 1862

## March

Colonel Walker Taylor, C.S.A., seeks Jefferson Davis's approval of a plan to capture Lincoln during one of his trips to Soldiers' Home, the president's summer White House on the outskirts of Washington, D.C. Davis disapproves the plan.

## September

Company K, 150 Pennsylvania Volunteer Infantry, assigned to the White House on guard duty. Principal function is to guard property, not the president.

# 1863

## January 1

Emancipation Proclamation takes effect.

## January 12

Jefferson Davis addresses Confederate congress stating that because of Lincoln's proclamation, "a restoration of the Union has now been rendered forever impossible."

## APRIL 24

General Order No. 100 issued by the War Department, clearly defining the laws and customs of land warfare. Order sanctions retaliation as a means to prevent future actions. Becomes the basis for justifying military tribunals.

## NOVEMBER 9

Lincoln and his wife attend Ford's Theatre to see John Wilkes Booth in *The Marble Heart*.

# 1864

## FEBRUARY 11

Confederate congress passes special act authorizing payment to individuals for destroying Union property.

## MARCH 3

Colonel Ulric Dahlgren killed during an attempt to sack Richmond and kill Jefferson Davis and members of his cabinet. Southern press calls for retaliation.

## MARCH 9

Confederate Secretary of War James A. Seddon authorizes Thomas E. Courtenay, inventor of the coal bomb, to employ up to twenty-five men "for secret service against the enemy." Courtenay forms a special "Bomb Squad" to facilitate destroying Union property with his explosive device.

## APRIL 27

Jefferson Davis sends Jacob Thompson and Clement C. Clay to Canada to oversee a series of clandestine operations designed to demoralize the people of the North and help defeat Lincoln's bid for reelection. Thompson carries a draft for $1 million in gold to support the operations.

## APRIL

Dr. Luke Pryor Blackburn initiates plot to introduce yellow fever epidemic in select northern cities.

## APRIL

A special cavalry unit from Ohio, the Union Light Guard, is assigned to the White House to guard the president as he travels about the city, and to and from Soldiers' Home.

## MAY 27

Jacob Thompson arrives in Montreal along with his secretary, William Cleary. Clay becomes ill and remains in Halifax, Nova Scotia, until he recovers before joining Thompson. Thompson sends Cleary to Toronto, which becomes the headquarters for the Confederate secret service operations operating out of Canada. Patrick C. Martin, already working from Montreal, becomes head of operations in that city.

## MAY 28

Booth ends his professional acting career, giving his last paid performance in *The Corsican Brothers* at the Boston Museum. He turns his attention to taking Lincoln hostage and turning him over to Confederate leaders.

## JUNE 10

Booth registers at McHenry House in Meadville, Pennsylvania. Looking to transfer oil interests.

## JUNE 29

Booth registers at McHenry House in Meadville, Pennsylvania, a second time. Looking to transfer oil interests.

## JULY

Confederate general Bradley T. Johnson proposes to his commander Wade Hampton a plot to capture Lincoln at Soldiers' Home. Plot is put on hold until after Confederate general Jubal Early's raid on Washington.

## AUGUST 9

Booth holds meeting in his room at Barnum's City Hotel in Baltimore with former school chums Samuel B. Arnold and Michael O'Laughlen. Booth outlines plans to capture Lincoln and invites Arnold and O'Laughlen to join him. Both agree.

### AUGUST 10–28

Booth contracts erysipelas infection in his right arm. Recovers in home of his brother Edwin in New York.

### AUGUST 31

Democratic convention in Chicago nominates Major General George B. McClellan for President and George H. Pendleton for Vice President.

### SEPTEMBER 2

Union troops enter Atlanta. General Sherman informs Lincoln, "Fairly won."

### SEPTEMBER 19

Major General Philip Sheridan defeats Jubal Early in Battle of Winchester, Virginia.

### SEPTEMBER 25

Confederate scout Thomas Nelson Conrad travels to Washington to reconnoiter White House in anticipation of capturing Lincoln while latter is traveling to Soldiers' Home. Conrad has support and financial backing of Confederate leaders. Booth begins transferring his assets to family members and oil partner, Joseph Simonds. When completed, all of his assets are transferred, leaving Booth with no assets and no source of regular income.

### OCTOBER

White House assigned four members of the (Washington) Metropolitan Police force to act as bodyguards to the president. Eventually, seven members of the police force will serve as bodyguards.

### OCTOBER 18–27

Booth visits Montreal over ten-day period. Registers at St. Lawrence Hall hotel, where he is seen meeting with Confederate agents Patrick C. Martin and George N. Sanders. In company of Martin, Booth purchases bill of exchange for 61 pounds, 12 shillings, 10 pence using $300 in gold. Opens bank account depositing $455 using check for $255 from Confederate money-changer by the name of Davis. Martin gives Booth a letter of introduction to

Drs. William Queen and Samuel A. Mudd, both living in Charles County, Maryland.

## OCTOBER 19

Confederate raiders ride across the border from Canada and attack the town of St. Albans, Vermont. Led by Lieutenant Bennett H. Young, twenty-five Confederate soldiers rob three banks of more than two hundred thousand dollars.

## OCTOBER

Mary Surratt moves her family into Washington and opens a boardinghouse at 541 H Street.

## NOVEMBER 1

Louis Wiechmann, friend of John Surratt, becomes a boarder at Mary Surratt's boardinghouse at 541 H Street in Washington.

## NOVEMBER 8

Lincoln reelected by substantial majority of both popular vote and electoral delegates. Lincoln wins 212 electoral votes, McClellan 21 electoral votes. Lincoln receives 116,887 soldiers' votes, McClellan 33,748 soldiers' votes.

## NOVEMBER 10

Thomas Nelson Conrad abandons plot to capture Lincoln after seeing him accompanied by Union Light Guard on his travels to Soldiers' Home.

## NOVEMBER 11

Booth visits Charles County, stays the night at Bryantown Tavern in Bryantown, Maryland.

## NOVEMBER 12

Booth stays at home of Dr. William Queen near Bryantown. Presents his letter of introduction to Queen. Booth seeks help in putting together his team of conspirators and laying out escape route through Southern Maryland.

## November 13

Booth attends services at St. Mary's Church in company with Dr. Queen's son-in-law. Following church Booth is introduced to Dr. Samuel Mudd, a member of the Confederate mail line that runs between Richmond and Canada.

## November 14

Booth returns to his room at National Hotel in Washington, writes letter to Bryantown Tavern manager Dominic Burch seeking to recover lost "item" (pistol) left on stagecoach during his return to Washington.

## November 16

Booth opens checking account in Jay Cooke & Co. bank in Washington depositing $1,500. Source of money unknown. Later deposits another $250 into account bringing total to $1,750.

## November 19

Booth tells his sister Asia he is smuggling quinine to the South. Jokingly refers to himself as "Dr. Booth."

## November 21

Booth writes his famous "To whom it may concern" letter explaining his proposed actions. He leaves letter with sister Asia in Philadelphia.

## November 24

Booth approaches fellow actor Samuel Knapp Chester asking him to join in capture plot. Chester declines, angering Booth.

## November 25

Booth appears in benefit performance in New York with brothers Junius Jr., and Edwin, in *Julius Caesar* to raise money for Shakespeare statue for Central Park.

## November 25

Canadian-based Confederate agents attempt to burn Manhattan by starting fires in nineteen New York hotels. The attempt fails when fires are extinguished before they can take effect. Robert Cobb Kennedy, a ringleader in the attempt, sets fire to P. T. Barnum's American Museum, which is saved from destruction by the New York Fire Department.

## NOVEMBER 29

Booth has carbuncle removed from the back of his neck by Dr. John Frederick May. The failure of the incision to heal properly leaves a characteristic scar that serves to identify the body taken at the Garrett farm as that of John Wilkes Booth.

## DECEMBER 9

Booth purchases two Spencer carbines, three pistols, daggers, and a set of handcuffs while in New York.

## DECEMBER 16

Booth travels to Charles County a second time. Spends night at Bryantown Tavern.

## DECEMBER 17

Stays at home of Dr. William Queen.

## DECEMBER 18

Booth attends services at St. Mary's Church in Bryantown, returns to home of Dr. Samuel Mudd. Mudd arranges meeting at Bryantown Tavern Sunday afternoon with Confederate agent Thomas Harbin. Mudd introduces Booth to Harbin, who agrees to join Booth's plot to capture Lincoln. Booth returns to Mudd home, where he spends the night as houseguest.

## DECEMBER 19

With Mudd's help, Booth purchases "one-eyed" horse from Mudd's nearest neighbor George Gardiner. Lewis Powell uses horse on night of the assassination.

## DECEMBER 20

"One-eyed" horse delivered to Booth at Bryantown Tavern by Gardiner's nephew. Booth has the horse shod by blacksmith Peter Trotter in Bryantown. Booth seen riding from Bryantown in company of Dr. Mudd. Returns to Washington later in the day after becoming lost along the way.

## DECEMBER 23

Booth back in Washington where he meets with Dr. Mudd for the purpose of bring introduced to John Surratt. Booth, Surratt, Louis Wiechmann, and Mudd return to Booth's room at the National Hotel.

## DECEMBER 25

Booth for the second time attempts to enlist Chester in the capture plan. Chester refuses again.

# 1865

## JANUARY 5

Booth deposits $250 in Jay Cooke bank account. The source of the money is not known. Booth and Lucy Hale, daughter of former senator John Hale, spend time in Booth's room at the National Hotel. Love affair develops.

## JANUARY 11

Booth leaves trunk with weapons he purchased in New York in the care of Arnold and O'Laughlen.

## JANUARY 14

John Surratt and Thomas Harbin recruit George Atzerodt into plot to capture president. Atzerodt skilled at ferrying people and arms across the Potomac. He is to serve as boatman ferrying a captured Lincoln across Potomac River.

## JANUARY 16

John Surratt pays Richard Smoot $250 for a rowboat, placing $125 in trust with Charles County attorney Frederick Stone—the balance to be paid upon use of boat. Surratt tells Atzerodt to hide boat until called for.

### JANUARY 18

Booth withdraws six hundred dollars from Cooke account, leaving a balance of only twenty-five dollars of the original $1,750. Booth disperses all but twenty-five dollars between November 16 and January 18.

### JANUARY 20

Booth plays benefit performance in *Romeo and Juliet* at Grover's Theatre in Washington.

### JANUARY 21

John Surratt and Louis Wiechmann travel to Baltimore, stay at Maltby House. Surratt visits Lewis Powell through his contact, David Parr. Powell is recruited into team of conspirators.

### JANUARY 24

Grant reinstates prisoner exchange. Confederate congress offers to reinstate prisoner exchange with the North. Grant, who ended prisoner exchange when he was appointed General of the Union armies in March, accepts.

### JANUARY 27

Arnold and O'Laughlen visit Booth in his room at the National Hotel. Booth introduces them to John Surratt.

### FEBRUARY 3

Lincoln and Seward meet with Confederate commissioners Stephens, Hunter, and Campbell at Hampton Roads, Virginia, to discuss peace terms. Conference fails when Lincoln insists on unconditional restoration of the Union.

### FEBRUARY 10

Lincoln, in company with Generals Ulysses S. Grant and Ambrose Burnside, attend Ford's Theatre to see *Love in Livery,* starring John Sleeper Clarke, John Wilkes Booth's brother-in-law.

Booth visits his sister Asia at her home in Philadelphia. He gives her envelope containing his "To Whom It May Concern" letter for safekeeping.

## FEBRUARY 13

Booth writes a special valentine for Lucy Hale. The romantic relationship continues to grow stronger.

## FEBRUARY 20

Atzerodt boards at Surratt House for the first time. Known to others staying there as "Port Tobacco." John Surratt and Booth meet in New York City.

## FEBRUARY 22

Mary Surratt asks Atzerodt to leave her house after finding several liquor bottles in his room.

## FEBRUARY 23

Lewis Powell visits Surratt boardinghouse and spends the night. He tells Mary Surratt he is a Baptist minister.

## MARCH 4

Lincoln inaugurated for a second term. Booth attends swearing-in ceremony with a pass he received from Lucy Hale.

## MARCH 5

Lucy Hale visits Booth in his hotel room. Writes poetry on envelope, "For all sad words from tongue or pen, the saddest are—it might have been. March 5, 1865 In John's room."

## MARCH 10

Powell arrested in Baltimore and questioned as a result of beating a black woman he claimed insulted him. Powell released after being held for a day.

## MARCH 13

Booth sends telegram to O'Laughlen in Baltimore telling him, "You had better come at once."

### March 14

Powell comes to Washington and stays at Mary Surratt's boardinghouse.

### March 15

Booth gives tickets to Ford's Theatre to Powell and Surratt, who take two of Mary Surratt's boarders with them. They sit in the presidential box. Later that evening Booth hosts dinner at Gautier's restaurant in Washington for Samuel Arnold, Michael O'Laughlen, David Herold, George Atzerodt, Lewis Powell, and John Surratt. Group discusses various plans to capture Lincoln.

### March 17

Booth conspirators abort plan to capture Lincoln on his scheduled return from visit to Campbell Hospital when he unexpectedly cancels trip. Herold takes weapons to village of T.B. near Surrattsville.

### March 18

Booth stars in benefit performance for John McCullough in *The Apostate* at Ford's Theatre. This is Booth's final appearance. Wiechmann, Surratt, Atzerodt, and Herold attend performance.

### March 27

Booth sends telegram to O'Laughlen telling him and Arnold to come to Washington. Lewis Powell arrives in Washington and stays at Herndon House. Samuel Arnold sends Booth the "Sam" letter, in which Arnold tells Booth he should check plans with "R—d."

### March 31

Arnold and O'Laughlen travel from Baltimore to Washington and meet with Booth in his hotel room. Booth tells them he is abandoning plot. Lends O'Laughlen five hundred dollars.

### April 2

Confederates evacuate Richmond.

## APRIL 3

Union troops occupy Richmond.

## APRIL 4

Lincoln visits Richmond, walks the streets with son Tad. Visits the White House of the Confederacy. John Surratt leaves Washington for Montreal carrying Confederate dispatches.

## APRIL 5

Seward badly injured in carriage accident in which he breaks his right arm and fractures his jaw.

## APRIL 7

Booth meets Samuel Chester and tells him he had an excellent opportunity to kill Lincoln at his inauguration. Told Chester he had spent four thousand dollars on capture plot.

## APRIL 9

General Lee surrenders the Army of Northern Virginia. Three major Confederate armies are still actively engaged in the field, totaling 80,000 troops. There remain on paper 160,000 Confederate troops scattered throughout the South.

## APRIL 10

Confederate torpedo agent Thomas Harney captured near Burke Station, Virginia. Some historians believe Harney was on a mission to blow up the White House and kill Lincoln and members of his cabinet.

## APRIL 11

Mary Surratt and Louis Wiechmann make trip to Surrattsville and meet John Lloyd while traveling along road. Mary tells Lloyd to have weapons ready. Booth hears Lincoln give speech to crowd on White House lawn proposing suffrage for certain Negroes. An enraged Booth tells Powell, "That is the last speech he will ever make."

## April 13

John Surratt arrives in Elmira, New York, on a secret mission for Confederate secretary of state Judah P. Benjamin.

Booth asks theater owner Leonard Grover if he intends to invite Lincoln to his theater that night.

General Grant arrives in Washington to clear up paperwork and meet with the president and cabinet.

## April 14

George Atzerodt registers at Kirkwood House early in the morning in preparation for attack on Vice President Johnson later that night, indicating plot is already in motion

Lincoln holds cabinet meeting with Grant as his guest. Grant later departs with his wife to visit young children in New Jersey.

Booth writes letter to the "Editors of the *National Intelligencer*" explaining his actions. He gives letter to fellow actor John Matthews, who will destroy it after reading it in the wake of Lincoln's assassination, but reconstruct it in 1881.

Booth asks Mary Surratt to take package (field glass) to Surrattsville tavern and tell Lloyd to have the "shooting irons" ready, as persons will be by later to pick them up. Louis Wiechmann takes Mary Surratt to Surrattsville in buggy paid for by Booth.

Booth meets with Lewis Powell, George Atzerodt, and David Herold in Powell's room at Herndon House at approximately 7:00 P.M. to go over assignments.

Booth assassinates Lincoln in Ford's Theatre at approximately 10:20 P.M. At the same time Powell enters Seward home and attacks Seward with a knife, attempting to kill him. Powell also injures several others, including Seward's male nurse, George Robinson, and Frederick Seward, the secretary's son. Atzerodt, assigned to kill Vice President Andrew Johnson, fails to carry out assignment.

## April 15

President Lincoln dies at 7:22 A.M. after lying comatose for nine hours as a result of Booth's gunshot to his brain. Booth and Herold cross Navy Yard Bridge and arrive at Surratt Tavern shortly after midnight Saturday; there they pick up a carbine, field glass, and whiskey before proceeding to Dr. Mudd's house.

Booth and Herold arrive at Dr. Mudd's house at 4:00 A.M. They remain until

7:00 P.M., when they leave for home of William Burtles. They change plans and pay Oswell Swan to lead them across swamp to home of Samuel Cox, where they arrive around Saturday midnight.

At 11:00 A.M. Chief Justice Salmon P. Chase administers oath of office to Vice President Andrew Johnson at the Kirkwood House, where Johnson is staying.

Members of the 13th New York Cavalry arrive in Bryantown around noon and establish headquarters.

John Surratt, still in Elmira, New York, learns of Lincoln's assassination and takes a train for Canandaigua, New York, where he registers at the Webster House using the alias John Harrison.

## APRIL 16

Booth and Herold remain at Cox's home until early morning, then are hidden in a pine thicket a mile from Cox's house. Cox sends for Confederate agent Thomas Jones and tells him to care for the two fugitives until he can safely put them across the Potomac River.

## APRIL 16–22

Booth writes in his diary (memorandum book) while hiding in pine thicket and later Nanjemoy Creek. The text consists of two main passages explaining what he had done and complaining about how he was being portrayed.

## APRIL 17

Edman Spangler, Samuel Arnold, Michael O'Laughlen, Mary Surratt, and Lewis Powell are taken into custody, suspected of being involved with Booth. Seventy-two hours after Lincoln is shot, five of the ten conspirators subsequently charged by the government with Lincoln's murder are in custody.

At the time of his arrest, Arnold tells detectives that Booth had a letter of introduction from a Confederate agent in Montreal to Drs. Queen and Mudd.

John Surratt arrives in Montreal and checks in to St. Lawrence Hall.

## APRIL 18

Detectives visit home of Dr. Mudd and question him and his wife.

John Surratt moves into the home of Confederate agent John Porterfield in Montreal.

## APRIL 19

Funeral services held in White House for President Lincoln. Booth remains in hiding in pine thicket in Charles County, Maryland.

## APRIL 20

George Atzerodt is arrested in the early morning hours at the Germantown (Montgomery County, Maryland) home of his cousin, Hartman Richter.

Booth and Herold attempt to cross Potomac River to Virginia. Thomas Jones provides Booth and Herold with a boat and sends them in the direction of Mathias Point, Virginia. The two fugitives fail to cross the Potomac River, winding up back on the Maryland shore at Nanjemoy Creek, where they spend the next day and a half waiting to cross the river.

John Surratt moves into rectory of Father Charles Boucher in St. Liboire, Quebec, thirty miles east of Montreal, where he will remain until leaving for England in September.

## APRIL 21

Detectives visit Mudd home a second time to question Mudd and his wife. They take Mudd into Bryantown, where he is questioned by Colonel Henry H. Wells. Mudd drafts voluntary statement. Lincoln's body leaves Washington for Baltimore and then on to Harrisburg, Pennsylvania.

## APRIL 22

Mudd returns to Bryantown for further questioning. Signs second statement based on his questioning.

## APRIL 22–23

Booth and Herold leave their hiding place at Nanjemoy Creek and successfully cross the river landing near the home of Elizabeth Quesenberry. Quesenberry sends for Thomas Harbin, who arranges for two horses and a guide, William Bryant, to take the two fugitives to the home of Dr. Richard Stuart. They arrive at Stuart's summer home, Cleydael, around 8:00 P.M. Stuart sends the two men to the cabin of William Lucas, a black. Booth and Herold spend the night in Lucas's cabin.

## April 24

Dr. Samuel A. Mudd is arrested at his home in Charles County.

William Lucas's son, Charley, conveys Booth and Herold to Port Conway, Virginia, on the Rappahannock River in the Lucas's wagon.

Booth and Herold meet up at Port Conway with three Confederate soldiers who accompany them across the Rappahannock to Port Royal, Virginia. The Confederate soldiers find refuge for Booth and Herold at the home of Richard Garrett, a Virginia tobacco farmer who lives a few miles south of Port Royal. Booth and Herold spend a comfortable night at the Garrett farm.

A troop of the 16th New York Cavalry, along with military detectives Everton J. Conger and Luther B. Baker, set out from Washington in pursuit of Booth and Herold Monday evening aboard the steamer *John S. Ide*.

## April 25

Members of the 16th New York Cavalry arrive at Port Conway in the afternoon and cross the river by ferry, regrouping on the Port Royal side of the river. They set out for Bowling Green, Virginia, a few miles south of the Garrett farm where Booth and Herold are hiding.

Arriving in Bowling Green around midnight, the detectives arrest Willie Jett, one of the Confederate soldiers who found the two fugitives lodging at the Garrett house. Jett agrees to lead the cavalry to the Garrett farm.

## April 26

Booth and Herold are cornered in the tobacco barn of Garrett. After failed negotiations, Booth is fatally wounded and Herold taken prisoner. Booth dies shortly after daybreak from a gunshot wound that causes paralysis from the neck down.

Confederate general Joseph E. Johnston surrenders his army to Union general William T. Sherman at Bennett House, North Carolina. Two major Confederate armies remain: E. Kirby Smith's in the Trans-Mississippi, and Richard Taylor's in Alabama and Mississippi.

## April 27

Booth's body is carried back to Washington, where it is placed aboard the monitor USS *Montauk*. An autopsy takes place and the body is transferred to the Washington Arsenal, where it is temporarily buried beneath the prison floor. With Herold's capture and Booth's death, the nine individuals accused by the government with Lincoln's death are in custody. Only John Surratt remains at large.

## May 1

President Andrew Johnson issues executive order establishing military tribunal to try those accused with Lincoln's murder.

## May 4

Lincoln funeral in Springfield, Illinois, at Oak Ridge Cemetery.

## May 6

Members of military tribunal appointed.

## May 10

Jefferson Davis captured near Irwinville, Georgia. Eight defendants are formally charged with conspiring to murder President Lincoln and others.

President Andrew Johnson proclaims armed resistance over.

## May 12

Testimony begins in trial of those charged with Lincoln's murder.

## May 29

President Johnson proclaims a general amnesty for those participating in the rebellion. The Lincoln conspirators are excluded.

## June 29

Defense completes its arguments. Tribunal members deliberate on the evidence in the case of each defendant.

## June 30

Tribunal members arrive at their findings and sentences for each of the accused. Mary Surratt, George Atzerodt, Lewis Powell, and David Herold sentenced to death by hanging. Samuel Arnold, Michael O'Laughlen, and Samuel Mudd sentenced to life at hard labor. Edman Spangler sentenced to six years hard labor.

### July 6

Major General John F. Hartranft, governor of the military prison, reads the Findings and Sentences to the four defendants sentenced to death.

### July 7

Four condemned prisoners are executed by hanging at the Washington Arsenal: Mary E. Surratt, Lewis T. Powell, George A. Atzerodt, and David Herold.

### July 17

Prisoners Samuel Arnold, Michael O'Laughlen, Edman Spangler, and Samuel Mudd transferred to the steamship USS *Florida* for transport to Fort Jefferson in Florida, where they will begin serving their sentences.

Last of prisoners being held in the Old Federal Penitentiary at Washington Arsenal transferred to other facilities, bringing to an end the temporary prison established especially for the prisoners accused in Lincoln's assassination.

### July 25

Samuel Mudd, Samuel Arnold, Michael O'Laughlen, and Edman Spangler arrive at Fort Jefferson to begin serving their sentences.

### Abbott, Dr. Ezra W. (1821–1907)

One of sixteen doctors who visited the Petersen house while Lincoln was dying. Dr. Abbott was the sixth physician on the scene, arriving shortly after Surgeon General Joseph K. Barnes and Assistant Surgeon General Charles H. Crane. Assisted by Dr. Albert F. A. King, Abbott kept a record of Lincoln's pulse and respiration between the hours of 11:00 P.M. and 7:22 A.M., when Lincoln died. In all, Abbott recorded fifty readings of Lincoln's pulse and twenty recordings of his respiration. His first record was made at 11:00 P.M., when he recorded a pulse of 44. Lincoln's pulse ranged from a low of 42 at 11:15 P.M. to a high of 95 at 1:30 A.M. Abbott also recorded visits by Mary Lincoln and Robert Lincoln to Lincoln's bedside. Mary Lincoln visited shortly after Vice President Andrew Johnson left at 1:30 A.M. and again at 3:00 A.M. She stayed in the room seated next to her husband for approximately twenty-five minutes on each visit. In the final hour before Lincoln died, five recordings were made, including notations that Lincoln's expirations were "prolonged and groaning" and his respiration "uneasy, choking and grunting." At 7:00 A.M., Abbott noted signs of imminent death, and at 7:22 A.M. he recorded the simple notation, "death."

Sources: L. C. Baker, *History of the United States Secret Service* (Philadelphia: L. C. Baker, 1867), 467; Louis A. Warren, ed., "Physicians at Lincoln's Bedside," *Lincoln Lore,* no. 627, April 14, 1941; W. Emerson Reck, *A. Lincoln: His Last 24 Hours* (Columbia, S.C.: University of South Carolina Press, 1987).

*See also:* King, Dr. Albert F. A.

### Adams, Austin

Owner of a tavern located in Newport, Maryland, two and a half miles east of Allen's Fresh and two miles north of the Wicomico River. Adams's employee James Owens gave a lengthy statement to Colonel Henry H. Wells admitting to rowing two Confederate agents across the Potomac River on Sunday, April 17. Authorities mistakenly believed that Owens's passengers were Booth and Herold, leading Secretary of War Stanton to authorize Lafayette Baker to send a troop of the 16th New York Cavalry after the two men. Although the two river passengers were not Booth and Herold, Owens's statement led to Booth and Herold being cornered at the Garrett farm, where Booth was killed and Herold taken into custody.

Sources: Statement of James Owens, NARA, RG 94, M619, reel 458, frames 412–15, and Statement of Lieutenant S. P. Currier to Colonel George A. Foster, NARA, M-599, reel 4, frames 228–30.

*See also:* Owens, James

## Aiken, Frederick Argyle (1837–1878)

Frederick Aiken, along with John W. Clampitt and U.S. senator Reverdy Johnson, served as defense counsel for Mary E. Surratt. At the time of her trial, Aiken and Clampitt were junior partners in Johnson's law firm. Aiken was a twenty-eight-year-old Baltimore attorney when he joined the Union army, in which he served as an aide on the staff of Major General Winfield Scott Hancock.

Reverdy Johnson, the senior senator from Maryland, agreed to accept the case of Mary Surratt, but after an acrimonious confrontation with Major General Thomas M. Harris, a member of the military commission, Johnson withdrew into the background, leaving the defense of Mary Surratt in the hands of Aiken and Clampitt. Their defense was primarily based on showing that Mary Surratt was a woman of good character and that her accusers were lying in an effort to save their own necks. Following Mary Surratt's conviction, Aiken, along with Clampitt, attempted to stay Mary Surratt's execution by appealing to Judge Advocate General Joseph Holt, the chief prosecutor. Holt refused. Aiken and Clampitt then prepared a writ of habeas corpus using the argument that Mary Surratt was a civilian illegally tried by the military. They took their writ to Judge Andrew B. Wylie at ten o'clock on the morning of the execution (July 7). Wylie endorsed the writ and U.S. marshal David Gooding served the papers on Major General Winfield Scott Hancock, commander of the Middle Military District, in charge of the Washington Arsenal and prison. Hancock appeared in Wylie's chambers at 11:30 A.M. and presented the judge with an executive order from President Andrew Johnson suspending the writ of habeas corpus in Mary Surratt's case. Wylie was powerless to act. Aiken and his associate had exhausted all hope of saving their client.

Sources: Elizabeth Steger Trindal, *Mary Surratt: An American Tragedy* (Gretna, La.: Pelican, 1996).

*See also:* Habeas Corpus Surratt, Mary Elizabeth

## Allen, William C.

Lieutenant William C. Allen was a member of the 151st New York Volunteer Infantry. Allen's name first surfaced as a witness to the events at the Garrett farm in 1937, twenty-nine years after his death. His widow attended a Grand Army of the Republic convention in Madison, Wisconsin, where she stole the show with her claim that her husband told her that the man killed at Garrett's farm was not Booth, but rather another man. None of the claims made by Mrs. Allen concerning Booth are supported by the known facts of her husband's service record.

Allen served in the 151st New York Volunteer Infantry for three years as a private. He enlisted on August 27, 1862. He was promoted to sergeant on October 22, 1862, and to second lieutenant on February 18, 1865. He ended his service on June 26, 1865, having served thirty-four months.

In July 1864, Allen was captured at the Battle of Monocacy during Jubal Early's abortive raid on Washington, D.C. He was taken to Libby Prison in Richmond, where he was exchanged on December 21, 1864, and returned to his regiment at Petersburg, Virginia, on March 4, 1865. The 151st served at Petersburg until it fell on April 2, and then chased Lee's retreating army to Appomattox Court House, where it was present at the surrender of the Army of Northern Virginia on April 9.

Following Lee's surrender, the 151st New York marched seventy miles south to Danville, Virginia, arriving on April 27, the day after Booth died. While the 151st New York was enroute to Danville, however, Lieutenant Allen was several hundred miles to the north at his home in LeRoy, New York. On April 20, Allen applied for emergency leave to return home and visit his ailing father, who was seriously ill and dying. Leave was granted on April 22 and Allen headed north to New York. There is nothing in the record to indicate that Allen decided to detour from his trip to New York and join the search for Booth one hundred and seventy-five miles to the northeast.

It should be noted that Allen never claimed he was present at the capture of Booth or that he saw Booth's body. All of the claims came from his widow twenty-nine years after his death. Her claims ran far afield, including the statement that her husband was in the Secret Service and worked for Lafayette C. Baker. She also claimed that her husband "was a living image of Wilkes Booth," so much so that the newspapers of the day, needing a photograph of Booth, used a photograph of her husband "taken only a week before . . . and printed it through the country captioned as the President's assassin." The reproduction of photographs in newspapers did not exist in 1865, further challenging the veracity of Mrs. Allen.

Mrs. Allen's story that her husband was present at Garrett's farm and later claimed the body was not that of John Wilkes Booth can be dismissed as another assassination myth fabricated by the elderly widow of a veteran who once served his country honorably.

Sources: Steven G. Miller, "Did Lieut. William C. Allen Witness the Shooting of John Wilkes Booth?," in Laurie Verge, ed., *The Body in the*

*Barn* (Clinton, Md.: Surratt Society, 1993), 35–42.

*See also*: Kenzie, Wilson D.; Zisgen, Joseph; Bates, Finis L.

## Allen's Fresh

Allen's Fresh was a small village located near the mouth of the Wicomico River in Charles County, Maryland. During the Civil War, it was a part of the Confederate mail line that ran between Richmond and various northern points on into Canada. It was situated approximately three miles due east of Huckleberry, the home of Thomas A. Jones, and five miles southeast of Rich Hill, the home of Samuel Cox.

While Jones looked after Booth and Herold in the pine thicket where they were hiding, Federal troops patrolled the area, making it impossible for Jones to send the two men safely across the Potomac River.

On Thursday, April 20, Jones rode to Allen's Fresh, where he visited Colton's store, a favorite drinking place for local farmers and Union soldiers. While in Colton's store, the soldiers received a report that Booth and Herold were seen in St. Mary's County several miles to the southeast. Jones watched as the Union troops rode away in the opposite direction from where Booth and Herold were hiding. Jones decided this was his best opportunity to put the two fugitives across the river. Leaving Allen's Fresh, he went directly to Booth and Herold and led them to a point on the Potomac River just north of Pope's Creek, where he put them in a rowboat and sent them on their way toward the Virginia shore.

Sources: Thomas A. Jones, *J. Wilkes Booth: An Account of His Sojourn in Southern Maryland after the Assassination of Abraham Lincoln, his Passage Across the Potomac, and his Death in Virginia* (Chicago: Laird & Lee, 1893).

*See also:* Jones, Thomas Austin; mail line

## American Knights, Order of

A paramilitary organization that was an outgrowth of the anti-Federal government Knights of the Golden Circle (KGC), formed by George Washington Lafayette Bickley in 1857. By the outbreak of the Civil War, the KGC had lost much of its membership and influence. In 1862, Emile Longuemare was sent to Missouri by Confederate president Jefferson Davis to organize a paramilitary organization in certain northern states for the purpose of overthrowing the Lincoln administration and opposing the civilian war effort in the North. Longuemare formed the American Knights (OAK), using the vestiges of the KGC as a base for the new organization. By 1864 the OAK had changed its name to the Sons of Liberty.

While the ostensible purpose of the

OAK was to support the Democratic Party in the northern states, the real purpose was to organize a clandestine paramilitary force to act against the Federal government and Union army. Chapters were organized within townships and followed strict rules of secrecy relying solely on verbal orders. The Knights engaged in a wide range of activity that included encouraging Union soldiers to desert, passing intelligence to the Confederacy, recruiting men for the Confederate army, supplying arms and ammunition to the Confederacy, and providing support to Confederate military raids into the North. The New York City draft riots, which occurred in July 1863, are believed by some historians to have been instigated by the OAK.

The organization operated mainly in Indiana, Illinois, Kentucky, and Ohio. In 1861, Cipriano Ferrandini, a Baltimore member of the former Knights of the Golden Circle, headed a plot to assassinate president-elect Lincoln during his stopover in Baltimore while on his way to Washington for his inaugural. The plot was uncovered simultaneously by Allan Pinkerton and the New York City Police Department. Lincoln changed his itinerary at the last minute, passing through Baltimore nine hours ahead of schedule and thus foiling the plot.

While most historians believe the Knights, along with the other clandestine organizations, were a serious threat to the North, historian Frank L. Klement views the OAK along with the KGC and Sons of Liberty as "paper-based organizations" devised by Republicans to discredit the Democratic Party. Although all three organizations are credited with far more success than they deserve, they were real, and played a role in various subversive activities in the North.

Sources: William A. Tidwell, James O. Hall, and David W. Gaddy, *Come Retribution* (Jackson: University Press of Mississippi, 1988); Frank L. Klement, *Lincoln's Critics: The Copperheads of the North* (Shippensburg, Pa.: White Mane, 1999).

*See also:* Baltimore Plot; Ferrandini, Cipriano; Knights of the Golden Circle; Sons of Liberty.

## Anacostia River

See Eastern Branch, Potomac River

## Anderson, Mary Jane

A witness called by the prosecution to testify at the conspiracy trial. She is identified in the trial transcript as "colored." Mary Jane Anderson claimed to know John Wilkes Booth by sight. She lived in a small house located on Baptist Alley in the rear of Ford's Theatre. Anderson claimed to have witnessed the events that took place in the rear of the theater on April 14. She told the military tribunal that she saw Booth during the morning at his stable behind the theater, and again between two and three o'clock in the afternoon talking to a (unidentified) lady. She told of standing at her gate and looking "right wishful at him." Later that same night she heard a horse clattering up the alley. She recognized the man leading the horse as Booth. Booth arrived at the rear door, where he called out four times for "Ned" (Edman Spangler). Anderson said three different men handled Booth's horse while he was inside the theater: James L. Maddox (Ford's property manager), Spangler, and a third, unidentified man (Peanut John Burroughs). She fixed the time from when Booth arrived at the rear of the theater until he burst through the door after shooting Lincoln to just under one hour. Her testimony was used by the prosecution to link Spangler directly to Booth and thereby to his conspiracy.

Sources: Testimony of Mary Jane Anderson in Ben Perley Poore, *The Conspiracy Trial for the Murder of the President*, 3 vols. (New York: Arno, 1972), vol. 1, 235–40.

*See also:* Maddox, James L.; Burroughs, John

## Anderson Cottage
*See* Soldiers' Home

## Antonelli, Cardinal Giacomo

The secretary of state for the Papal States in Italy, Cardinal Antonelli worked closely with Rufus King, the U.S. emissary to the Papal States, in arranging John H. Surratt's arrest and extradition to the United States. At the time of Lincoln's assassination, Surratt was in Elmira, New York, scouting the Union prison there for the Confederate head of operations in Canada, Brigadier General Edwin Grey Lee. Following Lincoln's assassination, Surratt had made his way to Canada and, with the help of agents there, to Italy, where he enlisted in the Papal Zouaves under the alias John Watson. He was discovered by a former schoolmate named Henri Beaumont de Sainte-Marie, who informed King, who in turn informed Secretary of State William Seward of Surratt's whereabouts. Although the United States and the Papal States had no extradition treaty, Cardinal Antonelli, acting on behalf of Pope Pius IX, agreed to honor the U.S. request for Surratt's extradition. Antonelli ordered the arrest of Surratt pending a formal request from the United States. Surratt was arrested in Veroli, Italy, and while in transit to Rome escaped his guards and made his way aboard a freighter to Alexandria, Egypt, where he was arrested a second time and returned to the United States.

A certain amount of intrigue surrounded the agreement to arrest and extradite Surratt to the United States. The Papal States were under threat of dissolution by the Italian unification forces. If this occurred the pope would need asylum, and a request was made of the United States. U.S. naval ships were sent to Italy ready to pick up Pope Pius IX and his entourage and bring them to the United States. Antonelli negotiated the arrangement whereby Surratt would be turned over to U.S. authorities in ex-change for asylum. A treaty was eventually signed establishing the Vatican as a separate authority known today as the Vatican.

Sources: Alfred Isacsson, *The Travels, Arrest, and Trial of John H. Surratt* (Middletown, N.Y.: Vestigium, 2003); Louis J. Wiechmann, *A True History of the Assassination of Abraham Lincoln and of the Conspiracy of 1865*, ed. Floyd E. Risvold (New York: Knopf, 1975).

See also: Surratt, John Harrison, Jr.

### Apostate, The

A play performed at Ford's Theatre on the night of March 18, 1865, as a benefit performance for the famous actor John McCullough. John Wilkes Booth played the leading part, Pescara, "a bloody villain of the deepest red." *The Apostate* was Booth's last performance. His last paid performance had occurred ten months earlier on May 28, 1864, at the Boston Museum, where he starred in *The Corsican Brothers*.

Booth gave several tickets to John Surratt, inviting him and his friends to see the play. Surratt, Louis Wiechmann, George Atzerodt, David Herold, and John Holahan, a boarder at the Surratt Tavern, attended the theater as Booth's guest.

The performance occurred the day after the abortive attempt to capture Lincoln on his return to the White House

A. LINCOLN,
died
April 15th 1865.

following his scheduled visit to the Campbell Hospital in northeast Washington. Lincoln canceled his visit at the last minute, thereby avoiding the attempt at his capture.

Sources: George J. Olszewski, *Historic Structures Report: Restoration of Ford's Theatre* (Washington, D.C.: U.S. Government Printing Office, 1963); William A. Tidwell, James O. Hall, and David W. Gaddy, *Come Retribution* (Jackson: University Press of Mississippi, 1988).

## Apotheosis

Apotheosis is the elevation of a person to a divine status, which is what happened to the nation's image of Lincoln soon after his murder. Henry Ward Beecher, along with dozens of his fellow preachers, drew parallels between Lincoln and Moses in a sermon given the day after Lincoln's death. Printmakers rushed their art to market with depictions of Lincoln ascending to heaven and into the arms of an angelic George Washington: the Father of the Country receiving the Savior of the Country. The deification of Lincoln soon replaced the common-man image. There were those, however, who dissented from this saintly view of Lincoln. One of the more vehement Lincoln haters was Lyon G. Tyler, son of former president John Tyler. Lyon Tyler wrote scathing commentary describing Lincoln's apotheosis as "the most amazing climbing vine in the garden of history."

Sources: Harold Holzer, Gabor S. Boritt, and Mark E. Neely, Jr., *The Lincoln Image* (New York: Scribner's, 1984); Merrill D. Peterson, *Lincoln in American Memory* (New York: Oxford University Press, 1994); Lyon G. Tyler, "An Open Letter," in *Confederate Leaders and Other Citizens Request the House of Delegates to Repeal the Resolution of Respect to Abraham Lincoln, the Barbarian* (Matthews Courthouse, Va.: Privately Printed, 1928).

## Arnold, Samuel Bland (1834–1906)

Samuel Arnold was a member of John Wilkes Booth's original conspiracy to capture Abraham Lincoln, and one of eight individuals charged with Lincoln's murder and tried by military tribunal. Arnold was found guilty and sentenced to life imprisonment at Fort Jefferson, Dry Tortugas, Florida. He was pardoned in March 1869 and returned to his home in Baltimore.

Booth recruited Arnold into his capture conspiracy during the second week of August 1864. The two had been schoolmates at St. Timothy's Hall in Catonsville, Maryland, in the early 1850s. Arnold lived for a time in a suburb of Baltimore known as "Hookstown," located along the present-day Reisterstown Road in northwest Baltimore, bordering on the present-day Pimlico Racetrack. He enlisted in Company C, First Maryland Infantry in 1861. Following the First Battle of Bull Run in July 1861, Arnold became ill and was discharged as no longer fit for service. He returned to Baltimore, where he convalesced at his parents' home. Fully recovered, he made his way south again and joined his older brother in Augusta, Georgia, in the Nitre and Mining Bureau, collecting nitre for making gunpowder. In 1864, Arnold returned to Baltimore after learning that his mother was critically ill.

Booth recruited Arnold and another Baltimorean and childhood chum, Michael O'Laughlen, as his first recruits at Barnum's City Hotel in Baltimore. Years later Arnold recalled the meeting:

I called upon him and was kindly received as an old schoolmate and invited to his room. We conversed together, seated by a table smoking a cigar, of past hours of youth, and the present war, said he had heard I had been south, etc., when a tap at the door was given and O'Laughlen was ushered into the room. O'Laughlen was also a former acquaintance of Booth's from boyhood up, so he informed me. I was introduced to him and this was my first acquaintance with O'Laughlen.

After a few minutes of conversation and several glasses of wine, Booth came to the point of his meeting: "Booth then spoke of the abduction or kidnapping of the President, saying if such could be accomplished and the President taken to Richmond and held as a hostage, he thought it would bring about an exchange of prisoners."

Samuel Arnold was particularly beguiled by Booth's charm. Reflecting back on their meeting, Arnold wrote in his memoir: "I found Booth possessed of wonderful power in conversation and became perfectly infatuated with his social manners and bearing." Arnold would justify their decision to capture Lincoln "as an act of honorable purpose, humanity and patriotism."

Frustrated with Booth, Arnold challenged him during a meeting on March 15, 1865, at Lichau's restaurant in Washington, telling Booth his plan to kidnap Lincoln at Ford's Theatre was totally impractical. The two argued in a threatening manner but soon calmed down and made amends. Two days later, the group reconvened at Booth's request to work out a plan to capture Lincoln on his return trip from Campbell Hospital, where he was scheduled to visit wounded soldiers. The plot fell through when Lincoln canceled his visit at the last minute, remaining in Washington. Frustrated at Booth's failure to carry through with a successful capture of Lincoln, Arnold took a job as a clerk in John W. Wharton's store located at Fort Monroe, Virginia, two weeks before the assassination. Arnold was still working in Wharton's store on the night of the assassination.

Early on the morning following the assassination, government detectives searched Booth's room at the National Hotel in Washington. Among several items found in Booth's trunk was a letter addressed to Booth, which was signed "Sam" and carried the address "Hookstown." The letter contained a critical piece of evidence apparently linking Booth to the Confederacy, "go and see how it will be taken in R—d." Neither "Sam" nor "Hookstown" registered with the detectives in Washington at the time of the letter's discovery.

Early Saturday morning, following Lincoln's murder, Voltaire Randall, one of Maryland provost marshal James McPhail's detectives, informed McPhail that Samuel Arnold and John Wilkes Booth were childhood friends. Arnold, a former Confederate soldier, had registered with McPhail's office on his return to Baltimore following his muster out as a Confederate soldier. He listed "Hookstown" as his place of residence. McPhail sent Randall and a second detective, Eaton Horner, to Hookstown after Arnold. McPhail then telegraphed the War Department in Washington: "Sir: Samuel Arnold and Michael O'Laughlen, two of the intimate associates of J. Wilkes Booth, are said to be in Washington. Their arrest may prove advantageous."

On reaching Hookstown, Randall and Horner learned from a "colored woman" that Arnold had taken a job at Fort Monroe in Virginia. The two detectives set out for Fort Monroe on Sunday evening and reached the fort the next morning and found Arnold. Under questioning, Arnold talked freely. He admitted to being a party to a plot to capture Lincoln but said he had withdrawn from the plot several weeks earlier. At one point, he told the detectives about a Dr. Mudd of Charles County, Maryland, who was intimate with Booth. Arnold said that Booth had visited Charles County in November 1864, carrying letters of introduction from a Confederate agent in Canada to Dr. Samuel Mudd and Dr. William Queen. Arnold pointed a finger at Samuel Mudd even before Mudd was a suspect.

Found guilty of aiding and abeting Booth, Arnold, along with Michael O'Laughlen and Samuel Mudd, was sentenced to life in prison. He was originally scheduled to serve in the Federal penitentiary in Albany, New York, but Secretary of War Edwin M. Stanton changed the prison to the military's Fort Jefferson in the Dry Tortugas off the Florida Gulf coast. In March 1869, President Andrew Johnson issued a full pardon to Mudd. Three weeks later, Johnson issued pardons freeing both Arnold and Spangler. Arnold returned to Baltimore, where his father operated a bakery and confectionery store at his residence on Fayette Street. In 1894 Arnold was employed as a butcher at Fells Point in Baltimore. By 1902 he was living in Friendship, Maryland, at the home of a close friend, Mrs. Ann Garner, whom he described as "a second mother." The Garner home provided a safe haven for the reclusive Arnold.

Sometime during the 1890s Arnold decided to record a memoir of his relationship with Booth and the conspiracy to capture Lincoln. His intention was to have the document published after his death in an effort to sway public opinion in his favor. His request was thwarted, however, when, in 1902, another man whose name was Samuel Arnold died. Several newspapers, assuming it was the Booth conspirator, wrote lengthy obituaries, which gave Arnold an opportunity to see just how he would be portrayed by the press after his real death. Accounts of his role with Booth were unflattering. Angered by what he read, Arnold agreed to allow the *Baltimore American* to publish his memoir; he believed it would vindicate him. The manuscript was published in serial form from December 2 to 20, 1902. As might be expected, Arnold's story was self-serving and filled with righteous indignation. In 1943 the original manuscript was published in a limited edition of 199 copies by an antiquarian book dealer who had purchased the memoir, and in 1995 the memoir was republished by Heritage Books.

Four years after publication, Arnold became seriously ill and in June 1906, he moved into the Baltimore home of his sister-in-law, where he died on September 21, 1906, at the age of seventy-two. He is buried in Green Mount Cemetery in Baltimore, where Michael O'Laughlen and John Wilkes Booth are also buried. Of the original ten conspirators, Arnold was survived only by John Surratt, who would live for another ten years before dying in 1916, the last of the conspirators tried for Lincoln's murder.

Sources: Pep Martin, "The Hookstown Connection," *Surratt Courier* 5, no. 7 (July 1980); Samuel Bland Arnold, *Memoirs of a Lincoln Conspirator*, ed. Michael W. Kauffman (Bowie, Md.: Heritage, 1995).

*See also*: Horner, Eaton; "Sam" Letter

### Artman, Enos R. (1838–1912)
Artman was a major in the 213th Pennsylvania Volunteers commanding the First Delaware Cavalry, stationed at Monocacy Junction near Frederick, Maryland, at the time of the assassination. Artman received information from an army undercover informant, James W. Purdom, that a suspicious character named Andrew Atwood (George Atzerodt) spoke knowingly of the assassination. Atwood was staying at the Germantown, Maryland, home of a man named Hartman Richter. At first, Artman did not act on the information, but reconsidering the situation ordered Captain Solomon Townsend to send a party of troopers to check out Purdom's information. Townsend ordered Sergeant Zachariah Gemmill to pick six troopers and go to Richter's house and investigate the situation. Gemmill and his men arrested Atzerodt and Richter around 4:00 A.M. on Thursday, April 20.

Major Artman was awarded $1,250 of the reward money for his actions leading to Atzerodt's capture.

Sources: Statement of E. R. Artman, NARA, M619, reel 456, frames 146–48.

*See also*: Atzerodt, George Andrew; Gemmill, Zachariah

### Ashmun, George (1804–1870)
A Massachusetts politician who served in the Thirtieth Congress with Abraham Lincoln (1847–1849). Like Lincoln, Ashmun was a Whig. He was chairman of the Republican Party in 1860 and visited Lincoln in Springfield, Illinois, to notify him of his nomination as the party's candidate for president. As a lawyer, Ashmun became involved in the seamy and unscrupulous contraband cotton trade, representing clients seeking to profit from captured Confederate cotton.

Ashmun visited Lincoln with one of his clients on the evening of April 14, 1865, for the purpose of gaining a favor in the cotton trade. Lincoln excused himself from meeting with Ashmun and his friend but agreed to see them the following morning. He penned a brief note that read, "Allow Mr. Ashmun & friend to come in at 9:00 A.M. tomorrow." It was Lincoln's last piece of writing before his assassination a few hours later.

Sources: Mark E. Neely, Jr., *The Abraham Lincoln Encyclopedia* (New York: McGraw-Hill, 1982).

## Assassination

A term derived from the Arabic word *hashshashin*, which refers to users of hashish, a narcotic drug extracted from the hemp plant. The Hashshashin were a Mohammedan sect of assassins, founded circa 1090 by Hasan-I Sabbah, which existed during the Crusades. Its members ritualistically drank extracts of hashish before they attempted to assassinate Christians who had invaded their territory.

Lincoln did not consider assassination a serious threat even though he was made aware of a plot to kill him in Baltimore in 1861. Secretary of State William Seward summed up the current belief when he wrote in 1862, "Assassination is not an American practice or habit, and one so vicious and so desperate cannot be engrafted into our political system." Seward felt so certain about his views that he pointed out, "The President . . . occupies a country house near Soldiers' Home . . . He goes to and from that place on horseback, night and morning, unguarded."

Cipriano Ferrandini, a member of the Knights of the Golden Circle in Baltimore, planned to assassinate president-elect Lincoln when he stopped over in Baltimore on his way to Washington for his inauguration. The plot was foiled when Lincoln learned of the plot and altered his schedule, passing through Baltimore nine hours earlier than planned.

Luke P. Blackburn, a Kentucky physician and member of the Confederates' Canadian operation, proposed to kill Lincoln by infecting him with yellow fever. Blackburn purchased several expensive shirts, which had been exposed to clothing taken from several victims who died of yellow fever. Blackburn intended to deliver the shirts as a gift, thereby exposing Lincoln to the dreaded disease. The plot failed when Blackburn's agent declined to deliver the shirts. Unknown to medicine at the time, yellow fever was not an infectious disease.

Lincoln's private secretary John Hay wrote of Lincoln keeping a bundle of around one hundred letters containing death threats. Hay wrote that Lincoln kept the letters tied with a ribbon in one of the pigeonholes in his White House desk.

Sources: Harold Holzer, ed., *Dear Mr. Lincoln: Letters to the President* (Reading, Mass.: Addison-Wesley, 1993), 20–21. Edward Steers, Jr. *Blood on the Moon* (Lexington: University Press of Kentucky, 2001), 16-26.

*See also:* Blackburn, Luke Pryor; Ferrandini, Cipriano

## Atwood, Andrew

See Atzerodt, George Andrew

## Atzerodt, George Andrew (1835–1865)

George Atzerodt was one of nine individuals charged by the government as a conspirator with John Wilkes Booth. Tried before a military tribunal, Atzerodt was found guilty and sentenced to death. Atzerodt, Lewis Powell, Mary Surratt, and David Herold were hanged at the Washington Arsenal on July 7, 1865.

Atzerodt was born in Thuringen, Germany, and immigrated with his parents to the small village of Germantown in Montgomery County, Maryland in 1844. Atzerodt and his brother, John C. Atze-

rodt, located in Port Tobacco, Charles County, Maryland, in March 1857. There they opened a carriage business, George working as a carriage painter.

Recruited in January 1865 by Thomas Harbin and John H. Surratt, Jr., as a member of Booth's conspiracy to capture Lincoln, Atzerodt was an important asset because of his experience in ferrying Confederate agents and contraband across the Potomac River between Maryland and Virginia. During the four years of war Atzerodt was never arrested as a result of his illegal activities on the river.

When Booth's capture conspiracy was converted to assassination, Atzerodt was assigned the task of killing Vice President Andrew Johnson. On the night of April 14, 1865, Johnson was boarding at the Kirkwood House, located at Twelfth and Pennsylvania Avenue, three blocks from Ford's Theatre.

Atzerodt had taken a room at the Kirkwood House on the morning of April 14 in anticipation of assassinating Johnson. At the assigned hour, Atzerodt walked into the bar of the Kirkwood and ordered a drink. Unable to carry out his assignment, he fled the scene and wandered the neighborhood around Ford's Theatre. Frightened by the commotion in the area, Atzerodt boarded a horse-drawn trolley car to the Navy Yard in southeast Washington, where he attempted to secure lodging in the room of a former acquaintance. Unsuccessful, Atzerodt rode the trolley back into the city and took a room at the Kimmel House (also known as the Pennsylvania House).

At approximately 6:00 A.M., Atzerodt left the hotel and walked to Georgetown, where he pawned his Colt revolver for ten dollars. After breakfasting with Lucinda Metz, an old acquaintance in Georgetown, Atzerodt boarded the stage for Rockville, Maryland. Reaching the military roadblock set up at the juncture of High Street (now Wisconsin Avenue) and Military Road, Atzerodt left the stage and made his way to the picket post where the military was screening the long line of persons attempting to leave Georgetown and enter Maryland.

Atzerodt bought drinks of hard cider for several of the soldiers at the roadblock. He then talked a farmer from Montgomery County, William Gaither, into giving him a ride in his wagon to Gaithersburg, just north of Rockville. Having successfully passed the army pickets, Atzerodt rode to Gaithersburg, where he left Gaither and walked several miles to the Clopper Mill near Germantown, where he spent the night with the mill operator. Easter Sunday saw Atzerodt invited to share dinner at the house of a Germantown farmer named Hezekiah Metz. During dinner the conversation turned to the assassination. Following the noon dinner, Atzerodt walked a short distance to the home of his cousin, Hartman Richter, where he remained until his capture early on the morning of April 20.

The arresting soldiers received a tip from another local farmer, James W. Purdom, who worked as an undercover Union army informant. Purdom learned from one of the dinner guests that Atzerodt talked freely about events surrounding the assassination. Purdom passed the information along to one of his army contacts, who reported the information to his superior officer. A search party was sent to Richter's house, where Atzerodt was arrested. He was taken to Washington and placed in the hold of the monitor USS *Saugus*, where he was interrogated before being transferred to a cell in the Old Federal Penitentiary at the Washington Arsenal.

While imprisoned on the USS *Saugus*, Maryland provost marshal James L. McPhail and John L. Smith visited Atzerodt at Atzerodt's request. Atzerodt gave a lengthy statement implicating both Samuel Mudd and Mary Surratt in Booth's conspiracy. The statement disappeared, only to be discovered among the papers of Atzerodt's attorney, William E. Doster, in 1979 by Joan L. Chaconas, former president of the Lincoln Group of D.C. and the Surratt Society.

Sources: William A. Tidwell, James O. Hall, and David W. Gaddy, *Come Retribution* (Jackson: University Press of Mississippi, 1988); Edward Steers, Jr., and James O. Hall, *The Escape and Capture of George A. Atzerodt* (Clinton, Md.: Surratt Society, 1980).

*See also:* Gemmill, Zachariah; Lost Confession; Purdom, James W.

## Atzerodt, John

Older brother of George Atzerodt. John, along with George, operated a carriage business in Port Tobacco, Charles County, Maryland, prior to the Civil War. When war came, John left Port Tobacco and the carriage business and applied for a job as a detective on the staff of Maryland provost marshal James L. McPhail, whose office was in Baltimore. Following Lincoln's assassination, John Atzerodt was on an assignment in Charles County. Learning that his brother was a suspect and had been arrested and imprisoned aboard the USS *Saugus*, John wired McPhail that his brother was known to frequent the Richter farm and suggested McPhail send detectives there to look for George. By the time McPhail's men reached the farm, George was already in custody and on his way to Washington. The detectives had missed capturing him by only a few hours.

Sources: Edward Steers, Jr., *Blood on the Moon* (Lexington: University Press of Kentucky,

2001), 167–69; James L. Swanson, *Manhunt: The 12-Day Chase for Lincoln's Killer* (New York: Harper Perennial, 2007), 219–21.

## Atzerodt Lost Confession
See Lost Confession

## Augur, Christopher Columbus (1821–1898)
Commanded the 22nd Army Corps (defenses of Washington, D.C.) at the time of Lincoln's assassination. Acting on information supplied by stable manager John Fletcher shortly after midnight (April 15), Augur ordered members of the 13th New York Cavalry to Southern Maryland in search of Booth. In just twelve hours after the assassination, his troopers arrived in Bryantown within five miles of Booth and Herold, who were holed up at Dr. Samuel Mudd's house.

Augur began the Civil War as commandant of cadets at West Point and after a few months was appointed a brigadier general of volunteers. He was given command of Franz Sigel's division in the Fifth Army Corps and severely wounded at Cedar Mountain. He was brevetted major general and assigned to command the left wing of Major General Nathaniel P. Banks's Army of the Gulf at the siege of Port Hudson in 1863. Following the subsequent Red River Campaign in Louisiana under Banks, Augur was given command of

Bridge sometime around 11:00 P.M., and that he was preceded by another man, presumably Atzerodt. Fletcher had no way of knowing the first man was Booth. This resulted in Augur sending a cavalry troop into Southern Maryland in the early hours of Saturday morning. Augur died on January 16, 1898, and is buried in Arlington National Cemetery.

Sources: Ezra J. Warner, *Generals in Blue* (Baton Rouge: Louisiana State University Press, 1964); William A. Tidwell, James O. Hall, and David W. Gaddy, *Come Retribution* (Jackson: University Press of Mississippi, 1988).

*See also:* Fletcher, John

the 22nd Army Corps, maintaining the defenses of Washington until the end of the war.

The one-eyed horse used by Lewis Powell with the saddle of George Atzerodt on his back was found wandering east of the Capitol and brought to the stables of the 22nd Army Corps next to Augur's headquarters around midnight on April 14. Identification of the saddle was made by Fletcher, manager of the stable where David Herold had rented his horse on April 14. Fletcher knew both Atzerodt and Herold and linked them together as friends. Fletcher told the detectives that Herold had passed over the Navy Yard

### Autopsy, Abraham Lincoln

Lincoln's body was brought back to the White House from the Petersen house and carried to one of the two guest rooms on the second floor. The room was located diagonally across from Mary Lincoln's bedroom, where the first lady lay in bed wailing in anguish. Two army surgeons, Drs. Joseph Janvier Woodward and Edward Curtis, performed the autopsy. Present were doctors Joseph K. Barnes, surgeon general; Charles H. Crane, assistant surgeon general; Charles Taft; Robert King Stone, family physician; and Assistant Surgeon William M. Notson; as well as Assistant Quartermaster General Daniel Rucker, whose men had escorted the body from the Petersen house to the White House.

The top of the skull was removed along with the brain so that the path of the bullet could be determined. Conflicting reports exist as to the actual path of the bullet. All agreed that the bullet entered "the skull to the left of the middle line, and below the line with the ear." At this point, the surgeons performing the autopsy stated that the bullet traveled through the left side of the brain, lodging behind the left eye. Barnes later testified that the bullet traversed diagonally through the brain, lodging behind the right eye. Later statements by the doctors were in disagreement as to which pupil was dilated and which was normal. Since this critical testimony is in conflict, it is impossible to know for certain the path of the bullet. However, because the president was sitting in a high-back rocking chair to the extreme left of the box, the only way he could have been shot in the lower left side of the back of the skull is if he turned his head to the left and was looking down into the orchestra area. If this were the case, as some eyewitnesses claimed, then the bullet would have traveled from left to right, lodging behind the right eye and not the left.

In an article published on June 17, 1865, in the journal *Lancet* by T. Long-more, professor of medical surgery at the Army Medical School, the bullet "passed obliquely across, from left to right, through the brain substance to the anterior lobe of the right hemisphere, in which it lodged, immediately over the right orbit."

The brain was weighed and found not to be above the average weight for a man of Lincoln's size. Following the autopsy, Dr. Charles D. Brown, of the firm of Brown & Alexander, embalmed the body.

The lead ball along with bone fragments were saved and deposited with the Army Medical Museum, where they reside on display today along with the Nélaton probe used to examine the path of the bullet.

Sources: Dorothy Meserve Kunhardt and Philip B. Kunhardt, Jr., *Twenty Days* (New York: Harper & Row, 1965); John K. Lattimer, *Kennedy and Lincoln: Medical and Ballistic Comparisons of Their Assassinations* (New York: Harcourt Brace Jovanovich, 1980); *The Medical and Surgical History of the War of Rebellion, 1861–65*, 4 vols. (Washington: Government Printing Office, 1870); T. Longmore, "Note on Some of the Injuries Sustained by the Late President of the United States," *Lancet*, June 17, 1865, 649.

**Autopsy, John Wilkes Booth**
Booth's body was transported from the Garrett farmhouse to Belle Plain, Vir-

ginia, where it was carried aboard the steamship *John S. Ide* to the Washington Navy Yard. Here it was transferred to the monitor USS *Montauk,* where it was placed on a carpenter's table located beneath a large canvas tent shading it from the sun. It was kept under a military guard until the next morning, when Surgeon General Joseph K. Barnes and his party arrived. Stanton and Secretary of the Navy Gideon Welles jointly drafted a letter to Admiral Augustus Fox, commandant of the Navy Yard, under whose jurisdiction the body was now being held. Fox had asked Stanton what should be done with the corpse. Stanton replied:

> You will permit Surgeon General Barnes and his assistant, accompanied by Judge Advocate Genl Holt, Hon. John A. Bingham, Special Judge Advocate, Major [Thomas] Eckert, Wm. G. Moore, Clerk of the War Department, Col. L. C. Baker, Lieut. [Luther] Baker, Lieut. Col. Conger, Chas. Dawson, J. L. Smith, [Alexander] Gardiner (photographer) + assistant, to go on board the Montauk, and see the body of John Wilkes Booth.
>
> Immediately after the Surgeon General has made his autopsy, you will have the body placed in a strong box, and deliver it to the charge of Col. Baker—the box being carefully sealed.

At the trial of the conspirators held one month later, Judge Advocate General Joseph Holt questioned Barnes as to the identification of the body. Barnes told the court about a distinctive scar on Booth's neck. The scar had resulted from an operation performed by Dr. John Frederick May of Washington.

Booth had developed a bothersome lump on his neck on the left rear side approximately three inches below the base of the skull; it was apparently an annoyance as well as a small disfigurement. Booth sought medical advice in the summer of 1863. May examined the lump and declared it a "fibroid tumor." May told Booth it should be removed and Booth consented. The minor operation resulted in a fine linear incision, which May cautioned Booth to protect so that it could heal properly. A few days after the removal Booth returned to May. The incision had been torn open by Booth's co-star, Charlotte Cushman, during a theatrical performance. Miss Cushman had thrown her arms around Booth's neck and hugged him so vigorously during the play that she tore the incision open. As a result, when the wound healed it left a large, circular mark whose new tissue gave the appearance of a "burn" scar. The new scar was described as "a broad, ugly-looking scar, produced by the granulating process." The scar took

on a marked appearance that served as an identifying characteristic.

Following May's examination of Booth's body on board the *Montauk*, Barnes and Woodward performed an autopsy, removing two cervical vertebrae and the damaged spinal cord from the neck. The path of the bullet was determined and the vertebrae and spinal cord were taken by Dr. Woodward to the Army Medical Museum as specimens. Barnes wrote a report of the autopsy that was submitted to Stanton the same day, April 27, 1865. In his report Barnes stated:

The left leg and foot were encased in an appliance of splints and bandages, upon the removal of which, a fracture of the fibula 3 inches above the ankle joint, accompanied by considerable ecchymosis, was discovered.

The cause of death was a gun shot wound in the neck—the ball entering just behind the sterno-cleido muscle—2-1/2 inches above the clavicle—passing through the bony bridge of fourth and fifth cervical vertebrae—severing the spinal cord and passing out through the body of the sterno-cleido of right side, three inches above the clavicle.

Paralysis of the entire body was immediate, and all the horrors of consciousness of suffering and death must have been present to the assassin during the two hours he lingered.

The last paragraph has less to do with objective medical observation and was probably added by Barnes to indicate to Stanton that Booth did not die easily or without the "horrors of . . . suffering and death."

Of all of the physical evidence associated with Booth's body, the scar left by Dr. May's surgery (and the denture work performed by Dr. William Merrill) clearly identified the body as matching the same physical characteristics of John Wilkes Booth. But there is one physical piece of evidence that was used for positive identification—the initials "J. W. B.," which occurred as a tattoo made with India ink. These initials were located on the back of the left hand in the crotch formed by the thumb and index finger. The most compelling evidence that such an identifying tattoo existed is found in the writings of Booth's older sister Asia: "across the back of one [of his hands] he had clumsily marked, when a little boy, his initials in India ink."

Following the examination and autopsy, the remains were sewn up in the same army blanket in which it had been placed at the Garrett farm. The body was then taken ashore at the Washington Arsenal. While rumors abounded at the time that the body was weighted and dropped overboard into a remote part of the Potomac River, it was taken to the arsenal.

A wooden box used to ship rifled muskets was used as a coffin. The box containing Booth's body was buried beneath the floor of a room in the arsenal that had been used to store ordnance. Both Lafayette Baker and Thomas Eckert were present at the burial and later testified to the event. After the body was buried, the floor was replaced and the heavy door to the building locked tightly and the key turned over to Stanton.

Sources: Laurie Verge, ed., *The Body in the Barn* (Clinton: Surratt Society, 1993); John Frederick May, "The Mark of the Scalpel" (Washington, D.C.: Columbia Historical Society, 1910); Terry Alford, ed., *John Wilkes Booth: A Sister's Memoir by Asia Booth Clarke* (Jackson: University Press of Mississippi, 1996), 45; *Medical and Surgical History of the War of the Rebellion, 1861–65*, 4 vols. (Washington: Government Printing Office, 1875), vol. 4, 452.

*See also:* May, John Frederick

## Baden, Joseph

A Confederate agent from King George County, Virginia, who worked for agent Thomas Harbin. When Booth and Herold reached the Virginia shore following their crossing of the Potomac River on the night of April 23, they arrived at the home of Mrs. Elizabeth Quesenberry, located at the mouth of Machodoc Creek. Quesenberry, a Confederate sympathizer and working with Confederate agents in the area, sent for Thomas Harbin and Joseph Baden, who turned the two fugitives over to William Bryant with instructions to take the pair to Dr. Richard Stuart's home, known as Cleydael.

Harbin and Baden had been in Charles County allegedly waiting for Booth with the captured Lincoln. When word arrived that Booth had murdered Lincoln, Harbin and Baden crossed the river to King George County, Virginia, on Sunday, April 16. Union officials searching the area mistakenly believed the two men were Booth and Herold and notified Secretary of War Stanton that the two men had crossed the Potomac. Union troops laying over at Allen's Fresh left the area, allowing Thomas Jones the opportunity to send Booth and Herold across the river to Virginia.

Sources: Thomas Jones, *J. Wilkes Booth* (Chicago: Laird & Lee, 1893); William A. Tidwell, James O. Hall, and David W. Gaddy, *Come Retribution* (Jackson: University Press of Mississippi, 1988).

*See also:* Stuart, Dr. Richard Henry; Quesenberry, Elizabeth

## Bainbridge, Absalom Ruggles (1847–1902)

Absalom Bainbridge, a seventeen-year-old private, served in Company B, Third Virginia Cavalry, before joining John Singleton Mosby's battalion of Rangers in March 1865 on detached service. On the morning of April 24, 1865, Bainbridge, along with Private Willie Jett and Lieutenant Mortimer Bainbridge Ruggles (Bainbridge's cousin), also of Mosby's Rangers, arrived at Port Conway on the Rappahannock River on their way to Caroline County following disbandment of Mosby's command. At Port Conway they came upon Booth and Herold, who were waiting for the ferry to carry them across the river to the village of Port Royal.

David Herold greeted the three Confederate soldiers while Booth stayed in the background. Herold told the soldiers that he and his injured brother, James W. Boyd, were heading south and asked if they could ride along with them. Neither Booth nor Herold had a horse. After several minutes Herold admitted who they were. Years later, Ruggles acknowledged in a magazine article that he had heard that Lincoln had been assassinated and that John Wilkes Booth was the assassin.

After some discussion, the three Confederate soldiers accompanied Booth and Herold across the river and subsequently found lodging for them at the home of Richard Garrett, a tobacco farmer who lived midway between Port Royal and Bowling Green, Virginia.

Sources: William A. Tidwell, James O. Hall, and David W. Gaddy, *Come Retribution* (Jackson: University Press of Mississippi, 1988).

*See also:* Jett, William Storck "Willie"; Ruggles, Mortimer Bainbridge

## Baker, Lafayette C. (1826–1868)

Lafayette C. Baker served as head of the National Detective Police (NDP) during

the Civil War. He was in overall charge of the Union force that cornered Booth and Herold at the Garrett farm near Bowling Green, Virginia. For his services, Baker received $3,750 of the reward money offered for Booth's capture, dead or alive.

Baker began the war as a spy working for Lieutenant General Winfield Scott, who was in command of all Federal forces (sixteen thousand men) at the outbreak of hostilities. It was at this time that Baker visited both Richmond and Manassas, Virginia, as an undercover agent gathering information for Scott. Shortly after returning to Washington he was appointed a special provost marshal with police authority.

During the first ten months of the war, internal security fell under the State Department, led by Secretary of State William H. Seward. In February 1862, it was transferred to the War Department, under Secretary of War Edwin M. Stanton. Under Stanton, Baker was appointed colonel of the First District of Columbia Cavalry in March 1862, and retained that command nominally throughout the war. Baker personally selected Lieutenant Colonel Everton J. Conger to undertake field command of the regiment while Baker remained in Washington carrying out his duties from his office. In the fall of 1862, Stanton created a special investigative unit within the War Department and appointed Baker as its head. The unit became known as the National Detective Police, which has frequently been mislabeled as the U.S. Secret Service. Baker first referred to himself as chief of the Secret Service in his memoir in 1867. The designation stuck. The National Detective Police was really a local agency and not national.

Baker quickly developed an unsavory reputation as a result of his dealings with fraud among government employees and contractors and subversive types known as Copperheads as well as pro-Confederate activists in Washington and Maryland. He was criticized for his police-state tactics, which his enemies claimed he used in his investigations into corruption. As was the case with his superior, Edwin M. Stanton, a great deal of the criticism of Baker fell into the category of misinformation generated by enemies.

Overall, Baker proved to be an effective operative especially in counter-espionage activities. While his arrests contributed heavily to the prison rolls in Washington, the great majority of those arrested were pro-Confederate operatives who actively engaged in disloyal practices. What seems strange in hindsight is that the majority of these subversives were soon released from prison on simply their taking the oath of allegiance, after which they returned to their disloyal practices.

Following Abraham Lincoln's assassination on April 14, 1865, Baker was instrumental in the capture of John Wilkes Booth and his accomplice, David Herold. As Booth and Herold made their way through Southern Maryland and across the Potomac River into Virginia, several law enforcement agencies were hard at work trying to capture them, but without success. For ten days Booth and Herold had managed to elude the hundreds of detectives and law enforcement officers searching for them. Then, on Monday, April 24, the government received a lucky break. Baker was in the War Department telegraph office when a telegram arrived from the military station at Chapel Point in Southern Maryland stating that two unidentified men had crossed the Potomac River on Sunday, April 16. The men were later identified as Thomas Harbin and Joseph Baden, two Confederate agents. Erroneously believing Harbin and Baden to be Booth and Herold, Baker received permission from Stanton to send a cavalry troop in pursuit. Baker chose Lieutenant Colonel Everton Conger and his cousin, Luther B. Baker, both agents working for Baker, and twenty-six men from the 16th New York Cavalry. Two days later the cavalry troop caught up with Booth and Herold at the farm of Richard Garrett near Bowling Green, Virginia, where they killed Booth and captured Herold.

Sharing in the reward and the glory, Baker retired from his post as head of the National Detective Police and returned to his home in Philadelphia, where he died in 1868 at the age of forty-two. The NDP detectives working under Baker either left the service and returned to civilian life or became part of the new Secret Service agency created on July 2, 1865, as part of the U. S. Treasury Department. Because of Baker's habit of embellishing his role in various undercover activities, it is difficult to separate fact from fiction when reading his personal account of the various activities he was involved in.

Sources: Edwin C. Fishel, *The Secret War for the Union* (Boston: Houghton Mifflin, 1996).

*See also:* National Detective Police

## Baker, Luther Byron (1830–1896)

Luther B. Baker was the junior officer assigned to the cavalry contingent that tracked John Wilkes Booth and David Herold to the Garrett farm. He was a cousin of Lafayette Baker and a member of the National Detective Police, which Baker commanded. Lafayette Baker assigned his cousin Luther and Lieutenant Colonel Everton Conger, both members of the NDP, to accompany twenty-six troopers of the 16th New York Cavalry under command of Lieutenant Edward P. Doherty in the pursuit of Booth. Lafayette Baker had to request a cavalry unit through Stanton since his own command was no longer in service. Baker said to his cousin Luther Baker, "Lieutenant, we have got a sure thing." He was right. It took another forty-eight hours to track down Booth and Herold, but in the end, Baker could claim credit for their capture.

Following Booth's death at the Garrett farm on the morning of April 26, 1865, Luther Baker accompanied the body back to Washington ahead of the troop of cavalry that captured him. On arriving back in Washington, Booth's body was transferred to the USS *Montauk*. Luther Baker carried a small carte-de-visite photograph of Booth with him and used it to help identify the corpse at the Garrett farm. Luther Baker, along with those at the Garrett farm, never had any doubt that the man killed in the tobacco barn was Booth.

For several years after the war, Luther Baker traveled the lecture circuit telling of the search and capture of Booth and Herold. He prepared a composite photograph, which included a picture of him seated on his horse "Buckskin," and pictures of Lincoln and of Booth, which he sold at his lectures to raise money.

Sources: George S. Bryan, *The Great American Myth* (New York: Carrick & Evans, 1940); William Hanchett, *The Lincoln Murder Conspiracies* (Urbana: University of Illinois Press, 1983).

*See also:* Baker, Lafayette C.; Conger, Everton Judson; Doherty, Edward Paul

### Balsiger, David, and Charles E. Sellier, Jr.

Writers and producers who published a book titled "The Lincoln Conspiracy" and produced a movie of the same title. The book and movie were based on the alleged missing pages from Booth's diary and the files of ficticious Secret Service agent Andrew Potter. The theme of *The Lincoln Conspiracy* centers on Secretary of War Edwin M. Stanton's supposed complicity with other powerful politicians and financiers in planning Lincoln's assassination. The second pillar of the book and movie is based on Booth escaping capture at the Garrett farm, leaving an innocent surrogate in his place. When the plotters of Lincoln's death discover they have killed the wrong man, a massive cover-up takes place in which Americans are duped and never learn of the horrific plot, that is, until Balsiger and Sellier expose it in their book and film.

The story is an old one that first emerged in 1937 with the publishing of *Why Was Lincoln Murdered?* by Otto Eisenschiml. As with most fabricated conspiracies, it is the internal evidence that exposes the plot as a fabrication. Wrong names, wrong dates, wrong places are part of the many inconsistencies that expose the "Stanton did it" and "Booth escaped" theories as false.

Sources: William Hanchett, *The Lincoln Murder Conspiracies* (Urbana: University of Illinois Press, 1983), 226–33.

*See also:* Missing Pages, John Wilkes Booth's Diary

### Baltimore, Maryland

At the time of Lincoln's assassination, Baltimore was a major seaport and thriving metropolis with strong ties to the Confederacy. Because of the Chesapeake Bay's inland dimension, Baltimore was two hundred miles closer to the major cities that lay to the west. With the coming of the Baltimore & Ohio Railroad in 1828, the city became even closer to western markets. Baltimore's importance as a commercial center with a major port linked her economically, and emotionally, with the southern states. By 1860, her population stood at 200,000. Of these, approximately 50,000 were free blacks, the largest number of free blacks of any city in the nation. When the Federal government finally accepted blacks into the military, Baltimore's black population contributed six regiments to the U.S. Colored Troops.

Baltimore had several connections with the assassination of Abraham Lincoln. The Booth family owned a home on Exeter Street, not far from the harbor. Young Booth as a child played with Michael O'Laughlen and his brother, whose family lived across the street. Samuel Arnold and Booth were schoolmates at St. Timothy's Hall in Catonsville, a suburb of Baltimore. John Ford owned the Holliday Street Theatre, where Booth and his brothers performed to sellout crowds. Lewis Powell spent time in Baltimore rooming at the boardinghouse of Mary Branson on Eutaw Street. David Preston Parr owned a china shop that served as a Confederate mail drop and safe house for agents moving between Canada and Richmond. Parr arranged for John Surratt to meet with Lewis Powell in his shop. As a result, Powell joined Surratt and Booth in their conspiracy.

In 1861, members of a subversive organization plotted to kill president-elect Lincoln on his stopover in Baltimore on his way to Washington. The plot failed when Lincoln altered his plans, passing through the city nine hours ahead

of schedule. Provost Marshal James McPhail had his office in Baltimore and was responsible for the rapid arrests of Samuel Arnold and Michael O'Laughlen. Stanton at first suspected that Booth was heading to Baltimore and sent a telegram at 3:00 A.M. to Brigadier General Morris, commanding the district of Baltimore, "to guard every avenue leading into Baltimore, and if possible, arrest J. Wilkes Booth."

On April 21, 1865, Lincoln's body, carried aboard a special funeral train, left Washington and arrived in Baltimore at 10:00 A.M. The coffin bearing Lincoln was placed on a hearse drawn by four horses wearing tall black plumes. Despite a heavy rainstorm the procession proceeded from the station, winding its way slowly through downtown Baltimore, passing within a block of the Booth home on Exeter Street before arriving at the Merchant's Exchange, where Lincoln lay in state for only one hour before continuing the sorrowful journey home to Illinois. Despite the brief time allotted for the viewing, ten thousand people passed by the open coffin to get one last look at the man who had saved the Union.

Sources: Scott Sumpter Sheads and Daniel Carroll Toomey, *Baltimore During the Civil War* (Baltimore: Toomey, 1997).

*See also*: Baltimore Plot

## Baltimore Plot

Members of a local chapter of the Knights of the Golden Circle (KGC) devised a plan to assassinate president-elect Lincoln during his stopover in Baltimore on his way to Washington for his inauguration in February 1861. Baltimore, the last of thirteen stops before Lincoln reached Washington, was a hotbed of secession activity. Members of the KGC were pro-Confederate and had planned on intercepting Lincoln on his arrival in Baltimore and killing him.

One of the principal meeting places for the anti-Lincoln forces in Baltimore was the bar located in Barnum's City Hotel. One of the principal anti-Lincoln members of the KGC was the Barnum's head barber, a Corsican immigrant named Cipriano Ferrandini. Ferrandini was a "captain" in the KGC and a passionate Confederate sympathizer. He was also an advocate of assassination as a means to further political aims. On learning that Lincoln would stop over in Baltimore to lunch with dignitaries before changing trains, Ferrandini hatched his plot to kill Lincoln.

Lincoln's train was originally scheduled to arrive at the Calvert Street Station in Baltimore shortly after noon on February 23. Lincoln was then scheduled to travel by carriage to a luncheon appointment in the city before reboarding a second train that would take him on to Washington. Ferrandini and his men planned on attacking Lincoln as he made his way through the terminal to his carriage. A fight would be staged to distract the police, leaving Lincoln unguarded and vulnerable to Ferrandini's attack. The plan was reasonable and had a good chance of succeeding. There was only one problem: members of Allan Pinkerton's detective agency had infiltrated the KGC and their plan was discovered in advance of Lincoln's scheduled arrival.

When Lincoln's train pulled into the Calvert Street Station on time, Lincoln was already in Washington, safely ensconced at the Willard Hotel having thwarted his would-be assassins. Lincoln had been warned of the plot the day before and secretly changed his schedule, passing through Baltimore nine hours earlier than planned. Because of clever detective work, the would-be killers found an empty coach.

Samuel M. Felton, president of the Philadelphia, Wilmington, & Baltimore Railroad, on learning of plots to sabotage his rail lines and block the movement of troops from New England to Washington, hired Allan Pinkerton to protect his railroad from attacks. Pinkerton was a well-known detective from Chicago whose agency was already famous for carrying out undercover operations in thwarting the activities of criminal elements. Hired by Felton, Pinkerton immediately set about infiltrating the Knights of the Golden Circle with several of his best agents. He soon learned of the plot by Ferrandini to assassinate Lincoln. After discussing his findings with Felton, Pinkerton met with members of Lincoln's entourage in Philadelphia, urging Lincoln to secretly change his schedule and go directly to Washington from Philadelphia, bypassing Harrisburg. Lincoln refused, stating that he was expected to take part in a special flag-raising ceremony at Independence Hall and later deliver an address in Harrisburg to the Pennsylvania state legislature.

While in Philadelphia, Lincoln was also visited by Frederick Seward, son of William Henry Seward, Lincoln's secretary of state designate and past governor of New York. Young Seward carried a message from New York City's superintendent of police, John A. Kennedy, informing Lincoln that Kennedy had uncovered the same plot that Pinkerton had discovered. Kennedy had sent word to William Seward in Washington. Seward sent his son to Philadelphia to warn Lincoln. Shortly after hearing Pinkerton's evidence Lincoln met with young Seward; convinced that the plot was serious, he decided to alter his schedule.

Lincoln's itinerary called for him to travel from Philadelphia to Harrisburg, where he would address the legislature and attend a dinner afterward. The following day he was scheduled to return to Philadelphia making connections aboard the Philadelphia, Wilmington, & Baltimore Railroad to take him to Baltimore, where he would arrive at noon in time for his luncheon. Following the luncheon, Lincoln was then scheduled to go on to Washington, arriving in the early evening. Pinkerton changed the schedule by arranging for Lincoln to leave the dinner in Harrisburg early and take a night train to Philadelphia.

Pinkerton had his agents cut the telegraph line from Harrisburg to Baltimore while placing his operatives in the Harrisburg and Philadelphia telegraph offices to make sure that no word of Lincoln's change in plans would leak. Lincoln arrived in Philadelphia, where Pinkerton was waiting in a carriage to take him to the Philadelphia, Wilmington, & Baltimore station. The train left Philadelphia at 10:55 P.M. and arrived in Baltimore at 3:30 A.M., a full nine hours ahead of schedule. Ferrandini and his henchmen were sound asleep, believing they still had several hours before setting out on their bloody work.

Arriving in Baltimore Lincoln's coach was transferred from the President Street Station to the Camden Station, where it was attached to the Baltimore & Ohio's morning train for Washington. Lincoln arrived in Washington at 6:00 A.M. on the morning of February 23, having left his assassins waiting in Baltimore. The first serious threat to Lincoln had been averted thanks to the professional work of Allan Pinkerton and his agents. It would not be the last threat to Lincoln's life, however.

Sources: Norma B. Cuthbert, *Lincoln and the Baltimore Plot, 1861* (San Marino, Calif.: Huntington Library, 1949); William A. Tidwell, James O. Hall, and David W. Gaddy, *Come Retribution* (Jackson: University Press of Mississippi, 1988).

*See also:* Ferrandini, Cipriano; Knights of the Golden Circle

## Barbee, David Rankin (1874–1958)

A journalist who became interested in Lincoln's assassination and devoted a great deal of time to studying it. The son of a Confederate chaplain, David Rankin Barbee began his career as a southern journalist working for papers in Memphis, Chattanooga, Montgomery, Mobile, and New Orleans before becoming a feature writer for the *Washington Post* in 1928. In 1933 he joined the Roosevelt administration as a public relations writer with the Federal Alcohol Administration. In 1942 he retired and took up historical research focusing on Abraham Lincoln, John Wilkes Booth, and the Confederate spy Rose Greenhow. By the time of his death in 1958, Barbee had accumulated an extensive collection of research material mostly devoted to the assassination. The papers contain three unpublished manuscripts along with correspondence, manuscripts, transcribed material, and photocopies of documents, newspaper clippings, and photographs.

On his death in 1958, Barbee's extensive collection of research notes and papers were donated to Georgetown University. Barbee's papers reside in the Special Collections section of the university library. The papers are organized into seven groupings, reflecting Barbee's interests: vol. 1, Abraham Lincoln; vol. 2, Death of Lincoln; vol. 3, Lincoln and Booth; IV: John Wilkes Booth; V: Conspirators; vol. VI, Rose O'Neal Greenhow; and vol. VII, American History.

Sources: http://library.georgetown.edu/dept/speccoll/cl145.htm.

### Barnes, Joseph K. (1817–1883)

Surgeon general of the United States from 1864 until 1883. Barnes was handpicked by Secretary of War Edwin M. Stanton in 1862 to replace Surgeon Gen-

eral William Hammond, who had fallen from Stanton's grace. Barnes served in an acting capacity until August 22, 1864, when he was permanently appointed surgeon general.

Shortly after arriving at the Petersen house on the night of April 14, 1865, Stanton sent for Barnes to come right away. When Barnes arrived he found Dr. Charles Leale, an army surgeon, already administering to Lincoln. Although he was Leale's commanding officer, Barnes deferred to Leale as the physician in charge of Lincoln's care until Lincoln's death at 7:22 A.M. on April 15. Barnes was also present at the autopsy, which was performed by two of his army surgeons, Drs. Joseph Janvier Woodward and Edward Curtis.

Stanton ordered Barnes to examine Booth's corpse and perform an autopsy. Barnes was called as a prosecution witness at the conspiracy trial and questioned about the identification of the body on the USS *Montauk*. Barnes told the court about the distinctive scar on Booth's neck, which had resulted from an operation performed by Dr. John Frederick May of Washington. Barnes assured the court that the body was John Wilkes Booth.

Sixteen years later Barnes was at the bedside of President James Garfield following his assassination by Charles Guiteau. Barnes retired on June 30, 1882, and died one year later on April 5, 1883. He is buried in Oak Hill Cemetery in Georgetown.

Sources: Ezra J. Warner, *Generals in Blue* (Baton Rouge: Louisiana State University Press, 1964); James L. Swanson, *Manhunt: The 12-Day Chase for Lincoln's Killer* (New York: Harper Perennial, 2007), 352–53.

*See also:* Autopsy, Abraham Lincoln

## Barnum's City Hotel

One of Baltimore's more upscale hotels, Barnum's was a favorite of John Wilkes Booth, who stayed there whenever in Bal-

timore. During the second week of August 1864, Booth sent word to two Baltimoreans to meet him at the Barnum. The two men had been good friends with Booth when all three were young boys growing up in Baltimore. Samuel Arnold and Booth had been schoolmates at St. Timothy's Hall in Catonsville in 1853. Michael O'Laughlen's family had lived across the street from the Booth home on Exeter Street and the young Booth was a playmate of the O'Laughlen brothers.

Agreeing to meet Booth, whom they had not seen since their youthful days, Arnold and O'Laughlen came to Booth's room in the Barnum. In later life, Arnold described the meeting: "Booth then spoke of the abduction or kidnapping of the President, saying if such could be accomplished and the President taken to Richmond and held as a hostage, he thought it would bring about an exchange of prisoners." After listening to Booth lay out the details of his plan, the two old friends agreed to join him.

Barnum's was also the place where the plot to assassinate president-elect Lincoln was hatched by Cipriano Ferrandini, a barber who worked at the Barnum.

Sources: Samuel Bland Arnold, *Memoirs of a Lincoln Conspirator*, ed. Michael W. Kauffman (Bowie, Md.: Heritage, 1995); Edward Steers, Jr., *Blood on the Moon* (Lexington: University Press of Kentucky, 2001).

## Bates, David Homer (1843–1926)

A cipher operator and manager of the War Department's telegraph office. Bates wrote a book titled "Lincoln in the Telegraph Office," which contained many reminiscences of Lincoln including some associated with the events of his assassination. Historian Otto Eisenschiml erroneously attributed to Bates the story that Stanton prevented Thomas Eckert from accompanying Lincoln to Ford's Theatre on the night of April 14 and thereby denied Lincoln an able bodyguard who would have protected him from Booth. In his memoir Bates writes that Stanton tried vigorously to dissuade Lincoln from attending the theater on security grounds, and that Eckert declined Lincoln's invitation in support of Stanton's protest.

Bates also wrote that Lewis Powell (alias Paine) had confided to Eckert that he was directly involved with the Confederate attempt to burn New York City in the fall of 1864. This story is untrustworthy, since Powell was serving with Mosby's Rangers in Virginia at the time of the fire attacks in New York.

Sources: David Homer Bates, *Lincoln in the Telegraph Office* (New York: Century, 1907); William Hanchett, *The Lincoln Murder Conspiracies* (Urbana: University of Illinois Press, 1983).

## Bates, Finis L. (1851–1923)

A Memphis, Tennessee, attorney who authored the book titled "The Escape and Suicide of John Wilkes Booth, Or the First True Account of Lincoln's Assassination, and Containing a Complete Confession by Booth, Many Years After the Crime." Bates published his personal account of having heard the confession of a Texas man who claimed to be the assassin of Abraham Lincoln. In 1872, while practicing law in Granbury, Texas, Bates was asked to listen to the dying confession of a local saloonkeeper named John St. Helen. St. Helen told Bates that he had been part of a plot that Vice President Andrew Johnson had engineered to kill Lincoln. Fortunately for St. Helen, he was not in the barn at the time the 16th New York Cavalry arrived. He had escaped earlier. In his place was another man by the name of "Ruddy."

"Ruddy," it turned out, was Franklin Robey, the overseer for Samuel Cox. It was Robey whom Cox told to hide Booth and Herold in a pine thicket near the boundary of his plantation. It was Robey who then led Thomas Jones to the thicket and showed him where he had hid the two fugitives. All of this, of course, was true. But here the truth ended.

According to Bates's story, it was Ruddy who safely piloted Booth and Herold over the Potomac and to Port Royal, where the three Confederate soldiers, Ruggles, Bainbridge, and Jett, were waiting for them. At this point, Booth, a.k.a. St. Helen, discovered that he had carelessly left several of his personal items, including his little memorandum book, in William Lucas's wagon. Booth–St. Helen asked Ruddy to return to Lucas' cabin and retrieve his lost items. Ruddy agreed. In the meantime, Booth, provided with a horse by one of the Confederate soldiers, safely made his escape south. The unfortunate Ruddy had retrieved Booth's lost articles and, attempting to catch up with Booth, made his way to the Garrett farm, where he stopped for the evening. Unable to find a place to sleep in the crowded farmhouse of Richard Garrett, Ruddy slept in the old farmer's tobacco barn.

It proved to be a fatal mistake. During the early morning hours members of the 16th New York Cavalry awakened him and before he could explain who he was, Sergeant Boston Corbett shot him. Meanwhile Booth made an escape that carried him to Mexico, then Texas and California, before he wound up in Enid, Oklahoma Territory.

After listening to St. Helen's incredible story, Bates left him for dead. Bates then decided to pursue a claim for part of the reward money set aside for the capture of Booth. In 1900, some twenty-eight years after hearing St. Helen–Booth's confession, lawyer Bates petitioned the U.S. government for the reward money. The government placed Bates's claim in its "crackpot file." As far as the government was concerned the case was closed. Why Bates had waited twenty-eight years after hearing St. Helen's confession before acting is not clear.

Having lost his claim for the reward money, Bates appears to have forgotten all about it—that is, until he read a claim in a newspaper by a woman named Mrs. E. C. Harper that John Wilkes Booth had only recently died in Enid, Oklahoma Territory, under the alias of David E. George. The story sparked Bates's interest. Could David E. George be the same man he knew as John St. Helen years earlier?

Bates set out from Memphis and, arriving in Enid, went straightway to the local undertaker, whom he asked to see the remains of the man named David E. George. It was the very same man Bates had listened to in 1872 in Granby, Texas, more than thirty years before, or so Bates said. David E. George was John St. Helen and John St. Helen was John Wilkes Booth.

Bates was ready to go after the government once again and the huge reward money offered for Booth's body, dead or alive. What Bates must have realized, but apparently ignored, was that the reward money had been disbursed thirty-five years earlier. At the very least, Bates would be sitting on an incredible story that he was ready to pursue with vigor.

To make matters even better for Bates, the body of George went unclaimed. For years it was kept in the back room of a furniture store owned by the undertaker who had embalmed George. Bates asked the undertaker, who had been appointed administrator of George's estate, if he could take the body. The undertaker agreed and Bates shipped the mummified body back home to Memphis.

For the next three years Bates hounded the government, offering to turn over the embalmed remains of the infamous Booth for the reward money. His offer was repeatedly rejected and his claims went nowhere. But Bates was determined. If he could not convince the government to make him a wealthy man, he would take his case to the American people and let them make him a wealthy man.

In between his lawyer duties, Bates began writing the book that would tell his amazing story of David E. George–John St. Helen–John Wilkes Booth. In 1907 Bates published his book, *The Escape and Suicide of John Wilkes Booth*. At first it created a mild sensation, selling some 75,000 copies, but soon became discredited by critics who wrote of its numerous flaws and inaccuracies. Bates had failed in his attempt to make his fortune based on a personal relationship with John Wilkes Booth. As a last resort he exhibited the body at county fairs as that of John Wilkes Booth.

Sources: William G. Shepherd, "Shattering the Myth of John Wilkes Booth's Escape," *Harper's Magazine,* November 1924; George S. Bryan, *The Great American Myth* (New York: Carrick & Evans, 1940).

*See also:* George, David E.

## Beall, John Yates

John Yates Beall, a master in the Confederate volunteer navy, was known in several quarters as "Mosby of the Chesapeake" as a result of his daring exploits against Union shipping on that body of water. He was a Virginia hero for his exploits. Yates's most spectacular feat occurred on September 19, 1864, when he destroyed four Federal schooners. By the fall of 1864, Beall was working as a Confederate agent under the direction of Jacob Thompson, head of Confederate espionage operations in Canada. Beall was in charge of a plan to capture the Union gunboat USS *Michigan*, operating on Lake Erie, and use the ship in a raid on the Union prison camp on Johnson's Island off Sandusky, Ohio, freeing the Confederate prisoners. The plan never materialized, presumably because the *Michigan* had been alerted and was prepared for an attack, causing the raiders to abort their mission. Seventeen of Beall's raiders refused to go through with the plan and Beall was forced to call it off.

Following the failure of the Johnson's Island raid, Beall headed an operation to intercept a train carrying seven Confederate general officers from Johnson's Island to Fort Lafayette in New York Harbor. The attempt failed and Beall was captured. Tried before a military tribunal as a spy, Beall was found guilty and sentenced to death by hanging. He was executed on February 24, 1865.

Sometime following Lincoln's death a story emerged that Booth had killed Lincoln out of revenge for Lincoln's failure to intercede in Beall's hanging. The story claims Beall and Booth were former schoolmates at the University of Virginia and that Booth was involved with Beall's sister. Booth, along with several prominent northerners, went to see Lincoln, where Booth got down on his knees and pleaded with Lincoln to spare Beall's life. Moved by Booth's pleading, Lincoln agreed to commute Beall's death sentence, only to reverse himself later. Booth, enraged by Beall's execution, swears he will kill Lincoln for his treachery. Almost everything in this little story is false, but it still persists in certain conspiracy circles and most likely will never die, as it should.

Booth and Beall may have met in Charles Town, Jefferson County, Virginia (now West Virginia) at the time of John Brown's hanging. Beall was born and raised in Jefferson County and was present at Brown's hanging as a member of the local militia. Booth was also present as a temporary member of the Richmond Grays. The two may have met and even exchanged sentiments on Brown, his hanging, slavery, and such. But there is no evidence that Booth took any steps to avenge Beall's hanging.

Sources: George S. Bryan, *The Great American Myth* (New York: Carrick & Evans, 1940); William A. Tidwell, *April '65: Confederate Covert Action in the American Civil War* (Kent, Ohio:

Kent State University Press, 1995); William A. Tidwell, James O. Hall, and David W. Gaddy, *Come Retribution* (Jackson: University Press of Mississippi, 1989); William A. Tidwell, "John Wilkes Booth and John Yates Beall," *Surratt Courier* 25, no. 11 (November 2000), 3–5.

## Beantown

A small community in Charles County, Maryland, located approximately two miles to the southeast of the present city of Waldorf. Samuel Mudd's house was located three and a half miles east of Beantown. Mudd, in his statements to Union authorities at the time of his arrest, said he lived in the small community of Beantown.

When John Wilkes Booth was stopped at the Navy Yard Bridge and questioned by Sergeant Silas T. Cobb as to his intended destination, Booth answered, "Beantown." This supports the view that Booth had intended to head for Dr. Mudd's house from the very beginning of his escape.

Source: Edward Steers, Jr., *His Name Is Still Mudd* (Gettysburg, Pa.: Thomas, 1997).

## Beckwith, Samuel

General Ulysses S. Grant's telegrapher. Beckwith had gone to lower Charles County to help in the search for Booth and Herold. While there he met with Provost Marshal James O'Beirne on Monday morning, April 24, and was informed by O'Beirne of James Owens's statement that he had rowed two agents across the Potomac River on Sunday, April 16, even though the two fugitives were still hiding in the pine thicket under Thomas Jones's care. Beckwith went to the telegraph station at Chapel Point, where he sent the information back to the War Department telegraph office. Colonel Lafayette Baker, head of the special National Detective Police, was in the telegraph office when Beckwith's message arrived. Baker took the message to Secretary of War Stanton, who authorized Baker to send a troop of cavalry to Northern Virginia in pursuit of Booth and Herold. Although the information was incorrect, it led to the capture of Herold and death of Booth at the Garrett farm near Port Royal, Virginia.

Sources: Statement of Samuel Beckwith to Joseph Holt, NARA, RG 94, M619, reel 458, frames 458–61; Statement of James R. O'Beirne, NARA, RG 153, M-599, reel 2, frames 523–24.

*See also:* Owens, James

## Bedee, Edwin E.

Bedee, a member of the 12th New Hampshire Infantry, was present at Ford's Theatre the night of the assassination. He made his way to the presidential box shortly after the fatal shot. According to the 12th New Hampshire regimental history, Bedee helped boost Dr. Charles Taft from the stage into the box, after which Bedee was boosted into the box. Inside the box he was handed papers taken from Lincoln's frock coat by one of the doctors and told to take them to the White House. He took them instead to the Petersen house, where he gave them to Stanton. Bedee returned to his unit in Virginia, where he was later arrested on April 18, at the instigation of Lincoln's secretary, John Hay. Hay thought Bedee had kept the papers but Hay was unaware that he had handed them over to Stanton, who kept them. The matter was quickly cleared up and General James A. Hardy, who originally ordered Bedee's arrest, sent Bedee a letter dated May 5, 1865, apologizing for his arrest: "I desire to express my serious regret at my action, and cheerfully make you the reparation of a full and free acknowledgment of my mistake, which is conceded, in the light of my present knowledge of the circumstances of the case, to have been an act of serious, tho' unintentional, injustice to yourself." Bedee ended his military service as a major having served in several battles of the Army of the Potomac.

Sources: James A. Hardy, letter to Edwin E. Bedee, April 18, 1865, James A. Hardy Papers, Library of Congress, Washington, D.C.; Edwin M. Stanton, telegram to Edwin E. Bedee, NARA, RG 107, M-473, War Department Telegrams, reel 89, frame 247; Asa W. Bartlett, *History of the Twelfth Regiment New Hampshire Volunteers in the War of the Rebellion* (Concord, N.H.: privately printed, 1897), 295–98, 651.

## Bel Air, Maryland

A small town located in Harford County, Maryland, approximately twenty miles northeast of Baltimore. In 1824, Junius Brutus Booth acquired 150 acres of densely wooded land near the small town. John Wilkes Booth and his younger brother, Joseph Adrian Booth, attended the Bel Air Academy, located in Bel Air, from 1846 until 1851.

Sources: Stanley Kimmel, *The Mad Booths of Maryland* (Indianapolis: Bobbs-Merrill, 1940).

*See also:* Bel Air Academy; Tudor Hall.

## Bel Air Academy

John Wilkes Booth and his younger brother, Joseph Adrian Booth, attended the academy located in Bel Air, Maryland, approximately twenty miles northeast of Baltimore. Booth attended the school from 1846 until 1851, or from the age of eight until he was thirteen. The director of the school, Dr. Edwin Arnold, described Booth as a very handsome boy "although slightly bowlegged." Although Arnold believed the young Booth was quite intelligent, he felt the youth was not interested in study except in those things that especially appealed to him. The school building still stands in Bel Air and is currently a private residence.

Sources: Stanley Kimmel, *The Mad Booths of Maryland* (Indianapolis: Bobbs-Merrill, 1940).

## Bel Alton, Maryland

Community located in Charles County, Maryland, two miles east of where the Port Tobacco River empties into the Potomac River. Rich Hill, the home of Samuel Cox, is located a short distance to the east of Bel Alton. It was in a pine thicket at the present site of Bel Alton that Cox had his overseer Franklin Robey hide Booth and Herold following their visit to his house early Sunday morning, April 16. From this spot, Thomas Jones led Booth and Herold approximately three miles to the south, where he put them in a boat and sent them out into the Potomac River. Bel Alton is reached today by highway 301.

Sources: Thomas Jones, *J. Wilkes Booth* (Chicago: Laird & Lee, 1893), 65–82.

## Bell, William

Black servant working in the William Seward household. On the night of the assassination, Lewis Powell arrived at Secretary of State William Seward's house accompanied by David Herold.

When Powell knocked on the door it was answered by Bell. Powell insisted on personally delivering medicine that he said Seward's doctor had prescribed. Bell resisted Powell's efforts and was knocked aside as Powell made his way up the steps to a landing where Seward's son Frederick met him.

After Powell attempted to murder Seward he fled east of the capitol, where he hid out for three days. On Monday night around eleven o'clock, Powell made his way to Mary Surratt's house at 541 H Street. Military detectives were already at the boardinghouse questioning Mary Surratt when Powell showed up pretending to be a laborer hired by Mary Surratt. When she was asked if she knew Powell she denied knowing him, stating she had never seen him before. Her denial of recognizing Powell was used against her at her trial, where prosecutors claimed she obviously lied. In her defense, it was claimed she had poor eyesight and could not see Powell that well in the dim light. Suspecting that Powell might be the man who attacked members of the Seward household, the detectives sent for William Bell. When Bell arrived he was asked to look over the men in the room and see if he recognized any of them. Bell did so, stopping at Powell, and according to a newspaper account pointed out Powell as the man who had attacked Seward.

Bell was called as a witness for the prosecution. He testified in detail to the events at Seward's house and at Mary Surratt's boardinghouse.

Sources: Statement of William H. Bell, NARA, RG 153, M-599, reel 4, frames 78–82; Poore, *Conspiracy Trial*, vol. 1, 471; Pitman, *Trial*, 154, 155.

*See also:* Powell, Lewis Thornton

## Belle Isle

Island located in the James River opposite Richmond, Virginia. Site of a major Confederate prison camp where Union enlisted men were held as prisoners. In July 1862, Confederates opened a prison camp using fifteen of the eighty-four acres on the island for the prison compound. Because of the policy of prisoner exchange, the prison camp closed in September 1862. With prisoner exchange suspended in 1863, the camp reopened and continued to grow until it held more than 8,000 Union prisoners. The conditions at the camp, originally set up to hold 3,000 prisoners, became deplorable. Starvation, exposure, and disease ravaged the prisoners. Word reached Washington, which led Lincoln to consider a plan to free the prisoners.

On February 28, 1864, the War Department planned a raid, consisting of 3,500 cavalrymen under the command of General Judson Kilpatrick, with the objective of freeing the Union prisoners held at Belle Isle and Libby Prison. Kilpatrick was to attack Richmond from the north while Colonel Ulric Dahlgren led a party of five hundred troopers around Richmond, entering from the south. Dahlgren and his men would free the Union prisoners held on Belle Isle and lead them into Richmond, where they would reunite with Kilpatrick. According to papers later found on Dahlgren's body, the plan was to burn the city and kill Jefferson Davis and members of his cabinet.

The raid failed due to Kilpatrick's failure to fully engage Confederate forces defending the northern approach to the city, and a swollen James River that prevented Dahlgren and his men from crossing and freeing the prisoners at Belle Isle. While attempting to retreat, Dahlgren and his men were ambushed and Dahlgren was killed.

Sources: Eli N. Evans, "Benjamin, Judah P.," in *The Confederacy*, Richard N. Current, editor in chief (New York: Simon & Schuster, 1993), 48–49; James O. Hall, "The Dahlgren Papers: Fact or Fabrication?," in *Civil War Times Illustrated*, November 1983, 30–39; Stephen W. Sears, "Raid on Richmond," *Quarterly Journal of Military History* (Autumn 1998), 88–96.

*See also*: Dahlgren Raid

## Belle Plain, Virginia

At the time of the assassination, Belle Plain was an abandoned military supply base used by the Army of the Potomac. It is located forty miles below Washington at the confluence of Potomac Creek and the Potomac River in King George County, Virginia. On Monday, April 24, members of the 16th New York Cavalry along with Colonel Everton J. Conger, Luther B. Baker, and Lieutenant Edward P. Doherty, steamed down the Potomac River from Washington aboard the *John S. Ide* in pursuit of Booth and Herold. Debarking at Belle Plain, they headed south toward the Rappahannock River at Fredericksburg, Virginia, where they turned east, working their way along the river to Port Conway, twelve miles to the southeast.

Following Booth's capture on April 26, his body was wrapped in an army blanket and carried in a wagon back to Belle Plain, where it was taken aboard the *Ide* back to Washington.

Sources: Statement of Luther B. Baker, NARA, M 619, reel 455, frames 665–86.

*See also*: Booth Capture and Death

## Benjamin, Judah Philip (1811–1884)

United States senator (Louisiana), Confederate States of America attorney general (1861), secretary of war (1861–1862), and secretary of state (1862–1865). While Confederate secretary of state, Benjamin was in charge of certain secret service operations. In May 1864, Jefferson Davis established a network of intelligence agents based in Canada under the supervision of Jacob Thompson. Thompson received financial support from a special fund authorized by Davis and controlled by Benjamin. Among Benjamin's corps of secret service agents was John Surratt. Surratt reported directly to Benjamin and served as a courier of papers and escort for female agents between Richmond and Canada. On the night of the assassination, Surratt was in Elmira, New York, on a mission for Benjamin.

At the end of the war, Benjamin escaped to Cuba and then to England, where he became a successful barrister eventually becoming Queen's Counsel, practicing before the House of Lords.

Sources: Eli N. Evans, "Benjamin, Judah P.," in *The Confederacy*, Richard N. Current, editor in chief (New York: Simon & Schuster, 1993), 49–54; William A. Tidwell, *April '65: Confederate Covert Action in the American Civil War* (Kent, Ohio: Kent State University Press, 1995), 31–34, 162.

*See also:* Surratt, John Harrison, Jr.

## Bickley, George Washington Lafayette (1823–1867)

Founder of the Knights of the Golden Circle. The organization, founded sometime between 1857 and 1858, was eventually taken over by ardent pro-Confederate men determined to overthrow the Union and gain independence for the Confederacy through subversive means. Remnants of Bickley's organization in Baltimore plotted the assassination of president-elect Lincoln in Baltimore in 1861.

Born July 18, 1823, in Russell County, Virginia, Bickley spent the first thirty-five years of his life in and out of a variety of schemes and con games. Bickley's original objective in forming the secretive Knights was the takeover of Mexico as a source of new territory for the United States and the expansion of slavery. The idea found favor with many Southerners, but was abandoned as secession and civil war approached. Following Lincoln's election to the presidency in 1860, the Knights turned their attention to supporting secession and overthrowing the Union through subversive tactics. Members of a Baltimore chapter led by Cipriano Ferrandini plotted the assassination of president-elect Lincoln as he passed through Baltimore on his way to Washington in February 1861.

By 1862 Bickley was considered a gadfly and the southern chapters of his organization were basically defunct. The northern chapters, however, were taken over by a New Orleans native, Phineas Wright, who used the existing chapters to form another subversive group known as the Order of American Knights. Bickley, who had lost control of the KGC, was imprisoned by the Union military in July 1863. He remained in prison until his release in October 1865. Bickley died two years later, on August 10, 1867, in Baltimore. The Baltimore undertaker, John Weaver, took charge of the body and placed it in the public vault in Green Mount Cemetery, where it remained until joined by the body of John Wilkes Booth on February 18, 1869. Cemetery records are silent on the final disposition of Bickley's body but presumably it still resides in Weaver's vault in Green Mount Cemetery.

Sources: James O. Hall, "A Magnificent Charlatan," *Civil War Times Illustrated* 18, no. 10 (February 1980), 40–42; Bethania Meredith Smith, "Civil War Subversives," *Journal of the Illinois State Historical Society* 45, no. 3 (Autumn 1952), 220–40.

*See also:* Knights of the Golden Circle

## Bill of Exchange

When John Wilkes Booth's body was searched soon after his death at the Garrett farm, several items were removed from his pockets. Among the items was a bill of exchange, for 61 pounds, 12 shillings, and 10 pence. Booth purchased the

Draft on the Ontario Bank (Montreal) for 61 pounds, 12 shillings, and 10 pence found on Booth's body at the time of his capture.

bill at the Ontario Bank in Montreal during his visit there in October 1864, using three hundred dollars in gold. The bill, dated October 27, 1864, was the equivalent of $660 in U.S. greenbacks. During the trial of the Lincoln conspirators, Robert Anson Campbell, first teller of the Ontario Bank, quoted Booth as saying, "I am going to run the blockade; and, in case I should be captured, can my capturers make use of this exchange?" Campbell told Booth the bill could only be cashed if Booth endorsed it first. The reason for the exchange and what Booth intended to use it for are not known.

Sources: Testimony of Robert Anson Campbell, in Poore, *Conspiracy Trial*, vol. 1, 87; Pitman, *Trial*, 45.

See also: Campbell, Robert Anson; Ontario Bank

### Bingham, John Armor (1815–1900)

Appointed special judge advocate in the trial of the Lincoln conspirators. Bingham, along with Judge Advocate General Joseph Holt, prosecuted the eight defendants accused of Lincoln's murder. Bingham began his Washington, D.C., career in 1854 when he was elected to the House of Representatives from Ohio. A Republican, Bingham served four consecutive terms before losing in 1862 to his Democratic opponent. Bingham's loss reflected the strong Democratic constituency in Ohio and the strength of the Copperhead element, which was prominent in the state,

as well as the general populace's op-position to the war. Lincoln appointed Bingham a judge advocate following his loss in 1862. Bingham worked closely with Holt until Bingham's reelection in November 1864. Bingham returned to Congress in March only to be appointed a special judge advocate several weeks, after Lincoln's murder.

Bingham was an accomplished law-yer who was highly respected for his intellect. The force of his examinations and summation at the end of the trial spelled doom for the defendants. While Holt was in charge of the prosecution of those accused of Lincoln's murder,

he deferred arguing most of the case to Bingham, who was a far better trial attorney. Bingham was a forceful pros-ecutor who effectively diminished the defense of each of the defendants, in-cluding the effort by General Thomas Ewing, Dr. Samuel Mudd's attorney, to gain a separate trial for Mudd. Bingham was so effective in his arguments that many historians have credited his vehe-ment attacks as securing Mary Surratt's death sentence. According to assas-sination historian William Hanchett, Bingham's closing statement, a lengthy summation of all the evidence against all eight conspirators, determined the outcome of the trial.

From the outset of the trial, Bingham maintained that assassination was the objective of the accused and that cap-turing Lincoln was nothing more than a ruse. In support of Bingham's claim, only Samuel Arnold mentioned an abduction plot at the time of his arrest and interro-gation. Several of the defendants admit-ted to being part of the abduction plot, but only after the trial was over. During the trial, only Samuel Knapp Chester gave testimony in support of a capture or kidnap plot.

After his strong attack on Mary Sur-ratt earned her a death sentence, Bing-ham drafted a clemency plea asking that her sentence be commuted to life in prison. President Andrew Johnson later claimed he was never made aware of the petition. Holt claimed he had shown it to Johnson, who ignored it. Bingham supported Holt in the controversy that arose following Mary Surratt's execution.

Sources: William Hanchett, *The Lincoln Murder Conspiracies* (Urbana: University of Illinois Press, 1983); Elizabeth D. Leonard, *Lincoln's Avengers: Justice, Revenge, and Reunion After the Civil War* (New York: Norton, 2004).

*See also:* Military Tribunal

### Bishop, Jim (1907–1987)

American journalist, author of *The Day Lincoln Was Shot*. Bishop's book was a bestseller providing most Americans with their understanding of Lincoln's assassination. The book contains numerous errors and is not a recommended source for those wishing to learn the factual account of Lincoln's death. Bishop first worked as a copy boy at the *New York Daily News*. In 1930 he became a reporter at the *New York Daily Mirror*, until leaving to join the staff at *Collier's* magazine. Bishop left *Collier's* to become executive editor at *Liberty* magazine, later became the director of the Music Corporation of America, and was founding editor of Gold Medal Books. Bishop wrote several "Day" books, including the bestselling *The Day Christ Died*.

Sources: http://en.wikipedia.org/wiki/Jim_Bishop

### Blackburn, Luke Pryor (1816–1887)

Luke Pryor Blackburn was a Kentucky physician who held a special devotion to the Confederacy and a passionate dislike for Lincoln and the Union. He was considered one of the leading medical experts on treating and controlling yellow fever. Blackburn, as did most of the medical community, erroneously believed the disease was infectious and could be spread by contact.

The belief that the disease was infectious led Blackburn to undertake a plan to infect select populations in the northern states, including Union troops stationed in the coastal towns of Norfolk, Virginia, and New Bern, North Carolina. In 1864, he devised a plan to collect and distribute clothing that had been exposed to victims of yellow fever. Blackburn's objective was to lower northern morale and support for the war and Lincoln's reelection. While subsequent history has treated Blackburn's yellow fever plot with skepticism, it was real, it was known at the highest levels of the Confederate government, and it was allowed to go forward.

As part of his plan of germ warfare, Blackburn specifically targeted President Lincoln. He purchased several elegant dress shirts, which he exposed to clothing taken from yellow fever victims. The shirts were then packed in a special valise that Blackburn tried to convince an agent to deliver to Lincoln at the White House. Afraid of the risk involved in personally delivering the valise to the White House, the agent refused.

In September 1867, Blackburn wrote to President Johnson from Canada requesting a pardon for his blockade-running activities and offering his services as a medical doctor to quell recent yellow fever outbreaks in Louisiana. Johnson refused to grant Blackburn a pardon because of his previous attempts to initiate epidemics among civilians. Blackburn, however, returned to the United States a few months later, slipping unnoticed into New Orleans. Returning to Lexington, Kentucky, he resumed his medical practice and helped fight a serious cholera epidemic in Lexington and yellow fever outbreaks in Natchez, Mississippi; New Orleans; and Hickman, Kentucky. In 1879 he was elected governor of Kentucky. His term as governor was controversial because of his institution of major prison reforms and generous pardon policies for men convicted of serious crimes.

He died September 14, 1887, and was buried in Frankfort (Kentucky) Cemetery in a plot overlooking the Ohio River. Four years later the state placed a large granite monument over his grave; it declares, "In his great soul justice, honor and mercy ruled." There is also a bronze plaque depicting him as "the good Samaritan." These words stand in stark contrast to those that appeared in the Bermuda *Royal Gazette* newspaper describing Blackburn's yellow fever efforts as "an act of cruelty without parallel."

Sources: Nancy Disher Baird, *Luke Pryor Blackburn* (Lexington: University Press of Kentucky, 1979); Edward Steers, Jr., "The Good Samaritan," *North & South* 3, no. 7 (July 2000).

*See also:* Black Flag Warfare

## Black Flag Warfare

A term used to describe tactics that fall outside the accepted practices and laws of war. The term *black flag* originally referred to the black skull-and-crossbones flag flown by pirates and first appeared during the Civil War, following the aborted raid on Richmond by Judson Kilpatrick and Ulric Dahlgren in which Dahlgren planned on entering an unprotected Richmond—"and once in the city [Richmond] must be destroyed and Jeff Davis and Cabinet killed."

The term appeared in the *Age*, a Philadelphia Democratic newspaper that denounced the raid on Richmond as beyond the accepted standard of civilized warfare. It was called "Black flag warfare."

Sources: Joseph George, Jr., " 'Black Flag Warfare': Lincoln and the Raids Against Richmond and Jefferson Davis," *Pennsylvania Magazine of History and Biography*, July 1991, 291–318; Edward Steers, Jr., "Terror—1860s Style," *North & South* 5, no. 4 (May 2002), 12–18.

*See also:* Dahlgren Raid; Blackburn, Luke Pryor

## Bodyguard, Lincoln's

Lincoln was noted for his disregard for his personal safety. On occasion, he stated that he believed no one wanted to kill him, and at other times he pointed out that if someone was determined to kill him at the risk of their own life, nothing could stop them.

Despite Lincoln's negative attitude toward his personal protection, Companies D and K of the 150th Pennsylvania Volunteer Infantry were initially assigned to the White House in the fall of 1862. Company D was later reassigned to other duty, leaving Company K as the sole bodyguard. This unit appears to have functioned little more than protecting the grounds of the White House and the president's summer retreat at Soldiers' Home. They did not appear to provide personal protection to the president as he moved about the area.

In December 1863, concerned over Lincoln's safety, Secretary of War Stanton ordered a cavalry detail assigned to the White House specifically to guard the president when he traveled about. Stanton did not seek Lincoln's approval but moved ahead on his own. Governor David Todd of Ohio raised a special unit specifically to guard Lincoln. This unit, known as the "Union Light Guard," was stationed near the White House on a piece of land known as the "White Lot," which adjoined the Treasury Department just to the southeast of the White House stables. The unit was meant to serve as a mounted escort to Lincoln as he traveled about the area. Beginning in the spring of 1864, troopers from this unit accompanied Lincoln whenever he traveled between the White House and his summer residence at Soldiers' Home, provided Lincoln notified them when he intended to leave. In keeping with his fatalistic nature, Lincoln disliked the guard, feeling it unnecessary and intrusive, and would slip off without informing his guards or aides that he was leaving. It was during these trips that Lincoln was at greatest risk of being harmed.

In October 1864, Lincoln finally acquiesced to Ward Hill Lamon's and Stanton's urging for personal police protection. Lamon requested the district's police superintendent, William Webb, to supply four men from the Metropolitan Police force for assignment to the White House. Webb agreed and on November 3 sent Sergeant J. R. Cronin and patrolmen A. T. Donn, T. F. Pendel, and A. C. Smith to Lamon. Subsequently, seven other members of the police force were assigned to the White House detail: W. H. Crook, Joseph Sheldon, W. S. Lewis, G. W. McElfresh, T. T. Hurdle, D. Hopkins, and John F. Parker. While a total of eleven members of the police force eventually served as special bodyguards, there were never more than five members assigned to the detail at any given time.

Police protection was afforded around the clock at the White House. The guards worked in shifts with two guards working the 8:00 A.M. to 4:00 P.M. shift, one from 4:00 P.M. to midnight, and one working from midnight to 8:00 A.M. On a hit-or-miss basis at least one officer accompanied Lincoln when he moved about the city visiting various sites—provided the president did not evade such protection or forget to notify the guards. There is no known record that describes the duties and responsibilities of these bodyguards and it remains unclear just what their precise duties were. From sketchy descriptions it seems their principal responsibility was to accompany the president while he traveled to and from various sites, but not attend the president while he was inside those sites.

These forms of protection, however, were at best limited. While discouraging some would-be assassins, they could not have prevented a well-planned attack against Lincoln, and he knew it. Lincoln found such protection more of a discomfort than a help. He acquiesced to bodyguards and cavalry escorts only to mollify Stanton and Lamon. More in jest than seriousness, Lincoln is reported to have stated that "some of [the cavalrymen] appear to be new hands and very awkward, so that I am more afraid of being shot by the accidental discharge of a carbine or revolver, than of any attempt upon my life by a roving squad of 'Jeb' Stuart's cavalry."

Sources: Edward Steers, Jr., *Blood on the Moon* (Lexington: University Press of Kentucky, 2001), 22–23; Robert W. McBride, *Lincoln's*

*Body Guard: The Union Light Guard of Ohio* (Indianapolis: Edward J. Hecker, 1911).

*See also:* Parker, John Frederick; Union Light Guard; Pendel, Thomas Francis

## Booth, Adelaide Delannoy (1792–1858)

The first wife of Junius Brutus Booth and mother of Richard Booth, the first child of Junius Brutus Booth. Adelaide Delannoy was born in Belgium, the youngest of three daughters. Junius Booth met Adelaide while touring Europe as an actor. They were married on May 8, 1815.

In 1820, after five years of marriage, Junius took up with a young flower girl by the name of Mary Ann Holmes. In April 1821, the two lovers made their way to the United States. Junius had decided on living a double life. After a voyage of forty-two days Junius and his new love landed in America. Two thousand miles away, Adelaide and her young son Richard were unsuspecting of Junius's double life.

In 1842, twenty-one years after Junius had arrived in America, his twenty-two-year-old son Richard visited him. It didn't take Richard long to learn of Mary Ann and the family on the Maryland farm. Richard wrote to his mother back in England telling her about his father and urging her to come to America as soon as possible and "establish his legitimacy."

Adelaide arrived in Baltimore and was met by Richard, who had rented a furnished house for her. Adelaide's anger on finding her husband with his illegitimate children living a second life with Mary Ann did not upset her rational thinking. Writing home to her sister, Adelaide revealed her plans for her unfaithful husband: "He [Junius] is just about to commence his winter tour. I don't want to do anything to prevent him from making money, so I shall wait until he comes to Baltimore, and as soon as he arrives my lawyer will fall on his back like a bomb."

Adelaide was true to her word. She waited for her husband to return from his acting tour and then pounced on him with fury. After a rancorous battle, waged almost entirely by Adelaide, a divorce was granted in Baltimore on April 18, 1851. Adelaide never returned to England but rather remained in the United States, never far from the Booths of Bel Air. She died in 1858 at the age of sixty-six and lies buried in New Cathedral Cemetery in Baltimore. On her tombstone are carved the words "Wife of Junius Brutus Booth, tragedian." Such was the powerful image of this great icon of the American stage that even in death the spurned Adelaide wished to be remembered as his wife.

Sources: Stanley Kimmel, *The Mad Booths of Maryland* (Indianapolis: Bobbs-Merrill, 1940).

*See also:* Booth, Junius Brutus

## Booth, Asia Frigga

See Clarke, Asia Booth

## Booth, Blanche DeBar (1844–1930)

Daughter of Junius Brutus Booth, Jr., and Clementine DeBar, an Irish actress who was eleven years older than Junius, Jr. Junius abandoned the girl and his wife, taking up with a prostitute and going to California. Ben DeBar, Blanche's uncle and a theatrical businessman in New Orleans, as well as a close friend of John Wilkes Booth, adopted Blanche. She established her own acting career with the help of DeBar. Wilkes Booth, also the girl's uncle, followed her career closely. Among his papers found at the National Hotel was a letter from DeBar extolling Blanche's "brilliant success" on the stage together with several clippings praising her acting ability.

Sources: Statement of Ben DeBar, NARA, RG 153, M-599, reel 2, frames 336; playbill of Blanche DeBar, NARA, RG 153, M-599, reel 2, frames 339–40; Stanley Kimmel, *The Mad Booths of Maryland* (Indianapolis: Bobbs-Merrill, 1940), 60–61, 345.

## Booth, Edwin Thomas (1833–1893)

The older brother of John Wilkes and one of ten children born to Mary Ann Booth and Junius Brutus Booth. Edwin succeeded his father Junius as America's leading tragedian. Edwin was born in

the Booth log home near Bel Air in Harford County, Maryland, on the night of November 13, 1833, during one of the century's most spectacular meteor showers. While a young boy, he accompanied his famous father around the country on theatrical tours. Young Edwin had his hands full caring for his father during his father's many bouts of alcoholism.

Edwin made his debut as an actor in 1849 and eventually rose to stardom as America's most famous actor and theatrical entrepreneur. Edwin and his brother, John, were close on most all things except politics. Edwin was a strong Unionist and supporter of President Lincoln, which brought the two brothers into conflict early during Lincoln's administration. Their arguments became so intense at times that they threatened family unity, and the two agreed not to discuss politics with each other. This brought a measure of peace between the two brothers until the night of April 14, 1865. On that fateful night Edwin was performing in Boston in a play, *The Iron Chest*. He learned of the assassination the following morning. In a letter to the manager of the Boston theater where he was performing, Edwin wrote: "I am oppressed by a private woe not to be expressed in words. But whatever calamity may befall me or mine, my country, one and indivisible, has my warmest devotion."

Edwin retired briefly from the stage following his brother's assassination of Lincoln, swearing never to act again. But pleas from his friends and the public convinced him to reconsider. The *New York Tribune* wrote: "No community could be so cruelly unjust as to allow the stigma of Wilkes Booth's crime to tarnish the fame of so true and loyal a citizen as Edwin Booth." He returned to the stage one year later, and by 1869 was the owner and manager of Booth's Theatre in New York. For the next five years, the theater hosted the world's leading actors and actresses in the greatest plays ever performed onstage. Success was short-lived, however, as the enterprise failed in the great panic in 1873 and Booth took to the road again, upholding his reputation as America's greatest actor. His last performance was as Hamlet in New York in 1891. He died in 1893 on the same day that the interior floors of Ford's Theatre collapsed, killing a number of federal employees who worked as War Department clerks, and the book written by Thomas A. Jones about Wilkes Booth's escape was released to the public. Edwin is buried in the famous Mount Auburn Cemetery in Cambridge, Massachusetts, far away from his brother and family, who are buried in Green Mount Cemetery in Baltimore.

Sources: Stanley Kimmel, *The Mad Booths of Maryland* (Indianapolis: Bobbs-Merrill, 1940).

### Booth, John Wilkes (1838–1865)

Assassin of President Abraham Lincoln. John Wilkes was the ninth child born to Mary Ann Holmes and Junius Brutus Booth. He was born on the family farm near Bel Air, Maryland. The first fifteen years of his life Wilkes would live on the Bel Air farm alternating between it and a second home Junius had purchased in Baltimore. Young Wilkes grew up in a happy and vibrant family, constantly challenged by the wit and wisdom of his older siblings. He and an older sister Asia grew inseparable during these years living in the Maryland countryside. De-

scribed by all who knew her as extremely bright and strong-minded, Asia assumed a dominant role over her younger brother. She hovered over him, schooling and encouraging him in those things she felt important. Booth historian Terry Alford described their relationship: "When the demanding common labor of house and farm was done, the two would pass their time in horseback riding, village dances, picnics, camp meetings and walks in the 'wild old woods nearby.'" It was an idyllic life.

Asia described Wilkes as an indifferent student who nevertheless survived each of the schools he attended. These included the private tutoring of Susan Hyde and Martin Kerney (1844–1846), the Bel Air Academy in Bel Air, Maryland (1846–1851), the Milton School for Boys in Cockeysville, Maryland (1851–1852), St. Timothy's Hall in Catonsville, Maryland (1853), and Bland's Boarding Academy in York, Pennsylvania (1854). It was while a student at St. Timothy's Hall in Catonsville that young Wilkes became friends with Samuel Bland Arnold.

As Booth grew older he grew more handsome and more charming. He captivated all who crossed his path. John Deery, a close friend and owner of Booth's favorite billiard establishment in Washington, remembered Booth in later years: "John cast a spell over most men . . . and I believe over most women." Others echoed Deery's assessment: "He was one of the best raconteurs to whom I ever listened. As he talked he threw himself into his words, brilliant, ready, enthusiastic. He could hold a group spellbound by the hour at the force and fire and beauty of him." His brother Edwin would remark wistfully, "John Wilkes had the genius of my father, and was far more gifted than I." He also showed other traits his father was infamous for.

Junius's lothario traits passed to young Wilkes, whose romantic affairs would eventually surpass even his father's. But unlike his father, whose exploits left bastard children in its wake, John Wilkes Booth was considerably more careful—or lucky, as far as history can determine. Although several spurious claims of Booth leaving offspring appear in the literature, none of them is supported by evidence. When John Wilkes Booth died at the Garrett farm he left several women to mourn him, but no sons or daughters.

In 1874, Asia Booth wrote her memoir of her brother and her family. Of Wilkes she wrote:

As a boy he was beloved by his associates, and as a man few could withstand the fascination of his modest, gentle manners. He inherited some of the

most prepossessing qualities of his father . . . he had the black hair and large
hazel eyes of his mother. These were
fringed heavily with long up-curling
lashes, a noticeable peculiarity as rare
as beautiful. He had perfectly shaped
hands, and across the back of one he
had clumsily marked, when a little boy,
his initials in India ink.

But Asia's flattering description of her
brother was not without its dark shadows. With his father dead, brothers June
and Ned on tour, and young Joe away at
school, it was a feminine world that surrounded young Wilkes. Its mores would
bond him even closer to the southern
culture he would passionately adopt in
his adult years. Asia described how her
younger brother bristled at the thought
of the women of Tudor Hall dining at
the same table as the white laborers. He
would have none of it. It simply wasn't
the southern way. After his father died
and the family moved into Tudor Hall,
Booth tried his hand at farming. It was
to no avail. While the spirit was willing,
the body was not. He was not a sower,
but a reaper. Let others do the sowing.
He had bigger plans.

In August 1855 the seventeen-year-old
Booth began his formal acting career. It
was at the same age that his father had
first played upon the stage in England.

Young John played the part of Richmond
in *Richard III* at the Charles Street Theatre in Baltimore. It was a flawed performance, perhaps premature, but the thrill
had overtaken him. He played to tolerant
reviews more out of respect for his father than for him. The truth was that his
poor performance was due to poor preparation. Determined not to ride on his
father's or brother's coattails, he billed
himself as "J. Wilkes," reserving his full
name until that day when he would do
it credit and not embarrassment. He told
Asia he would never be able to equal his
father. Perhaps not, but he would come
close. Very close. Over the next ten years
he would ascend to the heights of his father's profession and claim his own place
among America's matinee idols.

By 1858 Booth had accepted a position paying eleven dollars a week with
the Richmond Theatre in Richmond,
Virginia. He was still performing under
the name "J. Wilkes." Booth remained
in the employ of the Richmond Theatre
during the 1858–1859 season, and was,
therefore, well placed for one of the most
dramatic events in American history.

On October 16, 1859, John Brown
and his "liberation army" of eighteen
men seized the U.S. armory at Harpers
Ferry, Virginia. Brown had sought to foment a major slave uprising throughout
Virginia and elsewhere and begin the fi-

nal purge of slavery from American soil. The country was not ready for a violent overthrow of slavery. An aging captain in the U.S. Army named Robert E. Lee, together with his handsome young lieutenant, James Ewell Brown "Jeb" Stuart, were sent to the small village of Harpers Ferry, where they soon quelled the uprising and took Brown and his survivors prisoner.

Brown was placed on trial and charged with treason. The attack on a U.S. arsenal was considered a state crime. After a trial of one week Brown was found guilty and sentenced to hang on December 2, 1859. Two weeks after the trial ended, the Richmond Militia was ordered to Charlestown, the site of the hanging, to ensure order at the spectacle and to represent the capital city at the execution. Brown's hanging would be a special state event.

Booth was in Richmond fulfilling a theatrical contract and was able to persuade his military friends with his persuasive "force and fire and beauty" to allow him to join their ranks. He talked his way into accompanying the militia troops to Charlestown as a member of their outfit. Wearing a borrowed uniform, Booth climbed aboard the train and bundled with his new comrades in arms as they made their way into the Blue Ridge Mountains of Virginia.

During the next two weeks Booth took his turn standing sentinel and serving his adopted "state's cause." On the ill-fated day of Brown's execution, Booth stood with the Richmond troops encircling the scaffold that the great abolitionist would ascend to meet his maker. Booth could not help but admire the fire and passion of the old man's commitment to his cause. There was an attraction to Brown and his death that fixated the twenty-one-year-old Booth. He told his sister that Brown was a man inspired, "the grandest character of this century!"

From 1861 through 1864, Booth continued to ply his trade and emerged as a genuine star of the American stage. Under the "star" system, the finest actors and actresses toured the country performing at all the great theaters as headliners supported by local players who formed the theater's "stock" company. As a "star," Booth earned from hundreds to thousands of dollars a week including a percentage of the box office. At the height of his career he earned twenty thousand dollars in one year, equal to a huge sum in present-day dollars. Booth's star tours took him around the country, from Boston to New Orleans, from Richmond to Leavenworth, Kansas. Wherever he traveled and performed he was hailed as a good fellow and a great actor. By 1864, Booth had achieved all he could hope for in the field of acting. His star now formed its own constellation.

Eighteen sixty-four began to see changes in Booth, both in his acting and his behavior. During the year he began to experience difficulty with hoarseness. His throat problems have been attributed to a variety of sins ranging from improper care of his voice to bronchitis to syphilis, and are blamed by some writers for causing Booth to leave his acting career. His bouts of hoarseness were not persistent, however. His difficulty with his voice was episodic throughout 1864, and Booth appeared in several performances where laudatory reviews made no reference to any difficulty with his voice or ability to project.

Speculation claimed that Booth had developed a severe cold, which eventually turned into bronchitis as a result of becoming snowbound in St. Joseph, Missouri, in January 1864. Scheduled to perform in Breckenridge, Missouri, the following week, Booth was unable to travel by train because of the heavy snows. He promptly hired a four-horse sleigh and traveled sixty miles overland to Breckenridge under extremely severe conditions. Although Booth does not write in his letters of contracting a cold or bronchitis, some writers have speculated that his prolonged exposure to the subzero weather during the trip may have been the cause of his impaired speaking ability. While this may be true, it did not force Booth off the stage. Booth performed as late as March 18, 1865, in the very theater where he would murder Lincoln, and where he received his usual laudatory reviews for his performance. It was not bronchitis that drove John Wilkes Booth from the stage in 1865, it was his hatred for Abraham Lincoln and his obsession with removing him from office. Booth no longer had time for the stage. He had become consumed with only one passion, to get Lincoln.

In Chicago he was alleged to have exclaimed "What a glorious opportunity there is for a man to immortalize himself by killing Lincoln." Five years later, while standing on the lawn of the White House, Booth would listen to Lincoln speak of suffrage for the black soldier. Booth glared at the tall figure standing in the window above. He could scarcely believe his ears. He hissed the words through clenched teeth, "Now by God, I'll put him through!"

Sources: Stanley Kimmel, *The Mad Booths of Maryland* (Indianapolis: Bobbs-Merrill, 1940); Gene Smith, *American Gothic* (New York: Simon & Schuster, 1992); Terry Alford, ed., *John Wilkes Booth: A Sister's Memoir by Asia Booth Clarke* (Jackson: University Press of Mississippi, 1996).

### Booth, Joseph Adrian (1840–1902)

The brother of John Wilkes Booth and the youngest of the ten children born to Mary Ann Booth and Junius Brutus Booth. Joseph attended the Bel Air Academy (1846–1851) and St. Timothy's Hall (1851–1852) along with his brother John. Unlike the three older Booth brothers, Joseph decided to take up medicine as his profession rather than acting. He also differed from his older brothers in that he never drank heavily or womanized.

Joseph was a student at the Charleston Medical College when war broke out in April 1861. He immediately joined the staff of the Confederate Army as a physician and served briefly during the attack on Fort Sumter in Charleston, South Carolina. Following the surrender of the fort he traveled to Baltimore and was fearful of his association with the Confederate cause. During the war he traveled to Australia before settling down briefly in San Francisco where he worked for Wells Fargo & Company.

Following Lincoln's murder, Joseph was arrested along with other members of the Booth family and held briefly before being released. From 1868 until its failure in 1874, he served as treasurer of his brother Edwin's theater in New York City. In 1884 he resumed his medical studies at New York University and remained in New York where he practiced as a physician until his death in 1902.

In 1868, he traveled to Washington on behalf of the family to identify his brother's body, and take the remains back to Baltimore at the time President Johnson released the bodies of the conspirators to their families. He was the last survivor of the Booth children.

Sources: Stanley Kimmel, *The Mad Booths of Maryland* (Indianapolis: Bobbs-Merrill, 1940).

## Booth, Junius Brutus (1796–1852)

The *Concise Dictionary of American Biography* sums up Junius's entire life in one sentence, "Brilliant, erratic father of John W. and Edwin Booth." Junius Brutus Booth was born in London in 1796, the middle of three children. He made

his professional theatrical debut in 1813 at the age of seventeen, which was also the age at which he impregnated his first woman. Following an abortive attempt to escape his responsibilities by fleeing to America, Junius and his father appeared in court where the elder Booth pleaded a settlement with the pregnant paramour. Following his reprieve, Junius continued his thespian pursuits on the English stage and soon rose to prominence. Within a few short years Junius was recognized as one of England's up-and-coming young tragedians. It was during this period that he met his first wife, Adelaide Delannoy, while on tour in Belgium. Junius returned to England with his new prize and married Adelaide on May 8, 1815.

It took Junius all of five years and one son to return to his Lothario ways. In 1820, after five years of marriage, he took up with a young flower girl by the name of Mary Ann Holmes, whom he met outside the Covent Theatre in London. Junius was twenty-four and Mary Ann was eighteen. She was a beautiful young girl who adored the great actor. Her relationship, however, soon went beyond adoration. Within a year, Mary Ann informed Junius that she was pregnant. Caught between a wife and a pregnant mistress, Junius began looking for a way to leave Adelaide.

The portrait of George Washington, which hung prominently in his father's house, came back to him in a vision. Like father, like son, the lure of America called to the wayward Booth. Within the day he had secured passage on a ship bound for the United States. Junius swept up his pregnant mistress and set out for America. After a voyage of forty-two days Junius and his new love landed in Norfolk, Virginia. The American progenitor of the soon-to-be-famous Maryland Booths had arrived in his new country with his pregnant paramour and dreams of a new life. Two thousand miles away Adelaide and her young son Richard were unsuspecting of Junius's double life. Adelaide's ignorance would not last forever, however.

Two continents, two "wives," two children: Junius was just beginning to hit his stride. A year after his arrival in America he sought to find a safe place of seclusion; a retreat from which he could launch his American career and keep his new wife and son from prying gossip—gossip that he did not want to cross the Atlantic and reach Adelaide. He found his retreat on a beautiful piece of farmland twenty miles northeast of Baltimore near the little town of Bel Air, Maryland. Here he decided to settle with his young family. The date was June 4, 1824.

Junius became infamous for his erratic behavior, but his recognition as America's greatest tragedian caused his peers to overlook his many eccentric acts. A spasmodic alcoholic, the elder Booth alternated between bouts of drunkenness and brilliance as he performed his way across the American stage. To his audiences, he was a genius. His fits of crazy behavior only delighted them more.

As much as Junius's erratic behavior accompanied his professional life, there seemed to be none of it in his new family life. He was a doting father and faithful husband to Mary Ann and their children. He settled his family into a two-story log cabin on an adjoining farm. Junius eventually purchased the cabin and had it moved to his newly acquired property. He soon set about adding two wings to the cabin to accommodate the large family that he and Mary Ann brought into the new world. In all there would be ten children, including young Wilkes, who was born on the Bel Air farm on May 10, 1838.

All ten children were born out of wedlock. Of the ten, six would survive early childhood and grow to adults. Although Junius loved Mary Ann very much, he had failed to marry her. He could not, since he was still married to Adelaide. Adelaide would eventually rectify the situation once she found out about her husband's adulterous ways, but only after he had fathered ten children with Mary Ann.

In 1851, the elder Booth decided to begin construction of a fine brick home close to the old homestead in Bel Air. His stature and finances had outgrown the log home and he decided to build a home more fitting to his fame and family. He named it "Tudor Hall," a fitting title for the castle of a Shakespearean lord.

Junius would never see the home completed. He died on November 30, 1852, aboard a river steamer en route to a scheduled performance in Cincinnati. A year later Mary Ann moved into the unfinished construction with her three remaining children. Junius, Jr., and Edwin were in California, and Joseph was away at boarding school, leaving only Rosalie, Asia, and Wilkes at home with Mary Ann.

Junius Brutus Booth is buried in the beautiful family plot in Green Mount Cemetery in Baltimore, next to a large obelisk bearing the Booth name. All of the Booth children, except Edwin, are buried with their mother and father in the plot.

Sources: Stanley Kimmel, *The Mad Booths of Maryland* (Indianapolis: Bobbs-Merrill, 1940); Gene Smith, *American Gothic* (New York: Simon & Schuster, 1992).

## Booth, Junius (Jun) Brutus, Jr. (1821–1883)

Eldest son of Junius Booth and Mary Ann Holmes. Jun, as he was known to family and friends, followed his famous father into the theater. Jun never achieved the recognition that his father and two brothers achieved, but was a successful actor and gave rise to a family of actors and actresses of his own. What Jun lacked in acting skills he made up for in his managerial skills, which made him a success. He had business connections with several of the largest theaters in America and with many of the stage's more famous stars.

At the time of the assassination, Jun was appearing at the Pike Opera House in Cincinnati. Like his brother Edwin, he hid in his room from angry crowds that might have hanged him if they found him. Jun made his way to Philadelphia to his sister Asia Booth Clarke's home, where he was arrested on April 25. He was taken to Washington by train that same evening and put in the Old Capitol Prison. In the summer of 1864, Jun had written a letter to his brother Wilkes urging him to give up his oil speculations and return to acting. The government had drawn the conclusion that Booth's references to "oil" and the "oil business" were code words for Booth's assassination plot. The government got hold of Jun's letter and questioned him about it. Jun replied:

The letter I wrote was, substantially as follows; it urged him [John] to have nothing to do with the rebellion. Knowing his sympathy for the South I was very much afraid he might go over the lines and I begged of him not to be so foolish. I told him to follow his profession; to give up oil speculating and that I was expecting to meet him in New York City on the 22nd, Saturday, to play with his two other brothers. I then said, if he wished I would go with him to the oil regions and see how wells were being sunk there. I told him that this rebellion was now all over; Richmond had fallen; Lee had surrendered; Johnston would do the same shortly and all that there would be left would be a few bands of guerrillas to rove over the country, and these would very soon be routed out. In the postscript I said, "Give my love to Alice." That is all the letter contained.

The government eventually accepted Jun's plea that he had no knowledge of his brother's intentions and released him at the same time they released his brother-in-law, John Sleeper Clarke. Jun, like other members of the family, slowly returned to his private and professional life, shedding much of the stigma of John Wilkes Booth's heinous act.

Sources: Statement of Junius Brutus Booth, Jr., NARA, RG 153, M-599, reel 2, frames 257–60; Statement of Junius Brutus Booth, Jr., NARA, RG 153, M-599, reel 2, frames 261–68; Statement of Junius Brutus Booth, Jr., NARA, RG 153, M-599, reel 3, frames 741–46.

**Booth, Mary Ann Holmes (1802–1885)**
Second wife of Junius Brutus Booth and mother of John Wilkes Booth. Mary Ann met Junius in London while the famous actor was performing at the Covent Theatre where she was selling flowers at an adjoining market. Booth was six years older than Mary Ann at the time. Her youthful beauty smote the famous actor and she was enthralled by Booth's charm.

Junius soon adopted a dual life juggling two women and two homesteads. Junius solved his immediate dilemma by taking Mary Ann to America, where the two lovers arrived on June 30, 1821. Mary Ann would become Junius's American "wife" until his divorce in 1851. He married Mary Ann, legitimizing their common-law relationship of thirty years. All ten children born to Mary Ann and Junius were born out of wedlock.

Mary Ann was a devoted mother to her ten children and all ten loved her deeply. Wilkes wrote one of his last letters to his mother and reportedly said with his last breath, "Tell mother I die for my country."

Sources: Stanley Kimmel, *The Mad Booths of Maryland* (Indianapolis: Bobbs-Merrill, 1940); Gene Smith, *American Gothic* (New York: Simon & Schuster, 1992).

*See also:* Booth, Junius Brutus

## Booth Autopsy
See Autopsy, Booth

## Booth Capture and Death
After ten days of eluding their captors, a weary John Wilkes Booth and David Herold found rest at the home of Richard Garrett, a Virginia planter. During the early morning hours of April 26, Union cavalry finally caught up with the two men. How the cavalry wound up at Garrett's farm is an example of how wrong information can still lead to a correct conclusion. On Monday, April 24, the War Department telegraph office in Washington received a communication that Booth and Herold had been seen crossing the Potomac River on Sunday, April 16. Booth and Herald, however, were safely hiding in the pine thicket and had not crossed the river. It was a case of misidentification. The men crossing the river were two Confederate agents, Thomas Harbin and Joseph Baden.

Lafayette Baker, head of the National Detective Police (NDP), happened to be in the War Department's telegraph office when the message was received. Baker acted quickly. He went straight to Stanton and received permission to send a posse of twenty-six cavalrymen from the 16th New York along with his cousin, Luther B. Baker, and his ranking detective in the NDP, Everton Conger, in pursuit of the two men believed to be Booth and Herold.

Shortly after sundown on Monday, April 24, the troopers boarded the steamer *John S. Ide* and headed down the Potomac River some forty miles to the Union army's abandoned military base at Belle Plain, located near the western boundary of King George County. Belle Plain was only twelve miles as the crow

flies from Port Conway on the Rappahannock. The men were unloaded around 10:00 P.M. and headed south toward the Rappahannock River east of Fredericksburg. On reaching the river, they headed east toward Port Conway. They began beating on doors and hauling bewildered residents from their homes at gunpoint. Two men—one lame—were they here? Talk! It was not hard to get the truth.

At one point the party separated into two factions so they could cover more territory in less time than if they stayed together as a unit. The two posses met up again at Port Conway around noon on Tuesday morning, April 25. They found William Rollins and his wife, Bettie, tending to their store along with a black man by the name of Dick Wilson. The detectives questioned Dick Wilson, the free black who helped Rollins with his fishnets. He had been at Port Conway helping Rollins with his nets when Booth and Herold arrived. Wilson told the detectives he had seen two men fitting Baker's description the day before. Next, Conger and Baker interrogated Rollins.

Frightened by the cavalrymen, Rollins talked freely. Two men had crossed the river the afternoon before. One of the men was lame. Baker showed Rollins a photograph of Booth. Rollins said the injured man looked like the one in the photograph except he didn't have a mustache. The detectives knew Booth had shaved off his mustache at Mudd's house on April 15. Rollins told the detectives one more thing: three Confederate soldiers accompanied the two civilians. One of the soldiers was named Willie Jett. Rollins's young wife, Bettie, entered into the conversation. She knew that Jett was sweet on the Gouldmans' young daughter, Izora. Henry Gouldman operated the Star Hotel in Bowling Green. When the two men crossed the river they were in the company of the three confederates. Bettie Rollins told the soldiers if they wanted to find Willie Jett they should look for Izora Gouldman. Only sixteen years old, Izora was a very pretty girl, and she lived with her parents at the Star Hotel.

Conger told Rollins to get his horse. He would have to guide them to Bowling Green and the hotel. The troopers sensed they were getting close to their prey. On Monday morning they had been five days behind Booth and Herold; now it appeared they were less than a day behind.

Conger put three troopers in Rollins' boat and told them to cross the river and bring the ferry back over. Within thirty minutes the ferry was back on the Port Conway side. It took five crossings to-taling three hours before all twenty-six troopers and their horses could be carried over to the Port Royal side. In the meantime, two of the Confederate soldiers, Ruggles and Bainbridge, had decided to travel back in the direction of Port Royal after visiting friends near Bowling Green. As they crested the hill leading into Port Royal they saw the Union troopers crossing the river. The two Confederates concluded it was a search party looking for Booth and Herold. They wheeled around and headed back toward Garrett's house at a gallop.

Ruggles and Bainbridge had come dangerously close to riding into the 16th New York as it rode out of Port Royal. Riding hard, the two Confederates reached the Garrett place, where they found Booth relaxing on the porch. Ruggles alerted Booth of the approaching troopers, then headed out toward Bowling Green. The two fugitives were on their own now. Ruggles and his companions had done all they could do. Booth and Herold made a run toward the wooded area as Richard Garrett's son, Jack, watched in puzzlement. The two strangers were clearly avoiding the Union soldiers as if they were wanted men.

Another thirty minutes and the 16th New York came riding toward the Garrett farm, dust flying in their path. Upon reaching the far end of the lane that led to the house the posse continued on past the house. Within a few minutes they were gone, leaving Garrett wondering what the two men had done. About three miles south of Garrett's farm, the troopers came to a cabin known locally as the "Trap." Appropriately named, the Trap was a brothel that serviced soldiers without regard to their allegiance. The men reined up and Conger, Baker, and Doherty went inside. They found Mrs. Carter and her three daughters. Baker began questioning the women, but was having little luck. The Carter ladies were not very communicative. Loose talk could seriously hurt their business. Conger decided to try a ploy. He explained to the women that the reason they wanted to find the two men had nothing to do with the war. One of the men, Conger explained, had beaten and raped a young girl. It was an outrage that could not go unpunished. Conger hit a nerve among the Carter ladies. They talked freely. They told of being visited the day before by four soldiers on their way home. None of the men were lame, however. One man lived locally, a young man named Willie Jett. He was headed in the direction of Bowling Green. The ladies then said that three of the men had returned the next day heading back toward Port Royal. Willie Jett, however, was not one of them.

It wasn't clear to the detectives if Booth had been to the Trap, but certainly Jett had. Doherty reasoned that even if Booth had not accompanied Jett and the others to the Trap, Jett would know where Booth was. The men finally agreed to ride on to the Star Hotel in the hope of finding Jett.

It was near midnight when the 16th New York approached the small village of Bowling Green. A half mile outside of town the troopers stopped and dismounted. They continued the rest of the way on foot so as not to alert anyone of their presence. Arriving at the hotel the troopers surrounded the building, with orders to make sure no one escaped on foot. The three officers climbed the wooden steps of the porch and began pounding on the hotel door. Getting no response, Conger and Doherty walked around to the rear of the house, where they found a black man. Doherty asked if a man named Willie Jett was in the hotel. The man said he was in bed in an upstairs room. Doherty pounded on the rear door. After a few minutes the proprietor's wife, Mrs. Gouldman, opened the door. She escorted the two men into a front parlor. Doherty asked where her son was sleeping. She led the men to an upstairs bedroom, where her son and Jett were sleeping together in a bed. Rousing Jett from his sleep, the men took him back downstairs and began questioning him.

The eighteen-year-old Willie Jett concluded that the game was up. He was willing to cooperate with the search party. He told Doherty that the men they were looking for were staying at a farmhouse on the way to Port Royal. He would lead the troopers to the Garrett house but did not want to appear to be a willing accomplice. Conger obliged by having Jett cuffed as if he were under arrest.

Arriving at the farmhouse, the detectives soon learned that Booth and Herold were sleeping in one of Garrett's tobacco barns that was currently being used to store furniture from the surrounding farms to protect it from Union vandals. Surrounding the barn, the soldiers tried unsuccessfully to talk Booth into surrendering. Unable to convince him to voluntarily come out, they set fire to the barn in an effort to force him out. As the fire began to envelop the inside of the barn a shot was fired, striking Booth in the neck. The bullet severed part of Booth's spinal column, causing paralysis from the neck down.

Booth was dragged from the burning barn and carried to the porch of the farmhouse, where he was laid out on a straw mattress. The wound was mortal. Conger sent for a doctor from the surrounding neighborhood. Dr. Charles Urquhart arrived shortly after dawn from Port Royal, where Doherty's men had found him. Booth was still alive, though barely. Urquhart carefully examined Booth and then informed the three officers that it was hopeless. Booth could not live much longer. The paralysis was shutting down most of his vital functions. Soon it would shut him down completely. Even though paralysis had stilled his respiratory muscles, Booth's breathing continued slow and labored through the use of his diaphragm. As the men stood about watching his lifeless form, Booth opened his eyes. Conger noticed his lips quiver slightly as if he was trying to speak. Conger knelt down and placed his ear close to Booth's lips. The words came haltingly, "Tell . . . my . . . Mother . . . I . . . die . . . for my country." Conger repeated the words, asking Booth if that was what he had said. He signified "Yes."

It was a few minutes past seven o'clock when Booth died. His diaphragm had eventually shut down his respiration, and he died from asphyxia. It was twelve days since the night of April 14, when he had entered the box at Ford's Theatre and ended the life of Abraham Lincoln.

Sources: Edward Steers, Jr., *Blood on the Moon* (Lexington: University Press of Kentucky, 2001), 201–6; James L. Swanson, *Manhunt: The 12-Day Chase for Lincoln's Killer* (New York: Harper Perennial, 2007), 281–343.

*See also:* Baker, Luther B.; Conger, Everton Judson; Doherty, Edward Paul

## Booth Escape Route

Following his attack on President Lincoln at Ford's Theatre, Booth fled through a rear door that led into Baptist Alley. He was within seconds of being caught by a member of the audience who leapt onto the stage and followed after Booth into the alley. Booth's horse was being tended by a young man known as "Peanut John," a Ford's employee. After striking Peanut John on the head with his knife, Booth mounted his horse and galloped down the alley. Turning to his left, he passed through an open gate that led to F Street, where he turned right and headed for the Navy Yard Bridge and Southern Maryland only a few miles to the southeast.

The exact route Booth took through the city is not known, but it is believed he rode east along F Street and across the south grounds of the Capitol in the direction of Independence Avenue. It was close to 11:00 P.M. when Booth arrived at the Eleventh Street Bridge, located next to the Washington Navy Yard. On duty that night was Sergeant Silas T. Cobb, a member of the Third Massachusetts Heavy Artillery. Cobb questioned Booth, asking his name and where he was headed at such a late hour. Surprisingly, Booth gave his real name and told the guard he

was headed for "Beantown" in Southern Maryland. Both of these answers were true. Booth was headed for the home of Dr. Samuel A. Mudd, in a small community known as "Beantown." Booth told Cobb he had waited for the moon to rise so that he would have light to travel by. Moonrise that night was at 11:09 P.M.

Cobb allowed Booth to cross over the bridge despite orders to let no one leave the city without a proper pass. General Order No. 5, issued on January 24, 1863, was still in effect throughout the District of Columbia. It stated, "No person excepting General Officers will be passed over any of the several crossings between the hours of 9:00 P.M. and daylight without the countersign and a pass."

Once across the bridge, Booth turned onto Harrison Street (currently Good Hope Road) and galloped up the long incline. At the top of the hill the road passed between two army forts, Forts Baker and Wagner. It was a little past 11:00 P.M. when the hard-riding Booth passed the forts and headed south toward Surrattsville. He continued on for another five miles until he reached the high ground south of the city at a spot known as Soper's Hill. Soper's Hill appears to be the prearranged rendezvous spot for the conspirators since Herold told detectives following his arrest that it was at Soper's Hill where he met Booth. Herold put the time at approximately 11:30 P.M. The two men galloped off in the direction of their next stop, the Surratt Tavern.

Surratt Tavern was located thirteen miles southeast of Washington at the small village crossroads known as Surrattsville. It was here that Booth had sent two carbines, ammunition, a rope, a monkey wrench, and his field glass for safekeeping. Booth and Herold reached the tavern at a few minutes past midnight. Herold slid off of his horse, climbed onto the porch, and began pounding hard on the door. When John Lloyd, the tavern keeper, answered the door Herold said in a hurried voice, "Lloyd, for God's sake, make haste and get those things." Lloyd knew immediately what "those things" were. Later under questioning he would be asked an important question, "He [Herold] had not before that said to you what 'those things' were?" Lloyd was clear in his answer: "He had not." Lloyd continued his answer with a telling statement: "From the way he spoke, he must have been apprised that I already knew what I was to give him." This could only have come from someone who knew that Lloyd had been "apprised" earlier in the day. That someone was Mary Surratt. Lloyd testified at the trial that Mary Surratt had visited the tavern on the afternoon of April 14 and told him to have the "shooting irons" ready, as "there would be

some parties who would call for them."

Lloyd returned with the two carbines and Booth's field glass. Herold took one of the guns. Booth was offered the other. He refused it. His leg was broken and he was now experiencing considerable pain. He could not hold the carbine and ride his horse at the same time. Before leaving, Booth edged his horse forward slightly and, looking down at Lloyd, said, "I will tell you some news if you want to hear it. . . . I am pretty certain that we have assassinated the President and Secretary Seward."

Another fifteen miles brought them to the home of Dr. Samuel Mudd, a member of the Confederate mail line who had agreed back in November, and again in December, to help Booth in his plot to capture Lincoln and take him to Richmond. Booth was now in desperate need of a doctor. Mudd helped Booth into his house, and after examining his leg, told him it was broken and needed to be set. Preparing a splint, Mudd set the leg and put Booth to bed to rest while he and Herold rode into Bryantown to reconnoiter the area. Mudd would later tell his interrogator that he first learned of Lincoln's assassination while in Bryantown, Saturday afternoon, and that the assassin was a man named Booth. Returning home, Mudd sent Booth and Herold on their way. He surely must have cautioned

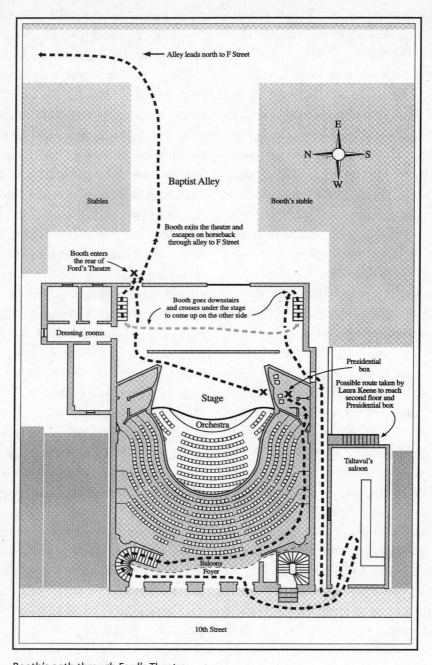

Booth's path through Ford's Theatre

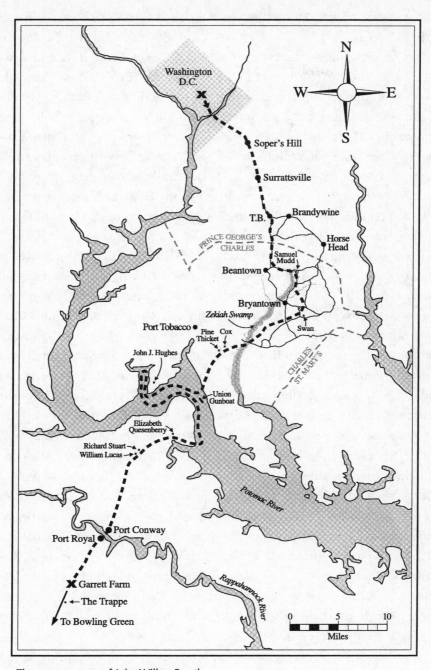

The escape route of John Wilkes Booth

them to circle east around Bryantown to avoid the soldiers.

Leaving Mudd's house the two men headed to the southeast, following a small farm road that led through the tobacco fields and ran near the edge of the Zekiah Swamp. Their destination was Hagan's Folly, the home of William Burtles, south of Bryantown. They soon became lost. An hour later they were seen at Oak Hill, the plantation of Mudd's father. Getting their bearings, Booth and Herold headed south, swinging east around Bryantown to avoid the soldiers stationed there. They eventually came to the house of a man named Joseph Cantor. Cantor, like his neighbors, had no use for Yankees. He pointed the pair down Cracklintown Road to where it intersected with the road from the Hughsville community. William Burtles's house was a short journey to the west of the intersection. They had been riding for close to two hours and had covered only six miles.

As Booth and Herold approached the juncture of the two roads they saw the light from a cabin. It was the home of a free black by the name of Oswell Swan. It was around 9:00 P.M. when they came across Swan standing outside his cabin.

By now, Booth and Herold were not sure of where they were or in what direction was Burtles's place. Booth offered to pay Swan two dollars to take

them to Burtles. The three men started out for Burtles, but after a short distance Booth asked Swan if he could take them to Samuel Cox's house instead. Booth would add five dollars to the fee. Cox's home, known as Rich Hill, was on the western side of the great swamp. Getting across it required an expert guide, especially at night. Booth upped the fee offering Swan another five dollars for his help. Swan agreed. He would guide them to Cox's place for twelve dollars.

With Swan as their guide the two men arrived at Rich Hill near midnight. They had now been traveling close to six hours since leaving Mudd's house. Cox invited the two men inside and gave them food and drink and allowed them to rest. They talked for nearly five hours. As dawn approached, Cox told them they would have to leave. He summoned Franklin Robey, his overseer and farm manager, and told Robey to take the two men to a pine thicket located a mile to the southeast of his home. Safely hidden, Robey told Booth that someone would soon come and take care of them. Back at Rich Hill, Cox sent word to Thomas A. Jones, his foster brother, who was his most trusted agent. Cox told Jones to see that Booth and Herold were safely put across the Potomac River to Virginia. The problem was that Union patrols were moving throughout the area, preventing Jones from putting the two men safely across the river.

On Thursday, April 20, Jones made his daily trip to the village of Allen's Fresh, located at the mouth of the Wicomico River. Most of the news from the surrounding area filtered through the local tavern. While Jones was sitting in the tavern, word came that Booth and Herold had been sighted in St. Mary's County a few miles to the southeast of Allen's Fresh. Jones knew Booth and Herold were several miles to the northwest of Allen's Fresh, the opposite direction. Within minutes a cavalry troop was mounted and riding hard to the southeast. Waiting until the last of the troopers rode out of sight, Jones mounted his horse and rode hard for the pine thicket. He gathered up the two men and told them it was time to cross the river. Following a brief stop at his house for food and drink, Jones led the pair down the long descent to the river. The path was steep and narrow in spots and Jones told Herold to help Booth off his horse. They would have to make the final descent on foot. With Booth leaning on Herold, Jones led them down the steep trail.

Reaching the shore, Jones found his boat where it had been hidden at the mouth of a small stream. It was a large, fourteen-foot, flat-bottom skiff. There were three oars carefully tucked under the seats. Jones helped Booth into the stern and gave him one of the oars, which he could use as a rudder by sculling over the stern. Herold seated himself amidships and carefully slid the oars into the pivot holes in the gunwales. Jones took a small compass from his pocket, and holding the candle over it showed Booth the course to steer. "Keep to that and it will bring you into Machodoc Creek," he said. "Mrs. Quesenberry lives near the mouth of this creek. If you tell her you come from me I think she will take care of you."

As they approached the Virginia shore they spotted a Union ship anchored in a direct line with their boat and Machodoc Creek. Herold quickly veered the skiff upriver, struggling hard to move out of the vision of the gunboat's watch. Hours later an exhausted Herold pulled the skiff into the mouth of Nanjemoy Creek some six miles upriver. After struggling against the current and wind they were back on the Maryland side not far from where they had started several hours earlier. It was too late to attempt another crossing that night. They would slip into the mouth of the Nanjemoy and come ashore on its eastern bank at a place called Indiantown. It was a large farm owned by Peregrine Davis, a local politician, and farmed by his son-in-law, John J. Hughes. Hughes gave the two men food and allowed them to stay in one of the outbuildings on the property. Booth and Herold laid over an extra day at Indiantown until Saturday night, April 22, when they once again attempted to cross the river. Why they waited until Saturday night is not clear, but Booth may have needed the extra day's rest, or Union gunboats may have been patrolling the river. After nine days of running and hiding, Booth and Herold finally reached Virginia early Sunday morning, April 23.

Elizabeth Quesenberry lived in a small house located on the inlet where Machodoc Creek emptied into the Potomac River. Leaving Booth to rest where they landed upriver, Herold set out for the widow Quesenberry's house. Quesenberry was not at home when Herold arrived, and he asked one of the young daughters if she could be sent for. After nearly an hour the widow finally appeared. Herold asked if she could furnish them with horses; they would pay her. She could not. She did, however, send for Thomas Harbin and Joseph Baden, two Confederate agents who were camped close by. Harbin and Baden had crossed the river the previous Sunday. She gave Harbin food for the two men and sent him off in the direction of Gambo Creek, where Booth was resting. Harbin was well acquainted with Booth, having been introduced to him at Bryantown Tavern by Dr. Mudd in December 1864. Years later, Harbin described how Booth explained his grand plot to capture Lincoln and asked Harbin to join him. Harbin agreed to help Booth. Now desperately in need of help, his introduction to Harbin by Mudd in December would pay off handsomely.

Booth told Harbin they needed horses and wanted to go to Dr. Richard Stuart's house. Stuart and his family were staying at Stuart's summer home called Cleydael and located fifteen miles inland from his plantation-style mansion located on the Potomac River south of Mount Vernon. Harbin sent for one of his subordinates, William Bryant, who brought two horses with him and agreed to lead the two men to Stuart's house.

The three men arrived at Cleydael shortly after dark. Herold, as he had done during the escape, did all of the talking. He told Stuart they came from Maryland and needed accommodations for the night. Stuart refused, telling the two men that his house was full with guests. Herold then told Stuart the injured man was his brother and had a broken leg. He needed Stuart's medical help. He told Stuart that "Dr. Mudd had recommended him." Stuart later told detectives, "I said that nobody was authorized to recommend anybody to me." Stuart obviously knew who the two men were and that Booth had assassinated Lincoln. Word traveled fast through the network of agents that stretched from Washington well into Virginia.

Although Stuart refused to give Booth and Herold shelter, he did tell Bryant to take them to the cabin of William Lucas, a free black located a short distance from Cleydael. Arriving at Lucas's cabin, Booth ordered Lucas and his wife and son out of the cabin. Booth would not sleep in the same room with blacks. He and Herold made themselves comfortable while Lucas and his family slept outside on the porch. When morning came Lucas's son Charley hitched up a pair of horses to their farm wagon and carted Booth and Herold the twelve miles to Port Conway on the Rappahannock River. They reached Port Conway sometime around ten o'clock. The once thriving community was now reduced to a few residences, a store, and an abandoned warehouse. William Rollins and his wife, Bettie, were able to make a modest living fishing and selling dry goods to their neighbors.

Herold helped Booth out of the wagon and over to a pier where he could rest comfortably. Rollins said he could take them across the river in his boat, but they would have to wait until he set out his fishing nets. While Booth and Herold waited for Rollins to return, three Confederate soldiers approached the pier on horseback. The youngest was Absalom Ruggles Bainbridge. He was a private in Company B of the Third Virginia Infantry. The next youngest was William S. Jett, known as Willie. Eighteen years old, Jett had served as a private in Company C of the Ninth Virginia Cavalry. Senior to the other two in both rank and age was Mortimer Bainbridge Ruggles, a lieutenant in the 43rd Virginia and son of General Daniel Ruggles. Bainbridge and Ruggles were cousins sharing the two family names.

Herold began talking to the three soldiers, telling them he and his wounded brother were from A. P. Hill's command. They were headed south to Orange County. On hearing that the three soldiers had recently served with Mosby, Herold decided to tell the truth. "I will tell you something," he said. "We are the assassinators of the President. That man sitting there is John Wilkes Booth." Herold said they needed help. They wanted to cross the river and needed a place to stay. Could the soldiers help? After a few minutes, they agreed to find the two men a place to stay.

It was near noon when the ferry returned from the Port Royal side of the river. Ruggles gave up his mount to Booth and climbed up behind Bainbridge. Herold rode double behind Jett.

The ferry with its passengers landed on the Port Royal side around two o'clock. The sun would be setting in a little over four hours and Booth needed a place to rest. Jett suggested they try the home of Randolph Peyton and his two sisters, a large house only two blocks from the ferry. Jett knew the family, or perhaps more important, the family knew Jett.

When they arrived at the house Jett found the two sisters, Sarah Jane and Lucy Peyton, alone. Their brother Randolph was away on business. It would not be appropriate to have two strange men, even though they may be Confederate soldiers, stay the night in the spinsters' home. Jett understood. He knew of another possibility. Just down the road was the farmhouse of Richard Garrett. Jett felt sure the two men would be welcome at Garrett's place.

When the three Confederate soldiers arrived at Garrett's farm on the afternoon of April 24 it was just after three o'clock. Jett asked Garrett if the two men could rest for a day or two before pushing on. The lame man, whom he introduced as James Boyd, had been injured at Petersburg before that city was abandoned. He was tired and worn out and his injury was bothering him. The old man did not hesitate. Of course the men could stay. They were welcome to stay as long as they wished. Booth and Herold

thanked the old man. They had been on the run for ten days.

Sources: Edward Steers, Jr., *Blood on the Moon* (Lexington: University Press of Kentucky, 2001); James L. Swanson, *Manhunt: The 12-Day Chase for Lincoln's Killer* (New York: Harper Perennial, 2007).

*See also:* Booth Capture and Death; Cobb, Silas T.; Lloyd, John M.; Mudd, Dr. Samuel Alexander; Swan, Oswell; Cox, Samuel; Jones, Thomas Austin; Quesenberry, Elizabeth Rousby; Harbin, Thomas Henry; Stuart, Dr. Richard Henry; Lucas, Charley; Rollins, William; Jett, William Storke "Willie"; Garrett, Richard; Soper's Hill

## Booth Funeral

Following the autopsy of Booth's body on board the monitor USS *Montauk*, the remains were sewn inside an army blanket then taken ashore to the Washington Arsenal grounds. A wooden box used to ship rifles was used as a coffin. The box, along with a bottle containing a slip of paper with Booth's name, was buried beneath the floor of a storage room inside one of the arsenal buildings. Colonel Lafayette C. Baker, head of the National Detective Police, and Assistant Secretary of War Thomas Eckert witnessed the burial and later publicly reported on it.

In 1867, the building was scheduled for demolition and Booth's body was removed to Warehouse No. 1 and reburied

there along with the bodies of Mary Surratt, George Atzerodt, David Herold, and Lewis Powell.

In February 1869, President Andrew Johnson, acting on a request from Booth's famous brother, Edwin, released the body to Edwin. Edwin contacted Baltimore undertaker John Weaver and asked him to take possession of the body, and arrange for its transfer to Baltimore for burial in the family plot in Green Mount Cemetery. Weaver made arrangements with Washington undertakers Harvey and Marr to accept the body from the government, and arrange its transfer to Baltimore.

In a strange irony, the body was moved to a storage shed used by Harvey and Marr that had been Booth's stable located on Baptist Alley behind Ford's Theatre. Its entrance faced onto the very alley where Booth made his escape from the rear of the theater after shooting Lincoln. From Harvey and Marr's facility the body was shipped to Weaver's establishment in Baltimore accompanied by Joseph Adrian Booth, John Wilkes's younger brother. While at Weaver's, the makeshift coffin was opened and the remains examined by Booth's mother, Mary Ann Booth, and his sister, Rosalie Booth, as well as brother Joe. Also present at the examination were John Ford, Charles Bishop, John Weaver, and Harry Clay Ford. All knew Booth intimately, and all agreed it was Booth's remains. Edwin Booth had specifically asked John Ford to be present and let him know when the body was safely in Baltimore. Ford sent a telegram to Edwin, "Successful and in our possession." The skull, hair, teeth, and broken leg were examined, as well as a filling in one of Booth's teeth. All agreed that the corpse was that of John Wilkes Booth.

The body was taken to Green Mount Cemetery in Baltimore and placed in Weaver's family vault until a spring funeral could be arranged. The funeral took place on Saturday, June 26, 1869. Pallbearers were members of the theatrical community who had known Booth. According to an article in the *Baltimore Sun* between forty and fifty people were in attendance, the majority out of respect for the famous Booth family. Reverend Fleming James, assistant minister at St. Luke's Hospital in New York performed the Episcopal service for the dead. When members of the hospital found out that James performed the burial service he was fired from his duties with the hospital.

Observers later noted that Booth was buried at the rear of the large marble obe-

lisk erected over Junius Brutus Booth's grave. The cemetery plot contains the remains of several members of the Booth family with the exception of Edwin who is buried in Cambridge, Mass.

On October 24, 1994, two amateur historians, believing Booth escaped the Garrett barn leaving a surrogate in his place, attempted to secure a court order allowing them to dig up the grave in an effort to prove it wasn't Booth's remains in the grave. The cemetery objected, and following a hearing in Baltimore Federal Court, the appeal was rejected and Booth remained in his grave unmolested.

Sources: George S. Bryan, *The Great American Myth* (New York: Carrick and Evans, Inc., 1940), 314–5; Edward Steers, Jr., *Blood on the Moon* (Lexington: University Press of Kentucky, 2001), 245–6, 256–9.

See also: Autopsy, Booth; Booth, Identifying the Body; Green Mount Cemetery.

## Booth, Identifying the Body

Of all the myths associated with Lincoln's assassination none is more widely known and believed than the myth that the man killed at the Garrett farm was not John Wilkes Booth, but rather an innocent surrogate who was in the right place at the wrong time. The claim that Booth escaped capture and lived for several more years in obscurity has several story lines.

In story, it was "Roby," the overseer of Samuel Cox the Confederate agent who hid Booth in a pine thicket. In the most widely believed story, it is a Confederate cavalryman turned Union agent named James W. Boyd. Booth lived on using the aliases David E. George, John St. Helen, and John B. Wilkes. He died in Guwahati, India, in 1883, and again in Enid, Oklahoma Territory, in 1903.

According to the conspiracy theorists, when Secretary of War Edwin M. Stanton realized that the body in Garrett's tobacco barn was not Booth, he set in place a government cover-up that lasted a hundred years and perverted American history to a shocking degree. Stanton, in league with Radical Republicans, northern financiers, and southern speculators, engineered a plot to murder President Lincoln thereby freeing them to virtually pillage the South and become instant millionaires.

Stanton must have been wary of myths claiming that the body brought back to Washington did not belong to Booth. He went to extra lengths to ensure a positive identification. On April 27, the day after Booth was killed, Stanton sent Surgeon General Joseph K. Barnes and assistant army surgeon Joseph Janvier Woodward to the USS *Montauk*, where Booth's body awaited. The two doctors performed an autopsy. Included in their report was the observation that the left leg of the corpse had been recently broken. Dr. John Frederick May, a surgeon who operated on Booth in 1864 removing a fibroid tumor from Booth's neck, identified the peculiar scar that the incision made. The last piece of forensic evidence was a small tattoo located on the back of the left hand in the crotch formed by the thumb and forefinger. Booth had formed the initials "JWB" using India ink. It left a permanent tattoo. Booth's older sister, Asia, confirmed the tattoo writing several years later, "across the back of the one [hand] he had clumsily marked, when a little boy, his initials in India ink."

There were eyewitness identifications. Sergeants J. M. Peddicord and Joseph H. Hartley were assigned to the *Montauk* as guards. Peddicord later wrote that when the body was brought aboard the monitor and left on deck with Peddicord as a guard, he examined the face, comparing it to a photograph, but more important, noticed the initials on the body's left hand. But there is one eyewitness who was present at the killing at the Garrett farm, David Herold, Booth's traveling companion. During his lengthy interrogation, Herold repeatedly referred to the man he accompanied, including into the tobacco barn, as "Booth."

In 1869, President Andrew Johnson released the bodies of the four conspirators executed by the government. Booth's remains were taken to Baltimore by Baltimore undertaker John Weaver acting on behalf of Edwin Booth, John Wilkes's older brother. Waiting at Weaver's establishment were Mary Ann Booth and Rosalie Booth, John Wilkes's mother and sister. Also present was Joseph Booth, Wilkes's younger brother. John T. Ford and Harry Clay Ford, close friends of John Wilkes Booth, were also present. Several weeks before the assassination Booth had visited a dentist and had one of his molars filled. Those present identified the peculiar plugged tooth. A close examination of the intact remains was made. The head was still covered with black curly hair. The plugged tooth, the black hair, the broken left leg, the old shoe from Dr. Mudd, and the long leather boot on the corpse's right leg left no doubt in the examiners' minds: the remains were those of John Wilkes Booth.

Source: Edward Steers, Jr., *Blood on the Moon* (Lexington: University Press of Kentucky, 2001), 243–67.

*See also*: Booth Capture and Death

## Booth Mummy

Claims that John Wilkes Booth was not killed at the Garrett farm on April 26 can be traced back to 1903, and the suicide death of an itinerant house painter in Enid, Oklahoma Territory, by the name of David E. George. George succumbed to a lethal dose of self-administered strychnine. A local woman named Mrs. E. C. Harper read of George's death in the obituary column of the local newspaper and recognized the name. She wondered if it could be the same man she had met three years earlier in El Reno, Texas. Mrs. Harper said she first met George while visiting a close friend in El Reno. George became ill and believed he was going to die. While waiting for the doctor to arrive, Mrs. Harper listened to the dying man's "confession." George told

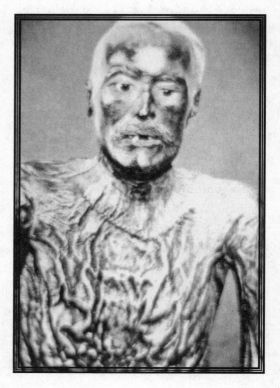

her that he was really John Wilkes Booth and that he had killed President Lincoln in 1865. Now that he was dying he had to tell someone his incredible secret.

Miraculously, George did not die that day in 1900, but recovered fully and lived another three years before finally succumbing to a lethal dose of self-administered strychnine. Mrs. Harper, now a resident of Enid, Oklahoma Territory, came to the conclusion that the corpse at the funeral home was indeed the very same David E. George, a.k.a. John Wilkes Booth, of El Reno.

The George-Booth story appeared in the local newspaper and soon was sweeping across the nation. It eventually reached Finis L. Bates, a lawyer practicing in Memphis, Tennessee. Bates claimed that he also had met a man who confessed to being John Wilkes Booth thirty years earlier, only his name was John St. Helen. Could David E. George be the same man Bates had known as John St. Helen? Bates took the train to Enid and went straight to the local undertakers, where he asked to see the remains of the man named David E. George. Bates claimed it was the very same man who had confessed to him thirty years earlier. David E. George was John St. Helen and since John St. Helen was John Wilkes Booth, George must be John Wilkes Booth, as he claimed on his deathbed.

The circle was closed and Bates saw a great opportunity.

As it turned out, the body of George went unclaimed. Bates took possession of the embalmed corpse and shipped it back home to Memphis. For the next three years Bates hounded the government, offering to turn over the embalmed remains of the infamous Booth for the reward money. His offer was repeatedly rejected and his claims went nowhere. Bates was not deterred, however, and he began writing a book in which he told the amazing story of David E. George–John St. Helen–John Wilkes Booth. In 1907 Bates published his book, *The Escape and Suicide of John Wilkes Booth, Or the First True Account of Lincoln's Assassination, and Containing a Complete Confession by Booth, Many Years After the Crime.*

After a brief success in which Bates sold seventy-five thousand copies of his book, the story quickly faded and Bates and his book were discredited. Bates next tried to interest automaker Henry Ford in buying his "mummified Booth." Ford had purchased the rocking chair that Lincoln was sitting in the night he was shot from the widow of John T. Ford. Ford then put the rocker on display in his museum village in Dearborn, Michigan. Bates thought that Ford's exhibit would be greatly enhanced by adding the mummy to the rocker. Ford was interested enough to put one of his private investigators on the case and asked him to find out what he could about the Bates mummy. Bates lost out again when the investigator reported back to Ford that the whole story was without foundation and bordered on the silly. Down, but not out, Bates was still not through. He took the mummy on the road, exhibiting it to thousands of wide-eyed spectators willing to be gulled by his fantastic tale. He showed the mummy at fairs and various circus sideshows until he became tired of the travel and sold the mummy to a small traveling carnival. The mummy eventually ran its show-business course and simply disappeared from sight sometime around 1940. There are people today who continue to search for the missing corpse, convinced it still exists. Such an object was probably too good to destroy.

Sources: C. Wyatt Evans, *The Legend of John Wilkes Booth Myth, Memory, and a Mummy* (Lawrence: University Press of Kansas, 2004). Blaine Haumes, "John Wilkes Booth and the Enid Mummy," *Lincoln Herald*, vol. 106, no. 1 (Spring 2001), 23–31.

*See also*: Booth Capture and Death

## Boutwell, George S. (1818–1905)

Member of the House of Representatives from Massachusetts (Republican), chairman of the House Committee on the Judiciary, charged by the House of Representatives to inquire into the nature of the evidence implicating Jefferson Davis and others in the assassination of Abraham Lincoln. Boutwell, a former Democratic governor of Massachusetts (1851–1852), was one of the organizers of the Republican Party in Massachusetts. Elected to the House in 1863, Boutwell was a Radical Republican. He was appointed a manager in the impeachment of President Andrew Johnson; he was secretary of the treasury, 1869–1873, and U.S. senator from Massachusetts, 1873–1877.

Sources: House Report 104, 39th Congress, First Session (1866), 1–29; Joseph G. E. Hopkins, managing editor, *The Concise Dictionary of American Biography* (New York: Scribner's, 1964), 94.

*See also:* Boutwell Report

## Boutwell Report

On April 9, 1866, one year after Lee's surrender, the House of Representatives asked its Committee on the Judiciary to hold an inquiry into the nature of the evidence implicating Jefferson Davis and others in the assassination of Abraham Lincoln. The House had become frustrated by President Johnson's apparent refusal to try Davis and his cohorts on any charges. Under the chairmanship of George S. Boutwell, hearings were held in which several witnesses gave testimony to personal knowledge of Davis's approval of Lincoln's assassination. The testimony of the key witnesses against Davis was eventually discovered to be false and Judge Advocate Joseph Holt withdrew all of the perjured depositions. The committee, relying only on the testimony of those witnesses who appeared not to have perjured themselves, concluded, "There is probable cause to believe that [Jefferson Davis] was privy to the measures which led to the commission of the deed [assassination]." The administration ignored the recommendation of the committee that Davis be brought to trial before a military tribunal. Davis was never brought to trial. He was released from prison in May 1867, two years after his capture.

Sources: House Report 104, 39th Congress, First Session (1866), 1–29; William Hanchett, *The Lincoln Murder Conspiracies* (Urbana: University of Illinois Press, 1983).

### Bowie, Walter "Wat" (1837–1864)

Known as "Wat" Bowie. A Confederate agent and later member of Mosby's Rangers, Wat Bowie was identified by prosecution witnesses at the Lincoln murder trial, along with John Surratt, as one of the men who frequented Dr. Mudd's farm and bivouacked in the woods near Mudd's house.

During the conspiracy trial in May 1865, several former Mudd slaves told the military tribunal of frequent visits by Wat Bowie to the Mudd farm, where he and other men in gray bivouacked in the woods behind the Mudd house and were carried food by the Mudd slaves. Bowie's escapades on behalf of Confederate espionage had brought him into contact with Samuel Mudd and his wife and Mudd's older brother, James Anthony Mudd. In 1863, James Mudd had been accused by several Mudd slaves of running ammunition and weapons through Charles County to Manassas, Virginia. In the summer of 1864, James Mudd traveled to Richmond on business. During his stay, he wrote a letter to a man in Charles County named "Wat" asking him to carry money from Mudd's father to him in Richmond. While the surname of "Wat" was revealed in Mudd's letter, it seems likely the correspondent was "Wat" Bowie.

Sources: James O. Hall, "Appointment in Samara," *North & South* 1, no. 3 (February 1998), 76–80.

### Bowling Green, Virginia

A small village located twelve miles southwest of Port Royal, Virginia, and the Rappahannock River. Booth and Herold had crossed the Rappahannock with the help of three Confederate soldiers at Port Royal. They stopped at the farmhouse of Richard Garrett, located midway between Port Royal and Bowling Green. They were finally caught by Federal troops at the Garrett farm, where Booth was killed and Herold taken prisoner. Willie Jett, one of the soldiers who found refuge for Booth and Herold at the Garrett farm, went on into Bowling Green, where he spent the night at the Star Hotel, owned by Henry Gouldman. Jett was attracted to Gouldman's daughter, Izora Gouldman, and decided to spend the night at her father's hotel. Following a tip that Jett might be found at the Star Hotel, Federal troops arrived there in the early morning hours of Wednesday, April 26. Taking Jett into custody, he led the troops back to the Garrett farm, where Booth and Herold were hiding out in a tobacco barn.

Sources: William A. Tidwell, James O. Hall, and David W. Gaddy, *Come Retribution* (Jackson: University Press of Mississippi, 1988).

*See also:* Booth Capture and Death

## Box

See President's Box, Ford Theatre

## Boyd, James W. (1822–1866)

Alias used by John Wilkes Booth at the time of his escape. The initials, J.W.B., are compatible with both names and conform to the initials that Booth placed as a tattoo on the back of his left hand in the crotch formed by his thumb and index finger. Several conspiracy theorists have claimed that the man killed at the Garrett farm was not John Wilkes Booth, but rather James Ward Boyd, a captain in the Sixth Tennessee Infantry, C.S.A., who was a former prisoner of war.

James W. Boyd was a real enough individual. Born in Hopkinsville, Kentucky, in 1822, he moved to Jackson, Tennessee, in the early 1840s. He married Caroline A. Malone in 1845 and together they had seven children (one died in infancy), all born between the years 1846 and 1862. At the outbreak of the war, Boyd enlisted in the Sixth Tennessee Volunteers (C.S.A.) and rose to the rank of captain. In July 1863 he was captured in Jackson and shuffled between several Union prison camps before winding up in the Old Capitol Prison in Washington, D.C. While in prison Boyd wrote to Stanton, offering valuable information about smuggling operations in Tennessee in exchange for his freedom. After taking the oath of allegiance, Boyd was released on February 15, 1865. All of the above is a matter of record and not in dispute. What happened after Boyd was released is where the "Booth escaped" authors differ sharply with other historians.

The first thing we learn from the documentary record is that James W. Boyd did not die on April 26, 1865, at the Garrett farm. He died in his hometown of Jackson, Tennessee, on January 1, 1866, eight months after his alleged death at the Garrett farm. On the Monday following his death a notice appeared in the *Daily Press and Times*, a Nashville newspaper:

On Monday before last, James W. Boyd, for more than twenty years a citizen of Jackson, Tennessee was shot and almost instantly killed by William Rowark [*sic*], a resident of McNairy County. The difficulty grew of an old grudge. Rowark [*sic*] was arrested, but managed to escape.

When James W. Boyd swore his oath of allegiance on February 15, 1865, he was required to sign a printed oath. Such oaths carry a description of the person. Boyd's oath, located in the National Archives by historian James O. Hall, carries the following description: "light complexion, grey hair, and blue eyes; and is 6 feet 2 inches high." John Wilkes Booth had black hair, dark brown to black eyes, and was five feet seven to eight inches in height. Booth was twenty-six years old in 1865, while Boyd was forty-three. With such differences in physical character-

istics, no one could have confused the identity of the two men.

The real James W. Boyd was almost a perfect substitute for John Wilkes Booth. The only problem is, he left too many vital records to escape detection by serious research.

Sources: William C. Davis, "Behind the Lines. Caveat Emptor," *Civil War Times Illustrated*, August 1977, 33–37; James O. Hall, "Unsolved Mysteries Revisited," *Surratt Courier* 16, no. 11 (November 1991).

### Boyle, John H.

Also known as the "Guerilla Boyle." John H. Boyle figured briefly in the assassination of Abraham Lincoln when he was erroneously identified as the attacker of William Seward and other members of the Seward household. Boyle's name was also invoked by Dr. Samuel Mudd's wife, who told investigating detectives that when Booth and Herold showed up at the Mudd house at four o'clock Saturday morning, they were fearful that it might have been Boyle and one of his men intent on assassinating Dr. Mudd. Why Mudd should have feared Boyle, a Confederate guerrilla, was never explained.

A Marylander by birth, Boyle enlisted in the Confederate army on June 1, 1861, at the age of eighteen. He was serving as an aide on the staff of Brigadier General George H. Stuart when he was captured at his father's home in Upper Marlboro. Exchanged four months later, Boyle eventually wound up back in Prince George's County, where he stole a horse belonging to the brother of Union Captain Thomas H. Watkins, also of Prince George's County. Boyle was finally apprehended by Watkins and taken into custody.

While en route to Union headquarters, Boyle escaped. The incident faded and Captain Watkins returned to his home following his muster from service in October 1864. On March 25, 1865, four months after Boyle's escape, he arrived at the Watkins farm looking for the former Union Captain. Shortly after 8:00 P.M. Boyle made his way into the Watkins house, where he fatally shot Watkins while the latter sat in his living room reading the evening paper.

The murder caused a sensation in the area and Maryland governor Augustus Bradford offered a five-hundred-dollar reward for Boyle's capture. At the time of Lincoln's murder on April 14, the search was still on and Boyle remained at large. Early on the morning of April 15, Major General C. C. Augur, commanding the 22nd Army Corps in the District of Columbia, sent a troop of cavalry under the command of Lieutenant David Dana into Southern Maryland in pursuit of Booth and Herold. In the course of his pursuit Dana sent word back to Washington that Seward's attacker was a man by the name of "Boyce or Boyd . . . who had killed Captain Watkins."

Boyle was arrested in Frederick, Maryland, on the morning of April 15 and taken to Annapolis, Maryland. He was indicted for horse stealing and the murder of Captain Watkins. Boyle was first tried on the counts of horse stealing and was found guilty. When he was brought to trial for the murder of Captain Watkins, his lawyer successfully had the trial postponed due to a quirk in the Maryland statutes that required a convicted felon to serve out his first conviction before standing trial on subsequent indictments. Boyle received a continuance for nine years, the length of his sentence for horse stealing. On March 1, 1872, seven years into his sentence, Maryland governor William Pinckney Whyte pardoned Boyle, setting him free. Boyle moved to Virginia, where, according to Watkins family legend, he was eventually killed by a former member of Captain Watkins's command in revenge for murdering Watkins.

Sources: James O. Hall, "The Guerilla Boyle," *Surratt Society Courier* 10, no. 4 (April 1985) and no. 5 (May 1985).

**Boynton, Thomas Jefferson (1838–1870)**

Federal judge who denied Samuel Mudd's petition for a writ of habeas corpus. Boynton upheld the military tribunal's legal jurisdiction to try Mudd. Following his conviction in 1865, Mudd began serving his sentence at Fort Jefferson in the Dry Tortugas near Key West, Florida. In 1866, Mudd's new lawyer, Andrew Sterrett Ridgely, petitioned Supreme Court chief justice Salmon P. Chase requesting a habeas corpus hearing. Ridgely based his request on the Judiciary Act of 1789 that read, in part, "either of the justices of the supreme court, as well as judges of the District Courts, shall have power to grant writs of HABEAS CORPUS for the purpose of an inquiry into the cause of commitment." The chief justice returned the petition to Ridgely with the following statement:

> Aside from questions of jurisdiction & of merits, the consideration of which I do not think it best to anticipate, there seemed to me sufficient reason for denying the application in the proposition that the petition should be addressed to a National Court or Judge of the United States in the District within which the prisoner is held.

Chase was not rejecting Ridgely's petition, but merely pointing out that the proper procedure for filing for a writ of habeas corpus was to first go to the Federal district court where Mudd was being held, namely Florida. Should the district court rule unfavorably on the petition, Ridgely could then appeal the decision to the Supreme Court.

In August 1868, Ridgely filed a petition on behalf of Dr. Mudd (and Samuel B. Arnold and Edman Spangler) with the U.S. District Court for the Southern District of Florida. Hearing the petition was a Lincoln appointee, Judge Thomas Jefferson Boynton. At the time of his appointment, Boynton was the youngest Federal judge in the country. Born on August 31, 1838, in Amherst, Ohio, he was admitted to the bar in 1858 at age twenty, and in July 1861, one month shy of his twenty-third birthday, was appointed by Abraham Lincoln to the position of district attorney for the Southern District of Florida. In January 1864 Lincoln made a recess appointment naming Boynton a Federal judge for the Southern District of Florida. He was twenty-five years old at the time.

Ridgely supported his jurisdictional argument by invoking an 1866 Supreme Court ruling known as *Ex Parte Milligan*. Milligan, a resident of Indiana, was tried in 1864 by a military tribunal in Indiana and found guilty of plotting to overthrow the local government by force and sentenced to hang. In 1866, while Milligan sat in prison awaiting his fate, his attorneys filed a petition for a writ of habeas corpus before the U.S. Supreme Court. In hearing the case the court ruled in favor of Milligan. It stated that Indiana was not under martial law, an invading army did not threaten it, and the civilian courts were open and functioning. Therefore, the military tribunal that convicted Milligan lacked jurisdiction.

Ridgely claimed the military tribunal that convicted Dr. Mudd was an illegal court based on the Supreme Court's ruling in *Milligan*. In an effort to cover all his bases, Ridgely added that if Boynton ruled that the tribunal did have jurisdiction, President Johnson's proclamation of July 4, 1867, granting general amnesty applied to the imprisoned conspirators and they should be set free immediately.

Boynton denied the petition, stating: "For the purpose of this application the prisoners are guilty of the charge on which they were convicted. . . . The question which I have to decide is whether the military tribunal had jurisdiction to try and sentence, and whether the [amnesty] proclamation of the President reaches their case."

On the first point, Boynton stated that Lincoln's assassination had a military objective: "It was not Mr. Lincoln who was assassinated, but the commander-in-chief of the Army for military reasons." Boynton went on to point out that "the President was assassinated not from any private animosity nor any other reason than a desire to impair the effectiveness of military operations and enable the rebellion to establish itself into a government." Boynton said that a sharp difference existed between the cases of Milligan and Mudd—the condition of Washington was not the condition of Indiana. Boynton considered Washington an active zone of combat. Hostile armies had threatened the city and martial law had existed since early in the war. Many of the police functions in the district were carried out by the military. And, Boynton added, the object of the conspiracy was to adversely affect the military operations of the government. In that context Mudd was an enemy belligerent.

In addressing Ridgely's claim that President Johnson's amnesty proclamation applied to the conspirators, Boynton pointed out that while the president's proclamation pardoned persons who had levied war against the United States (including those who had given aid and comfort to the enemy), it did not pardon persons who had committed offenses against the laws of war. More specifically, it excluded "all persons who were engaged directly or indirectly in the assassination of the late President."

Having followed Chief Justice Chase's advice and lost, Mudd's attorney filed a petition with the U.S. Supreme Court and arguments were heard on February 26, 1869. But because Mudd had been granted a presidential pardon eighteen days earlier, on February 8, 1869, his name was removed from the petition, leaving Samuel Arnold and Edman Spangler as the remaining petitioners. Before the Court could rule on the petition, President Johnson pardoned Arnold and Spangler on March 2, leaving the case moot. The Court dismissed the petition on March 19 without rendering an opinion. Although Samuel Mudd was granted his day in court, he chose to accept President Johnson's pardon instead of pursuing his appeal in the Supreme Court. This left Judge Boynton's original ruling in place.

Sources: Salmon P. Chase papers, Department of History, Claremont Graduate School, Claremont, Calif.; Beza Boynton Kaiser, "Annals of the John H. Boynton Family by One of Them," 1928, Family Papers, Thomas Gull, D-8; Edward Steers, Jr., "Thomas Jefferson Boynton and Ex Parte Mudd," *Lincoln Herald* 108, no. 4 (Winter 2006), 152–58.

**Branson, Margaret (Maggie)**
Maggie Branson was a friend of Lewis Thornton Powell. Maggie and her sister Mary lived with their mother in a fashionable town house at 16 North Eutaw Street in Baltimore. The Bransons were ardent Confederate sympathizers. Following the Battle of Gettysburg in July 1863, Maggie volunteered to work as a nurse caring for Confederate wounded who had been taken prisoner following the battle. It was while working as a nurse in Gettysburg that Maggie met Lewis Powell. Powell had been wounded in the right wrist on July 2 and was recuperating in a Union field hospital after being taken prisoner. The two became friends, perhaps romantically inclined.

In September 1863, Powell was transferred to a hospital in Baltimore, where Maggie soon followed. Within the week Powell had escaped from his hospital position with the help of Maggie Branson. Powell stayed at the Branson house briefly before heading south to Virginia, where he joined John Singleton Mosby's famous command.

In January 1865, Powell showed up at the Branson house in Baltimore where he became a boarder. Powell remained in Baltimore until the middle of March, when he made his way to Washington, D.C., having been brought into Booth's capture plot by John Surratt.

The Bransons appear to have been well connected to the Confederate underground in Baltimore and put Powell in touch with David Preston Parr, a china dealer whose Baltimore shop served as a safe house and drop for Confederate agents passing through the city. It was through Parr that John Surratt is believed to have been introduced to Lewis Powell, thereby bringing him into Booth's conspiracy.

Sources: Betty J. Ownsbey, *Alias "Paine": Lewis Thornton Powell, the Mystery Man of the Lincoln Conspiracy* (Jefferson, N.C.: McFarland, 1993).

See also: Parr, David Preston; Powell, Lewis Thornton

## Brawner Hotel

Located in the village of Port Tobacco in Charles County, Maryland. Site of meeting between Thomas A. Jones and mili-

tary detective William Williams. With Booth and Herold safely hidden in a pine thicket under his care, Thomas Jones rode into Port Tobacco on Tuesday, April 18, in an effort to find out whatever news he could about the government's efforts to capture the two fugitives. Jones went to the barroom of the Brawner Hotel, where local men met to exchange gossip. Here he met William Williams, a military detective on the staff of Washington provost marshal James O'Beirne. O'Beirne sent Williams to Southern Maryland to search for Booth. According to Thomas Jones's later recollection, Williams offered to pay the hundred-thousand-dollar reward to anyone (Jones) who could give him information leading to the capture of Booth. Jones replied "That is a large sum of money and ought to get him if money can do it." Whether or not the story is true, it has become a legend in Southern Maryland.

Sources: Thomas A. Jones, *J. Wilkes Booth* (Chicago: Laird & Lee, 1893).

See also: Port Tobacco; Jones, Thomas Austin

## Brenner, A.

A clerk in the firm of W. L. Wall, auctioneers. Brenner testified to auctioning the contents of several trunks of clothing for a Mr. J. W. Harris. Harris was the alias used by Confederate agent Godfrey

Hyams. Hyams worked under the direction of Dr. Luke P. Blackburn, a Confederate agent in Montreal who proposed using germ warfare against the North.

In the spring of 1864, Blackburn traveled to Bermuda, where a yellow fever epidemic was raging through the civilian population. Blackburn, a recognized expert on yellow fever, offered his services to the political leaders of Bermuda, who welcomed him with open arms. Blackburn used the opportunity to gather the soiled clothing and bed clothing from patients who had died from yellow fever. Blackburn erroneously believed yellow fever was contagious and hoped to initiate several epidemics of the disease in certain northern cities, including Washington. He shipped five large trunks back to Nova Scotia, where he assigned them to Hyams. Hyams took the trunks to Washington, where he hired the firm of W. L. Wall to auction off the contents. Brenner was a clerk working for Wall in charge of the financial arrangements. He was called as a prosecution witness and asked to describe his dealings with Harris (Hyams) as an example of the lengths Confederate leaders would go to in creating acts of terror against civilian populations in the North.

Sources: Testimony of A. Brenner, Poore, *Conspiracy Trial*, vol. 2, 420–22; Pitman, *Trial*, 57.

*See also:* Blackburn, Luke Pryor; Hyams, Godfrey Joseph

## Bridge Crossing

Booth left Washington after shooting Lincoln by way of the Navy Yard Bridge, located in southeast Washington. The Navy Yard Bridge spanned the Eastern Branch (currently the Anacostia River) of the Potomac River, ending at the road leading through Uniontown (currently Anacostia) to Southern Maryland.

Booth arrived at the gate guarding the bridge near 11:00 P.M. In charge of the detail guarding the bridge was Sergeant Silas T. Cobb. After a brief exchange in which Booth gave his real name and destination as "Beantown " (the community where Dr. Mudd lived), Cobb allowed him to cross over the bridge despite orders to let no one leave the city without a proper pass. General Order No. 5, issued on January 24, 1863, was still in effect throughout the District of Columbia. It stated, "No person excepting General Officers will be passed over any of the several crossings between the hours of 9:00 P.M. and daylight without the countersign and a pass."

A few minutes later David Herold rode up and after giving an alias and incorrect destination, was also allowed to pass. Five minutes later John Fletcher, manager of the stable where Herold had rented his horse, rode up in pursuit of Herold. Cobb told Fletcher he too could pass over the bridge, but could not return until morning. Fletcher returned to his stables in the city.

Cobb was apparently reprimanded by Major General Christopher C. Augur, but was not arrested or subjected to a court-martial for allowing Booth and Herold to pass over the bridge. This fact has led some authors to conclude that a greater conspiracy existed involving Secretary of War Edwin M. Stanton and others.

Cobb testified as to the events at the bridge that night:

> I was on duty Friday night, April 14, 1865 at the Navy Yard Bridge, at the Washington City end, from dark until one o'clock [sunset on April 14, 1865 was at 6:44 P.M.; twilight ended at 7:12 P.M.]. . . . About ten or eleven o'clock I noticed two horsemen pass the bridge from Washington. The first passed from twenty to twenty-five minutes of eleven; he was mounted on a bright bay horse, rather below medium size, dark legs, long tail and mane. . . . The man who rode the horse was medium-sized, five feet seven and a half or eight inches high, as near as I should judge, neither slight made nor stout, but snug-built and his motions indicated muscular power. He had on a soft black or dark brown felt hat. He had a pretty short black mustache of good shape and well trimmed and looking as though it had been recently colored. I noticed that his skin was white compared with the color of his mustache. He had clear white skin, not a sandy complexioned skin. I judge his age to be under twenty-five. His voice was rather light, and high-keyed. He had no gloves on. When first seen, he was riding rapidly, and as soon as he came up I halted him, and challenged him, when he said he was a friend. I asked his name, and he said it was Booth. I asked him where he was from and he replied, "I am from the city." I said, "Where are you going?" he said, "I am going down home, down in Charles's." I asked what town in Charles County. He said, "I don't live in any town, I live close to Beantown." I said I didn't know that place. He said "Good God! Then you never was down there." I said, "Well, didn't you know my friend, that it was against the laws to cross here after nine o'clock?" He said, "No, I haven't been in town for some time and it is new to me." Said I, "What is your object to be in town after nine o'clock when you have so long a road to travel?" Said he, "It is a dark road, and I thought if I waited a spell I would have the moon." The moon rose

about that time that night. I said, "I will pass you, but I don't know as I ought to." Said he, "Hell, I guess there'll be no trouble about that." He then turned and crossed the bridge; his horse was restive and he held him in and walked him across the bridge; he was in my sight until after passing the other side of the draw. I do not know with what speed he rode after that.

(A photograph of John Wilkes Booth was shown to the witness.)

That is the man I saw on the bridge. I will swear to that man.

(It was suggested to the witness that he was mistaken.)

The only thing that makes that different from the man is that the chin was a little narrower, and the cheek-bone were a little straighter down.

Between ten and fifteen minutes after this man had passed, another horseman came up. He asked me if a light roan horse had gone along, and I told him yes. He asked what kind of looking man, and I described him to him. He asked if he was going fast, and I told him not very. He said "God! I'm after him." I said, "How are you going to get back?" He asked "Why?" I said because—[interrupted] . . .

**Ques.** Now I want you to give a description of the second horse. After the first man passed how long was it before the roan horse passed?

**Ans.** From ten to fifteen minutes.

**Ques.** Describe the roan horse?

**Ans.** I think not as tall as the other one, but heavier than the bay, larger and seemed to be heavier; he carried his head forward more, and I think his head was dark colored.

**Ques.** What sort of a looking person was it who rode the horse?

**Ans.** He was a light complexioned man with little if any beard, if he had a mustache it was very light and very short, and I think his cheeks were hollowing a little; his cheek-bones were broad, prominent and wider than the lower part of his face. I did not notice anything peculiar about his eyes, except that his cheekbones appeared to be out even with his eyes. I should think he was from 25 to 27 years old. The man who had the roan horse was the heavier of the two; he was dressed in a light coat, light pants, and a snuff-colored felt hat, of rather a light shade. I halted him, and when challenged he answered "a friend." I asked him to advance and be recognized, and asked him where he was going. He said, "Home to White Plains." I asked, "where in White Plains?" He answered, "Down "[*sic*] I said "You can't pass; it is after 9 o'clock, it is against the rules." Said he, "How long have these rules been out?" I said, "Some time; ever since I have been here." He said, "I didn't know that before." I asked him, "Why weren't you out of the city before?" He said, "I couldn't very well; I stopped to see a woman on Capitol Hill, and couldn't get off before."

He did not ask anything about the man who had gone before him. The first one, who gave his name as Booth, seemed to be gentlemanly in his address and style and appearance, and what I thought was that he was some rich man's son who lived down there. His hands were very white, and he had no gloves on. The third man came along about fifteen minutes after the second. I think I would know him if I saw him.

(The livery stable man, John Fletcher, was here shown to witness.)

I recognize him as the man who came up with the third horse.

Sources: Statement of Silas T. Cobb, NARA, RG 153, M-599, reel 4, frames 41–43; Poore, *Conspiracy Trial*, vol. 1, 251; Pitman, *Trial*, 84; Testimony of Silas T. Cobb, NARA, RG 153, M-599, reel 4, frames 171–78; Joan L. Chaconas, "Crossing the Navy Yard Bridge," *Surratt Courier* 21, no. 9 (June 1996).

*See also:* Navy Yard Bridge

## Briscoe, Washington

An employee in the store at the Washington Navy Yard. Briscoe was an acquaintance of George Atzerodt. On the night of April 14, 1865, Atzerodt, after failing to carry out his assigned assassination of Andrew Johnson, boarded a horse-drawn trolley and road it to the end of the line at the Navy Yard. On board the trolley he met Washington Briscoe and asked Briscoe if he could sleep at the store where Briscoe worked. Briscoe refused.

Unable to stay at the store, Atzerodt boarded a second trolley and returned to the Kimmel House in Washington.

In his testimony during the trial Briscoe placed the time of his meeting with Atzerodt between 11:30 P.M. and midnight. He described Atzerodt as "excited." Called by the defense, Briscoe described Atzerodt as "a man of not much courage" and that he was considered by most people as a coward. The defense attempted to show that Atzerodt was a coward who could never kill another man, least of all the vice president of the United States.

Sources: Testimony of Washington Briscoe in Poore, *Conspiracy Trial,* vol. 1, 402, vol. 2, 507; Pitman, *Trial,* 145, 153; Statement of John P. Brophy, NARA, RG 153, M-599, reel 7, frames 399–402.

*See also:* Atzerodt, George Andrew

## Brophy, John P. (1842–1914)

A close friend of Mary Surratt. Brophy was serving as a school principal in Washington, D.C., at the time of the trial and execution of Mary Surratt. Brophy visited Mary at her request on the day of her execution. He was a firm believer in her innocence and worked hard to see her acquitted.

Brophy was well acquainted with Louis J. Wiechmann, one of the government's chief witnesses against Mary Surratt. Brophy claimed that Wiechmann had confessed to him that his testimony against Mary Surratt was made under duress and that he had feared for his own life if he did not testify against Mary. According to Brophy, Wiechmann agreed to write a letter to President Johnson explaining his situation but backed down when challenged by a member of Judge Advocate General Holt's staff. Brophy then prepared an affidavit that he submitted to the military tribunal telling of Wiechmann's admission. The tribunal failed to act on Brophy's affidavit and Brophy responded by publishing a pamphlet titled "Trial of Mrs. Surratt: Or, Contrasts of the Past and Present," signing it as "Amator Justitiae" (Lover of Justice).

Brophy's pamphlet, dated June 14, 1865, was reprinted in several newspapers. It accused the government of mistreating Mary physically and the newspapers of unfairly characterizing her in its articles. Brophy demanded that Mary be treated in a chivalrous manner. Wiechmann, in defending the military tribunal, described the pamphlet as "seditious and treasonable" and an affront to members of the tribunal.

The only known copy of Brophy's pamphlet is in the Library of Congress. The text is reprinted in an article written by historian Joseph George, Jr., in the *Lincoln Herald* (see Sources).

Sources: Joseph George, Jr., "Trial of Mrs. Surratt: John P. Brophy's Rare Pamphlet," *Lincoln Herald* 93, no. 1 (Spring 1991), 17–22; Statement of John P. Brophy, NARA, M-599, reel 7, frames 399–402.

## Brown, Dr. Charles D. (1817–1896)

Partner in the undertaking firm of Brown & Alexander. The firm was selected to embalm the body of Lincoln. Henry P. Cattell, a senior embalmer employed by Brown & Alexander, performed the actual embalming procedure. The Lincolns had used the services of Brown & Alexander to embalm their son Willie following his death in February 1862. Immediately after the autopsy was completed and while President Andrew Johnson and the doctors looked on, Cattell embalmed the body using chloride of zinc as a preservative.

Brown accompanied the body all the way to Springfield, Illinois, finding it necessary to cosmetically touch up the features of the president at several stops during the journey. It was the duty of Brown and the undertaker assigned to accompany Lincoln's body to see that the casket and corpse were kept in proper condition at all times during the long journey of 1,600 miles.

Sources: Victor Searcher, *The Farewell to Lincoln* (New York: Abingdon, 1965); Dorothy Meserve Kunhardt and Philip B. Kunhardt, Jr., *Twenty Days* (New York: Harper & Row, 1965).

## Brown & Alexander

A Washington, D.C., undertaking firm that was given the task of embalming Lincoln's body. Brown & Alexander were the undertakers that embalmed young William Wallace (Willie) Lincoln following his death in the White House on February 20, 1862.

Sources: Dorothy Meserve Kunhardt and Philip B. Kunhardt, Jr., *Twenty Days* (New York: Harper & Row, 1965).

*See also:* Brown, Dr. Charles D.; Lynch, Thomas

## Browning, William A. (1835–1866)

Private secretary to Vice President Andrew Johnson. Browning first served as Johnson's secretary when Johnson was elected to the U.S. Senate (1857–1862).

He returned with Johnson to Tennessee when Lincoln appointed Johnson military governor of that state (1862–1864). Browning continued to serve as Johnson's private secretary when Johnson served as vice president and after Johnson succeeded Lincoln as president on April 14, 1865.

Browning and Johnson both were staying at the Kirkwood House, located at Twelfth Street and Pennsylvania Avenue, following their return to Washington when Johnson became vice president. Sometime before 5:00 P.M. on April 14, Booth stopped by the Kirkwood House and placed a small card in Browning's message box that read, "Don't wish to disturb you. Are you at home? J. Wilkes Booth."

Browning, at the time of his testimony during the trial, stated that he believed the message was meant for Johnson and accidentally placed in his, Browning's, box. Most historians have accepted this explanation. It seems more likely, however, that the message was intended for Browning and not Johnson. Booth had met Browning in February 1864 when Booth was in Nashville performing in *Richard III*. Browning kept Johnson's appointment calendar and would have been more accessible to Booth than the new vice president. Booth was, in all probability, trying to find out if Johnson would be in his room later that night when Booth told Atzerodt to murder Johnson.

Sources: Testimony of William A. Browning, Poore, *Conspiracy Trial*, vol. 1, 240; Pitman, *Trial*, 70; obituary, *Washington Star*, March 2, 1866, 2, col. 4.

*See also:* Atzerodt, George Andrew

## Brownson, Orestes Augustus (1803–1876)

Brownson was a philosopher and author who espoused liberal views. A Unitarian minister, Brownson converted to Roman Catholicism in 1844 and began writing and publishing a journal, *Brownson's Quarterly Review* (1844–1865), which was among the more literate and widely respected journals of the mid-century period. Dr. Samuel Mudd was a subscriber to Brownson's journal. Upset with Browning's opposition to slavery and his support for Lincoln, Mudd wrote a revealing letter to Brownson dated January 13, 1862, criticizing him for his liberal views. Mudd wrote the letter after receiving a bill for a subscription that Mudd had previously canceled in protest of Brownson's views. In his letter Mudd severely criticized northerners, calling them among other things "Pharisaical, covert, stealthy, and cowardly." He challenged Lincoln's patriotism and wrote that if Lincoln were no longer president the "Revolution would immediately cease so far as the South is concerned." Mudd's letter to Brownson gives important insight into Mudd's views concerning Lincoln and slavery and reveals a darker side of his character, belying his claim that he was a "good Union man."

Sources: Arthur M. Schlesinger, *Orestes A. Brownson: A Pilgrim's Progress* (Boston: Little, Brown, 1939); Nettie Mudd, *The Life of Dr. Samuel A. Mudd* (1906; reprint, La Plata, Md.: Dick Wildes, 1975).

*See also:* Mudd, Dr. Samuel Alexander

## Bryant, William K.

A Confederate agent working with Thomas Harbin. When Booth and Herold reached the Virginia shore after crossing the Potomac River, they contacted the widow Elizabeth Quesenberry asking her help. Thomas Jones, the Confederate agent who had cared for the two men while they hid in a pine thicket, told Booth that Quesenberry would help him if he told her Jones had recommended her. Quesenberry sent for Thomas Harbin, the Confederate agent to whom Booth had been introduced by Dr. Mudd in December 1864. Harbin took Booth and Herold to the farm of William Bryant. Harbin instructed Bryant to lend two of his horses to the two men and take them to the summer home of Richard Stuart, a few miles inland from the river. When Bryant arrived at Stuart's house with Booth and Herold, Stuart refused to let the two men stay at his house, instructing Bryant to take them to the cabin of William Lucas, a free black who lived on the edge of Stuart's property. Bryant left the two men at Lucas's cabin and returned to his farm with his horses. Bryant was arrested and gave a lengthy statement describing his role in taking Booth and Herold to Stuart's, but did not mention Harbin or Quesenberry. Bryant feigned not knowing who the two men were, telling his interrogators that he thought the two men were soldiers and that the injured man wanted to go to Stuart's for medical help.

Sources: Statement of William L. Bryant, NARA, M-599, reel 4, frames 93–97; Edward Steers, Jr., *Blood on the Moon* (Lexington: University Press of Kentucky, 2001), 181–82.

*See also:* Booth Escape Route

## Bryantown, Maryland

A small village located five miles due south of the home of Samuel Mudd. Bryantown figures prominently in the Lincoln assassination story for it was at the Bryantown Tavern that John Wilkes Booth stayed on two of his visits to Charles County, and where Samuel Mudd agreed to introduce Booth to the Confederate agent Thomas Harbin on December 18, 1864.

The origin of the village is unknown but an early census taken between 1775 and 1778 lists six adult males with the surname of Bryan living at the crossroads later known as Bryantown. The village is believed to have taken its name from that of the innkeeper who operated a tavern in the heart of the village. The tavern building still exists today as a private residence.

Booth visited Bryantown on at least two occasions, November 11, 1864, and December 16, 1864. He spent both nights at the Bryantown Tavern before visiting with Drs. Queen and Mudd. On December 18, Mudd introduced Booth to the Confederate agent Thomas Harbin at the Bryantown Tavern. As a result of the meeting, Harbin agreed to help Booth with his plan to capture Lincoln and take him to Richmond. On December 19, Booth and Mudd visited the blacksmith shop of Peter Trotter in Bryantown. Booth wanted Trotter to replace the shoes on a horse Booth had purchased the day before from Mudd's neighbor, George Gardiner.

On the afternoon of April 15, 1865, Dr. Mudd traveled into Bryantown to mail letters received earlier from Confederate couriers but encountered troops of the 13th New York Cavalry, under Lieutenant

David Dana, who had set up their headquarters in the village. It was during this visit that Mudd later claimed he learned of Lincoln's assassination and that the assassin was a man named Booth.

On Friday, April 21, military detectives took Mudd to Bryantown, where Colonel Henry H. Wells interrogated him. Following his interrogation of Mudd, Wells drafted a statement summarizing Mudd's answers, which he asked Mudd to sign and date. Mudd also wrote out a voluntary statement while in Bryantown detailing his story of the events of April 15. These two statements are the basis of Mudd's testimony. Because Wells felt Mudd withheld vital information from these two statements, he was taken into custody and subsequently charged as an accomplice of Booth.

At the time Mudd and Booth visited Bryantown it was a center of local commerce. Included within the immediate vicinity of the village were six medical doctors, a constable, hotel, three blacksmiths, a wheelwright, coach maker, two bookmakers and shoemakers, three merchants, five mechanics, six schoolteachers, two millers, a magistrate, two lawyers, a carpenter, a Protestant Episcopal minister, and a Roman Catholic priest.

Sources: Jack D. Brown et al., *Charles County, Maryland: A History* (La Plata, Md.: Charles County Bicentennial Commission, 1976); Edward Steers, Jr., *Blood on the Moon* (Lexington: University Press of Kentucky, 2001), 77–79; James L. Swanson, *Manhunt: The 12-Day Chase for Lincoln's Killer* (New York: Harper Perennial, 2007), 181–83.

*See also:* Bryantown Tavern; Trotter, Peter; Harbin, Thomas Henry

## Bryantown Tavern

The Bryantown Tavern was the main hostelry located in the center of the small village of Bryantown in Charles County, Southern Maryland. The tavern was a scheduled stop for the stagecoach that ran from the National Hotel in Washington. Booth stayed at the tavern on November 11 and again on December 16, 1864. Dr. Mudd introduced Booth to the Confederate agent Thomas Harbin at the tavern on Sunday, December 18, 1864. As a result of the meeting, Harbin agreed to help Booth with his abduction plan.

The tavern became the headquarters for the 13th New York Cavalry after it arrived in the village shortly after noon on April 15. The military detectives brought Samuel Mudd to the tavern for questioning by Colonel Henry H. Wells on Friday, April 21, and again the following day. The tavern building survives as a private residence with little structural change to its appearance at the time of the assassination.

Sources: Jack D. Brown et al., *Charles County, Maryland: A History* (La Plata, Md.: Charles County Bicentennial Commission, 1976).

*See also:* Bryantown, Maryland; Mudd, Dr. Samuel Alexander

### Buckingham, John E., Sr. (1828–1912)

Buckingham was the doorkeeper at Ford's Theatre. A Baltimorean, Buckingham had come to Washington at Ford's urging and began working as his doorkeeper in 1862. Working nights and weekends at the theater, Buckingham worked at the Washington Navy Yard during the day as a gun carriage builder. He was attending the door to the lobby of the theater on the night of April 14, when Booth entered. Buckingham gave a statement to authorities on May 15, in which he stated that Booth first entered the lobby of the theater "about 10 o'clock." Buckingham described Booth as going into the parquet several times before climbing the stairs to the Dress Circle.

In an article that appeared in the *Washington Evening Star* on April 14, 1903, Buckingham wrote that he heard a pistol shot "about 20 minutes after 10 o'clock." He did not see Booth jump from the box but claimed to have seen him going across the stage holding a large knife in one hand and shouting "Sic Semper Tyrannis." Buckingham claimed to recognize the man instantly as John Wilkes Booth. He was called as a prosecution witness testifying to Booth's behavior just before the assassin went up to the Dress Circle.

In 1894, Buckingham published a small, illustrated booklet, *Reminiscences*

*and Souvenirs of the Assassination of Abraham Lincoln.*

Sources: Timothy S. Good, *We Saw Lincoln Shot: One Hundred Eyewitness Accounts* (Jackson: University Press of Mississippi, 1995); Edward Steers, Jr., ed., *The Trial* (Lexington: University Press of Kentucky, 2003), 73.

## Burch, Henry

A neighbor and friend of Samuel A. Mudd. Burch lived in Charles County, Maryland. He was accused, along with Samuel Mudd and Henry L. Mudd, Jr., Mudd's younger brother, of serving on a slave-capturing posse (referred to as "paddy rollers"), capturing and sending fugitive slaves south to Richmond to work in constructing defenses for the military.

Sources: Statement of Richard Washington et al., NARA, RG 109, M-416, Union Provost Marshal's File of Papers Relating to Two or More Civilians, file no. 6083.

*See also* Mudd, Dr. Samuel Alexander

## Burch, J. Dominic

Burch was manager of the Bryantown Tavern, where John Wilkes Booth stayed on his two visits to Charles County to see Dr. Samuel Mudd. Burch received a letter from Booth dated November 14, 1864, with the address "Washington, D.C."

The letter places Booth in Washington the very day that Dr. Mudd claimed Booth purchased the one-eyed horse from his neighbor George Gardiner.

This letter supports the claim that Booth was not only back in his hotel room on Monday the 14th, but that he returned to Washington by stagecoach and not on horseback as Mudd claimed in his statement to Colonel Henry H. Wells.

The Burch letter further supports the testimony of other witnesses that Booth visited Dr. Mudd a second time, in December 1864, and that it was during this second visit that Booth purchased the one-eyed horse from Gardiner, later riding it back to Washington. It was during this second visit in December that Booth was introduced by Mudd to Confederate agent Thomas Harbin at the Bryantown Tavern. Mudd compressed the two meetings, in November and December, into one, telling investigators that Booth was his overnight guest during Booth's November visit and it was at that time that Booth purchased a horse from Gardiner. Clearly, Mudd did not want the government to find out about the second visit and his introducing Booth to Harbin. Had the government learned of this second meeting, Mudd would in all likelihood have received a death sentence.

Sources: John Rhodehamel and Louise Taper, *"Right or Wrong, God Judge Me"* (Urbana: University of Illinois Press, 1997), 123; Edward

Steers, Jr., *Blood on the Moon* (Lexington: University Press of Kentucky, 2001), 75–76.

## Bureau of Military Information

Intelligence-gathering operation employed by the U.S. military under the command of colonel, later brigadier general, George S. Sharpe. This organization did not figure in the evidence-gathering phase of the Lincoln assassination.

## Bureau of Military Justice

Arm of the U.S. military that is responsible for adjudicating criminal law and procedure applicable to the armed forces of the United States. Joseph Holt was appointed judge advocate general of the U.S. Army and head of the Bureau of Military Justice by Abraham Lincoln in September 1862. The bureau assumed responsibility for the collection of evidence and subsequent military trial of those charged with Lincoln's murder. In a report to Secretary of War Edwin M. Stanton, Holt wrote that the bureau reviewed the records of 16,591 courts-martial and military commissions, a staggering number.

Sources: Elizabeth D. Leonard, *Lincoln's Avengers: Justice, Revenge, and Reunion After the Civil War* (New York: Wiley, 2004).

*See also*: Holt, Joseph; Burnett, Henry Lawrence

## Bureau of Special and Secret Service, C.S.A.

A special Confederate bureau created in March 1865, through a bill designated HR 361, to bring the various Confederate secret service agencies under one organization and place it under the secretary of state (Judah P. Benjamin). Although formed too late in the war to have a major impact, the newly established bureau was in place at the time of Lincoln's assassination. A major function that fell under the authority of the bureau was the Torpedo Bureau, under the command of Brigadier General Gabriel J. Rains. It was from the Torpedo Bureau that an alleged plot to blow up the White House was launched in April 1865 by Thomas F. Harney. The plot was prevented when Harney was captured along with members of Mosby's command on April 10, 1865.

Sources: William A. Tidwell, James O. Hall, and David W. Gaddy, *Come Retribution* (Jackson: University Press of Mississippi, 1988); William A. Tidwell, *April '65: Confederate Covert Action in the American Civil War* (Kent, Ohio: Kent State University Press, 1995).

*See also:* Torpedo Bureau; Harney, Thomas F.

## Burke, Francis P. (1827–1887)

The president's coachman who drove the Lincolns and their guests to Ford's Theatre on the night of the assassination. After dropping off President and Mrs. Lincoln and Major Rathbone and Clara Harris at the front door of the theater, Burke joined Charles Forbes, the president's valet and messenger, and John F. Parker, the president's bodyguard, for a drink in the Star Saloon, located next door to the theater. Burke returned to his carriage and waited for the play to end. He returned to the White House later that night.

Burke had acquired a reputation as a heavy drinker and was so drunk on one occasion that Leonard Grover, owner of the National Theatre, personally drove Lincoln back to the White House. Lincoln's tolerance and willingness to overlook certain failings in people saved Burke his job as coachman. Burke held various government positions following the assassination, eventually becoming captain of the watch in the State Department. He died of pneumonia in 1887 and is buried in Mount Olivet Cemetery in Washington, D.C.

Sources: George S. Bryan, *The Great American Myth* (New York: Carrick & Evans, 1940), 168, 175; Frederick Hatch, "Lincoln Assassination Encyclopedia," unpublished manuscript.

**Burnett, Henry Lawrence (1838–1916)**
Burnett served as special judge advocate during the military trial of the Lincoln conspirators. Prior to his selection as special judge advocate, he served in

the Second Ohio Cavalry in Missouri, Kentucky, and Kansas. He took part in the pursuit and capture of Confederate general John Hunt Morgan and his Confederate raiders in the summer of 1863. Burnett was called to Cincinnati in 1863 to serve as the prosecutor of General Ambrose Burnside's judge advocate, who was charged with committing a crime. He acquitted himself so well that he remained a judge advocate and served in that role in the Department of the Ohio and in the Northern Department. Burnett gained the further attention of the War Department for his prosecution of Clement L. Vallandigham in 1863 and his work in the trial of Lambden P. Milligan and his associates in 1864.

Burnett was serving as judge advocate in the trial of the Confederate agents who were charged with plotting to free the Confederate prisoners held in Camp Douglas, Illinois, when he was summoned to Washington to be special judge advocate in the trial of the Lincoln conspirators.

The appointment of Burnett was most likely at the request of Judge Advocate General Joseph Holt, the man who would prosecute the case against Lincoln's accused killers. Secretary of War Edwin M. Stanton was busy with military affairs and found it increasingly difficult to divide his attention between them and the pending trial. He resolved his dilemma by turning over the investigation to Holt, a man in whom he had complete confidence. Holt and Burnett developed a deep respect for each other's capabilities.

It became Burnett's responsibility to sift through all of the material pouring into the War Department and select the evidence needed to prosecute the case. He accomplished this by contacting every officer in the field collecting evidence and having them turn the material over to him immediately. He then set up a register containing the name of the person furnishing the statement, the date, and a summary of his statement, including the names of any persons referred to in the statement. Burnett next created a set of evidence books in which he recorded a synopsis of all the statements and documents that had been collected that might prove useful to the prosecution during the trial.

The materials gathered by Burnett and his staff are currently in the National Archives and Records Administration and are reproduced on a set of seven microfilm reels in M-599, known as the "Investigation and Trial Papers Relating to the Assassination of President Lincoln." For his outstanding service as a Judge Advocate, Burnett was brevetted brigadier general of volunteers.

Sources: U.S. National Archives and Records Administration, Investigation and Trial Papers Relating to the Assassination of President Lincoln, Pamphlet Accompanying Microcopy No. 599 (Washington, D.C.: General Services Administration, 1965).

*See also:* Investigation and Trial Papers

## Burroughs, John

Known as "Peanut John" or "Peanuts." Peanuts Burroughs was the young man who held John Wilkes Booth's horse in the rear of Ford's Theatre while Booth went inside to assassinate Lincoln. One of Burroughs's jobs at the theater was to attend the stage door located in the alleyway that separated the Star Saloon and the theater. He acquired the nickname "Peanuts" from selling peanuts at the theater. Burroughs also looked after horses Booth kept at various times in a stable behind the theater.

When Booth arrived at the rear door of the theater on the night of April 14, he left his horse in the care of Edman Spangler. Spangler, busy as a sceneshifter, turned the horse over to John Debonay while he went looking for Burroughs. Finding Burroughs, Spangler sent him to the rear of the theater and told him to take care of Booth's horse. At approximately 10:30 P.M. Booth burst through the rear door of the theater. According to Burroughs's statement, Booth put one foot in the stirrup and grabbing the reins from Burroughs, struck him on the head with the butt of his bowie knife. Burroughs fell to the ground as Booth mounted the horse and galloped off down the alley.

Burroughs was called as a prosecution witness at the trial of the conspirators. Many authors have assumed Burroughs was a Negro, but the usual designation "colored" does not appear next to his name in the trial transcripts, suggesting that he was Caucasian. Several years after the assassination, Edman Spangler told of an incident in which "Booth, Maddox, Peanut John and myself" went into the Star Saloon for drinks. It seems unlikely that Peanut John would have been allowed to drink along with white men had he been black.

Sources: Joan L. Chaconas, "Will the Real 'Peanuts' Burroughs Please Rise?," *Surratt Courier* 14, no. 6 (June 1989).

## Burtles, William

A member of the Confederate mail line operating in Charles County, Maryland. Burtles lived at Hagan's Folly located a few miles east of St. Mary's Catholic Church and Bryantown in a secluded area. The house was used to shelter Confederate agents moving between Richmond and points north along the Confederate mail line. In a statement given following his arrest, Oswell Swan said that when Booth and Herold stopped by his cabin after leaving Dr. Mudd's house on Saturday evening around 9:00 P.M. they asked him to lead them to the home of William Burtles. Booth changed his mind and offered Swan twelve dollars to guide them across the Zekiah Swamp to the home of Samuel Cox, another Confederate agent known to Booth. Swan agreed and the three men arrived at Cox's home (Rich Hill) around midnight or shortly thereafter. It seems clear that Booth and Herold had planned on having Burtles guide them to Cox's home, but used Swan instead.

Burtles, William

Sources: Statement of Oswell Swan, NARA, RG 153, M-599, reel 6, frames 227–9; William A. Tidwell, James O. Hall, and David W. Gaddy, *Come Retribution* (Jackson: Mississippi, University Press of Mississippi, 1988), 445–6; Edward Steers, Jr., "Dr. Mudd's Sense of Timing: The Trip Into Bryantown," *Surratt Courier* 24, no. 9 (September 1999), 4–8.

*See also:* Hagan's Folly; Cox, Samuel; Swan, Oswell

## Caldwell, John (1828–1909)

Employed as a clerk in the store of Matthews & Knowles, a dealer in fine teas and choice groceries, located at 49 High Street (now Wisconsin Avenue) in Georgetown, District of Columbia. On Saturday morning, April 15, 1865, around 8:00 A.M., George Atzerodt entered the store of Matthews & Knowles and pawned his navy Colt revolver with Caldwell for ten dollars. Atzerodt used part of the money to purchase a ticket on the Rockville stage, which he boarded in Georgetown and rode as far as Tennallytown, D.C. Caldwell explained in his statement, "On Saturday morning April 15th, about 8 o'clock, Atzerodt came into the store & told me he was going to Montgomery Co. & asked if I did not want to buy a watch. I said I had a watch of my own & did not want any. 'Well,' said he, 'I want to borrow $10; I have not any money; I am going to my uncle's; you let me have the $10 & I will leave my revolver with you, & I will send you the money or bring it to you next week.' I let him have the $10 & kept the revolver."

Sources: Statement of John L. Caldwell, NARA, RG 153, M-599, reel 3, frame 645–47; Poore, *Conspiracy Trial,* vol. 2, 148; Pitman, *Trial,* 148.

*See also*: Atzerodt, George Andrew

## Campbell, Robert Anson

Head teller at the Ontario Bank in Montreal. Campbell was called as a prosecution witness at the military tribunal testifying to Jacob Thompson's financial transactions between May 30, 1864, and April 11, 1865. Campbell was also questioned about Booth's financial transactions in October 1864. Booth purchased a bank draft using $300 in gold and opened a savings account, depositing $200 in Montreal bills and a check for $255 from a "Mr. Davis," a Confederate money broker with an office opposite St. Lawrence Hall hotel in Montreal. Campbell's testimony helped to tie Booth to the Confederate operations in Canada.

Sources: Edward Steers, Jr., ed., *The Trial* (Lexington: University Press of Kentucky, 2003), 45–46.

*See also:* Canadian Operation

## Campbell Military Hospital

A military hospital located near Soldiers' Home, approximately two miles north of the Capitol building in the District of Columbia. On March 17, 1865, Lincoln was scheduled to attend a special performance by a group of actors from Washington for the benefit of soldiers convalescing at the hospital.

Booth, on learning from a fellow actor of Lincoln's plan to visit Campbell

Hospital, gathered his band of conspirators to attempt to capture Lincoln on his trip back to the White House following the performance. Booth had his accomplices wait at a nearby restaurant while he reconnoitered the hospital to see when Lincoln was scheduled to leave, and whether guards would accompany him. Lincoln, however, canceled his visit at the last minute to attend a special ceremony in which the 140th Indiana Volunteer Infantry presented a captured Confederate battle flag to Oliver P. Morton, the governor of Indiana. The ceremony took place in front of the National Hotel, where Booth was staying at the time.

On learning that Lincoln had canceled his appearance, Booth joined his band in waiting and the plot was aborted. But the conspirators were scared. In their paranoia they believed the government had discovered their plot and canceled Lincoln's visit to avoid his capture. Returning to the Surratt boardinghouse, John Surratt burst into the room he shared with Wiechmann. He was extremely agitated, almost shouting, "I will shoot anyone that comes into this room." Soon Powell came into the room, followed by Booth. In seeing Wiechmann, Booth and his two conspirators went upstairs to Powell's room. The whole episode upset Wiechmann and got him to thinking that something serious was up. He ex-pressed his concerns in a letter to John B. Menu, his teacher and "father confessor" at St. Charles College, where he and Surratt had been students several years before. The episode soon died away and little was thought of it again.

Sources: Edward Steers, Jr., *Blood on the Moon* (Lexington: University Press of Kentucky, 2001), 85–87.

*See also:* Capture Plots; Menu, John B.

## Canadian Operation

In the spring of 1864, Jefferson Davis established a group of Confederate secret service agents in Canada. Their principal objective was to interfere with the Union war effort, wreaking as much havoc as possible throughout the North in an attempt to demoralize the civilian population and defeat Lincoln's bid for reelection in November 1864. Davis selected Jacob Thompson of Mississippi to head the operations, and Clement C. Clay of Alabama as Thompson's assistant. William Cleary served as Thompson's personal secretary. To this group, Secretary of State Judah P. Benjamin added James P. Holcombe, a professor of law at the University of Virginia. Davis supported the operations financially by authorizing $1 million in gold from a special secret service fund appropriated by the Confederate congress in February 1864.

Headquartered in Toronto, the operation had offices in Hamilton, St. Catharine's, and Windsor, Ontario, as well as in Montreal. Patrick C. Martin, the principal Confederate agent in Canada prior to Thompson's arrival, headed the Montreal office. Among the agents working out of Montreal was George N. Sanders, a notorious character who advocated assassination as an effective political tool.

Among the activities were plots to organize paramilitary uprisings in the Midwest, the burning of select northern cities, poisoning the water supply of New York City, and a plan to infect certain cities with smallpox and yellow fever. While all of the plots were undertaken, none of them succeeded nor had an apparent effect on northern morale and Lincoln's reelection.

On October 18, John Wilkes Booth arrived in Montreal and registered at St. Lawrence Hall hotel, where Martin and other Confederate agents were living at the time. Over the next ten days, Booth was seen in the company of several agents including Patrick Martin and George Sanders. Booth arranged with Martin to have his theatrical wardrobe shipped south on one of Martin's ships. Booth also accompanied Martin to Ontario Bank, where he purchased a bank draft for more than sixty-one pounds using $300 in gold and opened a bank account depositing $200 in Montreal bills and a check for $255 from a Confederate money broker in Montreal by the name of "Davis." The bank draft was recovered from Booth's body at the Garrett farm, and Booth's Ontario Bank book showing $455 was found at the Kirkwood House in George Atzerodt's room, where Atzerodt had registered on the morning of April 14—the day of the assassination. The bankbook was a direct link between Booth and Atzerodt.

On his return to Washington, Booth opened still another account, this one in Jay Cooke's Washington bank, where he deposited $1,750. Booth dispersed all of these funds between December 20 and March 16, a period of three months immediately prior to the assassination. The source of the funds in Booth's possession while in Canada and immediately after is not known, but it is reasonable to believe Booth received part, if not all, of the funds from Patrick Martin.

When Booth left Montreal on October 27, he carried with him a letter of introduction written by Patrick Martin to Drs. William Queen and Samuel Mudd. Three weeks later Booth arrived in Charles County, Maryland, where he met with Queen and Mudd for the first of two known visits. The agents involved in the Confederate operation in Canada, whether on their own authority or Richmond's, clearly facilitated Booth's plan to capture Lincoln and turn him over to Confederate authorities in Richmond. Both the money and letter of introduction proved vital to Booth's efforts to put a plan in place to remove Lincoln from office and derail the Union's war plans.

Sources: Oscar A. Kinchen, *Confederate Operations in Canada and the North* (North Quincy, Mass.: Christopher, 1970); William A. Tidwell, *April '65: Confederate Covert Action in the American Civil War* (Kent, Ohio: Kent State University Press, 1995), 107–59.

*See also:* Martin, Patrick Charles; Thompson, Jacob

### Canning, Matthew (1830–1890)

Canning owned several playhouses in the South and signed Booth in 1860 to perform as a member of Canning's stock company. In 1863, while Booth and Canning were in Washington, Canning noticed an unusual lump on the back of Booth's neck and took him to Dr. John Frederick May. May removed the tumor with Canning acting as his assistant. Cautioned to protect the incision until it healed properly, Booth, through carelessness, allowed the sutured wound to tear open, resulting in a large, noticeable scar.

John Jack, a former actor and good friend of Canning and Booth, arrested Canning at his home in New Jersey. Jack was a captain in the 186th Pennsylvania Volunteers, serving as provost marshal in Philadelphia at the time of the assassination. While traveling to Washington, Canning told Jack about the incident in 1863 when he had assisted Dr. May in removing the tumor from Booth's neck and the unusual scar resulting from it. Jack passed the information to detectives in Washington, who sent for Dr. May. May was brought to the *Montauk* and asked to identify the body. First, he described the scar on Booth's neck, then he examined the body. The scar was where May said it would be and had the exact appearance that May described. The unusual mark was taken as proof that the corpse taken from the Garrett farm was that of John Wilkes Booth.

Canning was involved in another unusual incident with Booth. During Booth's stay in Columbus, Ohio, as a part of Canning's stock company, the two men were staying at Cook's Hotel. While practicing a scene from one of the plays that involved a pistol, Canning was attempting to release the hammer slowly when his thumb slipped, causing the gun to discharge. The bullet hit Booth in the thigh, causing a flesh wound. The wound healed slowly, causing Booth to miss several performances.

Sources: Statement of Matthew W. Canning, Jr., NARA, RG 153, M-599, reel 2, frames 36–

39; Statement of John H. Jack, NARA, RG 153, M-599, reel 5, frames 49–57.

*See also:* May, Dr. John Frederick

## Cantor, Joseph

A resident of Charles County, Maryland, believed to be a member of the Confederate underground working in Southern Maryland. During the interrogation of David Herold by military detectives following his arrest, Herold said he learned of the murder of Lincoln from "a man named Canter [Cantor]" who lived "below Bryantown."

Joseph Cantor lived approximately two miles east of Bryantown, not far from the home of Oswell Swan where Booth and Herold eventually wound up around 9:00 P.M. on the night of April 15. Herold's claim that he first heard of Lincoln's assassination from Cantor appears to be an attempt to cover up his involvement with Booth. It is likely, however, that Booth and Herold did stop by Cantor's house to find out where they were and to get directions to the home of William Burtles, which was their original destination.

Sources: Statement of David E. Herold in Laurie Verge, ed., *From War Department Files* (Clinton, Md.: Surratt Society, 1980).

## Capitol Prison

See Old Capitol Prison

## Capture Plots

The idea of capturing Lincoln and delivering him to the Confederate leadership in Richmond, where he would be exchanged for prisoners being held in Union prison camps, did not originate with John Wilkes Booth. There were at least three capture plots that we know of that have credibility. They were proposed by Colonel Joseph Walker Taylor in 1862, by Thomas Nelson Conrad in 1864, and by Brigadier General Bradley T. Johnson in 1864. Each of the proposals called for a select group of cavalrymen to intercept Lincoln on one of his regular trips to Soldiers' Home. The cavalry would overwhelm Lincoln's escort, if he had one with him, and escape across the Eastern Branch of the Potomac River into Southern Maryland, then across the Potomac into Virginia and finally to Richmond.

Lincoln, like President Buchanan before him, made use of the facilities at the Soldiers' Home as an escape from Washington during the summer months. The facility was located three miles north of the Capitol. For several months in the spring and summer Lincoln would commute daily between the White House and the summer retreat. Although provided with a cavalry escort in 1864, Lincoln frequently left for Soldiers' Home without notifying his escort, making the trip alone on horseback, much to the consternation of those who tried to protect him from potential harm.

The trips to Soldiers' Home were clearly Lincoln's Achilles' heel, which became obvious to anyone who took the time to reconnoiter the president as he traveled around the district. Among those who first observed Lincoln's peculiar travel habits was Joseph Walker Taylor. Taylor, known as Walker by his family, had requested an audience with Jefferson Davis. The nephew of former president Zachary Taylor, Walker was closely connected to Davis through Taylor's favorite cousin, Sarah Knox Taylor, daughter of former president Taylor and Davis's first wife.

Wounded at Fort Donelson, Tennessee, Taylor escaped the night before the fort was surrendered and slipped into Washington, where he spent two weeks at his uncle's house convalescing from his wounds. His uncle, it turned out, was a Union general. Families divided by the war were not uncommon, and Taylor would never think of turning in his nephew, especially if all he wanted to do was recover from his wounds. When he recovered, Taylor headed for Richmond, where he visited Jefferson Davis at the White House of the Confederacy. During breakfast one morning, Taylor told Davis about his plan to capture Lincoln and bring him to Richmond. Davis asked

Taylor how he would carry out such an audacious plan. Taylor told Davis that Lincoln seldom left the White House until evening, or near twilight, and traveled alone or with only a driver when he took his carriage. Taylor proposed to take a select group of cavalrymen and capture Lincoln and bring him to Davis.

Davis listened intently to the details of the plan and why it would prove successful. When Taylor finished, Davis responded: "I suppose Lincoln is a man of courage . . . he would undoubtedly resist being captured . . . I could not stand the imputation of having let Mr. Lincoln be assassinated."

Davis then told his nephew: "No sir, I will not give my authority to abduct Lincoln."

The second plot to capture Lincoln occurred three years later, during the summer of 1864. Brigadier General Bradley T. Johnson, a Marylander familiar with the environs around Washington, came up with a plan to capture Lincoln. Like the two previous plans, Johnson would take one hundred of his best cavalrymen and capture Lincoln as he approached the Soldiers' Home. Johnson would take a small group of soldiers with him and the captured Lincoln while the majority of his cavalrymen headed west in the opposite direction as a feint to draw Union pursuers away and thus make them chase the wrong group. Johnson took his plans to his commanding officer, General Wade Hampton. Hampton passed Johnson's request on to General Jubal Early, who put the plan on hold until after Early's attack on Washington in July 1864. With Early's defeat and the reassignment of units from his destroyed armies, Johnson's plan was never initiated.

Two months after Johnson proposed his plan, Thomas Nelson Conrad, a Confederate secret service agent, slipped into Washington for the purpose of "reconnoitering the White House . . . to ascertain Mr. Lincoln's customary movements." Conrad had lived in Washington for more than five years and was familiar with the city and its environs. As with other capture plots, Soldiers' Home became the ideal venue for snatching up Lincoln.

Like Walker Taylor before him, Conrad was a credible person, well placed in the Confederate order of things and fully capable of carrying out such an operation. There was one difference, however. Conrad appeared to be on a mission that was connected directly to the government in Richmond. In his memoir Conrad tells of receiving two letters from Jefferson Davis to Secretary of War James A. Seddon and Secretary of State Judah P. Benjamin. These letters directed the transfer of Conrad to the secret service

department and provided him with the necessary funds to finance his operation in Washington.

While in Richmond, Conrad received a second letter from Seddon, which instructed Lieutenant Colonel John Singleton Mosby and Colonel Charles H. Cawood to "aid and facilitate the movements of Captain Conrad." Mosby commanded the 43rd Battalion of Virginia Cavalry, operating primarily throughout Loudoun County, Virginia, across the Potomac River from Montgomery County, Maryland. Cawood was in command of a signal corps camp in King George County, Virginia, situated across the Potomac River from Charles County, Maryland.

As with previous plots to capture Lincoln, this one also targeted Soldiers' Home as the likely place to grab the president. Conrad's scheme called for the four men to intercept Lincoln in his carriage as he arrived at the entrance to the Soldiers' Home. Overpowering the driver, the kidnappers would make their way over the Eastern Branch of the Potomac and head into Southern Maryland along the Confederate mail line used by agents of the Confederate secret service. While there were many similarities between Conrad's plan and Booth's later plan, including the route of escape into Virginia, there is no evidence that Conrad knew of Booth or what Booth was already planning.

Suddenly, without warning, Conrad noticed that Lincoln's carriage was accompanied by a troop of cavalry. Conrad was shaken by this sudden development. He scouted the White House for the next several days trying to find out if the cavalry escort was permanent and why it had been assigned to accompany Lincoln at this time. Conrad concluded that Lincoln's escort was a permanent addition to Lincoln's guard. He aborted the plan while musing that had Lincoln "fallen into the meshes of the silken net we had spread for him he would never have been the victim of the assassin's heartless, bloody and atrocious crime."

Booth's original plot to capture Lincoln and take him to Richmond emerged during the second week of August 1864, within the same time frame that Conrad and Johnson were trying to put their plots into play. While all three plots were actively being pursued, there is no evidence that the planners knew of the other plots. Precisely when Booth first decided to capture Lincoln is not clear, but by August 1864 he had met with two former school chums, Samuel Arnold and Michael O'Laughlen, at his room in Baltimore's Barnum Hotel. Both Arnold and O'Laughlen agreed to help Booth carry out his plan. In October, Booth traveled to Montreal, where he met with Patrick Martin, the principal secret service agent in charge of the Confederacy's covert activities in that city. After ten days Booth returned to Washington bearing letters of introduction from Martin to Drs. William Queen and Samuel Mudd. Over the next three months Booth filled out his action team, getting the cooperation of Samuel Mudd, John Surratt and Mary Surratt, David Herold, George Atzerodt, and Lewis Powell.

Dramatic changes were taking place. The surrender of Robert E. Lee's Army of Northern Virginia on April 9 sounded the death knell of the Confederacy. Although there were a substantial number of Confederate soldiers still in the field, the game was up. Booth, however, believed there was still hope. He was convinced "something decisive and great" must be done. Sometime between April 11 and 14, Booth decided to change his plot from capture to assassination. For those still in his capture plot, it was too late to back out. On the night of April 14, Booth struck, killing Lincoln as he sat watching a rollicking comedy in Ford's Theatre.

The four plots to capture Lincoln and hold him as a hostage for purposes of negotiation were not far-fetched schemes. The men involved were capable and possessed the wherewithal to carry out their abduction of Lincoln. Taking Lincoln south to Richmond, however, was another matter. Having captured Lincoln, it seems certain the escape party would have been confronted at some point between Soldiers' Home and Richmond. The outcome of such a confrontation is not clear.

Sources: William A. Tidwell, James O. Hall, and David W. Gaddy, *Come Retribution* (Jackson: University Press of Mississippi, 1988), 19–21; Edward Steers, Jr., *Blood on the Moon* (Lexington: University Press of Kentucky, 2001), 24–25.

*See also:* Taylor, Joseph Walker; Conrad, Thomas Nelson; Johnson, Bradley Tyler

## Carroll Prison, also Carroll Annex, Washington, D.C.

Originally a group of wooden row houses known as Carroll Row located in northeast Washington not far from the present U.S. Capitol. Carroll Row was a group of row houses that were adjacent to the Old Capitol building located at A and First streets, N.E. When the Old Capitol building was converted into a prison in 1861, the Carroll Row buildings were taken over as the prison annex. The complex became the largest and most important prison in Washington during the Civil War and was used to hold persons accused of being "disloyal" to the Union.

William P. Wood was appointed superintendent of Old Capitol Prison and Carroll Annex in 1862 and remained superintendent through the conspiracy trial.

Mary Surratt and her daughter Anna as well as Dr. Mudd were originally held in the Carroll Annex before being transferred to the Old Federal Penitentiary cell block at the Washington Arsenal, where the conspiracy trial was held.

Sources: Dorothy Meserve Kunhardt and Philip B. Kunhardt, Jr., *Twenty Days* (New York: Harper & Row, 1965), 189–91.

*See also:* Old Capitol Prison

## Carter Ladies

Mrs. Carter and her four daughters operated a tavern located midway between the Garrett farmhouse and Bowling Green in Caroline County, Virginia. The tavern was the type that "attracted men," which was a euphemism for prostitution. On the evening of April 24, 1865, three Confederate soldiers—Bainbridge, Ruggles, and Jett—together with David Herold visited the tavern after dropping John Wilkes Booth off at the home of Richard Garrett. They drank and otherwise amused themselves before going on to Bowling Green, where Jett and Ruggles rested for the night. Herold and Bainbridge proceeded on to the farm of Virginia Clarke, three miles south of

Bowling Green. Mrs. Clarke's son Joseph was a friend of Bainbridge. The next day, April 25, Bainbridge, Herold, and Ruggles headed back to the Garrett house, stopping once again at the Trap for refreshments. Returning to the Garrett farm, Bainbridge and Ruggles dropped off Herold and continued north toward Port Royal and the ferry.

Sources: William A. Tidwell, James O. Hall, and David W. Gaddy, *Come Retribution* (Jackson: University Press of Mississippi, 1988), 467–68, 474–75; Edward Steers, Jr., *Blood on the Moon* (Lexington: University Press of Kentucky, 2001), 191–200.

*See also*: Trap, Trappe

## Cartter, David Kellogg

Chief justice of the Supreme Court of the District of Columbia. In 1863, the district judiciary underwent a reorganization, establishing a four-member supreme court in place of the existing circuit court. Cartter was appointed chief justice of the new court. On the night of April 14, Secretary of War Edwin M. Stanton sent for Cartter to come to the Petersen house to assist in questioning witnesses to the assassination. Stanton sent for two other noted jurists to assist in the questioning: Judge Abram B. Olin, also a justice on the Supreme Court of the District of Columbia, and Britten

A. Hill, a highly respected law partner of General Thomas Ewing, the attorney who would later represent Samuel Mudd, Edman Spangler, and Samuel Arnold. The three men, with Stanton at their side, interviewed the first witnesses of the assassination.

Sources: Maxwell Whiteman, ed., *While Lincoln Lay Dying* (Philadelphia: Union League of Philadelphia, 1968), 4–5.

## Catholic Conspiracy

Mid-nineteenth-century prejudice against Roman Catholics among major segments of American society manifested itself shortly after Lincoln's assassination when George Alfred Townsend, a newspaper reporter, wrote that all of the conspirators were Roman Catholics. Townsend was wrong. Only the Surratts, Mary and John, and Samuel Mudd were Catholics. There is some evidence that Booth may have converted to Catholicism shortly before his death. The fact that three of the conspirators were Catholic fed the flames of anti-Catholic bigotry at the time of the trial and shortly thereafter. In 1886, an embittered former Catholic priest by the name of Charles Pascal Telesphore Chiniquy published a book, *Fifty Years in the Church of Rome*, in which he claimed Lincoln's assassination had been carried out by American Jesuits on the orders of Pope Pius IX.

Chiniquy had been defended by Lincoln in a slander suit in the 1850s, and later claimed in his book that he had visited Lincoln on three occasions in the White House. This is extremely doubtful and there is no documentation to support Chiniquy's claim. According to Chiniquy, Lincoln had come to believe that he was a target for assassination at the hands of Jesuits.

Several writers picked up Chiniquy's theory, including Thomas M. Harris, a member of the military commission that tried the Lincoln conspirators. These writers relied heavily on Chiniquy's book and have broadened the Catholic Conspiracy to include the murders of William Henry Harrison, Zachary Taylor, and even John F. Kennedy, the latter for refusing to take direction from the pope. Behind the pope's alleged reasoning for wanting to assassinate Lincoln was his fear of American democracy. As a republican democracy, the United States posed a continuous threat to autocratic forms of government, or so the theory goes.

There is no evidence of any Catholic complicity in the plot to capture Lincoln or in his assassination. Nor is there any evidence that Lincoln feared the Roman Catholic Church or the pope. As assassination historian William Hanchett has written, "The history of Lincoln's assassination is full of lunacies." The Catholic Conspiracy is only one of many ludicrous conspiracies that are scattered over the assassination landscape.

Sources: William Hanchett, *The Lincoln Murder Conspiracies* (Urbana: University of Illinois Press, 1983).

*See also:* Chiniquy, Charles Pascal Telesphore; Conspiracy Theories.

### Cattell, Henry Pratt (1838–1915)

Senior member of Charles D. Brown and Joseph B. Alexander firm. Cattell was the actual embalmer of President Lincoln. Born September 7, 1838, in Blackwoodtown, New Jersey, Cattell enlisted in the 20th Pennsylvania Volunteer Infantry. At the end of his ninety-day enlistment he joined the Washington firm of Brown & Alexander. Cattell embalmed young Willie Lincoln, the eleven-year-old son of President Lincoln, who died on February 20, 1862. According to an interview given by Cattell in 1901, he went alone to the White House where he embalmed Lincoln using "chloride of zinc" as a preservative. Present during the embalming was the new president, Andrew Johnson. Brown & Alexander were paid $260 for their services ($100 for the embalming and $160 to accompany the body to Springfield, Illinois).

Sources: Dorothy Meserve Kunhardt and Philip B. Kunhardt, Jr., *Twenty Days* (New York: Harper & Row, 1965).

*See also*: Brown & Alexander; Brown, Dr. Charles D.

## Cawood, Charles H.

Lieutenant Charles H. Cawood was the senior officer in the Confederate Signal Corps stationed in the Northern Neck of Virginia. Cawood operated a signal camp in King George County, which bordered the Potomac River. This placed him in proximity to the traffic that crossed the Potomac between King George County and Charles County, Maryland. On September 15, 1864, Cawood and Colonel John Singleton Mosby were issued an order from Confederate secretary of war James A. Seddon directing both men to give full cooperation to Captain Thomas Nelson Conrad, who was about to enter Maryland on a secret mission. Conrad's mission was to capture Lincoln in late September 1864 and carry him to Richmond. Cawood would be available to provide whatever assistance Conrad might need in crossing over the river and in bringing Lincoln back across the river to Virginia.

Sources: Thomas Nelson Conrad, *A Confederate Spy* (New York: J. S. Ogilvie, 1892); William A. Tidwell, James O. Hall, and David W. Gaddy, *Come Retribution* (Jackson: University Press of Mississippi, 1988).

*See also:* Conrad, Thomas Nelson

## Cedar Grove

The home of Dr. Richard Stuart. Located on the Potomac River in King George County, Virginia. During the summer months Stuart often moved to his other home, known as Cleydael and located several miles south of Cedar Grove. Stuart is buried in a small family cemetery located on the Cedar Grove property. The Confederate agent Reverend Kensey Johns Stewart stayed at Cedar Grove in October 1864 after crossing the Potomac River from the Maryland side.

Sources: William A. Tidwell, James O. Hall, and David W. Gaddy, *Come Retribution* (Jackson: University Press of Mississippi, 1988).

*See also:* Cleydael; Stuart, Dr. Richard Henry

## Celestino, Joao (John)

Joao Celestino, a Portuguese sea captain, was arrested in 1864 and imprisoned on suspicion of blockade running. His small ship was confiscated and later auctioned as a war prize. Celestino was released from prison and instructed to leave the country within ten days. He remained in the country, however, and was arrested on April 18, 1865, by Lafayette Baker's men on suspicion of being involved in Lincoln's murder, then thrown into Old Capitol Prison. He was later transferred to the Old Federal Penitentiary at the Washington Arsenal along with the other

Lincoln conspirators, where he remained until his release.

While incarcerated, Celestino's photograph was taken along with those of the other male conspirators and entered into the War Department files. The photograph of Celestino has been misidentified as being that of Thomas A. Jones.

Originally a suspect, there is no evidence linking Celestino to John Wilkes Booth or the plot to assassinate Lincoln.

Sources: Theodore Roscoe, *The Web of Conspiracy* (Englewood Cliffs, N.J.: Prentice-Hall, 1959).

## Charles County, Maryland

Charles County is part of a region made up of six counties collectively known as Southern Maryland. The region, and Charles County in particular, were dependent on the cultivation and sale of tobacco during the eighteenth and nineteenth centuries. The institution of slavery, so necessary to the production of tobacco, wed Charles County to her southern brethren financially and politically. By 1860, blacks accounted for almost two-thirds of the population. Charles County was strongly Confederate in its sympathies and vehemently anti-Lincoln. So passionate was the feeling against Abraham Lincoln that a special meeting was held for the purpose of expelling, by force if necessary, the one person who was considered a pro-Lincoln advocate among the six people in the county who voted for Lincoln in the 1860 election

Following the outbreak of war, 134 men from Charles County joined the Confederate military while only one enlisted in the Union army out of 1,862 male enrollments listed in the Maryland Hall of Records. Charles County raised four militia companies intent on defending Maryland against any coercive movement on the part of the Federal government.

Charles County became a principal avenue for people and materiel moving from the North across the Potomac River into the Confederacy. Three Confederate mail lines were established through Charles County, terminating on the shoreline of the Potomac River. Charles County was the home of Dr. Samuel A. Mudd, Samuel Cox, Thomas A. Jones, Thomas Harbin, Oswell Swan, and Dr. William Queen, all implicated in one way or another with John Wilkes Booth and his plot against Lincoln, and Booth's attempted escape.

Sources: Margaret Brown Klapthor and Paul Dennis Brown, *The History of Charles County, Maryland* (La Plata, Md.: Charles County Tercentenary, 1995); Edward Steers, Jr., "Maryland My Maryland: Charles County and the War of Northern Aggression," *North & South* 6, no. 2 (February 2003), 42–51.

*See also:* Southern Maryland

## Charley

Horse rented by David Herold on the night of the assassination from John Fletcher, manager of the stables owned by Washington Naylor located at 299 E Street between Thirteen-and-a-half Street and Fourteenth Street in the District of Columbia. Charley was never returned to his owner. According to legend, the horse was led into a swamp near the pine thicket where Booth and Herold were hiding and shot to avoid leading search parties to where the two fugitives were holed up. Inasmuch as Charley was

a valuable piece of property, it seems more likely that he lived out the remainder of his years anonymously on some Charles County farm.

Sources: Statement of John Fletcher, NARA, RG 153, M-599, reel 5, frames 414–21; Poore, *Conspiracy Trial*, vol. 1, 326; Pitman, *Trial*, 83, 145; Thomas A. Jones, *J. Wilkes Booth* (Chicago: Laird & Lee, 1893), 81–82.

## Chase, Salmon Portland (1808–1873)

Lincoln's secretary of the treasury, 1861–1864. Appointed chief justice of the U.S. Supreme Court by Lincoln shortly before the assassination. Chase was at home asleep in his bed when he was awakened and told the president had been shot. He allegedly said there was nothing he could do and would only get in the way. On Saturday morning he walked past the Petersen house and when informed Lincoln was still alive, kept on walking. He eventually made his way to the Kirkwood House, where Vice President Andrew Johnson was staying. On notification that Lincoln was dead, Chase administered the oath of office to Johnson.

A little-known fact of the Lincoln assassination story is that Chase was petitioned by Dr. Samuel Mudd's attorney, Andrew Sterrett Ridgely, to have the Supreme Court rule on the jurisdiction of the military commission that tried Mudd. Chase referred Mudd's attorney to the Federal Court for the Southern District of Florida.

Federal judge Thomas Jefferson Boynton ruled against Mudd, stating that the military commission that tried Mudd had legal jurisdiction. The attorneys for Mudd, Samuel Arnold, and Edman Spangler then filed a petition with the Supreme Court on February 19, 1869. The case was argued before the Court on February 26 without Mudd as a petitioner, since President Johnson had pardoned him. Subsequent to hearing the case and before rendering a decision, Samuel Arnold and Edman Spangler were also pardoned, causing the Court to rule the question moot.

In his Rockville Lecture in 1870, John Surratt referred to the abortive attempt to capture Lincoln on his return from Campbell Hospital on March 17, 1865. Lincoln canceled his scheduled visit at the last minute and remained in Washington, frustrating Booth and his conspirators. Surratt told his audience, "To our great disappointment, however, the President was not there, but one of the government officials—Mr. Chase, if I mistake not. We did not disturb him as we needed a bigger chase than he could have afforded us." Surratt was incorrect. Chase was not on the road leading back to Washington that day, and neither were the conspirators. They were waiting at a restaurant for Booth to return from the hospital and tell them that Lincoln was there and would be leaving soon.

Sources: James E. T. Lange and Katherine DeWitt, Jr., "Mudd Habeas Corpus," *Surratt Courier* 19, no. 1 (January 1994), 5–7; James E. T. Lange and Katherine DeWitt, Jr., "Ex Parte Mudd Confirmed," *Surratt Courier* 21, no. 3 (March 1996), 4–9; Dorothy Meserve Kunhardt and Philip B. Kunhardt, Jr., *Twenty Days* (New York: Harper & Row, 1965), 68.

*See also:* Boynton, Thomas Jefferson

**Chester, Samuel Knapp (ca. 1836–1921)**

An actor and friend of John Wilkes Booth. In a meeting with Booth in New York sometime in December 1864 or early January 1865, Booth revealed his plot to Chester to capture Lincoln and take him to Richmond. Booth asked Chester to join the conspiracy. His job would be to guard the rear door at Ford's Theatre and open it, allowing Booth and his cohorts to escape with the captured president. Chester refused and although Booth persisted for several weeks to enlist him, he continued to refuse.

In a lengthy statement following the assassination, Chester told of one meeting with Booth when Booth had been drinking heavy. At one point Booth slapped the table with his hand and said, "what a splendid chance I had to kill the President on the 4th of March." Booth was referring to Lincoln's inauguration, where, Booth claimed, he had stood not far from where Lincoln gave his famous inaugural speech.

Chester testified at the conspiracy trial about Booth's attempts to recruit him. Chester told of Booth sending him fifty dollars, which he later returned. According to Chester, when he returned the money to Booth, Booth had said that he was very short of funds and that "either himself or some of the party must go to Richmond to obtain means to carry out their designs." The government prosecutors used this statement to support their claim that Jefferson Davis and others in the Confederate government were behind Booth's plot to assassinate Lincoln.

Sources: Testimony of Samuel Knapp Chester, NARA, RG 153, M-599, reel, frames 17–19; Poore, *Conspiracy Trial*, vol. 1, 43; Pitman, *Trial*, 44.

**Chiniquy, Charles Pascal Telesphore (1809–1889)**

Made claims that Jesuit priests under orders from the pope engineered the assassination of Abraham Lincoln. Chiniquy had been a Catholic priest but left the church in 1860. Chiniquy became an anti-Catholic crusader who accused the Roman Catholic Church of numerous intrigues, including Lincoln's murder and instigation of the New York draft riots in 1863. In 1886 Chiniquy published a book, *Fifty Years in the Church of Rome*, in which he claimed the pope had ordered Lincoln's assassination.

In 1851, Chiniquy led a group of his followers to northern Illinois, where they founded the small village of St. Anne's. He soon became embroiled with his bishop and was sued for slander by a friend of the bishop in the Illinois courts. His attorney was Abraham Lincoln. Lincoln worked out a settlement, leading Chiniquy to believe he had been vindicated while Lincoln had drawn the hatred of the Catholic Church. According to Chiniquy, Lincoln's victory in court led to his death in 1865 at the hands of Jesuit priests who engineered the assassination.

Chiniquy left the Catholic Church in 1860 and began a crusade against it, culminating in his "popery" theory. Subsequent authors who continued the theme as late as 1963 linking John F. Kennedy's assassination to the grand Catholic Conspiracy picked up Chiniquy's claim that the Catholic Church was behind Lincoln's murder.

Sources: William Hanchett, *The Lincoln Murder Conspiracies* (Urbana: University of Illinois Press, 1983).

*See also:* Catholic Conspiracy

## Chubb, Lewis L.

Sergeant Chubb (13th Michigan Light Artillery) was in command of the picket post at the juncture of High Street (now Wisconsin Avenue) and Military Road on Saturday, April 15, 1865. Around noon on April 15, Atzerodt took the stage from Georgetown to Rockville, Maryland. He was headed for the small community of Germantown and his cousin Hartman Richter's farm. Arriving at the army's picket post at Military Road, the stage was held up by a long line of wagons undergoing inspection by the soldiers. The soldiers were ordered to search every wagon and arrest anyone who looked suspicious. Atzerodt left the stage and walked to the head of the line, where he engaged Chubb and several other soldiers in light banter. Atzerodt offered to buy Chubb and his men a round of hard cider using the money he had received on pawning his revolver. Chubb accepted. Finishing their drinks, Atzerodt talked his way onto the farm wagon of William Gaither, who had reached the head of the line. Atzerodt bid Chubb and his men good-bye and rode all the way to Rockville with Gaither.

Chubb was court-martialed on two charges stemming from Atzerodt's passing the picket post and thus escaping the military roadblock. Chubb was accused of being drunk while in charge of the picket post, and with disobedience of orders. He was found not guilty of the charges and returned to duty.

Sources: NARA, RG 153, Records of the Judge Advocate General's Office (Army), Court Martial File MM 2513

## Cipher

A message in code resulting in a ciphertext (the enciphered text as opposed to plaintext). Both Union and Confederate governments developed systems for encrypting messages. One common method used a cipher square consisting of horizontal and vertical rows of the alphabet. By writing a special "key phrase," letter for letter, beneath the message one could form a cipher message by selecting corresponding letters from the cipher square.

A cipher square of the type used by the Confederate state department in Richmond was found in Booth's Washington hotel room when it was searched on the morning of April 15, 1865. The cipher square was identical to one found in Confederate secretary of state Judah P. Benjamin's office after the fall of Richmond. The presence of the cipher square in Booth's possession was used by the government to support its claim that the Confederate leaders in Richmond were behind Booth and his plot to assassinate Lincoln.

Following Lee's surrender at Appomattox on April 9, 1865, the Confederates changed their key phrase from "Complete Victory" to "Come Retribution."

Sources: William A. Tidwell, James O. Hall, and David W. Gaddy, *Come Retribution* (Jackson: University Press of Mississippi, 1988).

## Clampitt, John Wesley (1839–1885)

Clampitt, a Washington, D.C., attorney, was a member of Mary Surratt's defense team along with Frederick A. Aiken and Maryland senator Reverdy Johnson. Clampitt was a graduate of Columbian College Law School (currently George Washington University) in the District of Columbia.

When Reverdy Johnson retired from an active role in Mary Surratt's defense, the task fell to Clampitt and Aiken, both young attorneys with little trial experience. Even so, the two attorneys acquitted themselves admirably. The thrust of their defense centered on Mary Surratt's good character and religious devotion. It proved too little in the face of damaging evidence implicating her directly in Booth's last-minute maneuverings. After learning of Mary's conviction and death sentence, Clampitt and Aiken tried to obtain a writ of habeas corpus from Judge Andrew Wylie. Working into the early morning hours of the day of the execution, Clampitt and Aiken drafted the petition. The two lawyers went to Wylie's house and arousing him from his sleep, presented him with their request. Wylie issued the writ ordering General Hancock to produce Mary Surratt in Federal court the morning of the execution. Hancock arrived in court without Mary Surratt. Instead he presented Wylie with an executive order from President Johnson suspending the writ and ordered Hancock to carry out the sentences handed down by the military tribunal.

In 1867, Clampitt received an appointment with the U.S. Post Office Department in the Western Territory. Coincidentally, Clampitt's partner was appointed auditor for the Treasury Department. Certain people interpreted these appointments as rewards from the government for deliberately failing to defend Mary Surratt adequately. Years later, Clampitt was working on a book that he hoped would exonerate his client. Before he could finish his house caught fire and burned to the ground, destroying all of his papers. Otto Eisenschiml, the writer who attempted to lay Lincoln's assassination on Secretary of War Edwin M. Stanton, believed the fire was caused by the government to destroy evidence damaging to its case against Mary Surratt.

After the trial, Clampitt discovered that his partner, Frederick Aiken, had forged Clampitt's name on checks. Clampitt immediately dissolved the partnership and filed charges against his former partner.

Sources: Elizabeth Steger Trindal, *Mary Surratt: An American Tragedy* (Gretna, La.: Pelican, 1996); Roy Z. Chamlee, Jr., *Lincoln's Assassins* (Jefferson, N.C.: McFarland, 1990).

*See also:* Aiken, Frederick.

## Clark, William "Willie" T. (1842–1888)

Clark rented the room in the Petersen house where Lincoln was taken from Ford's Theatre. The room was located at the end of a long hallway in the rear of the house. Clark, a former private in the 13th Massachusetts, was working as clerk in the Quartermaster's Department at the time. The room measured nine and a half feet by seventeen feet and had a small dresser, chair, and simple bed that had to be pulled away from the wall to accommodate the doctors and dignitaries who occupied the room. Clark was not in his room at the time Lincoln was brought there but returned shortly afterward to find the dying president in his bed.

On the Wednesday following Lincoln's death, Clark wrote a long letter to his sister describing the events following Lincoln's death. "Hundreds daily call at the house to gain admission to my room," he wrote. "Everybody has a great desire to obtain some memento from my room, so that whoever comes in has to be closely watched for fear they will steal something." He was taken by the fact that he slept the night of Lincoln's death in the very bed in which the president died.

Clark obtained a lock of Lincoln's hair, a swatch of the linen towel that covered the pillow "with a portion of his brain," and the suit of clothes removed from Lincoln's body. Clark returned the clothes to Mary Lincoln, who later gave them to Alphonso Donn, the White House doorman.

Sources: Osborn H. Oldroyd, *The Assassination of Abraham Lincoln* (1901; reprint, Bowie, Md.: Heritage, 1990); Dorothy Meserve Kunhardt and Philip B. Kunhardt, Jr., *Twenty Days* (New York: Harper & Row, 1965).

### Clarke, Asia Booth (1835–1888)

Older sister of John Wilkes Booth. Asia Booth was the fifth child born to Junius and Mary Ann Holmes Booth. Asia's unusual name was the whimsical choice of her father. After several months had passed without choosing a name, Junius wrote to his wife while on tour, "Call the little one Asia in remembrance of that country where God first walked with man."

Asia, three years his elder, formed a close bond with her brother John. Following Junius's death in 1852, only older sister Rosalie, Asia, and John lived in the Tudor Hall home in Bel Air, Maryland. Asia and John spent most of their hours together, and Asia nurtured young John. The two were inseparable during these years in the Maryland countryside. Described as extremely bright and strong-minded by all who knew her, Asia assumed a dominant role over her younger brother. She hovered over him, schooling and encouraging him in those things she felt important. Historian Terry Alford described their relationship: "The two would pass their time in horseback riding, village dances, picnics,

camp meetings and walks in the 'wild old woods' nearby." It was an idyllic life.

Asia resembled her father in many ways. Like her father, she was highly literate and loved poetry. She also loved to write and was an accomplished correspondent. Like all the Booth children, she inherited her father's love of classical literature and his personality quirks. Small trifles could send her off sulking. Her siblings were cautioned to leave her alone during these little fits. To one of her closest friends she wrote just before her twenty-first birthday, "Oh Jean, my Jean, all is vanity." Vanity was clearly a Booth family trait, especially in young Wilkes.

While attending the school of Miss Susan Hyde in Bel Air, Asia met John Clarke Sleeper, who would become her husband in 1859. By the time the two married, John Clarke Sleeper had achieved success as an actor and changed his name to John Sleeper Clarke. Over the next ten years Asia gave birth to seven children, much to the delight of Wilkes, who played his best role as doting uncle.

By 1865 John Clarke was on top of the theatrical world as both a comic actor and theater entrepreneur. Together with his brother-in-law, Edwin Booth, he purchased Philadelphia's Walnut Street Theatre. April 14, 1865, dramatically changed the lives of Asia and her husband. In her sixth month of pregnancy with twins, Asia was devastated by her brother's murderous act. In 1868, Asia and her children joined John Clarke in London, leaving the United States behind. At first Asia loved England and her new life in London, but by 1874 she hated everything about London. Her husband's career flourished in England and in 1878 he leased the famous Haymarket Theatre. For Clarke, these became the happiest years of his life while Asia grew increasingly despondent. By 1879 the couple had become very distant emotionally and physically, sleeping in separate rooms. In a letter to her brother Edwin, Asia wrote, "It is marvelous how he hates . . . but I am a Booth—that is sufficient."

Asia sought solace in her writing. In 1865 she began a memoir of her father, to which she added a biography of Edwin. She published the work in 1882 as part of the "American Actor Series" under the title "The Elder and the Younger Booth." In 1874 she wrote a memoir of her beloved brother John. In it she provides a sister's insight, painting a sympathetic picture of John while shedding light on the darker, more complex character of her brother. She kept the little memoir private, hoping it would be published one day, but only after her death. The manuscript passed to her close friend B. L. Farjeon. After Edwin's death in 1893 and

Clarke's death in 1899, Farjeon attempted to have the manuscript published, but without success. It passed to Farjeon's daughter, who edited the memoir adding an introduction and index. In 1938, G. P. Putnam published the manuscript under the title "The Unlocked Book: A Memoir of John Wilkes Booth by His Sister Asia Booth Clarke."

Asia died on May 16, 1888, and, by her dying wish, her body was returned to the United States, where she was buried in the family plot in Green Mount Cemetery in Baltimore. Asia joined her father and favorite brother back in the city where all three had shared many happy moments together.

Asia's memoir of her brother was written from memory, since no record or personal documents of John's remained with the family. The memoir gives an important insight to a side of John Wilkes Booth and his family that is lacking in other sources. While Asia's view may be biased in some respects, it is nevertheless insightful in describing Booth's early years.

Sources: Terry Alford, ed., *John Wilkes Booth: A Sister's Memoir by Asia Booth Clarke* (Jackson: University Press of Mississippi, 1996).

*See also*: Clarke, John Sleeper; Booth, John Wilkes

## Clarke, Henry Alexander (1818–1898)

Known as Alex, Henry Alexander Clarke was a first cousin of Dr. Samuel Mudd. Clarke owned a large wood and coal yard in the District of Columbia. On March 18, 1862, Mudd wrote a letter to Clarke asking him to intercede with the War Department in helping him get back two of his father's slaves who had escaped and were being sheltered in a Union army camp on the outskirts of Washington. Mudd had tried on two occasions to get the slaves back and was rebuffed both times by the camp commander. Cousin Alex apparently had some influence with the War Department and Stanton as a result of a contract to supply wood and coal to the army.

Sources: Samuel Mudd, letter to Henry A. Clarke, March 18, 1862, NARA, RG 107, Records of the Office of the Secretary of War, Letters Received, File M-353 (102); Statement of Henry A. Clark, NARA, RG 153, M-599, reel 2, frames 948–49; Poore, *Conspiracy Trial*, vol. 3, 331; Pitman, *Trial*, 197.

## Clarke, John Sleeper (1833–1899)

Husband of Asia Booth and brother-in-law of John Wilkes Booth. Born John Clarke Sleeper, Clarke changed his name to John Sleeper Clarke at the time he launched his professional career in 1852, because as an actor he did not want to be known as Sleeper.

Clarke was a Baltimore neighbor of the Booth family when they lived on Exeter Street in the 1850s. He first met Asia at the school run by Susan Hyde. He became fast friends with Edwin Booth, and the boys joined together to give a theatrical performance at the courthouse in Bel Air, Maryland.

Clarke pursued Asia and the couple married on April 28, 1859, in Baltimore. Over the next ten years Asia and John had seven children, including twins. By 1865, Clarke had achieved considerable success as a comedic actor and theatrical entrepreneur. It all came crashing down with the assassination of Abraham Lincoln. Although Clarke opposed the South and had little use for John Wilkes Booth, he was arrested along with several members of the Booth family and held in Old Capitol Prison for a month before being released on May 27. Clarke was badly shaken by the experience.

On February 10, 1865, Booth had left a packet of papers with his sister Asia asking her to keep them in a safe place, telling her, "if anything should happen to me—open the packet alone and send the letters as directed and the money and papers give to their owners." Asia gave them to her husband, who placed the papers in a safe, where they remained forgotten until the Monday following the assassination, April 17. Included in the packet were two letters written by Booth, one to his "Dearest beloved Mother" and a second dated 1864 and addressed "To whom it may concern." The second letter was a three-page explanation of Booth's reasoning why he did what he did. Clarke, now afraid for his own safety from Federal authorities, gave the "To whom it may concern" letter to U.S. Marshal William Millward, who unexplainedly turned it over to a reporter with the *Philadelphia Inquirer*. The letter, in its entirety, was published in the April 19, 1865, *Inquirer*. The letter disappeared and remained missing for 112 years, until 1977, when assassination historian James O. Hall found it among the papers of the Justice Department in the National Archives.

In 1867, Clarke traveled to London, where he continued his career as a comedic actor. A year later he was joined by Asia and their children taking up permanent residence in England. Within the next ten years the couple had grown distant and stayed out of each other's way, sleeping in separate rooms and seldom traveling anywhere together. As Clarke's career continued to improve the couple settled into separate lives and even discussed divorce at one point.

Clarke made regular visits back to the United States, always leaving Asia behind in London. Asia became critically ill in 1888 while Clarke was in America. He hastened home in time to be with her at the time of her death. Asia had made Clarke promise to ship her body back to Baltimore so she could be buried in the family plot in Green Mount Cemetery in Baltimore. John Sleeper Clarke died in 1899.

Sources: Terry Alford, ed., *John Wilkes Booth: A Sister's Memoir by Asia Booth Clarke* (Jackson: University Press of Mississippi, 1996); John Rhodehamel and Louis Taper, *"Right or Wrong, God Judge Me"* (Urbana: University of Illinois Press, 1997), 124–31.

## Clarvoe, John (1831–1879)

A police detective who visited Mary Surratt's boardinghouse around two o'clock on the morning of Saturday, April 15, three and a half hours after Lincoln was shot. Detectives James McDevitt, Daniel Bigley, and John Kelly accompanied him. Acting on a tip that John Surratt and John Wilkes Booth were good friends, the detectives went to the boardinghouse hoping to find him there. Surratt was in Elmira, New York, at the time of the assassination on an assignment for Brigadier General Edwin Grey Lee, head of the Confederate operation in Canada. No arrests were made that night, but on Monday, April 17, Colonel Henry H. Wells, provost marshal for the defenses south of the Potomac, had enough snippets of information to send detectives from the 22nd Army Corps to the boardinghouse with orders to thoroughly search the place and arrest all of the occupants.

Sources: Testimony of James A. McDevitt, Poore, *Conspiracy Trial*, vol. 3, 381–86; Pitman, *Trial*, 140.

See also: McDevitt, James

## Clay, Clement C. (1816–1882)

A senator from Alabama and Confederate agent in Canada. Clay resigned his U.S. Senate seat in January 1861 following Alabama's withdrawal from the Union on January 11. He was offered a cabinet post as secretary of war by Jefferson Davis but declined the position,

October 1864, Clay financed Lieutenant Bennett Young and twenty Confederate soldiers in their raid on the small border town of St. Albans, Vermont. Following the arrest of fourteen of the raiders by Canadian authorities, Clay provided six thousand dollars for their defense.

Following President Lincoln's assassination on April 14, 1865, Clay, along with several other Confederate agents operating out of Canada, was accused of being behind Booth and his assassination of Lincoln. Clay turned himself in to Federal authorities in Macon, Georgia, and was imprisoned along with Jefferson Davis at Fort Monroe. Clay was never brought to trial and was eventually released in May 1866 by order of President Johnson.

Sources: William A. Tidwell, James O. Hall, and David W. Gaddy, *Come Retribution* (Jackson: University Press of Mississippi, 1988); Richard N. Current, ed., *The Confederacy* (New York: Simon & Schuster Macmillan, 1993).

*See also*: Canadian Operation; Thompson, Jacob

### Cleary, William Walter (1831–1897)

Private secretary to Jacob Thompson, a Confederate commissioner in Canada. In June 1861, Cleary was wanted by Union authorities for a serious violation that remains unknown. Whatever it was

returning to Alabama, where he was elected to a two-year term as that state's senator in the Confederate congress.

Jefferson Davis appointed Clay and Jacob Thompson in April 1864 as his commissioners in Canada. Thompson was the senior commissioner, but Clay was more actively involved in designing and carrying out Confederate missions against the North. One of Clay's principal activities was an effort to disrupt the 1864 election using members of the Copperhead organization and Order of American Knights. Clay also masterminded an attempt to burn New York City. Several hotels were set on fire but the blazes were quickly discovered and contained and thus did little damage. In

was serious enough to cause Cleary to flee to Canada to avoid arrest. He later returned to the United States and eventually made his way to Richmond, where he worked in the auditor's office. In April 1864, Cleary returned to Canada to serve as private secretary to Thompson. As Thompson's secretary, Cleary was privy to much of the clandestine activity being sponsored by the Confederate agents in Canada. In May 1865, Confederate agent Luke Pryor Blackburn faced charges of violating Canada's Neutrality Act for his effort to initiate yellow fever epidemics among military and civilian populations. The prosecution dropped a bombshell into Blackburn's trial when it introduced a deposition from Cleary admitting he was well acquainted with Blackburn and Godfrey Joseph Hyams, having "met them on several occasions in Canada." Cleary told the court that Blackburn had told him "that he had [Hyams] employed to distribute . . . clothing which he had prepared, I think he said at Bermuda, infected with the yellow fever." Cleary confirmed Hyams's claim that Blackburn was involved in a yellow fever plot. Cleary's deposition left the impression that, while he knew about Blackburn's scheme, neither he nor Thompson had anything to do with it. The Confederate commissioners had clean hands, suggesting Blackburn acted alone in a rogue operation. According to Hyams's testimony, however, it was Thompson who paid Hyams one hundred dollars at Blackburn's request to distribute the infected clothing in certain cities in an attempt to start yellow fever epidemics. Fortunately, yellow fever is not an infectious disease, but one that is transmitted by a mosquito, not human contact. Blackburn's plot failed.

The evidence against Blackburn, although circumstantial, was considerable. Cleary's affidavit provides proof that the Confederate commissioners in Canada had knowledge of Blackburn's plot to undertake germ warfare against both military and civilian targets. Cleary was among the Confederate leaders charged at the conspirators' trial with conspiring with John Wilkes Booth and his associates to assassinate Abraham Lincoln. A ten-thousand-dollar reward was offered by the U.S. government for his capture. Cleary successfully evaded the authorities and was never tried as an accomplice to Lincoln's assassination.

Sources: William A. Tidwell, *April '65: Confederate Covert Action in the American Civil War* (Kent, Ohio: Kent State University Press, 1995), 107–59; "The Great Fever Plot," *New York Times*, May 26, 1865, 5, cols. 3 and 4.

*See also:* Blackburn, Luke Pryor

**Clemency Plea**

A recommendation of mercy for Mary Surratt by five members of the military tribunal. Following the sentencing of Mary Surratt to death by hanging, five members of the tribunal sent an appeal to commute her sentence to President Andrew Johnson that read:

> The undersigned members of the Military Commission detailed to try Mary E. Surratt and others for the conspiracy and the murder of Abraham Lincoln, late president of the United States, do respectfully pray the President, in consideration of the sex and age of the said Mary E. Surratt, if he can upon all the facts in the case, find it consistent with his sense of duty to the country to commute the sentence of death to imprisonment in the penitentiary for life.

David Hunter, August Kautz, Robert Foster, James Ekin, and Charles Tomkins signed the plea. Not signing were Lew Wallace, Albion Howe, Thomas Harris, and David Clendenin.

The plea soon developed into a major controversy involving Judge Advocate General Joseph Holt and President Johnson. Johnson later claimed Holt never showed him the plea document at the time he presented him with the sentencing document for his signature. Holt insisted he had shown Johnson the plea and that Johnson had simply ignored it, choosing not to commute Mary Surratt's sentence. The controversy continues to the present, with advocates on both sides of the question. It did Mary Surratt little good.

Sources: Roy Z. Chamlee, Jr., *Lincoln's Assassins* (Jefferson, N.C.: McFarland, 1990), 440–42.

**Clendenin, David Ramsey (1830–1895)**

A member of the military tribunal that judged those charged with Lincoln's assassination. Clendenin was chosen to replace Colonel Horace Porter, who was able to get himself removed from the tribunal. Born in Lancaster County, Pennsylvania, Clendenin was a graduate of Knox College in Galesburg, Illinois. At the time he was selected to serve on the military tribunal, Clendenin was Lieutenant Colonel of the Eighth Illinois Cavalry. He was one of four members of the military tribunal that did not sign a clemency plea on behalf of Mary Surratt.

Sources: Roger D. Hunt and Jack R. Brown, *Brevet Brigadier Generals in Blue* (Gaithersburg, Md.: Olde Soldiers, 1990).

**Cleydael**

Summer home of Dr. Richard Stuart, located in King George County, Virginia. After Booth and Herold crossed the Po-

tomac River on Saturday night, April 22, they made contact with the Confederate agent Thomas Harbin through the help of Mrs. Elizabeth Quesenberry. Harbin arranged for the two men to be supplied with mounts and taken to Cleydael by one of Harbin's agents, William Bryant. Booth had expected Stuart to provide him shelter and comfort for the night and to help him get to Port Royal on the Rappahannock River, where he could cross into Caroline County. According to David Herold, the two fugitives had been directed to Stuart's house by Dr. Samuel Mudd, leading them to believe Stuart would help them much as Mudd had.

Booth and Herold, led by Bryant, arrived at Cleydael late Sunday evening only to find Dr. Stuart unreceptive to their staying at his house. Stuart provided the two men with food and then told Bryant to take them to the cabin of a free black by the name of William Lucas, who lived a short distance from Cleydael. Booth and Herold spent the night at the Lucas cabin before continuing on to Port Royal on Monday morning.

Cleydael remains today as a private residence, nearly unchanged from its appearance in April 1865.

Sources: Edward Steers, Jr., *Blood on the Moon* (Lexington: University Press of Kentucky,

2001); Statement of Richard Stuart, NARA, RG 153, M-599, reel 6, frames 205–11.

See also: Stuart, Dr. Richard Henry

## Clinton, Maryland

Current name for Surrattsville, Maryland. Clinton is located in Prince George's County, Maryland, approximately thirteen miles from Washington, D.C. It is the site of the Surratt House and Museum and headquarters for the Surratt Society. Formerly the village of Surrattsville, the name was changed to Robeystown after Andrew V. Robey. Robey replaced John H. Surratt, Jr., who was removed as postmaster in 1863 presumably due to his Confederate underground activities. In 1878 the name was changed to its present designation of Clinton. The origin of the name Clinton is unknown.

Sources: Laurie Verge, "Why Clinton?," *Surratt Society News* 4, no. 6 (June 1979).

See also: Surrattsville

## Cloud, Daniel Mountjoy (1837–1871)

Partner of Confederate agent Thomas Nelson Conrad in plot to capture President Lincoln in the summer of 1864. As with previous plots to capture Lincoln, this one also targeted Soldiers' Home as the likely place to kidnap the president. To carry out his plan of capture, Conrad enlisted the help of three other individuals who were well-known to him. The first was Daniel Mountjoy Cloud. Cloud had been a classmate at Dickinson College and a good friend of Conrad. The two men had worked together previously and were confident of each other's capabilities.

Conrad's scheme called for intercepting Lincoln in his carriage as he arrived at the entrance to the Soldiers' Home. Conrad would be in the lead of the carriage while Mountjoy covered the rear. After capturing Lincoln the entourage would make its way over the Eastern Branch of the Potomac and head into Southern Maryland along the Confederate mail line used by agents of the Confederate secret service.

Conrad abandoned the plot after observing that Lincoln's carriage was accompanied by a troop of cavalry (members of the Union Light Guard from Ohio). He concluded, wrongly, that Lincoln was too heavily guarded to make a successful attempt to capture him.

Sources: Thomas Nelson Conrad, *The Rebel Scout* (Washington, D.C.: National, 1904), 118–19; William A. Tidwell, James O. Hall, and David W. Gaddy, *Come Retribution* (Jackson: University Press of Mississippi, 1988), 283.

See also: Conrad, Thomas Nelson

## Cloughley, Alfred

Clerk in the Second Auditor's Office in the District of Columbia. Cloughley was the first witness interviewed in the Petersen house on the night of the assassination. Cloughley was walking with a lady friend near the Seward home at the time Powell emerged. Cloughley ran after the man but he rode off on his horse. Cloughley testified that the man rode up "15th Street North" amid shouts of "murder & stop thief." Cloughley made his way into the Seward home and found Frederick Seward covered in blood. Believing Seward was dead, Cloughley ran to the White House, where he told the officer in charge of Lincoln's mounted guard that Seward was murdered and the killer was headed north along Fifteenth Street. He then headed toward Ford's Theatre, thinking he would get word to the president, only to learn that Lincoln had been shot. Despite witnessing Powell's flight from the Seward house, Cloughley was not called as a witness at the conspirator's trial.

Sources: Statement of Alfred Cloughley, NARA, M-599, roll 7, frames 473–80; Maxwell Whiteman, ed., *While Lincoln Lay Dying* (Philadelphia: Union League of Philadelphia, 1968).

## Coal Bomb

An explosive device intended to resemble a large lump of coal. The Torpedo Bu-

reau of the Confederate military had developed a large number of explosive devices collectively known as "torpedoes." Among these devices was one that was different from any other explosive device known to Union munitions experts. It was made of cast iron and resembled a large chunk of coal. These "coal" bombs were designed to be placed in bins with real coal and eventually make their way into furnaces and boilers in northern manufactories and ships. The U.S. Consul in Canada described one such coal bomb in his dispatch to Washington:

These torpedoes [an explosive mine] are covered with a mixture of broken coal & pitch, & resemble pieces of Bituminous coal—[the bombs] are made of thin cast iron of irregular shapes, hollow & are filled with powder—& covered with the preparation above mentioned . . . that they are to be thrown into coal bins in manufactories, steam boats, furnaces, etc. where they will without being noticed, be shoveled along with the coal into the fire, & effect the purpose for which they were designed.

The inventor of the coal bomb was Thomas Edgeworth Courtenay. In December 1863, Courtenay wrote to Jefferson Davis proposing to organize a "secret Service corps" for the purpose of "doing injury to the enemy." More specifically, Courtenay proposed to operate against Union shipping on the Mississippi River and its tributaries using principally his newly invented coal bomb. On March 9, 1864, Courtenay received authorization to employ a band of men not to exceed twenty-five. It is difficult to determine just how effective Courtenay's coal bomb and secret service corps was during the short period it operated. The clever concept of the coal bomb made its way into the U.S. Office of Strategic Services manual during World War II.

Union colonel Edward Hastings Ripley had found just such a coal bomb in a cabinet in Jefferson Davis's office in April 1865. Ripley commanded the first echelon of Union troops to occupy Richmond following its evacuation and took advantage of his situation by visiting the White House of the Confederacy, where he found a coal bomb left behind when Davis fled the capital. Intrigued by the device, Ripley sent it home to his father as a war souvenir.

Godfrey Joseph Hyams, a Confederate agent in Canada, first described coal bombs to Union authorities. Hyams gave important evidence against the Confederate agents operating out of Canada.

Sources: Thomas E. Courtenay, letter to Jefferson Davis, December 7, 1863, family papers, Thomas Thatcher; James A. Seddon, letter to Thomas Courtenay, March 9, 1864, family papers, Thomas Thatcher; Thomas E. Courtenay, letter to Laughlin A. Maclean, family papers, Thomas Thatcher; *New York Times*, May 18, 1865; David Thurston, U.S. Consular Dispatches, NARA, T-491, rolls 1, 3.

*See also:* Courtenay, Thomas Edgeworth; Hyams, Godfrey Joseph

## Cobb, Silas T. (1838–1867)

Cobb was in charge of the army detail guarding the Navy Yard Bridge on the night of April 14, 1865. Cobb allowed Booth, and later Herold, to cross over the bridge and out of Washington only minutes after Booth shot Lincoln. Cobb was a member of Company F, Third Massachusetts Infantry, stationed at Fort Baker located atop Good Hope Hill in the Anacostia region of the district. Orders specifically against allowing persons to pass over the bridge between the hours of 9:00 P.M. and daylight were still in effect on the night of April 14.

General Order No. 5, issued on January 24, 1863, stated, "No person excepting General Officers will be passed over any of the several crossings between the hours of 9:00 P.M. and daylight without the countersign and a pass."

Cobb was reprimanded by Major General Christopher C. Augur, but was not arrested or subjected to a court martial for allowing Booth and Herold to pass over the bridge. This fact has led some writers to conclude that a greater conspiracy existed involving Secretary of War Edwin M. Stanton and others. However, it appears the rules had been relaxed following General Lee's surrender five days earlier. The threat to the city, if there was one, came from individuals entering the city, not leaving it.

Sources: Edward Steers, Jr., *Blood on the Moon* (Lexington: University Press of Kentucky, 2001), 135–36; James L. Swanson, *Manhunt: The 12-Day Chase for Lincoln's Killer* (New York: Harper Perennial, 2007), 66–68.

*See also:* Bridge Crossing; Navy Yard Bridge

## Comstock, Cyrus Ballou

A member of the regular army at the outbreak of the war, Comstock rose to the rank of brevet major general for meritorious service during the campaign against the city of Mobile, Alabama. He was serving as an aide-de-camp on the staff of General Ulysses S. Grant when appointed to the military tribunal. He was deeply opposed to the military trial, writing in his diary, "They ought to be tried by civil courts." He further objected to what he believed would be a secret court behind closed doors. Comstock apparently clashed with chief prosecutor Joseph Holt, questioning the legal jurisdiction of the court. Comstock was soon replaced by Brevet Brigadier General James Ekin presumably because they were aides to Grant, who was an alleged target of the assassins.

Sources: Anthony Pitch, *"They Have Killed Papa Dead"* (Hanover, N.H.: Steerforth, 2008), 314–15.

*See also:* Porter, Horace

## Conger, Everton Judson (1834–1918)

The de facto leader of the military contingent that captured David Herold and killed John Wilkes Booth. Conger had served as lieutenant colonel of the First District of Columbia Cavalry under the command of Colonel Lafayette C. Baker.

When Secretary of War Edwin M. Stanton picked Baker to head up the National Detective Police (NDP), the First District Cavalry was assigned to Conger, who served as its commander. In September 1863, Conger, recently recovered from a wound in his side, was transferred from the Third West Virginia Cavalry to the First District Cavalry and promoted to lieutenant colonel. Wounded a second time while attempting to destroy a bridge over the Staunton River in Virginia, Conger was mustered out of service in November 1864 and Baker appointed him a detective with his NDP.

While visiting Major Thomas Eckert in the War Department telegraph office, Baker read a telegram that claimed that two men had crossed the Potomac River from Maryland to Virginia on Sunday, April 16. Although the two men were misidentified as Booth and Herold, Baker was able to secure a contingent of twenty-six troopers of the 16th New York Cavalry under the command of Lieutenant Edward P. Doherty. Baker attached his two top detectives, cousin Luther Byron Baker and Conger, telling Doherty that Conger would be in command of the contingent even though he was no longer in the military.

The party traveled down the Potomac River aboard the ship *John S. Ide* and landed at Belle Plain, Virginia. From here they made their way to Port Conway on the Rappahannock River and then to the Garrett farm near Bowling Green, where Herold was captured and Booth killed.

Conger came to Sergeant Boston Corbett's defense when critics accused him of violating strict orders not to shoot. "They had no orders to fire or not to fire," Conger told his superiors. Corbett told the military tribunal when questioned about the shooting, "I thought he would do harm to our men in trying to fight his way through that den if I did not."

After considerable negotiations on the part of congress, Conger received fifteen thousand dollars of reward money as a result of his role in capturing Booth. He later lost a portion of the reward money through a loan to Lafayette Baker for a hotel scheme that failed. Retiring from the NDP, Conger settled in Carmi, Ohio, before taking a position of associate justice of the Territory of Montana Supreme Court in 1884. He was removed from that position in 1884 due to an alleged drinking problem. He opened a law office in Dillon, Montana, and was elected prosecuting attorney in 1887 and again in 1892. Conger died of a stroke in 1918 at the age of eighty-four in Honolulu, Hawaii. His body was returned to Dillon for burial.

Sources: Statement of Everton J. Conger, NARA, RG, 94, M-619, reel 455, frames 691–703; William A. Tidwell, James O. Hall, and David W. Gaddy, *Come Retribution* (Jackson: University Press of Mississippi, 1988); Rob Wick, "'Blood on the Moon': Capturing Booth," *Carmi Times*, June 24, 1998, 1.

### Conness, John (1821–1909)

A U.S. senator from California. Born in Ireland, Conness emigrated to New York in 1833 and moved to California in 1849. Conness was elected to the U.S. Senate, serving from March 4, 1863, until March 3, 1869. An influential member of the Senate, Conness was made a part of the "Stanton murdered Lincoln" conspiracy and appeared in the fabricated "missing pages" from Booth's diary. Conness was further implicated in the conspiracy to murder Lincoln when an important and highly damaging entry from Indiana congressman George Julian's extensive Civil War journals was allegedly discovered, telling of a secret meeting in Stanton's office between Stanton, Conness, Julian, and Senator Zachariah Chandler of Michigan. Julian's alleged entry had the four men discussing the missing pages identifying all four of them as members of the murder conspiracy. The meeting resulted in covering up the conspiracy. The journal entry is believed by prominent historians and Lincoln scholars to be a fabrication. Conness moved to Boston after his Senate term expired and died in 1909 at the age of eighty-eight.

Sources: Edward Steers, Jr., and Joan L. Chaconas, "*Dark Union*: Bad History," *North & South* 7, no. 1 (January 2004), 12–30.

*See also:* Conspiracy Theories

### Conover, Sandford (ca. 1832–1900)

See Dunham, Charles A.

### Conrad, Thomas Nelson (1837–1905)

Thomas Nelson Conrad was head of a Confederate-backed plot to capture President Lincoln in the summer of 1864. Conrad taught at the Georgetown Institute in the District of Columbia until his arrest in June 1861 as a southern sympathizer. Conrad was arrested and imprisoned in the Old Capitol Prison in Washington, D.C. After several months he was paroled and made his way to Richmond, where he enlisted in Jeb Stuart's Cavalry Corps. A lay preacher, Conrad was appointed chaplain for the Third Virginia Cavalry. He spent most of his time functioning as a "scout."

In 1864, Conrad was plucked from his position with Stuart and placed in the employ of the Confederate secret service. In September of that year he slipped into Washington on a plan to capture Lincoln and carry him to Richmond. As with other capture plots, Soldiers' Home became the ideal venue for snatching up Lincoln. In his memoir, Conrad explained his mission:

> We had to determine at what point it would be most expedient to capture the carriage and take possession of Mr. Lincoln; and then whether to move with him through Maryland to the lower Potomac [Charles County] and cross or to the upper Potomac [Montgomery County] and deliver the prisoner to Mosby's Confederacy for transportation to Richmond. . . . [H]aving scouted the country pretty thoroughly . . . we

finally concluded to take the lower Potomac.

Conrad's mission, unlike those previously planned, appears to have been directed out of Judah Benjamin's office. In his memoir Conrad tells of receiving two letters from Jefferson Davis to Secretary of War James A. Seddon and Secretary of State Judah P. Benjamin. These letters directed the transfer of Conrad to the secret service department and provided him with the necessary funds to finance his operation in Washington.

While in Richmond, Conrad received a second letter from Seddon on War Department letterhead, dated September 15, 1864, that directed Lieutenant Colonel John Singleton Mosby and Colonel Charles H. Cawood to "aid and facilitate the movements of Captain Conrad." Mosby commanded the 43rd Battalion of Virginia Cavalry, operating primarily throughout Loudoun County, Virginia, across the Potomac River from Montgomery County, Maryland. Cawood was in command of a signal corps camp in King George County, Virginia, situated across the Potomac River from Charles County, Maryland. These two areas represented the "upper Potomac" and "lower Potomac" referred to by Conrad in his memoir. The two Maryland counties were avenues into Washington that Confederate agents used with great success throughout the war. Both were potential escape routes for a capturing party carrying the president from his summer quarters at Soldiers' Home to Virginia and the Confederate capital, Richmond. Seddon's letter was just one more dot making up the overall picture that tied Davis and his subordinates to an effort to remove Lincoln from the presidency.

Conrad's scheme called for the four men to intercept Lincoln in his carriage as he arrived at the entrance to the Soldiers' Home. The entourage would make its way over the Eastern Branch of the Potomac and head into Southern Maryland along the mail line used by agents of the Confederate secret service. While there were many similarities between Conrad's plan and John Wilkes Booth's later plan, including the route of escape into Virginia, Conrad's operation appeared to be independent of Booth's.

Conrad scouted the White House for the next several days. The cavalry troop assigned to accompany Lincoln on his trips to and from the Soldiers' Home worried Conrad. After reconsidering his chances of overcoming such a large cavalry unit, he aborted his plan. He couldn't help musing, however, that had Lincoln "fallen into the meshes of the silken net we had spread for him, he would never have been the victim of the assassin's heartless, bloody and atrocious crime."

Conrad's own account of his mission to Washington to observe Lincoln's movements for a capture operation seems authentic. The extant documents authorizing full support for his movements by Seddon and Benjamin suggest a direct link to Confederate leaders. It is doubtful that these two secretaries would be supporting Conrad without the knowledge and approval of Davis. Of importance, Conrad's activities were financed with Confederate secret service funds. On January 10, two months after he had aborted his capture mission, Conrad wrote to Secretary of War Seddon stating that he had received four hundred dollars in gold from Secretary of State Benjamin to cover his expenses over the past four months. Conrad further states in his letter that the gold was converted into one thousand dollars in northern funds (greenbacks). The authorization of gold payments from the special secret service fund required the authorization of Davis. That Lincoln was the target of a capture plot known by Jefferson Davis seems certain.

Sources: Thomas Nelson Conrad, *A Confederate Spy* (New York: J. S. Ogilvie, 1892); Thomas Nelson Conrad, *The Rebel Scout* (Washington, D.C.: National, 1904); William A. Tidwell, *April '65: Confederate Covert Action in the American*

*Civil War* (Kent, Ohio: Kent State University Press, 1995), 69–71.

*See also:* Capture Plots; Seddon, James Alexander

## Conspiracy Theories

Even before Abraham Lincoln's body was placed in the ground, conspiracy theories were taking hold in the public's mind. Thomas Harris, a member of the military tribunal, was a strong believer that Pope Pius IX had ordered Lincoln's assassination and chose American Jesuits to carry it out. Anti-Catholic bigotry was prominent at the time of the Civil War and it was an easy sell to those who already hated the Roman Catholics. Accusations were made that all of the conspirators were Catholic, and plotted under orders from Rome. In fact, only three of the conspirators were Catholic: Samuel Mudd, Mary Surratt, and her son, John. Asia Booth Clarke, John's sister, wrote in a letter to her close friend, Jean Anderson, that her brother John "was of that faith," but documentary proof is lacking. Michael O'Laughlen and Samuel Arnold were Methodists, George Atzerodt a Lutheran, and Lewis Powell a Baptist. The claim that the pope was responsible for Lincoln's murder still lives and can be found on the Internet.

The most widely believed conspiracy today claims that Lincoln's own secretary of war, Edwin M. Stanton, planned the president's death. In 1937, Otto Eisenschiml, a chemist turned historian, published his book, *Why Was Lincoln Murdered?* Eisenschiml posed a series of questions and carefully manipulated the data to show Stanton headed a group of powerful politicians and financiers who wanted Lincoln out of the way so they could plunder the South following the war. More recent authors have picked up Eisenschiml's thesis, and while they have changed the reasons for killing Lincoln, they still place the blame on Stanton.

The most controversial conspiracy theory is one that claims Lincoln's assassination can be traced to the Confederacy's president, Jefferson Davis. While there is no direct evidence linking Davis to Lincoln's death, there are several smoking guns that point in his direction. In the spring of 1864, Jefferson Davis selected Jacob Thompson of Mississippi to head a clandestine operation out of neutral Canada. Davis supported the operation by authorizing $1 million in gold from a special secret service fund appropriated by the Confederate congress in February 1864. Thompson established his headquarters in Toronto with offices in Montreal and the Ontario cities of St. Catharine's, Hamilton, and Windsor.

The main objective of the Canadian operation was to weaken northern morale such that Lincoln would be defeated in his bid for reelection in 1864. Davis knew that as long as Lincoln was in office there was little to no chance of an independent Confederacy. Among the various actions plotted were efforts to burn major northern cities, poison the water supply for New York City, liberate southern prisoners from northern prison camps, and unleash epidemics of smallpox and yellow fever in select cities. While all of these plots were attempted, none of them succeeded. With the fall of Atlanta in August 1864, along with the Confederate defeats at the battles of Winchester, Fisher's Hill, and Cedar Creek in Shenandoah Valley in September and October, northern morale never ran higher and Lincoln's reelection was assured.

Booth's connection to Davis's agents in Canada over a ten-day period in October is well documented. To what extent, if any, these agents helped Booth in preparing his capture plot is unclear. While there is circumstantial evidence linking Davis's agents to Booth, there is no evidence that the agents helping Booth did so with Jefferson Davis's approval or knowledge.

Sources: William Hanchett, *The Lincoln Murder Conspiracies* (Urbana: University of Illinois Press, 1983); William A. Tidwell, James O. Hall, and David W. Gaddy, *Come Retribution* (Jackson: University Press of Mississippi, 1988), 171–211.

*See also:* Canadian Operation; Catholic Conspiracy; Eisenschiml, Otto

## Conspirators

The government believed ten individuals were responsible for Lincoln's murder: Samuel B. Arnold, George A. Atzerodt, John Wilkes Booth, David Herold, Samuel A. Mudd, Michael O'Laughlen, Lewis T. Powell, Edman Spangler, John H. Surratt, Jr., and Mary E. Surratt. Booth was killed resisting arrest, and John Surratt escaped to Canada, where he was given sanctuary by several people before ending up at the rectory of Father Charles Boucher in St. Liboire, Quebec, some thirty miles west of Montreal. Surratt remained at Boucher's rectory throughout the trial and execution of his mother. He eventually made his way to Italy, where he served as a papal guard in the Vatican before his discovery and capture in 1867.

In addition to the eight conspirators in custody, the government charged several individuals not in custody as coconspirators of Booth: Jefferson Davis, George N. Sanders, Beverly Tucker, Jacob Thompson, William C. Cleary, Clement C. Clay, George Harper, and George Young. In an effort to make sure they did not overlook anyone, the government added to the charge "and others unknown." These individuals, with the exception of Jefferson Davis, were members of the Confederacy's secret service operation in Canada. The government was convinced that members of this organization, under orders from Jefferson Davis, had aided Booth. When the military tribunal began, none of these individuals was in custody. Davis was captured on May 10 but never brought to trial. Clement Clay turned himself in to authorities and was imprisoned along with Jefferson Davis, but was eventually released without being tried.

Within a few hours of Lincoln's assassination, several agencies of the U.S. government and local law enforcement groups were busy rounding up suspects. Over a period of two weeks, hundreds of individuals were swept up in the government's dragnet and thrown into prison, including those unlucky enough to be needed as witnesses in support of the government's case against the conspirators. Most of these individuals had no connection to Booth or to his plot to remove Lincoln from office. There were others, however, who were involved with Booth to varying degrees, enough to warrant their prosecution. Among these shadow conspirators were Samuel Cox, Thomas Jones, Thomas Harbin, William Bryant, Elizabeth Quesenberry, Richard Stuart,

and Patrick Martin (Martin died in December 1864, when the ship he was on, the *Marie Victoria*, sank near Bic, Quebec). Although these individuals were arrested they were eventually released. The government was unaware of their connection to Booth until many years later.

Sources: William A. Tidwell, James O. Hall, and David W. Gaddy, *Come Retribution* (Jackson: University Press of Mississippi, 1988).

*See also*: Cox, Samuel; Jones, Thomas Austin; Harbin, Thomas Henry; Bryant, William; Quesenberry, Elizabeth Rousby; Stuart, Dr. Richard Henry; Martin, Patrick Charles

## Cooke, Jay

Prominent Philadelphia financier and banker. John Wilkes Booth opened a checking account in Cooke's Washington bank shortly after returning from Canada, depositing $1,750 in all. Booth dispersed all of this money within three months of the assassination. The source of the funds is unknown but Booth had traveled to Canada in October 1864, one month before the deposit, where he was seen meeting with Confederate agents at St. Lawrence Hall hotel in Montreal. Some historians have speculated Booth received the money from these Confederate agents to help finance his capture operation. The funds were completely expended by March 16, 1865, one month before Booth assassinated President Lincoln.

Treasury Secretary Salmon Chase contracted with Cooke to broker large amounts of U.S. government bonds to help finance the war. Cooke was a major force in selling the bonds and raising money for the Union war effort. Both Jay Cooke and his brother Henry (dealing in the cotton trade during the war) are listed in the alleged missing pages of Booth's diary implicating both brothers in Booth's plot to kill Lincoln.

Sources: William A. Tidwell, James O. Hall, and David W. Gaddy, *Come Retribution* (Jackson: University Press of Mississippi, 1988); ledger sheet, Jay Cooke & Co. account with J. Wilkes Booth, manuscript collection, Chicago Historical Society.

## Copperhead

A derogatory term coined during the Civil War to describe northern "peace Democrats" who opposed the Lincoln administration and supported southern independence. The term was used to equate such Democrats with the poisonous snake of that name. *Copperhead* was used broadly to taint any Democrat who opposed Lincoln's policies irrespective of whether they supported the Confederacy. While the Democratic Party was divided into two camps, known as "peace Democrats" and "war Democrats," peace Democrats were vilified as disloyal to the Union and therefore Copperheads.

Several subversive paramilitary organizations arose during the war that were swept under the Copperhead umbrella. These included the Knights of the Golden Circle (KGC), the Order of American Knights (OAK), and the Sons of Liberty (SOL). While these organizations were pro-secession and anti-Lincoln, and therefore "Copperhead," there is no evidence that they were in any way connected with the legitimate Democratic opposition to Lincoln and his policies.

Sources: Jennifer L. Weber, *Copperheads* (New York: Oxford University Press, 2006).

*See also:* Knights of the Golden Circle; Order of American Knights

## Corbett, Boston

The man who shot John Wilkes Booth was Sergeant Boston Corbett, a member of the 16th New York Cavalry. He was one of the twenty-six cavalrymen chosen to accompany Everton J. Conger and Luther B. Baker under orders from Colonel Lafayette C. Baker in pursuit of Booth and Herold. Corbett openly admitted to shooting Booth and later told his superiors, "I immediately took steady aim upon him with my revolver and fired shooting him through the neck and head." Dur-

ing the conspiracy trial Corbett elaborated on his actions: "It was not through fear at all that I shot him, but because it was my impression that it was time the man was shot; for I thought he would do harm to our men in trying to fight his way through the den, if I did not."

Corbett's act would become part of the stuff that conspiracies are made of. It would be repeated over and over that Corbett carried secret orders from Edwin M. Stanton to make sure Booth could never talk or tell his story. Too many people would be dragged down if Booth had been allowed to live. Some would

say Conger shot Booth and that Corbett agreed to take the fall. Still others would claim Booth shot himself, committing suicide before he could be dragged back to Washington and exhibited like a crazy animal. They would all be wrong. Boston Corbett was telling the truth. He did shoot Booth and with reason, although not everyone can accept his reasoning.

With Booth cornered on Richard Garrett's tobacco farm near Bowling Green, Virginia, attempts to talk Booth into surrendering failed. The barn was set on fire and shortly thereafter a shot was fired, striking Booth in the neck and partially severing his spinal cord. The shot proved mortal. Corbett was placed under temporary arrest and taken back to Washington, where he was brought to Stanton. Lieutenant Edward P. Doherty, Corbett's commanding officer, defended Corbett, telling Stanton that Corbett was a brave and good soldier who volunteered to go into the barn and confront Booth. In fact, Corbett offered twice to Doherty to go into the barn and bring Booth out. Stanton decided to release Corbett, stating that "the rebel is dead; the patriot lives."

Corbett was born in England but soon came to Boston, where he underwent a religious experience becoming "born again." One evening after a religious meeting he castrated himself to remove all temptation by prostitutes. He adopted the name "Boston" presumably to honor the city of his "religious rebirth," pointing out that each of the disciples took new names after joining with Jesus. He was employed as a hatter at the time the war broke out and joined the 12th New York Volunteer Infantry on April 19, 1865. He reenlisted a total of three times, eventually winding up as sergeant in Company L of the 16th New York Cavalry.

After the war, Corbett moved around to several cities and occupations before landing the position of doorkeeper for the Kansas House of Representatives in 1887. His mental health slowly deteriorated. He was judged insane and committed to an asylum after waving a revolver and threatening several representatives in the Kansas state capitol. A year later, in 1888, he escaped from the asylum and disappeared, never to be heard from again. The gun Corbett shot Booth with was stolen from Corbett's tent.

Sources: Testimony of Sergeant Boston Corbett, Poore, *Conspiracy Trial*, vol. 1, 322–26; Pitman, *Trial*, 94–95; Earl C. Kubicek, "The Case of the Mad Hatter," *Lincoln Herald* 83, no. 3 (Fall 1981), 708; George S. Bryan, *The Great American Myth* (New York: Carrick & Evans, 1940).

## Corey, John

Corey, a private in Thompson's Battery C, Independent (Pennsylvania) Light Artillery, was one of four soldiers from that battery stationed at Camp Barry, on the outskirts of Washington, who attended *Our American Cousin* on the night of April 14, 1865. Corey, along with Privates Jacob Soles, Jake Griffiths, and William Sample, claimed to have carried Lincoln from the theater to the Petersen house. Corey, a resident of Pittsburgh, Pennsylvania, died in 1884 by drowning in the Allegheny River.

Sources: *Sunday Times-Telegraph* (Pittsburgh), February 12, 1928; *New York Tribune*, February 8, 1931.

*See also*: Griffiths, Jake; McPeck, William; Sample, William; Soles, Jacob

## Cottingham, George

A detective on the staff of Maryland provost marshal James O'Beirne, headquartered in Baltimore. Cottingham, along with detective Joshua Lloyd, was sent to Piscataway, Prince George's County, on Sunday, April 16, 1865, after O'Beirne learned that John Surratt and David Herold were most likely to go to Prince George's County in Southern Maryland to escape Washington. From Piscataway the detectives made their way to Surrattsville, known as Robeystown at the time, after the postmaster who replaced John H. Surratt, Jr. Robey expressed suspicions about John M. Lloyd, who had leased the Surratt Tavern from Mary Surratt in December 1864.

On Tuesday, April 18, Cottingham, along with several other military detectives including Lieutenant Alexander Lovett, arrested John M. Lloyd on the road near the village of T.B. Lloyd was brought to Surrattsville and placed in the charge of Cottingham until he was taken to Washington.

According to Cottingham's testimony during the conspiracy trial, Lloyd claimed that Mrs. Surratt "had come down to his place [Surratt Tavern] on Friday, betwixt four and five o'clock; and she told him to have the firearms ready; that two men would call for them at twelve o'clock." This is the same testimony Lloyd gave as a prosecution witness at the conspiracy trial. Cottingham recovered one of the two carbines that had been stored at the Surratt Tavern by John Surratt earlier.

Sources: Testimony of George Cottingham, Poore, *Conspiracy Trial*, vol. 2, 192; George Cottingham, letter to Major James O'Beirne, May 1, 1865, NARA, M-619, reel 458, frames 390–98.

*See also:* Lloyd, John M.

### "Coughdrop Joe" Ratto (1854–1946)

Giuseppe "Coughdrop Joe" Ratto was renowned around the environs of Ford's Theatre as a result of his claim to have held Booth's horse on the night of Lincoln's assassination. Born Giuseppe Ratto in Genoa, Italy, Coughdrop Joe immigrated to the United States at the beginning of the Civil War. He became a local character shuffling around the back alleys and streets of the District of Columbia. Not over five feet in height, "Coughdrop Joe" earned his nickname by selling strongly flavored Lewis's coughdrops to patrons in the saloon district who wanted to cover the smell of alcohol on their breath.

While Coughdrop Joe did not hold Booth's horse in the rear of Ford's Theatre on the night of April 14, 1865, he may well have held his horse on other occasions. Ratto frequented the alley behind Ford's Theatre during the time Booth was in Washington and playing at Ford's. He lived for many years at 411 Tenth Street, one block from the theater. The people of Washington came to recognize Joe as a fixture on the night streets. He spent the last four years of his life at the Sacred Heart Home in the district. Coughdrop Joe is another example of attaining a measure of fame by grabbing Lincoln's coattails. He is buried in St. Mary's Cemetery in the District of Columbia.

Sources: R. Gerald McMurtry, "Did 'Coughdrop Joe' Ratto Hold Booth's Horse?," *Lincoln Lore*, no. 1571 (January 1969).

## Courtenay, Thomas Edgeworth (1822–1876)

The inventor of the coal bomb. An example of the use of devices that cause indiscriminate killing. At the outbreak of the war Courtenay operated a cotton brokerage business in St. Louis. In December 1863, Courtenay wrote directly to Jefferson Davis offering his services and newly designed torpedo to the Confederate cause: "Sir, I propose to organize a 'secret service corps' to consist of such numbers of men as may from time to time be required. Said corps to be employed in doing injury to the enemy. . . . I propose to send a number of the 'corps' to the Northern States, West Indies Island and Europe, to operate on steam vessels, locomotives and all Federal property [where] steam is used."

Three months later, on March 9, 1864, Confederate secretary of war James A. Seddon wrote Courtenay authorizing him to employ up to twenty-five men "for secret service against the enemy." Seddon approved use of Confederate facilities and materiel for the production of Courtenay's unique device.

At the time Courtenay was authorized to form his special "bomb squad," Seddon specified that his men were to be paid for their work on a commission basis: "For the destruction of property of the enemy or injury done, a per centage shall be paid in Four per cent bonds in no case to exceed fifty per centum of the loss to the enemy. . . ."

Eighty years later, the ingenious device caught the eye of the U.S. Office of Strategic Services during World War II and a detailed description of Courtenay's coal bomb was included in one of their sabotage manuals. Some historians believe a coal bomb was responsible for the explosion of the steamboat *Sultana* on the Mississippi River in 1865.

Sources: Thomas E. Courtenay, letter to Jefferson Davis, December 7, 1863, manuscript letter in the possession of Thomas Thatcher, great-great-grandson of Thomas E. Courtenay; William A. Tidwell, *April '65: Confederate Covert Action in the American Civil War* (Kent, Ohio: Kent State University Press, 1995), 227, n32.

*See also:* Coal Bomb

## Cox, Samuel (1819–1880)

Booth and Herold arrived at Rich Hill, the plantation home of Samuel Cox, Sr., sometime around midnight on Saturday, April 15, 1865, five hours after leaving the home of Dr. Samuel Mudd. Cox provided food and shelter for the two fugitives, hiding them in a pine thicket near his home.

Cox was a major land and slave owner who commanded respect from nearly everyone in the region, and, most important, he was an ardent Confederate sympathizer and underground agent. One of the larger slave owners in the county, he owned thirty-seven slaves at the time of the slave census of 1860. At the start of the war he commanded a company of local volunteers organized to defend Maryland should she decide to secede along with her sister states. It was this activity that earned Cox the title of "Captain."

Cox was squat in build and had a round, heavily muscled face. He had a full head of hair and his beard was short-cropped running from ear to ear, his upper lip clean-shaven in Brethren style. He gave the appearance of a no-nonsense patrician.

Inside Cox's house the two fugitives gained a much-needed respite from their difficult travel through the swamp. They had covered nearly ten miles over difficult terrain at night and were tired. Cox gave the two men food and drink and allowed them to rest. They talked for nearly five hours before Cox told them they would have to leave. He would see that they were put into good hands. It was essential to get the two fugitives to a secure place before patrols started combing the area.

Cox told his overseer, Franklin Robey, to take the two men to a place where they would be safely concealed until he could send help to them. It was a small pine thicket located one mile to the southeast of his home, Rich Hill. The thicket was located just over the boundary of Cox's property.

On Sunday morning, Cox sent his son to bring Thomas Jones back to Rich Hill. Cox told Jones about the two men hiding in the pine thicket and asked Jones to care for the men and see that they safely crossed the river to Virginia. Jones agreed to take charge of the two fugitives and five days later put them in a boat and sent them out onto the river.

Samuel Cox, Sr., Thomas Jones, and Samuel Mudd were arrested and taken to Washington in connection with Lincoln's murder. Jones and Cox were eventually released and returned to their homes and old way of life. Samuel Mudd was not so lucky. He was held in the Carroll Annex until transferred to the penitentiary in the Washington Arsenal. The government could find no reason to keep Cox and Jones in jail any longer. They were lucky to have escaped with their lives.

Sources: Thomas A. Jones, *J. Wilkes Booth* (Chicago: Laird & Lee, 1893); William A. Tidwell, James O. Hall, and David W. Gaddy, *Come Retribution* (Jackson: University Press of Mississippi, 1988).

## Cox, Samuel, Jr. (1847–1906)

Adopted son of Samuel Cox, Sr., who lived at Rich Hill, where Booth and Herold stopped around twelve midnight on Saturday, April 15, 1865, after leaving Dr. Samuel Mudd's house. Left a written commentary on events surrounding Booth's stop at the houses of Mudd and Cox at the time of his flight from Washington. A free black named Oswell Swan escorted Booth and Herold to Cox's house.

Cox Jr. was an eyewitness to the events that occurred while Booth and Herold were at Cox Sr.'s house from Saturday midnight until 6:00 A.M. Sunday morning, when they were taken to a secret hiding place in a pine thicket just over the boundary line of Cox's property.

Cox Jr. left comments in the margins of his personal copy of a book written by Thomas Jones in 1893 describing Jones's role as a Confederate agent and in helping Booth escape over the Potomac River. The most revealing notations are those that refer to Samuel Mudd and his alleged admission to Cox Jr. that he knew his injured visitor was Booth and that Booth had assassinated Lincoln.

Cox wrote the following concerning Dr. Mudd:

In 1877, after Dr. Samuel A. Mudd's return from Dry Tortugas and when he and myself were canvassing this county as the Democratic candidates for the [State] Legislature, he told me he knew Booth but casually. That Booth had at one time sought an introduction to him [Mudd] through John Surratt on Penn. Ave., Washington. This was sometime prior to the assassination but he had refused and that Booth had forced himself on him shortly afterward and that subsequently Booth attended church at Bryantown where he spoke to him but he was particular in not inviting him to his house, but that Booth came that evening unsolicited. He told me he was not favorably impressed with Booth, and that when Booth & Herold, came to his home the night after the assassination they told him they were just from Virginia & that Booth's horse had fallen soon after leaving the river & had broken his leg. That he had rendered him medical assistance while in utter ignorance of the assassination. That after he had set the broken leg, he, Dr. Mudd went [into Bryantown with] letters he had but a short time gotten through the contraband [Confederate] mail for distribution, and that in going to Bryantown to mail them he was surprised to find the village surrounded by soldiers and upon being stopped by a sentry [missing] he was horrified when told the President had been shot the night before, and, upon asking who had shot him the fellow had answered Booth. He then told me his first impulse was to surrender Booth, that he had imposed upon him had twice forced himself upon him and now the third time, had come with a lie upon his tongue and received medical assistance which would be certain to have him serious trouble but he determined to go back and upbraid him for his treachery which he did. And that Booth had appealed to him in the name of his mother whom he professed to love so devotedly and that he acted and spoke so tragically that he told them they must leave his house which they then did and after getting in with Oswald Swan they were piloted to Rich Hill. Aug. 7, 1893. S Cox Jr.

The annotated book was donated by the grandson of Cox Jr. to the Maryland Historical Society, where it now resides.

Sources: Thomas A. Jones, *J. Wilkes Booth* (Chicago: Laird & Lee, 1893); William A. Tidwell, James O. Hall, and David W. Gaddy, *Come Retribution* (Jackson: University Press of Mississippi, 1988).

*See also:* Jones, Thomas Austin

## Cox, Walter Smith (1819–1900)

Attorney who represented Michael O'Laughlen during the military trial. Cox was a graduate of Georgetown College (now Georgetown University) and Harvard Law School. He was a law professor at Columbia College (now Columbia University) at the time of the conspiracy trial.

Cox began his defense argument of O'Laughlen by telling the tribunal he was not willing to connect his humble name to his defense unless he felt assured of their innocence. After hearing the evidence against O'Laughlen, Cox said, "there is no blood on his hands." Cox was forced to admit that O'Laughlen had conspired with Booth to capture Lincoln when Marshal James McPhail testified in court that Arnold had named O'Laughlen in a written confession that McPhail had obtained from Arnold. Cox's whole defense centered on separating the capture plan from Booth's murder of Lincoln. It was rejected by the tribunal, which relied on assistant judge advocate Bingham's claim that "whoever leagued in a general conspiracy, performed any part, however minute, or however remote, from the scene of action, are guilty as principals." It is the modern concept of "vicarious liability."

Cox was appointed a justice to the D.C. Supreme Court in 1879. In 1881, he was the presiding judge at the trial of Charles Guiteau, the assassin of President James Garfield.

Sources: John A. Bingham, "Argument," in Edward Steers, Jr., ed., *The Trial* (Lexington: University Press of Kentucky, 2003), 402; Edward Steers, Jr., and Harold Holzer, eds., *The Lincoln Assassination Conspirators: Their Confinement and Execution, as Recorded in the Letterbook of John Frederick Hartranft* (Baton Rouge: Louisiana State University Press, 2009).

## Crane, Charles Henry (1825–1883)

Assistant surgeon general. One of fourteen doctors who visited the Petersen house during the early morning hours of April 15, 1865. Crane's importance to the assassination story involves his role in the use of the photographic laboratories

of the surgeon general to make copies of Booth's photograph for distribution to military units searching for Booth.

When Lafayette C. Baker first learned that Booth was the assassin he requested use of the photographic facilities of the surgeon general's office. During the early hours of Saturday, April 15, he had several photographs of Booth reproduced for distribution to his agents and military posts. Just which image of Booth was used, and how it came into the hands of the military searching for him, has been the cause of confusion among several writers. Baker's use of the surgeon gen-

eral's photographic facilities is learned from a letter written by Crane that survives today in a private collection. In his letter Crane writes, "We still have hope that the murderer Booth will be captured. I send you his picture. We had a number struck off in our 'gallery' last Saturday [April 15] to distribute throughout the country." The "gallery" was the name of the surgeon general's photographic facility, and the picture Crane included with his letter is a particular image known today as "Gutman No. 35." The photograph had been taken by the Boston firm of Silsbee, Case & Company as one of two views taken during the same sitting. It subsequently became known as the "wanted poster view" because it was used on several of the wanted posters put out by the government.

Crane was present in the Petersen house when Lincoln died. He later observed Dr. Joseph Janvier Woodward and Dr. Edward Curtis, two army surgeons, perform the autopsy at the White House

Sources: Edward Steers, Jr., "Otto Eisenschiml, Samuel Mudd and the 'Switched' Photograph," *Lincoln Herald* 100, no. 4 (Winter 1998).

*See also:* Doctors

## Crane, Cordial

An official with the Boston Custom House who wrote a letter to Edwin M.

Stanton informing him of Booth's visit to Boston in July 1864.

While the trial of the conspirators was taking place in Washington, D.C., in May 1865, a government witness named Godfrey Joseph Hyams gave testimony about his exploits shipping Dr. Luke Blackburn's trunks, which contained soiled clothing exposed to yellow fever victims, past customs in Boston and on to Philadelphia. Upon reading Hyams's testimony, Crane's interest was aroused. He decided to check the register of the Parker House hotel in Boston to see if Hyams or his alias, J. W. Harris, had registered. Crane could find neither Hyams nor Harris in the register but was startled to find that John Wilkes Booth had registered at the Parker House on July 26. Crane noted that three men from Canada and one from Baltimore also registered on that day. Crane copied the names of the five men and sent a letter to Stanton calling his attention to what he felt was a strange coincidence. Whatever Stanton thought of Crane's observation, he failed to follow up on it and simply filed the letter away.

The authors of *Come Retribution* speculate that the presence of the men from Canada and Booth was more than a coincidence and may well have been a prearranged meeting. They write, "The inference is that agents of the Confeder-

ate apparatus in Canada had a need to discuss something with Booth. Capturing Lincoln?" They attempt to strengthen their case by pointing out that Booth met with Arnold and O'Laughlen two weeks later in Baltimore to initiate his capture plan.

Booth, at the time of his visit, was romantically involved with a Boston woman by the name of Isabel Sumner, which may explain his stopover in Boston.

Sources: Cordial Crane, letter to Edwin M. Stanton, July 26, 1865, NARA, RG 153, M-599, reel 3, frame 153; William A. Tidwell, James O. Hall, and David W. Gaddy, *Come Retribution* (Jackson: University Press of Mississippi, 1988).

*See also:* Parker House

## Crawford, A. M. S.

A lieutenant in the Veteran Reserve Corps stationed in Washington, D.C. Crawford was the second witness interviewed in the Petersen house by the special panel set up by Secretary of War Edwin M. Stanton immediately following the assassination. Crawford was seated in the Dress Circle, "about five feet from the door to the box." Seated immediately to Crawford's right was Captain Theodore McGowan. Booth passed Crawford and McGowan as he approached the box door. Crawford gave an accurate description of Booth's dress and his demeanor, remarking "what attracted my attention particularly was the glare in his eye." Hearing the gunshot, Crawford "jumped to the door" and tried to enter the box. Major Henry Rathbone, inside the box, removed the wood brace Booth had put in place and opened the door. Several people entered behind Crawford claiming to be surgeons. Rathbone then asked Crawford to block the door, admitting no one except a doctor.

Sources: Maxwell Whiteman, ed., *While Lincoln Lay Dying* (Philadelphia: Union League of Philadelphia, 1968), 30–33; Timothy S. Good, *We Saw Lincoln Shot: One Hundred Eyewitness Accounts* (Jackson: University Press of Mississippi, 1995), 41–44.

### Crook, William Henry (1839–1915)

One of the D.C. Metropolitan Police assigned to the White House as a bodyguard to President Lincoln. Crook replaced Thomas F. Pendel when Pendel became doorkeeper at the White House. Crook is listed as the author of two ghostwritten books about his service as a presidential bodyguard: *Through Five Administrations* (1910) and *Memories of the White House* (1911). Crook accused one of his associates, John F. Parker, of dereliction of duty in not protecting President Lincoln. Parker was on duty at the time Lincoln was shot. In his memoirs, however, Crook describes several incidents that are inconsistent with known facts. He writes of accompanying Lincoln through the streets of Richmond following its evacuation, of visiting Stanton in his office on the evening of April 14, and of Lincoln saying "Goodbye, Crook" shortly before leaving for Ford's Theatre on the night of the assassination. Crook wrote, "it startled me." "As far as I remembered he had never said anything but 'Good-Night, Crook' before."

Historian William Hanchett has shown that these recollections and other reminiscences Crook writes about fall into the myth category, related at a time late in Crook's life when there was no one left alive to refute them. None of the events took place. Because of this, Crook cannot be considered a trustworthy source on the events surrounding Lincoln's assassination.

Sources: William Hanchett, "Persistent Myths of the Lincoln Assassination," *Lincoln Herald*, 99 no. 4, 172–9.

*See also:* Parker, John Frederick

### Curtis, Dr. Edward G. (1838–1912)

One of fourteen physicians to visit Lincoln's bedside on the night of April 14–15, 1865, in the Petersen house. Lincoln was taken from the Petersen house Saturday morning shortly after his death to a guest room on the second floor of the White House where Curtis and Dr. Joseph Woodward performed the autopsy. In attendance were Surgeon General (army) Joseph K. Barnes; Dr. Robert Stone, the family physician; army surgeons Charles Crane, Charles S. Taft, and William M. Notson; Assistant Quartermaster General Daniel Rucker; and Lincoln's close friend from Illinois, Orville Hickman Browning.

Both Curtis and Woodward were army surgeons. Curtis described the scene:

> Dr. Woodward and I proceeded to open the head and remove the brain down to the track of the ball. The latter had entered a little to the left of the median line at the back of the head, had passed almost directly forward through the center of the brain and lodged. Not finding it readily, we proceeded to remove the entire brain, when, as I was lifting the latter from the cavity of the skull, suddenly the bullet dropped out through my fingers and fell, breaking the solemn silence of the room with its clatter, into an empty basin that was standing beneath. There it lay upon the white china, a little black mass no bigger than the end of my finger . . . the cause of such mighty changes in the world's history, as we may perhaps never realize.

Sources: John K. Lattimer, *Kennedy and Lincoln: Medical and Ballistic Comparisons of Their Assassinations* (New York: Harcourt Brace Jovanovich, 1980); Dorothy Meserve Kunhardt and Philip B. Kunhardt, Jr., *Twenty Days* (New York: Harper & Row, 1965); Edward Steers, Jr., *Blood on the Moon* (Lexington: University Press of Kentucky, 2001), 269–70.

*See also:* Doctors; Autopsy, Abraham Lincoln

## Dahlgren, Ulric (1842–1864)

See Dahlgren Raid

## Dahlgren Papers

Documents recovered from the body of Union colonel Ulric Dahlgren that called for the burning of Richmond and the killing of Jefferson Davis and his cabinet. Ulric Dahlgren, the son of Union admiral John Dahlgren, was part of a special cavalry raid against Richmond aimed at freeing several thousand Union prisoners from Belle Isle prison and Libby Prison.

On February 28, 1864, Brigadier General Judson Kilpatrick, commanding the Third Division, Cavalry Corps of the Army of the Potomac, set out to attack Richmond with 3,500 troopers from the north as a diversion while Colonel Ulric Dahlgren would lead a select group of 500 troopers around Richmond entering from the south. Dahlgren and his men would liberate the Union prisoners held in the Confederate prison camp on Belle Isle in the James River and lead them into Richmond, where they would free the prisoners held in Libby Prison.

Kilpatrick's attack was repelled and he turned back, failing to enter Richmond from the north as planned. Dahlgren was forced to abandon his plan to enter the city from the south when a swollen James River blocked his approach. Unable to find a fordable crossing, Dahlgren headed northeast in an attempt to hook up with Kilpatrick's men. Dahlgren was ambushed by Confederate soldiers and killed. Papers found on his body called for the burning of the city and killing Davis.

Among the papers recovered from Dahlgren's body were two sheets of official stationery with the designation "Headquarters, Third Division, Cavalry Corps" and containing the following words: "We hope to release the prisoners from Belle Isle first, and having them well started, we will cross the James River into Richmond, destroying the bridges after us and exhorting the prisoners to destroy and burn the hateful city." On a second sheet of the same stationery were the instructions "The men must keep together and well in hand, and once in the city it must be destroyed and *Jeff Davis and Cabinet killed*" (author's emphasis).

Confederate leaders, including Jefferson Davis, were convinced that Lincoln had authorized the raid. In his memoirs, Davis pointedly wrote about Lincoln: "The enormity of his offenses was not forgotten." The Confederate leaders felt that Lincoln had violated the laws of war and, in doing so, had lost whatever protection he had enjoyed under the civilized laws of war. If Jefferson Davis was fair game, then Abraham Lincoln was fair game. The effect of the Dahlgren Raid removed whatever restraints had existed on "black flag warfare."

The Confederate leadership decided to exploit the propaganda value of their find by producing photographic copies of the documents and distributing them to the southern press as well as sending copies to Major General George G. Meade. The northern press published accounts of the raid and the documents. Meade denied any knowledge of the documents or their alleged objectives, as did General Kilpatrick.

Historians have differed on the authenticity of the documents. One group of historians feels the papers are a fabrication made up by Confederate sources to embarrass Union officials while a second group feels the papers are authentic and that their objectives were known to Lincoln. The evidence comes down on the side of authenticity. The documents are not forgeries, but whether Lincoln knew about them and their call to assassinate Davis and his cabinet is unclear. It mattered little to Davis and his cabinet. They believed Lincoln knew and approved Dahlgren's mission.

Sources: James O. Hall, "The Dahlgren Papers: A Yankee Plot to Kill Jefferson Davis," *Civil War Times Illustrated* 22, no. 7 (November 1983), 30; Joseph George, Jr., "'Black Flag Warfare': Lincoln and the Raids Against Richmond and Jefferson Davis," *Pennsylvania Magazine of History and Biography*, July 1991, 291–318; Duane Schultz, *The Dahlgren Affair: Terror and Conspiracy in the Civil War* (New York: Norton, 1998); Stephen W. Sears, "Raid on Richmond," *Quarterly Journal of Military History* 11, no. 1 (Autumn 1998), 88.

*See also:* Dahlgren Raid, Black Flag Warfare

## Dahlgren Raid (Kilpatrick-Dahlgren Raid)

Cavalry raid against Richmond in March 1864 under the command of Brigadier General Judson Kilpatrick designed to liberate Union prisoners of war held on Belle Isle and Libby Prison, and burn Richmond, killing Confederate leaders including Jefferson Davis.

In early 1864 Lincoln received distressing reports about the deplorable conditions of Union prisoners on Belle Isle and in Libby Prison, and was anxious for their liberation. Lincoln also learned that the Confederate government was planning to remove the prisoners from Richmond to Andersonville in Georgia. If action were not undertaken soon these prisoners would be beyond the reach of any Union army and all hope for their safe return would pass. A military raid was planned that had three objectives: to free Union prisoners, to destroy public buildings and military facilities including arsenals and railroad equipage, and "to kill Jeff Davis and cabinet . . . on the spot." These objectives were written on a piece of paper that was an address from Colonel Ulric Dahlgren to his men.

On February 6, 1864, Brigadier General Isaac Wistar led a large body of Union cavalry on a special raid aimed at the lightly defended capital of Richmond. The Confederate military received advance word of Wistar's raid and he was stopped before he could breech the outer defenses of Richmond. The raid was aborted. Lincoln was disappointed at Wistar's failure.

Three weeks after Wistar's failure, Brigadier General Judson Kilpatrick, commanding the Third Division, Cavalry Corps of the Army of the Potomac, mounted a second raid. This operation was to consist of two parts: Kilpatrick with 3,500 troopers would attack Richmond from the north entering the city while Dahlgren, son of Rear Admiral John Dahlgren, would lead a select group of 500 troopers around Richmond, entering from the south. Dahlgren and his men would liberate the Union prisoners held in the Confederate prison camp on Belle Isle in the James River and escort them into Richmond, where they would free the prisoners in Libby Prison.

Kilpatrick's attack was quickly repelled. Dahlgren, unable to reach Belle Isle and cross the rain-swollen James River, abandoned his plan to enter the city from the south. Dahlgren tried to escape with his small band of men to the northeast and unite with Kilpatrick's command. Ambushed by Confederate soldiers, Dahlgren was killed and the papers on his body calling for the burning of the city and killing of Davis were discovered.

Sources: James O. Hall, "The Dahlgren Papers: Fact or Fabrication?," *Civil War Times Illustrated*, November 1983, 30–39; Jefferson Davis, *The Rise and Fall of the Confederate Government*, 2 vols. (1881; reprint, New York: Da Capo, 1990), vol. 2, 426; Joseph George, Jr., " 'Black Flag Warfare': Lincoln and the Raids Against Richmond and Jefferson Davis," *Pennsylvania Magazine of History and Biography*, July 1991, 291–318; Duane Schultz, *The Dahlgren Affair: Terror and Conspiracy in the Civil War* (New York: Norton,

1998); Stephen W. Sears, "Raid on Richmond," *Quarterly Journal of Military History* 11, no. 1 (Autumn 1998), 88–96.

*See also:* Dahlgren Papers, Black Flag Warfare

### Dana, David D. (1827–1906)

Commanded troops of the 13th New York Cavalry sent to Bryantown, Maryland, in search of John Wilkes Booth. At approximately two o'clock Saturday morning, April 15, three and a half hours after Booth shot President Lincoln, General C. C. Augur, commanding the 22nd Army Corps in Washington, ordered Dana and a troop of soldiers to Southern Maryland in search of Booth. Augur received information from John Fletcher, manager of Naylor's stables in Washington, that David Herold and another man had ridden over the Navy Yard Bridge, headed for Southern Maryland, around eleven o'clock. Herold was riding a horse rented from Fletcher on Friday afternoon and was long overdue. Augur did not know the second man was Booth but already had information linking Herold and Booth as well as George Atzerodt.

Dana, stopping first at Piscataway, continued on to Bryantown, arriving just before one o'clock Saturday afternoon. While at Piscataway he sent one of his men to the Chapel Point telegraph station to wire Washington that he had reliable evidence that Seward's attacker was the man who was already wanted for killing Captain Watkins (the guerrilla John Boyle). It was just one more piece of misinformation among the many that would plague the searchers. Dana established his headquarters at the Bryantown Tavern and informed the residents that Lincoln had been shot and the assassin was John Wilkes Booth. On Monday morning, George D. Mudd, Dr. Samuel Mudd's cousin, informed Dana that two suspicious strangers had visited Samuel Mudd's house on Saturday, and one of the men had a broken leg. For some unexplained reason, Dana did not act on George Mudd's information. He waited until Tuesday morning to tell the newly arrived Lieutenant Alexander Lovett about Dr. Mudd's guests. Lovett acted immediately. He sent for George Mudd, and with three military detectives, William Williams, Simon Gavacan, and Joshua Lloyd, set out for Mudd's house, five miles north of Bryantown.

Approximately thirteen hours after Booth shot the president, Dana and his troop of cavalry were within five miles of Booth and Herold, who were holed up at the Mudd house. By Saturday evening the opportunity to capture the two fugitives passed as Booth and Herold continued their escape, making a wide circle to the east of Bryantown and continuing on to their next stop at Samuel Cox's plantation, Rich Hill. Dana would not share in the reward money, but Lovett was awarded one thousand dollars for his quick action in following up on Dr. Mudd.

Sources: Testimony of David D. Dana, Poore, *Conspiracy Trial*, vol. 2, 67; Pitman, *Trial*, 88; Testimony of John Fletcher, Poore, *Conspiracy Trial*, vol. 1, 326; Pitman, *Trial*, 88; Edward Steers, Jr., *Blood on the Moon* (Lexington: University Press of Kentucky, 2001), 130–32, 133, 146–47; James L. Swanson, *Manhunt: The 12-Day Chase for Lincoln's Killer* (New York: Harper Perennial, 2007), 137.

### Davis, Jefferson (1808–1889)

President of the Confederate States of America. As the war was winding down with little to no hope for success, Jefferson Davis continued to fight on, grasping at every straw to save his Confederacy. In the spring of 1864 he sent Jacob Thompson and Clement Clay to Canada with instructions to establish a clandestine operation principally working out of Toronto and Montreal. Davis funded the organization with $1 million in gold from a special secret service fund. Several other agents already working in Canada soon joined Thompson and Clay. Their goal was to demoralize the people of the North, ending their support for the war and helping to defeat Lincoln's bid

for reelection in November 1864. Plots included the burning of northern cities; the poisoning of Croton Reservoir, which provided water to New York City; and the spreading of contagion in an effort to start smallpox and yellow fever epidemics.

The use of "black flag" warfare was not restricted to the Confederacy, however. In March 1864, the North launched a cavalry raid on Richmond with the express objective of freeing Union prisoners held there and burning the city and killing Jefferson Davis and members of his cabinet if possible. The reaction throughout the South was outrage toward Lincoln. Davis was convinced that

Lincoln had authorized the raid. In his memoirs, Davis pointedly wrote about Lincoln: "The enormity of his offenses was not forgotten." If Jefferson Davis was a fair target, then Abraham Lincoln was also. The gloves came off with the establishment of a secret service operation in Canada designed to carry out a series of operations well outside the accepted laws of war. Whether Davis was privy to all of the plots planned by his operation in Canada is not clear, but it appears he was made aware of the attempt to institute germ warfare and did not take steps to stop it.

Davis was forced to abandon Richmond on April 2, following Lee's abandonment of his defensive positions around that city and Petersburg. Attempting to make his way farther south and beyond Union lines, Davis was captured on May 10, near Irwinville, Georgia. Imprisoned at Fort Monroe, Virginia, Davis was never brought to trial although talk of such a plan continued long after his incarceration. Throughout the Lincoln conspiracy trial, Judge Advocate General Joseph Holt attempted to show that Lincoln's assassination had been planned and supported in Richmond by Confederate leaders, principally by Jefferson Davis. Holt's case quickly evaporated when his key witnesses were believed to have committed perjury. Holt and Assistant Judge

Advocate John A. Bingham shifted their efforts to the eight defendants in the dock, ignoring Davis. Davis was released from prison on May 13, 1867, without a trial being held.

Sources: Jefferson Davis, *The Rise and Fall of the Confederate Government*, 2 vols. (1881; reprint, New York: Da Capo Press, 1990). Richard N. Current, ed., *The Confederacy* (New York: Simon & Schuster Macmillan, 1993), 162–65; Edward Steers, Jr., "General Conspiracy," in Edward Steers, Jr., ed., *The Trial* (Lexington: University Press of Kentucky, 2003), xxix–xxxvii.

*See also:* Dahlgren Raid

## Davis, Peregrine

Owner of the farm known as Indianhead located along the Nanjemoy Creek in Charles County where Booth and Herold laid over following their failed attempt to cross the Potomac River on the night of Thursday, April 21. The farm was maintained by Davis's son-in-law, John J. Hughes. David Herold was well known to Hughes from his many hunting forays in the area. It is not known for sure what help, if any, Booth and Herold received from Hughes after landing along his shore early Friday morning. Family tradition holds that Hughes gave the two fugitives food and drink and allowed them to stay in one of the outbuildings.

It was while waiting to cross the river that Booth sat down and wrote in his diary once again, "After being hunted like a dog through swamps, woods, and last night being chased by gun boats till I was forced to return wet, cold, and starving, with every man's hand against me, I am here in despair." The two men set out on the night of Saturday, April 22, and successfully crossed to the Virginia shore landing at Gambo Creek. Authorities were unaware that the two had stayed at Hughes's two days and two nights.

Sources: William A. Tidwell, "Booth Crosses the Potomac: An Exercise in Historical Research," *Civil War History* 36 (April 1990), 325–33; Edward Steers, Jr., *Blood on the Moon* (Lexington: University Press of Kentucky, 2001), 183–85.

*See also*: Booth Escape Route; Hughes, John J.

## Dean, Mary Apollonia (1855–1894)

A young ten-year-old boarder at Mary Surratt's boardinghouse at 541 H Street in Washington. She was a student at St. Patrick's Institute, located nearby. On March 15, 1865, John Wilkes Booth, with Lewis Powell and John Surratt, took Mary and Nora Fitzpatrick, a seventeen-year-old girl who also boarded at the Surratt boardinghouse, to Ford's Theatre to see *The Tragedy of Jane Shore*. Booth presumably wanted to familiarize Powell and Surratt with the layout of the theater.

Sources: William A. Tidwell, James O. Hall, and David W. Gaddy, *Come Retribution* (Jackson: University Press of Mississippi, 1988), 413–14; Michael W. Kauffman, *American Brutus* (New York: Random House, 2004), 168, 179.

## DeBar, Benjamin (1821–1877)

Theatrical entrepreneur who owned theaters in New Orleans and St. Louis. DeBar was a good friend of John Wilkes Booth and uncle to Blanche DeBar, the daughter of Junius Brutus Booth, Jr. When Junius abandoned his wife and daughter, Ben DeBar adopted Blanche and became her guardian and benefactor. DeBar managed the St. Charles Theatre in New Orleans. At the outbreak of the Civil War he moved to St. Louis, where he was considered one of the most influential theatrical managers in the business. DeBar was strongly pro-Confederate and under surveillance by the military. He was arrested because of his close ties with John Wilkes Booth, who played at his theater. DeBar had corresponded off and on with Booth, but there is no evidence to link him to Booth's conspiracy to capture or kill Lincoln.

Sources: Statement of Ben DeBar, NARA, RG 153, M-599, reel 2, frames 417–20; William A. Tidwell, James O. Hall, and David W. Gaddy, *Come Retribution* (Jackson: University Press of Mississippi, 1988), 413–14; William Hanchett, *The Lincoln Murder Conspiracies* (Urbana: University of Illinois Press, 1983), 41.

### DeBar, Blanche (1844–1930)

Blanche DeBar was the daughter of Junius Brutus Booth, Jr., and Clementine DeBar, and niece of John Wilkes Booth. When Junius abandoned his wife and daughter, Ben DeBar adopted Blanche, assuming full responsibility for her. She reverted to using the DeBar name. Like her mother and father, she became an actress and played in her adopted father's theater in St. Louis. Also like her mother and father, she was strongly pro-Confederate and was quoted by a provost marshal in St. Louis as stating it would be right to kill President Lincoln.

A newspaper clipping among the evidentiary files best describes her success as an actress:

Miss Blanche De Bar, the now established favorite of St. Louis, had her benefit last night, which proved the greatest ovation of the whole season.... She introduced a beautiful song, which she executed admirably. At the end of this drama, Miss De Bar was loudly called for, when she appeared before the curtain amid a shower of bouquets and immense applause. When E. W. Decker, Esq., rose in the side box and, after speaking a very appropriate and flattering address, presented her, in behalf of a number of our citizens, a most elegant and costly present of a magnificent diamond ring and superb set of cameos, surrounded by pearls ... We are too much pressed for room today as much as we wish, so we will just conclude by congratulating Miss De Bar on her great and unparalleled success.

Sources: Ben DeBar, NARA, RG 153, M-599, reel 2, frame 336; Blanche DeBar, NARA, RG 153, M-599, reel 2, frames 421–25; William Hanchett, *The Lincoln Murder Conspiracies* (Urbana: University of Illinois Press, 1983), 41.

## DeBar, Clementine

Benjamin DeBar's sister, who married and later divorced Junius Brutus Booth, Jr. Junius and Clementine had one child, a daughter named Blanche. Following Junius's divorce of Clementine, Blanche reverted to using her mother's maiden name, becoming known on the stage as Blanche DeBar.

Sources: William A. Tidwell, James O. Hall, and David W. Gaddy, *Come Retribution* (Jackson: University Press of Mississippi, 1988), 413–14.

## Dent, George

Prominent resident and Confederate sympathizer in Charles County, Maryland, who helped pass materials along the Confederate mail line. On July 23, 1861, Cox wrote a letter to Mary Turner instructing her to place her correspondence to Confederate persons in the hands of Mr. George Dent. Dent would see that they made their way across the Potomac River care of Mr. Ben Grimes, who would then place them in the postal system and see to their delivery. In late 1861, Dent was arrested and put in the Old Capitol Prison along with Confederate signal agent Thomas Jones. Both men were eventually released and returned to their activities running the mail line and supporting the Confederacy in various ways.

Sources: William A. Tidwell, James O. Hall, and David W. Gaddy, *Come Retribution* (Jackson: University Press of Mississippi, 1988), 66–67.

*See also:* Mail Line

## Dent, Dr. Stoughton W.

A member of the Confederate mail line in Charles County, Maryland. Dent, along with George Dent, Thomas Jones, Samuel Cox, and Samuel Mudd, worked passing various documents and papers along the Confederate mail line through the county, across the river, to the Virginia side, where it was carried to Richmond. While most of the people were volunteers, Dent and chief signal agent Thomas Jones were reimbursed for their expenses from Confederate funds.

Because he was a doctor, Dent could move more freely about the county and carry large amounts of mail and medicines, which he could arrange for delivery across the river to the Grimes farm on the Virginia side. It was a highly successful arrangement that operated through most of the war.

Sources: William A. Tidwell, James O. Hall, and David W. Gaddy, *Come Retribution* (Jackson: University Press of Mississippi, 1988), 98; John M. and Roberta J. Wearmouth, *Thomas A. Jones: Chief Agent of the Confederate Secret Service in Maryland* (Port Tobacco, Md.: Stones Throw, 2000), 4–7.

## Deringer, Henry (1786-1868)

An American gunsmith who developed a small, single-shot pistol that was small enough to be easily concealed in a man's hand or coat pocket. The spelling of the weapon became corrupted to "derringer." The pistol became so popular that numerous types of derringer pistols came onto the market, but Deringer's little pistol remained the standard derringer. Approximately 15,000 of the .41 caliber pistols were manufactured between its introduction in 1852 and Deringer's death in 1868. Deringer is buried in Laurel Hill Cemetery located in Philadelphia.

John Wilkes Booth used one of Henry Deringer's pistols to murder President Lincoln on the night of April 14, 1865. The infamous pistol was later found on the floor of the box where Booth dropped it.

Sources: Wikipedia, http//en.wikipedia.org/wiki/Deringer. Statement of William T. Kent, NARA, RG 153, M-599, reel 5: frames 0129-31. Poore I: 257, Pitman 82.

*See also:* Derringer pistol

## Derringer Pistol

Invented in 1852 by Henry Deringer, the small, single-shot pistol became so pop-

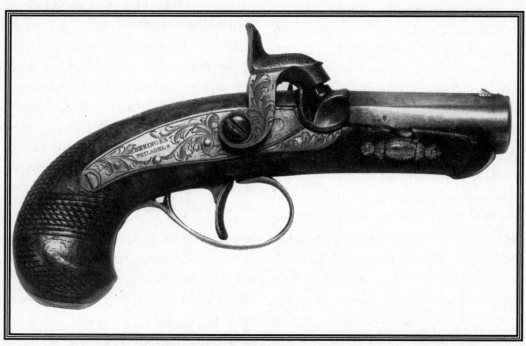

Booth's derringer pistol, used to assassinate President Lincoln

ular that several other companies manufactured knock-off models of the gun. The spelling soon became corrupted to "derringer" with two Rs. The pistol was small enough to fit in the palm of a man's hand and easily concealed in a vest or coat pocket. The gun was popular among military officers and soon became widely popular among civilians as a self-defense weapon. Introduced first by Deringer in 1852, a total of 15,000 "Philadelphia" derringers were manufactured by the time of Deringer's death in 1868.

John Wilkes Booth used a derringer to shoot Abraham Lincoln on the night of April 14, 1865. The small, .41 caliber lead ball, no larger than a pea, traversed Lincoln's brain leaving him comatose for nine hours before finally dying.

Booth's derringer was found on the floor of the box by William T. Kent, a clerk in the office of the paymaster general. Kent had entered the box shortly after the shooting and returned to Ford's Theatre looking for his apartment key, which he lost and believed was somewhere in the box. While searching the floor of the box he found the pistol. He turned it over to Lawrence A. Gobright, a reporter with the Associated Press, who turned it in to the Metropolitan police. The pistol was entered as an exhibit at the conspiracy trial and remained in the War Department until turned over to the National Park Service where it was placed on display at Ford's Theatre.

Sources: Timothy S. Good, We *Saw Lincoln Shot: One Hundred Eyewitness Accounts* (Jackson: University Press of Mississippi, 1995), 44; *Statement of William T. Kent*, NARA, RG 153, M-599, reel 5: frames 0129-31. Poore I: 257, Pitman 82.

*See also:* Deringer, Henry; Kent, William T.; Gobright, Lawrence A.

### Deveney, John A.

Called as a prosecution witness during the conspiracy trial. Deveney had served as a lieutenant in Company E of the Fourth Maryland Volunteer Infantry. He admitted going to Canada to evade the draft in 1863. While in Canada he testified to seeing John Wilkes Booth and the Confederate agent George N. Sanders talking in the lobby of the St. Lawrence Hall hotel in Montreal. Sanders was a rather notorious advocate of assassination as a means of bringing about political change.

Deveney was present at Ford's Theatre the night of the assassination and testified at the conspiracy trial as a prosecution witness. Deveney identified Booth right away. He told the tribunal he heard the words "Sic Semper Tyrannis" come from the presidential box seconds after he heard a gunshot. He also testified that Booth held a large bowie knife in his hand as he walked across the stage after jumping from the box.

Sources: Edward Steers, Jr., ed., *The Trial* (Lexington: University Press of Kentucky, 2001), 38; Timothy S. Good, *We Saw Lincoln Shot: One Hundred Eyewitness Accounts* (Jackson: University Press of Mississippi, 1995), 74–75.

## Devoe, Ely

A detective in the 22nd Army Corps in the office of Provost Marshal Henry H. Wells. One of several detectives sent by Wells on Monday night, April 17, with orders to arrest everyone in Mary Surratt's boardinghouse. Major Henry W. Smith, the officer in charge, ordered Devoe to go and bring a carriage to transport the ladies back to commanding general C. C. Augur's headquarters a few blocks west. While waiting for the occupants to gather their belongings, Lewis Powell unexpectedly arrived at the house seeking food and shelter. After questioning Powell he was placed under arrest. Devoe received five hundred dollars of the total award money set aside for the capture of Lewis Powell.

Sources: Statement of Ely DeVoe, NARA, RG 153, M-599, reel 2, frames 1090–92.

*See also*: Powell, Lewis Thornton; Surratt, Mary Elizabeth

## Devore, Eli

see Devoe, Ely

## Diary, John Wilkes Booth's

What is generally referred to as Booth's "diary" is in fact a small memorandum book for 1864 published by James W. Crawford, 54 Fourth Street, St. Louis. Booth purchased the book in 1864 while performing in St. Louis. The book is contained in a trifold leather cover measuring six inches by nine and one-eighth inches opened. The first dated page in the book begins with June 11; pages containing January 1 through June 10 (twenty-seven leafs) are missing. Booth made his first entry on the page dated Saturday, June 11, and ended on the page dated Friday, July 1; a total of fourteen pages or seven leafs. Two pages, one leaf, are blank: Friday, June 17 to Wednesday, June 22.

In 1977, the Federal Bureau of Investigation made a complete forensic analysis of the diary. This came about as a result of a National Park Service employee granting permission to a private individual to photograph the diary using various photographic techniques "for historical research purposes." The individual is controversial within the assassination community because of his claims that Booth was not killed at the Garrett farm and that the alleged papers

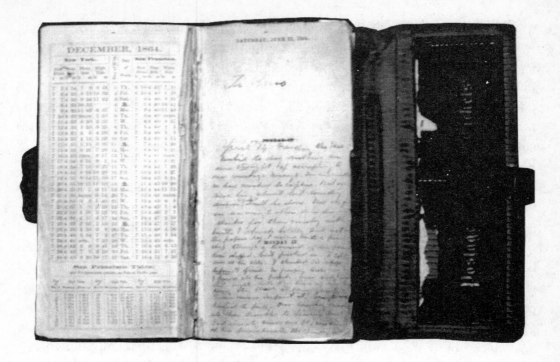

of a mysterious character place the blame for Lincoln's death on Secretary of War Edwin M. Stanton and other prominent northern politicians and businessmen.

Upon learning that a private individual had been granted such extraordinary access, assassination historian James O. Hall wrote to the Park Service expressing concern that the photographs could be used for personal gain and that historians had no way to independently verify any findings that might result from the individual's photo analysis. Hall urged the Park Service to subject the diary to a rigorous examination or allow another agency such as the National Archives or the FBI to undertake such an analysis.

The Park Service rejected Hall's request, stating the diary was now too fragile to subject it to further analysis and thus leaving the individual the sole possessor of the photographic copies of the diary. Undaunted, several individuals contacted Vice President Walter Mondale, Senator Hubert Humphrey, and Senator Wendell Anderson expressing their concerns about the photographs of the diary. The Park Service reconsidered its position and turned the diary over to the FBI for analysis. The FBI concluded its study by finding no secret writing or suspicious erasures, and affirmed that all of the writing in the diary was in John Wilkes Booth's hand.

The first twenty-four pages of the diary are printed with miscellaneous information. This is followed by sixty dated pages, with each page containing three dates, or six dates to a leaf. The first intact page in the diary is dated June 11. Assuming the first dated page in the diary began with January 1 and the last missing page ended with June 10, there would have been 162 dates. With six dates to a leaf (three to a page), there would have been twenty-seven leafs missing at the beginning of the diary.

Since Booth's first entry is on the page dated June 11, it suggests that the twenty-seven pages were already missing when Booth made his first entry. That entry is dated by Booth as April 14. It is not certain when Booth made his entries into the diary or that he made each separate entry on the date shown. Booth must have made his entries while hiding in the pine thicket waiting for Thomas Jones to send him across the Potomac River, and again while hiding at the farm of John J. Hughes. Of special interest is a hand-drawn calendar running from Monday, April 17, through Sunday, April 30. Booth crossed out each date for the 17th through the 25th (he was killed on the 26th). In the spaces of the calendar Booth writes "on Poto," meaning the Potomac River, over the "20"; "Swamp" over the "21"; and "Poto" over the "22." This leads to the conclusion that Booth set out on Thursday night, April 20 ("on Poto"), in his first attempt to cross the river only to return to Nanjemoy or "Swamp" on April 21. Booth set out a second time on Saturday, April 22 ("Poto"), and crossed the river to the Virginia side on Sunday, April 23.

Lieutenant Colonel Everton J. Conger found the diary on Booth's body following his death. Conger, a member of Colonel Lafayette C. Baker's National Detective Police, and the nominal head of the search party, removed the diary along with several other items from Booth's pockets and delivered them to Secretary of War Edwin M. Stanton.

The diary, and its missing pages, has become the centerpiece of considerable controversy over whether or not the missing pages still exist in the hands of a private person or were simply used by Booth and later discarded. The diary is on display in the museum at Ford's Theatre.[*]

Sources: Testimony of Everton J. Conger, Poore, *Conspiracy Trial*, vol. 1, 312; Statement of Everton J. Conger, NARA, RG 94, M-619, reel 455, frames 665–709; William Hanchett, "Booth's Diary," *Journal of the Illinois State Historical Society* 72, no. 1 (February 1979), 39–56; Edward Steers, Jr., *Lincoln Legends: Myths, Hoaxes, and*

[*] The text of the diary was first released to the press in May 1867.

*Confabulations Associated with Our Greatest President* (Lexington: University Press of Kentucky, 2007), 177–202.

*See also:* Missing Pages, John Wilkes Booth's Diary

## Dix, John Adams (1798–1879)

In charge of military operations in New York City. Commissioned a major general of volunteers on May 16, 1861, Dix outranked all other volunteer officers in the army throughout the Civil War. Sixty-three years old at the outbreak of the war, Dix was thought too old for combat service and assigned to garrison duties, becoming the commander of the military district of New York from 1863 to 1865. He achieved a certain fame in the North when, while serving briefly as secretary of the treasury in 1861, he sent a telegram to a treasury official in New Orleans saying that "if anyone attempts to haul down the American flag, shoot him on the spot."

In July 1863, Dix was in command during the New York draft riots, which he eventually suppressed. A few hours after Booth's shooting of Lincoln, Secretary of War Stanton sent Dix a telegram at 1:30 A.M. in which he gave details of the assassination without naming John Wilkes Booth as the suspected assassin. That wouldn't come until an hour and a half later, at 3:00 A.M., when Stanton wired, "Investigation strongly indicates J. Wilkes Booth as the assassin of the President."

When Lincoln's body arrived in New York City on April 24, 1865, it was placed on a black velvet catafalque specially built to hold the coffin inside the great rotunda of New York's city hall. Before the doors were opened to the general public, New York photographer Jeremiah Gurney, Jr., took a picture from high up in an alcove showing the open coffin with Admiral Davis and General Townsend standing at opposite ends of the coffin. When word reached Stanton he angrily ordered Dix to destroy all of the glass plates. Dix sent Stanton a print made from one of the plates to show him how unobjectionable the image was. Stanton, unmoved, renewed his order to destroy all the plates. The print Dix sent to Stanton survived, however, and was discovered among the Hay and Nicolay papers in 1952 by Ronald Reitveld, a fifteen-year-old boy.

Sources: Dorothy Meserve Kunhardt and Philip B. Kunhardt, Jr., *Twenty Days* (New York: Harper & Row, 1965), 162; Ezra J. Warner, *Generals in Blue* (Baton Rouge: Louisiana State University Press, 1964), 125–26.

## Dixon, Elizabeth

Mrs. Elizabeth Dixon, wife of Senator James Dixon of Connecticut. Soon after arriving at the Petersen house, Robert Lincoln sent for Mrs. Dixon to come immediately and sit with his mother. She stayed by Mary Lincoln's side all through the night until Lincoln's death at 7:22 A.M. on Saturday.

Mrs. Dixon accompanied Mary Lincoln back to the White House and stayed with her for two more hours before returning to her home. On leaving the White House, she started down the stairs from the second floor, where she met the military guard carrying the body of the president. Dixon wrote her sister: "I met the cortege bringing up the remains of the murdered President which were taken into the great State bedroom, wrapped in the American flag."

Sources: Elizabeth L. Dixon, letter to "My dear Louisa," reproduced in *Surratt Society News* 7, no. 3 (March 1982), 3–4.

## Doctors

Between the time Abraham Lincoln was shot and the time of his death nine hours later, sixteen physicians visited his bedside. They were Ezra W. Abbott, Joseph K. Barnes, Charles H. Crane, Edward Curtis, William Henry Ford, C. D. Gatch, Neal Hall, Albert F. A. King, Charles Augustus Leale, Charles Henry Lieberman, John Frederick May, W. M. Notson, Robert King Stone, Charles S. Taft, Lyman Beecher Todd, and Joseph Janvier Woodward.

Leale, a twenty-three-year-old army surgeon tending wounded soldiers at Armory Hospital in Washington, was the primary physician caring for Lincoln by virtue of his being first on the scene, even though he was outranked by several other physicians, including his superior, Surgeon General Joseph K. Barnes.

Sources: W. Emerson Reck, *A. Lincoln: His Last 24 Hours* (Columbia, S.C.: University of South Carolina Press, 1987), 151–55; George J. Olszewski, *Historic Structure Report: Restoration of Ford's Theatre* (Washington, D.C.: U.S. Government Printing Office, 1963); Charles A. Leale, *Lincoln's Last Hours* (New York: Privately printed, 1909).

## Dodd, Levi Axtell (1833–1901)

A member of Major General John F. Hartranft's staff charged with guarding the prisoners accused of murdering President Lincoln while imprisoned and on trial. Brigadier General Dodd was also in charge of the guard that accompanied the four conspirators to Fort Jefferson, Florida, following their conviction and sentencing. Dodd later filed a report with the War Department in which he claimed that while en route to Fort Jefferson, Dr. Mudd talked freely about his involvement with Booth. He was supported in his comments by Captain George Dutton and navy paymaster William Keeler, who were present at the time Mudd made his

November 8, 1865; Elizabeth D. Leonard, *Lincoln's Avengers: Justice, Revenge, and Reunion After the Civil War* (New York: Norton, 2004), 138–40.

*See also*: Dutton, George W.; Keeler, William F.

### Doherty, Edward Paul (1840–1897)

Officer in charge of the troop of twenty-six members of the 16th New York Cavalry that captured John Wilkes Booth and David Herold at the Garrett farm on Wednesday, April 26, 1865. Doherty, born in Ireland, was a company commander with the 16th New York Cavalry. On Monday, April 24, Doherty was relaxing in Lafayette Park opposite the White House when a messenger told him he was ordered back to his barracks. He was told to select twenty-six men, well

remarks. Mudd admitted, according to Dodd, "he knew Booth when he came to his house . . ." He also admitted that he had "been acquainted with Booth for some time, and that he was with Booth at the National Hotel on the evening referred to by Louis Wiechmann in his testimony before the military tribunal."

Sources: "The Assassins. Important Confession by Dr. Mudd—Statement of O'Laughlen and Sam Arnold," *Coldwater Union Sentinel*,

183

mounted, and report to Colonel Lafayette C. Baker. Baker told Doherty that he had reliable evidence that Booth and Herold were somewhere between the Potomac River and the Rappahannock River. Doherty was given several photographs of Booth and told to scour the countryside. Everton J. Conger and Luther B. Baker, detectives with Baker's National Detective Police, would accompany Doherty and his men. Although Conger and Baker were civilian detectives with the NDP, Conger, a former lieutenant colonel, acted as overall commander of the party, which rankled Doherty.

The search party boarded the steamer *John S. Ide* at the Sixth Street wharf in Washington and headed for Belle Plain, Virginia, where they disembarked. The two detectives with Doherty and his posse rode to the Rappahannock River about twelve miles west of Port Conway, and followed the course of the river east, reaching Port Conway around 2:00 P.M. on Tuesday, April 25. At Port Conway, they learned that two men answering Booth and Herold's description had crossed the river Monday in the company of three Confederate soldiers, one of whom was named Jett. It was also learned that Jett was courting the daughter of the owner of the Star Hotel in Bowling Green. After ferrying the men and horses across the river, the search party rode to Bowling Green, arriving around midnight. They found Jett, who agreed to lead the party to the Garrett farm where Booth and Herold were hiding. At the Garrett farm the troopers found the two fugitives. Herold surrendered, but Booth resisted and was shot, dying several hours later. Doherty proceeded back to Belle Plain with Herold and the two Garrett boys. Taking the *John S. Ide* back to Washington, Doherty turned Herold and the Garrett brothers over to Lafayette C. Baker.

For his part in the capture of Booth and Herold, Doherty received $5,250 of the reward money. Everton Conger received $15,000, Luther Baker received $3,000, and each of the twenty-six troopers under Doherty's command received $1,653.85.

Sources: Report of Lieutenant Edward P. Doherty, Official Records, Series I, vol. 46, Part I, 317–22; Statement of Edward P. Doherty, NARA, RG 153, M-599, reel 3, frames 92–95; Testimony of Edward P. Doherty, Poore, *Conspiracy Trial*, vol. 2, 92; Pitman, *Trial*, 95; Awards for the Capture of Booth and Others, NARA, RG 94, M-619, reel 456, frames 416–19.

## Donn, Alphonso

Doorkeeper at the White House. Donn accompanied young Tad Lincoln to Grover's National Theatre the night of the assassination to see the play *Aladdin! Or, the Wonderful Lamp.* Twelve years old, young Tad learned of his father's assassination when the manager of Grover's interrupted the play to announce the president had been shot. Tad was devastated, and Donn used all of his abilities to try to calm the young boy.

Mary Lincoln gave Donn the suit of clothes Lincoln was wearing at the time of his assassination. The Teamsters union purchased the clothes and donated them to the U.S. Park Service through the mediation of Iowa representative and Lincoln scholar Fred Swengel. The suit is on display in the museum at Ford's Theatre.

Sources: Dorothy Meserve Kunhardt and Philip B. Kunhardt, Jr., *Twenty Days* (New York: Harper & Row, 1965), 75.

### Doster, William E. (1837–1919)

Doster was hired by John Atzerodt to defend his brother, George Atzerodt. At the urging of Assistant Judge Advocate Henry L. Burnett, Captain Doster agreed to also represent Lewis Powell, who was unable to secure counsel. Doster, along with Thomas Ewing, was the most competent of the defense attorneys to appear before the military tribunal. He was a graduate of Yale and Harvard Law, and had served as provost marshal of District of Columbia during the war. While Doster was an able lawyer, he had a daunting task. Both of his clients were clearly involved with Booth and his conspiracy. There was no doubt about Powell. He freely admitted his attempt to kill Secretary of State William Seward, although he did not mean to harm anyone else and showed concern for Frederick Seward, whose skull he had fractured. Powell told Doster he wanted to apologize for what he did to Frederick Seward. Atzerodt was a different problem for Doster. He harmed no one. While he admitted to being a party to Booth's conspiracy to kidnap Lincoln, he did not attack Vice President Andrew Johnson, as he was supposed to do. In fact, it was Atzerodt's view that he saved Johnson's life by refusing to go through with his assignment. For this he should be thanked, not prosecuted.

Doster decided to defend Powell on grounds of insanity. He tried to emphasize the feeblemindedness of Powell, suggesting Powell had difficulty telling right from wrong in certain instances. He had been duped by Booth and was easily manipulated. Doster called two doctors who had examined Powell and felt he was insane at the time of his attack. Doster also called three prison guards who testified to Powell being deeply depressed and wanting to die. Powell, allegedly, had tried to bash his brains by beating his head against his cell wall.

The prosecution countered by calling Surgeon General Joseph K. Barnes and recalled one of the doctors who had originally testified for the defense. Barnes said Powell showed no signs of mental illness whatsoever. The other witness, Dr. James Hall, changed his testimony feeling that Powell was fully sane. Obviously, the government, or army superiors, had convinced Hall to reverse his previous testimony. Doster finally gave in and changed his defense strategy, claiming Powell's attack on Seward was an act of war. Powell was a soldier; Seward was an agent of the enemy. Powell's attack was that of a soldier attacking his acknowledged enemy. Certainly, this was within a soldier's duties and the laws of war. The strategy failed to convince anyone on the tribunal and Powell was found guilty and sentenced to death.

The prosecution had no problem linking Atzerodt to Booth and showing that Booth had assigned Atzerodt the job of killing Johnson. Atzerodt met with Booth on Friday along with Powell and Herold. What is more, Atzerodt went to the Kirkwood House at the appointed hour and was within a few steps of assassinating the vice president. The fact that he did not carry through his assignment did not save him. Had he gone to the authorities prior to Booth's mad act, he could have prevented Lincoln's murder by telling all to the police or to military authorities. He did not, and therefore he was held equally guilty—a case of vicarious liability. Atzerodt, like Powell, was found guilty and sentenced to death by hanging.

One of the more interesting things to come out of the trial involved a statement that Atzerodt made to Provost Marshal James McPhail and his assistant, John L. Smith. On May 1, while in custody, Atzerodt gave a seven-page statement. McPhail turned the statement over to Doster, who filed it among his papers, where it remained until discovered in 1977 by historian Joan L. Chaconas. The statement is significant in that Atzerodt implicates both Dr. Samuel Mudd and Mary Surratt in Booth's plot to capture Lincoln.

After the war Doster returned to his home in Bethlehem, Pennsylvania, and began a very successful career as an attorney. He died in 1919 and is buried in Bethlehem's Nisky Hill Cemetery.

Sources: Betty J. Ownsbey, *Alias "Paine": Lewis Thornton Powell, the Mystery Man of the Lincoln Conspiracy* (Jefferson, N.C.: McFarland, 1993); Edward Steers, Jr., "George Atzerodt," in Edward Steers, Jr., ed., *The Trial* (Lexington: University Press of Kentucky, 2003), lxvi–lxxi; Betty Ownsbey, "Lewis Thornton Powell alias Lewis Payne," in ibid., lxxii–lxxvii.

*See also:* Lost Confession

## Doyle, George
See Gardiner, Polk

## Drill, John
Desk sergeant on duty at the Metropolitan Police Headquarters on Tenth Street. Throughout the evening and early morning hours of April 14–15, 1865, Drill collected several items connected with the assassination. Chief among these was the small, single-shot derringer pistol Booth used to shoot Lincoln. Found on the floor of the box by William Kent, he turned it over to Associated Press writer Lawrence A. Gobright, who turned it in to Drill. Also turned in were Booth's slouch hat, a spur, an opera glass, and a hat believed to be Lincoln's.

Source: Michael W. Kauffman, *American Brutus* (New York: Random House, 2004), 55.

## Dry Tortugas
A group of small islands belonging to Florida located approximately seventy miles west of Key West. The name "Tortugas" means "turtles" in Spanish. In 1832, James Audubon visited the Dry Tortugas, describing its unusual wildlife. Strategically situated, the Dry Tortugas were considered the key to the Gulf of Mexico along the southern U.S. border. In 1846, the United States began construction of a fort that was never completed, but still served many purposes for the military.

Sources: Rodman Bethel, *A Slumbering Giant of the Past: Fort Jefferson, U.S.A. in the Dry Tortugas* (Hialeah, Fla.: W. L. Litho, 1979).

*See also:* Fort Jefferson

## Dunham, Charles A. (ca. 1832–1900)
Called as a prosecution witness in the conspiracy trial under the alias Sandford Conover and James Watson Wallace. Dunham claimed that he personally knew that Lincoln's assassination had been ordered by Jefferson Davis and planned in Canada.

Dunham (Conover) not only committed perjury, but also coached two other witnesses, Richard Montgomery and James Merritt, to commit perjury. The three witnesses testified to seeing John Wilkes Booth and John Surratt in Canada engaged in conversations with

Jacob Thompson, head of the Confederate's secret service operation there. Dunham went so far as to claim he was with Thompson when John Surratt delivered a letter to Thompson from Confederate secretary of state Judah P. Benjamin. On reading the letter, Thompson said, "This makes the thing right."

Dunham's claims on the witness stand were challenged almost immediately when the press in Canada and the United States wrote that he was a fraud and perjurer, and he recanted much of his testimony on his return to Canada. Chief prosecutor Joseph Holt had to recall Dunham to the witness stand in an effort to rehabilitate his testimony. Dunham, as one might expect, claimed the stories in the press were all false, including those that claimed he had recanted. Holt did not waiver. He stood by Dunham's testimony and carried on convinced that Jefferson Davis and his agents in Canada were behind Lincoln's assassination.

The effect of Dunham's perjured testimony, and that of Montgomery and Merrick, cast a suspicion over Holt's attempt to tie the Confederate leaders in Richmond and Canada to Booth's murder of President Lincoln. Not all of their testimony was false, and other, more reliable witnesses substantiated some of it. There is little doubt that Booth was in contact with Confederate agents in Montreal and that he may have received funds from them, which he used to support his capture scheme.

Dunham was a man with multiple personalities. Throughout his career as a charlatan, he used as many as nine aliases. The effect of Dunham's mastery of lying and fabricating carried over into modern times, dividing historians. David Rankin Barbee, after years of studying Dunham, concluded he was a secret agent working for Stanton while assassination historian William A. Tidwell concluded Dunham was working as a Confederate agent providing false testimony in the knowledge that it would be exposed and result in no one believing that the Confederate leaders in Richmond had had anything to do with Lincoln's assassination. Both roles are plausible, which shows just how effective Dunham was in convincing others that he was truthful. Dunham's success as a charlatan was a product of the Civil War. As his biographer, Carman Cummings, noted, "In ordinary times, Dunham night have ended up as a minor lawyer or confidence man."

Sources: Carman Cumming, *Devil's Game: The Civil War Intrigues of Charles A. Dunham* (Urbana: University of Illinois Press, 2004); Thomas R. Turner, *The Assassination of Abraham Lincoln* (Malabar, Fla.: Krieger, 1999), 49–51.

## Dutton, George W.

A captain in the Tenth Regiment, Veteran Reserve Corps. Dutton was in charge of the guard unit stationed at Old Aqueduct Bridge in Georgetown at the time of Lincoln's assassination. Among his papers in the Massachusetts Historical Society is a photograph of John Wilkes Booth (Gutman No. 35) with the notation: "This picture was sent to me at Aqueduct Bridge to be tacked upon the guard quarters to enable the guard to identify Booth if he passed this way." The photograph has four small pinholes, one in each corner. These photographs were hurriedly made

in the photograph facilities of the surgeon general under the supervision of Assistant Surgeon General Charles H. Crane, and distributed throughout the military. It is almost certain that detectives Everton J. Conger, Luther B. Baker, and Edward P. Doherty carried this photograph with them when searching for Booth.

Dutton played another important part in the assassination story. Following the conviction and sentencing of Samuel Mudd, Michael O'Laughlen, Samuel Arnold, and Edman Spangler, Dutton was in charge of the guard unit that accompanied them to Fort Jefferson, where they would be imprisoned. On his return to Washington, Dutton swore out an affidavit that stated in part, "during a conversation with Dr. Mudd, on the 22nd of July, he confessed that he knew Booth when he came to his house with Herold on the morning after the assassination of the President; that he had known Booth for some time . . . that he was with Booth at the National Hotel on the evening referred to by Wiechmann . . . that he came to Washington on that occasion to meet with Booth by appointment who wished to be introduced to John Surratt."

Dutton's claim that Mudd made such a statement was supported by navy paymaster William Keeler and army general Levi Axtell Dodd, who were present when Mudd made his statement.

Sources: Edward Steers, Jr., *Blood on the Moon* (Lexington: University Press of Kentucky, 2001), 76–77; Edward Steers, Jr., ed., *The Trial* (Lexington: University Press of Kentucky, 2003), 421.

*See also:* Dodd, Levi Axtell; Keeler, William F.

## Dye, Joseph M.

A witness at the conspiracy trial. Dye testified that he was in front of Ford's Theatre just before Booth fired the fatal shot. He told of three men meeting in front of the theater, one being Booth. Dye described the men's appearance. Two of the men were well dressed, obviously gentlemen, while the third was dirty and rough in appearance with a swollen face, typical of an alcoholic. Dye could not positively identify the rough-looking man from among the defendants. One of the men kept going into the lobby, then coming outside, announcing the time from a clock located inside the theater. He did this three or four times. At ten minutes past ten he announced the time and then hurriedly walked up the street while the second gentleman went into the theater and the rough-looking man went down the alley between the theater and the saloon next door to where the stage door was located.

The prosecution attempted to make the case that John Surratt was calling the time while Booth was waiting to go into the theater at the right moment and kill Lincoln. Spangler, being the rough-looking person, went down the alley. The effect of Dye's testimony is not obvious. John Surratt was in Elmira, New York, at the time, and Booth was in the rear alley behind the theater, while Spangler was inside the theater backstage, where he shifted scenes.

Dye was called again as a witness, this time in John Surratt's civil trial in the District of Columbia in June 1867. Dye gave essentially the same testimony as he had in 1865, the prosecution attempting to place John Surratt at the theater at the time of the assassination. Was Dye lying or simply mistaken about what he saw? Whatever the case, it does not comport with what we know based on the testimony of numerous other witnesses.

Sources: Testimony of Sergeant Joseph M. Dye, NARA, RG 153, M-599, reel 4, frame 36; Poore, *Conspiracy Trial*, vol. 1, 181; Pitman, *Trial*, 72; Statement of Joseph M. Dye, NARA, RG 153, M-599, reel 4, frames 270–76.

## Dyer, Jeremiah T.

A witness at the conspiracy trial called on behalf of Dr. Samuel A. Mudd Dyer was the brother of the doctor's wife, Sarah Frances Dyer Mudd. The defense used Dyer's testimony to refute the claim of several Mudd slaves that Samuel Mudd threatened to send them to Richmond if they did not behave or were caught trying to run away. Dyer also refuted the testimony that John Surratt and Walter Bowie (a Confederate soldier wanted by the Union authorities) were ever at Dr. Mudd's house. Dyer refuted the claim that several men wearing gray uniforms and short jackets camped in the woods behind Mudd's house on several occasions and that Mudd sent them food and blankets. Dyer said he and several other men hid in Mudd's woods in 1861 when Colonel William Dwight's regiment passed through Charles County. Word spread that Dwight was arresting all of the males, and so several of them hid until the regiment left the area. Dwight, however, was not in Charles County in 1864 and 1865, the time the witnesses claimed Confederate soldiers and John Surratt frequented the Mudd farm.

When Mudd was serving his sentence at Fort Jefferson, Dyer took over the management of his farm and saw that his wife and children were cared for.

Sources: Testimony of Jeremiah Dyer, Poore, *Conspiracy Trial*, vol. 2, 300, 329, 449; Pitman, *Trial*, 179–80.

*See also:* Simms, Mary

## Eastern Branch, Potomac River

A branch of the Potomac River that separates the community of Anacostia from the western area of the District of Columbia. Also known as the Anacostia River. When traveling to Southern Maryland, one must cross over one of the several bridges spanning the Eastern Branch. The Navy Yard Bridge (also known as the Eleventh Street Bridge) passed over the Eastern Branch into Uniontown (currently Anacostia). Booth used this bridge at the time of his escape after shooting Lincoln.

Sources: *DeLorme Maryland Delaware Atlas & Gazetteer*, 2000 ed., 47.

*See also:* Navy Yard Bridge; Booth Escape Route

## Eaton, William

A detective with the provost marshal's office in Washington, Eaton went to the National Hotel to Booth's room on Saturday, April 15, and took charge of the contents of Booth's trunk, including various papers and letters. He turned the material over to his superior, Lieutenant William H. Terry. Eaton was called as a prosecution witness at the conspiracy trial, telling the court about taking charge of Booth's papers, and his arrest of Edman Spangler at his boardinghouse on Seventh Street and H Streets.

Sources: Testimony of William Eaton, Poore, *Conspiracy Trial*, vol. 1, 419, 455; Pitman, *Trial*, 41, 98.

*See also:* Terry, William H.

## Eckert, Thomas (1825–1910)

Assistant secretary of war and head of the War Department's telegraph office. Eckert plays a major role in several of the odd conspiracy theories that claim Secretary of War Edwin M. Stanton was behind Lincoln's murder. At a cabinet meeting on the morning of April 14, Lincoln invited General and Mrs. Grant to accompany him and his wife Mary to Ford's Theatre. Grant accepted but later in the afternoon broke his engagement, telling Lincoln he and Mrs. Grant wanted to catch the early train to New Jersey so they might spend some time with their children. According to David Homer Bates, a telegrapher in the War Department telegraph office, Stanton persuaded Grant not to go with the Lincolns. He was afraid that Lincoln took unnecessary risks and asked Grant to urge Lincoln not to go to the theater.

Lincoln visited the telegraph office on the afternoon of April 14 while Stanton was there and asked Stanton if he could spare Eckert to accompany him to the theater later that evening. Stanton, still against Lincoln going to the theater, told Lincoln he could not spare Eckert; he had important work to finish. Lincoln

then went and asked Eckert if he couldn't put off his paperwork and join him. Eckert, realizing how strongly Stanton felt, turned Lincoln down, telling him he had to finish his work that evening, as it couldn't wait.

Conspiracy theorists make a great deal out of this little story, claiming Stanton wanted to be sure Lincoln was left unguarded to make it easier for the assassin to carry out his plan. Otto Eisenschiml, who wrote *Why Was Lincoln Murdered?*, suggested Stanton ordered Grant and Eckert to say no to Lincoln, leaving him unprotected that night, without either of the two men who might have stopped

Booth and saved Lincoln's life. Had Grant been present, the argument goes, his military guard would have protected the door leading into the box, thwarting Booth's ingress to Lincoln.

Such claims are baseless. In fact, evidence exists to the contrary. On February 10, just eight weeks prior to the assassination, Grant and Lincoln, along with Major General Ambrose Burnside, attended Ford's Theatre together and sat in the very same presidential box. The play starred John Wilkes Booth's brother-in-law John Sleeper Clarke in *Love in Livery*. No guards were posted from either Grant's or Burnside's staffs, and people were allowed to enter the box during the performance to deliver messages without being screened. More to the point, on the night of April 14, Simon P. Hanscom, editor of the Washington newspaper *National Republican*, entered the box and delivered a White House document to Lincoln. Charles Forbes, the president's messenger and footman, was seated closest to the box, and just as he would do twenty minutes later with Booth, waved Hanscom into the box.

At the moment Booth entered the box, Eckert was home preparing for bed. One of his telegraph operators ran to Eckert's house with the tragic news. Eckert quickly got dressed and headed straight for Stanton's house, where he found the secretary about to go to the home of William Seward. It was Eckert who later that night (12:20 A.M.) sent the telegram to Grant in Philadelphia with the words "The President was assassinated at Ford's Theatre at 10 30 tonight & cannot live."

The fact remains that Lincoln was readily accessible to all sorts of people, even when attending a play in a private box. Lincoln was in all probability the most accessible president of the nineteenth century, if not of all time.

Sources: David Homer Bates, *Lincoln in the Telegraph Office* (1907; reprint, Lincoln: University of Nebraska Press, 1995), 365–68; William Hanchett, *The Lincoln Murder Conspiracies* (Urbana: University of Illinois Press, 1983), 172–73.

## Eglent, Elzee

A former slave of Dr. Samuel Mudd. Eglent was an important prosecution witness against Samuel Mudd at the conspiracy trial. Eglent told of being shot in the leg by Dr. Mudd because he had not responded quickly enough to Mudd's orders. Eglent was described at the trial as being "obstreperous." Eglent also testified that Mudd would threaten his male slaves by telling them he would send them south to Richmond where they would be used to help build the defenses around Richmond. Eglent's testimony, along with Mary Simms's testimony that Mudd had

whipped her, causing her to run away, was used to portray Mudd as having a dark side that belied the defense's characterization of him as a kindly country doctor, a caring individual.

Eglent's testimony was also used to show that Mudd harbored Confederate soldiers in the woods behind his house, providing them with food and blankets. He also used his house as a safe house for Confederate agents such as John Surratt, who served as a Confederate courier working for Confederate secretary of state Judah P. Benjamin, carrying documents and escorting female agents between Canada and Richmond.

Sources: Testimony of Elzee Eglent, Poore, *Conspiracy Trial*, vol. 2, 157; Pitman, *Trial*, 171; Richard Washington et al., NARA, RG 109, M-416, Union Provost Marshal's File of Papers Relating to Two or More Civilians, File 6083.

*See also:* Simms, Mary

## Eisenschiml, Otto

Author of two major works on the assassination that claimed Lincoln was the victim of a "grand conspiracy" engineered by Secretary of War Edwin M. Stanton and other notable politicians and financiers. His sensational theory captured the American imagination and, although completely discredited by William Hanchett in his definitive study of

Lincoln assassination conspiracies, continues to survive in the minds of the general public, and has survived in several books, published as recently as 2004.

A professionally trained chemist turned avocational historian, Eisenschiml was the first to point an accusatory finger at Stanton, suggesting he was behind Lincoln's assassination. The motive for this treasonous act was to give the Radical Republicans a free hand in dealing with the defeated South and to allow a select group of people to profit from the spoils of war. In 1937, Eisenschiml published his first book, *Why Was Lincoln Murdered?*, in which he asked and answered several questions that led the reader to the false conclusion that Stanton engineered Lincoln's death. Much of Eisenschiml's "evidence" was false, fabricated, or carefully manipulated to support his thesis.

Among Eisenschiml's evidence were claims that the military telegraph was shut down during the critical hours immediately following Lincoln's murder; the bridge over which Booth escaped was kept open although all other avenues from Washington were closed down; Lincoln was denied protection when Stanton dissuaded General Grant and Assistant Secretary of War Thomas Eckert from accompanying Lincoln to the theater; and a derelict bodyguard was assigned who abandoned his post, thereby allowing Booth access to the presidential box. The bodyguard was never disciplined and remained in his position simply because he had done nothing wrong. The presence of either Grant or Eckert would have had no effect on Booth's act; he still would have had access to Lincoln. The military telegraph was in continuous operation throughout the night and early morning hours; it never shut down; only the commercial telegraph was shut down to allow the government time to gain control of the situation and avoid panic. Lincoln's bodyguard was not required to guard the entrance to the box, and Lincoln's footman and messenger was outside the box by chance, which allowed Booth to enter. Ingress and egress from Washington had been considerably relaxed following General Lee's surrender five days earlier. Eisenschiml is a prime example of an historian following the facts where he wanted them to lead him rather than following the facts wherever they might lead him. Eisenschiml's case against Stanton has been thoroughly refuted, principally by the research of James O. Hall and William Hanchett.

Despite their efforts, Eisenschiml's thesis has appealed to a segment of the population that continues to believe in an evil conspiracy within Lincoln's own family of friends and political supporters.

Sources: Otto Eisenschiml, *Why Was Lincoln Murdered?* (Boston: Little, Brown, 1937); William Hanchett, *The Lincoln Murder Conspiracies* (Urbana: University of Illinois Press, 1983); William Hanchett, "Persistent Myths of the Lincoln Assassination," *Lincoln Herald* 99, no. 4 (Winter 1997), 172–79.

### Ellsler, John

Manager of the Academy of Music in Cleveland and friend of John Wilkes Booth. In 1864, Ellsler and Thomas Mears became partners with Booth in the Dramatic Oil Company. Booth put up most of the capital in buying oil leases in Venango County, Pennsylvania. The three partners purchased rights to three and one-half acres of land on the Fuller farm along the Allegheny River at a time when oil was being discovered throughout western Pennsylvania. Booth brought in Joseph Simonds to act as business manager of the entire operation. Several productive oil wells were located close to the property of Booth and his partners, but as luck would have it, the Dramatic Oil Company was a loser. The summer of 1864 saw Booth lose interest in his failing oil investment. He asked Simonds to take care of assigning two-thirds of his interest in the well to his older brother Junius Brutus, Jr., and one-third to Si-

monds. Booth had other matters on his mind. In August he met with Samuel Arnold and Michael O'Laughlen in Baltimore and persuaded them to join his plan to kidnap President Lincoln. By the fall he had divested himself of all of his assets and devoted himself to his plan to capture Lincoln and present him to Jefferson Davis.

Sources: Ernest C. Miller, *John Wilkes Booth in the Pennsylvania Oil Region* (Meadville, Pa.: Crawford County Historical Society, 1987).

*See also:* Simonds, Joseph

### Elmira, New York

Site of Union prison camp for Confederate prisoners of war. On the day of Lincoln's murder, John H. Surratt, Jr., was in Elmira on an assignment for Confederate commissioner Brigadier General Edwin Grey Lee. Jefferson Davis had appointed Lee on December 6, 1864, to assume command of covert operations emanating from Canada. Surratt, a Confederate agent who reported directly to Confederate secretary of state Judah P. Benjamin, arrived in Elmira on April 13 with instructions to reconnoiter the Union prisoner-of-war camp and make sketches that could be used in freeing the Confederate prisoners held there. The war ended before any attempt could be mounted.

During Surratt's trial in 1867, the prosecution attempted to show that Surratt was in Washington on April 14. The defense rebutted the prosecution's witnesses by producing store clerks from Elmira who testified to Surratt's being in their establishment on April 14 buying shirts. The jury failed to bring in a verdict and Surratt was set free.

Sources: Alfred Isaccson, *The Travels, Arrest, and Trial of John H. Surratt* (Middletown, N.Y.: Vestigium, 2003); Joan L. Chaconas, "John H. Surratt, Jr.," in Edward Steers, Jr., ed., *The Trial* (Lexington: University Press of Kentucky, 2003).

*See also:* Surratt, John Harrison, Jr.

## Escape Route
See Booth Escape Route

## Ewing, Thomas (1829–1896)
Brevet Major General Thomas Ewing, along with civilian attorney Frederick Stone, represented Dr. Samuel A. Mudd at his trial. Ewing also represented Samuel Arnold and Edman Spangler. Ewing was born in Lancaster, Ohio, August 7, 1829. His mother, a Roman Catholic, converted him to Catholicism while a young child. Ewing entered Brown University, but left before he graduated to serve as private secretary to President Zachary Taylor from 1849 to 1850. He returned to Ohio, where he earned his law degree, and moved to Kansas in 1856 to become a member of the Leavenworth Constitutional Convention of 1858. An abolitionist, he worked hard to ensure Kansas entered the Union as a free state. As a result of his efforts he was elected chief justice of the Kansas Supreme Court. Ewing served as chief justice in 1861–1862. He resigned his position in 1862 to become colonel of the 11th Kansas Cavalry. His regiment fought as infantry in James G. Blunt's division in the battles of Fort Wayne, Cane Hill, and Prairie Grove. He was promoted to brigadier general and received a brevet appoint-

ment as major general for valor in February 1865. In March 1865, he resigned his commission and returned to civilian life. Ewing was the stepbrother of Union general William T. Sherman.

Ewing attempted to challenge the tribunal, claiming it lacked legal jurisdiction. The thrust of his challenge was that his clients were civilians and residents of a loyal state, Maryland, and should be tried in civil court, not a military court. The Constitution guaranteed such protection. Despite his efforts, the tribunal overruled Ewing's challenge. According to the rules established for military tribunals, the court was the sole arbiter on the question, and ruled in its own favor. Ewing was hampered in his defense of Samuel Mudd by his client's unwillingness to be truthful. Mudd denied knowing Booth, and denied meeting with him in Washington. Testimony during the trial clearly showed Mudd met with Booth on at least two occasions, once in Charles County, and once in Washington. Unknown to Ewing and the tribunal, Mudd met with Booth a third time, a fact that did not become known until after the trial ended. Mudd's joint counsel, Frederick Stone, said of Mudd at the time of Mudd's death in 1883, "His prevarications were painful. He had given his whole case away by not trusting even his counsel." Once the trial was over, Ewing no longer represented Mudd. Mudd turned to other attorneys in an effort to overturn the jurisdiction of the military tribunal.

Following the completion of the trial, Ewing remained in Washington practicing law from 1865 until 1871, when he returned to Lancaster, Ohio. He was elected to the U.S. House of Representatives, serving from 1877 to 1881. Ewing ran for governor of Ohio in 1879 but lost. Following his term in the House he settled in New York City, where he resumed his law practice. He died in New York on January 21, 1896.

Sources: Ezra J. Warner, *Generals in Blue* (Baton Rouge: Louisiana State University Press, 1964), 147; Edward Steers, Jr., "Samuel Alexander Mudd," in Edward Steers, Jr., ed., *The Trial* (Lexington: University Press of Kentucky, 2003), lxxix–lxxxvii.

*See also*: Stone, Frederick; Mudd, Dr. Samuel Alexander

## Farrell, Francis

A near neighbor of Samuel Mudd. On his return home from Bryantown on Saturday evening following Lincoln's assassination, and while Booth and Herold were still at Mudd's house, Mudd visited with Farrell and another neighbor, John Hardy. Both Farrell and Hardy were called as witnesses at the conspiracy trial and told the military tribunal that Mudd had told them about Lincoln's assassination, and that the assassin was a man named Booth. When they asked Mudd if it was the same Booth who had visited the area in the fall of 1864, Mudd replied that he thought it was the same man. Hardy also made the statement that when Mudd left for home the sun was only fifteen minutes above the horizon. Sunset on April 15 occurred at 6:44 P.M. If Hardy was correct, Mudd left Hardy's around 6:30 P.M. and arrived home near 7:00 P.M., and not between 4:00 and 5:00 P.M. as he later told detectives. This meant there were between two and three hours unaccounted for in Mudd's visit to Bryantown. Since Booth later said he was headed to the home of William Burtles, it seems likely that Mudd rode past Bryantown to Burtles's house to inform him that Booth and Herold would arrive later that night. This would take Mudd between two and three hours.

Hardy also testified that he saw Booth at St. Mary's Church on two occasions, not one as Mudd claimed; the first in November 1864 and the second in December 1864. The testimony of others clearly places Booth and Mudd together in December as well as November. Mudd never mentioned this December meeting.

Sources: Testimony of Francis Farrell, Poore, *Conspiracy Trial*, vol. 3, 418–23; Pitman, *Trial*, 218; Testimony of John F. Hardy, Poore, *Conspiracy Trial*, vol. 2, 434–36, vol. 3, 431–37; Pitman, *Trial*, 213, 218; James L. Swanson, *Manhunt: The 12-Day Chase for Lincoln's Killer* (New York: Harper Perennial, 2007), 160–61.

*See also:* Burtles, William; Hardy, John F.; Mudd, Dr. Samuel Alexander

## Farwell, Leonard J.

Inspector of patents and a former governor of Wisconsin who lived at the Kirkwood House hotel on Pennsylvania Avenue, where Vice President Andrew Johnson was rooming. The two men, both former governors, became good friends and visited with each other on numerous occasions. Farwell, on realizing President Lincoln had been shot by an assassin, feared for Johnson's life and rushed from Ford's Theatre to the Kirkwood House, where he alerted Johnson to what had happened. Farwell returned to the Petersen house, where he ran into

Provost Marshal James McPhail. Learning of Johnson's vulnerability, McPhail rushed to the Kirkwood House and arranged for detective John Lee to meet him in Johnson's room.

Sources: Mark E. Neely, Jr., *The Abraham Lincoln Encyclopedia* (New York: McGraw-Hill, 1982), 164–65; Michael J. Kauffman, *American Brutus* (New York: Random House, 2004), 30.

*See also:* Johnson, Andrew

## Ferguson, James

A witness for the prosecution. Told of finding a letter floating in the water near Morehead City, North Carolina. The letter was in cipher. A translation of the letter, addressed to "John," and dated April 15, was read into the court record. The substance of the letter makes coded references to killing Lincoln and others, including Generals Sherman and Grant. The letter appears to be a fabrication, but by whom and for what purpose is not clear.

Sources: Edward Steers, Jr., ed., *The Trial* (Lexington: University Press of Kentucky, 2003), 42.

## Ferguson, James P. (1828–1897)

Owner of restaurant adjoining Ford's Theatre on the north or upper side of the building, 452 Tenth Street. Ferguson was called as a prosecution witness at the trial. Ferguson was seated in the Dress Circle on the side opposite the presidential box and so had an excellent view of the president and his party. His testimony, recorded verbatim by James Tanner in the Petersen house a short time after the assassination, is considered the most detailed account of what happened. He told of seeing the flash of the pistol and heard Booth yell, "Revenge for the South." When Booth vaulted over the balustrade and landed off-balance on the stage he stood and shouted "Sic Semper Tyrannis." He described Booth as running across the stage before disappearing backstage.

Sources: James P. Ferguson, NARA, RG 153, M-599, reel 5, frames 384–99; Poore, *Conspiracy Trial*, vol. 1, 189; Pitman, *Trial*, 76; Poore, *Conspiracy Trial*, vol. 2, 537; Pitman, *Trial*, 106; Timothy S. Good, *We Saw Lincoln Shot: One Hundred Eyewitness Accounts* (Jackson: University Press of Mississippi, 1995), 78–79.

## Ferguson, William J. (1845–1930)

Worked as a stagehand at Ford's Theatre. Author of a booklet, *I Saw Booth Shoot Lincoln*. Ferguson wrote numerous accounts of what he saw the night of the assassination. According to Ferguson, Major Henry Rathbone was dressed in civilian clothes, not his military uniform as most histories state. Ferguson also claimed that the hole in the door leading

into the inner box was bored with a pen-knife, not a drill, and certainly not made by firing the ball through the door as James Gifford thought. An examination of the door on display at Ford's Theatre confirms this. The best account of what Ferguson related is found in Timothy S. Good, *We Saw Lincoln Shot: One Hundred Eyewitness Accounts*.

Sources: Timothy S. Good, *We Saw Lincoln Shot: One Hundred Eyewitness Accounts* (Jackson: University Press of Mississippi, 1995), 169–73.

### Ferree, Newton (1843–1928)

Found, on the floor of the presidential box in Ford's Theatre, Lincoln's shirt collar, which Dr. Charles Leale had removed while attending to Lincoln. Sometime after everyone had left the theater, Ferree and William T. Kent returned there to search the presidential box for Kent's keys, which he thought he had lost in the box earlier that evening during all the commotion. In searching the box, Kent found Booth's derringer on the floor, and Ferree found the president's collar stained with his blood. Ferree kept the collar while Kent gave the derringer to Lawrence Gobright, a reporter with the Associated Press who was also in the theater that night. Gobright turned the derringer in to the police.

Sources: Statement of William T. Kent, NARA, RG 153, M-599, reel 5, frames 129–31; Poore, *Conspiracy Trial*, vol. 1, 257; Pitman, *Trial*, 82.

*See also:* Kent, William T.

### Ferrandini, Cipriano

Ringleader of a plot to assassinate president-elect Lincoln during his stopover in Baltimore on his way to Washington on February 23, 1861. Born in Corsica in 1822, Ferrandini came to the United States and settled in Baltimore. A member of the Knights of the Golden Circle (KGC), Ferrandini worked as a barber at Barnum's City Hotel in Baltimore. The KGC was made up of anti-northern Confederate sympathizers located in several northern states. Ferrendini was an ardent Confederate who hated Lincoln for his antislavery views. He organized a plot to assassinate Lincoln during a stopover in Baltimore on his way to Washington in February 1861. Ferrendini's plot was discovered by agents working for Allan Pinkerton, who had infiltrated Ferrandini's circle of assassins. Undercover agents from the New York police force independently discovered the plot. The police commissioner of New York had learned of the plot and informed William Seward, Lincoln's secretary of state designate, who sent his son to meet with Lincoln in Philadelphia and inform him of the plot. Pinkerton told Lincoln what he had learned of the plot, urging Lincoln to alter his schedule. When Lincoln heard the same news from Kennedy's investigation, he concluded the plot was a real threat. Lincoln altered his schedule, passing through Baltimore nine hours ahead of schedule and thereby thwarting Ferrendini and his cohorts. Having failed, nothing more was heard of Ferrandini or the KGC in Baltimore. Ferrandini's plot was the first of several plots designed to remove Lincoln from office either by capturing him, or worse, killing him.

Ferrandini died on December 20, 1910, and was buried in the old Holy Cross Cemetery. Following abandonment of the old cemetery, Ferrandini's remains were reburied in the Holy Cross section of Woodlawn Cemetery in Baltimore.

Sources: Edward Steers, Jr., "MacLincoln's Highland Fling: The Baltimore Plot to Assassinate the President-Elect," *North & South* 6, no. 3 (April 2003), 50–59.

*See also*: Capture Plots

### Ficklin, Benjamin Franklin (1827–1871)

Arrested as a suspect in Lincoln's assassination. Ficklin served as a blockade runner early in the war. By 1864, blockade running was no longer profitable as a result of the navy's effective blockade, which cut off most of the sea lanes leading to the few Confederate ports that were still open. Ficklin found a more lucrative business in trading and selling cotton. The cotton trade cut across both northern and southern lines, finding strange partnerships all in the name of making money. Ficklin was one of the cotton traders who worked on both sides of the war.

The day after Lincoln's assassination, Ficklin wrote to an old friend and cotton trader, "In the meantime I am in constant dread of being arrested as a Southerner. When this is over I will go south to get out my cotton, unless some other terrible thing should happen which I do not now dream of."

Major James O'Beirne arrested Ficklin on April 16, 1865, convinced that Ficklin had a part in Lincoln's assassination. Ficklin had been in contact with George Atzerodt, and had stayed at the Kirkwood House on April 14. Both findings were true, but purely coincidental to the assassination. They had to do with Ficklin's cotton trading. Held for two months, he was released on June 16, as a result of former Illinois senator Orville H. Browning's intercession with Secretary of War Stanton.

Sources: Statement of Benjamin F. Ficklin, NARA, RG 153, M-599, reel 7, frames 69–74; William A. Tidwell, James O. Hall, and David W. Gaddy, *Come Retribution* (Jackson: University Press of Mississippi, 1988), 179–81.

### Fitzpatrick, Honora (1846–1896)

A boarder at Mary Surratt's Washington boardinghouse. Honora Fitzpatrick was seventeen years old at the time of the assassination. Her father arranged for her to board with Mary Surratt presumably because he thought Mrs. Surratt a pious woman of good character who would look after his daughter's well-being. She was the first of several boarders to live at the house. On the evening of March 15, Booth reserved the president's box at Ford's Theatre for Fitzpatrick and ten-year-old Mary Appolonia Dean, John Surratt, and Lewis Powell. Booth wanted Surratt and Powell to familiarize themselves with the box. Booth still had it in his mind to capture Lincoln while he sat in the box watching a play. Later that same evening, after the two young girls were taken home to the boardinghouse, Surratt and Powell met Booth, Herold, Atzerodt, Arnold, and O'Laughlen at Gautier's restaurant on Pennsylvania Avenue. Booth had rented a private dining room at the restaurant. It was during dinner that Booth went over his plan for capturing Lincoln at Ford's Theatre. Arnold objected, saying the scheme was impractical. They would never be able to kidnap Lincoln while he was in the box in full view of a crowded theater. The argument became heated and threats were exchanged. Booth, however, cooled down and made amends with Arnold and the others. Called as a witness, Fitzpatrick told the court about the evening at the theater.

Fitzpatrick was interviewed extensively and gave statements in addition to her interview. Perhaps the most important information she gave her interviewers was the fact that Booth visited the Surratt boardinghouse numerous times, and, Fitzpatrick said, times when John Surratt was not at home. Prosecutors interpreted this to mean that Booth visited the house specifically to see Mary Surratt. Called separately by the defense, she told the court that she knew Mary Surratt's eyesight was "defective." She often threaded a needle for her because she could not see to do it herself. Her testimony was meant to help support Mary Surratt's claim that she did not identify Powell the night he came to her house when detectives were there because her eyesight was poor.

Sources: Honora Fitzpatrick, NARA, RG 153, M-599, reel 5, frames 400–11; Poore, *Conspiracy Trial*, vol. 2, 89, 185; Pitman, *Trial*, 121, 132.

*See also*: Bell, William; Gautier's Restaurant; Powell, Lewis Thornton

## Flag

See Treasury Guard Flags

## Fletcher, John

Manager of Thompson Naylor's stables. On the night of the assassination Fletcher reported Herold to both the police and 22nd Army Corps headquarters as having stolen his horse, and that he fled over the Navy Yard Bridge. As a result, General C. C. Augur sent a troop from the 13th New York Cavalry to Southern Maryland after him.

Fletcher rented a horse to David Herold on the afternoon of April 14. Also on April 14, George Atzerodt stabled his horse with Fletcher that he rented earlier in the day from the stables of Keleher & Pywell, located on Eighth Street.

At 10:00 P.M. on the night of April 14, Atzerodt came by the stables and asked Fletcher to join him in a drink. The two men walked the short distance to the Union Hotel at Thirteen-and-a-half and E streets, where they drank whiskey together. Returning to the stables, Atzerodt took his horse and rode to the Kirkwood House at Twelfth Street and Pennsylvania Avenue and went inside and ordered a drink. Assigned to murder Vice President Andrew Johnson, Atzerodt could not bring himself to kill Johnson. He mounted his horse and rode off in the direction of Ford's Theatre.

Meanwhile, back at Naylor's stables, John Fletcher was looking for Herold, who was now overdue in returning Fletcher's horse. Fletcher walked up to Pennsylvania Avenue and looked around to see if he could see Herold. With uncanny luck, Fletcher saw Herold coming down Fourteenth Street shortly after fleeing the Seward House, where he had left Lewis Powell to fend for himself after attacking several members of the Seward household. Yelling at Herold to bring the horse back, Herold galloped back up Fourteenth Street, and turning east, raced toward the Navy Yard Bridge, where he crossed over the Eastern Branch of the Potomac River and into Uniontown.

Fletcher returned to his stables where he mounted a horse and took off after Herold. Arriving at the Navy Yard Bridge, Fletcher was told by Sergeant Cobb that a man crossed over several minutes before followed by a second man riding a horse that fit Fletcher's description of the horse he rented to Herold. Cobb told Fletcher he could cross over the bridge but could not return until daylight. Fletcher chose to return to the city and report his stolen horse to police headquarters located on Tenth Street near Ford's Theatre.

At police headquarters Fletcher was told that soldiers had recently found a stray horse wandering east of the Capitol, and had taken it to the stables of the 22nd Army Corps a short distance away. The police officer, Charles Stone, accompanied Fletcher to the stables, where Fletcher was shown the saddle taken from the stray horse. The saddle did not belong to Fletcher, but he recognized it as belonging to George Atzerodt. When Fletcher was shown the horse, he recognized it as one that he had seen Atzerodt riding. It was a distinctive horse in that it had lost an eye. The one-eyed horse was the horse that Booth had purchased, with Samuel Mudd's help, from George Gardiner, Mudd's nearest neighbor in Beantown. The horse had been ridden by Lewis Powell that very night and abandoned near Lincoln Hospital east of the Capitol.

As a result of Fletcher's information, the detectives were able to link David Herold and George Atzerodt, and later that day, linked Atzerodt to Booth as a result of searching Atzerodt's room at the Kirkwood House, where they found Booth's bankbook. Thus three men were quickly tied together, Booth, Herold, and Atzerodt, and the authorities knew at least one of these men, and perhaps two, had crossed the Navy Yard Bridge around 11:00 P.M., heading into Southern Maryland. Major General C. C. Augur, commander of the 22nd Army Corps, sent a troop of cavalry of the 13th New York Cavalry with orders to go to Southern Maryland and follow the trail of the two men who had fled over the bridge. The troop arrived in Bryantown around noon on Saturday. They were only five miles from where Booth and Herold were hiding at the home of Dr. Samuel A. Mudd.

Sources: Statement of John Fletcher, NARA, RG 153, M-599, reel 5, frames 414–21; Poore, *Conspiracy Trial*, vol. 1, 326; Pitman, *Trial*, 83, 145.

*See also:* Atzerodt, George Andrew; Herold, David

### Forbes, Charles (1835–1895)

Forbes served as Lincoln's messenger and footman. He accompanied President Lincoln and Mrs. Lincoln aboard their coach to Ford's Theatre on April 14. Forbes was seated in the Dress Circle closest to the president's box throughout the play (Section A, seat 300). John Wilkes Booth was seen talking with Forbes shortly before entering the outer vestibule of boxes 7 and 8. Eyewitnesses described Booth handing Forbes a card and then entering the vestibule. Booth wrote in his diary that he "was stopped, but pushed on." Once inside, Booth wedged a wooden bar between the door and a hole he had cut into the plaster earlier that day, securing the door so no one could enter from outside.

Forbes remains an enigma. He was not called as a witness at the conspiracy trial and did not give a statement to investigators as far as we know. On May 1, 1865, Superintendent A. C. Richards filed a formal charge against patrolman John F. Parker, the president's bodyguard on the night of April 14, stating that Parker "allowed a man to enter the President's private box and shoot the President." Charles Forbes witnessed the document.

It was Forbes, however, who allowed Booth to enter the president's box, and not Parker. Parker appeared before the Board of Metropolitan Police in answer to the charges of negligence. No transcript or record is known to exist of the hearing, and Parker was back on the job as one of the president's bodyguards. Apparently the board found nothing wrong in Parker's behavior and reinstated him. Nothing more is heard of Forbes. He continues to be the mystery man of that tragic night. Forbes died in 1895 and was buried in Congressional Cemetery. The Lincoln Group of the District of Columbia placed a tombstone on his grave in 1982.

Sources: James O. Hall, "The Mystery of Lincoln's Guard," *Surratt Society News* 7, no. 5 (May 1982), 4–6.

*See also:* Parker, John Frederick

### Ford, Blanche Chapman

Wife of Harry Clay Ford. In the 1930s, Mrs. Ford attempted to recover from the government the rocking chair Lincoln sat in the night he was murdered. The government refused. She then sued the government and was successful. The famous rocking chair was purchased from Mrs. Ford by automotive magnate Henry Ford, who placed it on display in the Edison Memorial Institute Museum in Dearborn, Michigan. The rocking chair on display in the box at Ford's Theatre is a replica.

Sources: Roy Z. Chamlee, Jr., *Lincoln's Assassins* (Jefferson, N.C.: McFarland, 1990), 558.

**Ford, Harry Clay (1844–1915)**

The younger brother of John T. Ford; treasurer of Ford's Theatre, supervised arranging the presidential box on the day of the assassination. Ford gave a lengthy statement on April 20, and was later called as a witness at the conspiracy trial. Ford's statement is valuable for its details of activity on April 14. On the morning of Lincoln's assassination Ford received a request from the White House asking that the presidential box be reserved for the president and his guests. Included on the guest list were Lieutenant General Ulysses S. Grant and his wife, Julia Dent Grant. Ford made sure boxes 7 and 8 were opened into a single, large box, which was appropriately decorated with flags.

Harry Ford was arrested, along with his brother James, on the night of the assassination. Ford told investigators about his conversations with Booth on the day of the assassination, including his telling of decorating the box by removing the partition that separated boxes 7 and 8, making one large box. He described the various employees of the theater and their duties. Ford also told of decorating the box with flags, including the regimental blue flag of the Treasury Guards. In his testimony Ford acknowledged speaking with Booth sometime near noon, but denied telling him that President Lincoln and General Grant would attend the performance that night.

Unlike his brother John, Harry was not considered a prime suspect in Lincoln's murder and was released. During the conspiracy trial, Ford was called as a defense witness on behalf of Edman Spangler. Ford died in 1915 and is buried in East Ridge Lawn Cemetery, Clifton, New Jersey.

Sources: Statement of Harry Clay Ford, NARA, RG 153, M-599, reel 5, frames 456–88; Poore, *Conspiracy Trial*, vol. 2, 548; Pitman, *Trial*, 99; George J. Olszewski, *Historic Structures Report: Restoration of Ford's Theatre* (Washington, D.C.: U.S. Government Printing Office, 1963).

## Ford, James Reed "Dick" (1840–1916)

Brother of John T. Ford and business manager of Ford's Theatre. Arrested on the night of the assassination, Ford was released along with his brother Harry without Stanton's approval. Although a serious violation of procedure, neither man was taken back into custody. Ford was called as a defense witness at the conspiracy trial on behalf of Edman Spangler. Ford died in 1916 in Baltimore and is buried in Loudon Park Cemetery there.

Sources: George J. Olszewski, *Historic Structures Report: Restoration of Ford's Theatre* (Washington, D.C.: U.S. Government Printing Office, 1963).

## Ford, John Thompson (1829–1894)

Owner of Ford's Theatre. Ford was born in Baltimore, where he lived his entire life. He worked for a brief period in the family's tobacco business and later as a bookseller before entering the theatrical business. While working in Richmond he wrote a satire on life in that city, which earned him a job as business manager of the *Nightingale Serenaders*. In 1854 he acquired the Holliday Street Theatre in Baltimore and his career in the theater business soared. In 1861 he took an option on the First Baptist Church, located on Tenth Street in Washington. Ford leased the theater to Christy's Minstrels, keeping a close eye on their attendance. Convinced that Washington was a profit-

able market for the theater business, Ford purchased the building and renovated it into a theater. The building was destroyed by fire on December 30, 1862. Ford completely rebuilt the theater and reopened it for business on August 27, 1863.

On the day of the assassination, Ford was in Richmond visiting his in-laws. During his absence the Washington theater was left in the care of his brother Harry Clay Ford. Ford was a close friend of Booth. He admired his acting ability and friendly nature. Ford allowed Booth essentially free rein about his theater, which proved to Booth's advantage when he decided to kill Lincoln.

Despite his prominence and loyal connections, Ford was arrested and held in the Carroll Annex of the Old Capitol Prison, where he languished for six weeks. While in prison, Ford met with Louis Wiechmann and John M. Lloyd, who were also being held as witnesses. Eventually cleared of any wrongdoing, Ford was released after being held for more than a month and returned to his theatrical business. On May 31, and again on June 9, he was called as a defense witness during the conspiracy trial on behalf of Edman Spangler. Although he never testified on Mary Surratt's behalf, Ford came to the conclusion she was innocent, as a result of his conversations with Wiechmann and Lloyd. He

continued to protest her conviction after her execution. Unable to operate his theater in Washington, Ford agreed to accept one hundred thousand dollars from the government for the building. The government converted it into offices.

Ford's theatrical business flourished. In 1879 he managed British musical comedy duo Gilbert and Sullivan during their American tour. Ford died of heart failure in 1894 at his home in Baltimore and is buried in Loudon Park Cemetery.

Sources: Statement of John T. Ford, NARA, RG 153, M-599, reel 5, frames 441–55; Poore, *Conspiracy Trial*, vol. 2, 527, vol. 3, 474; Pitman, *Trial*, 102, 104; Statement of John T. Ford, NARA, RG 153, M-599, reel 6, frames 510–12; Poore, *Conspiracy Trial*, vol. 2, 527, vol. 3, 474; Pitman, *Trial*, 102, 104; George J. Olszewski, *Historic Structures Report: Restoration of Ford's Theatre* (Washington, D.C.: U.S. Government Printing Office, 1963); Roy Z. Chamlee, Jr., *Lincoln's Assassins* (Jefferson, N.C.: McFarland, 1990).

**Ford's Theatre**
Built in 1833, the structure was originally occupied by the First Baptist Church of Washington, D.C. The building was abandoned as a church in 1859, and the trustees agreed to lease it to John Ford for a period of five years with an option to buy at the end of the lease. Ford rented the building to the Christy's Minstrels for two and a half months before renovating

the structure into a theater. Ford already owned the Holliday Street Theatre in Baltimore and the Academy of Music in Philadelphia.

Convinced the Washington market was profitable, Ford opened the renovated theater on March 19, 1862, producing plays until December 30, when a fire gutted the interior. Undaunted, Ford set about rebuilding the theater and opened it a second time on August 29, 1863. President Lincoln attended his first play at Ford's on May 28, 1862. Over the next three years he attended the theater on

at least twelve other occasions. The theater had a capacity of 2,400, and tickets ranged in price from twenty-five to seventy-five cents.

On April 14, 1865, tragedy struck again when John Wilkes Booth assassinated President Lincoln during a benefit performance for actress Laura Keene. The theater was closed and placed under a military guard by order of Secretary of War Edwin M. Stanton. The government paid Ford $1,500 a month until Congress appropriated funds to purchase the building. In 1866, Ford was paid $88,000 for the prop-

Ford's Theatre, as it looks today

erty, having already received $12,000 in rental fees, bringing the total sale amount to $100,000. The government converted the structure into a three-story office building. The building was used by various agencies of the U.S. government before being taken over by the Office of Records and Pensions of Civil War soldiers.

Tragedy struck for a third time when the interior structure of the building collapsed on June 9, 1893, killing twenty-two employees and injuring sixty-five. Rebuilt, the building continued in use by the government as office space until 1932, when it was transferred to the National Park Service and turned into the Lincoln Museum housing the collection of Osborn H. Oldroyd.

In 1964 Congress appropriated funds for the complete restoration of the building to its original configuration in 1865. On February 13, 1968, one day after Lincoln's birthday, the theater was opened to the public. The theater is an historic site as well as an active theater with seasonal plays. It remains a major attraction, drawing nearly a million visitors a year.

Sources: George J. Olszewski, *Historic Structures Report: Restoration of Ford's Theatre* (Washington, D.C.: U.S. Government Printing Office, 1963).

*See also:* Oldroyd, Osborn H.

## Fort Jefferson

Fort Jefferson is located in the Dry Tortugas islands off the Florida Keys. Built on Garden Key, the fort is sixty-eight nautical miles due west of Key West. Originally built to guard the Gulf Coast of the United States from foreign enemies, the fort was garrisoned in 1861 with nearly one thousand troops to secure it from falling into Confederate hands. It was also used as a military prison, holding as many as eight hundred prisoners by the end of the war. Federal soldiers sentenced to hard labor worked on the fort's construction, which wasn't completed until 1872.

Found guilty by a military tribunal in 1865, four of the eight conspirators were sent to Fort Jefferson to serve out their sentences. The sentences were originally to be served in the Federal penitentiary at Albany, New York, but were changed at the last minute by Secretary of War Edwin M. Stanton. By moving the prisoners to a military prison, Stanton maintained complete control over their incarceration.

Construction on the fort began in 1846 when Lieutenant Horatio G. Wright of the Army Corps of Engineers arrived on the small island that would hold the fort. It was the first engineering feat of its kind for the army

engineers. Foundations two feet thick and fourteen feet wide had to be constructed by building cofferdams to keep the ocean out. By 1862 the outer walls reached a final height of forty-five feet. The fort distilled its own water, converting seven thousand gallons of seawater to potable water every day. Food supplies, except for fish caught locally, were shipped in.

The most famous inmate at Fort Jefferson was Dr. Samuel A. Mudd. Convicted of aiding and abetting Booth in the assassination of President Lincoln, Mudd was sentenced to life at hard labor. Considerable myth has surrounded Dr. Mudd's life at Fort Jefferson. Life for Mudd and his co-conspirators has been described as a living hell, with the fort portrayed as an American Devil's Island. In 1936, Twentieth Century Fox released its own version of the story of Dr. Mudd. Produced by one of Hollywood's greatest filmmakers, Darryl F. Zanuck, and directed by John Ford, *The Prisoner of Shark Island* epitomized history as hoax. The movie takes its name from Hollywood's portrayal of Fort Jefferson as a fortress protected by a moat filled with man-eating sharks. In the film Dr. Mudd is beaten and threatened with being eaten alive by the sharks guarding the prison. Most Americans learned their history about Dr. Mudd from the movie. However, the film is a distortion of history. For most of his time Dr. Mudd worked in the fort's hospital assisting the post doctors, and in the carpentry shop, where he made a number of furniture pieces, some of which are on display at the Dr. Samuel Mudd House in Charles County, Maryland.

The summer of 1867 saw a major yellow fever outbreak at the fort that lasted into the fall. Of the 400 individuals at the fort, 270 contracted the disease and 38 of those died: 36 soldiers and 2 prisoners, one being Michael O'Laughlen. Among the fatalities were the post surgeon and four nurses. Dr. Mudd assumed command of the medical facility and helped the new surgeon, Dr. Daniel Whitehurst, in combating the epidemic. In 1869, President Andrew Johnson pardoned Mudd, citing in part Mudd's efforts during the yellow fever outbreak. Three weeks later Johnson pardoned Samuel Arnold and Edman Spangler.

By the end of World War I, the great fort had slipped into oblivion, forgotten by most. President Franklin D. Roosevelt saved it from destruction. On January 4, 1935, the fort was declared a National Monument. It was handed over to the National Park Service in 1993.

Sources: Rodman Bethel, *A Slumbering Giant of the Past* (Hialeah, Fla.: W. L. Litho, 1979); Edward Steers, Jr., *His Name Is Still Mudd* (Gettysburg, Pa.: Thomas, 1997).

*See also:* Mudd, Dr. Samuel Alexander; *Prisoner of Shark Island*

## Fort McNair
See Washington Arsenal

## Foster, Lafayette Sabine (1806–1880)
U.S. senator from Connecticut. President pro tempore of the U.S. Senate. Under the succession act of 1792, Foster would have become the acting president followed by Schuyler Colfax, Speaker of the House of Representatives, in the event of Vice President (later president) Johnson's death. Foster had a long political history, serving in the Connecticut state legislature 1839–1840 and 1846–1848 as speaker of the state house. In 1854 he was elected to the U.S. Senate. Strongly opposed to slavery, Foster joined the Republican Party in 1856 and was reelected to the Senate in 1860. He was elected president pro tempore of the Senate, serving from March 7, 1865, until March 2, 1867. He served on the Connecticut Supreme Court from 1870 until 1876. He died in 1880, all but forgotten to history, the man who would have become acting president had George Atzerodt followed through with Booth's assignment to assassinate Vice President Andrew Johnson.

Sources: James O. Hall, "Presidential Succession," *Surratt Society News* 7, no. 11 (November 1982), 4; James O. Hall, "Senator Atchison and Presidential Succession," *Surratt Courier* 16, no. 7 (July 1991), 2–3; James E. T. Lange and Katherine DeWitt, Jr., "Further Notes on Presidential Succession," *Surratt Courier* 16, no. 9 (September 1991), 6; Frederick Hatch, "Lincoln Assassination Encyclopedia," unpublished manuscript.

*See also:* Presidential Succession

### Foster, Robert Sanford (1834–1885)

A member of the military tribunal that tried the Lincoln conspirators. Foster entered the Civil War on April 22, 1861, as a captain in the 11th Indiana Volunteer Infantry. Foster rose to command a brigade and then a division, serving valiantly at Petersburg, where his division helped break the Confederate defenses at Fort Gregg at a cost of 714 casualties. Declining a position as lieutenant colonel in the regular army, Foster returned to civilian life in Indianapolis, where he held the offices of city treasurer, U.S. marshal, and president of the board of trade.

Sources: Ezra J. Warner, *Generals in Blue* (Baton Rouge: Louisiana State University Press, 1964), 158–59.

*See also:* Military Tribunal

### Funeral Car, the President's

The special car that carried the president's body back to his hometown of Springfield, Illinois, was built in the United States Military Car Shops at Alexandria, Virginia, between 1863 and 1865. It was completed two months before Lincoln's assassination. The special coach

was intended to serve as the official presidential car during Lincoln's second term. He never got to see it, although reports claimed that he was scheduled to examine it sometime that spring.

The coach was forty-eight feet in length and eight and one half feet in width. The inside of the car measured forty-two feet in length by eight feet in width. A corridor extended the full length of the car along one wall. The car as originally designed contained three large rooms: a stateroom, a drawing room with a small washroom, and a parlor or dining room. The stateroom was located in the center of the car and served as the president's quarters doubling as both his office and sleeping quarters. Considerably larger than the two end rooms, it contained four sofas, two of them seven and a half feet long with hinged backs that folded down making each sofa into a double bed large enough to accommodate the president's long frame.

The interior of the car was lined with black walnut and oak wood. The walls were upholstered from the seat rail to the headlining with crimson silk that had a tufted pattern. The clerestory above the headlining was painted zinc white and decorated with the coat of arms of all of the thirty-six states. The window curtains were made of a light-green silk. There were chandeliers made of cut glass and the floor was covered with wall-to-wall carpeting. Oil paintings depicting patriotic scenes decorated the interior spaces between the windows. In addition to the sofas there were folding upholstered chairs, and a desk for the president to work on.

The car's exterior was painted a rich chocolate brown rubbed with oil and rottenstone that produced a deep, shiny finish. A large five-and-a-half-foot oval, bearing the United States coat of arms, was located beneath the sixth and seventh windows on each side of the car. The car body set on four large trucks of four wheels each. The unusual construction using sixteen wheels has led some to believe the car was heavily armored for the president's protection, thus requiring the extra wheels to support the heavy weight due to the armor plate. Several of the men who worked on the car refute this idea. The twelve large windows each side of the car made it more vulnerable to attack.

Upon Lincoln's death, and his wife's insistence he be taken home to Springfield for burial, Myron H. Lamson, the assistant foreman overseeing the car's construction, suggested to Secretary of War Stanton that the special presidential car be converted to a funeral car for transporting Lincoln's body. Stanton agreed, and Lamson set to work converting the coach interior and building a catafalque that was mounted in the center of the stateroom. It contained a set of special clamps to hold the casket securely on the catafalque, and to allow for easy removal whenever the casket was removed for funeral parades and viewing.

Returned to the military car shops in Alexandria after delivering Lincoln's body to Springfield, the car was used again as a funeral coach in June 1865, when it carried the body of William H. Seward's wife back to Auburn, New York. The disposition of the car has an interesting and tragic history. Put up for auction by the government in April 1866, it was purchased by Lincoln's close friend and law partner, Ward Hill Lamon for $6,850. Stanton, however, objected to the sale apparently because he opposed any use of the car for exhibition purposes. Upon learning that Lamon was acting on behalf of the president of the Union Pacific Railroad who claimed to have purchased the car to keep it "away from speculators," Stanton approved the sale. The car was taken to Omaha, Nebraska, the home of the Union Pacific.

Used on rare occasions, the car was kept in a special shed constructed for it in Omaha. Its history over the next few years is controversial. One account states that it was painted Union Pacific yellow, stripped of its interior, and converted into a passenger coach. In 1874 it was sold to the Colorado Central Railroad. The car's next clouded history has it returning to the Union Pacific in 1878 and being used as a construction car. In 1886 it was converted into a bunk car, and later said to be used as a dining car for construction crews repairing and laying new track. In 1892, a group of New York men negotiated with the Union Pacific to purchase the car and exhibit it at the 1893 Columbian Exposition in Chicago, but the negotiations fell through.

In 1898, the car was cleaned up and exhibited at the Tran Mississippi Exposition in Omaha where over one and a quarter million people viewed it. Reports also claimed that the car, already in poor condition, was further damaged by souvenir hunters. By 1903, the vandalized car was purchased for two thousand dollars by a showman who partially refurbished it and exhibited it at the 1904 St. Louis World's Fair. Following the fair, the car briefly toured the country as a carnival exhibit. In 1905, a financial failure as an exhibit, it was auctioned to Thomas Lowry, president of the Minneapolis, St. Paul, and Sault Ste. Marie Railroad for eight hundred dollars.

Lowry tried unsuccessfully to convince the political leaders of Minneapolis to house the car in an appropriate museum building, and decided to use the car as a promotion to attract people to his land development park in Minneapolis, where viewers might then be induced to buy a home lot. Like all the other schemes that had gone before, this one also failed. The car was stored in a shed now abandoned following Lowry's death in 1909. On a March day in 1911, a small brush fire started by a young boy got out of control, and despite the efforts of several citizens from the surrounding area the shed and car were badly burned by the fire. Beyond salvaging, Lowry's land company gave its permission to the general public to come and take whatever souvenirs and relics they wanted from what was left of the car.

Sources: Raymond Borchers, "President Lincoln's Car," *Lincoln Herald*, vol. 86, No. 4 (Winter 1984), 212-216; H. Robert Slusser, "Mr. Lincoln's Railroad Car An Alexandria Artifact" (Alexandria, Virginia: *Alexandria Archeology Publications Number 76*, 1996); Edward Steers, Jr., *Blood on the Moon* (Lexington: University Press of Kentucky, 2001), 277–278.

*See also*: Lincoln Funeral; Funeral Train.

## Funeral Train

On April 21, Lincoln's casket was placed aboard a special train created just for the purpose of transporting his body back to his hometown of Springfield, Illinois. The train, under the control of the U.S. military, consisted of an engine and tender, and nine cars. Throughout the long 1,664-mile trip cars were added and removed in response to the number of dignitaries joining the entourage. An escort of twenty-nine soldiers drawn from the Veteran Reserve Corps was selected to act as pallbearers and escort to the body. These men traveled in a coach immediately in front of the funeral car, which was located next to last car in the queue. Car number one was a baggage car used to store materials involved in maintenance of the tracks and telegraph. Cars two through six were reserved for local, state, and national delegations. Car seven housed the members of the Veteran Reserve Corps. Car eight was the funeral car that carried the coffins of Lincoln and his young son Willie who died in the White House during Lincoln's first term as president. Car nine was reserved for members of the Lincoln family, high ranking military officers, and the guard of honor.

The incredible journey involved official stops in thirteen major northern cities, traveled over seventeen different company-owned railroad routes, and took thirteen days. The train traveled at speeds ranging from a low of five miles an hour when passing crowds gathered along the route, and twenty-five miles an hour when passing through rural coun-

President Lincoln's funeral train arrives in Harrisburg, Pennsylvania

tryside. Wartime regulations were still in effect and the special train would have priority over all other rail traffic, the trip being designated a "military necessity." Secretary of War Edwin Stanton appointed a commission of railroad men authorizing them to make all of the arrangements.

Once the route had been released, twenty-seven specially constructed memorial arches were built over the tracks at various locations beginning in Washington, D.C., and ending in Williamsville, Illinois. All along the journey thousands upon thousands of people turned out to stand at trackside or sit in their buggies and wagons solemnly waiting for the opportunity to see the train. In many instances, people turned out twenty-four hours in advance just to see the train

slowly pass. In some areas as many as ten thousand people were reported to line the tracks. In some areas young girls covered the rails with freshly cut flowers that inadvertently caused the engine's wheels to slip as it lost traction due to the flowers that were crushed by the train's wheels.

At each of the major cities where the train made an official stop elaborate funeral processions were scheduled with sermons, singing choruses, and public viewings of the open casket. An undertaker who accompanied the train was to make sure the president's appearance was refreshed cosmetically whenever necessary, which happened repeatedly over the thirteen days. The train completed its final leg of the 1,600-mile journey arriving in Springfield on May 3, at

9:00 A.M. only one hour behind schedule. In all, one million people were estimated to have viewed the remains of Abraham Lincoln as he lay in state while estimates approaching seven million people gathered along city streets and in country fields to pay their solemn respects as the funeral train made its way across the country. On May 4, funeral services were held at Oak Ridge Cemetery located on the outskirts of Springfield. Lincoln and his son's caskets were stored in the cemetery's public vault until an appropriate resting place could be constructed.

Sources: Victor Searcher, *The Farewell to Lincoln* (New York: Abingdon Press, 1965). Edward Steers, Jr., *Blood on the Moon* (Lexington: University Press of Kentucky, 2001), 268–293. Scott D. Trostel, *The Lincoln Funeral Train* (Fletcher, Ohio: Cam-Tech Publishing, 2002).

*See also:* Funeral Car; Lincoln Burial.

Lincoln reposes in the rotunda of New York City Hall

## Gaither, William (1824–1891)

Montgomery County farmer who gave George Atzerodt a lift aboard his wagon on Saturday, April 15. Gaither was returning from Washington, D.C., in his farm wagon when he was stopped for several hours in a long line of wagons waiting to be cleared by the military pickets stationed in Tennallytown on the main road from Georgetown to Rockville, Maryland. Atzerodt had walked from his hotel to Georgetown early Saturday morning. In Georgetown he purchased a ticket to ride the stage to Rockville. Atzerodt left the stagecoach he was riding in and walked to the head of the long line awaiting clearance. He found Gaither near the front of the line and talked him into giving him a ride as far as Rockville. Both Gaither and Atzerodt were allowed to pass the picket checkpoint. Atzerodt rode through the picket post at Tennallytown, thereby evading capture.

Sergeant Lewis L. Chubb, 13th Michigan Light Artillery, was in command of the guard unit that was screening the people who wanted to leave Washington. Chubb was court-martialed on two counts: "drunkenness on duty" and "disobedience of orders," for allowing Atzerodt to pass through Chubb's picket post. Atzerodt had bought Chubb and the soldiers under his command a round of hard cider before leaving on Gaither's wagon. Chubb was found not guilty of both charges.

Sources: Statement of William R. Gaither, NARA, RG 153, M-599, reel 3, frames 548–53.

*See also:* Chubb, Lewis L.

## Gambo Creek

A small creek on the Virginia side of the Potomac River where Booth and Herold stopped after crossing the river on Saturday night, April 22. The two men set out from Nanjemoy Creek on the Maryland side, where they spent Thursday and Friday nights waiting for the opportune moment to cross the Potomac. Having failed on their first attempt on Thursday evening, they were successful on the second try. They were looking for the home of Elizabeth Quesenberry, a short distance down the river from Gambo Creek. Mrs. Quesenberry had a small home on Machodoc Creek, Booth's original destination.

When they arrived on the Virginia side, Herold left Booth resting in the tall grass while he made his way to Mrs. Quesenberry's house. Finding the lady away, Herold waited for her return. When she returned she sent word to Confederate agent Thomas Harbin to come and take care of the two men. Harbin knew Booth, having been introduced to him by Dr. Mudd the previous December at the Bryantown Tavern. Gambo Creek now lies within the U.S. Navy's Dahlgren base.

Sources: William A. Tidwell, James O. Hall, and David W. Gaddy, *Come Retribution* (Jackson: University Press of Mississippi, 1988), 457.

*See also*: Quesenberry, Elizabeth Rousby

## Gardiner, George (1805–1882)

Nearest neighbor to Dr. Samuel Mudd. Gardiner owned the farm adjacent to Mudd's. With the help of Mudd, Booth purchased a horse from Gardiner on December 19, 1864. The horse was known as the "one-eyed" horse, having lost an eye. Lewis Powell used it on the night of the assassination. Gardiner had his nephew, Thomas Gardiner, deliver the horse to Booth on Monday in Bryantown. Booth took the horse to the town blacksmith, Peter Trotter, and had the horse shod with four new shoes. Trotter later said it was at this time that he noticed Dr. Mudd had accompanied Booth. Booth rode the horse back to Washington on Tuesday. In his flight from the Seward house, the horse threw Powell or stumbled and fell. He abandoned the horse east of the Capitol. It was later found that same night near the Lincoln Barracks, three-quarters of a mile east of the Capitol. The horse was brought to the army stables at the 22nd Army Corps headquarters in Washington the night of the assassination.

Sources: Testimony of Lieutenant John J. Toffey, *Conspiracy Trial*, vol. 1, 365, 418; Pitman, *Trial*, 159, 160; Statement of Dr. Samuel Alexander Mudd, NARA, RG 153, M-599, reel 5, frames 212–25; Statement of Thomas Gardiner, NARA, RG 153, M-599, reel 2, frames 925–26; Poore, *Conspiracy Trial*, vol. 1, 361, vol. 2, 422; Pitman, *Trial*, 71, 196.

*See also*: Gardiner, Thomas

## Gardiner, Polk

A young man who was on his way into Washington, D.C., the night of the assassination. Gardiner and George Doyle were riding together in a wagon heading into Washington when they met a man riding fast up Good Hope Hill in Anacostia (Booth). The man asked if a rider had passed by him and Gardiner said none had. A few minutes later a second rider came galloping up the road (David Herold), and stopping, asked Gardiner if he had seen a man ride past him. Gardiner said yes. He later told investigators that the two men must have been chasing each other. Gardiner told detectives that he saw the two men sometime near midnight and that they had asked the way to Upper Marlboro in Prince George's County. Gardiner was a witness for the prosecution.

Sources: Testimony of Polk Gardiner, NARA, RG 153, M-599, reel 4, frames 344–48; Poore, *Conspiracy Trial*, vol. 1, 255; Pitman, *Trial*, 85.

## Gardiner, Thomas

Nephew of George Gardiner, nearest neighbor of Dr. Samuel Mudd. Called as a witness at the conspiracy trial, Gardiner testified that he was present when Booth purchased the "one-eyed" horse from George Gardiner, and that he delivered the horse the "next day" to John Wilkes Booth at the Bryantown Tavern. Booth purchased the horse on a Monday and Gardiner delivered it to him on a Tuesday. This could only have taken place during Booth's second visit to Bryantown and Samuel Mudd's house on December 18–19, 1864. Booth took the horse to the town blacksmith, Peter Trotter, and had the horse shod with four new shoes. In an interview with Osborn H. Oldroyd in 1901, Trotter said that Dr. Mudd accompanied Booth on this visit to Bryantown, and that when the horse was shod, the two men rode away together.

Sources: Statement of Thomas Gardiner, NARA, RG 153, M-599, reel 2, frames 925–26; Poore, *Conspiracy Trial*, vol. 1, 361, vol. 2, 422; Pitman, *Trial*, 71, 196; Osborn H. Oldroyd, *The Assassination of Abraham Lincoln* (1901; reprint, Bowie, Md.: Heritage, 1990), 261.

## Gardner, Alexander

Former photographer under Mathew Brady who set up his own studio at Seventh and D streets in Washington. At the time Booth's body was brought to the Washington Navy Yard and placed aboard the monitor USS *Montauk*, an autopsy was performed. Gardner was invited to the *Montauk* with his assistant, Timothy O'Sullivan, by Secretary of War Edwin M. Stanton and asked to photograph the body. When he finished, Gardner returned to his studio accompanied by a military guard who had instructions to confiscate the photographic plate and subsequent prints and bring them directly to Stanton. It is not clear why Stanton would have allowed photographs to be taken and then not allow them to be seen by anyone else. Perhaps Stanton wanted to see Booth's corpse to satisfy himself that Booth was really dead.

For his effort, Gardner received permission from Stanton to photograph the hanging of the four conspirators condemned to death. In fact, the military commission issued his pass on July 5, two days before the public—or even the condemned—were informed of the conspirators' fate. Gardner and O'Sullivan arrived at the arsenal at 11:00 A.M. on July 7, and set up their cameras in two windows facing onto the front of the scaffold. It was an ideal location: inside a building shaded from the sun and separated from the crowd of people milling in the courtyard waiting for the proceedings to begin.

At some point during the day, Gardner persuaded the governor of the prison, Major General John F. Hartranft, to have himself and his staff pose for a photograph. Hartranft agreed, and assembled his staff in front of the brick wall enclosing the prison yard. Ironically, four of the men posed sitting in the very chairs that would be used soon thereafter by the condemned on the scaffold as they awaited their hanging.

Sources: D. Mark Katz, *Witness to An Era: The Life and Photographs of Alexander Gardner* (Nashville, Tenn.: Rutledge Hill, 1991), 160–92.

## Garrett, John Muscoe "Jack" (1840–1899)

Son of Richard Garrett, owner of the Garrett farm and tobacco barn where Booth was found hiding and killed. On Tuesday, April 25, the 16th New York Cavalry was closing in on Booth and Herold. After crossing the Rappahannock River the cavalry troop rode hard toward Bowling Green, passing by the Garrett farmhouse. Warned that Union cavalry were headed for the farm, Booth and Herold fled into the nearby woods.

Jack Garrett became suspicious that the two men were in some sort of trouble that might also endanger the Garretts and their house. He told Booth and Herold they would have to spend the night in the tobacco barn. Garrett feared that if the soldiers caught the two fugitives inside the house the soldiers would set it afire. Garrett and his brother, William, decided to sleep in a corncrib, taking turns keeping an eye on Booth and Herold. The brothers were afraid the two men would leave during the night and steal two of Garrett's horses.

When the cavalry returned to the Garrett farm, led by Confederate private Willie Jett, they threatened to hang Richard Garrett, the father, unless he gave up Booth and Herold. Jack Garrett stepped forward and told the soldiers the two men they were looking for were in the tobacco barn. Surrounding the barn, Lieutenant Doherty grabbed Jack Garrett and told him to go into the barn and bring out the two men. Garrett protested, saying the men in the barn would shoot him. Doherty told him that if he didn't go into the barn, *he* would shoot him. Garrett went into the barn and explained the situation to Booth. He was surrounded and couldn't possibly escape. Booth refused. Garrett then went back to the door and asked Luther Baker to let him come out.

After more negotiation Booth allowed Herold to surrender. Baker continued to try to talk Booth into surrendering, but the assassin refused and Baker ordered the soldiers to set the barn on fire. As the fire began to spread throughout the barn a shot rang out and Booth fell to the floor of the burning barn. Baker and Doherty rushed in and dragged Booth from the barn. Booth was carried to the porch of the Garrett house, where he died a few hours later.

Jack and his brother William were taken into custody and back to Washington, where they were held in the brig at the Washington Navy Yard until they were released and allowed to return home. Jack Garrett was held as a potential witness but was never called to testify. The prosecution relied on the Union officers who captured Booth and Herold to testify to the events that took place at Garrett's farm.

Sources: James L. Swanson, *Manhunt: The 12-Day Chase for Lincoln's Killer* (New York: Harper Perennial, 2007).

## Garrett, Richard Baynham (1854–1922)

Eleven years old at the time of Booth's capture, Richard Baynham Garrett was one of five children of Richard H. Garrett and his second wife. Years after the assassination, he described the scene he witnessed as a young boy in an article in the *Virginia Magazine of History and Biography*. He told of Jett introducing Booth as Mr. James W. Boyd, a Confederate soldier wounded at the Battle of Petersburg. Booth, he said, attempted to trade his civilian clothes for one of the Garrett boys' Confederate uniform, but the boy refused. On the day following his arrival Booth asked the young Garrett boy to take down the large map of the United States that hung over the fireplace and lay it on the floor. Booth then took a pencil and traced a route that passed through Norfolk, Virginia; Charleston, South Carolina; and Savannah, Georgia. When young Garrett asked Booth where he wanted to go he said Booth answered, "Mexico."

It wasn't until the morning of April 25 that they heard of Lincoln's assassination. Later that afternoon, two of the Confederate soldiers returned from Bowling Green and said that Union cavalry was crossing the river at Port Royal and heading down the road toward the Garretts' house. The young Garrett said the two men seemed "very much excited" and the wounded man sent him to his room to fetch his pistols. The two men then went into the nearby woods and hid. The soldiers rode past the Garrett farm, heading south toward Bowling Green. Now, suspicious of the two men, Jack Garrett asked them to sleep in the tobacco barn. Jack and his brother Will slept in a nearby corncrib, taking turns watching to make sure the two men didn't sneak off during the night with the Garretts' horses.

At two o'clock in the morning, soldiers came to the farmhouse and demanded to know where Booth and Herold were hiding. The father was threatened with hanging if he didn't tell, at which point Jack Garrett came from the corncrib and told the soldiers, "The men you seek are over there," and pointed to the tobacco barn. After several minutes of negotiation the barn was set afire and before Booth could act one way or another he was shot through the neck. According to young Garrett's recollections, it was not until Booth was laid out on the porch of the Garrett house that the Garretts learned he was John Wilkes Booth.

In 1880, Richard Baynham Garrett wrote to a relic collector, W. McKee Dunn, offering several relics of the events that took place at his father's house at the time of Booth's capture and death.

I have in my possession some very interesting relics of Jno. Wilkes Booth. It was at my father's house in Va. that he was killed and I have preserved the relics. Among them are the mattress upon which he died, a piece of the crutch which he used, and a lock of his hair, cut off after his death. Would any of these be of any value to you in your collection? I can satisfy you that the relics are genuine. I have also a map upon which he traced the route he said he was going to travel from Richmond to Mexico. I was with him for two days prior to his death, but did not know at the time who he was. I will be glad to give you any information upon the subject if it interests you. I am

Yours Respectfully

R. B. Garrett

Student S. B. Theological
Seminary

Louisville, Ky.

Sources: Betsy Fleet, ed., "A Chapter of Unwritten History: Richard Baynum Garrett's Account of the Flight and Death of John Wilkes Booth," *Virginia Magazine of History and Biography* 71, no. 4 (October 1963), 387–407; Richard Baynham Garrett, letter to W. McKee Dunn, January 13, 1880, NARA, RG 153, M-599, reel 7, frames 77–79.

See also: Booth Capture and Death

### Garrett, Richard Henry (1806–1878)

Owner of the farm and tobacco barn where Booth and Herold were cornered in the early morning hours of Wednesday, April 26, 1865. Shortly after midnight on Wednesday, April 26, the Garrett

farmhouse was surrounded by soldiers of the 16th New York Cavalry. Soldiers threatened to hang Garrett if he did not immediately tell them where Booth and Herold were hiding. A flustered Garrett was saved when his son Jack stepped up and told the soldiers the two fugitives were hiding in the tobacco barn. Booth was killed and Herold was captured.

Sources: Edward Steers, Jr., *Blood on the Moon* (Lexington: University Press of Kentucky, 2001), 201–2.

*See also:* Garrett, Richard Baynham

### Garrett, William "Will"

Son of Richard Garrett and brother of John "Jack" Garrett. Will, like his brother

Jack, was in the Confederate army and had only recently returned home. During afternoon dinner on Tuesday, April 25, the conversation around the dinner table centered on the reward money offered for Booth's capture. Will Garrett made a comment suggesting that if Booth were show up at the Garrett farm he would "catch him" and get the reward money. Booth, hearing that the reward money equaled $140,000, said he thought it would amount to $500,000. He did not give any indication that he was Lincoln's killer.

Will and Jack Garrett decided to sleep in a corncrib on the night of April 25–26, fearing Booth and Herold would steal two of the Garrett horses and continue their escape. It was Will Garrett who locked Booth and Herold in the tobacco barn that was used to store their neighbors' furniture, a safe haven from Yankee looters and burners. Both Will and Jack Garrett were arrested by Everton J. Conger and taken back to Washington, where they were confined in the Navy Yard brig.

Sources: Statement of John "Jack" Garrett, NARA, RG 94, M619, reel 457, frame 502.

*See also:* Garrett, John Muscoe "Jack"; Booth Capture and Death

### Garrett Farm

Known as the Locust Hill Farm. Located three miles south of the village of Port

Garrett's farm, roughly a year before its demolition in 1936

Royal along present U.S. highway 301. Richard Garrett, his wife, and nine children lived on the five-hundred-acre tract of land. Garrett was a tobacco farmer who agreed to give shelter and food to Booth and Herold. The farm no longer exists and the property is bisected by highway 301 and is, in part, the property of the U.S. Army's Fort A. P. Hill. Today, the site of the farmhouse where Booth died sits in the median strip separating the north and south lanes of the highway. An historical marker identi-fies the spot where the house existed.

Booth and Herold arrived at the Garrett farm the afternoon of Monday, April 24, accompanied by three Confederate soldiers. Private Willie Jett, known to Richard Garrett, asked if the two men might stay at the farm a day or two and rest. Jett introduced Booth and Herold as two Confederate soldiers recently from Petersburg, where one of the soldiers had been wounded. Garrett agreed to allow the two men to stay at his farm.

Sources: Edward Steers, Jr., *Blood on the Moon* (Lexington: University Press of Kentucky, 2001), 245–67.

## Gautier's Restaurant

Restaurant located at 252 Pennsylvania Avenue between Twelfth and Thirteenth streets in Washington, D.C. On the night of March 15, 1865, Booth rented an upstairs room at the restaurant and hosted a meeting with his gang of conspirators. Present were Lewis Powell, George Atzerodt, David Herold, Samuel Arnold, Michael O'Laughlen, John Surratt, and Booth. It was the first time that the seven cohorts of Booth had been together in the same place. Booth had ordered oysters, liquor, and cigars for his friends. The meeting began around midnight and continued until nearly 5:00 A.M. Booth outlined his plan for kidnapping Lincoln at Ford's Theatre while Lincoln was watching a play from the presidential box. Lincoln would be subdued by using chloroform to render him unconscious. He would then be lowered to the stage and carried out the rear door.

The reaction to Booth's plan was stunned disbelief. Arnold, in particular, thought the plan totally unrealistic. It was filled with danger, and what's more, would not work. They argued. Booth adjusted the role each would play, but still thought the plan a good one. Arnold continued to argue with Booth, causing Booth to threaten him. Arnold would not back down, and Booth relented, apologizing for threatening Arnold. The meeting ended around 5:00 A.M.

The important point to be taken from this episode is that all of the principal conspirators, save Mary Surratt and Dr. Mudd, met and were still in with Booth and his plan to kidnap Lincoln. Two days later on March 17, Booth called the group together once more on learning Lincoln would visit Campbell Hospital in northeast Washington. They all showed up, but the kidnap plan was aborted when Lincoln canceled his visit at the last moment to attend a flag presentation ceremony in front of the National Hotel in Washington.

Sources: Statement of John Thomas Miles, NARA, RG 153, M-599, reel 5, frames 289–94; Poore, *Conspiracy Trial*, vol. 1, 209; Pitman, *Trial*, 81; Edward Steers, Jr., *Blood on the Moon* (Lexington: University Press of Kentucky, 2001), 85–88.

See also: Campbell Hospital; Capture Plots

## Gavacan, Simon

Army detective on the staff of Maryland provost marshal James O'Beirne. Gavacan, along with Lieutenant Alexander Lovett and detectives William Williams and Joshua Lloyd, visited the Mudd farmhouse on Tuesday, April 18, and again on Friday, April 21, and interviewed Mudd as to the events of Saturday, April 15, when Booth and Herold were at Mudd's house. Gavacan was called as a prosecution witness on May 17, testifying to the questioning of Mudd on both days. His testimony supported that of Lovett, who testified on May 16. Gavacan said that Mudd at first denied two men had visited on Saturday, but on further questioning admitted they had been at the house. During the second visit, on Friday, April 21, Mrs. Mudd produced a boot with the name "J. Wilkes" written on the lining inside the top of the boot. The detectives were now convinced that Booth and Herold were at Mudd's house. They took Mudd into Bryantown for further questioning by Colonel Henry H. Wells. Mudd was arrested the following Monday, April 24, and taken to Washington, where he was held in the Carroll Annex of the Old Capitol Prison.

Sources: Testimony of Simon Gavacan; Poore, *Conspiracy Trial*, vol. 1, 301; Pitman, *Trial*, 89.

### Gayle, George Washington (1810–1875)

An Alabama lawyer who placed an advertisement in the Selma *Morning Dispatch* of December 1, 1864. The advertisement was introduced by the prosecution at the conspiracy trial as exhibit number 98. Gayle was arrested and held in Fort Pulaski for eighteen months. President Johnson pardoned him in 1867.

### ONE MILLION DOLLARS
### TO HAVE PEACE BY THE 1st OF MARCH.

If the citizens of the Southern Confederacy will furnish me with the cash, or good securities for the sum of one million dollars, I will cause the lives of Abraham Lincoln, Wm. H. Seward, and Andrew Johnson to be taken by the 1st of March next. This will give us peace and satisfy the world that cruel tyrants can not live in a "land of liberty." If this is not accomplished, nothing will be claimed beyond the sum of fifty thousand dollars in advance which is supposed to be necessary to reach and SLAUGHTER the THREE VILLAINS. I will give myself ONE THOUSAND DOLLARS TOWARDS THIS PATRIOTIC PURPOSE. Everyone wishing to contribute will address box X, Cahaba, Ala. December 1, 1864.

Sources: Edward Steers, Jr., ed., *The Trial* (Lexington: University Press of Kentucky, 2003), 51.

### Gemmill, Zachariah (1843–1922)

Sergeant in the First Delaware Cavalry who arrested George Atzerodt at the home of Atzerodt's cousin Hartman Richter in Montgomery County, Maryland. Captain Solomon Townsend of the First Delaware Cavalry, stationed at Monocacy Junction, received information from James Purdom, a Montgomery County farmer working as an undercover army detective, that a man recently arrived from Washington at Richter's farm talked knowingly about Lincoln's assassination. Townsend ordered Sergeant Gemmill to take six troopers and go to Richter's house and arrest the suspicious character. Gemmill arrived at the farmhouse shortly before dawn on Thursday, April 20, where he found Atzerodt sleeping. Gemmill arrested Atzerodt, Hartman Richter, and two farmhands working for Richter, and took them to Monocacy Junction. From Monocacy Junction they were taken to Relay, Maryland, and then by Baltimore & Ohio Railroad to Washington. For his effort Gemmill received $3,598.54 of the $25,000 offered for Atzerodt's capture. Purdom and each of the six soldiers accompanying Gemmill received $2,878.78.

Sources: Statement of Zachariah Gemmill, NARA, M-599, reel 2, frames 1014–19; Poore, *Conspiracy Trial*, vol. 1, 357; Pitman, *Trial*, 149; Awards for the Capture of Booth and Others, NARA, RG 94, M-619, reel 456, frame 416.

*See also:* Atzerodt, George Andrew; Purdom, James W.

## General Order No. 100 ✓

General Order No. 100 was a set of rules that set out in concise terms the international laws and customs of warfare as recognized by the United States during the Civil War. Major General Henry Halleck, commanding general of the Union army in 1862, appointed Dr. Francis Lieber, a Columbia College law professor, chairman over a board of general officers with instructions to draw up a code of war. General Order No. 100 was the result.

With Booth dead and Surratt in hiding, the eight individuals were placed on trial before a military tribunal established by an executive order of President Andrew Johnson based on a legal opinion of Attorney General James Speed. The choice of a military trial, however, was the decision of Secretary of War Edwin M. Stanton, who convinced others in Lincoln's cabinet that it was necessary. Only by using a military tribunal could the government control the proceedings and ensure what most people at the time felt was justice in the murder of their president.

The legal underpinning for using a military trial was based on General Order No. 100. The great majority of officers in the Union army were citizen volunteers, not professional or regular army officers. These officers knew little to nothing about the standard practices of military law or the customs of war. In April 1863, General Order No. 100 was issued to all members of the military. Henceforth, they would abide by this code of conduct.

The eight individuals accused of Lincoln's murder were charged with violating the laws of war while acting as unlawful enemy belligerents based on General Order No. 100.

Sources: Burrus Carnahan, "General Orders 100," in Edward Steers, Jr., ed., *The Trial* (Lexington: University Press of Kentucky, 2003), xcvii–c; Burrus Carnahan, *Act of Justice* (Lexington: University Press of Kentucky, 2007), 127–30.

*See also:* Military Tribunal

## George, David E.

Itinerant house painter and drifter who died by suicide in Enid, Oklahoma Territory, in 1903. Following his death, articles appeared in several newspapers stating that George had made deathbed claims

that he was John Wilkes Booth. According to Memphis attorney Finis L. Bates, the name David E. George along with the name John St. Helen were aliases used by John Wilkes Booth after he escaped from the Garrett farm, having left a surrogate in his place. George's alleged story is one of several that claim the man killed in Richard Garrett's tobacco barn on April 26, 1865, was not John Wilkes Booth. Booth allegedly escaped and the Federal government undertook a massive cover-up to deceive the American public.

David E. George's story began on January 13, 1903, with his death. George, who was prone to bouts of alcoholism, came to Enid two weeks before

his death. Mrs. E. C. Harper, on reading George's obituary in the local newspaper, believed he was the same man she had met three years earlier in El Reno, Texas, who, believing he was about to die, confessed to her that he was really John Wilkes Booth. The story soon made its way into newspapers around the country, including Memphis, Tennessee, where attorney Finis L. Bates read about it. Bates claimed that he met a man several years earlier by the name of John St. Helen who, believing he was dying, claimed to be John Wilkes Booth. Bates became convinced, or so he said, that David E. George and John St. Helen were the same man. Bates traveled to Enid, where he was able to claim the corpse of George, now mummified. Bates attempted to display the mummified corpse for an admission fee at various circus and fair sideshows.

In 1907, Bates wrote a book detailing the alleged adventures of George–St. Helen–Booth under the title "The Escape and Suicide of John Wilkes Booth; or, the First True Account of Lincoln's Assassination, and Containing a Complete Confession by Booth, Many Years After the Crime." At first the book created a mild sensation, selling seventy-five thousand copies, but it was soon discredited by critics who wrote of its numerous flaws and inaccuracies.

Bates then decided to pursue a claim for part of the reward money set aside for the capture of Booth. In 1900, some twenty-eight years after hearing St. Helen–Booth's confession, lawyer Bates petitioned the U.S. government for the reward money. The government placed Bates's claim in its "lunacy file." As far as the government was concerned the case was closed. Why Bates had waited twenty-eight years after hearing St. Helen's confession before acting is not clear.

When the government dismissed Bates's claim, he attempted to display his "mummified Booth" in circus sideshows with little financial success. He tried to interest automobile magnate Henry Ford in the mummy, thinking it would attract attention seated in the Lincoln rocking chair on exhibit in Ford's Dearborn, Michigan, museum. Ford had Bates and the mummy investigated by one of his detectives. The outcome was as expected. Bates was a charlatan and the mummy was not Booth. The mummy disappeared around 1940, never to be seen again.

The hoax continues to attract attention every so often when the story of Booth escaping emerges in the literature. Like most manufactured myths associated with Abraham Lincoln, the "Booth escaped" hoax fails the test of careful research.

Sources: C. Wyatt Evans, *The Legend of John Wilkes Booth: Myth, Memory, and a Mummy* (Lawrence: University Press of Kansas, 2004); Edward Steers, Jr., *Blood on the Moon* (Lexington: University Press of Kentucky, 2001), 245–67.

*See also:* Bates, Finis L.

## Georgetown, D.C.

Following Lincoln's assassination, George Atzerodt fled Washington for the safety of his cousin's farm in Germantown, Maryland. His first stop was in Georgetown, where he pawned his revolver for ten dollars. Georgetown is a neighborhood of Washington, D.C., located in the northwest section of the city. Established in 1751, before the creation of Washington, the community was annexed by the city in 1871. Georgetown University (formerly Georgetown College) is located within Georgetown. Dr. Samuel Mudd attended Georgetown College in 1852 but was expelled as a ringleader of a student riot that resulted in damage to school property.

On Saturday morning, April 15, George Atzerodt walked from the Pennsylvania House (Kimmel House) in Washington, where he had spent the night, to Matthews & Company's store on High Street (now Wisconsin Avenue) in Georgetown, where he pawned a navy Colt revolver for ten dollars. He then stopped to visit a widow named Lucinda Metz, and had breakfast there. Atzerodt, using part of the ten dollars, purchased a stagecoach ticket for Rockville, Maryland. He boarded the stage at the Montgomery House in Georgetown and rode as far as Tennallytown.

Sources: Statement of John L. Caldwell, NARA, RG 153, M-599, reel 3, frames 645–47; Poore, *Conspiracy Trial*, vol. 2, 148; Pitman, *Trial*, 148.

*See also:* Tennallytown; Chubb, Lewis L.; Caldwell, John

## Germantown, Maryland

Small community in Montgomery County, Maryland, located approximately twenty-five miles northwest of Washington, D.C. George Atzerodt was arrested at the home of his cousin Hartman Richter in the village of Germantown. The Atzerodt family along with the Richter family had immigrated to Germantown from Prussia in 1844. George Atzerodt was nine years old at the time. The Atzerodts were related to the Richters and together bought a farm in the vicinity of Germantown. In the 1850s, the Atzerodt family relocated to Westmoreland County, Virginia, but George Atzerodt kept his ties to the Richter family, visiting them on several occasions. It was at the Richter farm that Atzerodt was arrested during the early morning hours of Thursday, April 20, 1865. He was first taken to Monocacy Junction near Frederick, Maryland, where he was questioned. From Monocacy Junction he was taken to Relay, Maryland, outside of Baltimore where he was taken by train to Washington. Hartman Richter was also arrested, but eventually released when it was determined he knew nothing about the assassination, including Atzerodt's role.

Sources: Edward Steers, Jr., "George A. Atzerodt," in Edward Steers, Jr., ed., *The Trial* (Lexington: University Press of Kentucky, 2003), lxvi–lxxi.

*See also:* Gemmill, Zachariah

## Gifford, James J. (1814–1894)

Chief carpenter at Ford's Theatre in Washington, D.C. Gifford had a close connection with Booth. In 1851, he was in charge of building Junius Brutus Booth's home, named Tudor Hall, near Bel Air, Maryland. He was also the carpenter in remodeling Ford's Theatre in Washington both before and after the theater was gutted by fire in 1862. Gifford had longtime standing with John Ford. In 1864, while employed as Ford's chief carpenter and architect, he rebuilt a large shed in the alley behind the theater for John Wilkes Booth to keep his carriage and stable his horse. Gifford was asked by Secretary of War Stanton to re-create the presidential box at Ford's Theatre exactly as it was the night of the assassination. After Gifford finished his re-creation Mathew Brady photographed the box from the Dress Circle. We cannot be certain that the arrangement of the flags is exactly as it was the night of the assassination, because the flags borrowed by Harry Clay Ford were returned to their owners and Gifford had to get new flags. However, most historians accept the arrangement of the flags as accurate.

Gifford was called as both a prosecution witness and defense witness (for Edman Spangler) during the conspiracy trial. He testified that Jacob Ritterspaugh consulted him about "amending" his statement to authorities damaging to Spangler's defense.

Sources: Statement of James J. Gifford, NARA, RG 153, M-599, reel 4, frames 370–72; Poore, *Conspiracy Trial*, vol. 1, 458, vol. 3, 21; Pitman, *Trial*, 77, 109.

*See also:* Ritterspaugh, Jacob

## Gillette, Reverend Abram Dunn (1807–1882)

Baptist minister who comforted condemned conspirator Lewis Powell in his cell and on the gallows. Powell requested that Major Thomas Eckert, assistant secretary of war, ask Reverend Augustus P. Stryker, an Episcopal minister from St. Barnabas Church in Baltimore, to come and attend to Powell's spiritual care. Powell had heard Stryker give a sermon and was moved by his words. Eckert, afraid Stryker would not arrive in time, asked the Reverend Abram Dunn Gillette, pastor of the First Baptist Church in Washington, to visit Powell. Gillette attended Powell in his cell and accompanied him on the scaffold. He spoke briefly to the crowd, telling them that Powell wished to thank his captors, Major General John F. Hartranft and his staff, for the kind treatment they had given him. Stryker arrived at noon on July 7, in time to accompany Powell on the scaffold along with Gillette.

In his report to Major General Winfield Scott Hancock, military governor of the prison, Hartranft wrote, "I have the honor to report that in obedience to your orders, I did on July 6th, 1865 between the hours of 11:00 A.M. & 12:00 M., read the 'Findings & Sentences' of Lewis Payne [Lewis Powell], G. A. Atzerodt, David E. Herold and Mary E. Surratt to each of them and also delivered a copy of the same to each." When he finished, Hartranft handed each prisoner an envelope bearing the written findings and sentences of the tribunal. One of the envelopes that contained such a death warrant survives. Lewis Powell gave it to Reverend Gillette, who wrote on the back of the envelope: "This death warrant was given me by Payne [Powell] less than an hour before his execution. I was in his cell & with him the last moments of his life. A.D. Gillette."

Sources: Edward Steers, Jr., and Harold Holzer, eds., *The Lincoln Assassination Conspirators: Their Confinement and Execution, as Recorded in the Letterbook of John Frederick Hartranft* (Baton Rouge: Louisiana State University Press, 2009).

*See also:* Hartranft, John F.

### Gleason, Daniel H. L. (1841–1917)

Gleason worked as a clerk in the office of the Commissary General of Prisoners in the War Department. Working alongside Gleason was Louis J. Wiechmann, who became the government's chief witness. Wiechmann was a close friend of John Surratt, Jr., and boarded at the Surratt boardinghouse in Washington, D.C. Gleason admitted that three weeks before the assassination Wiechmann came to him and told him about the "strange doings of John Surratt" and several of his acquaintances. On March 20, 1865, Wiechmann told Gleason about John Surratt, Booth, and Powell coming into his room following their aborted capture plan. The three were highly agitated and talked in an excited and suspicious way. Wiechmann was sure something big was up and that it involved the president. In fact, Wiechmann revealed enough of his suspicions about Surratt and Booth to Gleason that had either one of them told the authorities they might well have prevented Lincoln's murder.

Modern-day conspiracy theorists believe Gleason told Secretary of War Stanton about Wiechmann's conversation prior to the assassination, and that Stanton suppressed it, wanting the plot to go forward. But a careful reading of the primary documents shows this not to be the case. Gleason came forward after the assassination, not before, and covered himself by claiming that Wiechmann subsequently recanted his story, leaving Gleason to believe it was nothing more than Wiechmann attempting to make himself look important. There was no truth to Wiechmann's claims.

Sources: Statement of Daniel H. L. Gleason, NARA, RG 153, M-599, reel 4, frames 373–80.

*See also*: Wiechmann, Louis

### Gobright, Lawrence A. (1814–1881)

A reporter working for the Associated Press. Gobright turned in Booth's derringer to the Metropolitan Police after it was found lying on the floor of the presi-

ized that he did not have his room key. Thinking he had lost it at the theater, he returned and was allowed by a guard to search the darkened box for his lost key. He came across Booth's derringer lying on the floor, and gave it to Gobright. Gobright turned the derringer in the next morning.

Sources: Timothy S. Good, *We Saw Lincoln Shot: One Hundred Eyewitness Accounts* (Jackson: University Press of Mississippi, 1995); Statement of William T. Kent, NARA, RG 153, reel 5, frames 129–131.

*See also:* Kent, William T.

## Gorsuch, Tommy

Youngest son of Edward Gorsuch, a Maryland slave owner killed at Christiana, Pennsylvania, in 1851. Gorsuch, along with seven other individuals including his son and nephew, set out to recover four of his slaves that ran away to Christiana, just over the border from Maryland. Christiana was known to the black community in the South as a safe haven for runaway slaves. A confrontation took place between Gorsuch's party and several free blacks living in Christiana. Along with the blacks were two white men, identified as Quakers. In the ensuing melee Gorsuch was killed and his son severely wounded. The event came to be known as the "Christiana Riot" and

dential box by William Kent. Gobright was at his office when a friend told him the president had been assassinated. He made his way to Ford's Theatre and, finding the theater near empty, was able to enter the presidential box and examine it so that he might be able to describe it in detail in his later dispatches. William Kent, a clerk in the office of the paymaster general, was sitting in the Dress Circle at the time of the assassination. He made his way to the box and entered shortly after the door was opened, admitting Dr. Charles Leale. Kent observed the president lying on the floor. He later described him as "insensible." Later that evening while walking home Kent real-

ended in a famous court case held in Independence Hall in Philadelphia.

Nine years later, John Wilkes Booth referred to the confrontation in a speech he wrote in 1860 while in Philadelphia. Booth told of a schoolmate from his youth, Tommy Gorsuch, and how abolitionists killed his father. Gorsuch became a martyr to slave owners throughout the South. To Booth, the young school chum lost his father because of antislavery agitators in the North, the very same agitators who were splitting the country apart and plunging it into Civil War.

Sources: Edward Steers, Jr., "Freedom Began Here," *North & South* 1, no. 4 (April 1998), 34–43.

## Gouldman, Izora (1847–1929)

Daughter of Henry Gouldman, owner of the Star Hotel in Bowling Green, Virginia. Izora was the sweetheart of Private Willie Jett at the time of Booth's escape. While questioning William Rollins and his wife Bettie in Port Conway, Virginia, Bettie Rollins told Union detective Everton J. Conger that Willie Jett was courting Gouldman's daughter Izora. Jett, Bettie told Conger, could in all likelihood be found at the Star Hotel in Bowling Green because of his romantic interest in the owner's daughter. After discussing strategy, the detectives decided to go to Bowling Green and find Jett, believing he could lead them to Booth and Herold. Shortly after midnight on April 26, members of the 16th New York Cavalry arrested Jett at the Star Hotel. After being threatened by the detectives, Jett agreed to lead the soldiers to the Garrett farm, where Booth and Herold were hiding. Booth was killed and Herold captured thanks to a romance between Jett and Izora and the keen observation of Bettie Rollins.

Sources: William A. Tidwell, James O. Hall, and David W. Gaddy, *Come Retribution* (Jackson: University Press of Mississippi, 1988), 75–76; Edward Steers, Jr., *Blood on the Moon* (Lexington: University Press of Kentucky, 2001), 189.

*See also:* Jett, Willie; Star Hotel

## Gouldman Hotel

See Star Hotel

## Gourlay, Jeannie (1844–1928)

Actress who played the part of Mary Meredith in *Our American Cousin* at Ford's Theatre the night of Lincoln's assassination. She married Robert Struthers and eventually settled in Milford, Pennsylvania. According to family tradition, Jeannie's father, Thomas Gourlay, took one of the flags that decorated the box at Ford's Theatre and kept it hidden away for several years. The flag descended through Jeannie to her son, V. Paul Struthers, who donated it to the Pike County His-

torical Society in Milford, Pennsylvania. The flag has achieved a special status as an icon of the assassination. Struthers died in 1928 and is buried in the Milford Cemetery in Milford, Pennsylvania.

Sources: Joseph Edward Garrera, *The Lincoln Flag of the Pike County Historical Society* (privately printed, 1996); Edward Steers, Jr., "Freedom Began Here," *North & South* 1, no. 4 (April 1998), 34–43.

*See also:* Lincoln Flag

### Gourlay, Thomas (1818–1885)

Stage manager for John Ford, and cast member of *Our American Cousin* on the night of Lincoln's assassination. When doctors in the presidential box called for water, actress Laura Keene, who was standing in the wings looking up at the box, grabbed a pitcher of water from the actors' green room and asked Thomas Gourlay to lead her to the box. Gourlay knew a rear passage that exited through a backstage door into the alleyway separating the theater from the Star Saloon, and up a staircase to the lounge area just off the Dress Circle. From the lounge it was only a few steps to the door that led into the outer vestibule of boxes 7 and 8, where the president was prostrate on the floor, being administered to by Drs. Leale and Taft.

Family tradition gives rise to the belief that Thomas Gourlay found the flag in the box and used it to cradle the president's head. The legend claims the flag remained under Lincoln's head while he was carried from the theater across the street to the Petersen house. Gourlay retrieved the flag and took it home, keeping it as a precious relic of the events of that night. The flag passed into the possession of Jeannie Gourlay Struthers on Thomas Gourlay's death.

In 1954, Jeannie Gourlay Struthers's son, Vivian Paul Struthers, donated the flag to the Pike County (Pennsylvania) Historical Society, where it resides today on display.

Sources: Joseph E. Garrera, *The Lincoln Flag of the Pike County Historical Society* (privately printed, 1996); Edward Steers, Jr., *Blood on the Moon* (Lexington: University Press of Kentucky, 2001), 121–22.

### Grant, Ulysses S. (1822–1885)

Lieutenant general and general in chief of the Union army. Grant and his wife, Julia, were invited to accompany the Lincolns to Ford's Theatre on the night of the assassination. Lincoln extended an invitation to Grant at the morning cabinet meeting held in Lincoln's office on April 14. Grant accepted with the proviso that Julia wanted to leave that evening and visit with their children, who were attending school in Burlington, New Jersey. Grant told Lincoln that if he was able to finish his paperwork early enough to catch the evening train to New Jersey, he and Julia would leave and visit the children. Lincoln said he understood.

Some authors have suggested that Grant's decision to turn down Lincoln's invitation was at the insistence of his wife. Julia Grant was the object of harsh words from Mary Lincoln while visiting the troops at City Point, Virginia, only the month before. Mary Lincoln became irrational on finding the wife of General Charles Griffin, commander of the Fifth Army Corps, sitting on a horse beside the president during the review of Griffin's corps. When Julia Grant attempted to calm Mary Lincoln, she was harshly accused of wanting to see her husband replace Lincoln in the White House. Julia Grant must have felt humiliated and yet she wrote of the incident in her memoirs excusing Mary Lincoln's behavior due to her exhaustion from travel. Julia, however, did not wish to attend the theater with Mary Lincoln and presumably told her husband to cancel his acceptance of Lincoln's invitation.

Whatever the reason for the Grants not attending the theater with the Lincolns, it had no bearing whatsoever on the events of that tragic night. Some argue that had Grant been with Lincoln, Booth could not have gotten past the military guards that attended Grant. It simply is not true. We know that Grant attended the theater on previous occasions without military escorts or guards. In fact, on the night of February 10, two months prior to the assassination, Grant attended the theater with Lincoln and General Ambrose Burnside without military guards or bodyguards of any sort. During the evening several people were able to enter the box without difficulty, there being no one to stop them.

Upon reaching Philadelphia, where the Grants stopped over for dinner, they received a telegram informing them that Lincoln had been assassinated and Secretary of State William Seward seriously wounded. Grant took the next train to Washington.

Sources: *Washington Evening Star*, February 11, 1865, 2, col. 4; Edward Steers, Jr., *Blood on the Moon* (Lexington: University Press of Kentucky, 2001), 98.

## Green, Thomas

Confederate sympathizer and covert agent living in Washington, D.C. Green's large Federal-style mansion located between Seventeenth and Eighteenth streets served as a safe house for Confederate agents during the war. Thomas Nelson Conrad, a Confederate agent who was in Washington to reconnoiter the White House and its environs in a plot to capture Lincoln in the fall of 1864, stayed at Thomas Green's mansion, using it as his base of operations.

Sources: Statement of Thomas Green, NARA, RG 153, M-599, reel 6, frames 515–40; William A. Tidwell, James O. Hall, and David W. Gaddy, *Come Retribution* (Jackson: University Press of Mississippi, 1988), 72–74.

## Greenawalt, John

Proprietor of the Kimmel (Pennsylvania) House located at 357–359 C Street in Washington, D.C., where George Atzerodt frequently stayed when in the city. Early on the morning of April 15, Atzerodt checked into the Kimmel House after wandering about the city. Greenawalt testified for the prosecution that Atzerodt came into the hotel between two and three o'clock Saturday morning in company with a man named Thomas (Samuel Thomas, who had no connection with the conspiracy but drew the suspicions of the government authorities), and that Atzerodt arose around five o'clock and left the hotel. Greenawalt also told the court that he had seen Atzerodt and Booth together in the lobby on various occasions in conversation. He also noted that he had seen them on the street in front of his house and in front of the National Hotel in conversation. Greenawalt clearly tied Atzerodt to Booth in more than a casual way, helping place a noose around Atzerodt's neck.

Sources: John Greenawalt, NARA, RG 153, M-599, reel 2, frames 1052–58; Poore, *Conspiracy Trial*, vol. 1, 341, 390; Pitman, *Trial*, 146; John Greenawalt, NARA, RG 153, M-599, reel 3, frames 529–30; Poore, *Conspiracy Trial*, vol. 1, 341, 390; Pitman, *Trial*, 146; John Greenawalt, NARA, RG 153, M-599, reel 3, frames 633–38; Poore, *Conspiracy Trial*, vol. 1, 341, 390; Pitman, *Trial*, 146.

*See also*: Atzerodt, George Andrew

## Green Mount Cemetery

Located in Baltimore and contains the Booth family burial plot as well as the graves of Michael O' Laughlen and Samuel Arnold. In 1869, President Andrew Johnson released Booth's remains to the family from their burial place in the Washington Arsenal. His corpse was placed in undertaker John Weaver's vault at Green Mount until burial could be arranged in the spring.

In 1995, two vocational historians who wanted to exhume Booth's remains in the hopes of proving that the body in the grave was not John Wilkes Booth filed a lawsuit in Baltimore County Circuit Court. The litigants had the approval of surviving Booth relatives. The relatives were not descendants of Booth but were believed to be the closest living relatives to Booth. The cemetery refused the request on the grounds that it had a legal obligation not to disturb the remains of any of the individuals under its care, except for legitimate reasons. The evidence, they claimed, clearly showed it was Booth that was buried in the grave and not a surrogate. Several well-known historians testified on behalf of the cemetery, supporting its claim that it was Booth buried in the grave. After several days of hearings, Judge Joseph H. Kaplan ruled that the overwhelming evidence supported the view that it was Booth who was buried in the grave, and the grave should not be disturbed. Had the remains been exhumed they might

well have put the question of who was buried in Booth's grave to rest once and for all.

Sources: Laurie Verge, ed., *The Body in the Barn* (Clinton, Md.: Surratt Society, 1993); Edward Steers, Jr., *Blood on the Moon* (Lexington: University Press of Kentucky, 2001), 245–67.

### Grillet, George

A witness called on behalf of Michael O'Laughlen. Grillet testified that he spent part of Thursday evening, April 13, in Washington with O'Laughlen and three other men. He also claimed to have been with O'Laughlen on Friday, April 14, between 8:00 P.M. and around 11:00 P.M. and midnight. He was with O'Laughlen when they heard of the assassination, establishing O'Laughlen's alibi at the time of the attack on Seward and shooting of Lincoln.

Sources: Testimony of George Grillet, Poore, *Conspiracy Trial*, vol. 2, 209; Pitman, *Trial*, 230.

*See also:* O'Laughlen, Michael

### Griffiths, Jake

Private Griffiths claimed to be one of the soldiers who carried Lincoln's body from Ford's Theatre across the street to the Petersen house. Griffiths was a member of Thompson's Battery C, Pennsylvania Artillery. Griffiths was at Ford's Theatre along with three other soldiers from Battery C on the night of the assassination. In later life Griffiths claimed the four soldiers helped carry Lincoln's body. The other three soldiers were Jacob J. Soles, John Correy, and William Sample. The people who carried Lincoln were never positively identified, and several made claims in later life. Certainly Dr. Charles Leale would be one along with Dr. Charles Taft. It probably took at least six individuals, and as many as eight, to carry the six-foot-four president, but precisely who they were remains conjecture.

Sources: *Sunday Times-Telegraph* (Pittsburgh), February 12, 1928; *New York Tribune*, February 8, 1921.

## Grimes (Grymes), Benjamin

An agent of the Confederate mail line operating through Maryland and Virginia. Grimes owned a farm on the Virginia side of the Potomac River that was directly opposite Confederate agent Thomas Jones's first house on the Maryland side. More often than not, Grimes received mail and people that Jones ferried across the river, all having business with the Confederacy. The high bluffs on the Maryland side cast long shadows across the river near sunset, making it difficult to see small boats on the river at that time of day. Boats carrying mail and other types of documents usually rowed across the river from Virginia side just before sundown and were deposited in hollowed-out tree trunks or under old stumps, where they were picked up and sent along their way to northern destinations. Grimes was an active player in this activity.

Sources: William A. Tidwell, James O. Hall, and David W. Gaddy, *Come Retribution* (Jackson: University Press of Mississippi, 1988), 66–67; John M. Wearmouth and Roberta J. Wearmouth, *Thomas A. Jones: Chief Agent of the Confederate Secret Service* (Port Tobacco, Md.: Stones Throw, 2000).

*See also:* Mail Line

## Grover, Leonard (1835–1926)

Owner of Grover's National Theatre, along with C. Dwight Hess, located on Pennsylvania Avenue. On the night of April 14, Grover was in New York leaving the theater operation to his partner. On the afternoon of the 14th, Booth met Hess standing in front of the theater. Booth asked Hess if the president would be attending the theater that night. Hess told him no, Mrs. Lincoln had declined his invitation. On that same night, young Tad Lincoln attended Grover's to see *Aladdin! Or, the Wonderful Lamp*, accompanied by Alphonso Donn, the White House doorkeeper, who was a favorite of Tad. Midway through the play Hess took the stage to announce that the president had been shot. Donn rushed Young Taddy back to the White House and stayed with the boy comforting him. Hess wanted the Lincolns to attend his theater, but lost out to friendly rival John Ford.

Sources: W. Emerson Reck, *A. Lincoln: His Last 24 Hours* (Jefferson, N.C.: McFarland, 1987).

*See also:* Grover's National Theatre

## Grover's National Theatre

On the afternoon of April 14, Booth dropped by Grover's National Theatre to see if the Lincoln party had accepted Grover's invitation to attend the evening performance. They had not, and Booth knew that Ford's would be the place where he could carry out his diabolical plan. On the night of April 14, Grover's was playing *Aladdin! Or, the Wonderful Lamp*. When word reached C. Dwight Hess he interrupted the show and announced to the audience that the president had been assassinated. Sitting in the audience was twelve-year-old Tad Lincoln and his chaperone, White House doorkeeper Alphonso Donn. Poor Tad screamed out loud, and Donn hustled him back to the White House where he sat with the young boy, comforting him through the terrible night.

Sources: W. Emerson Reck, *A. Lincoln: His Last 24 Hours* (Jefferson, N.C.: McFarland, 1987).

## Guerilla Boyle

See Boyle, John H.

## Gurley, Phineas Densmore (1816–1868)

Pastor of the New York Avenue Presbyterian Church located at New York Avenue and Thirteenth Street in Washington, D.C. The Lincolns rented a pew at the church and enrolled their two sons, Willie and Tad, in the church's Sunday school. Gurley was a favorite of Lincoln, who respected his intellect and enjoyed listening to his sermons.

The church has become a modern-day shrine of President Lincoln. On display is Lincoln's handwritten copy of a compensation bill by which Lincoln proposed paying slave owners in the border states for emancipating their slaves. He introduced the bill on July 14, 1862. The bill called for the transfer of 6 percent interest-bearing bonds of the U.S. Treasury to each state equal to the aggregate value of all the slaves within that state based on the census of 1860. Lincoln pointed out that "one half-day's cost of this war would pay for all the slaves in Delaware at four hundred dollars per head—that eighty-seven days cost of this war would pay for all the slaves in Delaware, Maryland, the District of Columbia, Kentucky, and Missouri at the same price." One day later, the border states rejected Lincoln's plan. The church also has on display a couch from Reverend Gurley's study used by Lincoln when attending midweek meetings.

Gurley was present at the Petersen house consoling Mary Lincoln while maintaining an all-night vigil over the dying president. On two occasions during the night, Gurley led the group of people around the bed in prayer. When Dr. Charles Leale proclaimed Lincoln dead, Secretary of War Edwin M. Stanton asked Gurley to offer a prayer. When Gurley finished, all present yielded up a spontaneous "Amen." Gurley partici-pated in the funeral services in the White House, where he spoke, and the Capitol building, where he offered a prayer, and later at Oak Ridge Cemetery in Springfield, Illinois.

Sources: Frank E. Edgington, *History of the New York Avenue Presbyterian Church* (Washington, D.C.: New York Avenue Presbyterian Church, 1961); Edward Steers, Jr., *Blood on the Moon* (Lexington: University Press of Kentucky, 2001), 268, 273, 279, 292.

*See also:* New York Avenue Church

### Gwynn, Bennett (1823–1897)

A neighbor of Mary Surratt in Surrattsville, Prince George's County, Maryland. On April 11, Mary Surratt and Louis Wiechmann traveled to Surrattsville from Washington, ostensibly to collect money that a man named John Nothey owed her. She and Wiechmann rode on to the home of Bennett Gwynn, where they had supper. On returning to the tavern they found Nothey waiting to see Mrs. Surratt. After some discussion, Mary and Wiechmann returned to Washington. Mary failed to recover the money Nothey owed her.

On April 14, Mary Surratt and Wiechmann again traveled to Surrattsville, this time to deliver a fateful message to the tavern operator John Lloyd to "have the shooting irons ready," as someone would call for them that night. She claimed the purpose of her second trip was to again speak to Nothey about the debt she claimed he owed her. Following his arrest, however, Nothey gave a different version: "On Friday she came I only saw her about 6 o'clock P.M. at Lloyds [Surratt Tavern]. Do not know how long she had been there that day. I did not see Lloyd or his horse. I was only there about five minutes." After supper, Mary Surratt returned to Washington.

Sources: Bennett F. Gwynn, NARA, RG 153, M-599, reel 4, frames 420–21; Poore, *Conspiracy Trial*, vol. 2, 190, 218, 294; Pitman, *Trial*, 126, 182.

*See also:* Nothey, John; Lloyd, John M.

## Habeas Corpus

Writ whose title means in Latin, "You have the body." President Andrew Johnson suspended the writ of habeas corpus in response to a petition by Mary Surratt's attorneys and issued by Justice Andrew Wylie. Habeas corpus is a writ issued by a court commanding the person holding another to produce the person in court to test the legality of the detention and not the innocence or guilt of the person. Upon learning of Mary Surratt's death sentence on July 6, her attorneys Frederick Aiken and John Clampitt met with Judge Andrew Wylie, a justice of the Supreme Court of the District of Columbia, and secured a writ of habeas corpus ordering Major General Hancock to bring Mary Surratt into his courtroom to determine if she was illegally detained. Hancock appeared before Wylie and handed him a presidential order suspending the writ in her case and that of the other conspirators. The legal jurisdiction of the military tribunal was controversial among certain jurists at the time and remains so today.

Sources: Henry Campbell Black, *Black's Law Dictionary* (1891; reprint, St. Paul, Minn.: West, 1983), 363; Thomas R. Turner, "The Military Trial," in Edward Steers, Jr., ed., *The Trial* (Lexington: University Press of Kentucky, 2003), xxi–xxviii.

*See also*: Military Tribunal; Surratt, Mary Elizabeth

## Hagan's Folly

The home of William Burtles in Charles County, Maryland. When Booth and Herold left Samuel Mudd's house Saturday evening at sundown they were headed for Hagan's Folly. Lost, they came upon the cabin of Oswell Swan, a free black whose farm was on the Cracklingtown Road near Hughesville and south of Bryantown. Booth and Herold made a wide swing around Bryantown to avoid the Union soldiers stationed there and in doing so came upon Swan's cabin. Swan later told detectives that Booth asked the way to William Burtles's house (Hagan's Folly). Burtles's home was located east of St. Mary's Church and Bryantown in a secluded area. The house was used to shelter Confederate agents moving between Richmond and points north along the Confederate mail line. After Swan gave the two men food and whiskey, Booth changed his mind and offered Swan twelve dollars to guide them across the Zekiah Swamp to the home of Samuel Cox, another Confederate agent known to Booth. Swan agreed and the three men arrived at Cox's home (Rich Hill) around midnight or shortly thereafter.

Sources: Statement of Oswell Swan, NARA, RG 153, M-599, reel 6, frames 227–29; William A.

Tidwell, James O. Hall, and David W. Gaddy, *Come Retribution* (Jackson: University Press of Mississippi, 1988), 445–46.

*See also:* Cox, Samuel; Swan, Oswell

## Hale, Charles B.

Called as a witness on behalf of Samuel B. Arnold at the conspiracy trial. Hale worked as a clerk along with Samuel Arnold for John Wharton, a sutler at Fort Monroe. Hale testified that Arnold had worked at Wharton's store every day since the later part of March and spent every night at Wharton's store during that time, establishing that Arnold was not in Washington, D.C., for a period of two weeks before the assassination.

Sources: Testimony of Charles B. Hale, Poore, *Conspiracy Trial*, vol. 3, 62–64; Pitman, *Trial*, 241.

*See also:* Arnold, Samuel Bland

## Hale, Lucy Lambert (1841–1915)

The daughter of abolitionist and former New Hampshire senator John Parker Hale. Lucy was romantically involved with John Wilkes Booth, much to her father's consternation. When Booth's body was searched following his death, a photograph of Lucy Hale was found in his wallet. According to Asia Clarke, Booth's sister, Booth sent Lucy a valentine he had made on February 14, 1865.

Booth and Lucy were dating, and would check into hotels as, "J. W. Booth & Lady." On March 5, 1865, the day after Lincoln's inauguration, Lucy was in Booth's room at the National Hotel in Washington, D.C. Lincoln appointed her father ambassador to Spain and he was taking Lucy with him. Lucy penned on the back of an envelope the words from a Whittier poem, "For all sad words from tongue or pen, The saddest are these, It might have been." Booth added the words, "Now, in this hour, that we part, I will ask to be forgotten, never, But in thy pure and guileless heart, Consider me thy friend, dear Ever. J. Wilkes Booth." Junius Jr., Booth's older brother, told investigators that his brother said to him that "he would not live in the oil regions for all the wealth in them & that he was in love with a lady in Washington & that she was worth more to him than all the money he could make." The "lady in Washington" was Lucy Lambert Hale.

Sources: Terry Alford, ed., *John Wilkes Booth: A Sister's Memoir by Asia Booth Clarke* (Jackson: University Press of Mississippi, 1996); Statement of Junius Brutus Booth, Jr., NARA, RG 153, M-599, reel 2, frames 261–68.

## Hall, James Otis (1912–2007)

Renowned assassination historian. Co-author of controversial book *Come Retribution*, which states the case for Jef-

ferson Davis and other high-ranking Confederate leaders' direct involvement in Lincoln's assassination. Born on June 30, 1912, in Afton, Oklahoma, Hall attended public schools and went on to earn a bachelor's degree in history and economics from Northeastern State College at Tahlequah. Following graduation Hall taught general education for two years in a public school. In the fall of 1940, he took the government's civil service exam and was hired as an investigator in the Department of Labor assigned to investigating violations of Federal labor laws.

Enlisting in the army in 1942, Hall used his investigative background to land a job in the army's criminal investigation division. He was sent to England, where he investigated crimes by the mili-

tary. He quickly realized he had a special aptitude for investigative work. He loved it, and following the war returned to the Labor Department. Then in 1950, he accepted a position in the Labor Department in Washington, D.C. It was while in Washington that Hall read an article in *Civil War Times* that claimed that Lincoln's secretary of war, Edwin M. Stanton, was involved in Lincoln's murder. Intrigued with what he read, Hall started digging into the various records available at the National Archives and the Library of Congress. Over the next fifty years Hall emerged as the premier historian on Lincoln's assassination. His contributions to the field were numerous and often unique. In the 1970s, he discovered the long lost "To whom it may concern" letter written by John Wilkes Booth explaining his reasons for killing Lincoln. Historians had come to suspect the letter was a fabrication made up for publication following Lincoln's assassination.

Over the years Hall narrated dozens of tours along Booth's escape route and lectured on the assassination from every angle. In 1988, he co-authored a book on the Confederate secret service and its involvement in Lincoln's assassination. The book, *Come Retribution*, contains a great deal of new information especially in the area of the Confederate secret service.

Although some of the book's conclusions remain controversial, it has stimulated a renewed interest among assassination historians and others and opened up fields of new research into Lincoln's murder. Hall generously shared his research with anyone who showed a genuine interest in Lincoln's assassination.

Hall died on February 26, 2007. His massive files, gathered over fifty years of research, now reside at the James O. Hall Research Center, a part of the Surratt House Museum located in Clinton, Maryland. It can be safely said that no study of Lincoln's assassination can be considered complete without a study of Hall's files.

Sources: Keiran McAuliffe, "Portrait of an Historical Detective," *North & South* 5, no. 3 (spring 2002), 74–80.

### Hancock, Winfield Scott (1824–1886)

Major general in the Union army commanding the middle military division, which encompassed the Washington Arsenal. Hancock was in overall charge of the prison following Lincoln's assassination, including the prisoners held there as well as the trial facilities. The day-to-day care of the prisoners, however, was delegated to Major General John F. Hartranft, who reported directly to Hancock.

On July 6, 1865, the day before the hanging, Hancock accompanied Hartranft as he visited the four condemned prisoners and read the "Findings & Sentences" to each of them, delivering a copy of the same to each. After Hartranft finished reading the sentences he asked each of them, with Hancock's approval, if they had any friends to send for or any special minister of the gospel whom they wished to see.

On the morning of the execution, Mary Surratt's attorneys prepared a draft seeking a writ of habeas corpus on her behalf, and presented it to Judge Andrew Wylie, a justice of the Supreme Court of the District of Columbia. Wylie endorsed it, ordering U.S. marshal David Gooding to serve the writ on Hancock. Hancock appeared in Wylie's chambers at 11:30 A.M. and presented Wylie with President Andrew Johnson's order suspending the writ in her case.

Prior to the hanging, Lewis Powell told Father Jacob Walter that Mary Surratt "was innocent of the murder of the President." Judge Advocate Joseph Holt told Hartranft to have Father Walter put the statement in writing and send it to him; Hartranft then added his own endorsement to the statement. General Hancock ordered Hartranft to explain his endorsement, and Hartranft did so, writing: "I believe Payne [Powell] had told the truth in this matter. In this, I did not by any means intend to express my own opinion of the guilt or innocence of Mrs. Surratt, but simply that I believed Payne had told the truth according to the best of his knowledge and belief." Hartranft's answer was sufficient and the subject was dropped without further action.

Source: Ezra J. Warner, *Generals in Blue* (Baton Rouge: Louisiana State University Press, 1964), 202–4; Edward Steers, Jr. and Harold Holzer, eds., *The Lincoln Assassination Conspirators: Their Confinement and Execution, as Recorded in the Letterbook of John Frederick Hartranft* (Baton Rouge: Louisiana State University Press, 2009).

*See also:* Hartranft, John F.

## Hanging of Conspirators

After deliberating for a day and a half, the nine members of the military tribunal found all eight defendants guilty. Four of the defendants, Mary Surratt, Lewis Powell, George Atzerodt, and David Herold were condemned to death by hanging. Dr. Samuel Mudd, Samuel Arnold, and Michael O'Laughlen were each given life sentences, while Edman Spangler was sentenced to six years. The date of execution was set for July 7. The only appeal was to President Andrew Johnson who endorsed each of the sentences meted out by the tribunal.

Major General John Frederick Hartranft, who served as military governor of the prison, was charged with oversight of the prisoners' well being throughout their incarceration. Now that the trial was over, Hartranft had the onerous duty of carrying out the death sentences. Hartranft selected Captain Christian Rath to fulfill the job of hangman. During his brief tenure as a provost marshal during the war, Rath had once before been in charge of a hanging. He secured a set of plans for a scaffold from the sheriff of Level Plains, Virginia, and set about overseeing the construction of a scaffold to hold the four condemned prisoners. Working throughout the night of July 6, the carpenters completed their work early on the morning of the execution.

The scaffold was twenty feet long by fifteen feet wide. The platform stood ten feet off of the ground, and consisted of two trapdoors or drops that measured six feet by four feet. Each drop was supported from beneath by a large upright beam held in place and guarded by two soldiers. At the appropriate signal, the guards would knock their beams away allowing the trapdoor to drop and the condemned to fall to their deaths. Four graves had been prepared immediately to the right of the scaffold. To one side of the graves four plain wooden boxes were stacked that would hold the bodies. A bottle containing a slip of paper with the name of the person was placed inside each box for future identification.

The executions were scheduled for between 1:00 P.M. and 2:00 P.M. of the 7th. By early morning, crowds had already begun to gather outside the main gate that led to the arsenal grounds. Only those with special passes signed by Secretary of War Edwin Stanton or Major General Winfield Scott Hancock (commander of the military district and the arsenal) were admitted to view the hanging. Even so, over one hundred people were admitted inside the grounds of the arsenal. Among those given special permission by Stanton was photographer Alexander Gardner and his assistant, Timothy O'Sullivan. The two photographers took a series of photographs documenting the entire procedure from start to finish including a photograph of Hartranft and his staff.

The day after the executions Hartranft filed his rather antiseptic report of the event with his superior officer, General Hancock:

Everything being in readiness at 1:00 P.M. 7th inst., the prisoners were conducted to the scaffold in the following order 1st Mary E. Surratt her guard and fathers Walters & Wiget. 2nd G. A. Atzerodt his guard & Rev. Mr. Butler. 3rd David E. Herold his guard and Rev. Mr. Olds. 4th Lewis Payne his guard and Rev. Dr. Gillette, each of the prisoners was seated in a chair on the platform while the ministers in attendance offered a prayer in their behalf. The prisoners were made to stand and everything in readiness. The drop fell at 1:30 P.M. Life was pronounced by the Board of Surgeons appointed for that purpose to be extinct in each of the bodies at 1:50 P.M. All officers and men on duty during the execution gave entire satisfaction.

The four prisoners had their arms and legs bound with white linen, and canvas hoods placed over their heads. The nooses were slipped over their heads and adjusted with the hangman's knot placed against the side of the neck. When the prayers were finished, and the necessary adjustments completed the prisoners were edged forward making sure they were standing squarely on the two trapdoors, and that everyone else stood clear. With everything in readiness waiting the final moment of execution, Mary Surratt suddenly spoke out in a trembling voice, "Please don't let me fall." George Atzerodt, shaking noticeably, addressed the others on the platform, "Good bye, gentlemen, who are before me now. May we all meet in the other world." And then as the noose was adjusted tighter around his neck cried out, "Don't choke me!"

Satisfied all was ready, Captain Rath clapped his hands three times. The soldiers guarding the uprights swung a pair of bludgeons forward striking the braces at their base knocking them free. As the uprights fell away from their supporting positions the two trapdoors fell with a screeching noise and the four bodies dropped with a snapping thud. The stain of innocent blood had been removed from the land.

Sources: Edward Steers, Jr., *Blood on the Moon* (Lexington: University Press of Kentucky, 2001), 227–30; Edward Steers, Jr., and Harold Holzer, eds., *The Lincoln Assassination Conspirators: Their Confinement and Execution as Recorded in the Letterbook of John Frederick Hartranft* (Baton Rouge: Louisiana State University Press, 2009), 48–53, 142–4.

*See also*: Arsenal, Washington; Hartranft, John Frederick; Rath, Captain Christian

## Hanscom, Simon P. (1820–1876)

Editor of the *National Republican* newspaper in Washington, D.C. On the night of April 14, during the third act of *Our American Cousin* at Ford's Theatre, Hanscom entered the president's box to deliver a document to Lincoln approximately twenty minutes prior to Booth entering the box. In his newspaper article the next day he wrote that the only person at the door to the box was Charles Forbes, the president's messenger and footman.

Sources: William Hanchett, *The Lincoln Murder Conspiracies* (Urbana: University of Illinois Press, 1983).

*See also:* Forbes, Charles

## Hansell, Emerick (1817–1893)

A State Department messenger present at the Seward house at the time of Lewis Powell's attack on Secretary of State William Seward. Hansell was stationed at the Seward home working as a messenger carrying messages to and from the State Department. When Powell fled the room where Seward was lying in a pool of blood, Hansell was on the staircase trying to flee. Powell caught up with him and slashed him across his back, pushing him aside as he ran down the stairs. Although wounded, Hansell survived Powell's knife attack.

Sources: James L. Swanson, *Manhunt: The 12-Day Chase for Lincoln's Killer* (New York: Harper Perennial, 2007), 60.

## Harbin, Thomas Henry (1833–1885)

Confederate agent from Charles County, Maryland, who aided Booth's attempt to escape by providing horses and a guide. Harbin had been introduced to John Wilkes Booth by Dr. Samuel Mudd in a prearranged meeting in Bryantown on December 18, 1864. Booth recruited Harbin into his capture plan. Before the war Harbin served as one of several postmasters of Bryantown. As such, he was well acquainted with the inhabitants of the county. He became a Confederate agent working the area the Virginia side of the Potomac River across from Charles County. On December 18, Harbin crossed the Potomac River from Virginia and met with Samuel Mudd and John Wilkes Booth at the Bryantown Tavern.

Harbin later told journalist George Alfred Townsend that Booth had outlined his plan to capture Lincoln and present him to Confederate leaders. Harbin, despite Booth's overly dramatic behavior, agreed to join Booth and help him take Lincoln to Richmond.

On Sunday, April 23, Booth and Herold successfully crossed the Potomac and made their way to the home of Elizabeth Quesenberry, a Confederate sympathizer. Thomas Jones had instructed Booth to seek out Quesenberry for help. Booth's meeting with Harbin paid dividends; Mrs. Quesenberry sent for Harbin. When he arrived he brought horses for Booth and Herold and arranged for one of his agents, William Bryant, to take the two fugitives to the home of Dr. Richard Stuart, where they expected to find food and shelter in continuing their escape.

Sources: William A. Tidwell, James O. Hall, and David W. Gaddy, *Come Retribution* (Jackson: University Press of Mississippi, 1988); *Cincinnati Enquirer*, April 18, 1885.

*See also:* Mudd, Dr. Samuel Alexander

## Hardy, John F.

A near neighbor of Samuel Mudd. On his return home from Bryantown on Saturday evening following Lincoln's assassination, and while Booth and Herold were still at Mudd's house, Mudd visited with Hardy and another neighbor, Francis Farrell. Hardy later was called as a witness at the conspiracy trial and told the military tribunal that Mudd had told him about Lincoln's assassination and that a man named Booth was the assassin. When Hardy asked Mudd if it was the same Booth that visited the area in the fall of 1864, Mudd replied that he thought it was the same man. Hardy also made the statement that when Mudd left for home the sun was only fifteen minutes above the horizon. Sunset on April 15 occurred at 6:44 P.M. If Hardy was correct, Mudd left Hardy's around 6:30 P.M. and arrived home near 7:00 P.M., and not between 4:00 and 5:00 P.M. as he later told detectives. This meant there were between two and three hours unaccounted for in Mudd's visit to Bryantown. Since Booth later said he was headed to the home of William Burtles, it seems likely that Mudd rode past Bryantown to Burtles's house to inform him that Booth and Herold would arrive later that night. This would take Mudd between two and three hours.

Hardy also testified that he saw Booth at St. Mary's Church on two occasions, not one, as Mudd claimed; the first was in November 1864 and the second in December 1864. The testimony of others clearly places Booth and Mudd together in December as well as November. Mudd never mentioned this December meeting.

Sources: Testimony of John F. Hardy, Poore, *Conspiracy Trial*, vol. 2, 434–36, vol. 3, 431–37; Pitman, *Trial,* 213, 218; James L. Swanson, *Manhunt: The 12-Day Chase for Lincoln's Killer* (New York: Harper Perennial, 2007), 160–61.

*See also:* Burtles, William; Mudd, Dr. Samuel Alexander

## Harney, Thomas F.

Employed as an agent in the Confederate Torpedo Bureau in Richmond. Sergeant Thomas F. Harney was expert in the use of various types of explosive mines, or torpedoes as they were called. On April 1, 1865, thirteen days before Lincoln's assassination, Harney was dispatched to John Singleton Mosby in Fauquier County, Virginia, where he was assigned to Company H. On April 8, a contingent of Companies H and D were ambushed by a detachment of the Eighth Illinois Cavalry at Burke's Station, Virginia. Harney was captured along with "ordinance" supplies that he was carrying.

On April 3, 1865, Richmond fell. One of the first units to march into Richmond was Colonel Edward Hastings Ripley of the Ninth Vermont Infantry. In his memoir, published after the war, Ripley wrote that a Confederate private working at the Torpedo Bureau in Richmond by the name of William H. Snyder, Company E, Second Virginia Cavalry, came to him and told of a plot by members of the Torpedo Bureau to blow up the White House in an attempt to kill Lincoln and members of his cabinet. Snyder was troubled by this "secret mission" and felt it a matter of conscience to alert Union authorities. Ripley took Snyder to Lincoln, who was then on board the *Malvern*, anchored in the James River. Lincoln listened to Ripley's account of the affair and ended it without actually talking to Snyder.

The authors of *Come Retribution* conclude that Harney was sent on a secret mission to assassinate Lincoln by blowing up a wing of the White House. A statement given by conspirator George A. Atzerodt supports their conclusion. In his statement given aboard the *Montauk*, Atzerodt said, "Booth said he had met a party in N. York who would get the Prest. Certain. They were going to <u>mine the end of the White House</u>, next to the War Dept." This statement, coupled with Snyder's statement, supports the theory that Thomas Harney was on his way to the White House when he and three other men with him were captured at Burke's Station.

Sources: William A. Tidwell, James O. Hall, and David W. Gaddy, *Come Retribution* (Jackson: University Press of Mississippi, 1988), 418–21; Edward Hastings Ripley, *The Capture and Occupation of Richmond, April 3, 1865* (New York: Putnam's, 1907), 23.

*See also:* Snyder, William H.; Torpedo Bureau

## Harper, Mrs. E. C.

Alleged to have heard the confession of David E. George of Enid, Oklahoma, in which he claimed to be John Wilkes Booth. Reading of George's death in a local newspaper, Mrs. Harper wondered if it could be the same man she had met three years earlier in 1900 in El Reno, Texas, who, believing he was about to die, confessed to her that he was John Wilkes Booth. The man did not die and Mrs. Harper forgot about the alleged confession until she read George's obituary. She sent her husband to the funeral parlor to examine the body. He told the funeral director he recognized the body as that of the same man who had confessed to his wife in El Reno. The George-Booth story quickly made its way into the local newspaper, and soon spread across the country. It reached a Memphis, Tennessee, attorney named Finis L. Bates, who came to Enid, claimed the body, and parlayed it into a book and sideshow attraction.

Sources: C. Wyatt Evans, *The Legend of John Wilkes Booth: Myth, Memory and a Mummy* (Lawrence: University Press of Kansas, 2004).

*See also:* Bates, Finis L.

## Harrington, George A.

Assistant secretary of the treasury, Harrington was entrusted by Secretary of War Edwin M. Stanton with the overall responsibility for the funeral procedures of President Lincoln. Benjamin B. French, Lincoln's appointed commissioner of buildings, was placed in charge of the corpse.

Under Harrington's supervision, an army of carpenters invaded the East Room of the White House and constructed the large catafalque that would hold Lincoln's coffin. Harrington also had his carpenters build a series of stepped platforms around the room so that the large number of dignitaries attending the White House funeral services would be able to stand several rows deep and still have an unobstructed view of the coffin and ceremonies taking place.

Sources: Dorothy Meserve Kunhardt and Philip B. Kunhardt, Jr., *Twenty Days* (New York: Harper & Row, 1965), 119–20, 123.

### Harris, Clara H. (1834–1883)

Lincoln's guest, along with her fiancé, Henry Rathbone, at Ford's Theatre on the night of Lincoln's assassination. Clara, the daughter of New York senator Ira Harris, later married Henry Rathbone, her stepbrother. Clara and her fiancée were not Mary Lincoln's first choice to accompany her and the president to the theater. General Ulysses Grant and his wife, Julia, were, but declined since they were planning to travel to New Jersey to visit their children. On Saturday, April 15, Clara Harris accompanied Judge Abram B. Olin, a justice on the D.C. Supreme Court and acting at the request of Secretary of War Stanton, to Ford's Theatre, where they went to the box. Judge Olin asked Clara to arrange the furniture in the box just as it was at the time Booth shot Lincoln, so he could envision the crime.

Clara Harris and Henry Rathbone married in 1867. In 1882, Henry was appointed consul to Germany and the

couple moved to Hannover, Germany. Henry's behavior became increasingly erratic and a year after their arrival in Hannover, Henry fatally shot Clara, then stabbed her several times before turning the knife on himself in an attempted suicide. Rathbone was judged insane and committed to an asylum in Germany, where he died in 1911. Clara's eldest son, Henry Riggs Rathbone, served as a U.S. congressman from Illinois and was instrumental in having legislation approved for the purchase of the Osborn H. Oldroyd collection of Lincoln memorabilia. The large collection is in the care of the U.S. National Park Service.

Sources: Thomas Mallon, *Henry and Clara* (New York: St. Martin's, 1994); Richard Bak, "An April Tragedy, Two Who Were There: The Eyewitness Accounts of Major Rathbone and Clara Harris," in Richard Bak, ed., *The Day Lincoln Was Shot* (Dallas: Taylor, 1998), 71–103.

*See also:* Rathbone, Henry Riggs

## Harris, Thomas Maley (1817–1906)

Member of the military tribunal. Published a book in 1892 in which he presented the evidence for convicting Jefferson Davis and his agents in Canada with Lincoln's assassination. In 1897, he published a booklet titled "Rome's Responsibility for the Assassination of Abraham Lincoln," in which he came to the conclusion that Lincoln's murder was a Roman Catholic plot ordered by Pope Pius IX and carried out by Jesuit priests in America, a theme that lives on today in some quarters.

Before the war Harris practiced medicine in Wood County, Virginia (now Ritchie County, West Virginia). When war broke out he recruited members of the Tenth West Virginia Cavalry, becoming a lieutenant colonel. By 1865, Harris had risen to the brevet rank of brigadier general of volunteers.

Harris questioned the moral fitness of Mary Surratt's defense attorney, Maryland senator Reverdy Johnson. During the 1864 presidential election, Johnson had opposed a law requiring qualified voters in Maryland to take a loyalty oath before they could vote. Johnson rightly challenged the requirement as unconstitutional. Harris claimed Johnson counseled Maryland voters to disregard the oath they were forced to take, and thus claimed Johnson ignored sworn oaths and therefore was unfit to serve as an attorney before the tribunal. After some debate, the commission overruled Harris's objection and accepted Johnson as counsel for Mary Surratt.

Harris firmly believed that the Confederacy under Jefferson Davis's leadership was behind Lincoln's assassination. He was a hard-liner with little patience for hearing the arguments of the defense attorneys. After the trial Harris published a book in support of his conclusion that Davis and those closest to him were behind the murder of the president. In 1897, Harris, agitated by Mary Surratt supporters who maintained she had been hanged because she was a Roman Catholic, published a pamphlet titled "Rome's Responsibility," in which he claimed there was a larger Catholic conspiracy to take over the world. Harris went so far as to claim the Catholic Church encouraged Catholics to emigrate to the United States, and that Catholics were secretly stockpiling weapons for use in taking over the country.

Sources: William Hanchett, *The Lincoln Murder Conspiracies* (Urbana: University of Illinois Press, 1983), 102–4, 238–39.

*See also:* Catholic Conspiracy; Conspiracy Theories

**Harrison, Burton Norvell (1838–1904)**
Private secretary to Confederate president Jefferson Davis. Imprisoned along with the eight accused prisoners at the Washington Arsenal. He was held in solitary confinement but never hooded. He was eventually released.

Harrison accompanied Davis on his flight from Richmond, and was captured along with him and imprisoned in the Washington Arsenal along with the conspirators. Harrison's only connection to Lincoln's assassination comes from a letter sent to Jefferson Davis by H. Waldeman Alston requesting a meeting with Davis to present a course of action on a plan that will "strike at the heart's blood of those who seek to enchain her [Confederacy] in slavery." Alston had served in the 11th Kentucky Cavalry and had been captured, only to escape to Canada. From Canada he made his way to Bermuda, where he contracted yellow fever. Convalescing in Virginia, he wrote the letter to Davis. The letter, introduced as Exhibit 64, bears the endorsement of Burton Harrison. It gives no hint as to Alston's plan. The prosecution believed Alston had proposed the assassination of Lincoln.

Sources: William A. Tidwell, James O. Hall, and David W. Gaddy, *Come Retribution* (Jackson: University Press of Mississippi, 1988), 238.

**Hartranft, John Frederick (1830–1889)**

Major general in the Union army, appointed by President Andrew Johnson as special provost marshal and governor of the military prison at the Federal arsenal in Washington, D.C. Hartranft was given the responsibility for the day-to-day care of the defendants charged with Lincoln's murder, and to the defense of the arsenal against an armed attempt to free the prisoners or create any disturbance that might prove disruptive. Hartranft made sure the accused were fed and clean, and that no one communicated with them except on the written orders of Secretary of War Edwin M. Stanton. Hartranft filed a daily report with Major General Winfield Scott Hancock, commander of the Middle Military District, detailing every aspect of the prisoners' daily lives. He kept copies in a letter book that clarifies many questions about the treatment of the accused.

Hartranft became involved in a minor difficulty over a statement concerning Mary Surratt's guilt or innocence. Prior to the hanging, Lewis Powell told Father Jacob Walter that Mary Surratt "was innocent of the murder of the President." Judge Advocate General Joseph Holt told Hartranft to have Father Walter put the statement in writing and send it to him; Hartranft added his own endorsement to the statement, causing difficulty with his superiors, who interpreted his endorsement as an official statement that he believed her innocent. General Hancock ordered Hartranft to explain his endorsement, and Hartranft responded by writing: "I believe Payne [Lewis Powell] had told the truth in this matter. In this, I did not by any means intend to express my own opinion of the guilt or innocence of Mrs. Surratt, but simply that I believed Payne had told the truth according to the best of his knowledge and belief."

Hartranft's most difficult assignment behind him, he returned home to Norristown, Pennsylvania. Entering the political arena, he was harassed by charges from the Democrats that he had behaved inhumanely in Mary Surratt's execution. In 1873, he was forced to deny John T. Ford's claim that he and Judge Holt cruelly kept Mrs. Surratt "in manacles . . . in presence of the court." In 1872, he secured the Republican gubernatorial nomination and won (he was reelected to a second term in 1876). Hartranft held several appointed positions within the Federal government. Suffering from Bright's disease, Hartranft died October 17, 1859, in his home in Norristown. He was two months shy of his fifty-ninth birthday.

Sources: Edward Steers, Jr., and Harold Holzer, eds., *The Lincoln Assassination Conspirators: Their Confinement and Execution, as Recorded in the Letterbook of John Frederick Hartranft* (Baton Rouge: Louisiana State University Press, 2009).

*See also:* Hancock, Winfield Scott; Powell, Lewis Thornton

## Harvey & Marr

Washington undertaking firm located at 335 F Street. Following President Andrew Johnson's order of February 15, 1869, to turn the body of John Wilkes Booth over to the Booth family, the undertaking firm of Harvey & Marr were hired by Baltimore undertaker John Weaver to receive the remains from the military and arrange to ship them to Baltimore. The box containing Booth's body was taken to the rear of Harvey & Marr's establishment and set on a pair of trestles. Ironically, the rear of the workshop opened onto Baptist Alley, the same alley that led up to the rear stage door of Ford's Theatre, where Booth had made his way that tragic night four years earlier.

Once inside the workshop, the box was opened and the body carefully examined by several witnesses to ensure it was Booth's remains. Transferred to a simple coffin, the body was placed aboard a train leaving Washington at 7:30 P.M. and arrived in Baltimore at 9:00 P.M. Baltimore undertaker John Weaver received the body and placed it in his own vault, located in Green Mount Cemetery, until spring, when a proper family burial could be held.

Sources: George S. Bryan, *The Great American Myth* (New York: Carrick & Evans, 1940).

*See also*: Weaver, John Henry

## Hawk, William Henry "Harry" (1837–1916)

Actor in John Ford's stock company. Played Asa Trenchard in *Our American Cousin*. On the night of the assassination, Hawk was alone on the stage when Booth fired the fatal shot into President Lincoln's brain. Hawk played an American backwoodsman who was visiting his English "cousins." As act 3, scene 2 was coming to an end, Hawk delivered the lines that always produced loud laughter from audiences: "Don't know the manners of good society, eh? Well I guess I know enough to turn you inside out, old gal—you sockdologizing old man-trap." It was at this moment that Booth fired the fatal shot into Abraham Lincoln's brain. Hawk stood frozen on the stage, alone, as Booth scrambled over the balustrade and landed on the stage not ten feet from where Hawk was standing. Rising to his feet, Booth turned toward the audience and shouted, "Sic Semper Tyrannis!" and ran across the stage and out the rear door into Baptist Alley. Hawk, fearing Booth might attack him, ran from the stage and up the small set of stairs leading to the flies. Booth slashed at Hawk with his bowie knife, cutting his vest and shirt, but not injuring Hawk.

Later that same evening, Hawk was interviewed in the Petersen house along with five other eyewitnesses. Stanton had asked lawyer B. A. Hill and Chief Justice of the Supreme Court of the District of Columbia David Kellogg Cartter to interrogate witnesses while James Tanner, a corporal in the Union army, recorded their testimony in a form of shorthand. In his statement he identified the man as Booth, stating at first, "I am not positive," but then later in his statement saying, "I do not have any doubt but that it was Booth."

Sources: Statement by William Henry Hawk, NARA, RG 153, M-599, reel 7, frames 485–86.

### Hay, John Milton (1838–1905)

Served as one of Lincoln's private secretaries along with John George Nicolay. The two men were very close to Lincoln, working diligently to screen his mail and visitors. They also prepared news summaries and provided Lincoln with their perspective on many issues. Hay had decided to leave the White House and had secured an appointment from Lincoln as secretary of legation in Paris but agreed to stay on until the new staff was trained. He was still in the White House when Lincoln was shot and was at his bedside in the Petersen house when Lincoln died. In the 1870s Hay and Nicolay teamed up to write the definitive biography with the blessing of Robert Lincoln, who controlled his father's papers.

Hay went on to have an illustrious career, serving as ambassador to England and later secretary of state under Presidents William McKinley and Theodore Roosevelt. He remained a steadfast admirer of Lincoln and described him as "the greatest since Christ."

Sources: Mark E. Neely, Jr., *The Abraham Lincoln Encyclopedia* (New York: McGraw-Hill, 1982).

### Headley, John W.

A lieutenant in the First Kentucky Cavalry, Headley was assigned to the Confederate secret service operating out of Canada. Headley wrote his memoir in 1906: *Confederate Operations in Canada and New York*. He was part of a group of agents who sought to free Confederate prisoners held in the Union prison camp on Johnson's Island in Lake Erie. He later became part of an organized effort to terrorize the population in certain northern cities in an effort to overturn support for Lincoln and cause his defeat in gaining reelection in 1864. This activity, described as "black flag warfare," involved an attempt to burn targeted northern cities, poison the water supply for New York City, and spread infective contagion among the civilian population. Tactics clearly in violation of the laws of war included targeting Abraham Lincoln for assassination. His memoir provides several interesting insights into the Confederate secret service operating out of Canada.

Sources: John W. Headley, *Confederate Operations in Canada and New York* (1906: reprint, New York: Time-Life, 1984).

*See also:* Black Flag Warfare

## Heiss, William H.

Manager of a public telegraph company in Washington. Two telegraph services were in operation at the time of Lincoln's assassination on April 14, 1865: the military telegraph, under the management of Assistant Secretary of War Thomas T. Eckert, and a commercial telegraph, known as the "People's Line of Telegraph," under the management of Heiss. Upon learning of Lincoln's assassination, Heiss deliberately shorted the transmission lines of the People's Line of Telegraph and did not reestablish service until the morning of April 15. Heiss later explained his action by stating that he was afraid the assassination was part of a general uprising and thought by closing down the commercial line, word of the assassination would not get out before the military throughout the country had been alerted and thereby "forearmed." Secondly, he was afraid that soldiers and northern citizens would take reprisals against southern citizens and their property. At no time was the military telegraph in Washington out of service.

Otto Eisenschiml, in his book, *Why Was Lincoln Murdered?*, erroneously claimed that there "was an interruption of all telegraphic communication between Washington and the outside world, lasting about two hours," leaving his readers to think that the telegraph lines were deliberately shut down to aid Booth in his escape. Eisenschiml never explained to his readers that service by the military telegraph was never interrupted and that messages were sent and received in the War Department throughout the night.

Sources: Arthur F. Loux, "The Mystery of the Telegraph Interruption," *Lincoln Herald* 81, no. 4 (Winter 1979), 234–37; Edward Steers, Jr., *Blood on the Moon* (Lexington: University Press of Kentucky, 2001), 129.

## Henry, Michael

Desk clerk and barkeep at the Kirkwood House, located at Twelfth Street and Pennsylvania Avenue in Washington. Henry told detective John Lee that a "suspicious character" (George Atzerodt) occupied room 126. On the morning of April 14, George Atzerodt registered at the Kirkwood House at the direction of John Wilkes Booth. He was later assigned by Booth the task of assassinating Vice President Andrew Johnson, who also boarded there. At the designated time Atzerodt showed up at the bar and after ordering a glass of whiskey lost his courage and fled, leaving Johnson safely in his room. Atzerodt was a willing cohort in capturing Lincoln but wanted no part in killing him or Johnson. The following morning, Henry told Lee that a "suspicious acting character" was staying in room 126 on the second floor above Vice President Johnson's room. On searching the room, Lee found a knife, pistol, bankbook issued to J. W. Booth, and several other items linking Atzerodt to Booth. The call went out to search for and arrest George Atzerodt. Henry's letter to the rewards committee explaining his actions in leading Lee to Atzerodt's room is in a private collection. A facsimile of the letter is published in the *Lincolnian*. Henry did not receive a share of the reward money offered for Atzerodt's capture.

Sources: Edward Steers, Jr., *Blood on the Moon* (Lexington: University Press of Kentucky, 2001); Edward Steers, Jr., "The Suspicious Character in Room 126," *Lincolnian* 1, no. 1 (September–October 1982), 5–6.

*See also:* Lee, John; Kirkwood House

## Herndon House

A boardinghouse located at the corner of Ninth and F streets in Washington, D.C.,

where Lewis Powell was living on April 14, and where Booth held a meeting sometime between six and seven o'clock on the evening of April 14. At that time Booth assigned Powell and Herold to kill Secretary of State William H. Seward, and George Atzerodt to kill Vice President Andrew Johnson. He would reserve killing the president for himself. The acts were coordinated to take place at approximately 10:30 that same evening. It was the last time all four conspirators would meet together. Booth apparently arranged for the four men to meet later that night on Soper's Hill, just south of Washington in Southern Maryland.

Sources: Betty J. Ownsbey, *Alias "Paine": Lewis Thornton Powell, the Mystery Man of the Lincoln Conspiracy* (Jefferson, N.C.: McFarland, 1993).

## Herold, David (1842–1865)

Conspirator, hanged as an accomplice in Lincoln's murder. Herold was Booth's close associate in Washington, D.C. Often described as a simple-minded boy, Herold was twenty-three years old at the time of Lincoln's assassination. He was the sixth of ten children born to Mary and Adam Herold, a middle-class family that lived in a row house on Eighth Street within a block of the Washington Navy Yard, where his father worked as a clerk. Herold studied pharmacy at Georgetown

College (later Georgetown University) and worked as a druggist's assistant. His pharmacy connections could give him easy access to chloroform, which Booth may have planned on using to subdue Lincoln. He was an avid hunter and spent a considerable amount of his time roaming the fields and marshes of Charles County, Maryland, where he became familiar with the people and geography of the region, making him an asset in maneuvering through difficult terrain at night. He was acquainted with both John Surratt and George Atzerodt. His knowledge of the people and places in Southern Maryland made him an ideal recruit for Booth in his plot to capture

Lincoln and take him south to the Confederate capital, Richmond, Virginia, as a hostage. When Booth's plot turned to murder, Herold was Booth's pathfinder, leading him through Southern Maryland on his attempted escape.

Booth first met Herold in 1863 while performing at Ford's Theatre. On the night of the assassination, Booth met with Herold, Atzerodt, and Lewis Powell at the Herndon House, located at Ninth and F streets only two and a half blocks from Ford's Theatre. During the meeting Booth revealed his plan to murder Lincoln and assigned Atzerodt the job of killing Vice President Andrew Johnson. Secretary of State William H. Seward was assigned to Powell, and Herold was given the task of acting as Powell's guide, leading him from Washington to a prearranged meeting point outside the city on Soper's Hill in Prince George's County, Maryland. The three attacks were to take place as near 10:15 P.M. as possible so as not to alert the authorities in time to prevent one or more of the attacks.

At the time of Powell's attack on Seward, Herold became alarmed by the shouts and screams coming from the Seward home and fled, leaving Powell and his unattended horse without a guide. Powell ran from the house, where he had seriously wounded five people in his attack. He mounted his horse and rode east past the Capitol, becoming lost in the region near a cemetery where he hid for three days.

Herold, leaving Powell behind to fend for himself, rode east past the Capitol to the Navy Yard Bridge. Arriving at the bridge only a few minutes after Booth, Herold convinced the army guard to let him pass. Unlike Booth, who convinced the guard to let him pass, Herold used an alias and gave the guard the wrong direction he and Booth were heading. Riding hard into Southern Maryland, Herold met up with Booth at a spot some five miles outside the city limits, at Soper's Hill. Together, the two fugitives continued their escape making their way through Prince George's and Charles counties, Maryland, over the Potomac and Rappahannock rivers before settling in at the farm of a Virginia planter named Richard Garrett.

On Wednesday morning, April 26, Herold and Booth were cornered in Garrett's tobacco barn by a troop of the 16th New York Cavalry. After a standoff of several minutes, Herold surrendered to the soldiers and Booth was mortally wounded. Herold was taken back to Washington and placed on board the monitor USS *Montauk*, where he was interrogated at length by special judge advocate John A. Bingham. While he was often described as mentally weak, Herold's answers to Bingham's interrogation show a cleverness that belies that description. Herold was, in fact, mentally quick and capable of maintaining his innocence. His lawyers, however, produced several witnesses at the conspiracy trial in an attempt to describe Herold as a mentally "light" or "trifling" boy who was easily duped by the cleverness of someone like Booth. The strategy failed, however, and Herold was found guilty and sentenced to hang. He was executed on July 7, 1865, eight days after the trial ended, along with coconspirators Lewis Powell, George Atzerodt, and Mary Surratt. He was buried on the grounds of the Washington Arsenal, and in 1869 his remains were turned over to his family. He was finally put to rest next to his father in Congressional Cemetery.

Sources: Statement of David E. Herold, NARA, RG 153, M-599, reel 4, frames 442–85; Terry Alford, "Testimony Relating to John Wilkes Booth, and Circumstances Attending the Assassination," in Edward Steers, Jr., ed., *The Trial* (Lexington: University Press of Kentucky, 2003), xxxviii–xlvi.

### Hess, C. Dwight

Owner, along with Leonard Grover, of the National Theatre (also known as Grover's National Theatre), located on Pennsylvania Avenue three blocks west of Ford's Theatre. Like John Ford, Hess considered himself a good friend of Booth. On April 13, the day before Lincoln's assassination, Booth stopped by the National Theatre to chat with Hess. Booth wanted to know if Hess intended to invite Lincoln to the theater. Booth had already decided to assassinate him. Hess told Booth that he intended to invite President and Mrs. Lincoln but had not yet sent the invitation to the White House. The Lincolns chose Ford's Theatre and *Our American Cousin*. Hess was featuring the play *Aladdin! Or, the Wonderful Lamp*. On the afternoon of the 14th, Booth met Hess standing on the sidewalk in front of Grover's and asked him if the president would be attending his theater later that night. Hess told Booth that Mrs. Lincoln had turned down his invitation. While the Lincolns attended Ford's Theatre, their young son, Tad, accompanied by Alphonso Donn, the White House doorkeeper, were at the National Theatre. The young boy learned of his father's murder when Hess interrupted the play to announce that Lincoln had been assassinated moments before at Ford's Theatre.

Hess appeared as a defense witness for Edman Spangler at the conspiracy trial but offered little of substance in Spangler's defense.

Sources: Statement of C. Dwight Hess, NARA, RG 153, M-599, reel 4, frames 381–84; C. D. Hess, NARA, RG 153, M-599, reel 3, frames 213–16; Poore, *Conspiracy Trial*, vol. 2, 538; Pitman, *Trial*, 99.

## Hill, Britten A.

A highly respected Washington, D.C., attorney who was a member of a panel interviewing witnesses at the Petersen house the night of the assassination. Shortly after arriving at the Petersen house on the night of April 14, Secretary of War Edwin M. Stanton set up a panel consisting of Chief Justice of the District of Columbia Supreme Court David K. Cartter, Judge Abram B. Olin, and attorney Britten A. Hill for the purpose of interrogating witnesses to the assassination. The panel interviewed six individuals and James Tanner recorded the testimony in an early form of shorthand.

Sources: Maxwell Whiteman, ed., *While Lincoln Lay Dying* (Philadelphia: Union League of Philadelphia, 1968).

## Historiography

While the evidentiary documents gathered by Colonel Henry L. Burnett and reproduced in microcopy M-599 provided the prosecution with its case against the accused conspirators, the files were unavailable to the general public for several decades. For more than seventy years, the War Department restricted access to them. It was not until the mid-1930s that the files were opened to historians and other researchers.

The earlier writers had to rely on the trial transcript and first-person reminiscences and newspaper accounts of the trial as their primary source of information, thereby missing out on important details. Three of the early writers who were personally involved in the aftermath of Lincoln's murder, Thomas Harris (a trial commissioner), Thomas Jones (co-conspirator who hid Booth), and William E. Doster (defense attorney), told their stories without benefit of the information contained in the documents in the War Department archives. Other early writers found themselves equally disadvantaged. David Miller Dewitt (*The Judicial Murder of Mary E. Surratt*, 1895, and *The Assassination of Lincoln and Its Expiation*, 1909), Osborn H. Oldroyd (*The Assassination of Abraham Lincoln: Flight, Pursuit, Capture and Punishment of the Conspirators*, 1901), Finis L. Bates (*Escape and Suicide of John Wilkes Booth, or the First True Account of Lincoln's Assassination*, 1907), Clara Laughlin (*The Death of Lincoln: The Story of Booth's Plot, His Deed and Penalty*, 1909), Burke McCarty (*The Suppressed Truth About the Assassination of Abraham Lincoln*, 1922), and Francis Wilson (*John Wilkes Booth: Fact and Fiction of Lincoln's Assassination*, 1929) all wrote their histories without the benefit of the evidence file.

Otto Eisenschiml, a chemist turned historian, was the first writer to have access to the files as part of his study. Unfortunately, it seems he did not examine the file carefully. In 1937 he published his seriously flawed book, *Why Was Lincoln Murdered?* Eisenschiml manipulated the data to lead his readers to the erroneous conclusion that Secretary of War Stanton was behind Lincoln's assassination.

Eisenschiml followed his 1937 study with a second book in 1940 (*In the Shadow of Lincoln's Death*), still maintaining that a northern conspiracy was behind Lincoln's murder. In that same year George S. Bryan published *The Great American Myth*, which challenged Eisenschiml's ridiculous theory and the earlier claim by Finis Bates that Booth escaped from the Garrett barn to eventually die by suicide in 1903. Bryan, unlike the authors before him, had access to the documents in the War Department but barely tapped the file to make his case, relying instead on secondary sources for his information. Nevertheless, Bryan's book became the standard for the next forty years.

The years that followed publication of Bryan's book were not much better when it came to delving into the collection of material amassed by Burnett and his staff. In the interim the documents were turned over to the National Archives and Records Administration as part of a major transfer of over 4,500 cubic feet of records from the Office of the Judge Advocate General (army) in 1943, where they became part of the Records of the Office of the Judge Advocate General (Record Group 153), where they reside today. Certain of the exhibits used in the trial of the conspirators were turned over to the National Park Service in 1940 and placed on display in the Lincoln Museum in Ford's Theatre. In 1965 the National Archives copied the files, along with the proceedings of the trial, onto microfilm, greatly facilitating public access to the records.

In 1982, historian Thomas R. Turner published the first book on Lincoln's assassination by a professional historian (*Beware the People Weeping: Public Opinion and the Assassination of Abraham Lincoln*). Turner's book focused on the public reaction to Lincoln's assassination and its aftermath. A year later historian William Hanchett published the second book by a professional historian demolishing the earlier false conspiracy theories by Eisenschiml and others who distorted and even manufactured evidence in support of their spurious claims (*The Lincoln Murder Conspiracies*, 1983). Both Turner and Hanchett relied heavily on primary sources.

In 1988, three historians, William Tidwell, James O. Hall, and David W. Gaddy, published their revisionist account of the assassination (*Come Retribution*), drawing on the evidence file now reproduced on reels 1 through 7 in M-599, setting themselves apart from previous writers. They concluded that the Confederate leadership, including Jefferson Davis, was behind Lincoln's assassination. Unlike previous conspiracy theories that were based on flawed, even fraudulent evidence, the authors of *Come Retribution* supported their claim with evidence drawn from the files of M-599 and other documents. While their conclusions failed to convince the majority of historians, their research has remained unchallenged. *Come Retribution* reinvigorated the debate over Lincoln's assassination.

The current file does not include all of the material originally collected by the War Department. Some of the documents were later used by the House of Representatives committee established to adjudicate the reward claims made by those who had participated in the capture of the conspirators (and some who did not participate) while others were used in the impeachment hearing of Andrew Johnson. An unknown number of these documents never found their way back to the original file. We cannot be sure of what was borrowed and what never returned. Nonetheless, the greater number of documents originally collected remained in the possession of the War Department until their archive was turned over to the National Archives and Records Administration.

It can safely be said that out of the hundred-plus books written on Lincoln's assassination only a handful have utilized the evidence file, and then sparingly.

Sources: William E. Edwards and Edward Steers, Jr., *The Lincoln Assassination: The Evidence* (Urbana: University of Illinois Press, 2009).

*See also:* M-599

## Holborn
See Harbin, Thomas

## Holloway, Lucinda Keeling Boulware (1831–1909)
Sister of Mrs. Richard Garrett and a boarder at the Garrett house at the time Booth and Herold arrived on the afternoon of April 24. Years later she wrote that she kneeled at Booth's side, took her handkerchief and dipped it in water, and moistened Booth's lips. Her remembrance contains numerous errors leading up to Booth's death but is an example of an "eyewitness account" of Booth's last moments.

Sources: Lucinda Holloway, "The Capture and Death of John Wilkes Booth by an Eye-Witness," published in Francis Wilson, ed., *John Wilkes Booth: Fact and Fiction of Lincoln's Assassination* (Boston: Houghton Mifflin, 1929), 209–17.

*See also:* Booth Capture and Death

## Holohan, John T. (1829–1877)
One of thirteen boarders who lived in Mary Surratt's boardinghouse in Washington, D.C. Holohan, his wife, and two children lived on the third floor. Holohan accompanied two of Superintendent of Police A. C. Richard's detectives and Louis Wiechmann to Montreal in search

of John Surratt following the assassination. Holohan had no authority to search Montreal for John Surratt or anything else connected with the assassination. His connection was as a boarder at the Surratt boardinghouse and as such was a witness to the goings and comings of various people, including John Wilkes Booth.

On his return from Canada, without John Surratt, Holohan was called as a prosecution witness. He testified to having seen Atzerodt, Payne (Lewis Powell), and John Wilkes Booth on several occasions at the house. He also claimed that a "Mrs. Slater" was present in the company of John Surratt. Sarah Slater was a known Confederate agent who moved between Richmond and Montreal on several occasions. Holohan also refuted the defense claim that Mary Surratt's eyesight was poor. Her defense lawyers claimed that when she denied knowing Lewis Powell when he came to her house on Monday evening, it was because her eyesight was poor and she did not recognize him in the darkened room. The prosecution contended she lied, and used Holohan to support their claim.

Sources: Statement of John T. Holohan, NARA, RG 153, M-599, reel 3, frames 379–80; Poore, *Conspiracy Trial*, vol. 3, 362; Pitman, *Trial*, 139; Statement of John T. Holohan, NARA, RG 153, M-599, reel 3, frames 1016; Poore, *Conspiracy Trial*, vol. 3, 362; Pitman, *Trial*, 139; Statement of John T. Holohan, NARA, RG 153, M-599, reel 3, frame 1301; Statement of John T. Holohan, NARA, RG 153, M-599, reel 3, frames 1302–4.

## Holmes, Mary Ann
See Booth, Mary Ann Holmes

## Holt, Joseph (1807–1894)

Judge advocate general from 1862 to 1875 and head of the U.S. Bureau of Military Justice. A Kentucky Democrat who supported the Union and the war, Holt became the chief prosecutor of the eight defendants charged with Lincoln's murder. He had served in the administration of President Buchanan as postmaster general (1859–1860) and secretary of war (January–March 1861). A southerner by birth, Holt was sympathetic to southern principals, but was a staunch supporter of the Union. Holt believed Jefferson Davis and members of his cabinet were directly involved in Lincoln's assassination. Appointed judge advocate general by Lincoln, Holt found himself in charge of the prosecution that tried the conspirators charged with Lincoln's murder. An able lawyer, Holt prosecuted with vigor and firmly believed that Davis was responsible for ordering Lincoln's death.

Sources: Elizabeth Leonard, *Lincoln's Avengers: Justice, Revenge, and Reunion After the Civil War* (New York: Norton, 2004).

## Hookstown

A small village located on the outskirts of Baltimore along the present-day Reisterstown Road. The family of Samuel Arnold had a small farm and country home in Hookstown. On returning from the Confederate army in 1864, Samuel Arnold spent most of his time at the Hookstown farm. It was here that he wrote his famous letter, signed "Sam," to Booth. In the letter, Arnold advises Booth to "go and see how it will be taken in R—D." The "it" was interpreted to mean "assassination," and the "R—D" was obviously "Richmond." This fed directly into the prosecution's contention that Jefferson Davis and other prominent Confederates sanctioned Booth's assassination.

On Monday morning, April 17, just two days after Lincoln's assassination, Eaton Horner and Voltaire Randall, two detectives working for Maryland provost marshal James O'Beirne, rode out to Hookstown to interrogate Arnold and arrest him, bringing him on the train to Baltimore.

Sources: Percy E. Martin, "Samuel Arnold and Michael O'Laughlen," in Edward Steers, Jr., ed., *The Trial* (Lexington: University Press of Kentucky, 2003), lxxxviii–xcv.

## Horner, Eaton

Military detective on the staff of Maryland provost marshal James McPhail in Baltimore. Arrested Samuel Arnold on Monday, April 17, at Fort Monroe, Virginia. On learning of Lincoln's assassination and that John Wilkes Booth was the assassin, McPhail sent Horner and Voltaire Randall, two of his better detectives, to track down Samuel Arnold, who McPhail knew was an old friend of Booth's from their childhood days in Baltimore. Horner learned from Arnold's father that Arnold was clerking for a sutler at Fort Monroe in Virginia.

Horner placed Arnold under arrest and interrogated him extensively. Arnold freely admitted his roll in Booth's capture plot and also told Horner that Booth had been given letters of introduction to Dr. Samuel Mudd and Dr. William Queen by Patrick Martin, a Confederate agent working out of Montreal. This revelation occurred on Monday, April 17, a full day before authorities in Washington or Charles County, Maryland, had learned about Booth stopping at Mudd's house on his escape.

While Arnold did not know who wrote the letter, the testimony of John C. Thompson, Dr. William Queen's son-in-law, provided the answer. Called as a defense witness on behalf of Dr. Mudd, Thompson testified that Booth carried a letter of introduction from a man by the name of Martin. Martin was Patrick C. Martin, a Confederate agent operating out of Montreal. Arnold's testimony that Booth carried a letter of introduction to Mudd is especially damaging to Mudd's claim that his initial meeting with Booth in November 1864 was accidental. It supported the prosecution's contention that Mudd was involved in Booth's conspiracy from the very beginning, by design.

Sources: Edward Steers, Jr., *His Name Is Still Mudd* (Gettysburg, Pa.: Thomas, 1997); Edward Steers, Jr., *Blood on the Moon* (Lexington: University Press of Kentucky, 2001).

## Howard's Livery Stable

Livery stables located near the corner of Sixth and G streets in Washington, D.C., operated by Brooke Stabler. Both John Surratt and Booth stabled horses at Howard's Livery. Booth, Surratt, and George Atzerodt frequently visited the stable throughout March and April 1865.

On April 14, Louis Wiechmann was given the afternoon off from work and arrived at the Surratt boardinghouse around 2:30 P.M., where he found Booth just leaving. He later testified he did not know why Booth was there. Mary Surratt told Wiechmann to go to Howard's and rent a buggy; she needed to go to the tavern in Surrattsville. She wanted Wiechmann to drive her to Surrattsville, ostensibly to see John Nothey about a debt he owed her. John Surratt stabled his horse at Howard's and sent a note to Stabler, which read: "Will please let the bearer Mr. Azworth [Atzerodt] have my horse whenever he wishes to ride also my leggings and gloves and oblige. Yours &c. J H Surratt." Surratt also sent a note to Stabler dated March 26, 1865, requesting Stabler to also let John Surratt's friend, "Mr. Booth," have the use of his horses.

Sources: Statement of Brooke Stabler, NARA, RG 94, M-619, reel 456, frames 379–85; Statement of Brooke Stabler, NARA, M-599, reel 4, frame 38; Poore, *Conspiracy Trial,*

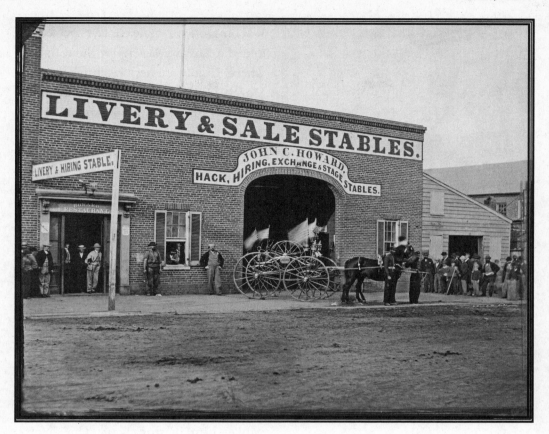

vol. 1, 176, 203; Pitman, *Trial,* 71; Statement of Brooke Stabler, NARA, RG 153, reel 4, frames 121-42; Poore, *Conspiracy Trial*, vol. 1, 176, 203; Pitman, *Trial*, 71.

*See also:* Stabler, Brooke

## Howe, Albion

One of the nine commissioners to serve on the military tribunal trying the eight conspirators charged with Lincoln's murder. Born in 1818 in Standish, Maine, Howe was a West Point graduate (class of 1841). A regular army officer, he saw service in the Civil War under McClellan in West Virginia, and later in the peninsula campaign. Receiving a brevet appointment as brigadier general, he commanded an infantry brigade at Fredericksburg and Chancellorsville. His unit was held at Gettysburg. In the fall of 1863 he was placed in charge of the Artillery Depot and the Office of Inspector of Artillery in Washington, D.C. He was brevetted major general and assigned to the honor guard over Lincoln's body. He retired from the regular army

as a colonel of the Fourth Artillery in 1882.

Howe died January 25, 1897, and is buried in Mount Auburn Cemetery in Cambridge, Massachusetts.

Sources: Ezra J. Warner, *Generals in Blue* (Baton Rouge: Louisiana State University Press, 1964), 239–40.

## Howell, Augustus S.

Confederate agent. Howell served as an agent along with John H. Surratt and visited the Surratt boardinghouse in Washington on at least two occasions, and the Surratt Tavern in Surrattsville, where Union soldiers arrested him on March 24. Howell served as an escort on occasion for the Confederate spy Sarah Slater, a French-speaking courier who also went under the name Kate Thompson. George Atzerodt, in his "lost confession," identified "Gus Powell" (Gus Howell) as an agent traveling from Richmond with John Surratt. Called as a defense witness on behalf of Mary Surratt, Howell never admitted his role as a Confederate agent or escort for Sarah Slater. He effectively dodged the prosecution's questions, claiming he only stayed at the Surratt boardinghouse because it was cheaper than a hotel. He also supported the defense's contention that Mary Surratt had poor eyesight and failed to recognize him in dim light. The defense used this to support her claim that she did not recognize Lewis Powell the night of her arrest when detectives asked her if she knew Powell. She denied she ever saw him before, which was used against her at her trial. He had no role in the assassination although he was arrested and held in prison for a while under suspicion of being involved.

Sources: William A. Tidwell, James O. Hall, and David W. Gaddy, *Come Retribution* (Jackson: University Press of Mississippi, 1988); Joan L. Chaconas, "Unpublished Atzerodt Confession,"

*Surratt Courier* 13, no. 10 (October 1988), 3–4; Testimony of Augustus Spencer Howell, in Edward Steers, Jr., ed., *The Trial* (Lexington: University Press of Kentucky, 2003), 133–34.

## Huckleberry

Charles County, Maryland, home of Confederate agent Thomas Jones at the time of Lincoln's assassination. Confederate agent Samuel Cox assigned Jones the task of safely putting Booth and Herold across the Potomac River. After hiding and caring for Booth and Herold in a pine thicket located between the home of Cox (Rich Hill) and Huckleberry, Jones decided he could safely send Booth and Herold across the river on the night of April 20.

Gathering up the two weary fugitives, Jones stopped at his home, Huckleberry, long enough to get some food and drink for the two men. He made them wait outside because of the risk to their being discovered to have been in his house. After giving them food and drink he led them to the shore of the Potomac River, where he placed them in a rowboat, giving Booth a compass and candle, and sending them on their way. Huckleberry still exists as a private residence at the edge of the Loyola Catholic Retreat.

Sources: Edward Steers, Jr., *Blood on the Moon* (Lexington: University Press of Kentucky, 2001).

## Hudspeth, Mrs. Mary

Witness called by the prosecution during the conspiracy trial. Mrs. Hudspeth testified to finding two letters on a New York streetcar in November 1864. The letter, addressed to "Dear Louis" and signed "Charles Selby," tells in rather dramatic terms that "Louis" has drawn the short straw and thus has the task of killing Lincoln—"*Abe* must *die*, and *now*. *You can choose your weapons*. The cup, the *knife*, the *bullet*." The second letter, addressed to "Dearest Husband," pleads for an errant husband to come home. There is nothing relating to the first letter or assassination in the second letter.

Mrs. Hudspeth turned the letters in to General John Dix, who forwarded them to the War Department in Washington. The interesting aspect of the two letters comes from their being found in Lincoln's desk in an envelope marked "Assassination." According to John Hay, Lincoln's young secretary, Lincoln kept around a hundred letters neatly tied together that foretold of his assassination. Accompanying the two letters sent by General Dix was a note by Dix that stated, "The Charles Selby letter is obviously a manufacture." Dix does not say why he believes the letter is fabricated. Both letters were entered as trial exhibits, numbers 2 and 3, respectively.

Sources: Testimony of Mrs. Mary Hudspeth, Poore, *Conspiracy Trial*, vol. 1, 25; Pitman, *Trial*, 39.

## Hughes, John J. (1825–1892)

Son-in-law of Charles County, Maryland, politician and landowner Peregrine Davis. Booth and Herold landed at Indiantown after attempting to cross the river on the night of April 20. After hours of struggling against the tide, the two fugitives neared the Virginia shore in their little rowboat. They were suddenly startled by the sight of a Union gunboat, the USS *Juniper*, anchored near their destination. Herold turned the small boat around and retreated back toward the Maryland shore and into the mouth of the Nanjemoy Creek. Herold knew the area and the farm owned by Peregrine Davis and farmed by his son-in-law, John J. Hughes. Nothing is known of the time the two fugitives stayed here from the early morning of Friday, April 21 until Saturday night, April 22. Family tradition tells that Herold visited with Hughes and received food and whiskey, but that Hughes did not let the two men sleep in his house or outbuildings for fear that if caught Hughes would be treated as an accomplice and the buildings would be burned by searching troopers.

Whatever happened over the thirty-six odd hours at Indiantown, Booth and Herold successfully crossed the river to Virginia landing at Gambo Creek on Sunday morning, April 23.

Sources: William A. Tidwell, "Booth Crosses the Potomac: An Exercise in Historical Research," *Civil War History* 36 (April 1990), 325–33; Edward Steers, Jr., *Blood on the Moon* (Lexington: University Press of Kentucky, 2001); James L. Swanson, *Manhunt: The 12-Day Chase for Lincoln's Killer* (New York: Harper Perennial, 2007), 147.

### Hunter, David

Major general in the Union army and good friend of President Lincoln. Stanton asked Hunter to preside over the trial of the conspirators. Like the other members of the tribunal, Hunter had seen considerable action during the war.

Born in Washington, D.C., in 1802, Hunter received an appointment to West Point and graduated with the class of 1822. He served in the army until 1836, when he retired briefly becoming involved in real estate in Chicago. He reenlisted in 1842 with the rank of major. He was invited by president-elect Lincoln to accompany him on his inaugural trip to Washington in February 1861. Hunter later accompanied the body of the dead president from Washington back to Springfield, Illinois.

Hunter had a spotty war record and is considered one of Lincoln's failed appointments early in the war. He was picked by Secretary of War Stanton to preside over the military tribunal even though he had a close and emotional connection to Lincoln.

Sources: Ezra J. Warner, *Generals in Blue* (Baton Rouge: Louisiana State University Press, 1964), 243–44.

## Hyams, Godfrey Joseph

Attempted to introduce germ warfare against the North in the Civil War. A Confederate agent recruited by fellow Confederate agent Luke P. Blackburn to distribute infected clothing among certain cities, including Washington, D.C., with the aim of spreading yellow fever among the civilian population. Hyams oversaw the shipping of several trunks of clothing and bedding collected from patients who had died from yellow fever during a major epidemic in Bermuda.

Blackburn and other medical experts of the period were unaware that yellow fever is spread through mosquitoes and not infected clothing. Blackburn had promised Hyams a substantial sum of money if he successfully carried out his assignment. Hyams was able to contract with the auction house of W. L. Wall in Washington to sell the clothing. Dissatisfied with not being paid, Hyams offered to expose the scheme along with other Confederate activities to U.S. authorities.

Hyams asked, and received, immunity, and an undisclosed sum of money. He gave details of the Confederate operations in Montreal and Toronto to the Federal authorities in Detroit and was a key witness during the conspiracy trial detailing the black flag warfare carried out from Canada against the North. He exposed bomb-making facilities in Toronto and plans to disrupt U.S. fishing off the Canadian coast by blowing up the fishing vessels. He was called as a prosecution witness and asked to describe his dealings with Blackburn as an example of the lengths to which Confederate leaders would go in creating acts of terror against civilian populations in the North.

Hyams's efforts have been largely ignored or dismissed in most accounts of the assassination, but germ warfare was a major effort on the part of Confederates operating out of Canada with the objective of demoralizing the people of the North and causing Lincoln's defeat in running for reelection in 1864. Hyams has been described as "an inglorious turncoat whose loyalties responded to money rather than a cause." This in itself supports the claim that Hyams was telling the truth regardless of the motive. Hyams's accusations turned out to be reliable in every instance.

Sources: Edward Steers, Jr., "Risking the Wrath of God," *North & South* 3, no. 7 (September

2000), 59–70; Edward Steers, Jr., *Blood on the Moon* (Lexington: University Press of Kentucky, 2001), 47–51.

*See also:* Blackburn, Luke Pryor; Wall, W. L.

## Hyde, Susan

A private tutor to John Wilkes Booth and his sister Asia and brother Edwin in Bel Air, Maryland. Hyde ran an "old-fashioned" school stressing the basics of education. Asia, Booth's older sister and very close to Booth, met her future husband, John Clarke Sleeper (he later changed his name to John Sleeper Clarke) at Mrs. Hyde's school when he entered show business.

Sources: Terry Alford, ed., *John Wilkes Booth: A Sister's Memoir by Asia Booth Clarke* (Jackson: University Press of Mississippi, 1996), 6–7.

I

## Indiantown, Maryland

Name of the farm owned by Peregrine Davis and farmed by his son-in-law, John J. Hughes. The farm was located in Charles County, Maryland, at the mouth of Nanjemoy Creek. On the night of April 20, 1865, Booth and Herold attempted to cross the Potomac River to Virginia. They were thwarted when they came upon a Union gunboat anchored near the spot where they attempted to reach shore. They returned to the Maryland shore at the mouth of Nanjemoy Creek and landed at Indiantown.

David Herold was well acquainted with Hughes from his many trips hunting in the area. A Hughes family tradition relates that the two men spent Friday and Saturday hiding at the farm before successfully crossing the river on Saturday night, April 22, reaching the Virginia shore Sunday morning near Gambo Creek.

While at Indiantown, Booth made another entry in his little diary. It begins:

> After being hunted like a dog through swamps, woods, and last night being chased by gun boats till I was forced to return wet cold and starving, with every man's hand against me, I am here in despair. . . .

Booth continues in a self-serving manner, comparing himself to Brutus and William Tell, "striking down a greater tyrant than they ever knew."

Sources: Statement of David E. Herold, NARA, RG 153, M-599, reel 4, frames 442–85; William Hanchett, "Booth's Diary," *Journal of the Illinois Historical Society* 72, no. 1 (February 1979), 39–56; William A. Tidwell, James O. Hall, and David W. Gaddy, *Come Retribution* (Jackson: University Press of Mississippi, 1988), 455–57.

*See also:* Hughes, John J.

## Ingraham, Timothy I. (1810–1876)

Provost marshal of the defenses north of the Potomac River with headquarters in Washington, D.C. Ingraham served as colonel, commanding the 38th Massachusetts Volunteer Infantry. The regiment served in the 19th Army Corps under Major General Nathaniel P. Banks in the Gulf region in 1862–1863 and in the Shenandoah Valley under Philip Sheridan in 1864. By the time he was appointed provost marshal in Washington, Ingraham was a battle-hardened veteran. After the assassination he sent Lieutenant William Tyrell and a squad of men to the National Hotel to search Booth's room and bring back everything they could find. Tyrell found a large trunk with the name "John Wilkes Booth" and "Theater" painted on the lid. Inside was a wealth of material, including the "Sam" letter written by Samuel Arnold to Booth and introduced as exhibit 43 at the trial. Ingraham later sent an inventory to Special Judge Advocate Henry L. Burnett that included in part: "No. 14 Package of private papers belonging to J. Wilkes Booth, seized at his room at the National Hotel by order of Col. J. H. Taylor, Chief of Staff. This package contains the secret cipher of the Confederate States Department, of the Confederate Govt. and a letter to Booth from 'Sam.'"

Sources: Timothy Ingraham, Inventory, NARA, RG 153, M-599, reel 2, frames 532–35; Papers of John Wilkes Booth, NARA, RG 153, M-599, reel 2, frame 290; Michael J. Kauffman, *American Brutus* (New York: Random House, 2004), 65–66.

## Investigation and Trial Papers Relating to the Assassination of Abraham Lincoln

The evidence file compiled by Special Judge Advocate Henry L. Burnett along with the trial proceedings are located in the National Archives and Records Administration (NARA) as part of Record Group 153, Records of the Office of the Judge Advocate General (Army).

Burnett was appointed special judge advocate and charged with collecting and managing all the evidence being gathered by the government in preparation for trying those accused of Lincoln's murder. It became Burnett's responsibility to sift through all the material pouring into the government and select the evidence needed to prosecute the case. He accomplished this by contacting every officer in the field and had them turn the material over to him immediately. He then set up a register containing the name of the person furnishing the statement, the date, and a summary of his or her statement, including the names of any persons referred to in the statement. Burnett then created a set of evidence books in which he recorded a synopsis of all the statements and documents that had been collected that might prove useful to the prosecution during the trial.

In 1965, the National Archives photocopied the entire evidence file, along with the trial proceedings, onto sixteen reels of microfilm (designated Microcopy No. 599). Reels 1 through 7 contain the evidence; reels 8 through 15 contain the proceedings of the trial, including the closing arguments and exhibits. Reel 16 contains issues of the Washington, D.C., newspaper *Daily National Intelligencer*, which published each day's verbatim trial transcript. Many of the ninety-eight trial exhibits were turned over to the National Park Service and are now on display at Ford's Theatre.

While the evidentiary documents in M-599 provided the prosecution with its case against the accused conspirators, the files were unavailable to the general public. For more than seventy years the War Department treated the files as secret, restricting access to them. It was not until the mid-1930s that the files were opened to researchers. The earlier writers had to rely on the trial transcript and first-person reminiscences and newspaper accounts as their only source of information, thereby missing out on important details. Three of the early writers who were personally involved in the aftermath of Lincoln's murder, Thomas Harris (a trial commissioner), Thomas Jones (co-conspirator who hid Booth), and William E. Doster (defense attorney), told their stories without benefit of the information contained in the evidence file in the War Department archives.

Other early writers found themselves equally disadvantaged. David Miller Dewitt, Osborn H. Oldroyd, Finis L. Bates, Clara Laughlin, Burke McCarty, and Francis Wilson all wrote their histories without the benefit of the evidence file.

It can safely be said that out of the hundred-plus books written on Lincoln's assassination only a handful have utilized the evidence file of M-599, and then sparingly. Listed below are the sixteen microfilm reels and their contents.

- Reel 1: Letters sent by Burnett, April 22 to July 3, 1865; Telegrams sent by Burnett, April 22 to June 30, 1865; Register of Letters Received by Burnett, April–August, 1865; Register ("Record Book") of the Military Commission, April–July, 1865; Endorsement Book of Burnett, April 22–July 1865; Letters Received by Burnett.
- Reel 2: File Nos. 1–359.
- Reel 3: File Nos. 360–751; Letters Received and Statements of Evidence Collected by the Military Commission.
- Reel 4: Pages 1–53.
- Reel 5: Pages 54–69.
- Reel 6: Pages 70–104; Letters Received by Burnett with Endorsements, May 9–June 9, 1865.
- Reel 7: Unregistered Letters Received by Burnett.
- Proceedings of the Court-Martial:
- Reel 8: May 9–15, 1865.
- Reel 9: May 16–18, 1865.
- Reel 10: May 19–25, 1865.
- Reel 11: May 26–29, 1865.
- Reel 12: May 30–June 3, 1865.
- Reel 13: June 5–10, 1865.
- Reel 14: June 12–16, 19, and 21–29, 1865; Defenses of Samuel Arnold, Edward [Edman] Spangler, Lewis Payne [Powell], and Michael O'Laughlen.
- Reel 15: Argument of John A. Bingham; Exhibits Used in the Court-Martial.
- Reel 16: Issues of the *Daily National*

*Intelligencer,* May 16–June 30, 1865; Miscellaneous Records Relating to the Court-Martial.

Sources: Pamphlet Accompanying Microcopy No. 599, *Investigation and Trial Papers Relating to the Assassination of President Lincoln* (Washington, D.C.: National Archives and Records Service, General Services Administration, 1965); William C. Edwards and Edward Steers, Jr., *The Lincoln Assassination: The Evidence* (Urbana: University of Illinois Press, 2009).

*See also*: Burnett, Henry L.

**Jackson, Susan Mahoney**

A free black woman employed by Mary Surratt approximately three weeks prior to the assassination. On Monday evening following Lincoln's death, Mrs. Jackson appeared at the headquarters of General C. C. Augur's 22nd Army Corps, where she was questioned. She claimed to have seen John Surratt at the boardinghouse on the morning of the assassination. She was mistaken. John Surratt was in Elmira, New York, but her statement sent the detectives back to the boardinghouse with orders to arrest everyone that lived there and bring them to headquarters for questioning.

While the detectives were at Mary Surratt's boardinghouse, Lewis Powell knocked on the door. Startled by the presence of soldiers, Powell recovered his composure and told the detectives he had been hired by Mary Surratt to dig a French drain alongside her house. When questioned, Mary Surratt denied knowing Powell. Both were arrested along with the other boarders present that night. Later, the detectives said that had it not been for Susan Jackson's statements about seeing John Surratt at the boardinghouse on the day of the assassination they never would have gone there on Monday evening. Perhaps, but there were other bits of information filtering into army headquarters that would have led detectives to the Surratt boardinghouse sooner or later.

Sources: Edward Steers, Jr., *Blood on the Moon* (Lexington: University Press of Kentucky, 2001), 177–78.

**James, Henry M.**

Employed as a stagehand by John Ford. James was backstage at Ford's Theatre in position to move the flats (scenery) when he heard a shot. While he did not witness the shooting, he was called as a defense witness on behalf of Edman Spangler. He testified that Spangler applauded the president when he entered the theater and that later, following the shot, he did not see Spangler do anything that could be interpreted as aiding Booth's escape. James also testified that he did not see Jacob Ritterspaugh, a prosecution witness, standing anywhere near Spangler at the time of the assassination, countering Ritterspaugh's damaging testimony against Spangler.

Sources: Testimony of Henry M. James, Poore, *Conspiracy Trial*, vol. 2, 542–45; Pitman, *Trial*, 105.

*See also:* Ritterspaugh, Jacob

**Jaquette, Isaac**

A witness called for the prosecution at the military trial. Jaquette was in the theater and witnessed the assassination. Shortly after Lincoln was carried from the theater, Jaquette entered the vestibule or outer hallway leading to the boxes and found the piece of music stand that Booth had used to secure the outer door so no one could follow behind him. Jaquette testified that the bar was covered with spots of blood, the implication being that the blood was Lincoln's. However, if there was any blood on the wood it in all probability came from Rathbone's serious wound. Jaquette took the piece of wood home as a souvenir, but later decided to turn it in to a government detective. The wooden bar was offered into evidence as exhibit 44 by the prosecution.

Sources: Testimony of Isaac Jaquette, Poore, *Conspiracy Trial*, vol. 1, 413; Pitman, *Trial*, 82.

## Jarboe, James Judson

Resident of Prince George's County, Maryland. Jarboe was arrested in the dragnet that swept through Southern Maryland shortly after the assassination. Detectives believed he had harbored John Boyle, a guerrilla who killed Union captain Thomas H. Watkins on March 24, 1865. In the initial hours following Powell's attack on Secretary of State William Seward, the detectives investigating the attack believed it was Boyle who had attacked Seward. In his statement given in Bryantown, Maryland, prior to his arrest, Dr. Samuel Mudd told investigators that he and his wife feared that the man at their door early Saturday morning, April 15, was John Boyle. Of course, Mudd had nothing to fear from Boyle, as both men worked on behalf of the Confederacy.

Jarboe was called as a defense witness on behalf of Dr. Samuel Mudd. Jarboe's testimony was of little value to either the defense or prosecution. He was cross-examined by both Judge Advocate General Holt and Assistant Judge Advocate Bingham, questioning his loyalty and thereby discrediting him as a witness.

Sources: Testimony of James J. Jarboe, Poore, *Conspiracy Trial*, vol. 3, 391–405; Pitman, *Trial*, 213.

## Jenkins, John Zadock (1822–1896)

Brother of Mary Surratt. Jenkins was called as a witness for the prosecution. Jenkins was at the Surratt Tavern in Surrattsville, Maryland, on the afternoon of April 14, 1865, when Mary Surratt arrived accompanied by Louis Wiechmann. Jenkins testified that Mary showed him a letter from George Calvert demanding payment of a debt due from her dead husband. Jenkins's testimony confirmed her claim that she came to Surrattsville on the afternoon of the assassination to collect a debt due her by John Nothey. According to Jenkins, she did come to see John Lloyd. He further testified to her giving milk, tea, and refreshments to Union soldiers passing by her house. Jenkins also supported Mary Surratt's claim that her eyesight was "defective." Mary told the detectives the night she and Powell were arrested that she did not know who he was when he showed up at her house claiming to be a workman hired by her to dig a ditch alongside her house. Jenkins's testimony failed to convince the tribunal that Mary had told the truth.

Sources: Testimony of John Z. Jenkins, Poore, *Conspiracy Trial*, vol. 2, 485, vol. 2, 386; Pitman, *Trial*, 127.

### Jett, William Storke "Willie" (1847–1885)

An eighteen-year-old private who served in Company C, Ninth Virginia Cavalry and in the 43rd Battalion, Virginia Cavalry, as a member of Mosby's Rangers. Jett, along with two comrades, Lieutenant Mortimer Bainbridge Ruggles and Private Absalom Bainbridge, arrived at the former village of Port Conway, located on the Rappahannock River, on the morning of April 24, 1865. Waiting near the dock for the ferry to take them across the river were John Wilkes Booth and David Herold. After some discussion, the three Confederate soldiers accompanied Booth and Herold across the

river to Port Royal on the southern side. Jett attempted to negotiate a place for the two fugitives to stay at the home of Randolph Peyton. Unable to do so, the five men road a few miles farther south to the home of Richard Garrett, a tobacco farmer known to Jett. Jett asked Garrett if the two men could stay at his house and rest for a day or two. Garrett agreed to take in Booth and Herold, believing they were Confederate soldiers on their way home. Jett told Garrett that Booth had been injured at Petersburg in the last days of the war.

Members of the 16th New York Cavalry arrested Jett in the early morning hours of April 26 at the Gouldman Hotel in Bowling Green, where he had been staying after dropping Booth and Herold off at Garrett's house. Jett agreed to lead the soldiers to the Garrett farm, where he said Booth and Herold were hiding. Without Jett's confession, the Federal troops would not have known that Booth and Herold were still hiding out at the farm.

Jett was taken into custody and under questioning gave a long and detailed statement describing the events that took place at Port Conway and the Garrett farm. He was called as a prosecution witness at the conspiracy trial, where he again described in detail his meeting with Herold and Booth at Port Conway. Jett was never charged with aiding Booth and Herold in their escape from Federal authorities.

Sources: Testimony of Willie S. Jett, NARA, RG 153, M-599, reel 5, frames 86–99; Poore, *Conspiracy Trial*, vol. 1, 308; Pitman, *Trial*, 90.

*See also:* Ruggles, Mortimer Bainbridge; Bainbridge, Absalom Ruggles; Booth Escape Route

## John S. Ide

A propeller-driven steamboat under contract to the military that was used to carry members of the 16th New York Cavalry along with Everton J. Conger and Luther B. Baker in their pursuit of Booth and Herold. The search party left the wharf in Washington, D.C., on the *Ide* near seven o'clock Monday evening, April 24, and headed down the Potomac River to General Grant's abandoned supply depot at Belle Plain, King George County, Virginia. The party disembarked and began their pursuit, heading southeast toward the Rappahannock River.

The *Ide* moored off of Belle Plain while the search party pursued the two fugitives. Following Herold's capture and Booth's death at the Garrett farm on Wednesday, April 26, the *Ide* carried Booth's body back to the Washington Navy Yard ahead of the search party. Arriving at the Navy Yard at 1:45 A.M., Booth's body was transferred from the *Ide* to the monitor USS *Montauk*, where it was placed on a carpenter's bench located on deck beneath a canvas awning.

Sources: William A. Tidwell, James O. Hall, and David W. Gaddy, *Come Retribution* (Jackson: University Press of Mississippi, 1988), 469–70; Edward Steers, Jr., *Blood on the Moon* (Lexington: University Press of Kentucky, 2001), 205–6.

## Johnson, Andrew (1808–1875)

Vice President Andrew Johnson was asleep in his room at the Kirkwood House when his friend Leonard J. Farwell, inspector

rank of brigadier general, was selected by Lincoln to be his running mate on the newly formed National Union (Republican) Party ticket in 1864. Lincoln sought to balance the ticket in the 1864 election with a war Democrat. Johnson fit the bill nicely.

On the night of the assassination, Johnson had retired to his room in the Kirkwood House hotel at Twelfth Street and Pennsylvania Avenue. Booth had assigned Atzerodt the job of killing Johnson. At the prescribed hour, Atzerodt went into the Kirkwood House, where he had checked into a room earlier that morning, and ordered a drink at the bar. Already under the influence of alcohol, Atzerodt decided not to kill Johnson and fled from the hotel, wandering about the city for the next few hours.

of patents, woke him with the news that the president had been shot. After asking Farwell to verify that both Lincoln and Seward had suffered mortal wounds, Johnson visited the Petersen house at approximately 1:30 A.M. According to Senator Charles Sumner of Massachusetts, who was present at the time, Johnson stayed only a few minutes, as Mary Lincoln wanted to come into the room again. Because she disliked Johnson so much, Sumner asked him to leave, which Johnson agreed to do. He never returned to the house, but remained in his room.

Johnson, a war Democrat and former military governor of Tennessee with the

Chief Justice Salmon P. Chase swore in Johnson as president shortly after Lincoln's death at 7:22 A.M. on Saturday, April 15, 1865. He was persuaded by Secretary of War Edwin M. Stanton to issue an executive order placing those accused of conspiring to murder the president under military authority and to be tried by a military tribunal. Although Johnson exercised his authority under the war powers presumably granted a president by the Constitution, it appears Stanton was setting policy for the new president. Attorney General James Speed issued an opinion upholding the legal authority of the military tribunal.

Johnson soon ran into conflict with the Radical Republicans in the Congress who were dissatisfied with his lenient policies toward reconstruction of the South. Johnson's defiance of the Radical members of Congress led to his impeachment by the House of Representatives, which he survived when the final vote in the Senate fell short of conviction by a single vote.

Shortly before leaving office, Johnson pardoned the surviving three conspirators serving their sentences at Fort Jefferson, Florida. Johnson pardoned Samuel Mudd in part because of Mudd's efforts during a yellow fever outbreak at Fort Jefferson, which killed the base surgeon. Mudd had stepped in and cared for the sick until the epidemic ended.

Johnson became embroiled in a controversy over the hanging of Mary Surratt. Five of the tribunal's nine commissioners recommended commuting her death sentence to life. The clemency plea was affixed to the findings of the court, which were presented to Johnson for his approval by Judge Advocate General Joseph Holt. Johnson later claimed Holt had never shown him the recommendation, but Holt claimed he did show it to Johnson, who, Holt said, ignored it. It still remains a question as to who was telling the truth. Regardless of whether

Johnson read the recommendation, Mary Surratt was hanged on July 7, 1865.

Johnson returned to the U.S. Senate in 1875, but died that same year.

Sources: Mark E. Neely, Jr., *The Abraham Lincoln Encyclopedia* (New York: McGraw-Hill, 1982), 164–5.

*See also:* Clemency Plea

## Johnson, Bradley Tyler

Brigadier general in the Confederate army. During the winter of 1863–1864, Johnson came up with a plan to select two hundred of his best troopers and make a surprise raid on Soldiers' Home in northeast Washington and capture Lincoln. Lincoln moved to Soldiers' Home during the summer months as a retreat from Washington's heat and unhealthy conditions. Johnson submitted his plan to his superior, General Wade Hampton. Hampton gave his approval and sent the proposal to his superior, General Jubal Early. Johnson was told to shelve his plan by Early until after Early's raid on Washington, scheduled for early July. Early had been sent to the Shenandoah Valley with an army of seventeen thousand men whose primary purpose was to drive General David Hunter from the valley and thus secure it and its rich supplies for the Confederate army. Once Hunter had been defeated, Early had orders to march on Washington from the north and attempt to sack the capital city. His action was intended to pull troops away from Grant, who had General Robert E. Lee surrounded at Richmond and Petersburg. Early was successful in pushing Hunter out of the valley but was unable to do more than demonstrate before the Washington suburbs because of Union reinforcements, not from Grant, but from the Sixth Army Corps just back from the Gulf.

Within four months, Early's army was destroyed in a series of engagements with General Philip Sheridan. Johnson's plan to capture Lincoln was canceled. Johnson spent the last months of the war in charge of the prison camp at Salis-

bury, North Carolina. After the war he practiced law in Richmond and served in the Virginia senate. He died in 1903 and is buried in Loudon Park Cemetery in Baltimore.

Sources: Ezra J. Warner, *Generals in Gray* (Baton Rouge: Louisiana State University Press, 1959), 156–57; John C. Brennan, "General Bradley T. Johnson's Plan to Abduct President Lincoln," *Chronicles of St. Mary's* 22 (November–December 1974), 1–3.

*See also:* Capture Plots

## Johnson, Edward

Confederate major general who became a defense witness called to impeach the testimony of Henry Von Steinacker. Mary Surratt's attorney, Frederick Aiken, called Johnson as a witness on her behalf. A graduate of West Point (1838), Johnson resigned his commission and joined the Confederate army on June 10, 1861. Rising to the rank of major general, he was captured at the Battle of Nashville, December 15, 1864, and held in the Old Capitol Prison until July 1865, when he was released.

One of the interesting sidelights of the trial was the objection to Johnson testifying because of his service as a Confederate officer. Brigadier General Albion Howe, a member of the military tribunal, objected to Johnson appearing as a witness on the grounds that he had violated his oath to the United States when he resigned his commission and joined the Confederate army. Violating his oath made him untrustworthy as a witness, Howe argued. Furthermore, "his hands [were] red with the blood of his loyal countrymen." Howe claimed Johnson was an "incompetent witness" and asked that he be barred from testifying. Brevet Brigadier General James Ekin seconded Howe's motion. Judge Advocate General Joseph Holt came to Johnson's defense. Holt pointed out that before a witness can be ruled incompetent he must first be convicted by a judicial proceeding and the record submitted as the basis for incompetence. Howe withdrew his motion and Johnson was allowed to testify.

Johnson's testimony was used by Aiken to refute the testimony of Henry Von Steinacker. Von Steinacker claimed he was an engineer on the staff of Johnson. Von Steinacker further claimed that while returning from leave to rejoin Johnson's division he had met with three men, one of whom was John Wilkes Booth. Later he claimed he saw Booth meeting with officers of the Second Virginia Infantry, a part of the Stonewall Jackson Brigade, and that the meeting was about sending a detached group of men to Canada to aid in various attacks against northern cities in league with the Knights of the Golden Circle and Sons of Liberty. Among the various acts planned was the assassination of President Lincoln.

Johnson's testimony had nothing to do with Mary Surratt, and only served to discredit Von Steinacker's claim that he served on Johnson's staff, and that Von Steinacker was a liar and therefore, an unreliable person.

Sources: Testimony of Edward Johnson, Poore, *Conspiracy Trial*, vol. 2, 471–8; Pitman, *Trial*, 64; Statement of Henry Von Steinacker, NARA, RG 153, M-599, reel 2: frames 462–65; Testimony of Henry Von Steinacker, Poore, *Conspiracy Trial*, vol. 1, 20; Pitman, *Trial*, 38.

*See also:* Von Steinacker, Henry

## Johnson, Charles H.

One of the eyewitnesses to Lincoln's assassination. Johnson was one of two eyewitnesses at Ford's Theatre to claim Booth ran across the stage with a "noticeable limp," supporting the notion that Booth broke his leg jumping from the presidential box to the stage. Johnson also stated that Booth "caught one of his spurs in the flag which draped the front of the box," and not in the Treasury Guard flag, as most people believe.

Sources: Timothy S. Good, *We Saw Lincoln Shot: One Hundred Eyewitness Accounts* (Jackson: University Press of Mississippi, 1995), 150–51.

## Johnson, Reverdy (1796–1876)

U.S. senator from Maryland (Democrat). Johnson served as one of Mary Surratt's defense attorneys along with Frederick Aiken and John W. Clampitt. At the time of the conspiracy trial, Johnson had accumulated a lifetime of honors. He had served as Maryland's deputy attorney general (1816–1817), as U.S. attorney general (1849–1850), and had represented the slave owners in the Dred Scott case in 1857. A Whig, Johnson became a Democrat when the Whig Party dissolved. Although he opposed Lincoln, he was a staunch Unionist, blaming the Confederate leaders for the breakup of the Union.

Johnson challenged the legal jurisdiction of the tribunal to try the conspirators, basing his claim on the fact that his client was a civilian resident of a loyal state and as such fell under the jurisdiction of the civil courts, not the military. He became embroiled in a bitter fight with Thomas M. Harris, one of the tribunal members, who questioned Johnson's right to appear before the tribunal. Harris maintained that Johnson had disregarded the loyalty oath by claiming that lawfully registered voters in the state of Maryland did not have to take the oath as a condition allowing them to vote. Johnson maintained that such an oath requirement violated the U.S. Constitution. The question was resolved when Harris, with Hunter's persuasion, agreed to recognize Johnson's right to represent Mary Surratt. It was pointed out that Johnson, as a U.S. senator, swore an oath of loyalty to the Constitution when seated as a senator. The fight left Johnson embittered and he avoided the trial, leaving the day-to-day defense to Aiken and Clampitt. However, his absence may have been because he doubted Mary Surratt's innocence.

Johnson filed an eloquent brief arguing against the jurisdiction of the military tribunal, which became a part of the official record. His argument, in brief, was that the military lacked jurisdiction because the defendant (Mary Surratt in his case) was a citizen of a loyal state in which the civil courts were open and functioning, and the Constitution guaranteed the accused to a trial by her peers. The tribunal, ruling on its own behalf, rejected Johnson's brief.

Sources: Edward Steers, Jr., "Introduction," in Edward Steers, Jr., ed., *The Trial* (Lexington: University Press of Kentucky, 2003), xi–xix; Reverdy Johnson, "Argument on the Jurisdiction of the Military Commission," in Edward Steers, Jr., ed., *The Trial* (Lexington: University Press of Kentucky, 2003), 251–63.

**Jones, Thomas Austin (1820–1895)**

Married Jane Harbin, the sister of Confederate agent Thomas Harbin. Jones became a paid principal agent of the Confederate Signal Service, being responsible for the mail line that ran north of the Potomac River through Charles County, Maryland, and for ferrying agents and other Confederate people across the Potomac River to Virginia. Jones was arrested in 1861 and held in Old Capitol Prison for disloyal practices. He was eventually released and returned to his clandestine activities.

In 1865, Jones lived in a small cottage known as Huckleberry, located near Pope's Creek in southern Charles County. On the morning of Sunday, April 16, Samuel Cox, Jr., the foster son of Confederate agent Samuel Cox, visited Jones at his home. He told him that Samuel Cox wanted to see him immediately. Meeting with Cox at his home, Cox told Jones that Booth and Herold were hiding in a pine thicket about a mile from Cox's house. Cox wanted Jones to care for the two fugitives and safely send them across the Potomac to Virginia. Jones provided food, drink, and newspapers to the two men for five days. Union soldiers were searching the area for Booth, and Jones felt it unsafe to move them until the coast was completely clear of soldiers. The opportunity came on the evening of Thursday, April 20, when the Union cavalry left the area on a false report that said Booth and Herold had been spotted in St. Mary's County, several miles south of where they were hiding. Jones led the two men down to the shore of the river. He gave Booth a compass and small candle and sent them on their way across the river. Jones returned to his home having fulfilled his job.

Jones was arrested along with several other people from Southern Maryland and held in Old Capitol Prison. The authorities were unaware of what Jones had done and never found out about his critical help. Unable to link Jones with Booth or Lincoln's assassination, Jones was released from prison in June 1865, and returned to Huckleberry. Jones was fortunate that Herold, in all of his lengthy statement given after his capture, never identified Jones as the man who had hidden them and helped put them across the Potomac. In 1893, Jones published a small book, *J. Wilkes Booth*, detailing his exploits as a Confederate agent and his role in helping Booth and Herold in their attempt to escape. Despite his admission, the government did not attempt to prosecute him. The sale of his book did poorly and original copies of it are rare today. Jones died in 1895 at the age of seventy-five, a poor man. His entire estate at the time of his death totaled $181.60.

Sources: Thomas A. Jones, *J. Wilkes Booth* (Chicago: Laird & Lee, 1893); William A. Tidwell, James O. Hall, and David W. Gaddy, *Come Retribution* (Jackson: University Press of Mississippi, 1988); John M. Wearmouth and Roberta A. Wearmouth, *Thomas A. Jones: Chief Agent of the Confederate Secret Service* (Port Tobacco, Md.: Stones Throw, 2000).

*See also:* Mail Line

## Julian, George Washington

A member of the Radical Republicans, Julian was a congressman from Indiana. He kept a journal throughout his entire political career, which his daughter, Grace Julian Clarke, destroyed after his death. Her actions were not sinister, but rather an effort to preserve family privacy, something that was not uncommon in her era. His journal has been used to support the conspiracy theorists who claim Stanton was behind Lincoln's assassination. A typescript copy of an alleged entry from Julian's journal dated April 24 (1865) tells of a meeting in Stanton's office between Stanton and three Radical Republicans: Julian, Senator Zachariah Chandler of Michigan, and Senator John Conness of California. The alleged copy quotes Julian as having "sensed something was amiss" at the time of the meeting. Stanton tells the three politicians, "We have Booth's diary, and he has recorded a lot in it."

Senator Conness, on scanning the pages, "moaned repeatedly, 'Oh, my God. I am ruined if this ever gets out.'" Stanton took the diary from Conness and asked Julian to look at it. Julian demurred. "I was better off not reading it," he wrote. Stanton pressed him in threatening language: "It concerns you for we either stick together in this thing or we will all go down the river together. We cannot let it [the diary] out."

The alleged entry clearly implicates all four men in Lincoln's murder. Fortunately, evidence exists showing the entry is a fabrication. Although Julian's daughter destroyed his journals, several entries were published in various periodicals prior to their destruction, including this entry:

> Monday, [April] 24th
> On Saturday last we had General Rosecrans before our committee, and his account of the campaign of Western Virginia makes McClellan look meaner than ever. On last Friday went with Indianans to call on President Johnson. Governor Morton transgressed the proprieties by reading a carefully prepared essay on the subject of reconstruction. Johnson entered upon the same theme, indulging in bad grammar, bad pronunciation and much incoherency of thought. In common with many I was mortified. ("The Assassination of Lincoln," *Indiana Magazine of History* 11, no. 4 [December 1915])

There is no mention of a meeting in Stanton's office, of Booth, or his diary, or its alleged claim of conspiracy. It is obvious the alleged entry is a fabrication by person or persons unknown.

Sources: William Hanchett, *The Lincoln Murder Conspiracies* (Urbana: University of Illinois Press, 1983), 229–30; Edward Steers, Jr., "Dark Union: Bad History," *North & South* 7, no. 1 (January 2004), 12–30.

*See also:* Balsiger, David, and Charles E. Sellier, Jr.

## *Juniper*, USS

A Union gunboat that was part of the Navy's flotilla patrolling the Potomac River in April 1865. On the night that Booth and Herold attempted their first crossing of the Potomac, the *Juniper* was anchored off Persimmon Point on the Virginia side of the river. The authors of *Come Retribution* attribute the gunboat's presence as forcing Booth and Herold to retreat back to the Maryland shore, where they wound up in the mouth of

Nanjemoy Creek at the farm of John J. Hughes. Because of the *Juniper*'s presence, the two fugitives were forced to make a second attempt to cross the river. On Saturday evening, April 22, Booth and Herold were able to cross the river, landing near Gambo Creek, Virginia, not far from their planned destination on Machodoc Creek.

Sources: William A. Tidwell, James O. Hall, and David W. Gaddy, *Come Retribution* (Jackson: University Press of Mississippi, 1988), 455.

## Kane, George Proctor (1817–1878)

Police commissioner of Baltimore. A Confederate sympathizer, Kane was arrested by order of General Winfield Scott and replaced by Colonel John R. Kenly of the First Maryland Volunteers. Eventually released, Kane left Baltimore and made his way to Montreal, where he worked as a Confederate agent plotting various schemes designed to break the morale of the northern people and thus lead to Lincoln's defeat in the 1864 election. Kane conspired with Patrick C. Martin and others to free the Confederate prisoners held in the Johnson's Island prison camp, in Lake Erie near Sandusky, Ohio. The plan was designed to take over the USS *Michigan* and turn its guns on the prison camp, demanding the release of some 2,500 soldiers held there. The plan failed when Union authorities learned of the plot and reinforced the garrison. For all his efforts, Kane accomplished little in attempting to win independence for the Confederacy.

Sources: Scott Sumpter Sheads and Daniel Carroll Toomey, *Baltimore During the Civil War* (Linthicum, Md.: Toomey, 1997); William A. Tidwell, James O. Hall, and David W. Gaddy, *Come Retribution* (Jackson: University Press of Mississippi, 1988), 330.

## Kautz, August Valentine (1828–1895)

A member of the military tribunal that presided over the conspirators' trial. Following his service in the Mexican War, Kautz received an appointment to West Point, where he graduated in 1852. He served for several years in the Pacific Northwest. At the outbreak of the Civil War, Kautz was appointed a captain in the Sixth U.S. Cavalry in the regular army. In 1862 he was appointed colonel in command of the Second Ohio Cavalry. By 1864, Kautz was promoted to brigadier general and commanded a cavalry division in the Army of the James. He was promoted to major general in 1865 and was among the first to enter the city of Richmond on April 3, 1865. Kautz served in various actions achieving the brevet rank of major general. He was selected to serve on the military tribunal in May 1865.

Kautz attempted to have himself removed from the tribunal, appealing to General Grant. His request was denied. He believed the evidence presented by Joseph Holt that Confederate leaders were behind the assassination. While he felt the prosecution failed to make their case against Dr. Mudd, he believed Mudd knew his injured patient was Booth, and failed to turn him over to pursuers when he had the opportunity. Kautz thought the prosecution had failed to make a convincing case that Mary Surratt knew about Booth's plan to murder Lincoln, but he believed she was fully aware of the plot to capture the president. Kautz was one of the five members of the tribunal to sign a clemency plea recommending mercy for Mary Surratt.

Sources: Ezra J. Warner, *Generals in Blue* (Baton Rouge: Louisiana State University Press, 1964), 257–58.

## Keckley, Elizabeth (ca. 1818–1907)

Confidante to Mary Todd Lincoln while living in the White House, Keckley provided comfort to Mary during her grief following Lincoln's assassination. Keckley became acquainted with Mary Lincoln when hired as her dressmaker and seamstress. Prior to the Civil War she established herself in Washington and also served Jefferson Davis and his wife, Varina. While she was working as a seamstress for Mary Lincoln, the two became very close, and following Lincoln's death, Keckley accompanied Mary back to Illinois and Chicago. However, she was later forced to return to Washington when Mary Lincoln could no longer pay for her services.

Keckley took part in an effort to sell many of Mary Lincoln's dresses, to no avail, an episode that caused Mary more grief and embarrassment. In 1868, Keckley agreed to allow a ghostwritten version of her life in the White House to be published by the firm of G. W. Carleton: *Behind the Scenes; Or, Thirty Years a Slave,* *and Four Years in the White House*. Keckley's memoir and the fiasco surrounding the selling of Mary's clothes resulted in a rupture of their friendship. Mary Lincoln had once referred to Keckley as her "best living friend" but now would only refer to her as "the colored historian." It was one more in a long list of individuals whom Mary Lincoln alienated.

Sources: Mark E. Neely, Jr., *The Abraham Lincoln Encyclopedia* (New York: McGraw-Hill, 1982), 171–72; Elizabeth Keckley, *Behind the Scenes; Or, Thirty Years a Slave, and Four Years in the White House* (1868; reprint, New York: Oxford University Press, 1988).

## Keeler, William F.

Paymaster, U.S. Navy. Keeler later wrote a letter to his congressman claiming Dr. Mudd had admitted to knowing Booth while at his house on Saturday, April 15, and that Booth had shot Lincoln. Keeler was aboard the USS *Florida*, which transported the four convicted conspirators to Fort Jefferson, off the Florida Keys, where they would begin serving their prison sentences. While living in Chicago in 1869, Keeler read an article in a Chicago newspaper to the effect that President Johnson was considering granting a pardon to Dr. Samuel A. Mudd. Keeler immediately wrote a letter (dated January 21, 1869) to his congressman, B. F. Cook, stating in part, "In conversation with myself, & I think with others on our passage down he admitted what I think the prosecution failed to prove at his trial—viz—that he knew who Booth was when he set his leg & of what crime he was guilty. I have thought it might be well to have these facts known if they are not." In a letter to his wife, Anna, Keeler wrote, "He is said to be a sharp shrewd man but I saw nothing about him to indicate it—he has a sort of cunning, foxy, look as if possessed of plenty of low cunning & a desire for concealment." Despite protests from men like Keeler, Johnson pardoned Mudd on February 8, 1869, but it took until March 8, 1869, before Mudd was released.

Sources: Robert W. Daly, ed., *Aboard the USS Florida: 1863–1865: The Letters of Paymaster William Frederick Keeler, U.S. Navy to his Wife, Anna* (Annapolis, Md.: U.S. Naval Institute, 1968); Edward Steers, Jr., *Blood on the Moon* (Lexington: University Press of Kentucky, 2001), 241–43.

### Keene, Laura (1826–1873)

Leading lady of the stage during her theatrical lifetime. Keene played the female lead opposite Harry Hawk in Tom Taylor's rollicking comedy, *Our American Cousin,* the night of Lincoln's assassination. The performance that evening was a benefit in which Keene was given the proceeds from the ticket sales. She had just finished her part in act 3, scene 2 and walked offstage when Booth fired the fatal shot that killed Lincoln. With the help of stage manager (and actor) Thomas Gourlay, Keene made her way up a back stairs to the Dress Circle and into the presidential box, where Lincoln lay on the floor as Dr. Charles Leale worked over him. Gourlay was familiar with the layout of the building and so was able to avoid the shocked crowd by leading Keene out of the stage door and up a back staircase to the offices of the Ford brothers. From there, Gourlay led Keene into the reception room adjacent to the Dress Circle and the presidential box.

Once inside the box, Keene asked Leale if it was all right to hold the president's head in her lap. Leale said yes and she carefully placed his head in her lap, trying to comfort the comatose Lincoln. Keene was one of the first people to positively identify Booth as the killer. That night she stayed at the Metropolitan Hotel a few blocks from the theater. She was taken into custody in Harrisburg, Pennsylvania, a few days after the assassination and taken to Cincinnati where she was soon released. Despite her presence in the theater the night of the assassination, and her familiarity with John Wilkes Booth, she was not called as a witness or even interviewed by the authorities. She suffered a stroke and died on November 4, 1873, and is buried in Greenwood Cemetery in New York City.

Sources: Edward Steers, Jr., *Blood on the Moon* (Lexington: University Press of Kentucky, 2001), 121–22.

### Keleher, James

Part owner of Keleher & Pywell stables, located at Eighth and F streets in Washington, D.C. George Atzerodt rented a horse from Keleher's stable the day of the assassination. Keleher testified at the conspiracy trial that Atzerodt rented a horse around two o'clock on Friday, April 14, and that the horse was back in his stable when he arrived for work early Saturday morning. Atzerodt had returned the horse at 11:00 P.M. and jumped on a streetcar headed for the Navy Yard. Keleher's testimony was of little value to either the prosecution or defense.

Sources: Testimony of James Keleher, Poore, *Conspiracy Trial*, vol. 2, 507; Pitman, *Trial*, 151.

### Kennedy, John Alexander (1803–1873)

Superintendent of the New York Metropolitan Police Force. Kennedy played a role in uncovering the plot in Baltimore to assassinate president-elect Lincoln on his arrival in that city before continuing on to Washington. With rumors flying about Washington, Baltimore, and New York that Lincoln was in danger of bodily harm, Kennedy sent detectives from his staff to both Washington and Baltimore much in the same manner as Pinkerton's detectives did working for Samuel L. Felton, president of the Philadelphia, Wilmington, & Baltimore Railroad.

Kennedy's men were able to pose as anti-Lincoln secessionists and gain information of a plot to assassinate Lincoln. Kennedy's principal detective, David Bookstaver, hastened to Washington, where he reported to Captain Charles P. Stone of General Winfield Scott's staff. Scott had Stone draft a report and give it to William Seward, Lincoln's secretary of state designee. Alarmed at what he read, Seward sent his son, Frederick, to intercept Lincoln in Philadelphia and give him the details of the plot. Unknown to Seward, and to Kennedy and his detectives, Allan Pinkerton had already met with Lincoln in the Continental Hotel in Philadelphia, where Lincoln was staying, and had briefed the president on the Baltimore plot. Pinkerton had advised Lincoln to change his schedule by passing through Baltimore hours before his published scheduled time. Hearing Pinkerton out and with Stone's report in his hand, Lincoln agreed to leave Harrisburg ahead of schedule and take a special train back to Philadelphia, then to Baltimore, arriving in that city nine hours ahead of schedule and thereby thwarting the assassins' plot.

Sources: Norma B. Cuthbert, ed., *Lincoln and the Baltimore Plot 1861* (San Marino, Calif.: Huntington Library, 1949); Victor Searcher, *Lincoln's Journey to Greatness* (Philadelphia: John C. Winston, 1960).

*See also:* Pinkerton, Allan

### Kent, William T.

Kent found Booth's derringer on the floor of the presidential box on the night of the assassination. He was employed as a clerk in the office of the paymaster general. On the night of the assassination Kent sat in the Dress Circle on the side opposite the presidential box. He had perhaps the best view of the box that evening. Following the shot and exit by Booth, Kent made his way around to the box and was able to enter it shortly after Dr. Charles Leale entered. While in the box he lent Leale his pocketknife, which the doctor used to cut Lincoln's collar from around his neck. Later, while walking home, he noticed he had lost his keys. Returning to the theater with Newton Ferree, he made his way to the box, where the guard allowed him to enter so he could look for his keys. While searching on the floor he found the derringer pistol that Booth had dropped. Finding no one in authority, he gave the pistol to Lawrence A. Gobright, an Associated Press reporter who had also returned to the theater that night. Gobright turned the derringer over to the Metropolitan Police. It was entered as exhibit 30 at the conspiracy trial.

Newton Ferree, who accompanied Kent to the theater, found Lincoln's bloodstained collar while helping Kent search for his keys. Ferree kept the collar, it having no evidentiary value.

Sources: Timothy S. Good, *We Saw Lincoln Shot: One Hundred Eyewitness Accounts* (Jackson: University Press of Mississippi, 1995), 44; Statement of William T. Kent, NARA, RG 153, M-599, reel 5: frames 129–31; Poore, *Conspiracy Trial*, vol. 1, 257; Pitman, *Trial*, 82.

*See also:* Gobright, Lawrence A.; Ferree, Newton

## Kenzie, Wilson D. (1844–1927)

A corporal in Battery A, First U.S. Artillery. In 1922 Kenzie swore out an affidavit in which he claimed to have been at the Garrett farm when Booth was cornered and killed. Kenzie swore that the man in the barn was not John Wilkes Booth, but another person altogether. Kenzie repeated his story over the next several years embellishing it with every new interview. He became one of the key witnesses for modern conspiracy buffs who believe Booth escaped and that the government conspired to make people believe Booth was killed at the Garrett farm. The problem with Kenzie's story, however, is that it is riddled with errors and inconsistencies. Kenzie may have met Booth in New Orleans in 1863, as he claimed, and he was well acquainted with one of the troopers who actually was at the Garrett farm and participated in Booth's capture. But the rest of his claims fall apart. In telling his story, he was unaware that the 16th New York Cavalry traveled to Belle Plain by steamboat. He stated that Booth was killed the day after Lincoln was shot and that it occurred on the outskirts of Washington, not near Port Royal, Virginia. He said the shooting took place in the afternoon, not in the early morning hours, and that because it wasn't Booth that was killed the government never paid out the reward money it offered (it paid out all of the reward money). Kenzie is one of several individuals who attempted to attach themselves to Booth's star late in life. Even a superficial search of the records will lead one to dismiss his claims as bogus.

Sources: Steven G. Miller, "Wilson D. Kenzie, the Linchpin of the Booth Escape Theories," in Laurie Verge, ed., *The Body in the Barn* (Clinton, Md.: Surratt Society, 1993), 25–33.

*See also:* Zisgen, Joseph

## Kerns, Francis

Driver of the stagecoach that ran between Washington, D.C., and Rockville, Maryland. Kerns made the Friday, April 14, 1865, trip to Rockville and decided to stay overnight. He turned the stage over to one of his drivers for the Friday return to Washington. The driver made the Saturday morning trip back to Rockville and Kerns started the return trip back to Washington Saturday morning. On the way he met William Gaither and George Atzerodt riding in Gaither's wagon. Atzerodt had taken the morning stage from Georgetown, intending to ride to Rockville. The stage was stopped at the military picket post in Tennallytown, just outside Washington. Atzerodt left the stage and climbed aboard Gaither's wagon, asking Gaither if he could ride with him the rest of the way to Rockville. Kerns told authorities that he met Gaither and Atzerodt midway between Georgetown and Rockville. Kerns knew Atzerodt, having seen him on several occasions hanging around the stable where he kept his horses. He gave the authorities a detailed description of what Atzerodt was wearing.

Sources: Statement of Francis Kerns, NARA, RG 153, M-599, reel 3, frames 518–23; NARA, RG 153, M-599, reel 3, frames 555–56

### Kilpatrick-Dahlgren Raid
See Dahlgren Raid

### Kimmel House
Also known as the Pennsylvania House. The hotel was located on the south side of C Street (357–359) between Fourth and Fifth streets. After failing to carry out his assigned assassination of Vice President Andrew Johnson, George Atzerodt wandered about the city, traveling to the Navy Yard and back before checking into the Kimmel House hotel at two o'clock Saturday morning. Atzerodt frequently stayed at the Kimmel House when in Washington. He was given room 53 along with five other guests.

Shortly after 5:00 A.M. on Saturday morning, Atzerodt left the Kimmel House without paying his bill and headed for Georgetown, where he would board the stage for Rockville, Maryland. Heading in the opposite direction of Booth and Herold, Atzerodt decided the safest place for him was the home of his childhood, now occupied by his cousin, Hartman Richter, in Germantown, Maryland, approximately twenty miles northwest of Washington.

Sources: Edward Steers, Jr., "George Atzerodt," in Edward Steers, Jr., ed., *The Trial* (Lexington: University Press of Kentucky, 2003), lxvi–lxxi.

### King, Dr. Albert F. A.
One of several doctors who made their way to the presidential box in Ford's Theatre after the president was shot. According to Drs. Leale and Taft, King helped in the examination of Lincoln and in the decision to move him to a more comfortable place. King assisted Dr. Ezra Abbott in monitoring Lincoln's pulse and respiration throughout the night and early morning hours of April 15.

Sources: Timothy S. Good, *We Saw Lincoln Shot: One Hundred Eyewitness Accounts* (Jackson: University Press of Mississippi, 1995), 22–24, 61, 64; W. Emerson Reck, *A. Lincoln: His Last 24 Hours* (Columbia, S.C.: University of South Carolina Press, 1987).

*See also:* Abbott, Dr. Ezra W.

## King, Rufus (1814–1876)

King served as U.S. minister to the Papal States from 1863 until 1867. During the first two years of the Civil War, King organized the famous "Iron Brigade" (Wisconsin). During the winter of 1861–1862, he commanded a division in the Third Corps. In 1863, he resigned his commission and was appointed minister to the Papal States. In 1865, King negotiated the extradition of John Surratt, who was serving as a papal Zouave under the name John Watson. Although no extradition treaty existed between the United States and the Papal States, King worked out a deal with Cardinal Giacomo Antonelli, secretary of state for Pope Pius IX, for the return of Surratt in exchange for the U.S. granting asylum to the pope should the Papal States be absolved.

Sources: Alfred Isacsson, *The Travels, Arrest, and Trial of John H. Surratt* (Middletown, N.Y.: Vestigium, 2003); Louis J. Wiechmann, *A True History of the Assassination of Abraham Lincoln and of the Conspiracy of 1865*, ed. Floyd E. Risvold (New York: Knopf, 1975).

*See also:* Antonelli, Cardinal Giacomo; Surratt, John Harrison, Jr.

## King George County, Virginia

King George County is located along the southern shore of the Potomac River opposite Charles County, Maryland. When Booth and Herold finally crossed the Potomac River on the night and early morning of Sunday, April 23, they landed in King George County. The county was the site of Dr. Richard Stuart's two homes, Cedar Grove and Cleydael, as well as the camps of Confederate agents Thomas Harbin and Charles Cawood. Booth and Herold spent Sunday night at the cabin of William Lucas, located in King George County a short distance from Cleydael.

Sources: William A. Tidwell, James O. Hall, and David W. Gaddy, *Come Retribution* (Jackson: University Press of Mississippi, 1988).

*See also:* Booth Escape Route

## Kirkwood House

Washington, D.C., hotel located on Pennsylvania Avenue and Twelfth Street. Vice President Andrew Johnson roomed at the Kirkwood House following his inauguration while awaiting better accommodations. On the morning of April 14, George Atzerodt registered at the Kirkwood under orders from John Wilkes Booth. Assigned room 126, Atzerodt spent most of the day wandering around the city. At approximately 7:00 P.M. that evening, Atzerodt met with Booth and Herold in Lewis Powell's room at the Herndon House, located at Ninth and F streets. Booth told his three accomplices that he was going to kill Lincoln that

night, assigning Powell to kill Secretary of State William Seward and Atzerodt Vice President Andrew Johnson.

Although Atzerodt later claimed he refused to kill the vice president, he did show up at the Kirkwood House at the assigned hour. After having a drink in the hotel bar, Atzerodt left the hotel and began wandering around the city. He never returned to the Kirkwood, checking into the Kimmel House instead.

Atzerodt left behind in his room at the Kirkwood hotel several items recovered by the authorities, including a bankbook belonging to John Wilkes Booth. The discovery was a major find linking Atzerodt to Booth. Michael Henry, the barkeep at the Kirkwood, reported to detective John Lee that a "suspicious character" was living in room 126, resulting in Lee discovering items of Booth and Atzerodt.

Sources: Edward Steers, Jr., "George Atzerodt," in Edward Steers, Jr., ed., *The Trial* (Lexington: University Press of Kentucky, 2003), lxvi–lxxi.

## Knights of the Golden Circle (KGC)

A secret society formed by a band of would-be adventurers whose primary objective was the conquest of Mexico and the entire region surrounding the Caribbean. Once complete, this "Golden Circle" of territory circling the Gulf of Mexico would become new land for the extension of American slavery. George Washington Lafayette Bickley, a charlatan and con man, claimed to have organized the order in Lexington, Kentucky, in 1854, but records indicate the order did not begin functioning until 1858. The order soon spread throughout the southern states, where its chief purpose by 1860 was to foster secession. Once secession became a reality, the order shifted its efforts into the border and "northwestern" states that remained in the Union.

The order consisted of local chapters known as "Castles," and members attained various "degrees" as they moved up the organization. Members of the first, or lowest, degree were nothing more than ordinary people who knew little and were entrusted with even less. They were more like members of a fraternal organization whose aims were social. Members of the higher degrees, however, were deep into anti-Union activity, which ran the gamut of disloyal practices.

Bickley was in Virginia at the outbreak of war and tried desperately to raise various military units for the Confederacy, but always failed. Confederate leaders soon dismissed him as a nuisance. Bickley soon faded and so did his Knights of the Golden Circle. At this point, Phineas C. Wright of St. Louis stepped in and reorganized the remnants of the KGC into the Order of American Knights (OAK). It eventually splintered in 1864, giving rise to the "Sons of Liberty." All three organizations sought to undermine the Union effort in the North and oppose President Lincoln and his policies whenever and wherever possible, by any means available.

Sources: James O. Hall, "A Magnificent Charlatan: George Washington Lafayette Bickley," *Civil War Times Illustrated* 18, no. 10 (February 1980), 40–42; Jennifer L. Weber, *Copperheads* (New York: Oxford University Press, 2006).

See also: Bickley, George Washington Lafayette; Order of American Knights; Sons of Liberty

meant to be used during Booth's escape to hinder pursuing cavalry by stringing it across the road, causing the pursuers' horses to stumble and fall.

Lamb was recalled by Spangler's defense regarding Jacob Ritterspaugh's testimony claiming Spangler slapped Ritterspaugh and said to him, "Don't say which way he [Booth] went." Lamb testified that Spangler did not make such a statement, and stated that what he heard him to say was "Shut up: What do you know about it? Hold your tongue."

Lamb designed and painted a new drop curtain for Ford's Theatre that was installed on August 29, 1864.

Sources: George J. Olszewski, *Historic Structure Report: Restoration of Ford's Theatre* (Washington, D.C.: U.S. Government Printing Office, 1963), 82, 116; Poore, *Conspiracy Trial,* vol. 3, 44–49, 57–60.

*See also*: Ritterspaugh, Jacob

## Lamb, James

An artist and scene painter who worked at Ford's Theatre from 1864 to 1865. Lamb appeared as a witness on behalf of Edman Spangler during the conspiracy trial. He was questioned by Thomas Ewing, Spangler's attorney, about a seventy- to eighty-foot rope found in Spangler's possession at the time of his arrest. The rope appeared to be "border rope" used in the theater to raise and lower canvases that occur along the border of the stage. The prosecution believed the rope was

## Lamon, Ward Hill (1842–1912)

Marshal of the District of Columbia, self-appointed bodyguard for Lincoln, and one of the president's closest friends. Born in Virginia (now West Virginia), Lamon moved in 1837 to Danville, Illinois, where he set up his practice of law. He became one of Lincoln's closest friends, riding the Eighth Judicial Circuit with Lincoln in the 1850s. He became a

partner with Lincoln, representing him in legal cases in Vermillion County, Illinois. Lamon accompanied Lincoln to Washington on his inaugural journey. He took it upon himself to act as Lincoln's bodyguard, even sleeping outside Lincoln's White House door to protect him from harm.

Lincoln appointed Lamon as Federal marshal of the District of Columbia in April 1861. The position was more ceremonial than real, although Lamon was in charge of the district's jail. In 1863, Lamon was appointed marshal in chief of the ceremonies at Gettysburg for the dedication of the cemetery.

Lamon constantly worried over Lincoln's safety and chastised Lincoln on more than one occasion about his disregard for his own safety. Lamon was in

Richmond the night Lincoln was assassinated, sent there by Lincoln to look into conditions for reconstruction of the state government. He returned to Washington and was placed in charge of the civil part of Lincoln's funeral procession.

Lamon purchased the notes that Lincoln's law partner William H. Herndon had accumulated in anticipation of writing a biography of Lincoln. Lamon called on his law partner's son, Chauncy Black, to do the actual writing. Lamon published the *Life of Abraham Lincoln* in 1872. The book attempted to tell the "true" story of Lincoln and wrote negatively about Lincoln's marriage, religion, and ancestry. It received scathing reviews and was attacked by many of Lincoln's friends, especially his son Robert. Lamon died in 1893 at the age of sixty-four. He is buried in a church cemetery in Gerrardsville, West Virginia.

Sources: Mark E. Neely, Jr., *The Abraham Lincoln Encyclopedia* (New York: McGraw-Hill, 1982), 177–79.

*See also:* Bodyguard, Lincoln's

### Laughlin, Clara

Author of a book on Lincoln's assassination published in 1909. Laughlin concluded Booth was the sole organizer of his plot to capture and then assassinate Lincoln. She defended John Surratt as sharing no responsibility for Lincoln's murder and defends Mary Surratt as well. Dr. Samuel Mudd was also an innocent victim, according to Laughlin. He may have been aware of a plot to capture the president, but bore no guilt for the assassination. Even if this were true, which it is not, Mudd would be considered a conspirator under the concept of vicarious liability.

Laughlin was a staff writer for *McClure's Magazine*, and publisher Samuel S. McClure assigned her the task of writing a history of Lincoln's assassination in anticipation of the Lincoln Centennial celebration. Her book, *The Death of Lincoln*, was released on February 12, 1909, right on schedule. It was her first book; two dozen others followed. Her book is unique in that it vigorously defends the innocence of John Surratt, Mary Surratt, and Dr. Samuel Mudd, although she believes Mudd was aware of the plot to capture Lincoln. Laughlin, like so many authors who followed her, separates the plot to capture Lincoln with Booth's actual assassination of Lincoln. The best that can be said about Laughlin's book is that it was written to meet a deadline and left her with little time to accurately investigate all of the intriguing aspects of the assassination.

Sources: Michael W. Kauffman, "Preface to the New Edition," in Clara E. Laughlin, *The Death of*

*Lincoln* (1909; reprint, Newport, Vt.: Vermont Civil War Enterprises, 1997), i–viii.

## Laws of War
See General Order No. 100

## Leale, Dr. Charles Augustus (1842–1932)

A young army surgeon who was the first doctor to reach Lincoln in the presidential box, thus making him the primary physician in treating the dying president. Leale was in charge of the officer's ward in Armory Square Hospital in Washington, D.C. After reading in the afternoon paper that Lincoln would be attending

Ford's Theatre, Leale took the evening off and went to the theater in hopes of seeing him. Leale was seated in the Dress Circle forty feet from the box. He later gave one of the more detailed accounts of the events that evening. He saw a man (Booth) in conversation with another man seated outside the outer door to the box (Charles Forbes). The man entered the box and moments later Leale heard the shot. When someone called for a surgeon, Leale made his way to the box and after identifying himself was admitted by Major Henry Rathbone, an occupant. He found Lincoln slumped in his chair motionless. With the help of two men (unidentified), Leale placed Lincoln on the floor. Noticing blood on his hand where he had held Lincoln by the shoulder, he assumed the president had been stabbed. Examining Lincoln he discovered the small wound to the rear of the skull and removed the blood clot that had formed. This restored Lincoln's breathing and pulse to a more regular rate.

Drs. Charles S. Taft and Albert F. A. King came into the box and offered Leale their help. After discussing Lincoln's condition they agreed to move him to more comfortable quarters, but also agreed he would not survive the difficult trip back to the White House. With the help of several soldiers who had been watching the play, Lincoln was carried down the stairs and outside the theater. Across the street a man beckoned the group and Lincoln was carried across the street and into the home of William Petersen. He was taken to a back room occupied by Private William T. Clarke. The bed was too short for Lincoln's long frame and so was pulled away from the wall; Lincoln's body was then laid diagonally across it. He was stripped of his clothing, and hot water bottles and mustard plasters were placed on his legs and chest to help his circulation.

Because he was first on the scene to treat Lincoln, Leale was acknowledged by the other doctors present to be in charge of the president's care. All the doctors agreed that the wound was mortal and all they could do was make the president as comfortable as possible and wait for the death that was sure to come. Leale held the president's hand all the while, in the hope that the president would sense he was in touch with humanity, as he lay comatose.

Years later, at the time of the U.S. centennial, Leale gave an address to the New York Loyal Legion, of which he was a member. His moving talk of those historic hours that he spent beside the dying president were published as a memorial pamphlet. It remains one of the more detailed and accurate accounts of those harrowing hours 44 years ago.

Sources: Charles A. Leale, *Lincoln's Last Hours: Address Delivered Before the Commandery of the State of New York Military Order of the Loyal Legion of the United States* (New York: Privately printed, 1909).

*See also:* Taft, Dr. Charles Sabin

## Leaman, James E., and Somerset Leaman

Two brothers who were invited to Easter dinner at the home of Hezakiah Metz in Germantown, Maryland, at the same time George Atzerodt visited Metz on Sunday, April 16, 1865. The Leaman brothers were called as defense witnesses on Atzerodt's behalf. The brothers told of Atzerodt's "confused" demeanor at Sunday dinner and his answers to questions about the assassination of Lincoln and attempt on Seward. When asked if General Grant had been assassinated, both brothers stated that Atzerodt said he didn't think so, that if Grant had been assassinated he would have heard about it. But Metz, the host at the dinner, claimed Atzerodt answered by saying, "If the man that was to follow him had followed him, it was likely to be so." Atzerodt's attorney, William E. Doster, was unable to undo the damage of Metz's statement through questioning of the Leaman brothers. Doster attempted to show that Atzerodt's "confused" behavior was the result of Metz's daughter rebuffing Atzerodt's advances toward her.

Sources: Testimony of James E. Leaman, Poore, *Conspiracy Trial*, vol. 2, 504; Pitman, *Trial*, 152; Testimony of Somerset Laman (Leaman), Poore, *Conspiracy Trial*, vol. 2, 501–4; Pitman, *Trial*, 152.

*See also*: Atzerodt, George Andrew; Metz, Hezekiah.

## Lee, Edwin Grey (1836–1870)

Brigadier General Edwin Grey Lee was appointed Confederate commissioner in Canada in December 1864, replacing Jacob Thompson and Clement Clay and taking over the clandestine operation.

In April 1865, Lee sent John Surratt on a mission to Elmira, New York, to reconnoiter the Union prison camp in that city. In his post as commissioner, Lee was in charge of the Confederate clandestine activities operating out of Canada against the Federal government. In April 1865, John Surratt, working as a Confederate agent for Secretary of State Judah P. Benjamin, was in Elmira gaining information about the Union prison camp for Lee. Lee was ostensibly planning a raid on the camp in hopes of freeing Confederate prisoners being held there. On learning of Lincoln's assassination, Surratt went to Lee in Montreal, where he was carefully protected by the Confederate secret service until he could be safely sent to Europe.

Sources: William A. Tidwell, James O. Hall, and David W. Gaddy, *Come Retribution* (Jackson: University Press of Mississippi, 1988); William A. Tidwell, *April '65: Confederate Covert Action in the American Civil War* (Kent, Ohio: Kent State University Press, 1995); Edwin Grey Lee, diary, 1864–1865, Accession 1456, Southern Historical Collection, University of North Carolina, Chapel Hill.

*See also:* Surratt, John Harrison, Jr.

## Lee, John

Army detective in the office of Washington provost marshal James O'Beirne. On Saturday morning, April 15, O'Beirne sent Lee to the Kirkwood House, where Vice President Andrew Johnson was staying, to make sure that Johnson was well protected in case there were an attempt on his life. George Atzerodt had been assigned to kill Johnson the night before and failed to do so when his courage evaporated and he fled the city. In questioning the barkeep, Michael Henry, Lee learned that a "suspicious character" had registered in room 126 the morning before. Lee asked Henry to take him to the room and let him in so he could examine it. Atzerodt had the only key to the room, so Henry allowed Lee to force the door open. Inside he found several items, including a coat. In the pocket Lee found a bankbook with the owner's name inside, John Wilkes Booth. The hotel register listed the occupant of the room as George Atzerodt. It was a major break for the authorities. Atzerodt had previously been identified as a close friend of David Herold. Now he was also linked to Booth, leading investigators to conclude that Herold and Atzerodt were part of Booth's conspiracy. Information from John Fletcher, manager of the stable where Herold had rented a horse earlier in the evening before fleeing over the Navy Yard Bridge moments after Booth, resulted in authorities sending a troop of the 13th New York Cavalry over the bridge and into Southern Maryland to search for the escaping fugitives.

Sources: Statement of John Lee, NARA, RG 153, M-599, reel 2, frames 523–24; Poore, *Conspiracy Trial*, vol. 1, 62; Pitman, *Trial*, 144; Statement of John Lee, NARA, RG 153, M-599, reel 2, frames 528–31; Poore, *Conspiracy Trial*, vol. 1, 62; Pitman, *Trial*, 144; Edward Steers, Jr., *Blood on the Moon* (Lexington: University Press of Kentucky, 2001), 131–33.

## Letter of Introduction

On October 18, 1864, John Wilkes Booth traveled to Montreal, where he registered at the St. Lawrence Hall hotel. He remained in Montreal for a total of ten days. During that time he was seen meeting with Confederate agent Patrick C. Martin in the St. Lawrence Hall lobby and at Ontario Bank. When Booth left Montreal on October 27, he returned to Washington carrying a letter of introduction from Martin to Drs. William Queen and Samuel Mudd in Charles County, Maryland.

Three weeks later, on Friday, November 11, Booth took the stagecoach to Bryantown in Charles County, where he spent the night at the Bryantown Tavern. The next day he was taken to the home of Dr. Queen. According to Queen's son-in-law, John C. Thompson, Booth showed the letter to Queen. The following morning Booth attended services at St. Mary's Church near Bryantown. After church services ended, Booth was introduced to Dr. Mudd by Thompson. The letter obviously introduced Booth to Queen, and to Dr. Mudd. Booth's introduction to Mudd served him well. Three weeks later Mudd arranged a meeting at the Bryantown Tavern, where he introduced Booth to Thomas Harbin, a Confederate agent. A week later Mudd met Booth in Washington, where he introduced him to John Surratt at Booth's hotel room. Booth was able to convince both Harbin and Surratt to join his plot to kidnap Lincoln. Harbin and Surratt then met with George Atzerodt, who agreed to join the group.

The letter of introduction was an important step in helping Booth gain access to important people in Southern Maryland who were essential to Booth's kidnap plan, and to gain access to the Confederate mail line, over which Booth intended to take Lincoln to Richmond after capturing him.

Sources: Statement of Samuel B. Arnold, NARA, RG 94, M-619, reel 458, frames 305–12; Testimony of Eaton Horner, Poore, *Conspiracy Trial*, vol. 1, 423; Pitman, *Trial*, 234; Edward Steers, Jr., *Blood on the Moon* (Lexington: University Press of Kentucky, 2001), 171–72.

*See also:* Mudd, Dr. Samuel Alexander

## Lincoln, Abraham (1809–1865)

Abraham Lincoln was elected sixteenth president of the United States in November 1860, with only thirty-nine percent of the popular vote, the smallest percentage in American history. The results, however, were sufficient to win him 60 percent of the Electoral College despite the fact that he was not even on the ballot in ten southern states. So great was the fear that the new president's policies would inevitably lead to the abolition of slavery, seven southern states had already passed ordinances of secession by the time of Lincoln's inauguration on March 4, 1861. Two months later four more states had seceded and joined the newly formed Confederate States of America.

While he urged the seceded states to return to the Union peacefully, President

Lincoln was prepared to use military force to maintain the Union and protect its interests. To Lincoln, the Union was perpetual, a sacred contract not to be broken under any circumstances. Unwilling to compromise on the critical question of union, Lincoln let war come rather than accept disunion. In June 1862, Lincoln made his position clear in a letter to William Seward, his secretary of state, "I expect to maintain this contest until successful, or until I die, or am conquered, or my term expires, or Congress or the country forsake me."

As the war progressed it became clear to Confederate President Jefferson Davis and his close associates that a restoration of the Union was no longer possible as long as Lincoln was president. Neither side was willing to accept the conditions proposed by the other, especially on the issue of slavery. In September 1862, Lincoln decided to use his war powers as president to issue his Emancipation Proclamation, changing the objectives of the war and blunting possible foreign intervention on the side of the Confederacy. To many in the Confederacy it was a heinous act. Davis described the proclamation as the "most execrable measure recorded in the history of guilty man." It was, in Davis's opinion, "an incitement to slave revolt with the inevitable consequence of the massacre of innocent women and children." Confederate leaders knew that Lincoln, not the Union army, was their greatest enemy. If they were to succeed in their quest for independence, Lincoln had to lose his bid for reelection in November 1864.

In March 1864, Union General Judson Kilpatrick launched a raid against weakly defended Richmond. Accompanying Kilpatrick was Colonel Ulric Dahlgren, son of Union admiral John A. Dahlgren. The raid failed and Dahlgren was killed in an ambush by Confederate soldiers. Nothing would have been made of the raid except for an incredible document found on his body. The document contained written instructions from Dahlgren to his men that stated, "The men must keep together and well in hand, and once in the city it must be destroyed *and Jeff Davis and cabinet killed*" [emphasis added]. The publication of the document was a major propaganda coup for the Confederacy and outraged both the military and the people of the South. Targeting Davis and his cabinet was considered a gross violation of the laws of civilized warfare and Lincoln was held directly responsible. If Davis was a legitimate target was Lincoln not also a target?

In April 1864, seven months before the presidential election in the North, Jefferson Davis sent former United States Senators Jacob Thompson and Clement Clay to Canada with instructions to establish a clandestine organization and engage in various actions designed to demoralize the North and bring about Lincoln's defeat in the upcoming election. The efforts failed and Lincoln's reelection to a second term signaled the death knell for the Confederacy.

As Union war efforts improved and victories outnumbered defeats, efforts to remove Lincoln from office by abduction or assassination increased. Despite repeated warnings about his safety and pleas that he accept protection, Lincoln dismissed the idea of assassination as improbable. Lincoln acknowledged that an attack by anyone willing to risk his own life could not be prevented. Nevertheless, he finally acquiesced to an around the clock bodyguard drawn from the Washington, D.C., Metropolitan Police force. Protection, however, was limited at best. Lincoln did not help matters by his seeming indifference to protection; he often would leave the White House without notifying his protectors thereby leaving himself exposed to possible attack.

In all, there were eight plots that we know of directed against Lincoln from the time of his election to the night of his death. By the summer of 1864, the Confederates had two separate plans to capture Lincoln, one under Brigadier General Bradley T. Johnson and a second under Confederate agent Thomas Nelson Conrad. Both plots never fully materialized and were abandoned. Then in August of 1864, actor and Confederate sympathizer John Wilkes Booth decided to make his own move against Lincoln. He met with two former Baltimore childhood friends and ex-Confederate soldiers, Samuel B. Arnold and Michael O'Laughlen, and enlisted their participation in a plot to capture Lincoln and take him south to Richmond. Booth's team of conspirators soon expanded as a result of his visit to Canada where he met with Confederate agents and received help in his recruitment. Returning to

Southern Maryland, Booth enlisted the aid of several Confederate sympathizers and agents, including John Surratt, Dr. Samuel Mudd, George Atzerodt, and Lewis Powell. After an abortive attempt to capture Lincoln in March 1865, Booth decided to kill Lincoln along with Vice President Andrew Johnson, and Secretary of State William Seward. If successful, the plan might well have created enough chaos in the North to give the Confederate forces time to regroup.

Lincoln's love of the theater coupled with Booth's pathological hatred of Lincoln came together on the night of April 14, 1865, at Ford's Theatre. Booth, a nationally acclaimed actor, chose Ford's Theatre as the place to carry out his plan. His familiarity with the theatre and fame as an actor gained him access that few others possessed.

Conspiracy theorists who believe Lincoln was deliberately exposed on the night of April 14, are seriously mistaken. Lincoln attended the theatre on numerous occasions. He attended Ford's Theatre on at least thirteen occasions, including the evening of February 11, 1865, eight weeks before his assassination. On that occasion, Lincoln was accompanied by Generals Ulysses S. Grant and Ambrose P. Burnside. As on other occasions, there were no Metropolitan Police bodyguards or military guards protecting the president and his famous generals. Persons freely entered the box on at least two occasions during the performance without impediment. Such was the protection afforded the president in 1865, and such was the case on the night of April 14.

Lincoln's death came too late to have an impact on the war and the Confederacy's dream of independence. Although there were still over 120,000 Confederate troops and three Confederate armies still in the field at the time of Lincoln's assassination, the war was lost for the Confederacy and only weeks from ending. Had the assassination occurred prior to Lincoln's election to a second term, the outcome may have been quite different.

Sources: Mark E. Neely, Jr., *The Abraham Lincoln Encyclopedia* (New York: McGraw-Hill, 1982), 97–102; Joseph George, Jr., " 'Black Flag Warfare': Lincoln and the Raids Against Richmond and Jefferson Davis," in *The Pennsylvania Magazine of History and Biography*, July 1991, 291–318; William A. Tidwell, *April '65. Confederate Covert Action in the American Civil War* (Kent, Ohio: Kent State University Press, 1995), 107–59; Edward Steers, Jr., *Blood on the Moon* (Lexington: University Press of Kentucky, 2001), 39–46.

*See also:* Canadian Operation; Conspiracy Theories; Dahlgren Papers; Dahlgren Raid; Davis, Jefferson

## Lincoln, Mary Todd (1818–1882)

Wife of Abraham Lincoln. Accompanied Lincoln to Ford's Theatre on night of the assassination. Contrary to modern popular belief, Mary Lincoln did not want to go to the theater on April 14, 1865, but was persuaded by her husband, who she said insisted, as "his mind was fixed upon having some relaxation & bent on the theater."

Mary was born in Lexington, Kentucky, to the wealthy Robert Smith Todd and his first wife, Eliza Parker. Robert Todd fathered a total of fourteen children who lived to adulthood. Mary was one of four girls and two boys, born to Robert's first wife, and five girls and three boys born to her father's second wife, Elizabeth Humphreys. A slave owner living in Kentucky, Robert's family was staunchly pro-Confederate, a situation that caused Mary considerable grief. Her brother George Rogers Clark Todd served as a surgeon in the Confederate army. Three of her half brothers served in the Confederate infantry, and two of her brothers-in-law were Confederate officers. Mary's favorite stepsister, Emilie Todd, married Ben Hardin Helm, a brigadier general in the Confederate army.

Mary's siblings' Confederate connections gave rise to one of the uglier myths attached to her and her husband in the White House. The myth, which first appeared in 1905, told of rumors spreading throughout Washington that Mary was passing military secrets to the Confederacy. Her alleged treasonable behavior resulted in the Joint Committee on the Conduct of the War meeting in secret session to investigate her behavior. Lincoln, upon hearing of the committee's investigation, surprised its members by showing up unannounced to testify on his wife's behalf. The stunned committee members sat silent as Lincoln spoke: "I, Abraham Lincoln, President of the United States appear of my own volition before this committee of the Senate to say that I, of my own knowledge, know that it is untrue that any of my family holds treasonable communication with the enemy."

The entire story is false, having survived in such literary mainstays as Carl Sandburg's monumental biography *Abraham Lincoln: War Years*, and Margaret Leech's award-winning *Reveille in Washington*. Mary Lincoln's loyalty was beyond reproach and she viewed all Confederates as traitors.

The considerable hostility to Mary Lincoln by Confederate sympathizers in Washington was minor compared to Mary's personal grief. In 1862, her twelve-year-old son "Willie" (William Wallace Lincoln) became ill with what was probably typhoid fever and died on February 20. Willie's death pushed Mary to the brink of insanity. She was preyed upon by spiritualists who claimed to be in contact with her son.

Mary was plagued by money matters due to her own behavior, which also brought her husband's wrath on more than one occasion. Despite her change in mood and difficult ways, Mary's husband was able to protect her when necessary and comfort her when she needed it most. On the day of the assassination, Mary and Lincoln took a relaxing carriage ride to southeast Washington. She later remarked that he seemed so cheer-ful, almost playful. With Lee's surrender, it was only a matter of days before the terrible war would finally be over. That evening the couple had planned on attending Ford's Theatre to see the rollicking comedy *Our American Cousin*. Mary had developed another of her headaches and wanted to stay home, but the president told her a night out of relaxation would do them both a world of good. They arrived at the theater late. The play had started a half hour earlier. Making their way up the lobby steps to the Dress Circle, they were greeted by applause from the audience. Making their way to the presidential box, President and Mrs. Lincoln, along with their guests, Major Henry Rathbone and his stepsister and fiancée, Clara Harris, entered the box and took their seats. The president sat in a large rocking chair taken from John Ford's office and set in the box especially for the president. Mary sat in a small padded chair at his side. Near the end of scene 2 in act 3, the lone figure on the stage spoke the lines that would become infamous: "Don't know the manners of good society, eh? Well, I guess I know enough to turn you inside out, old gal—you sockdologizing old man-trap." Mary Lincoln laughed along with the rest of the audience. Suddenly there was a sharp bang. The president slumped forward, his chin dropping down against his chest. A shout. A struggle. Arms flaying. A man scrambled over the balustrade and dropped to the stage. Mary screamed. The president had been shot.

The next several hours were a nightmare for Mary Lincoln. She accompanied her husband's body to the Petersen house across the street from the theater. She was taken to the front parlor, where her son Robert joined her and Mrs. Elizabeth Dixon, a close friend and wife of Senator James Dixon of Connecticut. Her periodic visits to her husband's bedside became difficult. She moaned, cried, and pleaded, to no avail. Finally, Mrs. Dixon was asked to take her to the front parlor and keep her there. Moments before the end she was allowed back in the room for a final visit. The president breathed his last breath at 7:22 on the morning of April 15, 1865. Mary Lincoln's world turned upside down.

His assassination plunged her into deep despair. So distraught was she that she remained in her bedroom secluded from the world outside. She took no part in any of the funeral ceremonies in Washington or Springfield, Illinois, remaining in seclusion.

When she finally emerged from her self-imposed seclusion five weeks after the assassination, she took young Tad and went to Chicago. Although Lincoln had left her financially well-off, Mary Lincoln was beset by money worries in her own mind. She tried to sell some of her elaborate dresses in New York, a humiliating experience. Her trusted friend, Elizabeth Keckley, wrote a book about her life and her experiences in the White House as Mary's confidante. Mary took exception to some of the things Keckley wrote and became embittered, shunning her friend. In 1868 she and Tad went on a trip to Germany and didn't return until 1871, then only to see Tad die from tuberculosis at the young age of eighteen. Mary sank even deeper into despair.

In 1875, her son Robert found it necessary to have his mother committed to a sanitarium. A trial was held and Mary Lincoln was declared insane for purposes of administering her day-to-day living. She was institutionalized for four months, then released. She went to live at the home of her sister, Elizabeth Todd Edwards, and brother-in-law Ninian Edwards in Springfield. She remained in her room secluded as her health worsened. On July 16, 1882, she died. She is buried in a crypt in the Lincoln Monument in Oak Ridge Cemetery in Springfield, Illinois.

Sources: Mark E. Neely, Jr., *The Abraham Lincoln Encyclopedia* (New York: McGraw-Hill, 1982), 180–84; Mary Lincoln, letter to Francis Bicknell Carpenter, November 13, 1865, in Justin G. Turner and Linda Levitt Turner, eds.,

*Mary Todd Lincoln: Her Life and Letters* (New York: Fromm International, 1987), 283–85; Edward Steers, Jr., *Blood on the Moon* (Lexington: University Press of Kentucky, 2001), 119–34.

## Lincoln, Robert Todd (1843–1926)

Oldest of four sons of Abraham and Mary Lincoln. Robert was a captain serving on the staff of General Ulysses S. Grant, and had visited his parents at the White House following Robert E. Lee's surrender on April 9, 1865. Invited to accompany his parents to Ford's Theatre on April 14, Robert declined, saying he was extremely tired and wanted to get a good night's sleep.

Robert, preparing to retire for the night, was told by C. C. Bangs, a member of the Christian Commission (similar to the modern Red Cross), that his father had been shot and that his mother wanted him to come back with him to the Petersen house right away. He spent the rest of the night trying to comfort his mother and stayed by the bedside while his father's life slipped away.

With his mother refusing to leave her bedroom in the White House for weeks, Robert was present at all of the ceremonies in the East Room of the White House and the U.S. Capitol. Robert accompanied his father's body on the long, mournful train ride back to Springfield, Illinois.

With the death of young Tad in 1871, Mary Lincoln's behavior grew more and more erratic. In 1875, Robert, consulting with two of his father's closest friends, John T. Stuart and David Davis, had his mother tried in court for insanity. The court ruled her insane and she was committed to a private sanitarium, where she remained for four months before being released to the custody of Ninian Edwards and his wife. Robert and his mother remained estranged until 1882, when she made peace with Robert.

After the war, Robert practiced law. In 1881, President James Garfield appointed Robert secretary of war. In 1884 and again in 1888 there were movements to gain Robert the Republican nomination for president, but both failed. The following year, President Benjamin Harrison appointed him ambassador to England. Robert returned to his law practice in 1893 and stayed there until 1897, when he became the president of the Pullman Company, which he led until 1911.

Always mindful of his father's image, Robert agreed to help John G. Nicolay and John Hay write their monumental biography of Lincoln, giving them access to Lincoln's private papers but censoring what they could print. He willed the papers to the Library of Congress with the stipulation they not be made public until twenty-one years after his death. Robert's personal life had its share of tragedy. Losing his father to an assassin, his three brothers to disease, his mother's insanity and estrangement, his wife's suffering from neurasthenia (chronic fatigue and depression), and his only son, Jack, dying from blood poisoning as a young boy all plagued Robert throughout his adult life.

Robert retired to a beautiful home in Georgetown and spent his summers at his summer home, Hildene, in Manchester, Vermont. He lived long enough to attend the dedication of the Lincoln Memorial in Washington in 1922. Robert Lincoln died in 1926 and is buried in Arlington National Cemetery along with his son Abraham "Jack" Lincoln.

Sources: Mark E. Neely, Jr., *The Abraham Lincoln Encyclopedia* (New York: McGraw-Hill, 1982), 184–86.

## Lincoln, Thomas "Tad" (1853–1871)

The Lincolns' youngest surviving son at the time of the assassination. Named after Abraham Lincoln's father, the boy was given the nickname "Tad" as a baby because his father said his large head made him look like a tadpole. Twelve-year-old Tad was at the Grover's National Theatre a few blocks from Ford's, watching the magical play, *Aladdin! Or,*

the Wonderful Lamp. Alphonso Donn, the White House doorkeeper and a favorite of Tad, had taken him to the theater. Tad learned of his father's assassination when the theater manager, C. Dwight Hess, interrupted the play to notify the audience. Donn took the grief-stricken young boy back to the White House, where he took care of the boy until Mary Lincoln returned the next morning.

The Lincoln children were overindulged by their parents, having the run of the White House much to the displeasure of the workers and guests. Following older brother Willie's death in 1862, his parents were even more lenient on Tad. He basically did whatever pleased him. At times he was charming and at other times he was a little terror. Unable to read or write at an age when other children could, Tad was protected by his parents, who looked after his every care or want. After his father's death, Mary Lincoln kept him close to her at all times. With Robert away, Tad was all Mary had left of her once-vibrant family. Two of her children had died in childhood and her husband had been murdered as he sat by her side.

Mary Lincoln took Tad to Germany when she visited that country from 1868 to 1870. Spending part of 1871 in England, she returned to the United States with an increasingly ill Tad. A few months after their return, Tad died of what was believed to be tuberculosis. He was buried in the family crypt in Oak Ridge Cemetery in Springfield, Illinois.

Sources: Mark E. Neely, Jr., *The Abraham Lincoln Encyclopedia* (New York: McGraw-Hill, 1982), 188–89.

## Lincoln Flag

An American flag made of wool bunting and measuring twelve feet, nine inches by eight feet, eight inches is believed to have been in the president's box at Ford's Theatre on the night of the assassination. Family tradition claims that Ford's stage manager, Thomas C. Gourlay, who was also a member of the cast performing *Our American Cousin*, found the flag in the box and used it to cradle the president's head both in the box and while carrying him across the street to the Petersen house. Mr. Gourlay retrieved the flag and took it home, keeping it as a precious relic of the events of that night. The flag passed to Jeannie Gourlay Struthers on Thomas Gourlay's death. Jeannie Gourlay's only son, Vivian Paul Struthers, donated the flag to the Pike County Historical Society in Milford, Pennsylvania, in 1954. It is on permanent display there.

Sources: Joseph E. Garrera, *The Lincoln Flag of the Pike County Historical Society* (privately printed, 1996); Edward Steers, Jr., *Blood on the Moon* (Lexington: University Press of Kentucky, 2001), 121–22.

*See also:* Gourlay, Thomas; Treasury Guard Flags

**Lincoln Funeral**
Shortly after Abraham Lincoln died in the Petersen House across the street from Ford's Theatre, Secretary of War Edwin Stanton sent for a contingent of soldiers from the Veteran Reserve Corps to escort the body back to the White House. Arriving at the White House mid-morning the body was taken upstairs to one of the guest rooms where it was carefully placed on a table that had been es-pecially set up for the autopsy. Following the autopsy, the body was turned over to Charles D. Brown of the Washington undertaking firm of Brown & Alexander. The body was cleaned and embalmed, and then dressed under Secretary of War Edwin Stanton's supervision using the same Brooks Brothers suit Lincoln wore at his second inaugural.

The first of several funeral services was scheduled for Wednesday noon on April 19 in the great East Room of the White House. Assistant Secretary of the Treasury George A. Harrington was selected for supervising the overall procedures for the funeral. Under Harrington's guidance, a team of carpenters built a large catafalque in the center of the room to hold the president's coffin. After allowing the public to pass through the building and view the president the carpenters reentered that same evening and working all night built a series of raised steps around the edge of the room allowing the dignitaries to be able to view the catafalque and funeral service scheduled for the next day.

Shortly after 11:00 A.M. selected officers of the government, members of the Senate and House, state governors, prominent members of the military, the diplomatic corps, foreign representatives, and members of various committees and commissions entered the great room and took their places on the el-

Funeral procession on Broadway, New York City

evated steps. At 12 M. President Andrew Johnson entered followed by his cabinet, and sixty members of the clergy. Reverend Thomas, pastor of Epiphany Episcopal Church in Washington, began the formal service reading from the Gospel of St. John, "I am the Resurrection and the Life saith the Lord; he that believeth in Me, though he were dead, yet shall live, and whosoever liveth and believeth in Me shall never die."

Timed to coincide precisely with the beginning of the service in the White House, churches all across the Northern states began their own services. At the end of the service in the White House the casket was placed on a hearse drawn by six white horses, and taken to the U.S. Capitol where it was placed on a second catafalque and once again the public made its way slowly past the coffin to view their dead president.

On April 21, the casket was escorted to the Baltimore & Ohio Railroad's Depot located a few blocks north of the Capitol where it was carried aboard the special funeral car and locked onto another catafalque where it would rest during the long trip back to Springfield.

A few minutes past 9:00 o'clock on the morning of May 1, after an arduous trip of 1,664 miles taking thirteen days, the train arrived in Springfield. The casket was escorted to Oak Ridge Cemetery on the outskirts of Springfield. Leading the procession was a military escort consisting of members selected from several units of the army. These were followed by the "surgeons and physicians of the deceased," the Guard of Honor, and the hearse. In an added touch of sentimentality, Lincoln's favorite horse, "Old Bob," draped in a large black blanket with silver fringe followed the hearse. Next were members of the family (Mary Lincoln remained absent still in deep mourning), then more military, civil authorities, religious groups, Free Masons, Fraternities,

Firemen, and last, "Colored Persons."

The ceremony was held at the public vault where Lincoln's coffin, along with that of his young son, Willie, who died while in the White House, was stored until an appropriate memorial could be erected. The service opened with a prayer followed by a hymn and several scriptural readings. Lincoln's second inaugural address was then read to the gatherers followed by the funeral oration delivered by Methodist Bishop Matthew Simpson, one of America's leading religious figures. Simpson told the attentive crowd that no person, "so identified with the heart of the people—and the people knew it." Reverend Phineas Gurley, pastor of the Lincolns' church in Washington offered a closing prayer bringing an end to the long, emotional trip that led from Washington to Springfield over twenty days and 1,664 miles.

Lincoln's body, like John Wilkes Booth's, was moved several times before coming to permanent rest. Following an aborted attempt to steal Lincoln's body, it was placed in a special grave beneath the massive memorial and covered with tons of cement encased in steel bars assuring everyone that Lincoln's body was forever beyond reach.

Sources: Edward Steers, Jr., *Blood on the Moon* (Lexington: University Press of Kentucky, 2001), 268–93; Thomas J. Craughwell, *Stealing Lincoln's*

*Body* (Cambridge, Massachusetts: The Belknap Press of Harvard University Press, 2007).

*See also*: Funeral Train

## Lincoln Rocker

The rocking chair President Lincoln was sitting in at the time he was shot by John Wilkes Booth. The chair was part of the furniture in John Ford's office complex in Ford's Theatre. Harry Clay Ford had the chair carried from the office to the presidential box, where it was placed inside the door to box 7 in the narrow angle of the box.

The chair was confiscated by the military on April 22. It was kept in Secretary of War Edwin M. Stanton's office until 1867, then removed to the Department of Interior. The chair was then sent to the Smithsonian Institution. It was on display in the Petersen house along with the collection of Osborn H. Oldroyd from 1893 until 1896, when it was placed in storage.

In 1927, Harry Clay Ford's widow, Blanche Chapman Ford, asked the government to return the chair, since it was still the property of the Fords. The government refused and Mrs. Ford filed a lawsuit demanding its return. She was awarded the chair and offered to sell it to Henry Ford for his museum in Dearborn, Michigan. Presumably feeling her asking price too high, Ford declined and Mrs. Ford then placed it in an auction. Henry Ford's representative was the winning bidder at $2,400. Henry Ford placed it on display at the Ford Museum in Dearborn, where it remains today.

The chair on display at Ford's Theatre is a replica. The stains that appear on the rocking chair at head level were caused by hair grease, not Lincoln's blood, which many people have assumed.

Sources: Frederick Hatch, "Lincoln Assassination Encyclopedia," unpublished manuscript.

## Lindsley, George G.

Sergeant in Company D, First Delaware Cavalry, stationed at Monocacy Junction near Frederick, Maryland. He reported information on whereabouts of George Atzerodt to his superior, Captain Solomon Townsend. On Wednesday, April 19, Private Frank O'Daniel, also of the First Delaware, traveled to Clarksburg, a small farm community located in Montgomery County, Maryland. While there he learned from James Purdom, a local farmer serving as an army informant, that George Atwood (George Atzerodt) was talking freely about Lincoln's assassination and it sounded as if the man had inside knowledge of the events surrounding the murder. O'Daniel returned to camp that same evening and passed the information he received from Purdom to Sergeant Lindsley, who reported it to Captain Townsend. The captain did nothing at first, but on reflection decided to send a troop of six men under the command of Sergeant Zachariah Gemmill to the Richter house and arrest the suspicious man and bring him to Monocacy Junction. Gemmill and his men road to Purdom's house and with Purdom as their guide arrived at the Richter house early Thursday morning before dawn and arrested Atzerodt and Richter, along with two laborers, Somerset and James Leaman. Lindsley did not share in the reward money offered for Atzerodt's arrest.

Sources: Statement of Sergeant George Lindsley, NARA, RG 153, M-599, reel 2, frames 233–34.

## Lloyd, John M. (1824–1892)

Lloyd leased the Surrattsville tavern from Mary Surratt for six hundred dollars a year when she moved into Washington, D.C. He became the principal witness against her during the conspiracy trial in 1865. In November 1864, Mary Surratt decided to lease the tavern in Surrattsville and move her family to the house at 541 H Street in Washington. It was a move that cost her her life.

Following the aborted attempt to kidnap Lincoln after a performance at Campbell Hospital in Washington, John Surratt left two carbines, a box of ammunition, a monkey wrench, and a length of rope with John Lloyd, telling him to hide the items among the rafters over the kitchen.

On April 11, three days before the assassination, Mary Surratt asked Louis Wiechmann, one of her boarders in Washington, to take her to the tavern in Surrattsville. She wanted to speak with John Nothey about a debt he owed her. On the way to the tavern, Wiechmann and Mary Surratt met John Lloyd coming from the other direction and heading toward Washington. The two buggies stopped, and according to

Wiechmann, Mary spoke in hushed or guarded tones to Lloyd. While Wiechmann was not sure of what was said during the conversation, Lloyd testified that Mary Surratt told him to have the "shooting irons" (carbines) ready as persons would come by soon to pick them up. After the two parted, Mary continued on to the tavern, where she sent word to Nothey. Nothey came to the tavern and Mary presumably asked him for the money due her for seventy-five acres of land her husband had sold him several years earlier.

On April 14, the day of the assassination, Mary again asked Wiechmann to take her to the tavern so she could attempt to collect her money from Nothey. Before leaving Washington, John Wilkes Booth stopped by Mary Surratt's H Street boardinghouse with a small package he asked her to carry to the tavern and give to John Lloyd. Wiechmann agreed and the two reached Surrattsville around 4:30 P.M. Lloyd was away in Upper Marlboro, Maryland, attending a trial. Nothey was not at the tavern and Mary made no attempt to meet with him. Instead she waited for Lloyd to return from Upper Marlboro, which he did a little after 5:00 P.M. Lloyd later testified that once again Mary told him to have the shooting irons ready and this time was more specific, telling Lloyd that "there will be parties here to-night who will call for them." Lloyd also said that the package Mary carried from Booth contained a field glass, which he was also to give to Booth.

Lloyd's testimony was especially damaging to Mary Surratt's defense. Unknown to prosecutors at the time, but subsequently revealed in a statement to Maryland provost marshal James McPhail, was Atzerodt's statement that "Booth told me that Mrs. Surratt went to Surrattsville to get out the guns which had been taken to that place [Surratt Tavern] by Herold [and John Surratt on March 17]." While Mary told authorities she wanted to collect the debt owed to her, she delivered the field glass and the message that resulted in her conviction. Both were important pieces of evidence used by the prosecution to prove she had gone to Surrattsville at Booth's behest.

Sources: Statement of J. M. Lloyd, NARA, RG 153, M-599, reel 4, frame 45; Poore, *Conspiracy Trial*, vol. 1, 115, 137; Pitman, *Trial*, 85, 87; Statement of John M. Lloyd, NARA, RG 153, M-599, reel 5, frames 148–83; Statement of John M. Lloyd, NARA, RG 153, M-599, reel 2, frames 199–209; Edward Steers, Jr., *Blood on the Moon* (Lexington: University Press of Kentucky, 2001), 139–43.

## Lloyd, Joshua

A detective on the staff of Major James O'Beirne, a District of Columbia provost marshal. On Sunday, April 16, O'Beirne sent Captain George Cottingham and detective Lloyd to Surrattsville, Maryland, to search the area since he had learned that John Surratt and David Herold frequently visited the area. It was Joshua Lloyd who advised O'Beirne that the two men were seen around that area.

After tracking down John Lloyd (no relation) and arresting him, they sent word back to O'Beirne for more men to help them canvas the area. O'Beirne sent a contingent of troopers from the Provisional cavalry. These men wound up in Bryantown, Maryland, where they joined the contingent from the 13th New York Cavalry that arrived there Saturday noon.

On Tuesday, April 18, Lloyd accompanied Lieutenant Alexander Lovett to the Mudd farm, where they interviewed both Mrs. Mudd and Samuel Mudd. He visited the Mudds again on Friday, April 21, and interviewed them a second time. As a result of the two interviews Mudd was asked to come to Bryantown on Saturday, April 22, and meet with Colonel Henry H. Wells. As a result of these meetings, Mudd prepared a written statement and signed a second statement summarizing his answers to the interviews he gave to the detectives. Mudd was arrested on Monday, April 24, and taken back to Washington, where he was held in the Carroll Annex of the Old Capitol Prison.

Lloyd testified at the conspiracy trial about the interviews with Mudd. He clearly supported the prosecution position that Mudd had lied repeatedly during his interviews and described Mudd as "very much excited" at the time Booth's boot was discovered at the Mudd house.

Sources: Testimony of Joshua Lloyd, Poore, *Conspiracy Trial*, vol. 1, 273–81; Pitman, *Trial*, 90.

## Lost Confession of George A. Atzerodt

Statement of George A. Atzerodt sequestered by his attorney, William E. Doster. On May 1, 1865, while in custody aboard the monitor USS *Montauk*, George Atzerodt gave a seven-page statement to Maryland provost marshal James L. McPhail that was recorded by McPhail's assistant John L. Smith. This statement is the "confession" referred to by McPhail during his testimony concerning Atzerodt. The statement disappeared, only to surface in 1977 among the personal papers of William E. Doster, Atzerodt's attorney.

Atzerodt clearly implicates Dr. Samuel Mudd and Mary Surratt with the statements "I am certain Dr. Mudd knew all about it, as Booth sent (as he told me) liquors & provisions for the trip with the President to Richmond, about two weeks before the murder to Dr. Mudd's" and "Booth told me that Mrs. Surratt went to Surrattsville to get out the guns (two carbines) which had been taken to that place by Herold, this was Friday."

Joan L. Chaconas, a past president of the Surratt Society and Lincoln Group of the District of Columbia, discovered the handwritten statement during her research. The complete statement was published in the *Surratt Courier*, the newsletter of the Surratt Society located in Clinton, Maryland, and in Edward Steers, Jr., *His Name Is Still Mudd*. The statement is currently in a private collection.

Sources: Testimony of James L. McPhail, Poore, *Conspiracy Trial*, vol. 1, 396; Pitman, *Trial*, 148; Edward Steers, Jr., *His Name Is Still Mudd* (Gettysburg, Pa.: Thomas, 1997), Appendix 6.

## Lucas, Charley

Son of William Lucas. After spending the night in the cabin of William Lucas, Booth paid Lucas's wife twenty dollars to have her son drive Booth and Herold to Port Conway, Virginia, on the Rappahannock River. Lucas was a free black who lived a short distance from Dr. Richard Stuart's house in King George County, Virginia. Stuart refused to put Booth and Herold up for the night, but sent them to Lucas's cabin located a short distance away, where the two men spent the night of Sunday, April 23. Charley Lucas used his father's farm wagon and took the two men to Port Conway, arriving shortly before noon on Monday, April 24.

Sources: Statement of William Lucas, NARA, RG 153, M-599, reel 5, frames 144–47; William A. Tidwell, James O. Hall, and David W. Gaddy, *Come Retribution* (Jackson: University Press of Mississippi, 1988).

*See also*: Lucas, William

## Lucas, William

A free black whose cabin was located near the summer home of Dr. Richard Stuart in King George County, Virginia. On Sunday afternoon, April 23, Booth and Herold were led to the summer home of Dr. Stuart. After being turned away by Stuart, who refused to let the two men sleep in his already crowded house, Booth and Herold were taken to the cabin of William Lucas. Booth ordered Lucas, his wife, and son Charley out of their cabin so he and Herold could sleep there. On the morning of April 24, Booth and Herold awoke and offered Lucas twenty dollars to take them to Port Conway in Lucas's farm wagon. After a heated discussion, Charley Lucas agreed to drive the pair the ten miles to Port Conway, on the Rappahannock River.

Sources: Statement of William Lucas, NARA, RG 153, M-599, reel 5, frames 144–47.

*See also:* Lucas, Charley

## Lynch, Joseph

Dealer in rare manuscripts and Americana. Lynch claimed to have discovered the whereabouts of the alleged missing pages from Booth's diary in the possession of one of Secretary of War Edwin M. Stanton's great-granddaughters. Never able to produce a single original page from the little memorandum book, the only thing Lynch could provide was a typescript of the pages. On examination the typescript contained substantive errors that easily showed the missing pages to be fabrications from a highly imaginative mind. Even so, the pages were the stuff that conspiracy buffs relish and the rights to use the material were purchased by David Balsiger and Charles E. Sellier, Jr. of Sunn Classic Pictures. The price was allegedly thirty-nine thousand dollars. The final product was a paperback book and movie, *The Lincoln Conspiracies,* both released in October 1977. The conclusion drawn from the typed pages was the age-old plot whereby Lincoln's secretary of war, Edwin M. Stanton, in cahoots with northern financiers and businessmen as well as greedy politicians, needed Lincoln out of the way so they could plunder the reconstructed South. Who better to accomplish this than John Wilkes Booth? The story is a modern retread of Otto Eisenschiml's 1937 trashy work, *Why Was Lincoln Murdered?*

Lynch faded from the scene and died before he could produce the actual missing pages. There were no missing pages. The only recourse conspiracy buffs have now is to find a spiritualist who is able to communicate with Lynch's spirit and convince him to reveal the name and whereabouts of Stanton's great-granddaughter in the hope of convincing her to release the original pages so historians can pass final judgment. Don't hold your breath.

Sources: Richard Sloan, "The Case of the Missing Pages," *Journal of the Lincoln Assassination* 9, no. 3 (December 1995), 38–44; Edward Steers, Jr., "The Missing Pages from Booth's Diary," in *Lincoln Legends: Myths, Hoaxes, and Confabulations Associated with Our Greatest President* (Lexington: University Press of Kentucky, 2007), 177–202.

*See also:* Balsiger, David, and Charles E. Sellier, Jr.

## Lynch, Thomas

Thomas Lynch was a Springfield, Illinois, undertaker who was invited by Dr. Charles D. Brown to assist in preparing Lincoln's body for viewing in Springfield. According to Lynch, Lincoln's features had become severely discolored, requiring him to apply a mixture of chalk and rouge "coloring the President's features."

Source: Dorothy Meserve Kunhardt and Philip B. Kunhardt, Jr., *Twenty Days* (New York: Harper & Row, 1965).

*See also*: Brown, Dr. Charles D.

## M-599

The designation given to the National Archives microfilm publication *Investigation and Trial Papers Relating to the Assassination of President Lincoln*. The file consists of sixteen reels of microfilm relating to the investigation of persons suspected of having participated in the assassination of President Lincoln. Reels 1 through 7 contain all of the evidence collected by various individuals and agencies and used by the government in prosecuting the case. Reels 8 through 15 consist of the trial proceedings, exhibits, and final argument of Special Judge Advocate John A. Bingham. Reel 16 contains issues of the Washington, D.C., *Daily National Intelligencer* from May 16 through June 30, 1865, carrying verbatim transcripts of the trial proceedings. The majority of records are dated between April 15 and July 3, 1865. The records are filed in Record Group 153, the Records of the Office of the Judge Advocate General (Army).

By Sunday, April 16, 1865, evidence was coming in so fast and in such volume that it was difficult to manage. Secretary of War Edwin M. Stanton solved the problem by appointing three officers with investigative experience from the War Department to take charge of the incoming evidence: Colonel Henry H. Wells, Lieutenant Colonel John A. Foster, and Colonel Henry S. Olcott. Stanton then sent a telegram to Colonel Henry L. Burnett, judge advocate in the Northern Department with headquarters in Cincinnati, directing him to come to Washington immediately to take charge of the evidence and assist in the prosecution of the conspirators.

The appointment of Burnett was most likely at the request of Judge Advocate General Joseph Holt; the man who would prosecute the case against Lincoln's accused killers. Stanton turned over the investigation to Holt, a man he had complete confidence in. Holt and Burnett had worked together on several important trials in Indianapolis and developed a deep respect for each other's capabilities. Holt made it Burnett's responsibility to sift through all of the material pouring into the War Department and select the evidence needed to prosecute the case.

Sources: Pamphlet Accompanying Microcopy No. 599, *Investigation and Trial Papers Relating to the Assassination of President Lincoln* (Washington, D.C.: National Archives and Records Service, General Services Administration, 1965); Kenneth W. Munden and Henry Putney Beers, eds., *The Union: A Guide to Federal Archives Relating to the Civil War* (Washington, D.C.: National Archives and Records Administration, 1962).

*See also:* Burnett, Henry L.

## M-619

The letter and numerical designation given to the National Archives and Records Administration microfilm publication containing the records of the Commission on Rewards for the Apprehension of Lincoln Assassins and Others. The file consists of four reels of microfilm designated 455–58. The files appear in Record Group 94, Records of the Adjutant General's Office.

The government offered reward money in the amount of one hundred thousand dollars for the apprehension of those implicated in the assassination of President Lincoln. So many individuals and conflicting claims were made that the Adjutant General's Office issued an order directing all persons having claims on the reward money should file their claim along with proof with the office before January 1, 1866. Reward money was offered for the apprehension of John Wilkes Booth, Lewis Payne (Powell), George Atzerodt, David Herold, and Jefferson Davis. A commission was formed to review the claims and recommend which claims were valid and how the money was to be distributed. The commission consisted of Assistant Adjutant General Edward D. Townsend and Judge Advocate General Joseph Holt. The total amount of reward money awarded was $105,000.

Sources: Kenneth W. Munden and Henry Putney Beers, eds., *The Union: A Guide to Federal Archives Relating to the Civil War* (Washington, D.C.: National Archives and Records Administration, 1962).

*See also:* Reward Money

## Maddox, James L.

Property manager at Ford's Theatre and later a prosecution witness at the conspiracy trial. Maddox was standing backstage at Ford's Theatre with one of the sceneshifters when he heard the shot from Booth's derringer. His eyewitness account offers little to the event of Lincoln's assassination. He testified at the conspiracy trial about Edman Spangler's movements.

Earlier in the afternoon of April 14, Maddox and William J. Fergueson went with Booth to the Star Saloon located next door to Ford's to have a drink. Maddox testified at the conspirators' trial that he arranged to rent a small stable behind Ford's for Booth to keep his horse. He also testified that he saw Joe Simms (a Ford employee) carry a rocking chair from John Ford's office to the box. He also said that the passageway by which Booth escaped was normally kept clear and not obstructed. Maddox told the court that Spangler was in his proper position as a sceneshifter, and that if Spangler had left and gone somewhere else he would have noticed his absence.

Sources: Edward Steers, Jr., ed., *The Trial* (Lexington: University Press of Kentucky, 2003), 75–76; Timothy S. Good, *We Saw Lincoln Shot: One Hundred Eyewitness Accounts* (Jackson: University Press of Mississippi, 1995), 90–91.

*See also:* Spangler, Edman

## Mahoney, Ella V.

Author of the book *Sketches of Tudor Hall and the Booth Family* (1925). In 1878, Ella Mahoney and her husband purchased the Booth home, Tudor Hall, in Bel Air, Maryland, from Mary Ann Booth, Junius Brutus Booth's wife and the mother of John Wilkes Booth. In her little book, Mahoney describes the building and its history as well as that of the grounds. Mahoney then attempts to relate the story of Lincoln's assassination and Booth's escape and capture, and refutes the claim that Booth escaped and was not killed in the Garretts' tobacco barn, all subjects she was ill equipped to discuss.

Sources: Ella V. Mahoney, *Sketches of Tudor Hall and the Booth Family* (Bel Air, Md.: Privately printed, 1925).

*See also:* Tudor Hall

## Mail Line

A route running from Washington, D.C., through Prince George's and Charles counties, Maryland, across the Potomac River to Virginia and the capital of the Confederacy, Richmond. Local people working as Confederate agents serviced the line. Intelligence was vital to the success of the Confederacy. A communications link was necessary between Richmond and points as far north as Canada. Charles County became a key conduit to the Confederacy's communications link. Within months of the outbreak of war, a "mail line" had been established that ran from the southern boundary of Charles County north to Washington and beyond. This line ran due north from Richmond through Bowling Green and Port Royal on the Rappahannock River to a spot on the Virginia side of the river near Mathias Point. Here it crossed the river and continued on just east of Port Tobacco, Maryland, to Surrattsville. From Surrattsville it made its way directly into Washington.

Closely attending these routes were the prominent leaders of Charles County, men whose names would have slipped into obscurity had it not been for John Wilkes Booth. Principal among them were Thomas Jones, William Queen, Samuel Cox, Thomas Harbin, and Samuel Mudd. All five men would become intimate with Booth and his plan to capture Lincoln, and Mudd, Cox, Jones, and Harbin would aid Booth in his attempt to escape.

Thomas Jones, the chief agent in Charles County, had labored long and hard in service to the Confederate cause as the person in charge of the mail route, and in ferrying people across the Potomac River to Virginia. John H. Surratt, Jr. was also key to the operation of the mail line. He lived in Prince George's County, although he used the Mudd home as well as the Surratt Tavern as "safe" stops when traveling along the mail line.

Sources: David W. Gaddy, "The Surratt Tavern—A Confederate 'Safe House?,'" in Laurie Verge, ed., *In Pursuit of . . . Continuing Research in the Field of the Lincoln Assassination* (Clinton, Md.: Surratt Society, 1990), 129; Edward Steers, Jr., "Maryland My Maryland," in *North & South* 6, no. 2 (February 2003), 42–51.

## Marble Heart, The

*The Marble Heart* was a play performed at Ford's Theatre on November 9, 1863, starring John Wilkes Booth. President Lincoln attended the performance and was seated in the presidential box. It is the only known instance that Lincoln witnessed Booth on the stage. Booth performed that year at Ford's from November 2 through November 14, appearing in twelve plays, including playing Richard III on two of those occasions.

Source: George J. Olszewski, *Historic Structures Report: Restoration of Ford's Theatre* (Washington, D.C.: U.S. Government Printing Office, 1963), 109.

## Martin, Patrick Charles (1817–1864)

A blockade-runner and Confederate agent located in Montreal who helped Booth assemble his team of conspirators. On October 18, John Wilkes Booth traveled to Montreal, where he registered at the St. Lawrence Hall. The hotel was home to several Confederate agents working out of Canada. Among these agents was Patrick C. Martin. Booth was in Montreal for ten days, from October 18 through the 27th. During that time he was seen meeting with Martin and another agent, George N. Sanders. Martin, a former liquor merchant from Baltimore, gave Booth letters of introduction to two Charles County men, Drs. William Queen and Samuel Mudd. Two weeks later, on November 11, Booth made his first trip to Charles County, where he was introduced to Samuel Mudd at St. Mary's Church near Bryantown. He was introduced to Mudd by Queen's son-in-law, John C. Thompson, using Martin's letter of introduction as an entree.

Booth's trip to Montreal and his receiving a letter of introduction to Samuel Mudd is important. It ties both Booth and Mudd to the Confederate operation in Montreal. For a letter of introduction to have had any significance, Mudd must have known Martin and Martin must have known Mudd. Booth's meeting with Mudd was key to Booth's kidnap conspiracy. Mudd arranged for Booth to meet John Surratt and Thomas Harbin. It was Surratt who brought Atzerodt and Powell into Booth's conspiracy.

Before Booth left Montreal, he made arrangements with Martin to ship his trunk of theatrical costumes south aboard one of Martin's schooners, the *Marie Victoria*. The ship was destroyed in a violent storm, and everyone aboard drowned, including Patrick Martin. Booth's trunk was later recovered and sent to Edwin Booth. Edwin burned the trunk and its contents.

Sources: William A. Tidwell, James O. Hall, and David W. Gaddy, *Come Retribution* (Jackson: University Press of Mississippi, 1988), 330–31.

*See also:* Letter of Introduction; Mudd, Dr. Samuel Alexander

## Mathews, John (1836–1905)

An actor and close friend of John Wilkes Booth. Booth had approached Mathews in January attempting to convince him

to join his kidnap plan, but Mathews refused. Booth was angry with Mathews, later calling him a coward. His anger subsided and on the afternoon of the assassination Booth gave Mathews a letter he had written earlier in the day justifying his killing Lincoln. He asked Mathews to give it to the editor of the *Daily National Intelligencer* the next day (Saturday, April 15). On hearing of Lincoln's murder by Booth, Mathews read the letter, then burned it, fearing he would be implicated with Booth. Sixteen years later, Mathews would attempt to reconstruct the letter from memory for an article published in the *Washington Evening Star* of December 7, 1881. The reconstructed letter is nearly identical to Booth's "To Whom It May Concern" letter that Booth wrote in November 1864 and gave to his sister Asia Booth Clarke to hold for safekeeping. It is not likely that Mathews could have remembered the content of the letter sixteen years later. He in all likelihood used the text of Booth's "To Whom It May Concern" letter to reconstruct the burned letter.

Sources: Statement of John Mathews, NARA, RG 153, M-599, reel 5, frames 302–14; John Rhodehamel and Louise Taper, *"Right or Wrong, God Judge Me"* (Urbana: University of Illinois Press, 1997).

*See also:* "To Whom It May Concern" letter.

## May, Dr. John Frederick (1812–1891)

Doctor who operated on John Wilkes Booth and was asked to identify the body on board the USS *Montauk* following the assassin's death at the Garrett farm in Virginia. May examined the corpse and identified it as that of John Wilkes Booth. May relied in part on a unique scar on Booth's neck.

In 1863, approximately eighteen months prior to his death, Booth came to Dr. May about a medical problem. He had developed a bothersome lump on his neck on the left rear side, approximately three inches below the base of the skull. It was an annoyance as well as a disfigurement, and so Booth sought May's advice. May examined the lump and told Booth it was a "fibroid tumor." He said it should be removed. Booth agreed. The minor operation resulted in a fine linear incision, which May cautioned Booth to protect so that it could heal properly. A few days after the removal, Booth returned to May's office. The new scar had been torn open, leaving "a broad, ugly-looking scar, produced by the granulating process." The scar took on a distinctive appearance and so served as an identifying characteristic.

Certainly the scar was obvious to anyone carefully examining the body, as it lay stretched out on the monitor. Dr. May was asked to come to the Navy Yard to identify a body. Arriving on board the ship, May and his young son, William, were met by Surgeon General Joseph K. Barnes. Barnes escorted the two over to the table where Booth's body had been laid out under a tarpaulin. Before exposing the body, Dr. May described the identifying scar to Barnes. May told Barnes that if the body under that tarpaulin was the body of John Wilkes Booth, there would be a scar on the back of his neck, and described its unusual appearance. Barnes replied, "You have described the scar as well as if you were looking at it." The judge advocate general then questioned May while still on board the monitor:

> Q. Do you recognize the body as that of J. Wilkes Booth from its general appearance, and also from the particular appearance of the scar?
> A. I do recognize it, though it is very much altered since I saw Booth. It looks to me much older, and in appearance much more freckled than he was. I have no doubt it is his body. I recognize the features.

In January 1887, Dr. May wrote an essay titled "The Mark of the Scalpel." In it he recounted his experiences of Booth coming to his office and of his removing the fibroid tumor, the resulting scar altered by the vigorous hug of Charlotte Cushman, and of positively identifying the unusual scar that resulted. May then gave the proponents of the conspiracy theory more fuel for their smoky fire. He said the corpse had a broken *right* leg. Of course it was Booth's left leg that was broken, not his right leg. The conspiracy theorists who claim Booth escaped thus seized on May's error and used it to shore up their erroneous theory. Forget the scar, the black hair, the physical appearance; and the tattoo "JWB" on Booth's hand. And yet, May was asked point blank, "Do you recognize the body as that of J. Wilkes Booth . . . ?" May answered, "I do recognize it. I have no doubt it is his body."

Sources: John Frederick May, *The Mark of the Scalpel* (Washington, D.C.: Columbia Historical Society, 1910); Statement of John Frederick May, NARA, RG 153, M-599, reel 4, frames 361–65.

## McDevitt, James (1836–1912)

A Washington, D.C., Metropolitan Police detective. McDevitt, having received a tip that John Surratt and John Wilkes Booth were friends and often seen together, took detectives John Clarvoe, Daniel Bigby, and John Kelly with him to the boardinghouse at 541 H Street looking for John Surratt. It was two o'clock on Saturday morning, just three and a half hours since Lincoln was shot. McDevitt searched the house thoroughly for any sign of John Surratt or Booth but came up dry. One and a half days later, Colonel Henry H. Wells sent Captain William M. Wermerskirch and three other military detectives to the Surratt boardinghouse with orders to arrest everyone in the house. Wells acted on a tip from Susan Mahoney Jackson, a black servant who had been working for Mary Surratt. While the detectives were gathering up the boarders, Lewis Powell showed up and was arrested as well.

Sources: Testimony of John McDevitt, Poore, *Conspiracy Trial*, vol. 3, 381–82; Pitman, *Trial*, 140; Edward Steers, Jr., *Blood on the Moon* (Lexington: University Press of Kentucky, 2001), 173–75.

*See also:* Jackson, Susan Mahoney; Wermerskirch, William M.

## McGowan, Theodore

Captain Theodore McGowan of the Veteran Reserve Corps sat in a chair in the rear of the Dress Circle of Ford's Theatre when John Wilkes Booth approached the president's box. As Booth attempted to approach the closed door he found his path blocked by McGowan. The officer pulled his chair forward, making room for Booth to pass by. McGowan, called as a witness for the prosecution, recalled what took place:

I was sitting in the aisle leading by the wall toward the door of the President's box, when a man came and disturbed me in my seat, causing me to push my chair forward to permit him to pass; he stopped about three feet from where I was sitting, and leisurely took a survey of the house.... He took a small pack of visiting-cards from his pocket, selecting one and replacing the others, stood a second, perhaps, with it in his hand, and then showed it to the President's messenger [Charles Forbes], who was sitting just below him. Whether the messenger took the card into the box, or, after looking at it, allowed him to go in, I do not know; but, in a moment or two more, I saw him go through the door of the lobby leading to the box, and close the door.... I know J. Wilkes Booth, but, not seeing the face of the assassin fully, I did not at the time recognize him as Booth.

Sources: Testimony of Theodore McGowan, Poore, *Conspiracy Trial*, vol. 1, 194; Pitman, *Trial*, 78; Timothy Good, *We Saw Lincoln Shot: One Hundred Eyewitness Accounts* (Jackson: University Press of Mississippi, 1995), 80–81.

*See also:* Forbes, Charles

## McPeck, William

A private in the Union army who, along with Private John Weaver, claimed to be at Ford's Theatre seated in the Dress Circle the night of the assassination. As Dr. Charles Leale and the soldiers carried Lincoln's body from the box, across the back of the Dress Circle, they decided to reverse Lincoln's position and carry him down the stairs to the lobby feet first. Years later, McPeck claimed he and Weaver stepped forward and volunteered to help carry Lincoln.

Sources: *Sunday-Times Telegraph* (Pittsburgh), February 12, 1928; *New York Tribune*, February 9, 1931; Edward Steers, Jr., *Blood on the Moon* (Lexington: University Press of Kentucky, 2001), 122–23.

*See also:* Soles, Jacob; Griffiths, Jake; Corey, John; Sample, William

## McPhail, James L. (1816–1874)

Maryland provost marshal with office in Baltimore. McPhail played a key role in hunting down and capturing members of Booth's conspiracy. McPhail's alertness and quick action led to the arrest of Samuel Arnold and Michael O'Laughlen on Monday, April 17, and came within a few hours of capturing George Atzerodt.

McPhail's office was in the thick of the hunt for all the conspirators. On Monday, April 17, he engineered the arrests of Samuel Arnold and Michael O'Laughlen. McPhail's efforts were a model of efficient detective work. Following the abortive capture plot on March 17, Sam Arnold had returned to Baltimore frustrated with Booth and his antics. He applied for a job as clerk in the store of John W. Wharton at Fort Monroe, Virginia. At the time Lincoln was shot Arnold was working at the fort apparently oblivious to what Booth had done.

McPhail received word shortly after midnight on Friday, April 14, that Lincoln had been shot by Booth. One of McPhail's detectives, Voltaire Randall, told McPhail that Sam Arnold and John Wilkes Booth were old friends from their Baltimore days. Perhaps there was a connection. McPhail also remembered that Michael O'Laughlen had lived across the street from the Booth family in Baltimore, and that the two men were boyhood friends. McPhail was a shrewd enough detective to realize that these two Baltimoreans just might be connected to Booth and that even if not, they might still know where to find him. He immediately telegraphed the War Department in Washington: "Sir: Samuel Arnold and Michael O'Laughlen, two of the intimate associates of J. Wilkes Booth, are said to be in Washington. Their arrest may prove advantageous."

McPhail didn't wait for Washington to respond. He swung into immediate action. As a former Confederate soldier Arnold was required to register his address with McPhail's office on returning from the military. Checking his register, McPhail found the word "Hookstown" next to Arnold's name. McPhail sent Randall and a second detective, Eaton Horner, to Hookstown to find Arnold. At Hookstown the two detectives learned from a "colored woman" that Arnold had taken a job at Fort Monroe. Randall and Horner returned to Baltimore, where they visited Arnold's father at his bakery, located less than a half mile from McPhail's headquarters. It was at this time that the detectives learned of the "Sam" letter from the morning papers. They were now convinced that Arnold was a conspirator in Lincoln's murder. Arnold's father confirmed that his son was working at Fort Monroe. Randall and Horner set out Sunday morning for the fort.

On reaching the fort, the two detectives took Arnold into custody. It was a major collar and showed how efficient McPhail had been in his investigation. He was well ahead of his counterparts in Washington.

After taking Arnold into custody, Horner began questioning him about his relationship with Booth. Stonewalling at first, Arnold soon realized that the detectives knew a great deal about him and his relationship with Booth as a result of the damaging "Sam" letter. Arnold began talking freely. He told Horner about a Dr. Mudd of Charles County, Maryland, whom Booth had visited in November 1864. Booth, he said, carried a letter of introduction from someone in Canada. Horner later testified at the conspiracy trial about his arrest and questioning of Arnold, telling the court of Arnold's statement about the letter of introduction. When Horner was asked to whom the letter was directed, he answered bluntly: "[Arnold] said that [Booth] had a letter of introduction to Dr. Mudd and to Dr. Queen." The testimony severely damaged Mudd's case.

Returning to Baltimore with Arnold, Horner turned him over to McPhail. By now McPhail had learned of the letter found in Booth's hotel room in Washington that was signed "Sam." The "Sam" letter contained a reference to another of Booth's friends by the name of "Mike." Arnold had written in the "Sam" letter, "I called also to see Mike, but learned from his mother he had gone out with you, and had not returned." Washington was as much in the dark about "Mike" as they were about "Sam." But McPhail was ahead of Washington here also. He had known the O'Laughlen family for thirty years, and his office was located only a short distance from the O'Laughlen home. McPhail's earlier investigation had also turned up the name of Mike O'Laughlen. McPhail sent his men out to look for O'Laughlen.

Word soon reached the O'Laughlen family in Baltimore that the authorities were looking for their son Mike. On Monday afternoon, April 17, O'Laughlen turned himself in to McPhail to spare his mother the pain of seeing her son arrested in her home. By the evening of the 17th, Samuel Arnold and Michael O'Laughlen were in the custody of McPhail and on their way to Washington.

McPhail came within a whisker of also bagging George Atzerodt. McPhail, acting on a tip from Atzerodt's own brother, John Atzerodt, sent out a posse to the Richter farm in Germantown. John Atzerodt was McPhail's deputy and had been on an assignment in Charles County when Lincoln was shot. On learning that the government was looking for his brother, John Atzerodt suggested McPhail check out the Richter farm. By the time McPhail's men reached the Richter farm it was too late. Atzerodt was already in custody, but McPhail's quick action was only a few hours behind the men of the First Delaware Cavalry who arrested Atzerodt early Thursday morning, April 20. McPhail's men would lose

out on the twenty-five thousand dollars of reward money that had been allotted for Atzerodt's capture.

Sources: Benjamin B. Hough, letter to Edward D. Townsend, December 20, 1865, NARA, RG 94, M-619, reel 458, frames 162–70; Testimony of John W. Wharton, Poore, *Conspiracy Trial*, vol. 3, 340; Pitman, *Trial*, 241; Memorial of James L. McPhail, Voltaire Randall, and Eaton Horner, in John B. Horner, *Lincoln's Songbird* (Gettysburg, Pa.: Horner, 1991), 37–48; Percy E. Martin, "Surprising Speed in the Identification of Two Baltimore Conspirators," in Laurie Verge, ed., *In Pursuit of . . . Continuing Research in the Field of the Lincoln Assassination* (Clinton, Md.: Surratt Society, 1990), 167; Testimony of Eaton G. Horner, Poore, *Conspiracy Trial*, vol. 1, 423–35; Pitman, *Trial*, 234.

*See also:* Arnold, Samuel Bland; O'Laughlen, Michael

## Menu, John B.

A Catholic priest on the faculty of St. Charles College, where both John Surratt, Jr., and Louis Wiechmann studied for the priesthood. Wiechmann considered Menu his "father confessor." Among the papers found in Booth's trunk in his room at the National Hotel in Washington was a letter by Menu dated March 19, 1865. The letter was written to Louis Wiechmann in a response to a letter Wiechmann wrote to Menu, in which

Wiechmann appears to have expressed concerns about John Surratt and his rebel activities. Menu wrote, "You speak in a obscure way of Mr. Surratt, as if he were a rebel; could you not have said openly what is the perilous trip point which he is soon to depart?"

How the letter wound up in Booth's trunk is not known, but someone must have intercepted it and turned it over to Booth. The logical choice would seem to be Mary Surratt, but there is no evidence to support this. The date of the letter is two days after the aborted kidnap attempt on Lincoln by Booth and his team of conspirators, including John Surratt. Menu's letter suggests Wiechmann wrote him as a result of the failed attempt, expressing concern about Surratt's activities and knowing that Menu was deeply fond of Surratt. The prosecution team considered the letter "unimportant."

Sources: Letter of John B. Menu, NARA, RG 153, M-599, reel 2, frames 381–82.

## Merrick, Henry E.

Worked as a clerk at the National Hotel, where Booth was a regular guest. Merrick was called as a defense witness on behalf of Edman Spangler. He testified that on March 7, 1865, he, with his wife and friends, attended the play at Ford's Theatre using box 8. Thomas Raybold, in charge of the house, took Merrick and his party up to box 8 and found the door locked. Unable to find the key, Raybold forced the door, breaking the lock loose. It remained broken on the night of April 14, 1865. Although it was highly unlikely that the door would have been locked when President Lincoln used the box on April 14, the defense wanted to make sure Spangler did not break the lock and thereby aid Booth in his entry into the box.

Sources: Testimony of Henry E. Merrick, Poore, *Conspiracy Trial*, vol. 2, 42; Pitman, *Trial*, 111.

*See also:* Raybold, Thomas J.

## Merritt, James B.

The government's three chief witnesses to a general conspiracy involving Confederate leaders were James B. Merritt, Richard Montgomery, and Sandford Conover. All three witnesses claimed to have been in Canada at a crucial time, and to have been taken into the confidence of the Confederate leaders there, particularly Jacob Thompson and George N. Sanders. Thus all three had intimate knowledge of the Confederate leaders' alleged relationship with Booth, and his plot to eliminate Lincoln. Their testimony came under a cloud when the press and others claimed all three had committed perjury.

Of the three witnesses, Conover proved to be the most sensational in linking the Confederacy to Lincoln's death. Conover, alias James Watson Wallace, and whose real name was Charles A. Dunham, claimed that he had actually seen Booth together with Thompson and Sanders in Canada and that Thompson had told him that Booth had been authorized by Richmond to kill Lincoln. Merritt reiterated what Conover said, then went further, claiming that Davis had actually authorized the killing in writing. Montgomery confirmed both Conover's and Merritt's testimony that a plot to assassinate Lincoln was in the works and that Thompson had only awaited approval from Richmond. The three witnesses claimed to have seen Booth, Powell, and Herold in Canada and that Booth, Surratt, and Atzerodt were among the band of conspirators assigned to murder Lincoln. Montgomery claimed to have seen Lewis Powell in Canada in close conversation with Thompson's second in command, Clement C. Clay. Conover's testimony placing Booth in the presence of Confederate agents was the link prosecutors had been looking for. Then the government's case took a dramatic turn for the worse.

Canadian newspapers published stories stating that Conover had recanted his testimony in Canada. Charges were made that Conover had coached the other two witnesses what to say on the witness stand. Judge Advocate General Joseph Holt had to recall Conover in an attempt to rehabilitate his earlier testimony. Conover attempted to cover himself by telling the tribunal his life had been threatened if he did not recant his charges. A year later, William Campbell, a witness before the House Judiciary Committee, admitted under oath that he had been coached by Conover with a promise of money and that his deposition had been false.

Because part of the testimony of Conover and Montgomery and Merritt proved to be perjured, most historians have concluded that the charge of Confederate involvement was without merit. The public, however, had little difficulty with the government's case. Despite the perjury, the public believed there was enough evidence to indict the Confederate leaders, including Jefferson Davis. Holt, having struggled with his grand conspiracy case, turned his undivided attention to the eight defendants in the dock. With them, he had substantial evidence that held up under scrutiny.

Sources: Testimony of Richard Montgomery, Poore: *Conspiracy Trial*, vol. 3, 83–94; Pitman, *Trial*, 24, 26, 28; William Hanchett, *The Lincoln Murder Conspiracies* (Urbana: University of Illinois Press, 1983), 72–74, 78–81; Thomas R. Turner, *Beware the People Weeping* (Baton Rouge: Louisiana State University Press,

1982); Thomas R. Turner, *The Assassination of Abraham Lincoln* (Malabar, Fla.: Krieger, 1999), 49–51.

## Metz, Hezekiah

A Germantown, Maryland farmer who entertained George Atzerodt on Easter Sunday at time of his attempted escape. Easter Sunday following Lincoln's murder, George Atzerodt visited the Metz farm while on his way to his cousin Hartman Richter's house in Germantown. Metz invited Atzerodt to stay for the noonday dinner. Joining the family were the two Leaman brothers, Somerset and James, and a local farmer, Nathan Page. During the dinner, the conversation turned to the assassination. Atzerodt spoke knowingly of the circumstances, telling the other guests that Grant was also a target. Atzerodt appeared nervous raising suspicions as he talked about the assassination. When dinner was over, Atzerodt left the Metz house and continued on the few miles to his cousin's house where he stayed until his arrest early Wednesday morning, April 20. Page later told an army undercover detective about Atzerodt's strange behavior ultimately leading to Atzerodt's arrest. Metz became a witness for the prosecution in their case against Atzerodt.

Sources: Testimony of Hezekiah Metz, Poore, *Conspiracy Trial*, I, 353; Pitman, *Trial*, 149. Edward Steers, Jr., *Blood on the Moon* (Lexington: University Press of Kentucky, 2001), 169–170.

*See also:* Leaman, James E., and Somerset Leaman

## Miles, John T.

A witness for the prosecution. Miles worked at Ford's Theatre assisting with scene changes by working in the "flies" above the stage. Miles testified that Booth came to the theater around three o'clock in the afternoon of April 14. He came up the back alley (Baptist Alley) and left his horse in his stable behind the theater. At the time Edman Spangler and Jim Maddox were with him. Miles saw Booth again between nine and ten o'clock that night. This time he called for Spangler to hold his horse while Booth went inside the theater. Miles then told the prosecution that Spangler, busy with the play, called for "John Peanuts" (John Burroughs) to hold Booth's horse.

Sources: Poore, *Conspiracy Trial*, vol. 1, 209–16; Timothy S. Good, *We Saw Lincoln Shot: One Hundred Eyewitness Accounts* (Jackson: University Press of Mississippi, 1995), 81.

## Military Commission

See Military Tribunal

## Military Justice

See Uniform Code of Military Justice; General Order No. 100

Standing left to right: General Thomas M. Harris, General Lew Wallace, General August V. Kautz, and Special Judge Advocate Colonel Henry L. Burnett. Seated left to right: Colonel David R. Clendenin, Colonel Charles Tompkins, General Albion P. Howe, Colonel James Ekin, General David Hunter (President), General Robert S. Foster, Assistant Judge Advocate General John A. Bingham, and Judge Advocate General Joseph Holt.

## Military Tribunal

On May 1, newly installed president Andrew Johnson issued an executive order placing those accused of participating in the conspiracy to assassinate President Lincoln under the legal jurisdiction of the military, to be tried by a military tribunal. The decision would be fraught with controversy then and now.

Johnson was bolstered in his decision by the opinion of Attorney General James Speed, who justified a military trial by describing the accused as "enemy belligerents" who had violated the laws of war. The use of a military trial, however, appears to have been the decision of Secretary of War Edwin M. Stan-ton, who persuaded Johnson and others, including Speed, that a military trial was the only way to ensure control over the investigation and trial proceedings.

Sitting in judgment as military commissioners were nine Federal army officers appointed by Johnson, but clearly the selection of Secretary of War Edwin M. Stanton and Judge Advocate General Joseph Holt. They were Major General David Hunter (president of the tribunal), Major General Lew Wallace, Brevet Major General August Kautz, Brigadier General Albion Howe, Brigadier General Robert Foster, Brevet Brigadier General Cyrus B. Comstock, Brigadier General Thomas Harris, Brevet Colonel

Horace Porter, and Lieutenant Colonel David Clendenin. Within twenty-four hours, Comstock and Porter were relieved from serving as commissioners and replaced by Brevet Brigadier General James Ekin and Brevet Colonel Charles Tomkins. Porter and Comstock were replaced on May 10. Both officers were members of Grant's staff and requested removal. It was thought inappropriate for them to serve since Grant had been a target of Booth's assassination plot. Privately, however, they appeared to not want to be a part of the military tribunal and so had Grant intercede for them. All nine of the officers had seen combat service during the war. All of them had shown qualities of leadership in their various capacities during the war. Included among the nine were four graduates of West Point who remained professional soldiers, a former U.S. marshal, a medical practitioner, two lawyers, and a schoolteacher.

The use of a military trial resulted in dissent from certain quarters, including members of Lincoln's (now Johnson's) cabinet and certain members of Congress. Stanton, however, prevailed and the trial went forward. One year after the trial the U.S. Supreme Court issued a ruling in an unrelated case that defined, in part, the jurisdiction of military tribunals. The justices in the case, known as *Ex Parte Milligan*, concluded that a

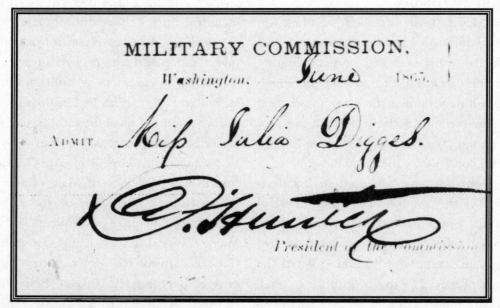

Entry pass to the military tribunal

military tribunal could not try civilians where the civil courts were open and functioning and *no threat by an enemy army existed*.

Not all jurists are in agreement as to the applicability of the Milligan case to the Lincoln military tribunal. In 1868, a Federal court for the Southern District of Florida upheld the jurisdiction of the military tribunal that had tried the Lincoln conspirators. In 1942, and again in 1946, the U.S. Supreme Court, in two separate cases stemming from World War II, upheld the jurisdiction of military tribunals even though two of the defendants were U.S. citizens. And in 2001, a Federal court in the District of Columbia upheld the jurisdiction of the Lincoln military tribunal to try U.S. citizens in a lawsuit brought by Dr. Samuel Mudd's grandson.

Despite misconceptions about the trial and the alleged denial of due process under military jurisdiction, the military tribunal followed civil procedures throughout and in every instance, both the prosecution and defense cited precedents from civil cases.

Sources: Edward Steers, Jr., "Introduction," in Edward Steers, Jr., ed., *The Trial* (Lexington: University Press of Kentucky, 2003), xi–xx; Thomas R. Turner, *Beware the People Weeping* (Baton Rouge: Louisiana State University Press,

1982), 138–64; Thomas R. Turner, *The Assassination of Abraham Lincoln* (Malabar, Fla.: Krieger, 1999), 49–51.

*See also:* Milligan, Lambden P.

## Milligan, Lambden P.

Principal defendant in the famous case before the U.S. Supreme Court in 1866. Milligan, tried and convicted by a military trial, had his conviction overturned by the Supreme Court in *Ex Parte Milligan*. The case was cited by Dr. Samuel Mudd's attorneys in filing an appeal of his conviction with the District Court of Southern Florida in 1867.

Milligan had been arrested by the military and tried before a military commission in Indiana on charges of attempting to disrupt the military operations in that state by violent means. Milligan was found guilty and sentenced to hang. He was able to bring his case before the U.S. Supreme Court in the fall of 1866 thanks to the cooperation of Supreme Court associate justice David Davies. In what has come to be known as a landmark decision, the Supreme Court ruled that U.S. citizens cannot be tried by military tribunal in those jurisdictions where the civilian courts are open and functioning, and no military threat exists. The Court ruled that Indiana was not a war zone, had not been invaded by a hostile force, nor had been threatened with invasion by a hostile force, and that martial law, therefore, could not exist under such conditions. Milligan was set free.

The supporters of Dr. Mudd have cited the Milligan decision that the court that convicted had lacked jurisdiction. Mudd's attorneys filed a brief with the U.S. Supreme Court, but the petition was returned by Chief Justice Salmon P. Chase directing Mudd to first take his case to the closest Federal court. If denied a hearing, or a negative ruling, Mudd could then petition the Supreme Court. Mudd was able to successfully appeal his conviction in the Federal court for Southern Florida, but was denied relief, the judge upholding the tribunal's 1865 ruling. Mudd then filed his brief with the U.S. Supreme Court, which agreed to hear the case. Arguments were heard, but the Court ruled the case moot when Mudd, and his two fellow conspirators Spangler and Arnold, were granted full pardons by President Johnson. History will never know what the Court might have ruled had it not been for President Johnson's eleventh-hour pardons.

Dr. Mudd's grandson, and subsequently, great-grandson, sued the U.S. Army in Federal court, hoping to overturn Mudd's conviction. Mudd lost when the judge upheld the original ruling of the 1865 military tribunal. The Mudd family appealed the ruling to the Appellate Court for the District of Columbia, only to lose once again. It was the final step in the case of Dr. Samuel Mudd and his and his descendants' attempts to seek relief based on the Milligan decision. The case had run from 1865 to 2001 before it was finally settled.

Sources: Thomas R. Turner, "The Military Trial," in Edward Steers, Jr., ed., *The Trial* (Lexington: University Press of Kentucky, 2003), xxi–xxviii; Edward Steers, Jr., "Introduction," in Edward Steers, Jr., ed., *The Trial* (Lexington: University Press of Kentucky, 2003), xi–xx.

*See also:* Military Tribunal

## Millward, William

U.S. marshal based in Philadelphia. On April 19, 1865, five days after the assassination, Booth's brother-in-law, John Sleeper Clarke, remembered that Booth had left a packet of papers with his sister Asia, Clarke's wife, for safekeeping. Among the papers were two letters written by Booth: one to his "Dearest beloved Mother" and a second dated 1864 and addressed "To whom it may concern." The second letter was Booth's attempt to explain his feelings about Lincoln and his effort to destroy Booth's beloved Confederacy. Clarke, afraid for his own safety from Federal authorities, gave the "To whom it may concern" letter to U.S. marshal William Millward, who unexplain-ably turned it over to a reporter with the *Philadelphia Inquirer*. The letter was published in its entirety by the *Inquirer* on April 19, 1865. Millward was chastised by Secretary of War Stanton and ordered to retrieve the letter and bring it to Washington immediately. The letter disappeared and remained missing for 112 years, until 1977, when assassination historian James O. Hall found it among the papers of the Justice Department in the National Archives.

Sources: John Wilkes Booth, NARA, RG 153, M-599, reel 2, frames 616–18; John Rhode-hamel and Louis Taper, *"Right or Wrong, God Judge Me"* (Urbana: University of Illinois Press, 1997), 124–31; Anthony Pitch, *"They Have Killed Papa Dead"* (Hanover, N.H.: Steerforth, 2008), 177–83.

*See also:* Clarke, John Sleeper; "To whom it may concern" Letter

## Missing Pages, John Wilkes Booth's Diary

When Booth's body was searched following his death on the porch of the Garrett house, several items were removed and noted. Booth had a pocket knife, a compass, a draft note for sixty-one-plus pounds drawn on the Ontario Bank in Montreal, greenbacks totaling about one hundred dollars, two Colt revolvers in holsters on a belt, a carbine, a box of cartridges, wood shavings, a map, and a diary, or more accurately, a small memorandum book. Colonel Everton J. Conger removed several items from Booth's pockets. He later made a statement in which he said, "I took some papers, trinkets, and a pocket book from the person of Booth, and myself delivered all of them to Secretary Stanton." The diary was placed in Stanton's vault and did not appear again until 1867, during the impeachment hearing of President Andrew Johnson.

At the time of Johnson's impeachment hearing, Lafayette C. Baker, head of the National Detective Police, testified that there were pages missing from the diary: "I think there was a great deal more of the original diary than appears here now." Baker's statement has become the stuff that conspiracy theories are built on. Beginning in 1937 with historian Otto Eisenschiml's book *Why Was Lincoln Murdered?* and continuing to 1975, claims were made that the missing pages from Booth's diary contained proof that Stanton and high-ranking officials in the government and financial world had conspired to murder Lincoln.

There are indeed, missing pages from Booth's little diary. The question is, who removed them? The answer accepted by the majority of historians is that Booth removed them during the year he used the memorandum book as a source of notepaper. Because there are stubs of every page removed, it is easy to count the number of pages missing. In all, there are forty-three full sheets, or eighty-six pages, missing from the diary.

In November 1975, rumors spread that the missing pages were in the possession of a Stanton descendant, and that they were filled with incriminating evidence not only resurrecting Eisenschiml's 1937 theory of Stanton's role in Lincoln's murder but also naming dozens of other high-ranking politicians and prominent people as accomplices.

As word of the missing pages spread, a motion picture studio in Salt Lake City, Sunn Classic Pictures, expressed an interest in obtaining the rights to the missing pages for use in a major motion picture about the Lincoln assassination. Eventually a full transcript of the missing pages was produced, although the originals were kept locked away, and their owner refused to allow historians to examine them—the Stanton heir would not permit anyone to see them, claiming they were kept in a bank safe deposit box. She further claimed she was anxious about having government property that might be considered stolen. In October 1977, Sunn Classics released the movie and a paperback book, *The Lincoln Conspiracy*.

The movie is almost entirely historical fiction.

In analyzing the transcript, there are several things to consider. First is the alleged "Stanton heir" who claimed to own the missing pages. When the known descendants of Edwin M. Stanton were contacted, none of them was aware of the missing pages, or any other documents relating to Lincoln's assassination. When historians failed to find a Stanton heir who had such pages, the alleged owner claimed to be the descendant of an illegitimate child of Stanton's who had been kept hidden from public view. The second consideration is the internal evidence of the transcript. Even the best of fabricators make mistakes. The transcript of the alleged missing pages contains numerous errors of fact, including wrong names, dates, and places. It is not difficult to show that the transcript, while clever, is a fabrication.

There can be no doubt that Booth had the diary on him when he was killed. The missing pages are pure fabrications in support of the myth that Stanton engineered Lincoln's assassination. Just who was responsible for creating the missing pages remains a mystery. It isn't even clear when they were written, although it seems likely that they are twentieth-century fabrications. Like the other myths associated with Abraham Lincoln, the myth of the missing pages and Stanton's complicity in Lincoln's death will continue to live on, finding new believers in future generations.

Sources: David Balsiger and Charles E. Sellier, Jr., *The Lincoln Conspiracy* (Los Angeles: Schick Sunn Classic, 1977); Edward Steers, Jr., "The Missing Pages from Booth's Diary," in *Lincoln Legends: Myths, Hoaxes, and Confabulations Associated with Our Greatest President* (Lexington: University Press of Kentucky, 2007), 177–202.

*See also:* Diary, John Wilkes Booth's

### Monroe (Munroe), Frank (1842–1877)

A captain in the Marines, Frank Monroe was in charge of the prisoners held aboard the USS *Saugus*. Monroe was called as a defense witness on behalf of George Atzerodt. Atzerodt was initially held on the *Saugus* before he was transferred to the cell block in the Washington Arsenal. While on the *Saugus*, Atzerodt gave a statement to Monroe. He told the captain that Booth had ordered him to kill Vice President Andrew Johnson and that he had refused. Booth then threatened to "blow his brains out," and Atzerodt still refused. In Atzerodt's mind he really saved Johnson's life by refusing to follow Booth's orders, and therefore was not guilty. In fact, Atzerodt viewed himself as some-thing of a hero who had saved the vice president's life.

Defense attorney William Doster wanted to put Monroe on the witness stand to get him to introduce Atzerodt's statement before the tribunal. It was a clever ploy, but Judge Advocate General Joseph Holt was too smart to allow Atzerodt to testify through a surrogate. In 1865, the accused were not allowed to testify. They were considered "incompetent witness[es]." Prohibiting them from testifying was for their own protection, the fear being they would say something while on the stand that would incriminate them. Hence the rule was meant to protect the accused from self-incrimination. Doster gave up his effort to have Atzerodt speak for himself on the record.

Sources: Statement of Frank Monroe, NARA, RG 153, M-599, reel 2, frames 45–47; Poore, *Conspiracy Trial*, vol. 2, 514; Pitman, *Trial*, 150; Edward Steers, Jr., "George Atzerodt," in Edward Steers, Jr., ed., *The Trial* (Lexington: University Press of Kentucky, 2003), lxvi–lxxi.

*See also:* Atzerodt, George Andrew

### *Montauk*, USS

A U.S. Navy monitor at anchor in the Eastern Branch of the Potomac River offshore from the Washington Navy Yard. The body of John Wilkes Booth was placed aboard the *Montauk* under a canvas awning on April 26, 1865. It was kept under guard the entire time up to when it was buried beneath the floor of the warden's office at the Washington Arsenal. Several individuals were brought to the *Montauk* and asked to identify the body, including John Frederick May, a Washington doctor who had performed surgery on a benign tumor on Booth's neck. Following identification, Surgeon General Joseph K. Barnes and army surgeon Joseph Janvier Woodward performed an autopsy. Booth's body was then taken inside the Washington Arsenal and buried.

The *Montauk* was also used as a holding pen for the accused conspirators George Atzerodt, Edman Spangler, David Herold, and a Portuguese ship captain thought to be involved with Booth, Joao Celestino.

Commissioned on December 17, 1862, the *Montauk* served in the shelling of several Confederate forts and engaged the CSS *Nashville* in February 1863. Decommissioned in 1865, she was sold for scrap on April 14, 1904.

Sources: Charles O. Paullin, "The Navy and the Booth Conspirators," *Journal of the Illinois State Historical Society* 33, no. 3 (September 1940), 269–77.

*See also: Saugus*, USS

## Montgomery, Richard

Witness for the prosecution during the conspiracy trial. Montgomery was the first of three witness called by the prosecution in an attempt to tie John Wilkes Booth and his assassination plot directly to Jefferson Davis and the Confederate leaders in Canada; the other two being Sandford Conover and James B. Merritt.

Montgomery testified to being in Canada during the summer of 1864 and off and on up to two weeks before the assassination occurred. During that time he had several conversations with the head of Confederate operations Jacob Thompson, as well as overhearing conversations between Thompson and others, about having Lincoln "put out of the way." Montgomery identified virtually all of the major agents in Canada, including Thompson, William Cleary, Clement C. Clay, and George N. Sanders, and claimed they were waiting for the word to go ahead and kill the president. While Montgomery did a great deal of name-dropping, he did not mention Jefferson Davis by name. Of the three key witnesses whom Judge Advocate General Joseph Holt called to show Lincoln's murder was given the go-ahead by Richmond, only Sandford Conover (alias James Watson Wallace, real name Charles Dunham) testified to Davis's involvement. Conover claimed John Surratt carried a dispatch from Confederate secretary of state Judah P. Benjamin and Davis. After reading the dispatch, Conover claimed Thompson said, "This makes the thing all right."

As damaging as the testimony of Montgomery and the others appeared to have been, it fell apart when all three came under attack by the press, which claimed all three men had committed perjury. Their stories began to unravel when reporters could not verify most of their claims. Wrong dates, wrong places, even wrong names discredited their testimony. While Holt continued to believe that Confederate leaders, including Davis, were involved in Lincoln's murder, perjured witnesses tainted the evidence. The court soon turned its attention to the eight defendants in the dock.

Sources: Thomas R. Turner, *The Assassination of Abraham Lincoln* (Malabar, Fla.: Krieger, 1999), 48–50; William Hanchett, *The Lincoln Murder Conspiracies* (Urbana: University of Illinois Press, 1983), 71–75, 81.

*See also:* Dunham, Charles A.; Merritt, James B.

## Morgan, Richard C.

A detective working for Colonel Henry Olcott, and one of three army officers picked by Secretary of War Stanton to manage the large amount of evidence being gathered in the first days of the investigation into Lincoln's murder. On Monday night, April 17, 1865, Olcott ordered Morgan and three other detectives to go to the Surratt boardinghouse at 541 H Street in Washington, D.C., and arrest all of the occupants. In charge of the detectives was Major Henry B. Smith. Morgan was called as a witness by the prosecution during the conspiracy trial and asked to describe the events surrounding the arrests. He went into considerable detail describing the arrest of Lewis Powell and Mary Surratt's denial of knowing Powell, who claimed he had come to the house at Mary Surratt's request. Morgan also told of another detective finding an image of John Wilkes Booth hidden behind another image.

Sources: Testimony of R. C. Morgan, Poore, *Conspiracy Trial*, vol. 2, 9–14; Pitman, *Trial*, 122; Edward Steers, Jr., *Blood on the Moon* (Lexington: University Press of Kentucky, 2001), 175–77.

*See also:* Surratt, Mary Elizabeth

## Mudd, Dr. George Dyer (1826–1899)

Second cousin of Dr. Samuel A. Mudd, sharing the same great-grandfather. Testified at the conspiracy trial on behalf of Dr. Samuel A. Mudd. A graduate of the University of Maryland Medical School in Baltimore, George Mudd, seven years

Samuel Mudd's senior, sponsored his cousin Samuel Mudd for his doctorate in medicine. George Mudd was one of a handful of Unionists in Charles County, Maryland. As such, he was held in favor by the Union military that operated throughout the county.

Samuel Mudd and George Mudd attended Easter services (April 16, 1865) at St. Peter's Church, a few miles east of Samuel Mudd's house. On the ride home after church, Samuel Mudd told George Mudd of the two "strangers" at his house on Saturday. Mudd said he was suspicious of their behavior and was worried they might have something to do with the assassination. He asked George if he would go into Bryantown and inform the military stationed there about the two strangers. George agreed, but waited until Monday morning to tell Lieutenant David Dana of the 13th New York Cavalry. On Tuesday morning, Lieutenant Alexander Lovett, a detective on provost marshal James O'Beirne's staff in Washington, arrived in Bryantown. Dana told Lovett about George Mudd's message and Lovett sent for George Mudd. Lovett, with detectives William Williams, Simon Gavacan, and Joshua Lloyd, with George Mudd showing the way, went to Mudd's house, where the first in a series of interrogations took place, resulting in Samuel Mudd's arrest on Monday, April 24.

George Mudd testified at considerable length on the events surrounding his cousin's request and his visit to Bryantown to tell Lieutenant Dana about his cousin's visitors.

Sources: Testimony of George D. Mudd, Poore, *Conspiracy Trial*, vol. 2, 386, vol. 3, 486; Pitman, *Trial*, 206, 210; Statement of Samuel Mudd, NARA, RG 153, M-599, reel 5, frames 212–25.

### Mudd, Henry Lowe (1798–1877)

Father of Dr. Samuel Alexander Mudd and patriarch of the Mudd family during the Civil War. Henry Lowe Mudd was one of the largest landowners in Charles County, Maryland. His property totaled over 1,700 acres. He was also among the largest slave owners in Charles County, owning eighty-nine slaves worth an estimated ninety thousand dollars in 1860 or approximately $1 million in today's terms. Henry Mudd's land was divided into smaller parcels for his sons Anthony Mudd and Samuel Mudd. Although his oldest son, Anthony, and middle son, Samuel, worked large adjoining farms on their own, the land was deeded in the name of Henry Lowe Mudd.

Samuel Mudd's ownership of the land he farmed became an issue during his trial in 1865. Mudd's attorneys attempted to show that the reason Booth visited Mudd in November (and again in December in

Washington) was that Booth wanted to buy some of Samuel Mudd's land. And Mudd had an interest in selling. The prosecution was able to determine that Samuel Mudd didn't own any of his farm or any other farmland in Charles County and therefore could not sell land to Booth. Only Henry Lowe Mudd could sell the land.

On Saturday afternoon, April 15, Samuel Mudd and David Herold stopped by Henry Lowe Mudd's home to see if they could borrow one of his farm wagons. Samuel Mudd's younger brother, Henry Lowe, Jr., told them there was no working wagon available. Mudd and Herold continued on to Bryantown.

Sources: Testimony of Henry L. Mudd, Jr., Poore, *Conspiracy Trial*, vol. 2, 431–34; Pitman, *Trial*, 198; Edward Steers, Jr., *Blood on the Moon* (Lexington: University Press of Kentucky, 2001).

## Mudd, Henry Lowe, Jr. (1844–1903)

Younger brother of Dr. Samuel Alexander Mudd. Testified as a defense witness for his brother, Samuel Mudd. Henry Lowe, Jr., lived at his father's plantation home, Oak Hill, located a quarter mile from Samuel Mudd's house. Together with Samuel Mudd and James Anthony Mudd, Henry belonged to a slave-capturing posse (known as "paddy rollers") that regularly patrolled Charles County for runaway slaves.

On Saturday, April 15, 1865, shortly after one o'clock in the afternoon, Mudd and David Herold rode over to the home of Henry Lowe Mudd, Samuel Mudd's father. They met Henry Mudd, Jr., and tried to borrow an old farm wagon to carry the injured Booth to their next stop in their escape, the home of Samuel Cox, known as Rich Hill. (William Burtles may have been the next stop, but Booth later changed his mind and asked guidance to Cox's home.) Henry Jr. told his brother that the spare wagon was broken and needed repair. Mudd and Herold then rode on toward Bryantown.

Sources: Richard Washington et al., NARA, RG 109, M-416, Union Provost Marshal's File of Papers Relating to Two or More Civilians, File 6083; Statement of Samuel Mudd, NARA, RG 153, M-599, reel 5, frames 212–25.

## Mudd, James Anthony (1829–1903)

Older brother of Dr. Samuel Alexander Mudd. James Anthony, along with Henry Lowe Mudd, Jr., and Samuel Mudd, was part of a group of able-bodied white men and slave owners who formed slave-capturing posses known as "paddy rollers" that patrolled Charles County on a regular basis, hunting down runaway slaves passing through. The provost marshal's office in Washington recorded the testimony of several ex-slaves from Charles County who claimed that the Mudd brothers, along with a neighbor, Henry Burch, captured a slave by the name of George Hawkins, who "was beaten unmercifully" and thrown into a holding pen until he could be shipped across the river to Richmond to work in the defenses surrounding that city.

In the fall of 1861, George W. Smith, sheriff of Charles County, also a Union informer, filed a statement with the provost marshal of the District of Columbia accusing James Anthony Mudd and Thomas Jones with subversive activities. Mudd, the statement claims, conveyed men and boxes of munitions from Baltimore and the surrounding area to Thomas Jones, who then transported them across the Potomac River to Virginia using his own boat and his own Negroes. In the summer of 1863, five runaway slaves from the Mudd family leveled charges against James Anthony and Samuel Mudd and their sister, Mary Clare Mudd. Two of the former slaves claimed that Samuel Mudd hid a quantity of arms and accoutrements on his property, which were then taken to Samuel Cox, who arranged for their shipment south to Virginia. The arms included swords. The former slaves also claimed that while a Union cavalry troop was searching the area, "Mudd's wife ran into the kitchen and threw a bundle of Rebel mail into the fireplace" and burned it before the troops arrived at their house.

Sources: Union Provost Marshal's File of Papers Relating to Two or More Civilians, NARA, RG 109, M-416, File 6083.

### Mudd, Mary Clare (1838–1882)

Sister of Dr. Samuel Alexander Mudd. Mary Mudd was named by one of Samuel Mudd's slaves, Elzee Eglent, and two of Henry Lowe Mudd, Sr.'s slaves of collecting and sending arms to Samuel Cox for the Confederate army. The arms were identified as several swords. She testified as a witness on behalf of her brother at his trial, identifying various dates that her brother was home and visited her at their father's house. She also testified to seeing John Wilkes Booth in "Dr. Queen's pew" at St. Mary's Church in the "fall or winter" last. It was at the time he bought a horse from Mr. Gardiner, her brother's neighbor.

Sources: Union Provost Marshal's File of Papers Relating to Two or More Civilians, NARA, RG 109, M-416, File 6083; Testimony of Mary Clare Mudd, Poore, *Conspiracy Trial*, vol. 3, 451; Pitman, *Trial*, 195–96.

### Mudd, Mary Eleanor "Nettie" (1878–1943)

Youngest of nine children of Samuel Mudd and his wife. In 1906, Nettie Mudd edited a collection of her father's letters to his wife from Fort Jefferson, where he was serving a life sentence for complicity in President Lincoln's murder. The book is an important source of material on Dr. Mudd and his association with John Wilkes Booth. While the book was meant to exonerate Dr. Mudd, it contains information damaging to his claim of innocence as well as an insight into his deep-seated racism.

At the time of Mudd's trial, his lawyer, Thomas Ewing, denied that Booth ever stayed at Mudd's house, stating that he "never was at Mudd's house, or in his immediate neighborhood prior to the assassination, except once, and on his first visit [November 1864]." Ewing continued his argument by attacking the testimony of Louis Wiechmann and the claim that Mudd and Booth met with John Surratt and Wiechmann in Washington, and that Mudd introduced Booth to Surratt. Ewing told the commission "there is no reliable evidence that he [Mudd] ever met Booth before the assassination but once on Sunday, and once the day following, in November last." On this point Mudd lied to his own attorney, putting Ewing in a difficult position. Mudd later admitted to such a meeting, doing so while in prison at Fort Jefferson one month after the trial ended. In an affidavit dated August 28, 1865, and reproduced in Nettie Mudd's book, Mudd wrote: "I did confess to a casual or accidental meeting with Booth in front of one of the hotels on Pennsylvania Avenue, Washington, D.C., on the 23rd of December, 1864. . . . Booth, on that occasion, desired me to give him an introduction to Surratt."

Within a few months of his imprisonment, Mudd attempted to escape aboard a supply ship. He was caught and returned to prison. Mudd's defenders claim he was trying to reach Key West, where he could obtain a writ of habeas corpus in Federal court and have his conviction overturned. Mudd himself told a different story for his attempt to escape. Shortly before the attempt, the 161st New York Infantry, a white regiment, was replaced with a colored regiment (USCT). In a letter to his wife reproduced in Nettie Mudd's book, *The Life of Dr. Samuel A. Mudd*, Mudd explains the real reason for his attempt to escape: "[I]t is bad enough to be a prisoner in the hands of white men, your equals under the Constitution, but to be lorded over by a set of ignorant, prejudiced and irresponsible beings of the unbleached humanity, was more than I could submit to. . . ." Three days later Mudd wrote to his brother-in-law, citing "the humiliation of being guarded by an ignorant, irresponsible, & prejudiced Negro Soldiery, before an Enlightened People" as a justification. "We are now guarded entirely by Negro soldiers & a few White officers a skins difference. . . . [C]ould we have had a White

Regiment, the 161st N.Y.V. to guard the place no thought of leaving should have been harbored for a moment."

Sources: Nettie Mudd, *The Life of Dr. Samuel A. Mudd* (1906, reprint; La Plata, Md.: Dick Wildes, 1991), 42; Argument of Thomas Ewing, Jr., in Edward Steers, Jr., *The Trial* (Lexington: University Press of Kentucky, 2003), 323.

*See also:* Mudd, Dr. Samuel Alexander

## Mudd, Richard Dyer (1901–2002)

Grandson of Dr. Samuel Alexander Mudd. A physician by training, Richard Mudd devoted a lifetime to exonerating his grandfather. As a recent graduate of medical school, Richard Mudd visited Fort Jefferson, the place where his grandfather was imprisoned for nearly four years. It spurred him to try to reverse the conviction of his grandfather, a project that lasted more than seventy years.

Mudd's principal effort was directed at the president, asking him to reverse the tribunal's conviction based on the belief that his grandfather was a civilian resident of a loyal state and, as such, could not be tried by a military tribunal. In parallel with his efforts to pursue every president beginning with Franklin D. Roosevelt, Mudd also waged an effective campaign in the print media, and later television, basically turning his grandfather into an American folk hero wrongly convicted and persecuted by a vengeful government simply for following his Hippocratic oath in rendering medical aid to Booth.

Although Mudd was successful in getting President Carter, and later President Reagan, to respond in writing to his requests, neither president could offer any legal help to Mudd, pointing out that President Andrew Johnson pardoned Mudd, making any future appeals moot. Richard Mudd then changed tactics and approached the Army Board for the Correction of Military Records (AB-CMR) in asking that his grandfather's conviction be overturned because the military lacked jurisdiction to try him. The ABCMR is a civilian review board charged with reviewing the record of army personnel for the purpose of *advising* the secretary of the army on the appropriate action to take regarding appeals of personal actions taken against army personnel. In Mudd's case, the ABCMR concluded that the military tribunal lacked jurisdiction in trying and convicting Samuel Mudd. The secretary of the army declined the board's recommendation, concluding the board had no business reviewing cases of a historical nature and that such deliberations were best left to historians.

Richard Mudd next sought relief in the District of Columbia Federal Court,

asking that the secretary of the army be ordered to act on the ABCMR's ruling. The court upheld the military tribunal's original findings and stated it had jurisdiction to try and convict Samuel Mudd. The case was then appealed to the District of Columbia Court of Appeals, where once again the court ruled against Mudd, stating that Samuel Mudd's case should never had been heard by the ABCMR since its mandate was to receive cases of military personnel, and since Samuel Mudd was not in the military his case was wrongly heard. The court dismissed the appeal, bringing the Mudd family's efforts to a close after 137 years.

Sources: Edward Steers, Jr., "Samuel Alexander Mudd," in Edward Steers, Jr., *The Trial* (Lexington: University Press of Kentucky, 2003), lxxx–lxxxvii; Thomas R. Turner, "The Military Trial," in ibid., xxi–xxviii.

*See also:* Military Tribunal

## Mudd, Dr. Samuel Alexander (1833–1883)

Key conspirator in Booth's plot to kidnap Lincoln and take him south to Richmond. Tried by a military tribunal, Mudd was found guilty and sentenced to life in prison at hard labor. At the time of Abraham Lincoln's death, Samuel Alexander Mudd was a thirty-two-year-old tobacco farmer and part-time physician who lived in Charles County, Southern Maryland, with his wife and four young children. Samuel Mudd represented the seventh generation of American Mudds. He was born in 1833 on the family plantation within a half mile from where he would live his entire life. In 1847, at age fourteen, Mudd attended St. John's College in Frederick, Maryland, where he met his future wife, Sarah Frances Dyer. From 1850 until 1852 he attended Georgetown College in the District of Columbia. Although a good student, Mudd was expelled in his third year for being one of the ringleaders in a school riot.

After he returned home to his father, Mudd's education was taken un-

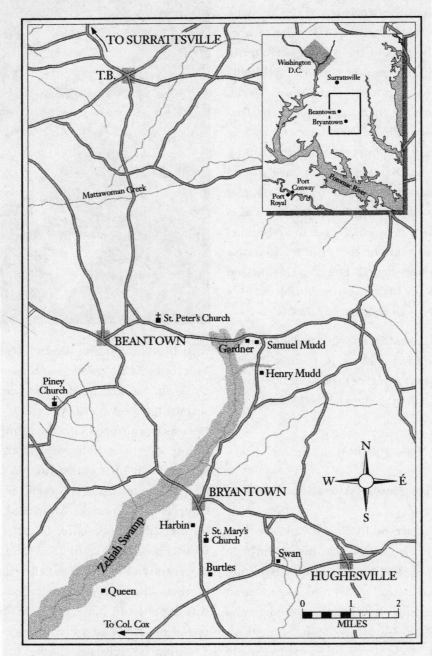

Dr. Mudd's Neighborhood, 1865

der the wing of his cousin, Dr. George Dyer Mudd, seven years Mudd's senior. George sponsored his cousin Sam at the University of Maryland Medical School in Baltimore, where Mudd graduated in 1856 at the age of twenty-three. One year later he married his childhood sweetheart, Sarah, or "Frank," as family members affectionately knew her. Within the year, Sam and his wife began farming a 218-acre tract of his father's prime land and in 1859 the couple moved into their newly built house, which still stands today as an historic site.

Mudd's farm was located thirty miles southeast of Washington and fifteen miles due south of Surrattsville, where Mary Surratt owned a tavern. From Mudd's house to the Potomac River where John Wilkes Booth would cross in his escape was another twenty-five miles. In all, the route from Ford's Theatre to the Potomac River was a little over fifty-five miles, with Mudd's house located equidistant from Ford's Theatre and the river.

Five and a half hours after shooting Abraham Lincoln, Booth and his cohort, David Herold, arrived at Dr. Mudd's house ostensibly seeking medical treatment. Booth had broken the fibula or small bone in his left leg as a result of jumping from the box onto the stage at the theatre. Mudd treated the broken leg and after a stay of approximately fifteen hours, Booth and Herold left the Mudd home on their continued escape from military authorities.

On Sunday, April 16, Dr. Mudd asked his cousin, George Mudd, to visit the military authorities that had set up headquarters in Bryantown, Maryland, and tell them about the two men who had been at his house. George Mudd visited Bryantown on Monday and told Lieutenant David Dana, the officer in command, about the two visitors to Samuel Mudd's house. Dana delayed visiting Mudd's house and waited to pass the information on to Lieutenant Alexander Lovett.

Suspecting that Booth had crossed over the Navy Yard Bridge shortly after shooting Lincoln, Major General C. C. Augur sent Dana and a troop from the 13th New York Cavalry into Southern Maryland with orders to search for Booth and arrest anyone who appeared suspicious. Dana set up headquarters at the Bryantown Tavern, located five miles south of Mudd's house.

Lovett, a member of the Veteran Reserve Corps stationed in Washington, had been ordered to go to Charles County along with military detectives Simon Gavacan, Joshua Lloyd, and William Williams on Tuesday morning, April 18. Arriving in Bryantown around noon on Tuesday, Lovett reported to Dana. Dana told Lovett that George Mudd had told of two strange men having been at the home of Dr. Samuel Mudd on Saturday. Lovett and the three detectives, along with George Mudd as their guide, rode to Mudd's house to question Mudd and his wife.

When Lovett finished questioning Mudd on Tuesday, he had a feeling something was not quite right. Concluding that the injured man was Booth, Lovett rode back to Washington on Thursday, April 20, and informed Colonel Henry H. Wells, provost marshal for the defenses south of the Potomac, of the information he had learned from interrogating Samuel Mudd. Wells immediately went to Secretary of War Edwin M. Stanton and informed him that Booth was positively seen in the Bryantown area and that his leg was broken. Stanton ordered Colonel Wells to go to Bryantown immediately and follow up on the information that he had received from Lovett. In the meantime, Lovett was ordered to return to Bryantown to pick up the hunt. Not satisfied with Mudd's answers during their first meeting, Lovett set out Friday morning for Mudd's house, where he questioned Mudd a second time.

Lovett's suspicions were again aroused and he told Mrs. Mudd that his men would have to search her house, whereupon Dr. Mudd remembered the boot that he had removed from the injured man's leg. Mudd explained that it had been accidentally shoved under the bed and was only later discovered while cleaning the room. Lovett examined the boot and noticed an inscription on the inside of the upper margin of the boot that read *J. Wilkes*. Lovett showed Mudd the inscription and Mudd said he had not noticed it before.

Dissatisfied with Mudd's evasiveness and his highly nervous demeanor, Lovett took Mudd into Bryantown for further questioning by Colonel Wells. Wells questioned Mudd extensively, during which time Mudd wrote out a voluntary statement reiterating what he had told Lovett. Wells then told Mudd he could return home but he wanted him to return to Bryantown the next morning, Saturday.

When Mudd returned to Bryantown the next morning, Wells presented him with a statement that Wells had drafted gleaned from Mudd's answers the day before. Wells asked Mudd to read over the statement and, if he agreed with it, to sign and date it. Mudd signed the statement.

Wells, like Lovett, suspected Mudd had lied about not recognizing his visitor as Booth. On Monday, April 24, Wells, now convinced Mudd was connected to Booth and his conspiracy, ordered Lovett to return to Mudd's house and arrest him and take him to Washington where he was put in the Carroll Annex of the Old Capitol Prison. From the Carroll Annex, Mudd was transferred to the Old Federal Penitentiary, now located within the Washington Arsenal in southeast Washington. Mudd was formally charged with conspiring with Booth and others to kill the president and with aiding and abetting Booth in his attempt to escape from the military authorities.

Samuel Mudd was found guilty on all charges except conspiring with Edman Spangler and harboring "Lewis Payne, John H. Surratt, Michael O'Laughlen, George A. Atzerodt, Mary E. Surratt, and Samuel Arnold." He was sentenced to life in prison. Mudd avoided the death penalty by a single vote when the commission voted five to four in favor of hanging. The death sentence required six votes.

A great deal of mythology has emerged around Dr. Mudd's time in prison at Fort Jefferson. For most of his time, Mudd worked in the prison hospital and prison carpentry shop, where he made several pieces of furniture, some of which are on display at the Dr. Samuel A. Mudd House in Charles County. Among the items on display are a "ladies work box," an "inlaid table," a presentation "cane," "wreaths and flowers made of collected shells," and several "cribbage boards." Even after his attempted escape a few weeks after his arrival, Mudd was dealt with leniently. In a letter to his wife he wrote, "I am taking my present hardship as a joke. I will soon assume my former position, or one equally respectable. I have no labor to perform, yet I am compelled to answer roll call, and to sleep in the guardhouse at night. This will not last longer than this week."

President Andrew Johnson pardoned Mudd on February 8, 1869, after he had served just over three and a half years of his life sentence. Mudd returned to his home and wife and children and picked up his life where it was so abruptly changed by his involvement with John Wilkes Booth. Over the next nine years he fathered five children. He died on January 10, 1883, at the age of forty-nine. He is buried in St. Mary's Cemetery in Charles County, Maryland.

Following Mudd's death, journalist and author George Alfred Townsend interviewed Frederick Stone, who along with Thomas Ewing acted as Mudd's defense attorney. Stone made a shocking statement to Townsend: "The court very nearly hanged Dr. Mudd. His prevarications were painful. He had given his whole case away by not trusting even his counsel or neighbors or kinfolks. It was a terrible thing to extricate him from the toils he had woven about himself. He had denied knowing Booth when he knew him well. He was undoubtedly accessory to the abduction plot, though he may have supposed it would never come to anything. He denied knowing Booth when he came to his house when that was preposterous. He had even been intimate with Booth."

Sources: Statement of Dr. S. A. Mudd, NARA, RG 153, M-599, reel 5, frames 226–39; Statement of Dr. S. A. Mudd, NARA, RG 153, M-599, reel 5, frames 212–25; Elden C. Weckesser, *His Name Was Mudd* (Jefferson, N.C.: McFarland, 1991), 193–94; Edward Steers, Jr., *His Name Is Still Mudd* (Gettysburg, Pa.: Thomas, 1997).

## Mudd, Sarah Frances Dyer "Frank" (1835–1911)

Wife of Dr. Samuel Alexander Mudd. Sarah Frances Dyer was born on March 15, 1835, in Charles County, Southern Maryland, to one of the early families to settle that region. Affectionately known to family and friends as "Frank," she first met her future husband in Frederick, Maryland, in 1847 when the two teenagers were attending school there. Just when the courtship first started is not known, but the couple set their wedding date after Samuel Mudd graduated from medical school. They were married on November 11, 1857, at the bride's home in Bryantown, Maryland, not far from where the couple would take up permanent residence.

Frank would give birth to nine children between 1858 and 1878, of which eight would live to adulthood. At the time of the assassination, the Mudds had four children ranging in age from fifteen months to seven years.

When military detectives first visited the Mudd farm on Tuesday, April 18, Mrs. Mudd was interviewed before her husband had returned to the house from his farm, where he was tending to his tobacco crops. She told the detectives one piece of information that later proved troublesome to her husband. She said that the man with the injured leg wore a false beard. She noticed the beard had come loose on one side of his face. Dr. Mudd never mentioned this important piece of information when the soldiers interviewed him later that same morning, raising suspicions. When one of the detectives finally asked Mudd if the man with the injured leg wore false whiskers, Mudd replied that he didn't know if they were natural or false even though the detectives knew his wife had told him on Saturday evening after Booth and Herold left the Mudd house. This and other inconsistencies resulted in Mudd's arrest.

There is no record of Mrs. Mudd visiting her husband while he was in the Old Federal Penitentiary (in the Washington Arsenal) or during the trial. Admission to visit with a prisoner required the permission of Secretary of War Stanton and such visits were recorded by Major General John F. Hartranft, governor of the military prison and in charge of the prisoners while incarcerated. Permission was granted to family members and friends of several of the other prisoners.

Mrs. Mudd died at the home of her daughter Rose de Lima Mudd Gardiner on December 29, 1911, at the age of seventy-six.

Sources: Richard D. Mudd, *The Mudd Family of the United States*, 2 vols., (privately printed, 1951), vol. 1, 529–34.

*See also:* Mudd, Dr. Samuel Alexander

## Mudd House

Home of Dr. Samuel Alexander Mudd and place where John Wilkes Booth and David Herold stayed from four o'clock Saturday morning, April 15, until nearly seven o'clock that evening.

The home, once owned and lived in by descendants of the Mudd family, is now an historic site, restored to its original condition and operated by the Samuel A. Mudd Society.

## Mudd Society

Taken from the Dr. Samuel A. Mudd Society website: "The Society was founded June 22, 1976 as The Society for the Restoration of the Dr. Samuel A. Mudd Home. The home was placed on the Register of Historical Places, Oct. 1, 1974. The property was deeded to the Society by the Maryland Historical Trust, March 3, 1983. On March 26, 1981 the name was changed to the Dr. Samuel A. Mudd Society, Inc. The Society is dedicated to the preservation and interpretation of the historic Dr. Samuel A. Mudd Home. The Society encourages research into the role that this historic site played at the time of the assassination of President Abraham Lincoln."

Sources: www.somd.lib.md.us/MUSEUMS/Mudd/purpose.html

## Nanjemoy Creek

Major creek located in Charles County, Maryland, whose mouth empties into the Potomac River. On April 20, 1864, John Wilkes Booth and David Herold set out from Pope's Creek, a short distance to the southeast of Nanjemoy Creek, with the help of Thomas Jones in their attempt to row across the Potomac River. Their objective was Machodoc Creek on the Virginia side of the river, and the home of Elizabeth Quesenberry. They failed to reach the Virginia shore and wound up back on the Maryland shore, where the Nanjemoy Creek enters the Potomac River. The designation "creek" is misleading, as the mouth of Nanjemoy Creek is a wide expanse of water. There is much speculation as to why the two men returned to the Maryland side. The most likely explanation is given by the authors of *Come Retribution*. As they approached the Virginia shore, they encountered a Union patrol boat anchored offshore. They turned around and in their attempt to avoid the ship, found themselves back on the Maryland side of the river at Nanjemoy Creek. Entering the mouth of the creek they landed at the farm managed by John J. Hughes. The two fugitives waited until Saturday night, April 22, to attempt a second crossing. Setting out from Nanjemoy Creek, they successfully crossed the river, reaching the Virginia shore at Gambo Creek. From this point they made their way to the home of Elizabeth Quesenberry, a Confederate sympathizer, who sent for agent Thomas Harbin.

Sources: William A. Tidwell, James O. Hall, and David W. Gaddy, *Come Retribution* (Jackson: University Press of Mississippi, 1988), 454–57.

*See also:* Hughes, John J.; Harbin, Thomas Henry

## National Detective Police

A secret service police organization within the War Department. Detectives from the NDP cornered Booth and Herold at the Garrett farm in Virginia.

In the fall of 1862, Secretary of War Edwin M. Stanton created a special investigative unit within the War Department reporting directly to him, and appointed Colonel Lafayette C. Baker as its head. This unit adopted the official name of National Detective Police (NDP), which became the U.S. Secret Service shortly after the war.

The designation "National" is a misnomer. The organization spent most of its time within the environs of greater Washington, investigating corruption stemming from government contracts, bribery, graft, and the activities of Confederate agents and southern sympathizers operating within the nation's capital. Under Baker, the NDP became the investigative arm of the War Department.

On Monday, April 24, at 11:00 A.M., the assistant secretary of war, and head of the War Department's telegraph office, Thomas Eckert, received a telegraph message from Chapel Point, Maryland, that two men had crossed the Potomac River on Sunday, April 16. The two men were erroneously believed to be Booth and Herold. They were, in fact, Thomas Harbin and Joseph Baden, two Confederate agents. The wrong identification, however, spelled doom for Booth and Herold. Baker was in Eckert's office when the message came in and immediately went to Secretary of War Stanton and requested authorization to send a search party into King George County, Virginia. Stanton gave his approval and Baker sent two of his top agents, Everton J. Conger and Luther B. Baker, together with troopers from the 16th New York Cavalry in pursuit.

Sources: William A. Tidwell, James O. Hall, and David W. Gaddy, *Come Retribution* (Jackson: University Press of Mississippi, 1988), 468–69.

*See also:* Baker, Lafayette; Conger, Everton Judson

## National Hotel

John Wilkes Booth's place of residence when in Washington. The National was one of Washington's largest and finest hotels. Located on the corner of Sixth Street and Pennsylvania Avenue, the National had been the hotel of choice for southerners before the war (the Willard Hotel was the choice of northerners). Booth was staying at the National on March 17, 1865, when he gathered his cohorts in an attempt to capture Lincoln on his return to the White House following his visit to Campbell Hospital in northwest Washington to see a play staged for the convalescing soldiers. Booth had his team of conspirators gather at a restaurant not far from the hospital while he verified Lincoln was at the hospital. Lincoln had canceled his visit at the last minute to attend a ceremony in front of the National Hotel at the invitation of Indiana governor Oliver P. Morton. Morton accepted a captured Confederate battle flag from the 140th Indiana Volunteers, and Lincoln wanted to show the soldiers his support for their service to the Union.

On Saturday morning, April 15, 1865, government detectives were at the National Hotel searching Booth's room. They found a trunk in which Booth

kept his personal belongings, including a cache of letters, among which was the famous "Sam" letter written to Booth by Samuel Arnold on March 27, 1865.

Sources: Edward Steers, Jr., *Blood on the Moon* (Lexington: University Press of Kentucky, 2001), 170–71.

## National Volunteers

A secretive paramilitary organization whose core members were closely linked to the pro-Confederate, anti-Lincoln Knights of the Golden Circle. Both groups had as their objective the overthrow of the Federal government. The Baltimore members of the organization, led by Cipriano Ferrandini and William Byrne, a Baltimore barber and a businessman, respectively, had developed a plan to assassinate president-elect Lincoln during his stopover in Baltimore on February 22. On learning of the plot, Lincoln changed his plans, arriving in Baltimore nine hours ahead of his scheduled time and thus thwarting the assassin's plans. As the war progressed these anti-Lincoln, anti-Union organizations carried out various attempts to destroy Union and Federal property but failed in their main objectives to help the Confederacy gain independence and to defeat Lincoln's re-election in 1864.

Sources: Norma Cuthbert, *Lincoln and the Baltimore Plot 1861* (San Marino, Calif.: Huntington Library, 1949).

## Navy Submarine Battery Service, Confederate

The Navy Submarine Battery Service's main function was to protect the major ports of the Confederacy by laying minefields blocking access by the Union fleet. It was formed in the fall of 1862 and initially placed under the command of Matthew Fontaine Maury. Maury strongly believed that the most effective, and cheapest, way to defend southern ports was by mining the harbors. Maury experimented with several devices and developed the first electrical detonator. In 1862, Maury was sent to England as a secret agent and the navy replaced him with Lieutenant Hunter Davidson. Because the operation was clandestine, personnel were required to sign a security agreement.

Sources: William A. Tidwell, *April '65: Confederate Covert Action in the American Civil War* (Kent, Ohio: Kent State University Press, 1995), 49–50.

*See also:* Torpedo Bureau

## Navy Yard Bridge

Bridge crossing the Eastern Branch of the Potomac River near the Washington Navy Yard (the branch is known as the Anacostia River today). Booth crossed over the bridge shortly before 11:00 P.M. following his flight from Ford's Theatre. The bridge was the last obstacle Booth faced in fleeing Washington following his assassination of Lincoln.

This bridge, and other bridges leading into and out of the District of Columbia, were guarded by the military. Sergeant Silas T. Cobb, Company F, Third Massachusetts Heavy Artillery, stationed at Fort Baker, was head of the provost guards on the bridge that night. They were stationed at the Washington end of the bridge, where, shortly before 11:00 P.M., Booth arrived at the bridge. Cobb challenged him. After a brief exchange, Cobb allowed Booth to pass over the bridge. Approximately five minutes later, David Herold arrived at the bridge and was also permitted to pass over. A few minutes after Herold crossed the bridge, John Fletcher, manager of Naylor's Stables in Washing-

ton, where Herold had rented his horse that day, arrived as well. He was told he could cross over but would not be allowed back before daylight. Fletcher chose not to cross the bridge and went to Metropolitan Police Headquarters, located on Tenth Street, where he reported his stolen horse. While Cobb was reprimanded by Major General C. C. Augur, who commanded the defenses of Washington, he was not subject to court-martial.

Interestingly, Sergeant Lewis L. Chubb, 13th Michigan Light Artillery, who was in command of the picket post at the juncture of High Street (now Wisconsin Avenue) and Military Road on Saturday, April 15, was subject to court-martial for dereliction of duty for allowing George Atzerodt to pass through his picket post. Chubb was found not guilty and returned to his duties.

Sources: Joan L. Chaconas, "Crossing the Navy Yard Bridge," *Surratt Courier* 21, no. 9 (October 1996), 5–7.

*See also:* Cobb, Silas T.; Booth Escape Route

## Naylor, Thompson

Owner of Washington, D.C., livery stables located on E Street just south of Pennsylvania Avenue between Fourteenth and Thirteen-and-a-half streets. George Atzerodt visited the stables on April 14, at one o'clock in the afternoon, when he stabled his horse that he had rented earlier in the day from the stables of Keleher and Pyewell on Eighth Street. He returned just before seven o'clock that evening and took his horse out for a short ride, presumably to the Herndon House, where Booth met with Lewis Powell, David Herold, and Atzerodt to go over plans for that night. Atzerodt returned to the stable at 10:00 P.M. and asked the manager, John Fletcher, to have a drink with him at the Union Hotel at the corner of E and Thirteen-and-a-half streets. The two men then returned to the stable and Atzerodt took his horse out again and rode over to the Kirkwood House, where he had been assigned by Booth to assassinate Vice President Andrew Johnson.

David Herold also rented a horse from Naylor's stable earlier in the day and had failed to return it at the designated hour, leading stable manager John Fletcher to go looking for him.

Sources: Statement of John Fletcher, NARA, RG 153, M-599, reel 5, frames 414–21; Poore, *Conspiracy Trial*, vol. 1, 326; Pitman, *Trial*, 83, 145.

*See also:* Fletcher, John

## New Cathedral Cemetery

Cemetery located in Baltimore. Its most famous assassination internment is John H. Surratt, Jr., who died in 1916. Also buried in New Cathedral are Henry W. Mears, the funeral director who helped identify the corpse of John Wilkes Booth when it was released to the family in 1869, and Edward Murphy, a friend of Michael O'Laughlen who appeared as a witness at the conspiracy trial and testified to his accompanying O'Laughlen to Washington the day of the assassination.

Sources: John Muranelli and Edward Steers, Jr., *The Lincoln Assassination Underground: A Selection of Graves of People Associated with the Assassination of Abraham Lincoln* (Clinton, Md.: Surratt Society, 2008).

## Newman, Littleton P. D.

A witness for the prosecution. Newman, a neighbor of the Arnold home in Hookstown, Maryland, a suburb of Baltimore, testified that in September 1864, Arnold was helping to thresh wheat when a letter was brought to him. It was from John Wilkes Booth, and contained a fifty-dollar bill. Newman said Arnold gave him the letter to read, but Newman said he could not understand the "half dozen lines," as they were "very ambiguous." Newman handed the letter back to Arnold and asked him what it meant. Arnold "remarked that something big would take place one of these days, or be seen in the paper, or something to that effect."

Sources: Statement of L. P. D. Newman, NARA, RG 153, M-599, reel 2; frames 927–28; Poore, *Conspiracy Trial*, vol. 1, 423; Pitman, *Trial*, 239.

### Newport, Newport Tavern

A small community situated a few miles east of Allen's Fresh and the mouth of the Zekiah Swamp. Austin Adams and his wife operated the Newport Tavern, where Confederate agents such as Thomas Harbin, Joseph Baden, and Thomas Jones would meet. James Owens, an employee of the Adamses at the tavern, was arrested and interrogated by Colonel Henry H. Wells at the tavern. Owens later admitted that he had rowed Harbin and Baden across the Potomac River to Virginia on Sunday, April 16. At the time, the two were mistaken for Booth and Herold, leading Colonel Lafayette C. Baker, head of the National Detective Police, to go to Secretary of War Edwin M. Stanton and request a troop of cavalry to go after the two fugitives. On Monday, April 24, Stanton authorized Baker to send a troop from the 16th New York Cavalry across the river and into Virginia after Booth and Herold. Baker assigned his two top detectives, Everton J. Conger and Luther B. Baker, to accompany the detachment. It was the false identification that resulted from Owens rowing Harbin and Baden across the Potomac that ultimately led to Booth's demise at the Garrett farm on Wednesday, April 26.

Sources: Statement of James Owens, NARA, RG 94, M-619, reel 458, frames 412–15.

*See also:* Owens, James

### New York Avenue Church

The New York Avenue Presbyterian Church, also known as the Lincoln Church. Located within walking distance of the White House at New York Avenue and Thirteenth Street in Washington, D.C., its pastor, Phineas Gurley, was a favorite of Lincoln.

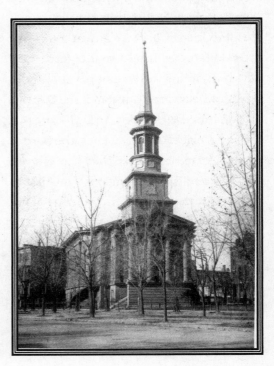

Lincoln admired Gurley for his intellect. The Lincolns rented a pew at the church shortly after coming to Washington, and enrolled their two sons, Willie and Tad, in the church's Sunday school.

The church has become a modern-day shrine of Lincoln. On display is Lincoln's handwritten copy of a compensation bill by which Lincoln proposed paying slave owners in the border states for emancipating their slaves. He introduced the bill on July 14, 1862. The bill called for the transfer of 6 percent interest-bearing bonds of the U.S. Treasury to each state, equal to the aggregate value of all the slaves within that state based on the census of 1860. Lincoln pointed out that "one half-day's cost of this war would pay for all the slaves in Delaware at four hundred dollars per head—that eighty-seven days cost of this war would pay for all the slaves in Delaware, Maryland, the District of Columbia, Kentucky, and Missouri at the same price." One day later, the border states rejected Lincoln's plan. The church also has on display a couch from Gurley's office that was used by Lincoln during his midweek visits to the church.

Sources: Frank E. Edgington, *History of the New York Avenue Presbyterian Church* (Washington, D.C.: New York Avenue Presbyterian Church, 1961).

*See also:* Gurley, Phineas

## Nicolay, John George (1832–1901)

Secretary to President Lincoln. Nicolay was away from Washington on the night Lincoln was assassinated. He returned immediately, staying on in his position organizing the president's papers. At the time of the funeral services, held in the East Room of the White House on April 19, Nicolay, along with Lincoln's other secretary, John Hay, stood alongside Robert Todd Lincoln, who sat at the foot of the president's coffin. Having strained relations with Mary Lincoln, Nicolay had sought a foreign appointment and on March 11, 1865, Lincoln had appointed him consul in Paris. Nicolay, along with John Hay, wrote a multivolume biography of Lincoln, *Abraham Lincoln: A History,* using Lincoln's papers, which were under the strict control of Robert Lincoln.

Sources: Mark E. Neely, Jr., *The Abraham Lincoln Encyclopedia* (New York: McGraw-Hill, 1982), 224–25.

*See also:* Hay, John

## Nothey, John

Witness at the conspiracy trial for Mary Surratt. Nothey, a neighbor of Mary Surratt in Surrattsville, Maryland, owed an unspecified sum of money to Mary Surratt and asked her for payment. On April 11 and April 14, she traveled from Washington to the Surratt Tavern in Surrattsville, her lawyers said, in an effort to collect the money Nothey owed her. It was at the time of these two visits that John Lloyd claimed she told him to have the "shooting irons" (carbines) and other items ready, as they would be picked up very soon. On April 14, the day of the assassination, Mary Surratt arrived at the tavern around 4:30 P.M., and finding Lloyd away in Upper Marlboro, waited for him to return. He returned shortly after 5:00 P.M. According to Lloyd's testimony, Mary gave him a package from Booth that contained Booth's field glass and told Lloyd to have "those shooting irons" ready, since persons would be by later that evening to pick them up. She made no effort to send for Nothey and returned to Washington after speaking with Lloyd. Lloyd's testimony, along with Louis Wiechmann, condemned Mary in the eyes of the tribunal.

Sources: John Henry Nothey, NARA, RG 153, M-599, reel 4, frames 411–12, Poore, *Conspiracy Trial*, vol. 2, 250; Pitman, *Trial*, 126; Statement of John M. Lloyd, NARA, RG 153, M-599, reel 5, frames 162–83; Poore, *Conspiracy Trial*, vol. 1, 115, 137; Pitman, *Trial*, 85, 87.

See also: Lloyd, John M.

## Notson, Dr. William M. (1836–1882)

One of twelve physicians present at Lincoln's bedside at the Petersen house as

he lay dying, and present at the autopsy in the guest room of the White House on Saturday, April 15.

Sources: W. Emerson Reck, A. *Lincoln: His Last 24 Hours* (Columbia, S.C.: University of South Carolina Press, 1994), 169; Edward Steers, Jr., *Blood on the Moon* (Lexington: University Press of Kentucky, 2001), 269 n25, 331 n1.

## Nott, Joseph T.

Bartender at the Surratt Tavern in Surrattsville, Maryland. Called as a witness at the conspiracy trial on behalf of Mary Surratt. Nott testified to Lloyd's drinking most of the day on April 14, the day Mary Surratt visited him at the tavern. The defense attempted to discredit Lloyd's damaging testimony against Mary Surratt by making it appear he was an alcoholic who was drunk on April 14, and whose observations could not be trusted. Nott failed to mention that while yes, Lloyd had been drinking that day, he was sober enough to repair a broken spring on Mary Surratt's rented buggy, which allowed her and Wiechmann to return to Washington, D.C.

Sources: Testimony of Joseph T. Nott, Poore, *Conspiracy Trial*, vol. 2, 482, vol. 3, 156; Pitman, *Trial,* 126, 127.

## Oak Hill

Charles County, Maryland, plantation of Henry Lowe Mudd, father of Dr. Samuel Mudd. Little was heard of Samuel Mudd's father during the time of Samuel Mudd's arrest and trial. Henry Mudd owned more than 1,700 acres of land in Charles County and eighty-nine slaves, making him and his sons among the largest slave owners in the county. Oak Hill was located a short distance from Samuel Mudd's house along the road to Bryantown.

David Herold and Samuel Mudd went to Oak Hill on Saturday, April 15, in the hope of borrowing a carriage to transport the injured Booth and his companion to their next stop in their attempt to escape to the South. Told there were no carriages in good repair available, Herold and Dr. Mudd continued on toward Bryantown. As they approached the outskirts of the village the two men saw Union soldiers milling about. Herold made a quick retreat back to Dr. Mudd's house, avoiding capture by the soldiers searching the area for Booth.

Sources: Edward Steers, Jr., "Samuel Alexander Mudd," in Edward Steers, Jr., *The Trial* (Lexington: University Press of Kentucky, 2003), lxxix–lxxxvii.

## O'Beirne, James Rowen (1838–1917)

Washington provost marshal. On Saturday morning, April 15, O'Beirne sent detective John Lee to the Kirkwood House hotel to check on Vice President Andrew Johnson, soon to be sworn in as president. Michael Henry, the barkeep and desk clerk, told Lee that the occupant of room 126 was acting in a suspicious manner. Lee went to the room, and forcing the door, entered and searched the room thoroughly. He found, among other things, a bankbook belonging to John Wilkes Booth. Between the findings of Lee and stableman John Fletcher, the authorities were able to link Atzerodt with Booth and Herold.

On Monday, April 17, O'Beirne sent detective Alexander Lovett, with nine troopers and two of O'Beirne's detectives, William Williams and Simon Gavacan, to Bryantown, Maryland, to aid in the search for Booth. Lovett arrested Mudd after several interrogations and took him back to Washington, where he was held in the Old Capitol Prison until transferred to the Federal penitentiary cell block at the Washington Arsenal. O'Beirne received two thousand dollars of the reward money offered for the capture of Booth.

Sources: Edward Steers, Jr., *Blood on the Moon* (Lexington: University Press of Kentucky), 132–33; Official Act of Congress, NARA, RG 94, M-619, reel 456, frames 416–19; Statement of James R. O'Beirne, NARA, RG 153, M-599, reel 2, frames 523–24.

## O'Daniel, Frank

Private in Company D, First Delaware Cavalry, stationed near Monocacy Junction, Maryland. O'Daniel played a role leading to the arrest of George A. Atzerodt. O'Daniel was in Clarksburg, Maryland, on the evening of April 19, 1865, ostensibly to recover an overcoat he left there the previous night. Around four o'clock that afternoon he met James Purdom, a local farmer who was an undercover informant for the Union army. Purdom told O'Daniel that a suspicious character using the name "Andrew Atwood" (George Atzerodt) had been talking during dinner at the house of Hezekiah Metz on Easter Sunday in a manner that implicated him in Lincoln's assassination.

O'Daniel took the information back to camp, where he told Sergeant George Lindsley, who told their commanding officer, Captain Solomon Townsend. Around nine o'clock that night, Townsend sent a troop of six men under command of Sergeant Zachariah W. Gemmill with orders to go to the Richter farm where Atwood (Atzerodt) was staying and arrest him. Gemmill, after picking up Purdom as a guide, rode to the home of Hartman Richter near Germantown, Maryland, and arrested Atwood, learning a short time later that he was George Atzerodt.

Although O'Daniel applied for a share of the reward money offered for Atzerodt's capture, his claim was denied.

Sources: Statement of Frank O'Daniel, NARA, RG 94, M-619, reel 455, frames 835–38.

*See also:* Gemmill, Zachariah

## Offutt, Emma

Sister-in-law of John Lloyd, operator of the Surratt Tavern in Surrattsville, Maryland, at the time of the assassination. Offutt testified at the conspiracy trial that she was riding to Washington, D.C., with Lloyd on April 11 when they met Mary Surratt and Louis Wiechmann traveling on the road to Surrattsville. Offutt supported Lloyd's testimony that Mary Surratt engaged Lloyd in hushed conversation, but said she did not hear the content of what was said. She also testified to being at the Surratt Tavern on April 14, when Mary Surratt came to the tavern with Louis Wiechmann and again engaged Lloyd in conversation. Offutt again claimed not to hear any of the conversation, but did confirm Lloyd's claim that Mary Surratt twice spoke with him the week prior to Lincoln's murder. Mrs. Offutt also testified that Lloyd "was very much in liquor, more so than I have ever seen him in my life." Offutt's statement, along with others, that Lloyd was heavy into alcohol was used to discredit him as a reliable witness against Mary Surratt.

While Lloyd may have been drinking heavily, he was sober enough to repair the broken wagon spring in the buggy that Mary Surratt and Louis Wiechmann used to come from Washington to the tavern, and presumably sober enough to remember what Mary Surratt told him.

Sources: Testimony of Mrs. Emma Offutt, Poore, *Conspiracy Trial*, vol. 1, 304–7; Pitman, *Trial*, 121, 125.

*See also:* Lloyd, John M.

### O'Laughlen, Michael (1840–1867)

A conspirator with John Wilkes Booth. O'Laughlen was convicted and sentenced to life in prison for his role in the assassination of President Lincoln. He contracted yellow fever at Fort Jefferson, Florida, while serving his sentence and died. O'Laughlen was born in Baltimore in 1834 and lived with his mother and younger brother Samuel William on Exeter Street across from the Baltimore home of the Booth family. O'Laughlen was an early playmate of John Wilkes Booth. The two boys eventually parted ways, only to meet again in August 1864, when Booth sent messages to O'Laughlen and Samuel Arnold to come to Barnum's City Hotel in Baltimore. It was during this meeting at the Barnum that Booth told O'Laughlen and Arnold about his plans to capture Lincoln and take him to Richmond. Both men agreed to help Booth carry out his plot.

On Monday, April 17, 1865, just two days after Lincoln's assassination, detectives from Provost Marshal James McPhail's office in Baltimore searched for Arnold and O'Laughlen. McPhail knew both families and knew the two men were acquaintances of Booth. Arnold was arrested on Monday, April 17, at Fort Monroe, Virginia. Word soon reached the O'Laughlen family in Baltimore that the authorities were looking for their son Mike. On Monday, April 17, O'Laughlen made arrangements to turn himself in to the Baltimore police to spare his mother the pain of seeing her son arrested in her

home. By the evening of the 17th, Samuel Arnold and Michael O'Laughlen were in the custody of McPhail and on their way to Washington, D.C. That same evening detectives were making their way to the boardinghouse of Mary Surratt armed with new information and new questions for the lady of the house.

Arnold's letter to Booth contained a reference to another of Booth's friends that the government added to their list of suspects, a man by the name of "Mike." Arnold had written in the "Sam" letter, "I called also to see Mike, but learned from his mother he had gone out with you, and had not returned." Washington was as much in the dark about "Mike" as they were about "Sam." But McPhail was ahead of Washington here also. He had known the O'Laughlen family for thirty years and his office was located only a short distance from the O'Laughlen home. McPhail's earlier investigation into Arnold had also turned up the name of O'Laughlen in association with Booth. Through the "Sam" letter, O'Laughlen was directly linked to Arnold.

Sources: Percy E. Martin, "Samuel Arnold and Michael O'Laughlen," in Edward Steers, Jr., *The Trial* (Lexington: University Press of Kentucky, 2003), lxxxviii–xcv.

*See also:* Arnold, Samuel Bland; "Sam" Letter

## Olcott, Henry S. (1832–1907)

One of three army officers picked by Secretary of War Edwin M. Stanton to manage the large amount of evidence being gathered in the first days of the investigation into Lincoln's murder. By Sunday, April 16, evidence was coming into the War Department so fast and in such volume that it was difficult to manage. Stanton solved the problem by appointing three officers with investigative experience from the War Department, asking them to take charge of the incoming evidence: Colonel Henry H. Wells, Lieutenant Colonel John A. Foster, and Colonel Henry S. Olcott. A few days later Stanton appointed Colonel Henry L. Burnett to take over the evidence-gathering operation and sort through all of the material and provide the prosecuting team with such evidence as might be useful in prosecuting the government's case against the eight conspirators on trial. Olcott, the most experienced of the three investigators, turned over several statements to Burnett that proved useful.

Sources: Statement of Henry Steel Olcott, NARA, RG 153, M-599, reel 5, frames 492–501; Statement of H. S. Olcott, NARA, RG 153, reel 3, frames 394–98; Statement of H. S. Olcott, NARA, RG 153, M-599, reel 3, frames 88–91.

## Old Capitol Prison

A building located near the U.S. Capitol that was used as the temporary capitol following the British occupation of Washington and the burning of several buildings, including the Capitol. During the Civil War the building was taken over by the War Department and used as a prison, hence its name, "Old Capitol Prison."

The complex was used mostly to hold persons accused of being "disloyal" to the Union. Several of the people in Southern Maryland who helped Booth in his effort to organize a plan to capture Lincoln, and helped him escape follow-ing the assassination, were arrested and held in the Old Capitol Prison. Unable to tie them to the murder of Lincoln, they were eventually released and returned to their homes, having escaped the hang-man's noose. William P. Wood was ap-pointed superintendent of Old Capitol Prison and Carroll Annex in 1862 and remained superintendent through the conspiracy trial.

Sources: Dorothy Meserve Kunhardt and Phil-ip B. Kunhardt, Jr., *Twenty Days* (New York: Harper & Row, 1965), 188–90.

*See also:* Carroll Prison

## Old Federal Penitentiary

Both the penitentiary where the prisoners were held and the military tribunal courtroom where they would be tried were located on the grounds of the Washington Arsenal, located in southwest Washington. Back in 1791, Pierre L'Enfant, the designer of the Federal City, had designated a section of local land known as Greenleaf Point as a military base. The site was ideally situated on the southernmost tip of the city. Bounded by the Potomac River to the west and the Eastern Branch of the Potomac to the east, it was surrounded on three sides by water. The army developed the site as an arsenal in 1803. In 1831, a Federal penitentiary was built there, boasting 160 cells in a building 120 feet in length and fifty feet in width. The cells, each measuring seven feet by three and a half feet, with seven-foot ceilings, were arranged in four tiers. The upper tier was originally intended for female prisoners, but a separate addition was added to the central cell block, especially for female prisoners.

It was in this addition that the Lincoln conspirators were held during their trial. Under Major General Winfield Scott Hancock's instructions, a door was cut into an adjoining room that had once served as the deputy warden's quarters. By this arrangement the prisoners were moved from their cells directly into the adjoining courtroom without exposing them to onlookers. At its peak, the prison complex was three hundred feet long and fifty feet wide, boasting cells for 220 prisoners. It was widely considered one of the best facilities in the country. No less vigilant an observer than Dorothea Dix, one of the era's most outspoken prison reformers, gave her approval to the facility, donating money to the prison library.

With the coming of the Civil War in 1861, however, the demands of the arsenal far outweighed the need for a Federal penitentiary, and President Lincoln ordered that it be turned over to the War Department to be used as additional space for the arsenal. The prisoners were transferred to the Federal penitentiary in Albany, New York.

Sources: Edward Steers, Jr., and Harold Holzer, eds., *The Lincoln Assassination Conspirators: Their Confinement and Execution, as Recorded in the Letterbook of John Frederick Hartranft* (Baton Rouge: Louisiana State University Press, 2009).

*See also:* Washington Arsenal

## Oldroyd, Osborn H. (1842–1930)

An early Lincoln collector whose extensive assassination-related memorabilia is displayed at Ford's Theatre. As a young man working at a newspaper stand in his hometown of Mount Vernon, Ohio,

Oldroyd became a fan of President Lincoln and began acquiring various items pertaining to his election campaign and presidency. He enlisted in the 20th Ohio Volunteer Infantry at eighteen and served throughout the war. After the war he held various administrative positions, all the while collecting Lincolniana. In 1883, Oldroyd moved to Springfield, Illinois, and rented the Lincoln home, where he put his growing collection on display. In 1893, he moved his collection to Washington, D.C., and displayed his collection in the Petersen house, where Lincoln died.

As Oldroyd grew older and found it increasingly difficult to maintain his collection, he offered to sell it to the U.S. government. The government declined, but Henry Ford offered to buy the collection for fifty thousand dollars. Oldroyd wanted to keep the collection in Washington and sought the help of Republican congressman Henry R. Rathbone, the son of Lincoln's guest the night he was assassinated in Ford's Theatre. Rathbone introduced legislation authorizing the Congress to purchase the collection. In 1932, the collection was purchased by the U.S. government and moved into Ford's Theatre, where it was on display until the restoration of the theater in 1964. Following restoration, only select pieces of the collection were displayed, the great bulk of the collection placed in storage on the second floor at Washington's Union Station, a poor environment for maintaining artifacts. The collection was eventually moved to the U.S. National Park Service facilities near Landover, Maryland.

Oldroyd died in 1930 and is buried in Oak Ridge Cemetery in Springfield, Illinois, where he rests alongside many of Lincoln's friends.

Sources: Mark E. Neely, Jr., *The Abraham Lincoln Encyclopedia* (New York: McGraw-Hill, 1982), 228.

## Olds, Reverend Dr. Mark

Family minister to the Herold family. Minister at Christ Episcopal Church in Washington, D.C. Herold's mother and seven sisters attended the church. Reverend Olds visited Herold in his prison cell prior to his execution. He did not accompany Herold on the scaffold at his execution.

Sources: Roy Z. Chamlee, *Lincoln's Assassins: A Complete Account of Their Capture, Trial, and Punishment* (Jefferson, N.C.: McFarland, 1990), 455.

*See also:* Walter, Father Jacob Ambrose; Wiget, Father Bernadine F.; Gillette, Reverend Abram Dunn

## Olin, Abram B. (1808–1879)

Justice on the Supreme Court of the District of Columbia. As Lincoln lie dying in the rear bedroom of the Petersen house, Secretary of War Edwin M. Stanton set up a court of inquiry in an adjoining parlor. He asked David Kellogg Cartter, chief justice of the Supreme Court of the District of Columbia, to take charge of questioning witnesses as they were brought to the Petersen house. He then sent for two other jurists to assist in the questioning: Judge Abram B. Olin, and Britten A. Hill, a highly respected law partner of General Thomas Ewing, the attorney who would later represent Samuel Mudd, Edman Spangler, and Samuel Arnold. The three jurists interviewed six witnesses whose statements were recorded verbatim by James Tanner, an employee in the Ordnance Bureau of the War Department.

Sources: William C. Edwards and Edward Steers, Jr., eds., *The Lincoln Assassination: The Evidence* (Urbana: University of Illinois Press, 2009).

*See also:* Cartter, David Kellogg; Hill, Britten A., Tanner, James

## Ontario Bank

Canadian bank located in Montreal and used by Booth in several financial transactions. On October 27, 1864, Booth opened a savings account in the Ontario Bank depositing $200 in Canadian bills and a check from a Confederate money broker by the name of Davis for $255, for a total of $455. Booth also purchased a draft on the Ontario Bank for 61 pounds, 12 shillings, and 10 pence with $300 dollars in gold. The draft was still on Booth's body when examined following his death at the Garrett farm. Together, the transactions were equal to $1,115 U.S. greenbacks or the equivalent of approximately $13,000 in current spending power.

On April 15, while searching George Atzerodt's room at the Kirkwood Hotel in Washington, D.C., detective John Lee found Booth's bankbook from the On-

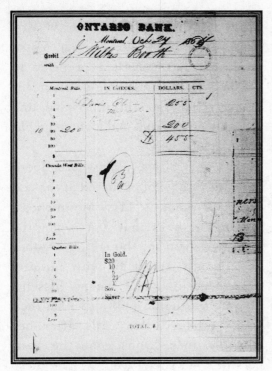

Booth's bank account (Canada)

tario Bank showing a balance of $455. The book linked Atzerodt to Booth. During the conspiracy trial, Robert Anson Campbell, head teller at the bank, testified to Booth's transactions, and also testified to the Confederate agents in Montreal opening an account in the amount of $649,973.28, money used to finance Confederate covert operations in the northern states.

Sources: William A. Tidwell, James O. Hall, and David W. Gaddy, *Come Retribution* (Jackson: University Press of Mississippi, 1988), 334; Testimony of Robert Anson Campbell, Poore,

*Conspiracy Trial*, vol. 2, 83–89; Pitman, *Trial*, 45–47.

*See also*: Bill of Exchange; Campbell, Robert Anson

## Order of American Knights

Prior to the Civil War, an organization called the Knights of the Golden Circle (KGC) existed throughout the southern states. Its purpose was to have the United States annex a major part of Mexico and allow slavery to extend into the newly acquired territory. By the time the Civil War erupted, the KGC was a moribund organization. The leaders of the newly formed Confederate States of America sent emissaries into certain northern and western states in an effort to revive the KGC and garner support for the Confederacy using any means possible, including terrorist-style tactics. Using the remnants of the KGC, a new organization was formed, the Order of American Knights (OAK). While its stated purpose was to bolster the recently beaten Democratic Party in the North, its real purpose was to organize the local chapters into a paramilitary organization that could aid in overthrowing the local and state governments and setting up organizations that would support the Confederacy.

The Confederacy saw part of its objective come to realization when the OAK helped foment the draft riots in New

York City in the summer of 1863. There were many problems in being able to organize activities on a larger, more national scale, and historians have debated the effectiveness of the OAK. There is no doubt, however, that the organization existed and was widespread. It tried to cause revolution in more than one state.

Sources: William A. Tidwell, James O. Hall, and David W. Gaddy, *Come Retribution* (Jackson: University Press of Mississippi, 1988), 182–85.

*See also:* Knights of the Golden Circle; National Volunteers

### Our American Cousin

Popular comedy by English playwright Tom Taylor, written in 1852. President Lincoln attended the Friday, April 14, 1865, evening performance of the play at Ford's Theatre, where he was assassinated. The play was a spoof on British aristocracy and the American "backwoodsman." Taylor sold the play to American actress and theatrical businesswoman Laura Keene for a thousand dollars. Keene first performed the play in 1858 in New York, where it was a huge success.

The male lead character, Asa Trenchard, played by Harry Hawk in the April 14 production, is a coarse, uneducated bumpkin who visits his English cousins where he is mistaken for a wealthy suitor for the daughter of Mrs. Mountchessington, an English matriarch. Asa has inherited property in England and travels there to claim his property. He forgoes his inheritance and gives his money to a maid whom he has fallen in love with.

The part of the play where Booth fired his fatal shot occurred at the end of act 3, scene 2. Mrs. Mountchessington discovers that Asa is not the wealthy cousin she thought, but rather an uncouth American with nothing to offer her daughter except "hisself." Mountchessington upbraids Asa, then walks offstage. Asa calls after her with the lines, "Don't know the manners of good society, eh? Well I guess I know enough to turn you inside out, old gal—you sockdologizing old mantrap." The line always generated loud laughs from the audience and it is believed that Booth used the moment in the play to cover the report of his pistol. They were the last sounds heard by Lincoln.

Sources: Tom Taylor, *Our American Cousin* (New York: Samuel French, 1869); Edward Steers, Jr., *Blood on the Moon* (Lexington: University Press of Kentucky), 117–18.

### Owens, James

An employee at James Adams's Newport Tavern in Charles County, Maryland.

Owens, along with Adams and his wife, was arrested on April 28. Interrogated by Colonel Henry H. Wells, Owens gave a lengthy statement admitting to rowing two Confederate agents across the Potomac River on Sunday, April 17. Owens's two passengers were mistaken for Booth and Herold and resulted in Stanton authorizing Colonel Lafayette C. Baker to send a troop of the 16th New York Cavalry after the two men. As a result, Booth and Herold were cornered at the Garrett farm, where Booth was killed and Herold taken into custody. Thus, a mistaken identity proved to be Booth's undoing.

Sources: Statement of James Owens, NARA, RG 94, M-619, reel 458, frames 412–15.

*See also:* Adams, James

## Page, Nathan

Montgomery County, Maryland, farmer who informed Union army undercover agent James Purdom of George Atzerodt's suspicious behavior, which information led to his capture. Page lived near Germantown and the home of Hezekiah Metz. On Easter Sunday, April 16, 1865, Page stopped by Metz's house, where he was invited for the noonday dinner. George Atzerodt was also invited for dinner that day, having spent Saturday night at Clopper's Mill, not far from the Metz house. During the dinner, Atzerodt made the statement that "if the man that was to follow [General Ulysses S. Grant] had followed him, it was likely to be so" (that Grant would have been shot as well as Lincoln). Later that evening Page ran into James Purdom, a local farmer who served as a Union army informant, and told him about Atzerodt's comments. Purdom passed the information on to Private Frank O'Daniel of the First Delaware Cavalry, stationed at Monocacy Junction, who then passed the information on to his sergeant, George Lindsley. Lindsley told his commanding officer, Captain Solomon Townsend, who sent a troop of cavalry under the command of Sergeant Zachariah W. Gemmill to the Richter farm with orders to arrest Atzerodt and anyone else who seemed suspicious. Gemmill arrived at the Richter farm with Purdom as guide and arrested Atzerodt and Hartman Richter. Purdom received $2,878.78 as his share of the reward money offered for the capture of Atzerodt. Page, O'Daniel, and Lindsley did not receive any of the reward money despite their part in Atzerodt's capture. Page is buried in the small cemetery next to the Riffleford Baptist Church near Darnstown, Maryland.

Sources: Statement of Nathan Page, NARA, RG 94, M-619, reel 455, frame 563; Statement of Sergeant George Lindsley, NARA, RG 153, M-599, reel 2, frames 233–34; Testimony of Hezekiah Metz in Poore, *Conspiracy Trial*, vol. 1, 353; Pitman, *Trial*, 149; Statement of James W. Purdom, NARA, RG 153, M-599, reel 2, frames 227–29.

*See also:* Atzerodt, George Andrew; Lindsley, George G.; Metz, Hezekiah; Purdom, James W.

## Paine, Lewis

Paine was the alias that Lewis Powell used in signing his oath of allegiance in March 1865. Lewis Powell used the name "Powell," and not "Paine," while serving with Mosby's Rangers in 1864.

Sources: Betty J. Ownsbey, *Alias "Paine": Lewis Thornton Powell, the Mystery Man of the Lincoln Conspiracy* (Jefferson, N.C.: McFarland, 1993), 33.

*See also:* Powell, Lewis Thornton

## Parker, John Frederick (1830–1890)

A member of the District of Columbia's Metropolitan Police force assigned to the White House as President Lincoln's bodyguard. Parker was one of eleven men who served as bodyguard to the president during his tenure in office. On the night of April 14, Parker accompanied the Lincolns and their guests to Ford's Theatre. Once there, he was basically on his own until the play was over and the Lincolns were ready to return to the White House. Accounts by historians that Parker was somehow derelict in his duty or had abandoned his post are wrong. It was Parker's duty to accompany the president to and from, not stay with him inside the theater or any building. In fact, he was principally a White House guard, not a bodyguard in the modern sense.

No one knows exactly where Parker was at the time Booth shot Lincoln. Wherever he was, he was not outside the presidential box. Seated closest to the door leading into the hallway outside the box was Charles Forbes, the president's messenger and personal valet. It was Forbes whom Booth encountered before entering the box, and it was Forbes who allowed Booth to enter. Following the assassination, Parker was charged with allowing the president to be shot. A hearing was held in camera and no record survived the hearing. Parker was exonerated of any responsibility, and returned to duty on the Metropolitan Police force. He was subsequently dismissed three years later for violating the rules of the police force.

Sources: James O. Hall, "The Mystery of Lincoln's Guard," *Surratt Society News* 7, no. 5 (May 1982), 4–6; Timothy H. Bakken, "Mary Lincoln's Fatal Favor," *Rail Splitter* 8, nos. 1–2 (Summer–Fall 2002), 1, 7–9; Edward Steers, Jr., *Blood on the Moon* (Lexington: University Press of Kentucky, 2001), 23–24.

## Parker House

Hotel in Boston, Massachusetts, believed to be the meeting place for Confederate agents with John Wilkes Booth. On July 26, 1864, Booth registered at the Parker House. The authors of *Come Retribution* make a case for a clandestine meeting there with four individuals they believe were Confederate agents from Montreal. The four individuals—Charles R. Hunter, (Toronto), A. J. Bursted (Baltimore), H. V. Clinton (Hamilton, Ontario), and R. A. Leech (Montreal)—registered at the same time as Booth and left at the same time as well. Two weeks later, Booth was in Baltimore recruiting Samuel Arnold and Michael O'Laughlen into his plot. All attempts by the authors of *Come Retribution* failed to locate the men in directories and census reports, leading them to believe the names in the hotel registry were aliases. The evidence in support of their theory is thin, and it is not certain that such a meeting took place.

Another explanation for Booth's presence in Boston was his courting Isabel Sumner, a young and attractive girl who lived in that city with her parents.

Sources: William A. Tidwell, James O. Hall, and David W. Gaddy, *Come Retribution* (Jackson: University Press of Mississippi, 1988), 262–63.

## Parr, David Preston (1819–1900)

A china dealer with a shop in Baltimore that served as a safe stop and conduit for Confederate secret service agents and activities. Parr was a Confederate agent whose shop was also a Confederate mail drop. On January 13, 1865, Lewis Powell took the oath of allegiance in Alexandria, Virginia, and made his way to Baltimore. On January 21, Parr arranged for John Surratt ("Harrison" Surratt) to meet with Lewis Powell in his shop. As a result, Powell joined Surratt and Booth in their conspiracy. On March 14, 1865, John Surratt sent a telegram to Parr telling him to send Powell to Washington, D.C., to Mrs. Surratt's boardinghouse on H Street. Parr was arrested under suspicion of being involved in Booth's plot but eventually released for lack of evidence.

Sources: Statement of David Preston Parr, NARA, RG 153, M-599, reel 5, frames 517–41; Statement of David Preston Parr, NARA, RG 153, M-599, reel 3, frames 213–14; Statement of David Preston Parr, NARA, RG 153, M-599, reel 6, frames 18–27.

*See also:* Powell, Lewis Thornton; Surratt, John Harrison, Jr.

## Payne, Lewis

Alias used by Lewis Thornton Powell. Powell said he used the names "Payne" and "Paine" so that his parents would not know how he died if he were killed while attempting to assassinate Seward. He wanted them to think he died on the battlefield. Powell was referred to through most of the trial as "Payne." His real name, Powell, did not become known until late in May, several weeks after the trial began.

Sources: Betty J. Ownsbey, *Alias "Paine": Lewis Thornton Powell, the Mystery Man of the Lincoln Conspiracy* (Jefferson, N.C.: McFarland, 1993), 33.

*See also:* Powell, Lewis Thornton

## Peanut John

See Burroughs, John

## Peddicord, John M. (1843–1921)

Peddicord was a sergeant in the marines detailed for duty on the monitor USS

*Montauk,* on which the conspirators were temporarily held in April 1865, before their transfer to the cell block in the Washington Arsenal. Peddicord was on duty when the *John S. Ide* pulled alongside the monitor and the body of John Wilkes Booth was brought on board. The body was placed on a carpenter's bench under an awning to protect it from the hot rays of the sun. While the body was on board the *Montauk* several persons came on board to identify it. Army surgeon general Joseph K. Barnes performed an autopsy on the body before taking it to the Washington Arsenal for burial.

Several years after these events Peddicord would read the story in the newspapers that claimed the body on board the *Montauk* was not that of Booth, but another man. Peddicord knew better and, realizing his special place in history, wrote an article about his experience of April 27, 1865, that was published in the *Roanoke Evening News:*

> I turned out on deck where [Sergeant Hartley] was along side a carpenter's bench on which lay the body of a man wrapped about in a soldier's blanket. . . . It was the body of the assassin, John Wilkes Booth, which had been brought up the river during the night by the detachment of troops who had captured him. . . . [W]e unwrapped the face and

compared it with a photograph, and I also remember the letters in India ink on the back of his hand in pale straggling characters, "J.W.B.," as a boy would have done it.

Peddicord was one of several witnesses who positively identified the body on the *Montauk* as that of John Wilkes Booth. He noted it had the distinctive mark of initials tattooed on the left hand in the base of the V formed by the index finger and thumb, just as Booth's sister, Asia, described it in her memoir about her brother.

Sources: James O. Hall, "The Body on the Monitor," in Laurie Verge, ed., *The Body in the Barn* (Clinton, Md.: Surratt Society, 1993), 70.

*See also:* Autopsy, John Wilkes Booth

## Pendel, Thomas Francis (1825–1909)

One of the members of the Metropolitan Police force assigned to the White House as a bodyguard for President Lincoln. Born in Washington, D.C., in 1824, Pendel joined the Washington Metropolitan Police in 1862 at the age of thirty-eight. On November 3, 1864, Pendel, along with John R. Cronin, Alphonso T. Donn, and Andrew C. Smith, was assigned to the White House. Subsequently, seven other members of the police force were assigned to the White House detail including John F. Parker. Parker relieved Pendel on the evening of April 14, 1865. There is no known record that describes the duties and responsibilities of these guards. On a hit-or-miss basis at least one officer accompanied Lincoln when he moved about the city—provided Lincoln alerted them to his travels or didn't simply slip out of the White House without notifying them.

Sources: Thomas F. Pendel, *Thirty-six Years in the White House* (Washington, D.C.: Neale, 1902), 9–13, 26–29, 32–33, 38–45; Edward Steers, Jr., *Blood on the Moon* (Lexington: University Press of Kentucky, 2001), 23–24.

*See also:* Bodyguard, Lincoln's

## Pennsylvania House

See Kimmel House

## Petersen House

The house where Lincoln died. It is located across the street from Ford's Theatre and is open to the public, under the administration of the National Park Service. Built in 1849 by William Petersen (1816–1871), a German-born tailor, the house has its entrance above street level and is reached by a curving stairway of ten risers. There is also a basement entrance in the front that led to Petersen's tailor shop, which was located in the front basement room. The house was home to several tenants on the first and second floors, who were accommodated in eleven rooms. The basement area has two rooms, the first floor contained a front and back parlor and a rear bedroom (where Lincoln died), the second floor consisted of three rooms, and the third floor also contained three rooms. On entering the front of the house on the first floor, a narrow hallway passed by the two parlors on the left before ending at the doorway to the rear bedroom.

Lincoln was taken to the room at the end of the hall on the first floor. The

room was small, measuring nine and a half feet wide by seventeen feet long and had a small dresser and two chairs in addition to the bed. The room was occupied by a young Union soldier named William Clark (known as "Willie"). Clark worked in the quartermaster general's office in Washington. The front parlor served as a mourning room during the deathwatch and it was here that Mary Lincoln waited between visits to her husband. The rear parlor served as the war room, where Secretary of War Edwin M. Stanton assumed control of the only two activities the government would concern itself with for the next nine hours: assassination and war, in that order.

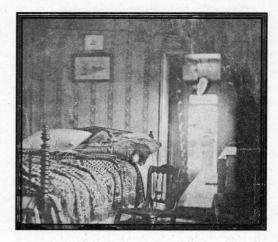

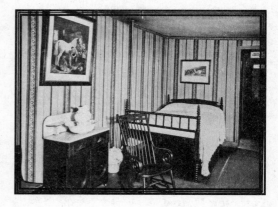

The bed in the room was too small to accommodate Lincoln's six foot four frame. Clark's bed was pulled away from the wall, allowing doctors access from both sides of the bed. The president's body was then laid diagonally across the bed, placing his head closest to the door and his feet closest to the wall. Throughout the night various dignitaries and friends visited the Petersen house to see the dying Lincoln. As best as can be determined, fifty-seven people visited the dying president, but there were never more than a dozen people in the room at any one time. Artists and printmakers went to work representing the death chamber, fitting in as many important people as they could put on the canvas or printer's block. The artists' renditions were so crammed with people that Willie Clark's bedroom became known as "the rubber room." Lincoln died in Clark's rear bedroom at 7:22 A.M. on the morning of April 15, 1865.

In 1893, Osborn H. Oldroyd moved into the house, where he displayed his vast collection of Lincoln memorabilia. In 1896, the Federal government purchased the building, allowing Oldroyd to continue to display his collection. The Park Service restored the house to the way it was on the evening of the assassination. In 1932, the government purchased Oldroyd's collection and moved it into Ford's Theatre, turning the Petersen house back closer to its layout at the time of Lincoln's death.

Sources: George J. Olszewski, *House Where Lincoln Died: Furnishing Study* (Washington, D.C.: U.S. Government Printing Office, 1967); Mark E. Neely, Jr., *The Abraham Lincoln Encyclopedia* (New York: McGraw-Hill, 1982), 235–36; Edward Steers, Jr., *Blood on the Moon* (Lexington: University Press of Kentucky, 2001), 123–24.

*See also*: Clark, William "Willie" T.

## Phillips, Henry B. (1819–1896)

An actor and member of John Ford's stock company. Phillips was one of the six persons interviewed in the Petersen house the night of the assassination. He told the special panel he was backstage dressing for his singing performance between acts. Phillips said he spoke with Harry Hawk, who was on the stage at the time of the shooting. Hawk told Phillips, "that was Wilkes Booth who rushed past me. I could say it if I was on my death bed." Phillips also told the panel, "I have been a very dear friend of Mr. Booth almost from infancy."

Sources: Henry B. Phillips, NARA, RG 153, M-599, reel 7, frames 490–92; Maxwell Whiteman, ed., *While Lincoln Lay Dying* (Philadelphia: Union League of Philadelphia, 1968).

## Pinkerton, Allan (1819–1884)

A private detective who infiltrated a conspiracy to assassinate president-elect Lincoln in Baltimore, and thereby averted his murder. Pinkerton worked in the first year of the war as a Union spy. He became one of the most famous detectives in American history. Born in Scotland in 1819, Pinkerton moved to America in 1842. He founded a private detective agency and had as his clients several prominent railroads and the Adams Express Company. He was hired by the Philadelphia, Wilmington,

& Baltimore Railroad in 1861 to protect its rail lines from sabotage by Confederate sympathizers and subversive groups intent on supporting Confederate independence. In the course of his investigation learned of a plot to assassinate president-elect Lincoln during a planned stopover in Baltimore on his way to Washington. When Lincoln and his party reached Philadelphia, Pinkerton told Norman Judd, traveling with Lincoln, about the plot. Judd arranged for a meeting in Philadelphia's Continental Hotel, where Lincoln patiently listened as Pinkerton urged him to change his schedule, bypassing Baltimore and going directly to Washington.

Unknown to Pinkerton, detectives from the New York Police Department had also learned of the Baltimore plot and informed Major General Winfield Scott, who informed secretary of state designate William H. Seward. Seward sent his son Frederick to Philadelphia with the information. Hearing each presentation separately, Lincoln became satisfied the plot was real and agreed to alter his schedule, but only after fulfilling a commitment to speak in Harrisburg, Pennsylvania.

Following his speech in Harrisburg, Lincoln attended a dinner. Midway through the dinner Lincoln excused himself and along with Pinkerton agents boarded a special train that took him back to Philadelphia. Here he transferred to a train that took him to Baltimore, where he arrived at 3:00 A.M. at the President Street Station nine hours ahead of schedule. Lincoln's coach was then pulled through the streets of Baltimore by a team of horses to the Camden Yards Station of the Baltimore & Ohio Railroad, where the car with Lincoln and Pinkerton's agents was attached to the train for Washington. Lincoln arrived in Washington at 6:00 A.M., leaving his would-be assassins back in Baltimore waiting for the twelve o'clock train without Lincoln on board.

Sources: Norma B. Cuthbert, *Lincoln and the Baltimore Plot 1861* (San Marino, Calif.: Huntington Library, 1949); Allan Pinkerton, "Allan Pinkerton's Unpublished Letter," *American Magazine* 75, no. 4 (February 1913), 18–22.

*See also:* Baltimore Plot; Ferrandini, Cipriano

## Pitman, Benn (1822–1910)

The official court recorder of the proceedings of the military tribunal that tried the Lincoln conspirators. Pitman had a staff of recorders who alternated recording testimony and transcribing it at the end of each day's session. Pitman was the brother of English-born Isaac Pitman, the man who developed a system

of shorthand known as phonography in 1837. Benn Pitman emigrated from England to the United States in 1852 and established the Phonographic Institute in Cincinnati. By 1865, Pitman had already served the Federal government in several instances as a court recorder, his most famous trial being the Indiana Treason Trial, which eventually wound up before the Supreme Court of the United States in a case known as *Ex Parte Milligan*. He was hired again by the government to record, transcribe, and reproduce the daily testimony at the Lincoln conspiracy trial, for which he eventually received approval to publish the transcripts he produced. The only stipulations placed upon Pitman were that the production of such a publication result in no cost to the government and that it "adhere to strict accuracy."

The Rules of Proceeding specified that a copy of each day's testimony be provided to the judge advocate general and to "the counsel of the prisoners." While it is not likely that Pitman provided transcribed copies to each of the defense attorneys, he did make his transcriptions available as revealed by defense attorney Thomas Ewing's statement in the trial record. Ewing commented before the commission: "I will state that the reporters are not able to furnish us immediately with an official copy of the record; it is behind-hand always a day or more: but inasmuch as the record is published quite accurately in the 'intelligencer,' and in fact published, I think from the notes of the reporters . . ." Ewing's reference to the *Intelligencer* refers to the *Daily National Intelligencer*, a major Washington, D.C., paper of the day. Pitman supplied "press copies" to the *Intelligencer* and to commercial telegraphers who transmitted the content of the copies to Philadelphia at the end of each day for publication in the *Philadelphia Inquirer*. Thus, both the *Intelligencer* and *Inquirer* published verbatim copies of the trial testimony daily.

Pitman carefully edited and collated the 4,300 pages of transcribed testimony by defendant and indexed the arranged testimony by name, date, whether the witness was a prosecution or defense witness, and a one-line summary of what the witness testified to. Herein lies the strength of the Pitman version. Thus all of the testimony relating to Dr. Samuel Mudd is grouped together in one section, and each witness is identified as a prosecution or defense witness. What Pitman lacks, however, is a verbatim transcription of the trial testimony. Pitman frequently merged the witnesses' response to multiple questions by the prosecutors and defense attorneys summarizing the testimony into a single, often long response. Where the testimony is unclear or in controversy, Pitman gives the testimony verbatim. Pitman's version compares favorably with the verbatim transcript and shows that Pitman tried very hard to adhere to the essence of the testimony. The last feature found in the Pitman version, which is lacking in the three-volume version published by Ben Perley Poore, are the final arguments by the attorneys. This is a major difference. There are important facts to be gleaned from these arguments, and their absence from the Poore version places a limitation on that one's use.

Sources: Edward Steers, Jr., *Blood on the Moon* (Lexington: University Press of Kentucky, 2001), 123–24; Edward Steers, Jr., "Introduction," in Edward Steers, Jr., ed., *The Trial* (Lexington: University Press of Kentucky, 2003), xiii–xiv.

*See also:* Poore, Ben Perley; Press Copy, Trial Transcriptions

## Playbill, *Our American Cousin*

There are two versions of the playbill for April 14, 1865. Henry Polkinhorn, the theater's printer, began running off copies of version one when word came that the president would attend the evening performance. It was decided to mark the occasion by having actress Laura Keene sing H. B. Phillips's special song, "Honor to Our Soldiers." Circumstances were such, however, that Keene did not sing the special tribute scheduled between the second and third acts.

Polkinhorn was already in the process of printing the playbills when he received word from Ford's Theatre to stop. He interrupted the print run and prepared a second playbill inserting thirteen new lines, including an eight-line stanza from Phillips's song:

***Patriotic Song and Chorus, "Honor to Our Soldiers"***
Honor to our soldiers,
Our Nation's greatest pride,
Who neath our Starry Banner's folds,
Have fought, have bled and died:

They're nature's noblest handiwork,
No King so proud as they,
God bless the heroes of the land,
And cheer them on their way.

*Words by H.B. Phillips; Music Composed
and Arranged by Prof. William
Withers, Jr., Solos by Miss M. Hart, H.B.
Phillips and George M. Arth
And the Ladies and Gentlemen of the
Company*

The initial print run without the inserted words is the first version, and the playbill with the inserted words shown above announcing the special song is the second version.

John E. Buckingham, the doorkeeper on the evening of the assassination, produced a "souvenir" copy of version one, thus adding a third copy that has confused collectors on more than one occasion. This copy by Buckingham is easily distinguished from the two authentic versions by several anomalies: the letter *e* at the end of "Keene" is poorly printed, the blurred printing of the number 6 in "Night 196" makes it appear as "Night 191," and "orchestra chairs" is changed to "orchestra." The Buckingham copy was printed by Polkinhorn making it as near a perfect copy as one can get. After 1865, several copies of the playbill were produced, but none on Polkinhorn's press using his type.

Original specimens of the playbill are rare and highly sought after by collectors and museums alike.

Sources: Theodosia Kichorowsky, "Library Catalogs Playbills from the Night of Lincoln Assassination," *Library of Congress Information Bulletin* 40, no. 45 (November 6, 1981), 390–92.

## Polkinhorn, Henry (1813–1890)

Printer used by Ford's Theatre for printing playbills. Polkinhorn printed two versions of the playbill announcing *Our American Cousin* starring Laura Keene in a benefit performance on April 14, 1865. Polkinhorn was one of several investors in John Ford's rebuilt theater following its destruction by fire in December 1862.

Sources: Paula Degrin, ed., *Ford's Theatre and the Lincoln Assassination* (Washington, D.C.: Parks and History Association, 2001), 27; Theodosia Kichorowsky, "Library Catalogs Playbills from the Night of Lincoln Assassination," *Library of Congress Information Bulletin* 40, no. 45 (November 6, 1981), 390–92.

*See also:* Playbill, April 14, 1865

## Poore, Ben Perley

Newspaper journalist in Washington. Poore published the verbatim trial transcript in three volumes. Shortly after the assassination conspirators' trial ended, three separate hardback versions of the testimony were published. The first version to become available to the public was by Peterson & Brothers of Philadelphia, using the transcripts published in the *Philadelphia Inquirer*. These transcripts were wired to the *Inquirer* each day from Washington. It appeared in paperback on July 10, 1865, and in hardback on July 19. Boston newspaper journalist Ben Perley Poore published the second version. Using the transcripts, which appeared daily in the Washington, D.C., *Daily National Intelligencer*, Poore published the transcript in three volumes containing 1,584 pages. He released two volumes almost immediately and didn't publish his third volume until 1866. Poore, like Peterson & Brothers, also published a paperback version in sixteen separate segments. Pitman, the originator of the trial transcript, was the last to publish. He produced a 421-page "summary" version in November 1865.

The three versions differ in several ways. The first two versions published, Peterson's and Poore's, were copied from the daily newspaper accounts and lack editing and commentary of any sort. They also lack the closing arguments of the prosecution and defense counsels. Most important, however, they lack indexing, which makes it impossible to locate testimony by specific witnesses without familiarizing yourself with the entire transcript. Witnesses did not appear at the same time on the same subject, but were occasionally called out of sequence, thus making it difficult to read the testimony as it relates to a particular defendant unless one is thoroughly familiar with the contents of the three volumes.

Sources: Edward Steers, Jr., *Blood on the Moon* (Lexington: University Press of Kentucky, 2001), 123–4; Edward Steers, Jr., "Introduction," in Edward Steers, Jr., ed., *The Trial* (Lexington: University Press of Kentucky, 2003), xiii–xiv.

*See also:* Pitman, Benn; Press Copy, Trial Transcriptions

## Port Conway, Virginia

A small village located on the northern shore of the Rappahannock River east of Fredericksburg, Virginia, and site of a ferry owned and operated by William Thornton. At one point in the nineteenth century, Port Conway was one of the busiest communities in Virginia. It received hundreds of hogheads of tobacco, which were then rolled onto steamers and taken to distant ports. By April 1865, the village was reduced to a few homes and a store owned by William Rollins.

John Wilkes Booth and David Herold had spent Sunday night, April 23, in the cabin of William Lucas after being turned away by Dr. Richard Stuart.

When morning came, Booth negotiated with Lucas to take him and Herold to Port Conway in Lucas's farm wagon. Lucas demurred, explaining that his wife was ill and he did not want to leave her. After some discussion in which Booth threatened Lucas, Lucas's son Charley agreed to take the men to Port Conway. Booth gave twenty dollars to Lucas's wife in payment for the trip.

The three men arrived at Port Conway on Monday morning, April 24, between ten and eleven o'clock. The ferry was on the south side of the river and Herold asked Rollins if he would row the two men across the river. Herold repeated the story that he and his brother (Booth) were headed for Orange County, Virginia. Rollins said he would row them across but had to set his shad nets in the river first. While the two fugitives waited, three Confederate soldiers rode up, also looking to cross the river. They were on their way to Caroline County to the south. The youngest soldier was Absalom Bainbridge. He was seventeen years old and a private in Company B of the Third Virginia Cavalry. The next youngest was William S. Jett, known as "Willie." He was a private in Company C of the Ninth Virginia Cavalry. The oldest of the three men was Mortimer Ruggles, a lieutenant who was second in command to Thomas Nelson Conrad in his spy operation in Northern Virginia. By the end of the war all three were serving in Mosby's Rangers.

Herold approached the soldiers and introduced himself and Booth, using the alias "James Boyd" for his companion. He said his brother had injured his leg at Petersburg, and after further conversation, admitted that he and the other man were the "assassinators of the President." Herold asked the Confederates to help them find accommodations for the night. The soldiers agreed to help. It was near noon when the ferry returned to the northern shore of the river. Booth, Herold, and the three Confederate soldiers then crossed the river to the Port Royal side. They were now traveling as a team.

Sources: Statement of Willie S. Jett, NARA, RG 153, M-599, reel 5, frames 86–99; Poore, *Conspiracy Trial*, vol. 1, 308; Pitman, *Trial*, 90; Edward Steers, Jr., *Blood on the Moon* (Lexington: University Press of Kentucky, 2001), 23–24.

### Porter, George Loring (1838–1919)

Army surgeon assigned to the medical care of the prisoners on trial for the murder of President Lincoln. On April 30, Stanton ordered Dr. Porter to report to Major General John F. Hartranft, governor of the prison facility that was reopened in the Washington Arsenal to hold the conspirators. Porter, a twenty-seven-year-old army surgeon, was al-

in a warehouse section in the old penitentiary building.

On June 17, Edman Spangler began to show signs of mental stress. Hartranft wrote in his daily report that Spangler's mind seemed to wander. Hartranft summoned Porter, who advised that Spangler be taken into the prison yard where he could get fresh air. As a result of Spangler's apparent mental suffering, Porter recommended that all the prisoners be allowed to walk in the yard at least once a day. In his daily report, Hartranft wrote Major General Winfield Scott Hancock, who commanded the Middle Military District, including the arsenal, to urge that the prisoners be allowed in the yard and provided with a chew of tobacco after meals. Stanton approved the request.

Sources: Mary Porter, *The Surgeon in Charge* (Concord, N.H.: Rumford, 1948), 8–9; Edward Steers, Jr., and Harold Holzer, eds., *The Lincoln Assassination Conspirators: Their Confinement and Execution, as Recorded in the Letterbook of John Frederick Hartranft* (Baton Rouge: Louisiana State University Press, 2009).

## Port Royal, Virginia

Small village located on the southern shore of the Rappahannock River opposite Port Conway. On Tuesday, April 25, 1865, shortly before noon, members of the 16th New York Cavalry, along with Detectives Everton J. Conger and Luther

ready stationed at the arsenal where he and his wife had been living for the past year. His duties would now include the daily medical inspection of the prisoners. While Porter could answer medical or health questions from the prisoners, he was instructed not to answer any questions that were not directly related to their medical examinations.

On the night Booth's body was brought to the arsenal by Colonel Lafayette C. Baker, Porter was one of two officers who witnessed his temporary burial

B. Baker, arrived at Port Conway. Learning that Booth had crossed the river Monday afternoon, the search party ferried across the river to Port Royal. It took most of the afternoon to ferry the men and horses over to the Port Royal side.

Unlike Port Conway, Port Royal was still an active community. Booth and Herold and the three Confederate soldiers accompanying them had reached the Port Royal side of the river around 2:00 P.M. on Monday, April 24. A short distance up the hill from the ferry was the home of Randolph Peyton and his two spinster sisters. Willie Jett suggested they try to find shelter for the two fugitives there. Arriving at the house, Jett found the two sisters, Sarah Jane and Lucy Peyton, alone. Their brother Randolph was away on business. Jett told the two women that Booth and Herold were Confederate soldiers looking to rest overnight before continuing on their journey. At first the ladies felt obliged, but looking over the two travel-worn men, they had second thoughts. They demurred, explaining that their brother was away and it wouldn't be proper for the two strangers to spend the night. Jett understood. The five men then continued south on the road to Bowling Green. Jett had one more possibility in mind. It was the home of Richard Garrett, a Virginia tobacco farmer who lived five miles down the road.

Sources: Edward Steers, Jr., *Blood on the Moon* (Lexington: University Press of Kentucky, 2001), 189–90, 196–97.

## Port Tobacco, Maryland

A major colonial seaport located in Charles County, Maryland, at the mouth of the Port Tobacco River. Founded in 1727, Port Tobacco became the county seat. While the village was a thriving port in colonial days, the mouth of the river slowly silted in, such that the village was left high and dry. A fire completely destroyed the courthouse in 1892, resulting in a special election approving the moving of the county seat to the town of La Plata, four miles to the northeast.

George Atzerodt and his brother John established a carriage shop in Port Tobacco in 1857. They continued in the business through the start of the Civil War when John Atzerodt took a job as a detective in Marshal James McPhail's office in Baltimore. George was a southern sympathizer and became adept at ferrying men and materiel across the Potomac River. George Atzerodt was given the nickname of "Port tobacco," having lived and worked in the small village at the time he was recruited by John Surratt to join the Booth conspiracy.

Sources: Jack D. Brown, *Charles County, Maryland: A History* (South Hackensack, N.J.: Custombook, 1976), 56–59.

## Porter, Horace

An aide to General Ulysses S. Grant who was awarded the Medal of Honor for his heroism at the Battle of Chickamauga, Georgia, in 1863. Porter was appointed to the military tribunal by Secretary of War Edwin M. Stanton. Both Porter and Cyrus Comstock, another aide to Grant, were soon removed and replaced with Brevet Brigadier General James Ekin and Brevet Colonel Charles Tomkins, another Medal of Honor winner. Comstock wrote in his diary, "We were both very much delighted."

Sources: Anthony Pitch, *"They Have Killed Papa Dead"* (Hanover, N.H.: Steerforth, 2008), 314–15.

*See also:* Comstock, Cyrus Ballou

## Potter, Andrew (1840–1932)

A case of historical fabrication. Andrew Potter is a fictitious character touted as a member of the National Detective Police (NDP) and believed by proponents of the "Booth escaped" theory to have uncovered the "real" persons involved in the murder of Abraham Lincoln. The character Andrew Potter appears for the first time in the book *The Lincoln Conspiracy* by David Balsiger and Charles E. Sellier, Jr., published in 1977. Potter is alleged to be head of the Secret Service Division of Colonel Lafayette C. Baker's NDP. By the end of the war Potter and his equally fictitious brother Earl retired from Federal service, taking all of their Secret Service files with them. Once in civilian life they joined a private agency known as the "United States Detective Service."

According to an unpublished autobiography of Potter, it was while working for the Detective Service that he and Earl undertook their most important assignment. Following the deaths of several important people in government service, President Ulysses S. Grant secretly authorized an investigation to determine whether any of the deaths were from other than natural causes. The man Grant allegedly asked to take charge of the investigation was former general Lew Wallace, one of the commissioners who had sat in judgment of the Lincoln conspirators, and a friend of Grant. Wallace hired the Potter brothers to handle the fieldwork of the investigation.

The two brothers set about the country interviewing persons believed to have pertinent information relating to the assassination of President Lincoln and the deaths of certain government officials. Many of these individuals were never questioned or interviewed at the time of the assassination, hence the Potters were breaking new ground. They logged more than two hundred interviews over a four-year period.

At the end of their investigation the Potters turned their files over to Lew Wallace. Wallace, after evaluating the information, concluded that the risk of proceeding with prosecution was too great. He wrote Grant, "who knows what direction testimony might take and just what previously undisclosed secrets might be dislodged by an astute defense." Wallace recommended "the report be sequestered." Grant agreed. There were too many powerful individuals involved in Lincoln's murder to proceed any further.

Andrew Potter, through his investigations and interviews, concluded that another man, James W. Boyd, was killed in Booth's place at the Garrett farm, and that Booth eventually made his way to India, where he died in 1883. Following Booth's escape, the government, under Stanton's leadership, engaged in a massive cover-up. Witness after witness provided Potter with enough scurrilous accusations to indict dozens of former Federal officials for complicity in a plot to kidnap Lincoln, and the cover-up of his murder, and General Lew Wallace and President Ulysses S. Grant for obstruction of justice.

The hard evidence, however, does not support any of the claims made. Andrew Potter and his brother Earl were created by an inventive mind. As with most historical fabrications, there are numerous facts woven into the story that are true, but there are enough important errors to show the story to be a fabrication.

Based on the above information on Andrew Potter, a search was undertaken of several record groups in the National Archives where records pertaining to the persons and activities associated with Lafayette Baker and the NDP reside. As a control, a parallel search of the same records was made for known individuals such as Lafayette Baker, and NDP detectives Luther B. Baker and John F. Baker. The results of the search failed to find a single record or reference to Andrew (or his brother Earl). The control searches, however, produced numerous references to the control individuals.

Of importance to the question of Andrew Potter's role as an NDP detective, five separate payroll disbursement records for the years 1862–1863 were discovered in Record Group 110, entry 95, Secret Service Accounts in the National Archives. These accounts listed the names of every employee of Baker's NDP along with their position, pay, and signatures. The name Potter was not among the detectives listed.

While the Potter brothers may have "spirited" their own files away when they left government service, they could not take the files of other offices and agencies in the Federal government. Yet no record could be found of these important men who allegedly ran Lafayette Baker's operation for three years and later uncovered a diabolic plot to remove Lincoln as president.

One can only conclude that this Andrew Potter does not exist outside the collection of typescripts that now reside at Indiana State University. He is unique among even the most secret of secret service agents. His entire life of ninety-two years has left no trace of his existence in any public record. It is simply beyond belief that so important an individual would go through life without leaving a trace of his existence outside of a private collection.

Sources: David Balsiger and Charles E. Sellier, Jr., *The Lincoln Conspiracy* (Los Angeles: Schick Sunn Classic, 1977); Leonard F. Guttridge and Ray A. Neff, *Dark Union* (New York: Wiley, 2003); Edward Steers, Jr., and Joan L. Chaconas, "Dark Union: Bad History," *North & South* 7, no. 1 (January 2004), 12–30.

*See also:* Potter Papers; Balsiger, David, and Charles E. Sellier, Jr.

## Potter, Earl
See Potter, Andrew

## Potter Papers

A collection of documents containing notes, interviews, biographies, correspondence, and reports from the files of Andrew Potter, alleged secret service agent with the National Detective Police and postwar investigations. The papers make up the bulk of the Neff-Guttridge Collection housed in the Rare Book and Special Collections Department, Cunningham Library at Indiana State University. The documents provide all of the evidence for the revisionist claims that maintain Lincoln's murder was the result of a diabolical conspiracy emanating from within his own cabinet and crossing party and sectional lines. All of the documents are typescript copies of alleged originals that no longer exist. Once the documents were transcribed, the originals were destroyed. Allegedly, a variety of physical calamities seriously damaged or destroyed the original holographic documents in every single case. In other instances, the originals from which typescript copies were made cannot be traced leaving only the copy as proof of their existence. NDP detective Andrew Potter created the core of the papers over a period of several years. This subset of documents housed at Indiana State are referred to as "The Potter Papers." Space does not permit an analysis of all of the documents in this large collection of papers. Suffice it to say that all of them appear to be fabricated along with Andrew and Earl Potter. By whom, and when, this considerable effort was perpetrated is unclear at this time.

Sources: Edward Steers, Jr., and Joan L. Chaconas, "Dark Union: Bad History," *North & South* 7, no. 1 (January 2004), 12–30.

*See also:* Potter, Andrew; Balsiger, David, and Charles E. Sellier, Jr.

### Powell, Lewis Thornton (1844–1865)

One of Booth's conspirators, assigned to kill Secretary of State William H. Seward at his home, where Seward was confined to bed as he recovered from a carriage accident. Powell, alias "Paine" or "Payne," is often described as the "muscle" in John Wilkes Booth's team of conspirators. He is also portrayed as weak-minded or slow-witted. Powell, however, demonstrated clever behavior under stress during his interrogations. He appears anything but slow-witted.

Powell was twenty-one years old at the time of the assassination. He enlisted in Company I of the Second Florida Infantry at the age of seventeen in May 1861. He was wounded on the second day of the battle at Gettysburg, then captured and taken to the Union army's makeshift hospital at Pennsylvania College, now Gettysburg College. Here he met Baltimorean Margaret "Maggie" Branson, who worked as a volunteer nurse in the Confederate ward. Powell recovered quickly from his wound and worked as a nurse alongside Maggie. In September 1863, Powell was transferred to the West Buildings Hospital in Baltimore. He made his escape with the help of Maggie and hid out at the Branson boardinghouse located at 16 North Eutaw Street in Baltimore.

Powell left Baltimore and headed south to Northern Virginia in hopes of finding his old regiment, now a part of Longstreet's Corps. He arrived one evening at the home of John Scott Payne near Warrenton, Virginia. Hearing that

John Singleton Mosby's 43rd Battalion was in the area, he signed on with Company B of Mosby's Rangers. Powell participated in escorting several prisoners that Mosby captured to Richmond. On his return he took part in the capture of six Union cavalrymen fighting under Brigadier General Alfred Torbert.

In January 1865, Powell left Mosby's Rangers and made his way to Fairfax Courthouse, where he acquired civilian clothes, sold his horse, and was conveyed to Alexandria, Virginia, where he signed an oath of allegiance to the United States on January 13, 1865. He then made his way to Baltimore and returned to the Branson home on Eutaw Street.

While at the Branson boardinghouse Powell became involved with David Preston Parr, the Baltimore china dealer whose shop was a safe house for Confederate agents and a mail drop for Confederate documents and papers. Parr was well connected with the clandestine operations of the Confederacy's agents, including John Surratt. Parr's relationship with Surratt can be traced to a series of telegrams between him and Parr. On January 21, 1865, John Surratt made a trip to Baltimore and delivered three hundred dollars to a "private party" who was in all probability Parr. A few weeks after Surratt's visit to Baltimore, Powell left the Branson boardinghouse and headed to Washington, D.C., where he showed up at the Surratt boardinghouse at 541 H Street. From here Powell becomes an important part of John Wilkes Booth's team assembled to capture Lincoln and take him to Richmond.

Failing to capture Lincoln, Booth rolled his plot over to assassination. On Friday, April 14, 1865, Booth, along with David Herold and George Atzerodt, gathered in Powell's hotel room at the Herndon House located on the corner of Ninth and F streets, where Booth had moved Powell from the Surratt boardinghouse. Booth laid out his plan to the three cohorts. He would kill Lincoln. Powell, with David Herold as his guide, would kill Secretary of State Seward, and Atzerodt would kill Vice President Andrew Johnson. The plan was designed to decapitate the Federal government and throw it into a state of chaos, thereby allowing the Confederacy desperately needed time to regroup. The diabolical plan, if carried out, would undoubtedly cause some chaos, but would not derail the Union juggernaut as long as Secretary of War Edwin M. Stanton was alive. Nevertheless, Booth's plan was a good one, and what else was left to save a dying Confederacy?

At ten o'clock that night Powell, with Herold at his side, arrived at the Seward home. Seward was in an upstairs bedroom recovering from a serious carriage accident. Powell approached the front door, leaving Herold to tend to his horse. Powell gained entrance posing as a messenger from Seward's doctor with a bottle of medicine that Seward needed. When he was denied admittance to Seward's bedroom, an argument broke out and Powell pulled out his revolver and attempted to shoot Seward's son Frederick. The revolver misfired and Powell struck young Seward on the head, fracturing his skull. Breaking into Seward's bedroom, Powell, now brandishing a large bowie knife, pushed aside Seward's young daughter, Fanny, and grappled with Seward's male nurse, George F. Robinson. Knocking Robinson aside, Powell fell on top of Seward and began stabbing him with the knife. Robinson got to his feet and pulled Powell off Seward. Just then, Seward's eldest son, Augustus, came into the room and grabbed Robinson in the confusion. Powell broke loose, ran down the stairs, and bolted outside looking for Herold and his horse.

Herold, hearing the screams and shouts coming from inside the house, let go of Powell's horse and galloped off, leaving Powell to his own devices. Powell mounted his horse and sped off, heading east toward the Capitol. Abandoning his horse somewhere near Lincoln Hospital, Powell hid out all day Saturday, and Sunday, and Monday. On Monday night near midnight, Powell made his way to the Surratt boardinghouse. Knocking on the door he was momentarily startled when the door opened and a man in uniform stood before him. Asked what he wanted, Powell showed his cleverness when he made up a story that the owner of the house had hired him to dig a French drain alongside her house. Powell said he wanted to begin early in the morning and wanted to check with the lady where she wanted the drain. Powell was pulled into the house and brought into the front parlor where Mary Surratt was being interrogated by several Union detectives. Asked if she knew the man, Mary Surratt denied ever having seen him. Powell, along with the occupants of the house, including Mary Surratt, was arrested.

At the conspiracy trial, Powell's court-appointed lawyer, Captain William E. Doster, attempted to mount a temporary insanity plea for his client. When that failed, Doster attempted to justify Powell's attack on the grounds that Powell was a soldier carrying out an attack against a Union official and was no guiltier of attempted murder than a soldier on the battlefield would be. All of Doster's valiant attempts failed and Powell was convicted and condemned to death by hanging. The sentence was carried out on July 7, 1865, when Powell, together with Mary Surratt, David Herold, and George Atzerodt, was hanged at the Washington Arsenal, outside the building where their trial had been held.

Sources: Betty J. Ownsbey, *Alias "Paine": Lewis Thornton Powell, the Mystery Man of the Lincoln Conspiracy* (Jefferson, N.C.: McFarland, 1993).

*See also*: Branson, Margaret; Herold, David; Seward, William Henry

## Presidential Succession

The order of succession should the president and vice president die while in office is one of the major misconceptions associated with Lincoln's assassination. Secretary of State William H. Seward was not the constitutional successor should both Lincoln and Johnson have died. Article II, paragraph 6 of the Constitution states that the Congress shall provide for the absence of both president and vice president. On March 1, 1792, Congress established that the president pro tempore of the Senate would become the acting president until the Electoral College selected a new president. Secretary of State Seward was not the next in line to succeed the vice president. In fact, none of the cabinet officers was in line to succeed to the presidency.

The succession act determined that the president pro tempore of the Senate would succeed after the vice president, followed by the Speaker of the House. On January 19, 1886, the Congress established a new line of succession. The secretary of state would succeed the vice president followed by secretary of the treasury, followed by each cabinet post in the order in which it was created. In 1947, the Congress changed the law again. The Speaker of the House of Representatives succeeds the vice president, followed by the president pro tempore of the Senate, followed by the members of the cabinet in order of their creation. In 1964, the Congress amended the Constitution, affirming the law passed in 1947. This requires a constitutional amendment in the future if anyone wishes to change the line of succession.

On April 15, 1865, the president pro tempore of the Senate was Lafayette S. Foster; a senator from Connecticut who would have become acting president, presumably until the Electoral College selected a new president. The law specifies that the Electoral College will be called into service by the secretary of state, and provides no remedy should the secretary of state die prior to calling the electors together. No provision of the act gives the acting president the power to appoint a new secretary of state. Barring decisive action on the part of an acting president, the country could have found itself in a serious dilemma. Realistically, the war would have proceeded without disruption under Secretary of War Stanton and General Grant.

Sources: James O. Hall, "Presidential Succession," *Surratt Society News* 7, no. 11 (November 1982), 4; James O. Hall, "Senator Atchison and Presidential Succession," *Surratt Courier* 16, no. 7 (July 1991), 2–3; James E. T. Lange and Katherine DeWitt, Jr., "Further Notes on Presidential Succession," *Surratt Courier* 16, no. 9 (September 1991), 6.

## President's Box, Ford's Theatre

The box at Ford's Theatre, used by President Lincoln on the night of April 14, 1865, was actually a double box. It was always reserved for those occasions when the president attended the theater. There were eight boxes located on either side of the stage, four on the first level and four on the second level. The Lincolns used the upper two boxes located stage left. On the night of the assassination, a partition, seven feet high and three inches thick, separating boxes 7 and 8 was removed, creating a double box. Access to the two boxes was through a narrow vestibule or corridor four feet wide and ten feet long, which led off the Dress Circle. A single door led into the vestibule from the Dress Circle. Once inside the vestibule there were separate doors, which opened into each box. The boxes were normally rented at ten dollars each.

When the president attended the theater, additional furniture was placed in the box to accommodate him and his guests. On the night of April 14, a beautiful red tufted sofa, large rocking chair, and two upholstered chairs were added to the box from the private living quarters of Harry Clay Ford on the third floor. The box was lighted by a large chandelier located outside of the box and suspended from a twelve-foot beam centered over the top of the box.

President Lincoln sat in the large rocking chair located on the far left of the box, with Mary Lincoln seated in a cane chair immediately on his right. The president's guests, Clara Harris and Major Henry Rathbone, sat to the far right in box 8. Miss Harris sat in one of the tufted armchairs while Major Harris sat on the sofa directly behind Miss Harris.

The door to box 7 was closed, but the door to box 8, according to Henry Rathbone, was open. The door to the box where President and Mrs. Lincoln were sitting contained a small hole in the corner of one of the panels, approximately three feet above the floor. While most people have concluded that Booth made the hole on the afternoon of April 14 for the purpose of observing the president before entering the box, Frank Ford, the son of Harry Clay Ford, insisted that the

hole was bored by his father to allow the president's guard to peer through the hole to observe the president without opening the door.

Not all historians are in agreement as to which door Booth went through when he stepped into the box and shot Lincoln. Both doors would place Booth in close proximity to Lincoln. The majority of historians believe Booth entered through the door to box 7, the one with a hole bored through it. A minority believe it was through the already open door to box 8. Floor diagrams of boxes 7 and 8 show that either door would have put Booth in a position to shoot Lincoln. The trajectory through Lincoln's brain and the position he was seated in at the time the shot was fired does not give a clue as to which door Booth stepped through.

The current box was restored to its original condition at the time the theater was restored in 1964. The furniture, with the exception of the Lincoln rocker, which was purchased by Henry Ford from the widow of John Ford, is original. The Assam Wallpaper Company of Washington, D.C., using an original fragment as a pattern, reproduced the wallpaper. The door with the hole is on display in the museum located on the lower level of the theater.

Sources: George J. Olszewski, *Historic Structures Report: Restoration of Ford's Theatre* (Washington, D.C.: U.S. Government Printing Office, 1963); Michael W. Kauffman, "Door Number 7 or Door Number 8?," *Surratt Courier* 33, no. 2 (February 2008), 3–4.

*See also:* Ford's Theatre

## Press Copy, Trial Transcriptions
The term used to describe the process of making copies from originals. Often confused as copies distributed to the press corps covering the trial. Pitman supplied "press copies" to the prosecution and defense attorneys as well as the Washington, D.C., *Daily National Intelligencer* and to commercial telegraphers who transmitted the content of the copies to Philadelphia at the end of each day for publication in the *Philadelphia Inquirer*. Thus, both the *Intelligencer* and *Inquirer* published verbatim copies of the trial testimony daily. The accounts published in the *Inquirer* were plagued by numerous typographical errors, which the Washington newspaper did not experience. This probably resulted from errors in transmission by the telegraphers, who every evening wired the words from the large number of transcribed pages to their editor. The *Intelligencer* worked directly from the "press copy," thereby experiencing few transcribing errors.

The term "press copy" has caused a certain amount of confusion among some authors who misunderstand its meaning as used in 1865. While the term in twentieth-century parlance refers to a hard copy passed out to members of the press corps, it had a different meaning in the mid-nineteenth century. The term *press* did not refer to the media but rather to the physical process by which verbatim copies were produced. The transcription of shorthand notes was made with ink and later copies were "lifted" from the original ink transcriptions by laying a piece of tissue paper over the ink transcription and backing it with a damp cloth, followed by the application of pressure. In this way a "copy" was lifted off the original transcription onto the tissue paper by transferring some of the ink. The use of tissue paper allowed the image to read through the transparent tissue. In skilled hands, the process was extremely effective.

Pitman was assisted in his operation by two army privates assigned to his care specifically to aid in "lifting" copies from the original ink transcriptions. The process allowed Pitman to make several sets of press copies of each day's transcriptions. One copy was made available to the *Intelligencer* and to telegraphers who transmitted the record by using Samuel Morse's ingenious code, while other copies were made available to the attorneys.

Sources: Edward Steers, Jr., "Introduction," in Edward Steers, Jr., ed., *The Trial* (Lexington: University Press of Kentucky, 2003), xxiii–xiv.

### *Prisoner of Shark Island*

In 1936, Twentieth Century Fox released its own version of the story of Dr. Samuel Alexander Mudd. Produced by one of Hollywood's greatest filmmakers, Darryl F. Zanuck, and directed by John Ford, *The Prisoner of Shark Island* epitomized history as hoax. The film starred Warner Baxter as Dr. Mudd and Gloria Stuart as Mrs. Mudd. Mr. Warner and Miss Stuart were supported by an outstanding cast including John Carradine, Harry Carey, and Frank McGlynn, Sr., one of the early actors noted for his portrayal of Abraham Lincoln. A recent filmography of dramas depicting Abraham Lincoln described the film as "accurately depicting the real-life experiences of Samuel Mudd, the doctor who was sentenced to life imprisonment for treating John Wilkes Booth's broken ankle." The portrayal, in fact, was far from the actual events and real people.

The movie takes its name from Hollywood's portrayal of Fort Jefferson prison, located in the Dry Tortugas off Key West, Florida, as a fortress protected by a moat filled with man-eating sharks. The cruel Sergeant Rankin (John Carradine) taunts Dr. Mudd, daring him to try to escape, so the guards can watch as the sharks tear him into little pieces in a feeding frenzy. The mean guard then tells Mudd he will welcome the sharks by the time he gets through torturing him. Before the film ends, Sergeant Rankin does an about-face and adds his name to a petition pleading with President Johnson to free Dr. Mudd for his heroism in overcoming the yellow fever epidemic that killed many of the people living inside the fort.

Two years after the film's release, the popular radio show *The Lux Radio Theatre* staged a re-creation of the story. Gary Cooper portrayed Dr. Mudd while Fay Wray (of *King Kong* fame) appeared as "Peggy" Mudd. Her real name was Sarah Frances and the family knew her as "Frank." This was only one of dozens of errors in the script. What is interesting about this particular production was the guest appearance of Dr. Mudd's youngest child, Mary Eleanor "Nettie" Mudd Monroe. Mrs. Monroe, author and editor of a book about her father, read a statement during the show's intermission about her father, who had died when she was four and a half years old.

Both the movie and radio portrayal helped to perpetuate the myth of Dr. Mudd as a simple country doctor who was persecuted for nothing more than observing his Hippocratic oath. Mudd

was Booth's key conspirator along with John Surratt.

Sources: Edward Steers, Jr., "A Remarkable Voice from the Past: Mrs. Nettie Mudd Monroe Speaks of Her Father as 'The Prisoner of Shark Island,'" *Surratt Courier* 26, no. 11 (November 2001), 3–4; Mark S. Reinhart, *Abraham Lincoln on Screen: A Filmography, 1903–1998* (Jefferson, N.C.: McFarland, 1999), 222–24.

*See also:* Mudd, Mary Eleanor "Nettie"

## Pumphrey, James W. (1833–1871)

Pumphrey owned a livery stable on C Street in Washington, D.C., just behind the National Hotel where Booth stayed when he was in town. Booth became a patron of Pumphrey's, renting horses from him on several occasions, including the night of the assassination. Booth stopped by Pumphrey's stable shortly after noon on April 14, asking to reserve a particular horse, and to have it ready at four o'clock that afternoon. When Booth stopped by the livery the horse had already been rented to someone else and Booth had to settle for a bay mare. Pumphrey was a prosecution witness at the conspiracy trial. He told of Booth going to Grover's National Theatre on the afternoon of April 14 to write a letter. Booth's first visit was in the company of John Surratt, who vouched that Booth would pay his bill.

Sources: Testimony of James W. Pumphrey, Poore, *Conspiracy Trial*, vol. 1, 175; Pitman, *Trial*, 72; Statement of James W. Pumphrey, NARA, RG 153, M-599, reel 4, frames 32–35.

## Purdom, James W.

A Montgomery County, Maryland, farmer who worked as an informant for the army. On Easter Sunday, April 16, George Atzerodt stopped by the home of Hezekiah Metz after fleeing Washington, D.C. He was invited to join the family and others for the dinner meal. He spoke about the assassination in terms that made the other guests suspicious. One guest, Nathan Page, reported Atzerodt's conversation to Purdom on Wednesday afternoon, April 19. Purdom passed the information along to Private Frank O'Daniel of the First Delaware Cavalry, stationed at Monocacy Junction near Frederick, Maryland. The information was passed up the chain of command and resulted in a troop of cavalry being sent to Purdom's farm; Purdom led the troop from there to the Richter farm, where Atzerodt was staying. Atzerodt was arrested on Thursday morning, April 20, and taken to Monocacy Junction and then to Relay, Maryland, and on to Washington by railroad. Purdom received $2,878.78 as his share of the reward money offered for the capture of Atzerodt.

Sources: Statement of James W. Purdom, NARA, RG 153, M-599, reel 2, frames 227–29.

*See also:* Atzerodt, George Andrew; Page, Nathan

## Queen, Joseph

Son of Dr. William Queen. When John Wilkes Booth visited Charles County in Southern Maryland on Friday, November 11, 1864, he stayed the first night at the Bryantown Tavern. The following morning, Saturday, he was met by Joseph Queen and taken to the home of Queen's father, Dr. William Queen, where he spent Saturday night. The following morning, Sunday, Joseph Queen took Booth to St. Mary's Church, outside Bryantown, where he was introduced to Dr. Samuel Mudd by Queen's son-in-law, John Thompson. It was the first of four meetings between Booth and Mudd. Like his father, Joseph Queen was an active member of the Charles County Confederate underground.

Sources: Testimony of John C. Thompson, Poore, *Conspiracy Trial*, vol. 2, 268, vol. 3, 405; Pitman, *Trial*, 130, 178; Edward Steers, Jr., *Blood on the Moon* (Lexington: University Press of Kentucky, 2001), 74–76.

See also: Thompson, John C.

## Queen, Dr. William (1789–1868)

Elderly physician living approximately six miles south of Bryantown, Charles County, Maryland. Queen was a respected member of the community and an ardent Confederate supporter. When John Wilkes Booth first visited Charles County a few weeks after visiting Montreal in October 1864, he carried a letter of introduction to Dr. Queen and Dr. Mudd. Confederate agent Patrick C. Martin had given Booth the letter of introduction during Booth's stay at the St. Lawrence Hall hotel in Montreal. Booth spent Saturday, November 12, 1864, as Queen's houseguest and the following morning, Sunday, November 13, Booth was taken to St. Mary's Church near Bryantown, where John Thompson, Dr. Queen's son-in-law, introduced him to Dr. Mudd. As a result of this meeting, and Martin's letter of introduction, Mudd agreed to help Booth in putting together his team of conspirators.

Booth visited Charles County a second time in December 1864 and again was a houseguest of Dr. Queen. He attended church services a second time at St. Mary's on December 18 and returned to Dr. Mudd's house following services, where he was an overnight guest. The following morning, Mudd took Booth to see Mudd's neighbor, George Gardiner. Booth purchased a one-eyed horse from Gardiner. Gardiner's nephew, John Gardiner, delivered the horse to Booth at the Bryantown Tavern on Tuesday morning. Booth then took the horse to a local blacksmith, Peter Trotter, and had the horse shod. According to Trotter,

Booth then rode off in the company of Dr. Mudd.

Sources: Edward Steers, Jr., *His Name Is Still Mudd* (Gettysburg, Pa.: Thomas, 1997); Edward Steers, Jr., *Blood on the Moon* (Lexington: University Press of Kentucky, 2001), 74–76.

## Quesenberry, Elizabeth Rousby (1826–1896)

A widow of a Virginia farmer who lived at the mouth of the Machodoc Creek in King George County, Virginia. When Booth and Herold arrived on the Virginia shore near Gambo Creek on Sunday morning, April 23, after crossing the Potomac River, they made their way to the home of Elizabeth Quesenberry. Absent, her daughters sent for her, and when she returned home she provided the two fugitives with food and rest while she sent word to Thomas Harbin, a Confederate signal agent (secret service). Harbin provided the two men with horses and assigned another Confederate agent, William Bryant, to take the two men to Dr. Richard Stuart, who was living at his summer home, Cleydael, not far from Quesenberry's.

Mrs. Quesenberry was later arrested and brought to Washington, where she was questioned and released. The Federal authorities never suspected her role in aiding Booth and Herold.

Sources: Statement of Elizabeth Rousby Quesenberry, NARA, RG 153, M-599, reel 5, frame 556; Statement of William L. Bryant, NARA, RG 153, M-599, reel 4, frames 93–97.

*See also:* Harbin, Thomas Henry

## Rains, Gabriel J.

Brigadier general in charge of the Confederate Torpedo Bureau. An expert in the use of various explosive devices. During the Peninsula Campaign in 1862, Rains, serving under General James Longstreet at the time, had planted a number of pressure-sensitive shells along the road that the Union army was marching on near Yorktown, Virginia. It was the first such use of explosive devices as hidden antipersonnel weapons. The effort drew protests from Union commanders and even from Longstreet, who opposed the use of antipersonnel mines. As a result of Longstreet's objection, Confederate secretary of war George W. Randolph established the Torpedo Bureau within the War Department and appointed Rains superintendent of the newly created agency.

Working in the Torpedo Bureau under Rains was Sergeant Thomas F. Harney. Harney was expert in the use of various types of explosive mines, or torpedoes as they were called. On April 1, 1865, thirteen days before Lincoln's assassination, Harney was dispatched to Lieutenant Colonel John Singleton Mosby in Fauquier County, Virginia, with a letter directing Mosby to aid Harney in his mission. Harney and his assistants were assigned to Company H of Mosby's command. On April 8, a contingent of Companies H and D was ambushed by a detachment of the Eighth Illinois Cavalry at Burke's Station, Virginia. Harney was captured along with "ordnance" that he was carrying on him.

On April 3, 1865, the Confederate capital, Richmond, Virginia, fell. One of the first units to march into Richmond was Colonel Edward Hastings Ripley of the Ninth Vermont Infantry. In his memoir, published after the war, Ripley wrote that a Confederate private working at the Torpedo Bureau in Richmond by the name of William H. Snyder, Company E, Second Virginia Cavalry, came to him and told of a plot by members of the Torpedo Bureau to blow up the White House in an attempt to kill Lincoln and members of his cabinet. Snyder was troubled by this "secret mission" and felt it a matter of conscience to alert Union authorities. Ripley took Snyder to Lincoln, who was then on board the *Malvern*, anchored in the James River. Lincoln listened to Ripley's account of the affair and ended it without actually talking to Snyder.

The authors of *Come Retribution* conclude that Harney was sent on a secret mission to blow up the White House killing Lincoln. Their conclusion is based in part on a statement given by conspirator George A. Atzerodt, who stated "Booth said he had met a party in N. York who would get the Prest.

Certain. They were going to <u>mine the end of the White House</u>, next to the War Dept." This statement, coupled with Snyder's, supports the idea that Thomas Harney was on his way to the White House when he and three other men with him were captured at Burke's Station.

Sources: William A. Tidwell, James O. Hall, and David W. Gaddy, *Come Retribution* (Jackson: University Press of Mississippi, 1988), 418–21; Edward Hastings Ripley, *The Capture and Occupation of Richmond, April 3, 1865* (New York: Putnam's, 1907), 23.

*See also:* Harney, Thomas F.; Torpedo Bureau; Lost Confession.

## Randall, Voltaire (1828–1902)

Military detective on the staff of Maryland provost marshal James McPhail in Baltimore who arrested Samuel Arnold. On learning of Lincoln's assassination and that John Wilkes Booth was the assassin, McPhail sent Randall and Eaton Horner, two of his better detectives, to track down Samuel Arnold, who McPhail knew was an old friend of Booth's from their childhood days in Baltimore. Randall and Horner learned from Arnold's father that Arnold was clerking for a sutler at Fort Monroe in Virginia.

Randall and Horner placed Arnold under arrest and interrogated him exten-sively. Arnold freely admitted his role in Booth's capture plot and also told the detectives that Booth had been given letters of introduction to Dr. Samuel Mudd and Dr. William Queen by Patrick C. Martin, a Confederate agent working out of Montreal. This occurred on Monday, April 17, a full day before authorities in Washington or Charles County, Maryland, had learned about Booth stopping at Mudd's house on his escape.

Randall did not share in the reward money.

Sources: Edward Steers, Jr., *His Name Is Still Mudd* (Gettysburg, Pa.: Thomas, 1997); Edward Steers, Jr., *Blood on the Moon* (Lexington: University Press of Kentucky, 2001).

*See also:* Arnold, Samuel Bland; Horner, Eaton

## Rappahannock River

A river in Virginia that posed the last obstacle to Booth and Herold who crossed on Monday, April 24, 1865, two days before Booth's death and Herold's capture. The river has its origin in the Blue Ridge Mountains of Virginia and flows approximately 210 miles southeast before emptying into the Chesapeake Bay. Port Conway and Port Royal are situated on opposite shores eighteen miles southeast of Fredericksburg, Virginia. On Monday, April 24, following an overnight stay at the cabin of William Lucas, Booth and

Herold arrived at Port Conway sometime close to noon. They crossed the river on ferry, continuing their attempt to escape Union authorities.

Sources: Marion Severynse, ed., *The Houghton Mifflin Dictionary of Geography* (Boston: Houghton Mifflin, 1997), 323.

## Rath, Christian

Loosely referred to as the hangman in charge of carrying out the technical details of the hanging. Captain Christian Rath was a member of the 17th Michigan Volunteer Infantry (First Division, Ninth Army Corps) assigned to the staff of Major General John F. Hartranft at the Old Federal Penitentiary at the Washington Arsenal. On assuming his command in May, Hartranft requested that Rath be assigned to his staff. At the time neither man had envisioned their future roles as executioners for the tribunal. Now, two months later, Hartranft found himself in charge of the execution details, while Rath was given the job of hangman. Rath had once before built a scaffold while serving as a provost marshal. He obtained a set of the plans from the sheriff of Level Plains, Virginia, and, using them as a guide, set about sketching plans for the new scaffold. Rath's crew worked throughout the night of July 6 and completed the job by the morning of the 7th.

The scaffold was twenty feet long, fifteen feet wide, and ten feet high to the floor of the scaffold, and twenty feet high to the beam that held the ropes. The platform consisted of two drops, each six feet by four feet, supported by an upright beam that could be knocked away on command.

On July 7, 1865, Rath prepared the nooses for the four conspirators, and gave the final signal with three claps of his hands, which signaled to the soldiers waiting beneath the scaffold to knock away the posts supporting the floor of the scaffolding. The condemned conspirators dropped six feet to their deaths.

Sources: John K. Lattimer, *Kennedy and Lincoln: Medical and Ballistic Comparisons of Their Assassinations* (New York: Harcourt Brace Jovanovich, 1980), 116; Edward Steers, Jr., and Harold Holzer, eds., *The Lincoln Assassination Conspirators: Their Confinement and Execution, as Recorded in the Letterbook of John Frederick Hartranft* (Baton Rouge: Louisiana State University Press, 2009).

## Rathbone, Henry Riggs (1837–1911)

Union army major whom, along with his fiancée and stepsister, Clara Harris, were guests of the Lincolns at Ford's Theatre the night of Lincoln's assassination. Upon the death of her husband, Pauline Rathbone, Henry's mother, married Senator Ira Harris, Republican of New York. Harris had a daughter, Clara Harris, who became Henry Rathbone's stepsister. Booth seriously wounded Rathbone while attempting to subdue him after he shot Lincoln. Booth had a large bowie knife and stabbed Rathbone in the left arm. Booth broke free of Rathbone's grip, swung his legs over the balustrade, and dropped to the stage below. Realizing that Lincoln was severely injured, Rathbone went into the vestibule, where he found the door braced with a piece of wood. Removing the brace, Rathbone opened the door and admitted Dr. Charles Leale, who on briefly examining Rathbone, determined his injury was not life threatening. Leale then went to the president, who was slumped in his rocking chair.

Two years later, on July 11, 1867, Rathbone and Clara were married. They had three children. Rathbone's behavior had become increasingly erratic since the night of the assassination. Even so, President Grover Cleveland appointed Rathbone consul to Hannover, Germany, in 1893. The following year Rathbone's mental state deteriorated to such an extent that one night, in a fit of unjustified jealousy, he fatally shot his wife, then stabbed her several times before turning the knife on himself in an attempted suicide. He was convicted in a German court and committed to an asylum for the criminally insane, where he died in 1911.

Sources: Mark E. Neely, Jr., *The Abraham Lincoln Encyclopedia* (New York: McGraw-Hill, 1982).

*See also:* Harris, Clara

## Raybold, Thomas J.

A witness at the conspiracy trial. Raybold was in charge of overseeing any work that was needed around Ford's Theatre. He testified that he was the person who broke the lock on the door to box 8. On March 7, 1865, Raybold was asked to find seats for Mr. Merrick, clerk at the National Hotel, and his guests, who arrived at the theater late. Raybold said he took them to the presidential box, but finding the door locked, used his foot to break it open. After examining both locks, to 7 and 8, Raybold testified, he found that the lock on the door to box 7 was also forced, but he was unaware of when or by whom it had been done. He told of placing the rocking chair in the triangular corner of box 7 for the president. Raybold was a witness for the defense on behalf of Edman Spangler.

Sources: Statement of Thomas J. Raybold, NARA, RG 153, M-599, reel 3, frames 682–85; Testimony of Thomas Raybold, Poore, *Conspiracy Trial*, vol. 3, 29, 159; Pitman, *Trial*, 109, 111.

*See also:* Merrick, Henry E.

## Reed, David

Reed was called as a witness by both the prosecution and the defense in regard to John H. Surratt. That practice was not uncommon during the conspiracy trial. Reed testified that he saw John Surratt on the day of the assassination walking past the Grover's National Theatre on Pennsylvania Avenue. Reed claimed to have known John Surratt as a boy, and identified a photographic image at the trial as being Surratt and the man he had seen in Washington, D.C. Surratt was in Elmira, New York, on a mission for the Confederacy on April 14, 1865, and not in Washington.

Sources: Joan L. Chaconas, "John H. Surratt, Jr.," in Edward Steers, Jr., *The Trial* (Lexington: University Press of Kentucky, 2003), lx–lxv.

*See also:* Surratt, John Harrison, Jr.

## Reford, J. J.

While Reford is not known to have a role in the assassination of Abraham Lincoln, he does have a role in the evidence file, where a letter from Reford dated "N.Y. 20th Feby/65" is addressed to J. W. Booth. It was found among Booth's papers in his trunk left in his room at the National Hotel in Washington. The letter is quoted in *Come Retribution*, a major work on the assassination, whose authors describe the letter as a loosely coded message between Reford and Booth concerning Lewis

Powell, the co-conspirator who attacked William H. Seward. A crucial part of the letter was transcribed in the book to read: "As Lewis [Powell] anxious to have a conversation with you relative to the order for shipping the horses, as well as the Ile [oil] question." "Horses" and "ile" are believed to be code words, leading the authors of *Come Retribution* to conclude that the letter is an important piece of evidence supporting a wider conspiracy involving Reford with Powell and Booth.

A careful reading of the original document, however, resulted in the editor transcribing the quote to read, "As I was anxious . . ." rather than "As Lewis anxious . . ." This changes the whole meaning of the sentence. While the letter may still be a loosely coded message from Reford to Booth, one cannot conclude from it that Lewis Powell wanted to get in touch with Booth concerning Booth's plot.

Sources: Letter of J. J. Reford to J. W. Booth, NARA, RG 153, M-599, reel 2, frames 353–57; William A. Tidwell, James O. Hall, and David W. Gaddy, *Come Retribution* (Jackson: University Press of Mississippi, 1989), 404; William C. Edwards and Edward Steers, Jr., eds., *The Lincoln Assassination: The Evidence* (Urbana: University of Illinois Press, 2009).

## Reward Money

Under the direction of Secretary of War Edwin M. Stanton, the government offered rewards totaling $100,000 in the sums of $75,000 for John Wilkes Booth, $5,000 for Lewis T. Powell, and $25,000 for George A. Atzerodt. The claims for the reward money were so great that a committee of two was established to hear all claims and recommend how and to whom the money should be distributed. Judge Advocate General (army) Joseph Holt and Adjutant General Edward D. Townsend examined all claims and reported their findings and recommendations to the War Department. The recommendations were then sent to the Congress for approval. The Congress adjusted the recommendations, having the final word on who would receive what amount.

Booth pursuit and capture: Everton J. Conger, detective NDP, $15,000; Lafayette C. Baker, detective NDP, $3,750; Luther B. Baker, detective NDP, $3,000; Lieutenant Edward P. Doherty, commanding 16th New York Cavalry, $5,250; James R. O'Beirne, provost marshal, $2,000; Colonel Henry H. Wells, Sergeant George Cottingham, Lieutenant Alexander Lovett, detectives, $1,000 each; Sergeant Boston Corbett, Sergeant Andrew Wendell, Corporal Charles Zimmer, Corporal Michael Uniac, Corporal John Winter, Corporal Herman Newgarten, Corporal John Walz, Corporal Oliver Lonpay, Corporal Michael Hormsbey, Privates John Myers, John Ryan, William Byrne, Philip Hoyt,

Martin Kelly, Henry Putnam, Frank Mc-Daniel, Lewis Savage, Abraham Genay, Emery Parady, David Baker, William McQuade, John Millington, Frederick Dietz, John H. Singer, Carl Steinbrugge, and Joseph Zisgen, each $1,653.85. Total $75,000.

Atzerodt capture: Major E. R. Artman, 213th Pennsylvania Infantry, $1,250; Sergeant Z. W. Gemmill, First Delaware Cavalry, $3,598.54; Privates (First Delaware Cavalry) Christopher Ross, David H. Baker, Albert Bender, Samuel J. Williams, George W. Young, James Longacre, and private citizen and army informant James W. Purdom, each $2,878.78. Total $25,000.

Powell capture: Major H. W. Smith, $1,000; Detectives Richard C. Morgan, Eli Devore, Charles H. Rosch, Thomas Sampson, W. M. Wermerskirch, $500 each; J. H. Kimball, citizen, $500; J. H. Kimball, citizen, $250; P. M. Clark, citizen, $250; Susan Jackson (Mahoney), citizen (colored), $250; Mary Ann Griffin, citizen, $250. Total $5,000.

The total amount of reward money awarded was $105,000.

The claims filed along with supporting documents are part of Record Group 94, Records of the Adjutant General in the National Archives and Records Administration. They have been photocopied and are part of microcopy 619, reels 455–58.

Sources: Official Documents Relating to the Rewards, NARA, RG 94, M-619, reel 456, frames 416–19.

### Reynolds, William (1843–1866)

Reynolds's letters to his mother in England tell of his taking part in the capture of George Atzerodt. Reynolds was an Englishman who had entered the Royal Navy in 1857 at the age of fifteen years. When, in the autumn of 1862, his ship was moored in Halifax, Nova Scotia, Reynolds was found guilty of a misdemeanor that warranted him being sent ashore to spend twenty-eight days in the local penitentiary. After completing his sentence, Reynolds returned to his ship, but his presence there was short. Within a few days he had "jumped" ship. He made his way into the United States, where he enlisted in the Union army.

Reynolds saw active service in Louisiana. He received a leg wound during the Red River campaign of 1864 and, as a result, was invalided out of the army. He then became a coal miner in a remote part of Pennsylvania, but in March 1865, being unable to make ends meet, Reynolds decided to reenlist, entering the ranks of the 213th Pennsylvania Volunteers as a corporal.

The following month, William Reynolds's company was stationed at Fort Dix, Relay, Maryland, guarding a strategically important location on the Baltimore & Ohio Railroad, nine miles west of Baltimore. Following the president's assassination, Secretary of War Edwin M. Stanton alerted authorities in the vicinity of Washington and Baltimore—including those at Relay—to be on the lookout for the conspirators. Five months later, William Reynolds penned a very poignant farewell letter to his widowed mother in Portsmouth, England, telling her he was dying from consumption. In this letter he wrote:

> . . . after the President was killed a party of our men were immediately ordered in search of the assassin. I, being an old soldier, (it was a green regiment) was ordered in charge of twelve men. They sent us without tents or overcoats and told me not to return until the murderer was either killed or taken. I started and for three days it never ceased to rain, but there was no back out. I pushed ahead with hopes of success, two or three men gave out first, then another and another until I only had five men. The fourth day we met a few cavalry scouting and they requested my aid to capture Atzerodt. I cheerfully consented and to our satisfaction captured him, he was given over to my charge and I yanked him back to the Relay House.

If Reynolds's account is true, and there is no good reason to doubt his words, then the cavalry to which he refers would have been the posse of troopers from the First Delaware Cavalry, based at Monocacy Junction. The six troopers, under the leadership of Sergeant Zachariah W. Gemmill, had been sent out specifically to apprehend Atzerodt—correctly suspected of being in hiding on his cousin's farm in Germantown, Maryland—on the orders of Major Enos Artman. Interestingly, Artman was an officer of the 213th Pennsylvania Volunteers, William Reynolds's regiment, and was in overall command of the Union soldiers at Monocacy Junction. Moreover, if Reynolds's words are to be believed, then they immediately throw into question the recognized version of events that has long been accepted and emerges from the contemporary accounts and statements of key players involved in the instigation and conduct of George Atzerodt's arrest and his conveyance to Relay.

Nowhere in those depositions is there mention of a depleted party of infantrymen from Fort Dix, Relay. Artman, James Purdom, Gemmill, and the six troopers were ultimately recipients of reward money offered for the apprehension of Atzerodt. If, as he claimed, Reynolds was

party to the capture of the conspirator, then it is sadly ironic that nine months later he died in comparative poverty. Yet, as consumption took its grip on him, he was at least able to tell his mother that a patriotic old doctor had befriended him and taken him under his charge gratuitously because he had served the country. William Reynolds died in Philadelphia in January 1866 at the age of twenty-three.

Sources: William Reynolds letters to his mother, A. J. Hoare Collection, Hildenborough, England.

*See also:* Purdom, James W.; Artman, Enos R.; Gemmill, Zachariah W.

## Rich Hill

The home of Samuel Cox, located in Charles County, Maryland. Originally, the name applied to six hundred acres of rich farmland located on the east side of the Wicomico River near its mouth. Booth and Herold visited Cox, a Confederate agent, whose home was situated on the Confederate mail line, around midnight on Saturday night, April 15. The two fugitives had spent most of the day resting at the home of Samuel Mudd. After a stay of five or six hours, during which time the two men rested and were fed, Cox turned them over to his overseer, Franklin Robey, with orders to hide them in a pine thicket approximately one half mile south of the village of

Cox's Station. Cox next told Thomas Jones, an agent under Cox's command, to care for the men and put them across the Potomac River to Virginia at the earliest possible moment when it was safe. Jones waited five days before deeming it safe. On April 20, Jones put Booth and Herold in a boat and sent them toward the Virginia shore and Thomas Harbin. Rich Hill stands today much the same as it did in 1865, except for the attached kitchen wing, which was removed several years ago.

Sources: Edward Steers, Jr., *Blood on the Moon* (Lexington: University Press of Kentucky, 2003), 156, 159.

*See also:* Cox, Samuel

## Richards, Almarin Cooley (1827–1907)

Superintendent of the Washington Metropolitan Police from 1864 to 1878. Born in Cummington, Massachusetts, in 1827, Richards moved in 1851 to Washington, D.C., where he worked as a schoolteacher until he was appointed superintendent of police by President Lincoln on December 1, 1864.

Richards telegraphed provost marshal James McPhail in Baltimore that Booth may well be heading to Baltimore to hide out among his many friends. This alerted McPhail to send his own detectives after Booth's known acquaintances, which included Samuel Arnold and Michael O'Laughlen. In 1885, Richards claimed he had entered Ford's Theatre shortly before the shooting and was sitting in the Dress Circle. He also claimed that he followed Booth's escape through the rear door of Ford's into Baptist Alley, where he encountered Peanut John Burroughs and J. B. Stewart, the man who tried to capture Booth as he fled from Ford's Theatre. Richards gave several statements in the forty years following the assassination, all filled with inconsistencies and errors. Interestingly, in none of his statements does he mention Stewart, who did follow

Booth into the alley. If Richards was in the theater and chased after Booth, which is doubtful, he added nothing to our knowledge of what transpired.

Richards remained superintendent of the district police force until resigning on January 28, 1878, under a cloud of scandal. He practiced law from 1882 until 1893, when he moved to Florida to take up citrus farming. He carried on a correspondence with Louis J. Wiechmann supporting the latter in his defense against those who claimed he had lied on the witness stand to save himself from being charged as a conspirator.

Sources: Gary R. Planck, *The Lincoln Assassination's Forgotten Investigator* (Harrogate, Tenn.: Lincoln Memorial University Press, 1993).

### Richter, Ernest Hartman (1834–1920)

Cousin of George A. Atzerodt. In 1844, Richter's father, Johann Richter, and Atzerodt's father, Henry Atzerodt, purchased a small farm near Germantown in Montgomery County, Maryland. A few years later, Henry Atzerodt sold his interest in the farm to Johann, his brother-in-law, and moved his family to Westmoreland County, Virginia. George Atzerodt periodically visited the old homestead and his cousin. On the morning of April 15, 1865, Atzerodt decided to visit the Richter farm, where he thought he would be safe. Arriving Sunday eve-

ning, Atzerodt spent the next three days strolling around the farm doing odd jobs to earn his keep. Around 5:00 A.M. on April 20, Union soldiers rudely awakened Atzerodt. Atzerodt and Hartman Richter, as he was known, were taken under military guard to Monocacy Junction, south of Frederick, Maryland. From there they were taken to Relay, Maryland, and then by train to Washington, D.C. Richter and Atzerodt were placed aboard the monitor USS *Saugus* and held there until transferred to the Old Federal Penitentiary, at the Washington Arsenal. Richter was finally released, no longer believed involved in Booth's conspiracy.

Sources: Edward Steers, Jr., *Blood on the Moon* (Lexington: University Press of Kentucky, 2003), 167–69; Edward Steers, Jr., "George Atzerodt," in Edward Steers, Jr., ed., *The Trial* (Lexington: University Press of Kentucky, 2003), lxvi–lxxi.

*See also:* Atzerodt, George Andrew

## Ripley, Edward Hastings

Colonel commanding the Ninth Vermont Infantry. On April 2, 1865, Ripley and his regiment were the first to occupy Richmond following its evacuation on April 2. On April 4, Ripley interviewed Confederate private William H. Snyder and learned of a plot by members of the Torpedo Bureau to blow up the White House in an attempt to assassinate President Lincoln. Ripley took the information to President Lincoln. Lincoln listened to Ripley recount Snyder's claim, but did nothing about it. It was one more example of Lincoln's laissez-faire attitude toward his personal safety.

Sources: Edward Hastings Ripley, *The Capture and Occupation of Richmond, April 3, 1865* (New York: Putnam's, 1907); Edward Steers, Jr., *Blood on the Moon* (Lexington: University Press of Kentucky, 2003), 90.

## Ritterspaugh, Jacob (1840–1926)

A sceneshifter at Ford's Theatre. Ritterspaugh was behind the stage ready to shift the large flats between scenes. He heard the shot and saw Booth run to the rear door. Ritterspaugh testified at the trial as a prosecution witness. He claimed that Edman Spangler, who was standing backstage, struck him in the face with the back of his hand, saying, "Don't say which way he went" and "For God's sake, shut up." His testimony helped convict Spangler.

Sources: Jacob Ritterspaeh [Rittersback, Ritterspaugh], NARA, RG 153, M-599, reel 6, frames 47–49; Poore, *Trial*, vol. 2, 32, 460; Pitman, *Trial*, 97.

## Robey, Franklin A. (1831–1896)

Overseer for Samuel Cox. On the morning of April 16, 1865, Cox, after hosting Booth and Herold for several hours, sent for Robey. He told Robey to hide the two fugitives in a pine thicket just beyond the boundary of his land. Robey told them that someone would come later to care for them (Thomas Jones). So that they would recognize him, "they agreed upon a signal," a peculiar whistle. Thomas Jones, the man caring for Booth and Herold in the thicket, told them to get rid of their horses, which might give away their hiding place. According to Jones's account, Robey and Herold led the two animals into the swamp and shot them. They sank beneath the surface, where no one would find them. Robey's part in hiding the two men was not discovered until many years later.

Sources: Thomas A. Jones, *J. Wilkes Booth* (Chicago: Laird & Lee, 1893), 73–82.

## Robinson, George F. (1832–1907)

A member of the Invalid Corps stationed in Washington, D.C., Robinson was assigned as a nurse to attend Secretary of State William H. Seward in his convalescence from a carriage accident.

Robinson enlisted in Company B of the Eighth Maine Volunteer Infantry. He was severely wounded in his left leg in the Battle of Ware Bottom Church, Virginia, on May 20, 1864. He eventually was sent to Washington, where he was detailed as Seward's nurse beginning April 12. On the night of April 14, he was in Seward's room when Lewis Powell burst through the door and flung himself on Seward, attempting to kill him with a large bowie knife. Robinson and Powell grappled for several moments before Powell knocked Robinson and fled from the room, down the steps, and out the front door. Powell mounted his horse. Herold had fled the scene at the first sound of screams, leaving Powell to find his own way.

Robinson, cut about the forehead and face, returned to the hospital in Washington and convalesced for several weeks from his stab wounds. Once recovered, he testified at the trial as a prosecution witness. In his testimony he identified Powell as the man who had attacked him and Seward. According to Robinson, Powell reconnoitered the house on April 13, and again, on the morning of the 14th. In a statement that did not make it into the trial record, Robinson said, "A man came to the window of the dining room of Mr. Seward's house on the morning of the 13th and 14th of April and inquired each day of the health of the Secretary." Robinson identified the man as Lewis Powell. This statement shows that Booth was planning his murderous attacks at least as early as April 13.

In 1871, Congress awarded Robinson a special gold medal along with five thousand dollars, to honor him for saving Seward's life.

Sources: Statement of George Foster Robinson, NARA, RG 153, M-599, reel 6, frames 94–96; Poore, *Conspiracy Trial*, vol. 1, 479, vol. 2, 3, 31; Pitman, *Trial*, 155, 156.

*See also:* Powell, Lewis Thornton

## Rollins, Bettie

Wife of William Rollins of Port Conway, Virginia. Bettie Rollins tipped off detective Everton J. Conger that Willie Jett could be found at the Star Hotel in Bowling Green. On Tuesday, April 25, 1865, the 16th New York Cavalry, along with Conger and Luther B. Baker, arrived at Port Conway, where they interrogated William Rollins. Rollins told

Conger that two men, one with a lame leg, had crossed over the Rappahannock River around noon on Monday. Three Confederate soldiers, one of whom was Willie Jett, accompanied them. Rollins told Conger he didn't know where they were headed. At this moment, Bettie Rollins volunteered that Jett was "sparking" Izora Gouldman, the young daughter of Isaac Gouldman. Gouldman owned the Star Hotel in Bowling Green, a few miles down the road. Mrs. Rollins told the soldiers that if they wanted to find Jett they should find Izora, for Jett was, in all probability, at the hotel with Izora. She was right. Conger and Baker and the troopers of the 16th New York headed for Bowling Green and found Willie Jett.

Sources: Statement of William Rollins, NARA, RG 153, M-599, reel 6, frames 76–77; Statement of William Rollins, NARA, RG 153, M-599, reel 6, frames 78–82; Edward Steers, Jr., *Blood on the Moon* (Lexington: University Press of Kentucky, 2001), 197–200.

## Rollins, William (1833–1901)

Owner of a small store located in Port Conway, on the Rappahannock River in Virginia. On Monday afternoon, April 24, 1865, Booth and Herold arrived at Port Conway in the wagon of Charley Lucas. Rollins was taken into custody and interrogated. He told his interrogator:

That on Monday, the 24th of April, about 12 M [midday], two men came here in a wagon driven by a colored man named [Charley] "Lucas," who lives near Dr. Stewart's [Richard Stuart]. One of the men was lame; had his ankle bandaged; had crutches; offered me, ten dollars to be taken in my wagon to Bowling Green. Afterwards told me they had made different arrangements. They had met friends who would help them; one of the men I knew to be Willie Jet and two other men names not known who belonged to Mosby. This picture of Booth is the likeness of one of the men. He, however, has his mustache off [Booth shaved his mustache off at Dr. Mudd's]. The other one is Herold. They started from here to go to Bowling Green. The friends whom they met were Willie Jet and two of Mosby men.

The soldiers were Lieutenant Mortimer Bainbridge Ruggles, and privates Willie Jett and Absalom Ruggles Bainbridge. The three soldiers agreed to accompany Booth and Herold across the river and find them a place to stay. After being turned down by the Peyton sisters in Port Royal, Jett found them lodging at the farm of Richard Garrett.

On the morning of April 25, members of the 16th New York Cavalry along with National Detective Police detectives Everton J. Conger and Luther B. Baker arrived at Port Conway. They interrogated William Rollins and his wife, Bettie, and learned that two men fitting the description of Booth and Herold had crossed the river on Monday at around noon, accompanied by three Confederate soldiers, one of whom was Willie Jett. Bettie told the detectives that Jett was "sparking" young Izora Gouldman,

whose father owned the Star Hotel in Bowling Green, located not far down the road. She had no doubt they would find Jett at the Star Hotel, and she was right.

Sources: Statement of William Rollins, NARA, RG 153, M–599, reel 6, frames 76–77; Statement of William Rollins, NARA, RG 153, M–599, reel 6, frames 78–82.

## Ruggles, Mortimer Bainbridge (1844–1902)

Ruggles, a cousin of private Absalom Bainbridge, was the son of Confederate brigadier general Daniel Ruggles, commander of the Virginia forces in the Fredericksburg area. Lieutenant Ruggles was a member of Thomas Nelson Conrad's spy group, located in King George County, Virginia. He was Conrad's second in command.

Ruggles, along with Bainbridge and Willie Jett, escorted Booth and Herold to the home of Richard Garrett midway between Port Royal and Bowling Green, Virginia, on April 24. Booth and Herold were finally caught up with two days later at the Garrett farm, where Booth was killed and Herold taken into custody. Ruggles, who was not at the Garrett farm when Booth was killed, later claimed that Booth had shot himself rather than be taken alive. Ruggles's statement became the basis for the subsequent false belief that Booth committed suicide. Ruggles, as well as Bainbridge and Jett, was never tried for aiding Booth and Herold in their attempt to escape Federal authorities.

Sources: William A. Tidwell, James O. Hall, David W. Gaddy, *Come Retribution* (Jackson: University Press of Mississippi, 1988), 461–67.

### Rutherford, George V. (1835–1893)

Was present at the Petersen house when Lincoln died. Rutherford, along with Colonel Thomas McCurdy Vincent, a member of Secretary of War Edwin M. Stanton's staff, Maunsell B. Field, assistant secretary of the treasury, and Dr. Charles Leale, all swore they had placed two large coins on Lincoln's eyes to keep the eyelids shut.

Sources: Edward Steers, Jr., *Blood on the Moon* (Lexington: University Press of Kentucky, 2001), 268–69.

## Safford, Henry S. (1839–1917)

A boarder at the Petersen house, where Lincoln died. Safford, awakened by all the commotion outside the house, went to the front steps to see what was causing all the noise. Seeing the crowd parting for the soldiers carrying Lincoln's limp body, Safford called out, "What's the matter?" The reply stunned him: "The President has been shot!" Safford called out to the group of men struggling with Lincoln's long frame, "Bring him in here." Safford then led them down the narrow hall to the rear bedroom, where his friend, William "Willie" Clark, roomed. Dr. Leale, the physician in charge due to his being the first doctor on the scene, told Safford to go to the kitchen and start boiling water and fill as many bottles as he could find, to place next to the president's legs in an effort to warm them.

Sources: Dorothy Meserve Kunhardt and Philip B. Kunhardt, Jr., *Twenty Days* (New York: Harper & Row, 1965).

*See also:* Clark, William "Willie"

## "Sam" Letter

Letter written by Samuel Arnold to John Wilkes Booth dated March 27, 1865, with the address of "Hookstown."

Early Saturday morning on April 15, 1865, government detectives were searching Booth's room at the National Hotel in Washington. Among several items found in a trunk in the room was a letter addressed to Booth that was signed "Sam" and carried the address "Hookstown." Neither "Sam" nor "Hookstown" registered with the detectives in Washington at the time of the letter's discovery. Hookstown, it turned out, was the name of a small community in northwest Baltimore where Sam's father, George William Arnold, had purchased a farm in 1848. When Samuel Arnold returned home from Confederate service in 1864, he spent part of his time living on the old farm. At the time Arnold wrote his letter to Booth from "Hookstown" he was staying at the old Arnold farmhouse in northwest Baltimore.

The letter tied Arnold and Michael O'Laughlen directly to Booth's plot. It also supported the government's contention that Confederate leaders were involved in Booth's conspiracy. Arnold writes in the letter, "Do not act rashly or in haste. . . . Go and see how it will be taken at R—d." The "it" was interpreted to mean "assassination," while the "R—d" was obviously "Richmond." The letter took on great importance to the prosecution. It was introduced into the trial record as exhibit 43.

Sources: H. W. Smith, Package of private papers belonging to J. Wilkes Booth, NARA, RG

153, M-599, reel 2, frames 532–35; Percy E. Martin, "The Hookstown Connection," *Surratt Courier*, July 1980, 5–6; Edward Steers, Jr., *Blood on the Moon* (Lexington: University Press of Kentucky, 2001), 172–73.

*See also:* Arnold, Samuel Bland

## Sample, William

A member of Thompson's Battery C, Independent Pennsylvania Artillery. Sample, along with three other members of Battery C, claimed in later life to have helped Dr. Charles Leale carry Lincoln's body from Ford's Theatre across the street to the Petersen house.

Sources: *Sunday Times Telegraph* (Pittsburgh), February 12, 1928; *New York Tribune*, February 8, 1931.

*See also:* Corey, John; Griffiths, Jake; Soles, Jacob

## Sanders, George Nicholas (1812–1873)

A Confederate agent working out of Canada. Sanders was named in the charge and specification against the eight defendants tried before the military tribunal. Sanders was a Kentuckian who had a fanatical devotion for the Confederacy and a fanatical hatred for Lincoln. He was a strong advocate of political assassination as a tool to bring about change. Appointed U.S. consul in London in 1853 by President Franklin Pierce, Sanders

played host to Europe's famous revolutionary heroes such as Lajos Kossuth of Hungary, Giuseppe Garibaldi of Italy, and Aleksandr Ivanovich Herzen of Russia.

Sanders was in Montreal for part of the time that John Wilkes Booth visited there from October 18–27, 1864, and was reported in company with Booth during Booth's stay at the St. Lawrence Hall hotel in Montreal. Earlier that year, in July, he had been party together with Clement C. Clay and James P. Holcombe, both Confederate commissioners in Canada, to hold a peace conference at the Clifton House on the Canadian side of Niagara Falls. The overall purpose was to embarrass Lincoln and influence the 1864 election. Lincoln ignored attempts to send representatives and the conference failed.

Sanders's role in the assassination is without any direct evidence other than that he would favor Booth's plans and undoubtedly encourage him. Following the war he traveled to Europe, where he remained until 1872. He returned to the United States, where he died on August 12, 1873.

Sources: William A. Tidwell, James O. Hall, and David W. Gaddy, *Come Retribution* (Jackson: University Press of Mississippi, 1988), 330–33.

## *Saugus*, USS

A monitor used, along with the USS *Montauk*, as a prison ship to hold suspects in Lincoln's assassination. The two monitors were anchored in the Eastern Branch of the Potomac River at the Washington Navy Yard. Michael O'Laughlen was the first prisoner held on the *Saugus*, arriving on April 17. Lewis Powell arrived on the 18th, followed by Samuel Arnold the next day. George Atzerodt and his cousin Hartman Richter arrived on the 20th. Edman Spangler was also held on the *Saugus*. The prisoners were transferred on April 29 to the Old Federal Penitentiary cell block at the Washington Arsenal.

Sources: Dorothy Meserve Kunhardt and Philip B. Kunhardt, Jr., *Twenty Days* (New York: Harper & Row, 1965), 190–91, 199.

## Secret Service, Confederate

See Bureau of Special and Secret Service, C.S.A.

## Secret Service, United States

See National Detective Police

## Seddon, James Alexander (1815–1880)

Seddon served as the Confederate secretary of war from 1862 to 1865. His letter directing Colonel John Singleton Mosby and Colonel Charles H. Cawood to aid Confederate spy Thomas Nelson Conrad in a plan to capture President Lincoln is one example of Confederate involvement in plans to remove Lincoln from office in 1864.

Conrad was head of a Confederate-backed plot to capture President Lincoln in the summer of 1864. Conrad's mission, unlike those previously planned, appears to have been directed out of Confederate secretary of state Judah P. Benjamin's office. In his postwar memoir Conrad tells of receiving two letters from Jefferson Davis: one to Secretary of War James A. Seddon and another to Secretary of State Benjamin. These letters directed the transfer of Conrad to the Secret Service department, and provided him with the necessary funds to finance his operation in Washington.

While in Richmond, Conrad received a second letter from Seddon on War Department letterhead, dated September 15, 1864, that directed Lieutenant Colonel John Singleton Mosby and Colonel Charles H. Cawood to "aid and facilitate the movements of Captain Conrad." Mosby commanded the 43rd Battalion of Virginia Cavalry operating primarily throughout Loudoun County, Virginia, across the Potomac River from Montgomery County, Maryland. Cawood was in command of a signal corps camp in King George County, Virginia, situated across the Potomac River from Charles County, Maryland. These two areas represented the "upper Potomac" and "lower Potomac" referred to by Conrad in his memoir. The two Maryland counties were avenues into Washington, D.C., that Confederate agents used with great success throughout the war. Both were potential escape routes for a capturing party carrying the president from his summer quarters at Soldiers' Home to Virginia and the Confederate capital, Richmond. Seddon's letter was just one more "dot" making up the overall picture that tied Davis and his subordinates to an effort to remove Lincoln from the presidency.

Sources: Thomas Nelson Conrad, *The Rebel Scout* (Washington, D.C.: National, 1904), 94–95, 118–19; Thomas Nelson Conrad, *A Confederate Spy* (New York: J. S. Ogilvie, 1892), 56; William A. Tidwell, *April '65: Confederate Covert Action in the American Civil War* (Kent, Ohio: Kent State University Press, 1995), 69–71.

*See also:* Conrad, Thomas Nelson; Johnson, Bradley T.; Taylor, Joseph Walker

**Sessford, Joseph S. (unknown—1901)**
Ticket seller at Ford's Theatre on the night of the assassination. Sessford was on duty in the ticket seller's box having started work at 6:00 P.M. He was called as a witness for the defense during the trial of the conspirators. He testified that only the President's box was reserved for the evening performance. The remaining six boxes (two upper and four lower)

remained empty. Harry Clay Ford, in his statement dated April 20, 1865, told of a conversation the Wednesday before the assassination in which Booth was present along with Joseph Sessford and Thomas Raybold. Booth lamented the result of Lincoln's policies, "We are all slaves now." He further expressed being upset that whites were no longer the superior of blacks, and that insulting a black would result in being knocked down by the black without recourse, to which Sessford and Raybold told Booth that if that were the case he should not insult a negro. Sessford is buried in Congressional Cemetery located in Washington, D.C.

Sources: William C. Edwards and Edward Steers, Jr., eds. *The Lincoln Assassination: The Evidence* (Urbana, Ill.: University of Illinois Press, 2009), 516, 519, 520.

### Seward, Augustus (1826–1876)

Eldest son of Secretary of State William H. Seward. In 1858, Seward's daughter, Frances Adeline Seward, or "Fanny," began a journal as a way to fulfill her writing ambitions. She graphically described the horror of the night her father was attacked: "My screams awakened Gus [Augustus]. . . . The first recollection I have of seeing Augustus—except when the assassin broke away from him, was

with his forehead covered with blood." Although Augustus Seward was bloodied by Lewis Powell's knife attack, his wounds were superficial and he quickly recovered. On Tuesday, April 18, Augustus visited the monitor *Saugus*, where Powell was being held. He positively identified Powell as the man who had attacked him and his father on Friday night.

Sources: Patricia Carley Johnson, ed., "'I have supped full on horrors,'" *American Heritage* 10, no. 6 (October 1959), 60–65, 96–101.

*See also:* Seward, William Henry

### Seward, Francis Adeline "Fanny" (1844–1866)

The Sewards' only daughter, twenty-year-old Fanny Seward, was sitting by

her father's bedside when Lewis Powell forced his way to the bedroom on April 14, 1865. Fanny kept a journal beginning on Christmas Day, 1858, and continued her entries until October 7, 1866, twenty-two days before her untimely death. Her health declined steadily from the night of the attack on her father, Lincoln's secretary of state, until her death. Her entry for April 14, 1865, begins with her father's condition improving after a recent carriage accident. She sat by his bedside reading "Legends of Charlemagne" to him. She heard voices outside in the hall and, thinking it was someone important or perhaps the president wishing to visit Seward, she went to the door and opened it, saying to her brother Frederick, "Fred, father is awake now." It was a terrible mistake. Standing in the hall with Fred was Lewis Powell, intent on finding William Seward and killing him. Fanny gave away her father's location. Inside the room with Fanny was George Robinson, a convalescing soldier assigned as a nurse to Secretary Seward. The door opened and Powell and Fred came into the room struggling. Powell broke loose and "seemed rushing toward the bed. In the hand nearest me was pistol, in the right hand a knife. I ran beside him to the bed imploring him to stop." Powell fell on top of Seward and knocked him to the floor, stabbing him several times. Robinson and Fred Seward grappled with Powell while Fanny stood watching in horror. "My screams awakened Augustus." The three men continued grappling with the powerful assassin, who broke loose and fled down the stairs and out the front door. David Herold, who had been outside holding Powell's horse, was now nowhere in sight, having fled when he heard the screams coming from the house. "It seemed to me that every man I met had blood on his face," Fanny recalled. Fanny ran back to her father's room. "Where's father?" she screamed seeing an empty bed. Looking around, she saw a pile of bedclothes next to the bed and suddenly realized it was her father. "As I stood my feet slipped in a great pool of blood."

Powell left behind five injured members of the household, two badly injured: Fred Seward had a fractured skull and stab wounds, and George Robinson had several severe stab wounds, requiring hospitalization. Fortunately, William Seward and Augustus Seward were not seriously wounded. Emerick Hansell, a State Department employee, was knifed when he got in the way of the fleeing Powell.

Sources: Patricia Carley Johnson, ed., " 'I have supped full on horrors,' " *American Heritage* 10, no. 6 (October 1959), 60–65, 96–101.

*See also:* Seward, William Henry

## Seward, Frederick William (1830–1915)

Second born of three sons of William H. Seward and Adeline Seward. Frederick assumed some of the administrative duties of his father while the latter recovered from a serious carriage accident. Frederick Seward confronted Lewis Powell on the night of April 14 when Powell forced his way past one of the servants and made his way up the stairs to the second floor, where the secretary of state was convalescing in bed. When Frederick refused to allow Powell to continue farther, Powell drew his Colt revolver and fired point blank at Seward. The gun misfired and Powell struck Seward on the head, fracturing his skull. Seward recovered and continued to grapple with Powell, receiving several stab wounds. Powell rushed into William Seward's bedroom when Fanny Seward opened the door to see what the commotion was. Frederick and an army nurse both grappled with the powerful Powell, who was able to break free and fall on top of William Seward, stabbing him several times and knocking him to the floor. Powell fled the scene and escaped from the Seward house, heading east of the Capitol and abandoning his horse somewhere near Lincoln Hospital. He was arrested on Monday night, April 17, at the Surratt House in Surrattsville, Maryland, where he came hoping to find solace. He found military detectives instead.

Within a few hours of the attack, Frederick Seward had lost all ability to speak, and he soon became comatose. His recovery was slow but after a month he was returning to normal. His father improved, too, and by May was making visits to his office. Frederick continued to serve his father as assistant secretary of state. In 1891 he published a three-volume biography of his father, which although eulogistic, contained many of his father's more important state papers.

Sources: Patricia Carley Johnson, ed., "'I have supped full on horrors,'" *American Heritage* 10, no. 6 (October 1959), 60–65, 96–101; John M. Taylor, *William Henry Seward: Lincoln's Right Hand* (New York: HarperCollins, 1991).

### Seward, William Henry (1801–1872)

Secretary of state under Abraham Lincoln, Seward was attacked in his home at approximately the same time as Booth shot the president at Ford's Theatre. Booth's plan was apparently an attempt to decapitate the head of the Federal government, throwing it into a chaotic state and thereby giving the Confederate leaders and their army time to regroup. The plan was not without some merit in view of a dying Confederacy. There were few alternatives, yet even if Booth had succeeded in killing President Lincoln, Vice President Andrew Johnson, Secretary of State Seward, and General Ulysses S. Grant, as originally envisioned, the Federal government and her military would have continued on their course of defeating what was left of the Confederate armies struggling to stay alive.

At approximately 10:15 P.M. on April 14, 1865, Lewis Powell and David Herold arrived at the Seward home opposite Lafayette Square in Washington, D.C. Powell had been assigned the task of killing Seward. Herold's role was to act as Powell's guide, presumably to lead him to Southern Maryland, where the two would rendezvous with Booth

(and possibly George Atzerodt). Powell went to the front while Herold held Powell's horse, the one-eyed horse Booth had purchased from Dr. Samuel Mudd's neighbor George Gardiner on December 18, 1864, during Booth's second visit to Charles County and Dr. Mudd.

William Bell, a house servant, answered the door at Seward's home. Powell told Bell he had been sent by Seward's physician, Dr. Tullio Verdie, with medicine he was instructed to give to Seward personally. Bell argued and Powell pushed his way past him and started up the stairs to the second floor, where Seward's bedroom was located. Fred Seward, the second-eldest son and acting in his father's stead while the secretary convalesced, met Powell at the top of the stairs and engaged Powell, telling the intruder his father could not be disturbed and to leave the medicine with him. After arguing further, Powell turned as if to go back down the steps, but suddenly wheeled around and aimed his Colt revolver at Fred Seward. The gun misfired so Powell bludgeoned Seward over the head and pushed past him. As Seward attempted to recover and block Powell, Fanny Seward, the daughter of William Seward, opened the father's bedroom, where she had been seated reading to him. She said to Fred that Seward was awake, thus giving Powell the location of the bedroom. Powell rushed into the room with Fred Seward on his back. George Robinson, a male nurse assigned to Seward who was seated in Seward's room, sprang to his feet and tried to help Fred restrain Powell. At some point Powell was able to break free and lunged on top of William Seward, stabbing him several times and knocking him from his bed to the floor.

Powell, assuming he had done his job, fled from the room and out of the house. Herold was gone, having fled at the first sound of screaming coming from the house. Powell mounted his horse and fled east of the Capitol, abandoning his horse somewhere near Lincoln Hospital. Powell hid out all day Saturday, Sunday, and Monday.

William Seward survived Powell's brutal knife attack but was badly scarred for life. He continued on as President Johnson's secretary of state. As if the attack on him by Powell were not debilitating enough, Seward lived to see his wife die on June 21, nine weeks after Powell's attack, and his beloved daughter Fanny die on October 29, 1866, of tuberculosis. William H. Seward died on October 10, 1872.

Sources: Patricia Carley Johnson, ed., " 'I have supped full on horrors,' " *American Heritage* 10, no. 6 (October 1959), 60–65, 96–101; John M.

Taylor, *William Henry Seward: Lincoln's Right Hand* (New York: HarperCollins 1991).

*See also:* Powell, Lewis Thornton

## *Sic Semper Tyrannis*

Exclamation made by John Wilkes Booth at the time he assassinated President Lincoln. The Latin phrase translates, "Thus always to tyrants." It was the motto of the state of Virginia at the time Booth shouted it from the president's box at Ford's Theatre. The motto was replaced following the Civil War because of its heinous association with Booth's murderous act. From 1865 to 1873, the motto was replaced by the words "Liberty and Union." By 1873, the Pierpont administration was gone and the state was again under the control of "native and true Virginians" who promptly restored the old Latin motto, *Sic Semper Tyrannis*. "Liberty and Union" was found to be objectionable to the segment of Virginians who had supported the Confederacy. "Liberty" had been restored to that segment of the population that had been slaves, and "Union" was forced on those that did not want it.

Sources: Edward Steers, Jr., "Liberty and Union: The Motto on the Great Seal of the Commonwealth of Virginia," *Surratt Courier* 25, no. 1 (January 2000), 3–4.

## Simms, Mary

Former slave owned by Dr. Samuel Mudd. Mary Simms was one of the principal witnesses for the prosecution's case establishing Mudd as a southern sympathizer and conduit for passing mail and documents along the Confederate mail line. Simms testified that John Surratt was a frequent visitor at Mudd's house, where he often stopped when coming from or going to Richmond. She also claimed that soldiers often slept in the woods behind Mudd's house and that Mudd provided them with food, instructing Simms and other of his slaves to stand lookout for Union soldiers patrolling the area. According to Simms, Mudd received letters from Virginia (Richmond) that he passed on in addition to sending letters he received from persons in the North, which he sent on to Richmond. She told of Mudd deliberately shooting her brother, Elzee Eglent, in the leg for failing to heed Mudd's orders in a timely way, and that Mudd whipped her in December (1864), resulting in her leaving the farm and running away to Washington. She described several men in gray pants and jackets with yellow stripes camping out in Mudd's woods under Mudd's care.

Sources: Testimony of Mary Simms, Poore, *Conspiracy Trial*, vol. 2, 150–57; Pitman, *Trial*, 170.

See also: Eglent, Elzee; Mudd, Dr. Samuel Alexander

## Simonds, Joseph

Close personal friend of John Wilkes Booth. Booth hired Joseph Simonds to manage his oil ventures in Venango County, Pennsylvania. Simonds's previous job was as a bank teller in Boston. Simonds testified at the conspiracy trial that Booth had lost his entire six-thousand-dollar investment by the fall of 1864. Part of the trouble was Booth's apparent distraction with his growing desire to do something great for his beloved Confederacy. On February 21, 1865, Simonds wrote to Booth, beginning his letter with a perceptive inquiry: "Your strange note of the 16th Rec'd. I hardly know what to make of you this winter. So different from your usual self. Have you lost all your ambition or what is the matter." Booth's noticeable change in demeanor was brought about by his preoccupation with removing Lincoln from office. Simonds continued, "Don't get offended with me, John, but I cannot but think you are wasting your time spending the entire season in Washington doing nothing when it must be expensive to live and all for no other purpose beyond pleasures."

Called as a witness at the conspiracy trial, Simonds explained Booth's "oil business" to the members of the tribunal. "In accordance with your request, I am happy to give you correct information with regard to the property of J. Wilkes Booth in this section, more especially as newspaper rumor has assigned to him extensive and valuable interests here. The first time he was ever in Venango County was in January 1864 when he made a small investment in connection with two gentlemen of Cleveland in a lease on the Allegheny River directly opposite Franklin. He owning an undivided third interest in the same. During the summer the lease was placed in my hands for management and at that time on the occasion of his second visit here in June last he made an investment of $1000 in a property on Pithole Creek owned by an association of gentlemen in Boston, the management of whose affairs here was also placed in my hands."

Simonds kept writing to Booth to urge him to come to Venango County and settle down: "If you have nothing else to do and get hard up just come out here and stop with us. We will guarantee to support you." Booth had been a good friend to Simonds, who readily told Booth how grateful he was: "Let me assure you I shall never forget all your kindness to me."

Eighteen sixty-four would mark a turning point in Booth's short but illustrious life. His last paid appearance occurred on May 28 with a matinee performance in *The Corsican Brothers* at the Boston Museum. Although he would appear three more times in benefits, his career was over. He would turn away from the stage and toward the role he believed destiny had thrust upon him. At the same time, he began transferring all of his assets over to his mother, his older brother Junius, and his sister Rosalie. He instructed Simonds to take care of the transfer of his oil holdings. At the same time he transferred a lucrative lot he owned in the Back Bay area of Boston to his mother. Simonds told his interrogators, "On May than [Booth] requested me to prepare deeds conveying all his title and interest in the Allegheny River property to his brother, Junius Brutus Booth, two thirds and to myself one third, and all his interest in the Pithole property to his sister [Rosalie], he giving as a reason that his oil speculations had proved unprofitable and he wished to dispose of every interest he had in this section as they served to draw away his mind and attention from his profession to which he intended to devote all his faculties in the future." Of course, Booth would withhold his plan to capture Lincoln, using the reason for the transfer that he wanted to get them off his mind.

Simonds was called as a witness at the conspiracy trial and explained Booth's business transaction in the "oil business," which some still believed was a code word for "assassination." Simonds never saw Booth again after his last visit in September 1864.

Sources: Statement of Joseph H. Simonds, NARA, RG 153, M-599, reel 2, frames 317–19; Testimony of Joseph H. Simonds, Poore, *Conspiracy Trial*, vol. 1, 39; Pitman, *Trial*, 45; Statement of Joseph H. Simonds, Nara, RG 153, M-599, reel 2, frames 738–40; Statement of Joseph H. Simonds, NARA, RG 153, M-599, reel 7, frames 31–42.

### Slater, Sarah (1843–1880)

A mysterious lady described as an exotic young French-speaking Confederate courier who moved between Montreal and Toronto and the capital of the Confederacy, Richmond, Virginia. Slater also used the alias "Kate Thompson." On several occasions, John Surratt accompanied her in her travels between Canada and Richmond. Slater showed up at the Surratt boardinghouse in Washington, D.C., on a couple of occasions, and was joined by Mary Surratt, who accompanied her to the Surratt Tavern in Surrattsville, Maryland. While no direct connection exists to tie her into Booth's conspiracy to capture, and later kill, Lincoln, her associations with John Surratt and his mother, Mary, are one more link that bring John and Mary Surratt and

Booth in direct contact with Confederate agents.

Sources: James O. Hall, "Saga of Sarah Slater," *Surratt Society News* 7, no. 1 (January 1982), 3–6, and *Surratt Society News* 7, no. 2 (February 1982), 2–6.

## Sleichmann, John F.

Assistant property manager at Ford's Theatre. Called as a witness for the prosecution in the case of Edman Spangler. Sleichmann testified that he was standing backstage when Booth entered the rear of the theater and spoke to Spangler. Booth said, "Ned, you'll help me all you can won't you?" To which Spangler replied, "Oh yes." He further testified that he saw Spangler approximately fifteen minutes after the shooting, standing with a white handkerchief in his hand. He was "very pale, and wiping his eyes." The testimony was used in an attempt to show that Spangler had helped Booth escape the theater after shooting Lincoln.

Sources: Testimony of John F. Sleichmann, Poore, *Conspiracy Trial*, vol. 1, 216; Pitman, *Trial*, 73.

*See also:* Ritterspaugh, John

## Smith, Henry W.

A detective working for provost marshal Henry H. Wells. Wells, having gathered sufficient evidence to tie John Surratt

and his mother to Booth, ordered Major Smith and four of his detectives, Ely Devoe, R. C. Morgan, Charles W. Rosch, and William M. Wermerskirch, to go to the Surratt boardinghouse in Washington, D.C., and arrest all of the occupants. While at the boardinghouse, Lewis Powell suddenly showed up, knocking on the door. Taken by surprise to find several army detectives there, Powell attempted to pretend, but to no avail, that he had the wrong house. Smith began interrogating Powell as well as Mary Surratt, who claimed she had never seen Powell before and did not know who he was. Smith quickly became convinced that both Mary Surratt and Lewis Powell were in some way connected to the assassination, and so took them and the other boarders to the 22nd Army headquarters. Smith received a thousand dollars of the reward money for Powell's arrest while the other detectives received five hundred dollars each.

Sources: Edward Steers, Jr., *Blood on the Moon* (Lexington: University Press of Kentucky, 2001), 174–79.

*See also:* Powell, Lewis Thornton; Reward Money; Surratt, Mary Elizabeth

## Smith, John L.

Detective under Maryland provost marshal James McPhail and brother-in-law of George A. Atzerodt. While Atzerodt was held as a prisoner in the Old Federal Penitentiary cell block inside the Washington Arsenal, he requested to see McPhail and Smith. The two men were granted permission by Secretary of War Edwin M. Stanton and visited Atzerodt on May 1. During the visit, Smith took down a seven-page statement by Atzerodt that contained several important points relative to Lincoln's murder. Atzerodt told the two men that "Booth said he had met a party in N. York that would get the Prest. Certain. They were going to mine the end of Pres. House, next to War Dept. They knew an entrance to accomplish it through. . . . Booth said if he did not get him quick the N. York crowd would." Atzerodt implicated Dr. Samuel Mudd when he told his interrogators, "I am certain Dr. Mudd knew all about it [capture plan], as Booth sent (as he told me) liquors & provisions for the trip with the President to Richmond, about two weeks before the murder to Dr. Mudd's." He then went on to implicate Mary Surratt: "Booth told me that Mrs. Surratt went to Surrattsville to get out the guns (two carbines) which had been taken to that place by Herold, this was Friday."

McPhail, surprisingly, handed the statement over to William E. Doster, Atzerodt's attorney, who filed it among his personal papers. It was never mentioned during the conspiracy trial. The statement was discovered 112 years later in 1977 by historian Joan L. Chaconas among Doster's personal papers in the family's possession. Known as the "Lost Confession," it is currently in a private collection, although photocopies of the statement were made and distributed among assassination historians.

Sources: Edward Steers, Jr., " 'Lost Confession' of George A. Atzerodt," in Edward Steers, Jr., ed., *The Trial* (Lexington: University Press of Kentucky, 2003), civ–cvi.

See also: Lost Confession

## Smoot, Richard Mitchell (1833–1906)

A tobacco farmer in Charles County, Maryland. Smoot was part owner along with James Brawner of a good-size fishing skiff needed by Booth's conspirators. On January 14, 1865, John Surratt and Thomas Harbin, both working with Booth in his conspiracy to capture President Lincoln, went to see Smoot in Port Tobacco. They negotiated with him to purchase the skiff, agreeing to pay Smoot $250, half down and the balance later. The $125 balance was deposited with attorney Frederick Stone, another Charles County resident, who agreed to hold the money until told to release it to Smoot.

Smoot wanted to use the boat before turning it over to Surratt, but Surratt told him "he would want possession right away, as the need of the boat would be the consequence of an event of unprecedented magnitude in the history of the country." The skiff was turned over to George Atzerodt, who hid the boat in Goose Creek and later in a small tributary of Nanjemoy Creek. Booth never used the skiff.

Sources: Richard M. Smoot, *The Unwritten History of the Assassination of Abraham Lincoln* (Clinton, Mass.: W. J. Coulter, 1908); William A. Tidwell, James O. Hall, and David W. Gaddy, *Come Retribution* (Jackson: University Press of Mississippi, 1988), 339.

## Snyder, William H.

A private in the Confederate army assigned to work in the Torpedo Bureau under the command of General Gabriel J. Rains. On April 4, 1865, the day after Richmond was evacuated and occupied by the Ninth Vermont Infantry under command of Colonel Edward Hastings Ripley, Snyder sought an interview with Ripley. Snyder alerted Ripley to a plot that placed "the head of the Yankee government . . . in great danger of violence." Snyder said that a party "had just been dispatched from Rains's torpedo bureau on a secret mission . . . and he wanted to put Mr. Lincoln on his guard." Snyder could not give Ripley the names of the people in the party, since their mission was secret, but he emphasized to Ripley that "the President of the United States was in great danger."

Snyder's warning fits nicely with a statement given by George Atzerodt that Booth "met a party in N. York who would get the Prest. Certain. They were going to mine the end of the White House, next to War Dept." The object was to blow up the section of the White House where Lincoln's office was located and where cabinet meetings were held.

On April 2, two days before Snyder's revelation, Thomas Harney, a Confederate agent working in the Torpedo Bureau, left Richmond with a cache of special ordnance and linked up in Loudoun County, Virginia, with Colonel John Singleton Mosby's Rangers. Harney was assigned to Company H, and on April 10, Harney and several of Mosby's men were ambushed by a patrol of the Eighth Illinois Cavalry at Burke Station, just fifteen miles from Washington, D.C., and captured. The action report states that Harney was captured with ordnance in his possession.

Snyder's revelation and the timing of a plot against Lincoln emanating from the Torpedo Bureau are remarkably coincidental. Atzerodt's statement along with Snyder's claim and Harney's movements fit neatly together. However, until more information is uncovered, the link remains speculative.

Sources: Edward Hastings Ripley, *The Capture and Occupation of Richmond, April 3, 1865* (New York: Putnam's, 1907), 23; William A. Tidwell, James O. Hall, and David W. Gaddy, *Come Retribution* (Jackson: University Press of Mississippi, 1988), 89–91.

*See also*: Torpedo Bureau; Harney, Thomas F.; Ripley, Edward Hastings

## Sockdologer, Sockdologizing

From the play by English playwright Tom Taylor, *Our American Cousin,* performed at Ford's Theatre on the night of Lincoln's assassination. At the end of act 3, scene 2, actor Harry Hawk delivered the lines that always produced loud laughter from audiences: "Don't know the manners of good society, eh? Well I guess I know enough to turn you inside out, old gal—you *sockdologizing* old man-trap." It was at this moment that Booth fired the fatal shot into Abraham Lincoln's brain.

*Sockdology* is believed to be a corruption of *doxology*, which refers to a hymn sung near the end of a church service. The definition of *sockdologer* (also spelled *sockdolager*) in most modern dictionaries is along the lines of "That which finishes or ends a matter; a settler; a poser, as a heavy blow, a conclusive answer, and the like" (*Webster's Revised Unabridged Dictionary*, 1913). This does not fit well with its use in *Our American Cousin*. But the word had another meaning common in

the 1840s that has long since fallen from use: "A combination of two fish hooks which close upon each other, by means of a spring, as soon as the fish bites." This fits nicely with its use in the play.

Sources: Jeffrey Kacirk, *Forgotten English* (New York: William Morrow, 1997), 168–69.

*See also: Our American Cousin*

## Soldiers' Home

Site of President Lincoln's summer White House, located three miles north of the Capitol building in the outskirts of Washington, D.C. Lincoln spent most of the summer months from 1862 to 1864 at the Soldiers' Home. At least three plots were proposed that involved capturing Lincoln while he was traveling to or from the place. Established by an act of Congress on March 5, 1851, the property consisted of two hundred acres of land and a large, two-story farmhouse owned by wealthy Washington banker and financier George Washington Riggs. The property was located three miles due north of the White House in what was then rural farmland beyond the residential limits of Washington. The funds to purchase the property came from a levy by Major General Winfield Scott on the officials of Mexico City as payment in lieu of pillage during the Mexican War. Scott received $150,000, which he used

to establish a refuge for old soldiers. A main administration building and two stone cottages were added to the existing farm residence.

In 1858, President James Buchanan and his secretary of war, John B. Floyd, spent the summer months in the two smaller stone cottages, thereby establishing a precedent for future presidents. In 1862, President Lincoln, along with Secretary of War Edwin M. Stanton, moved into the two stone cottages during the summer months and again in 1863. In 1864, Lincoln and his family moved into the larger farmhouse, which had been the original home occupied by the Riggs family, and was named after Robert Anderson, the original administrator of the Soldiers' Home. Anderson Cottage was the site where Lincoln prepared the first draft of the Emancipation Proclamation.

Lincoln would, on occasion, ride to and from the Soldiers' Home without notifying his cavalry escort, causing alarm among certain members of his administration. On one occasion his hat was shot off his head as he approached the main gate. In 1862, Confederate colonel Joseph Walker Taylor, nephew of former president Zachary Taylor, sought Jefferson Davis's approval to capture Lincoln while he was en route to the home.

In 1864, Thomas Nelson Conrad, with Confederate leaders' approval, reconnoitered Lincoln's movements with the intention of capturing him. Again in 1864, Confederate general Bradley T. Johnson proposed to capture Lincoln at Soldiers' Home. His plan was put on hold until Jubal Early completed his planned raid of Washington in July 1864.

Sources: Edward Steers, Jr., *Blood on the Moon* (Lexington: University Press of Kentucky, 2001), 23–26; Edward Steers, Jr., *His Name Is Still Mudd* (Gettysburg, Pa.: Thomas, 1997), 10–15.

*See also:* Taylor, Joseph Walker; Conrad, Thomas Nelson; Johnson, Bradley T.

## Soles, Jacob (1845–1936)

A member of Thompson's Battery C, Independent Pennsylvania Artillery. Soles, along with three other members of Battery C, claimed in later life to have helped Dr. Charles Leale carry Lincoln's body from Ford's Theatre across the street to the Petersen house. Although there are eight individuals who made such claims, there are no records that definitively confirm who carried Lincoln's body from the theater into the Petersen house.

Sources: *Sunday Times Telegraph* (Pittsburgh), February 12, 1928, and *New York Tribune*, February 8, 1931.

*See also:* Corey, John; Griffiths, Jake; Samples, William

## Sons of Liberty

A derivative of a larger organization known as the Knights of the Golden Circle (KGC). One of several fifth column organizations that operated in the northern states in support of Confederate independence by paramilitary means.

In 1864, the KGC changed its name for the third time, to the Sons of Liberty. The Sons of Liberty, as well as the Knights of the Golden Circle and Order of American Knights, were organized as paramilitary organizations located in the northern states with the objective of working on the Confederacy's behalf to overthrow the Federal government whether through nonviolent or violent means. A principal objective was to defeat Lincoln's reelection, using dirty tricks as well as outright terror.

The history of the Sons of Liberty is murky. Confederate agent Thomas Hines reported that the leaders were not united in support for the Confederacy and desired the war to cease. Jacob Thompson, head commissioner of the Confederate secret service organization in Canada, anticipated uprisings by the Sons of Liberty on several occasions that never materialized. Thompson remained upbeat despite the inactivity that the Sons of Liberty, with aid from his organization, could successfully stage an uprising to a Northwestern Confederacy composed of Illinois, Indiana, Ohio, Kentucky, and Missouri. Thompson even sent a request to Jefferson Davis urging Davis to send a Confederate force into Kentucky and Missouri that would aid the uprising. It never came about. Thompson ordered Hines and his associates to give aid to the Sons of Liberty in a planned uprising at the time of the Democratic convention in Chicago, hoping to bring about a general uprising. But, once again, the ineptness of the organizers, including those of the Sons of Liberty, were never able to muster enough strength and support to carry out their plan. The Sons of Liberty eventually faded away, playing little if any part in hindering Lincoln's reelection or Union victory.

Members of the KGC–Sons of Liberty in Baltimore, under the leadership of Cipriano Ferrandini, plotted to assassinate president-elect Lincoln during his stopover in that city on February 23, 1861, on his way to Washington. The plot was thwarted when Lincoln changed his schedule and passed through Baltimore nine hours ahead of schedule.

Sources: James O. Hall, "A Magnificent Charlatan: George Washington Lafayette Bickley," *Civil War Times Illustrated* 18, no. 10 (February 1980), 40–42; Larry E. Nelson, *Bullets, Ballots, and Rhetoric: Confederate Policy for the United States Presidential Contest of 1864* (Tuscaloosa, AL: University of Alabama Press, 1980).

*See also:* Knights of the Golden Circle; Order of American Knights; Ferrandini, Cipriano

## Soper's Hill

A point in Prince George's County, Maryland, approximately eight miles southeast of the Navy Yard Bridge in the District of Columbia. Booth and David Herold met there after fleeing from the city on the night of the assassination of President Lincoln at Ford's Theatre. The spot was obviously a prearranged meeting place for the conspirators following the planned assassinations of that night. Booth arrived first and waited for the other conspirators to arrive. Only Herold showed up. George Atzerodt failed in his assignment and wandered aimlessly around the city before checking in to the Kimmel Hotel on C Street around two o'clock in the morning. Lewis Powell, abandoned by Herold and left on his own, made his way east of the Capitol building, and hid out until he became desperate for food and comfort and made his way to Mary Surratt's boardinghouse at 541 H Street, where detectives arrested him on Monday evening, April 17.

After rendezvousing at Soper's Hill, Booth and Herold continued on for another five miles to the Surratt Tavern in Surrattsville.

Sources: James O. Hall, *John Wilkes Booth Escape Route: Notes by James O. Hall* (Clinton, Md.: Surratt Society, 1980), 4; William A. Tidwell, James O. Hall, and David W. Gaddy, *Come Retribution* (Jackson: University Press of Mississippi, 1988), 444.

## Southern Maryland

A region of Maryland encompassing the six counties of Montgomery, Prince George's, Calvert, St. Mary's, Charles, and Anne Arundel. The last five are situated to the south and east of the District of Columbia. They form a large peninsula bounded on the west and south by the Potomac River and on the east by Chesapeake Bay. The entire western border, consisting of seventy-five miles of shoreline, lies opposite the state of Virginia. At its narrowest point less than two miles separates the two shores. Southern Maryland had ideal soil and weather conditions for cultivating tobacco. So lucrative was the tobacco trade with England that many of the plantation owners in the region established residences in London to facilitate their sales, cutting out the middleman in the process. By the outbreak of the Civil War, the border states of Missouri, Kentucky, and Maryland accounted for half of the nation's production of tobacco, and of that half, Southern Maryland outproduced Missouri and Kentucky combined.

The institution of slavery, so necessary to the labor-intensive cultivation of tobacco, wed the region to the other southern states culturally and economically. The region was strongly pro-Confederate, and following the outbreak of war three routes were established that the Confederacy referred to as "mail lines" and that ran from Richmond across the Potomac River through Charles County to various points in the north and on to Canada, where the Confederacy had a substantial clandestine organization. People, documents, and a variety of materiel passed from points north along this mail line, carefully managed by the residents of Charles County and Prince George's County.

Southern Maryland was ideal for Booth's avenue of escape. Booth planned on using the principal mail line as his escape route with a captured President Lincoln, drawing on the aid of Confederate agents in the area, including Thomas Jones, Samuel Cox, and Dr. Samuel A. Mudd.

Sources: William A. Tidwell, James O. Hall, and David W. Gaddy, *Come Retribution* (Jackson: University Press of Mississippi, 1988), 328–45; Edward Steers, Jr., "Maryland My Maryland," *North & South* 6, no. 2 (February 2003), 42–51.

*See also*: Mail Line; Charles County, Maryland

**Spangler, Edman (1825–1875)**

A sceneshifter and general handyman at Ford's Theatre at the time of the assassination of President Lincoln on April 14, 1865. Spangler held Booth's horse before turning it over to Peanut John Burroughs. He was tried as a conspirator of John Wilkes Booth and sentenced to six years in prison at Fort Jefferson, Florida.

Spangler was born in York, Pennsylvania, in 1825 and later moved to Baltimore, where he was living at the outbreak of the Civil War. He married a Baltimore woman who died soon after the wedding. Spangler took up the trade of carpentry and worked on Tudor Hall, the home of Junius Brutus Booth, where Spangler first met the young John Wilkes Booth. When war broke out, Spangler made his way to Washington, where he was employed as a carpenter and sceneshifter at John Ford's theater.

Spangler and Booth renewed their friendship while both were working at Ford's Theatre. Spangler's primary duties were to assist in changing scene backdrops during plays, which kept him backstage and aware of the time. On the night of the assassination, Booth walked his horse up Baptist Alley to the rear door of the theater. Spangler, in a statement given to Justice Abram B. Olin, described what happened that night:

I did not see anything of Booth after that until he came back between nine and ten o'clock and haloed for me. I was in the theater on the stage attending to my business. Mr. Deboney [an actor in John Ford's stock company] said to me Booth is calling you. I then went out to the back of the theater in the alley. I then saw Mr. Booth holding a mare to the best of my knowledge the same one that he had brought there that afternoon. Says he to me "hold this mare for ten or fifteen minutes." Says I, "I have not time, but I would call Peanut John [John Burroughs]." I sent word in for him to come out and took hold of the mare. I held the mare until he came out. Booth said she would not stand tying, she had to be held. When he told me to hold her ten or fifteen minutes he went into the theater. As soon as Peanut John came out I went back to my work. As near as I could come to it, ten or fifteen minutes after Booth left the horse and went into the house I heard the shot while I was on the stage. Immediately after the shot was fired, I saw some person, [unintelligible word] on the stage run out at the prompter's side through the exit at the left hand side of the stage. And communicating directly with the door in the rear near which the man was standing when I went into the theater.

When I went out I could only hear the clatter of the hoofs in the distance. The person who went out went out through the same door through which Booth went in when I took the horse.

Jacob Ritterspaugh, a carpenter working at Ford's Theatre, was called as a prosecution witness against Spangler. Ritterspaugh testified that Spangler slapped him across the face, saying "Don't say which way he went" only seconds after Booth fled the theater. When Ritterspaugh asked Spangler why he slapped him in the face, Spangler replied, "For God's sake, shut up!" The testimony helped convict Spangler as an accomplice of Booth. Curiously, none of the other people who were presumably within hearing distance of Ritterspaugh and Spangler claimed they heard Spangler warn Ritterspaugh.

Spangler was arrested on Monday evening, April 17, and taken to Old Capitol Prison before transfer to the USS *Montauk,* where he joined Lewis Powell, George Atzerodt, Michael O'Laughlen, and Samuel Arnold. Found guilty by the tribunal, Spangler was sentenced to six years and imprisoned at Fort Jefferson along with Mudd, Samuel Arnold, and O'Laughlen. He was pardoned by President Andrew Johnson along with Arnold and Mudd (O'Laughlen died of yellow fever).

Spangler returned to John Ford's employ and worked for him until 1873, when poor health forced him to leave. He was taken in by Mudd and lived on the Mudd farm in an outbuilding until his sudden death on February 7, 1875. He is buried at St. Peter's Church Cemetery near the home of Samuel Mudd. His unmarked grave finally received a burial marker in 1983. It was placed there by members of the Surratt Society.

Sources: Statement of Edman Spangler, NARA, RG 153, M-599, reel 6, frames 201–4; Statement of Jacob Ritterspaeh [Rittersback, Ritterspaugh], NARA, RG 153, M-599, reel 6, 47–49; Poore, *Conspiracy Trial,* vol. 2, 32, 460, and vol. 3, 49, 107; Pitman, *Trial,* 97.

*See also:* Ritterspaugh, Jacob

## Speed, James (1812–1887)

U.S. attorney general at the time of the assassination and conspiracy trial. The older brother by two years of Joshua Speed, Lincoln's best friend in Springfield, Illinois, Lincoln appointed James attorney general after Joshua turned him down. At the time of the conspiracy trial, President Johnson asked Speed for his legal opinion on the jurisdiction of a military trial to try the defendants accused of Lincoln's murder. Just when Speed wrote his opinion and delivered it to Johnson is unclear. Critics point to the publication date of July and claim Speed wrote it after the trial had ended. Those who favor the use of a military tribunal disagree. There is no evidence in any record discovered and studied to date that Stanton coerced Speed or demanded he write an opinion upholding the tribunal's jurisdiction. A xerographic copy of the original order (in private hands) is reproduced in the *Lincolnian*, a newsletter of the Lincoln Group of the District of Columbia.

Speed's opinion, which has been upheld in test cases, concluded that the military had jurisdiction. Speed wrote that the accused were "enemy belligerents" whose alleged offenses were violations of the laws of war and had a military objective—to adversely affect the war effort of the North. Johnson had assumed the presidency on April 15; two and a half hours after Lincoln had died, and although officially in charge of the federal government, Secretary of War Edwin M. Stanton controlled much of its operations. Stanton wanted to keep control of the trial under the military and away from the civil courts. An accomplished lawyer, he knew such an undertaking required the blessing of the Justice Department. Having obtained Speed's approval, Stanton drafted the executive order in his own hand on War Department stationery for President Johnson.

Sources: Edward Steers, Jr., "To Remove the Stain of Innocent Blood from the Land," *Lin-*

*colnian* 1, no. 2 (November–December 1982), 4–5; Thomas R. Turner, "The Military Trial," in Edward Steers, Jr., *The Trial* (Lexington: University Press of Kentucky, 2003), xxi–xxviii.

*See also:* Military Tribunal

## Stabler, Brooke

Manager of Howard's Livery Stable, located at Sixth and G streets in Washington, D.C. John Surratt stabled his horses at Howard's Stable. Called as a prosecution witness at the conspiracy trial, Stabler testified to seeing John Wilkes together with John Surratt and George Atzerodt at his stable on several occasions, and that Surratt stabled two horses, including the one-eyed horse purchased by Booth from Dr. Mudd's neighbor, George Gardiner, on December 19, 1864. Stabler also produced a note he had been holding: "Please let the bearer Mr. Azworth [Atzerodt] have my horse whenever he wishes to ride also my leggings and gloves and oblige. Yours &c. J H Surratt." Later in a second note Surratt wrote, "If Mr. Booth my friend should want my horses let him have them, but no one else. If you should want any money on them he will let you have it." The testimony was to show that the three men were intimate with one another. Another link in the chain tying the conspirators together.

Source: Statement of Brooke Stabler, NARA, RG 94, M-619, reel 456, frames 379–85; Statement of Brooke Stabler, NARA, M-599, reel 4, frame 38; Poore, *Conspiracy Trial,* vol. 1, 176, 203; Pitman, *Trial,* 71; Statement of Brooke Stabler, NARA, RG 153, M-599, reel 6, frames 121–42; Poore, *Conspiracy Trial,* vol. 1, 176, 203; Pitman, *Trial,* 71.

*See also:* Howard's Livery Stable

## St. Helen, John

See George, David E.

## St. Lawrence Hall

Hotel in Montreal where Confederate agents had their unofficial headquarters and where John Wilkes Booth stayed as a guest, in room 150, October 18–27, 1864. While in Montreal, Booth was seen meeting with Confederate agents Patrick C. Martin and George N. Sanders in the lobby of the hotel, and later with Martin in the Ontario Bank. Booth opened a savings account using $200 in Canadian twenty-dollar bills and a check for $255 from a Confederate moneychanger by the name of Davis. He also purchased a draft for 61 pounds, 12 shillings, and 10 pence with $300 in U.S. gold. Before Booth left St. Lawrence Hall, Martin gave him a letter of introduction to Dr. William Queen and Dr. Samuel Mudd of Charles County, Maryland. Three weeks later Booth traveled to Charles County, where he met

with Queen and Mudd. Presumably the letter of introduction paved the way for Booth in seeking help from the two for his capture plan.

Sources: William A. Tidwell, James O. Hall, and David W. Gaddy, *Come Retribution* (Jackson: University Press of Mississippi, 1988), 331–35.

*See also:* Martin, Patrick Charles; Letter of Introduction

### St. Mary's Church

Church located near Bryantown, Maryland, where John Thompson, Dr. William Queen's son-in-law, first introduced John Wilkes Booth to Dr. Samuel Mudd on Sunday, November 13, 1864. Booth returned a second time in December 1864 and attended church services, after which he returned to Mudd's house, where he spent the night.

Armed with Patrick C. Martin's letter of introduction, which Booth was given while visiting Martin in Montreal in October, Booth took a stage from Washington, D.C., to Bryantown on Friday, November 11. He spent the night at the Bryantown Tavern where he was met on Saturday and taken to the house of Dr. Queen, where he spent that night. The next morning, Sunday, November 13, he was taken to St. Mary's Church, where he was introduced to Dr. Mudd.

Mudd's presence at St. Mary's Church on this particular Sunday appears to have been by arrangement, since the Mudd family were members and regularly attended St. Peter's Church a few miles west of the Mudd farm and a little over seven miles northwest of St. Mary's. While Mudd's statement before his arrest in April 1865 claimed that Booth stayed Sunday night, November 13, at his home and bought a horse the following day from Mudd's neighbor, he did not. Booth was back in his room at the National Hotel on Monday, November 14.

On December 18, Booth returned to St. Mary's Church, where he met with Dr.

Mudd again, and was an overnight guest of the Mudds. On Monday, the 19th, Booth purchased the one-eyed horse from George Gardiner and had the horse delivered to him in Bryantown on Tuesday, the 20th.

St. Mary's Church appears to have been a safe gathering place for those Confederate agents doing business in Charles County. Attending church was a normal activity and drew little suspicion. On Booth's two trips to Charles County that we know of, he attended church services at St. Mary's.

Sources: Statement of Dr. S. A. Mudd, NARA, RG 153, M-599, reel 5, frames 226–39; Statement of Dr. S. A. Mudd, NARA, RG 153, M-599, reel 5, frames 212–25; Testimony of John Thompson, Poore, *Conspiracy Trial*, vol. 2, 268–74; Pitman, *Trial*, 130.

See also: Mudd, Dr. Samuel Alexander

### St. Peter's Church

The Mudd family were members of St. Peter's Church, located two miles west of Dr. Mudd's house. The Mudd family normally attended St. Peter's except on those times when Dr. Mudd attended St. Mary's Church to meet John Wilkes Booth. The two Catholic churches were in separate parishes. St. Peter's Church had its own priest in residence, Father Peter B. Lenaghan. Sarah Frances Dyer and Samuel A. Mudd were married by Father Lenaghan at St. Peter's and their four children born before 1865 were baptized there. It is not a coincidence that Dr. Mudd attended St. Mary's Mass the two times that Booth attended St. Mary's Mass. The meetings were intentional.

Sources: Testimony of John Thompson, Poore, *Conspiracy Trial*, vol. 2, 268–74; Pitman, *Trial*, 130.

See also: St. Mary's Church

### St. Timothy's Hall

A boys' school located in Catonsville, Maryland, a suburb of Baltimore. The significance of the school lies in the fact that John Wilkes Booth and Samuel B. Arnold were schoolmates there in 1853. Wilkes and his brother Joe, also a student at St. Timothy's Hall, appear in a baptismal book that indicates both boys were baptized at St. Timothy's Episcopal Church on January 23, 1853. The Reverend Libertus Van Bokelen established the school in 1845. According to Booth's sister Asia, he and Samuel Arnold took part in a student rebellion at the school.

Sources: Terry Alford, ed., *John Wilkes Booth: A Sister's Memoir by Asia Booth Clarke* (Jackson: University Press of Mississippi, 1996), 44–45.

### Ste. Marie, Henri Beaumont de

A schoolmate of John H. Surratt, Jr., and Louis J. Wiechmann who notified authorities that Surratt was serving as a papal guard at the Vatican. Applied for and received financial compensation for the information.

In 1862, Ste. Marie, a young, well-educated teacher, was hired by Father William Mahoney to teach in the latter's Catholic school, near Texas, Maryland. It was while teaching at Mahoney's school that Ste. Marie met Surratt and Wiechmann, then students at St. Charles College in Ellicott, Maryland (later Ellicott City). Wiechmann, at Ste. Marie's urging, found him a teaching position at St. Matthew's School in Washington, D.C.

Ste. Marie claimed to have served as a substitute for Edward D. Porter in the Seventh Delaware Infantry. However, there is no record of Ste. Marie's service. Alfred Isacsson, a Surratt biographer, believes much of Ste. Marie's biographical claims are not trustworthy. The one thing that is trustworthy is Ste. Marie's service as a papal guard and his exposing Surratt's whereabouts to Federal authorities.

Ste. Marie became a member of the Ninth Company of papal Zouaves serving in Sezze, Italy, at the same time that Surratt was serving in the papal guards under the alias of John Watson. Ste. Marie recognized Surratt and informed the U.S. minister to the Vatican, Rufus King, that Surratt was a papal guard. King went to Cardinal Giacomo Antonelli, secretary of state for the Papal States, and told him where Surratt was working. Antonelli ordered the arrest of Surratt pending a formal request from the United States. Surratt was arrested in Veroli, Italy, and while in transit to Rome escaped his guards and made his way aboard a freighter to Alexandria, Egypt, where he was arrested a second time. From there he was returned to the United States.

Sources: Alfred Isacsson, *The Travels, Arrest, and Trial of John H. Surratt* (Middletown, N.Y.: Vestigium, 2003); C. Wyatt Evans, *The Legend of John Wilkes Booth: Myth, Memory, and a Mummy* (Lawrence: University Press of Kansas, 2004).

*See also:* Surratt, John Harrison, Jr.

## Stanton, Edwin McMasters (1814–1869)

Secretary of war. Early on the afternoon of April 14, Ellen Stanton, wife of Edwin M. Stanton, visited the War Department to see her husband. She reminded him that they had been invited to go with the Lincolns to the theater that evening. Stanton told his wife to decline the invitation if she wished. Stanton was very much opposed to the president's theatergoing and had no

interest in accompanying him there. On the way home from his office he stopped by the home of Secretary of State William Seward to see how he was recovering from his carriage accident. After a short chat with Seward, Stanton returned home, where he was greeted by a group of War Department clerks who had come to serenade him. There was a great spirit of joy among everyone. The feeling of victory seemed almost boundless.

It was a few minutes past ten o'clock when Stanton locked up the house and went to his bedroom. As he began to undress he was startled by his wife's scream from the floor below: "My God! Mr. Seward has been murdered!" Stanton's first reaction was one of disbelief. He had left Seward a little over an hour ago and the man had been resting comfortably despite his serious injury. Stanton quickly pulled on his clothes and hurried downstairs. An excited messenger stood in the front hallway. It was true: Seward had been murdered. Stanton told the soldiers standing guard outside to accompany him to Seward's house, a few blocks away.

As Stanton arrived at the Seward home, Gideon Welles, secretary of the navy, appeared, too. Welles had been also preparing for bed when a messenger yelled up to him that Lincoln had been shot and Seward murdered. Welles asked where the president was shot. The messenger said at Ford's Theatre. Welles told the man that he must be mistaken. Seward was confined to bed and could not possibly be at the theater with Lincoln. He decided to go to Seward's house immediately. He met Stanton at the door. The two secretaries found Seward lying in bed, attended to by Seward's family physician, Dr. Tullio Verdi. The bedsheets were saturated with blood.

Although seriously wounded, Seward was alive. Satisfied that Seward would survive, the two men decided to go to the theater immediately. At this point Major General Montgomery Meigs joined the pair along with Judge David Kellogg

Cartter of the District of Columbia Supreme Court. Meigs climbed in the carriage next to Stanton and Welles while Cartter climbed up alongside the driver. As they were about to depart, Major Thomas Eckert rode up on horseback. Eckert tried to talk Stanton from going near Tenth Street, telling him it would be too risky. Welles and Stanton ignored Eckert's pleas and ordered the driver to hurry. Eckert followed closely behind. Arriving at Tenth Street the men were told that the president was no longer in the theater. He had been taken to a house across the street.

It was a little past eleven o'clock when the two secretaries stepped down from their carriage and made their way into the tailor's house. Viewing the president, Stanton became alarmed. Lincoln's labored breathing was like a death rattle to the secretary. He knew the president's life was slipping away with each passing minute.

Stanton set up his acting government in the rear parlor of the house. For the next several hours Stanton assumed the role of acting president. He was without constitutional authority, but such times called for action, not debate. Often maligned by his critics for his vigorous prosecution of the war, Stanton fulfilled his enemies' characterization of him as a usurper of power. In actuality, he stepped into the breach at a moment of national crisis and brought a steadying influence. Both the president of the United States and his secretary of state seemed to be dying and the belief that a major conspiracy was still in the process of unfolding was widespread.

Stanton and Cartter sat at a small table in the rear parlor with one of the army clerks acting as a recorder. They were soon joined by two others to assist in the questioning: Judge Abram B. Olin, also a justice on the Supreme Court of the District of Columbia, and Britten A. Hill, a highly respected law partner of General Thomas Ewing, the attorney who would later represent Samuel Mudd, Edman Spangler, and Samuel Arnold.

The three men, with Stanton at their side, began interviewing witnesses. They soon realized they were unable to record the testimony in longhand fast enough. A call went out for a clerk with shorthand skills. A young army soldier named James Tanner was a boarder in the house next door. Tanner was proficient in a type of shorthand widely used at the time. He joined the men in the rear parlor shortly before midnight and began recording verbatim the testimony of witnesses to the events of that fateful night.

By 1:30 A.M., the questioning was over. Six individuals had been interviewed, four of whom were present in the theater at the time Booth shot Lincoln. Their testimony would be folded into the great body of evidence collected by the Bureau of Military Justice and later used against the eight defendants charged with Lincoln's murder.

Stanton was engaged in considerably more than hearing the testimony of the six witnesses who appeared at the Petersen house early Saturday morning. He was issuing orders to his subordinates throughout the country. By the time Horace Greeley's *Daily Tribune* hit the streets of New York, a dozen dispatches had been issued. One fact that most writers ignore is that Stanton did not listen to the testimony of each witness in its entirety or continuously. He was interrupted constantly and had to make numerous decisions and issue orders. Coupled with this was his compulsion to visit the president at periodic intervals between midnight and 1:30 A.M., when the testimony finally ended.

Seven o'clock came and went, and the silent pauses between beats and breaths grew longer; when they did resume, they were feebler. Sitting opposite Dr. Charles Leale at the head of the bed was Surgeon General Joseph K. Barnes. As Leale held the president's hand he placed his forefinger over its pulse. For nearly a minute he felt nothing. The breathing stopped. Leale looked across at Barnes and the two men seemed to close their eyes in unison. It was over. Barnes carefully crossed Lincoln's hands across his breast and whispered, "He is gone."

To several of those in the room it seemed that several minutes passed in utter silence. Then Stanton quietly said to the Reverend Dr. Phineas Gurley, "Doctor, will you say anything?" Gurley knelt by the bedside and waited as each of the men sank to their knees. All placed their hands on the bed along with Gurley as if to connect with the lifeless body of their president. Gurley prayed for the nation, beseeching God to heal the wounds and restore a united country. He asked that God accept his humble servant Abraham Lincoln into His glorious Kingdom. When he finished, the men rose to their feet with "a fervent and spontaneous amen." Stanton, tears streaming down his cheeks, spoke the six words that would become immortalized: "Now he belongs to the angels." Or did he say, "Now he belongs to the ages"? Historians are not in full agreement on which word Stanton used, *angels* or *ages*.

Stanton remained on as President Johnson's secretary of war, becoming embroiled in a series of conflicts with Vice President Andrew Johnson and General William T. Sherman. He was determined to see that the conspirators

503

who killed Lincoln were punished. He proposed they be tried by a military tribunal and convinced others to agree. While Stanton was the moving force behind the military trial, he did not interfere with the proceedings, satisfied that Joseph Holt and John Bingham would successfully prosecute the defendants. Stanton was busy with military matters and the growing conflict with President Johnson. Exhausted physically and financially, having traded his income as a lawyer for that of secretary of state, he resigned in 1868. He was too ill to take up the law. President Ulysses S. Grant appointed him to the U.S. Supreme Court in 1869, but he died before he could take his place on the Court.

Stanton became a target for all of the bizarre conspiracy theories, beginning with Otto Eisenschiml in 1937 and continuing right up to the present. His position as secretary of war and his vigorous, some say ruthless, prosecution of the war made him an easy target. A number of books, articles, and media presentations have painted Stanton as the man behind Lincoln's murder. Together with powerful politicians and financiers, both northern and southern, Stanton arranged for Lincoln to be removed from office, thereby allowing sinister interests to plunder the South financially and physically. Nothing could be further from the truth. While Lincoln and Stanton differed in their personalities, the two were in basic agreement on policies, including Reconstruction. Stanton grew to admire Lincoln and loved him as a friend by the end of the war. He grieved for months over Lincoln's death.

Sources: Benjamin P. Thomas and Harold M. Hyman, *Stanton: The Life and Times of Lincoln's Secretary of War* (New York: Knopf, 1962); Mark E. Neely, Jr., *The Abraham Lincoln Encyclopedia* (New York: McGraw Hill, 1982), 287–89.

## Star Hotel (Gouldman's Hotel)

Hotel owned and operated by Henry Gouldman in the small Virginia village of Bowling Green, located twelve miles to the southwest of the Rappahannock River. Willie Jett, one of the three Confederate soldiers who accompanied Booth and Herold over the Rappahannock River on Monday, April 24, at the time of their escape, spent the nights of April 24 and 25 at the Star Hotel. Federal troops under command of Lieutenant Edward Doherty, and detectives Everton J. Conger and Lieutenant Luther B. Baker of the National Detective Police, arrived at the hotel around 2:00 A.M. on the morning of April 26. They arrested Jett after receiving a tip from Bettie Rollins of Port Conway that he would be staying there because of his interest in Izora Gouldman, the hotel owner's sixteen-year-old daughter.

Sources: William A. Tidwell, James O. Hall, and David W. Gaddy, *Come Retribution* (Jackson: University Press of Mississippi, 1988), 467–68.

*See also:* Booth Capture and Death; Jett, William Storke "Willie"

## Star Saloon

Saloon located adjacent to the south side of Ford's Theatre on Tenth Street in Washington, D.C. Booth frequently drank in the Star Saloon. Peter Taltavul was the proprietor and was called as a prosecution witness at the conspiracy trial. He testified that Booth came into his saloon on the evening of April 14 and ordered whiskey and water. After drinking the whiskey and water, Booth placed the money on the bar, walked out of the saloon, and entered the theater. Taltavul claimed he heard screams coming from the theater approximately ten minutes after Booth left his establishment.

Contrary to popular accounts of Booth's interchange with a customer in Taltavul's saloon that evening, Booth did not say, "When I leave the stage I'll be the most famous man in America." It appears that apocryphal statement first appeared in Eleanor Ruggles's book *Prince of Players*.

Sources: Statement of Peter Taltavul, NARA, RG 153, M-599, reel 6, frames 368–72; Poore, *Conspiracy Trial*, vol. 1, 179; Pitman, *Trial*, 72.

*See also:* Taltavul, Peter

## Starr, Ellen

Also known as Nellie Starr, Ella Turner, Fannie Harrison. A nineteen-year-old Baltimore prostitute who was a favorite of John Wilkes Booth. On December 12, 1864, Booth brought her from Baltimore to Washington, where he put her up in her sister's bordello on Ohio Avenue. At the same time, Booth was courting Miss Lucy Hale, daughter of Senator John P. Hale of New Hampshire. Picked up by detectives following Lincoln's murder, Starr told her interrogators, "I have known John Wilkes Booth about three years. He was in the habit of visiting the house where I live, kept by Miss Eliza Thomas, No. 62 Ohio Avenue, City of Washington. The house is one of prostitution." One of her love notes to Booth became part of the evidence file: "My darling Boy, Please call this evening or as soon as you receive this note & I'll not detain you five minutes—for god's sake come Yours Truly E. S. If you will not come send a note the [unintelligible word] etc." Her statement also claimed Booth had kind words about the president: "I have never heard him speak unfavor-able of the President. I heard him speak of the President as being a good man just as other people did." This statement is completely at odds with many of Booth's derogatory statements about Lincoln.

Sources: Statement of Ellen Starr, NARA, RG 153, M-599, reel 2, frames 358–59; Statement of Nellie [Ellen] Starr, NARA, RG 153, M-599, reel 6, frames 258–59.

## Stewart, Joseph B.

A lawyer and major in the Union army, Stewart chased after Booth into Baptist Alley behind the theater as Booth fled after shooting Lincoln. He came closest of anyone to apprehending Booth.

Stewart was a witness for the prosecution at the conspiracy trial. His testimony was long and greatly detailed as to the events immediately following Booth's exit from the theater into the alley behind Ford's. He also testified to Edman Spangler's standing by the rear door and said he had noticed nothing unusual in Spangler's behavior.

On the night of the assassination, Stewart was seated in the orchestra section on the right side as one faces the stage of Ford's Theatre. He was the first person to react to the shooting. Stewart jumped to his feet, scrambled through the orchestra pit, climbed onto the stage, and followed Booth down the small passageway that led to the rear door. Stewart was unable to reach Booth and so watched as he galloped down Baptist Alley, turning left into the narrow alley that led to F Street.

Sources: Statement of Joseph B. Stewart, NARA, RG 153, M-599, reel 4, frames 58–63; Poore, *Conspiracy Trial*, vol. 2, 70; Pitman, *Trial*, 79; Statement of Joseph B. Stewart, NARA, RG 153, M-599, reel 2, frames 546–52.

## Stewart, Kensey Johns

Episcopal minister who became a Confederate agent working from Canada. In a letter in 1864 addressed to Jefferson Davis, Stewart indirectly confirmed that efforts to engage in germ warfare against civilian populations in the North were taking place, and Stewart asked Jefferson Davis to stop them.

At the outbreak of the war, Stewart was officiating at St. Paul's Episcopal Church in Alexandria, Virginia. After minor trouble with Union officials Stewart went to Richmond, where he was appointed chaplain in the Sixth North Carolina Infantry. In late 1862 he was reassigned as chaplain for Union prisoners, and in March 1863, Stewart traveled to England, where he spent a year putting together a special edition of the Episcopal prayer book for the Confederacy. Stewart returned to Richmond in 1864 and, after a visit with Jefferson Davis, traveled to Canada, where he became one of Davis's agents.

Stewart was in Toronto when he wrote a letter to Davis complaining about the "miserable failures" and "useless annoyances" that some of Davis's other agents were engaged in. Stewart pointed out that these ineffectual activities did little more than engender a "thirst for revenge" on the part of the Confederacy's enemies; they had no real effect toward winning the war. In simpler words, Stewart felt Davis had a few loose cannons rolling around in Canada, which cannons should be spiked. Stewart went on to call Davis's attention to one particular activity that he felt the Confederate president should order stopped immediately. Stewart wrote:

> I cannot regard you as capable of expecting the blessing of God upon, or being personally associated with instruments & plans such as I describe below. As our country has been and is entirely dependent upon God, we cannot afford to displease him. Therefore, it cannot be our policy to employ wicked men to destroy the persons & property of private citizens, by *inhumane & cruel acts* [emphasis added]. I name only one. $100.00 of public money has been paid here to one "Hyams," a shoemaker, for services rendered by conveying and causing to be sold in the city of Washington at auction, boxes of small-pox clothing. . . . There can be no doubt of the causes of the failure of such plans. It is only a matter of surprise that, God does not forsake us and our cause when we are associated with such misguided friends.

Stewart was speaking of Confederate agent Joseph Godfrey Hyams, who was working with another Confederate agent, Dr. Luke P. Blackburn, in an attempt to create yellow fever and smallpox epidemics in select northern cities. The objective was an attempt to lower morale and weaken Lincoln's efforts for reelection. Stewart's reference to "$100.00 of public money" paid to 'Hyams,' a shoemaker" is clear confirmation of Hyams's testimony at the conspiracy trial that Dr. Blackburn tried to introduce germ warfare into the war. Stewart's letter not only confirmed Blackburn's plot and supported Hyams's claim that Thompson paid him, but placed the whole affair on the desk of Jefferson Davis.

Four months after Stewart's letter to Davis, the trunks had not been destroyed and the plot was still going forward despite Stewart's plea to Davis. The project failed only because yellow fever is not contagious and is transmitted through mosquitoes. The introduction of testimony telling of a yellow fever plot was part of the prosecution's effort to show that Davis and other leaders of the Confederacy were capable of committing heinous acts, including the assassination of President Lincoln.

Sources: Edward Steers, Jr., *Blood on the Moon* (Lexington: University Press of Kentucky, 2001), 46–54; Edward Steers, Jr., "Risking the Wrath of God," *North & South* 3, no. 7 (September 2000), 59–70.

*See also:* Blackburn, Dr. Luke P.; Hyams, Joseph Godfrey

## Stone, Frederick (1820–1899)

Charles County lawyer who defended Dr. Samuel A. Mudd and David E. Herold. Stone was a member of one of Charles County's more illustrious families. His great-uncle was Thomas Stone, a signer of the Declaration of Independence and a wealthy plantation owner. Stone would become a judge after the war and serve _____ was retained _____ udd to de- _____. During _____ Stone's _____ of her _____ Mary _____ nced _____ life _____ in _____ rk

given his whole case away by not trusting even his counsel or neighbors or kinfolk. It was a terrible thing to extricate him from the coils he had woven about himself. He had denied knowing Booth when he knew him well. He was undoubtedly accessory to the abduction plot, though he may have supposed it would never come to anything. He denied knowing Booth when he came to his house when that was preposterous. He had even been intimate with Booth.

Sources: Edward Steers, Jr., *Blood on the Moon* (Lexington: University Press of Kentucky, 2001), 72–84.

## Stone, Dr. Robert King (1822–1872)

Lincoln family physician. Once Dr. Charles Leale stabilized Lincoln at the Petersen house, he sent notes to several people telling them to come to the house. Stone arrived and joined the other physicians that were there in assessing the president's condition. He was sitting at the foot of the bed when Leale declared Lincoln dead. Stone accompanied the body back to the White House and was present when the autopsy was performed by army assistant surgeons Joseph Janvier Woodward and Edward Curtis. In all, fourteen physicians appeared at Lincoln's bedside at various times throughout the night.

Sources: Edward Steers, Jr., *Blood on the Moon* (Lexington: University Press of Kentucky, 2001), 125, 133, 269.

## Stuart, Dr. Richard Henry (1808–1889)

Medical doctor who owned a summer home in King George County, Virginia. On Sunday evening April 23, 1865, John

Wilkes Booth and David Herold were taken to Cleydael, the summer home of Dr. Richard Stuart, by William Bryant. When the two fugitives crossed the Potomac River, reaching the Virginia shore and home of Mrs. Elizabeth Quesenberry, the Confederate agent Thomas Harbin was sent for. Harbin arranged for horses for Booth and Herold and instructed one of his agents, Bryant, to take the two men to the home of Dr. Richard Stuart.

Arriving at Stuart's summer home around eight o'clock Sunday evening, Booth and Herold were refused refuge in the house. Stuart did provide the two men with food and drink and had Bryant take them to the cabin of William Lucas, located a short distance from Stuart's house. After evicting Lucas and his wife and son, Charley, from the cabin, Booth and Herold spent Sunday night to Monday morning inside it.

When morning came, Booth attempted to persuade William Lucas to take Herold and himself to Port Conway on the Rappahannock River. After some discussion, Charley Lucas, William Lucas's twenty-year-old son, agreed to take the two men in his father's wagon. Booth gave a twenty-dollar bill to Lucas's wife in payment for the trip.

Before leaving, Booth wrote out an insulting note to Stuart on a page cut from his memorandum book (diary). Booth wrote, "It is not the substance, but the manner in which a kindness is extended that makes one happy in the acceptance thereof. 'The sauce in meat is ceremony; meeting were bare without it.'" He signed the note, "Stranger." Of course, Booth was telling Stuart that the latter's treatment of the two "strangers" that had come to his door seeking aid was more insult than kindness. Stuart had heard through the underground grapevine of Lincoln's assassination and that Booth was the assassin. Not wanting to endanger his home or family by harboring Booth and Herold, he denied them the use of his house overnight, resulting in Booth's note. To further add insult, Booth attached a five-dollar bill as "compensation" for Stuart's giving them food and drink. Thinking better of it, Booth scribbled a second note adding $2.50 to it and put the first note into his memorandum book.

It was this substituting of one note for another that helped Stuart when he was later arrested and interrogated by Union detectives. Stuart claimed he did not harbor Booth and Herold. The note found in Booth's diary and the note in Stuart's possession showed that Booth felt insulted and was poorly treated by Stuart. Stuart also implicated Dr. Samuel Mudd when he told the detectives interrogating him, "they said Dr. Mudd had recommended them to me." This statement implicated Mudd, and the fact that Mudd did not admit to such a recommendation in his own statement to detectives supported the conclusion that he had been lying all along about his relationship to Booth. Stuart was eventually released from custody and returned home.

Sources: Statement of Richard H. Stewart [Stuart], NARA, RG 153, M-599, reel 6, frames 205–11.

## Succession, Presidential
See Presidential Succession

## Surratt, Elizabeth Susanna "Anna" (1843–1904)
Daughter of Mary Elizabeth Surratt. Known as "Anna" Surratt. Anna was twenty-two years old at the time of her mother's trial and execution. She lived with her mother in the boardinghouse at 541 H Street and was present on Monday, April 17, when the military detectives arrived with orders to arrest all of the occupants of the house. Of course, the military was primarily after John Surratt, Jr. Mary Surratt was of secondary interest at the time, but the case against her would quickly grow to equal those of the principal defendants in the president's murder.

Louis J. Wiechmann, the boarder and close friend of John H. Surratt, Jr., described Anna as a "tall, well-proportioned, and fair-complexioned young woman." There is nothing in the evidentiary file to suggest Anna Surratt knew much of anything about John Wilkes Booth's conspiracy to capture the president, and she certainly knew nothing about his decision to kill Lincoln.

The military detectives took everyone in the house that Monday evening into custody, including Lewis Powell, who arrived shortly after the detectives. Powell was placed aboard the monitor *Saugus*, where he was held deep in the bowels of the ship. Mary and Anna were taken to the Carroll Annex of the Old Capitol Prison. Anna was questioned extensively about the various people who visited the boardinghouse and about her brother

John's activities. She basically denied knowing much of anything, and said she didn't like Lewis Powell, whom she knew only as Mr. "Wood," a Baptist minister.

Anna was never charged with any crime and was released from custody on May 11, nearly one month after her arrest. Her mother, however, was charged as an accomplice in Booth's murder of Lincoln. The eight defendants were transferred to the women's cell block in the Old Federal Penitentiary, inside the Washington Arsenal. The arrangement was such that the defendants could walk from their cells into the courtroom and back again without ever passing outside the building.

During the first weeks of the trial Anna was granted permission to meet with her mother. The meetings took place in the courtroom either before or after the proceedings. Mary Surratt's health continually deteriorated and on June 20, Major General John F. Hartranft requested and received permission to move her to a room immediately adjacent to the courtroom. Her living conditions improved but her health did not. Hartranft requested that her daughter Anna be permitted to stay with her mother and care for her. His request was approved and Anna moved in with her mother for the duration of the trial.

On May 30, Anna was called as a witness on behalf of her mother. Her testimony did little to help, or hinder, her mother's defense. She downplayed the various visits and meetings of several of the accused at her mother's boardinghouse. She explained why a photograph of Booth was hidden behind another picture on the parlor mantel (she was hiding it from her brother, who had told her to get rid of it), and said her mother's eyesight was very bad, which explained why she said she had never seen Powell and did not know who he was the night of April 17, when he showed up at the boardinghouse with the military detectives about to take the occupants into custody.

The trial completed, Mary Surratt waited to hear the verdict of the court. On July 6, between the hours of 11:00 A.M. and noon, Hartranft, acting as jailer, visited each of the condemned prisoners and read them the "Findings & Sentences" of the court. Mary Surratt, Lewis Powell, David Herold, and George Atzerodt were found guilty and sentenced to death by hanging, the sentence to be carried out the following day.

Anna was not present when Hartranft visited Mary Surratt. With less than twenty-four hours before her mother was to hang, Anna tried to see President Andrew Johnson in an effort to plead for her mother's life, but was denied entrance. She next went to Judge Advocate

General Joseph Holt, the prosecutor of the case. Holt agreed to meet her at the White House, but when she arrived, he told her "the President is immovable."

On July 9, two days after her mother's execution, Anna wrote to Hartranft requesting "the pillow upon which her head rested and her prayer beads, if you can find them—these things are dear to me." Anna went on to write, "Remember me to the officers who had charge of Ma and I shall always think kindly of you."

Anna married Dr. William Tonry, a chemist who worked in the surgeon general's office, on June 18, 1869. Tonry was dismissed from his government job, and the couple moved to Baltimore and began life anew. Anna was mother to four children: William, Albert, Reginald, and Clara. Anna died on October 24, 1904, and was interred in Washington's Mount Olivet Cemetery, where her mother is also buried.

Sources: Statement of Anna E. Surratt, NARA, RG 153, M-599, reel 6, frames 212–16; Poore, *Conspiracy Trial*, vol. 2, 496–501; Pitman, *Trial*, 496; Elizabeth Steger Trindal, *Mary Surratt: An American Tragedy* (Greta, La.: Pelican, 1996).

See also: Surratt, Mary Elizabeth

## Surratt, Isaac Douglas (1841–1907)

Oldest son of Mary Surratt and brother of John H. Surratt, Jr. Isaac Surratt had gone to Texas shortly before the war began, and enlisted in the Confederate army in Company A, 33rd Texas Cavalry, Texas Partisan Rangers, shortly after the shelling of Fort Sumter in Charleston, South Carolina. He was promoted to sergeant in 1863. The 33rd Texas spent most of the war on the lower Rio Grande. He remained a member until paroled in September 1865.

Isaac apparently never heard of his mother's plight until well after she was dead. He was present when her body was turned over to the family and her burial at Mount Olivet Cemetery in Washington, D.C., in 1869. Isaac, like his brother John, was employed by the Old Bay Line, a Baltimore steam packet company. He never married, dying a bachelor at age sixty-six on November 3, 1907. He is buried in Mount Olivet Cemetery.

Sources: Elizabeth Steger Trindal, *Mary Surratt: An American Tragedy* (Greta, La.: Pelican, 1996); Laurie Verge and Joan L. Chaconas, *Surratt House Museum* (Clinton, Md.: R. L. Ruehrwein, 1997).

## Surratt, John Harrison, Jr. (1844–1916)

John H. Surratt, Jr., was one of Booth's more capable conspirators. A member of the capture plot, Surratt was in Elmira, New York, at the time of Lincoln's assassination. Surratt, born April 13, 1844,

John H. Surratt, Jr. in his Zouave uniform

in Washington, D.C., was the youngest of Mary Surratt's three children. In 1852, the family moved into their newly built tavern and home, where John's father, John H. Surratt, Sr., became a tavern keeper and postmaster. The vicinity immediately around the Maryland crossroads where the tavern was located became known as Surrattsville (present-day Clinton). In 1859, young John attended St. Charles College in Ellicott Mills, a few miles southwest of Baltimore. Also a student at the Roman Catholic seminary was Louis J. Wiechmann, the government's prime wit-

ness against him and his mother, Mary Surratt.

With John Surratt's father's death in August 1862, John returned home from school and assumed his father's duties as tavern keep and postmaster. On February 17, 1863, Surratt was removed from his position as postmaster for "disloyalty." It was probably during this period that John was recruited by the Confederacy as a secret service agent. In that role he spent most of his time carrying messages and escorting other agents between Richmond, Virginia, and Canada. Surratt worked out of the offices and reported directly to Confederate secretary of state Judah P. Benjamin.

In the fall of 1864, Mary Surratt, under financial strain, moved her family to the Washington house at 541 H Street (now 604 H Street). It would prove a fatal move for the widow. It was while John was living at the H Street boardinghouse that he was introduced to John Wilkes Booth. On December 23, 1864, Surratt and former schoolmate Louis Wiechmann were walking down Seventh Street in Washington when they ran into Dr. Samuel Mudd and Booth. Dr. Mudd introduced Booth to John Surratt and the four men returned to Booth's room at the National Hotel, a few blocks away. It was at this time that Booth recruited Surratt into his plan to capture Lincoln and take him south to Richmond.

The introduction to Booth by Dr. Mudd proved fruitful for Booth. Surratt introduced George Atzerodt into Booth's team and later played a role in bringing Lewis Powell into the plot. John took part in the aborted kidnap plot of March 17, 1865, when Lincoln failed to attend a scheduled play held at Campbell Hospital in northeast Washington. On the day of the assassination, April 14, 1865, Surratt was in Elmira, New York, after visiting Canada at the direction of Judah P. Benjamin. Arriving in Canada, Surratt was sent to Elmira by Brigadier General Edwin Grey Lee, Confederate commissioner in Canada since December 1864, to survey the situation at the Union prison camp for a possible raid freeing the Confederate prisoners being held there. On learning of Lincoln's assassination, and the government's offer of a twenty-five-thousand-dollar reward for his capture, Surratt fled to Montreal, and from Montreal, Surratt was taken to the village of St. Liboire thirty miles east of Montreal. He was placed under the care of several individuals who housed him and saw to his safety. In August, Surratt returned to Montreal, where passage was arranged for him aboard the *Montreal*, which carried him to Quebec City, where he transferred to the *Peruvian*, headed for England.

From England, Surratt made his way to the Vatican, where he secured a position with the papal guards, using the alias "Watson." Discovered by an old schoolmate, Henri Beaumont de Ste. Marie, who was also a papal guard, Surratt was arrested on November 7, 1866, only to make a heroic escape aboard a steamer headed for Alexandria, Egypt. Word reached Alexandria that Surratt was aboard the *Tripoli,* and on landing he was taken into custody. He was returned to the United States and put on trial in civil court in June 1867.

The prosecution attempted to prove that Surratt was a close conspirator with Booth, which he was, and that he was in Washington on the night of April 14, 1865, which he was not. The defense produced witnesses to show that Surratt was in Elmira, New York, the day of the assassination. The trial ended in a hung jury, probably due to strong Confederate sympathies on the part of certain jurors. The government attempted to bring Surratt back to trial, securing indictments based on the District of Columbia's treason statute of 1862. Surratt was released when the court ruled that the statute of limitations made the indictment null and void. The district had a two-year limitation on all crimes except murder and fraud.

A free man, Surratt moved to Rockville, Maryland, where he taught in a girl's academy. While in Rockville, he gave a lecture at the Montgomery County Courthouse admitting his role in Booth's conspiracy to capture Lincoln, but denying any knowledge of Booth's decision to murder Lincoln. Surratt eventually wound up in Baltimore, where he married Mary Victorine Hunter in 1872. That same year he hired on with the Old Bay Line shipping company, becoming treasurer and auditor. He outlived all of the conspirators, dying on April 16, 1916, at the age of seventy-two. He is buried in New Cathedral Cemetery in Baltimore.

Sources: Elizabeth Steger Trindal, *Mary Surratt: An American Tragedy* (Greta, La.: Pelican, 1996); Joan L. Chaconas, "John H. Surratt, Jr.," in Edward Steers, Jr., ed., *The Trial* (Lexington: University Press of Kentucky, 2003), lx–lxv; Alfred Isacsson, *The Travels, Arrest, and Trial of John H. Surratt* (Middletown, N.Y.: Vestigium, 2003).

*See also:* Mudd, Dr. Samuel Alexander

## Surratt, John Harrison, Sr. (1813–1862)

Husband of Mary Surratt. John died in August 1862, leaving Mary with the tavern in Surrattsville, Maryland; a house in Washington, D.C.; and several unpaid debts that would ultimately cause Mary Surratt grief. John had been troubled his entire adult life with alcoholism and bad debts. Still, he acquired four hundred acres of land in Prince George's County, Maryland, as well as the tavern in Surrattsville and house in Washington.

Sources: Joan L. Chaconas, "John H. Surratt, Jr.," in Edward Steers, Jr., ed., *The Trial* (Lexington: University Press of Kentucky, 2003), lx–lxv.

## Surratt, Mary Elizabeth (nee Jenkins) (1823–1865)

Mother of conspirator John H. Surratt and owner of a boardinghouse at 541 H Street in Washington, D.C., and a tavern in Surrattsville, Maryland (now Clinton, Maryland). Mary Surratt was convicted of conspiring with John Wilkes Booth and others in the assassination of President Lincoln and was sentenced to death by hanging for her part. She was hanged along with Lewis Powell, George Atzerodt, and David Herold on July 7, 1865.

Mary Elizabeth Jenkins was born in 1823 in Prince George's County, Maryland. At the age of twelve her mother placed her in a Catholic boarding school in Alexandria, Virginia. While a student at the Sisters of Charity School, Mary converted to the Roman Catholic faith, adopting the confirmation name of Eugenia. In 1840, at the age of seventeen, she married John Harrison Surratt, also from Prince George's County. He was ten years her senior. The couple had three children: Isaac Douglas, born in 1841;

Elizabeth Susannah (known as Anna), born in 1843: and John Harrison, Jr., born in 1844.

John Surratt, Sr., was troubled his entire adult life by alcoholism and bad debts. Even so, he managed to acquire four hundred acres of farmland in Prince George's County, built a substantial home and hostelry in 1852, a town house in Washington in 1853, and acquired several slaves. In 1854 the hostelry and tavern became a post office and John Surratt was commissioned a postmaster, the area around his tavern adopting the name Surrattsville. Despite his alcoholism, John Surratt managed to stay ahead of his creditors, at least for a while. As his alcoholism took over much of his life, maintaining the hostelry and caring for the children fell entirely on Mary. In 1858, Mary wrote a letter to a priest begging his help: "O, I hope dear Father, you will try to get him [Isaac] something to do as it will be so much better for him to be out of sight of his Pa, as he is drunk almost every day & I fear there is little hope of his ever doing better."

John Surratt died suddenly in August 1862, leaving Mary to manage the properties and her children. When war broke out in 1861, Isaac went to Texas, where he enlisted in the Confederate army. John, Jr., was away at St. Charles College boarding school near Ellicott City in Howard County, Maryland, where he had enrolled in 1859 to study for the priesthood. It was there that he became good friends with Louis Wiechmann, a friendship that would bring tragedy to both John and his mother.

On his father's death, young John Surratt returned home to the hostelry and tavern and assumed the role of helping with the business, to his mother's relief. He took over his father's job as postmaster in September 1862. In addition, John Jr. took up another profession that fit nicely with the location of the tavern: he became a Confederate agent and courier, an activity that resulted in

Mary Elizabeth Surratt

his dismissal as postmaster a year later, on November 17, 1863. John's frequent absence due to his courier duties placed virtually the entire burden of managing the hostelry and tavern back on Mary Surratt's shoulders. In November 1864, Mary decided to give up the business and leased the tavern and hostelry to John M. Lloyd. She moved herself and her family to Washington, into the house at 541 H Street, a decision that would send her to the gallows.

In August 1864, John Wilkes Booth began recruiting members into his conspiracy to capture President Lincoln. Eight weeks later, in October, he traveled to Montreal, where he met with several Confederate agents, including Patrick C. Martin, who gave Booth a letter of introduction to Drs. William Queen and Samuel A. Mudd, both living in Charles County, Maryland. In November, Booth traveled to Charles County, where he was introduced to Dr. Mudd. The following month, while in Washington, Booth met with Dr. Mudd, who introduced him to John Surratt. As a result of this meeting, Surratt agreed to join Booth in his conspiracy. Subsequently, John Surratt introduced the charismatic actor to his mother. Booth became a frequent visitor to Mary Surratt's boardinghouse.

In March 1865, with his team of conspirators now assembled, Booth planned to capture Lincoln following a scheduled visit to a hospital on the outskirts of Washington. The plan was aborted when it was learned that Lincoln canceled his scheduled visit and stayed in Washington. John Surratt took the weapons and other paraphernalia to the tavern in Surrattsville, where he told John Lloyd to hide them away in safekeeping for a future effort. Booth's capture plan soon fell apart as a result of the fall of Richmond and the subsequent surrender of General Robert E. Lee's army on April 9, 1865. Booth decided to roll his capture scheme over to one of murder.

On learning that Lincoln would attend an evening performance at Ford's Theatre on April 14, Booth decided to strike. He assembled what was left of his team and assigned them the task of killing Vice President Andrew Johnson and Secretary of State William H. Seward. During the day he called on Mrs. Surratt and spoke with her. Later that afternoon she made a trip, along with Louis Wiechmann, to the tavern in Surrattsville. On arriving at around four o'clock, she found John Lloyd away in Upper Marlboro. On his return she gave him a package that Booth had asked her to deliver, and according to Lloyd's later testimony, told him to have "the shooting irons ready," as persons would stop by later to pick them up.

On the Monday following the assassination, detectives were at the Surratt boardinghouse interviewing the several people who lived there, including Mary Surratt. They had received information that led them to believe John Surratt was a good friend of Booth. While they were interviewing Mary Surratt, Lewis Powell, the conspirator assigned to kill Seward, knocked on the door. Brought into the parlor, he was asked why he had come to this particular house so late at night. He answered that he was hired by Mrs. Surratt to dig a drain alongside her house. Mary Surratt was asked if she knew the man. She vigorously denied knowing him or ever having seen him before. She, along with Powell and the other boarders in the house, was arrested.

At her trial the prosecution attempted to show that Mary Surratt was well acquainted with Booth and several of his coconspirators and that some had even boarded at her house. The most damaging evidence against her came from John Lloyd, who said she had told him at the time of her visit on April 14 to have the guns ready, as there would be persons stopping by that evening to pick them up along with the package containing Booth's field glass that she had delivered that afternoon. Another witness, Louis Wiechmann, John Surratt's old school mate and a boarder as well, supported Lloyd's testimony. Wiechmann told of various visits by Booth to the boardinghouse, Booth's private conversations with Mary Surratt, and the two trips with Mrs. Surratt to the tavern, where she had engaged Lloyd in conversation.

Mary Surratt was found guilty and sentenced to death by hanging. Five members of the nine-member tribunal that condemned her drafted a statement to President Andrew Johnson to spare her life. Johnson did not, and later maintained he had never been shown the clemency plea. Mary Surratt was hanged on July 7, 1865. She was the first woman to be executed by the U.S. government. She is buried in Mount Olivet Cemetery in Washington, D.C.

Sources: Elizabeth Steger Trindal, *Mary Surratt: An American Tragedy* (Greta, La.: Pelican, 1996); Laurie Verge and Joan L. Chaconas, *Surratt House Museum* (Clinton, Md.: R. L. Ruehrwein, 1997); Laurie Verge, "Mary Elizabeth Surratt," in Edward Steers, Jr., ed., *The Trial* (Lexington: University Press of Kentucky, 2003), lii–lix.

*See also:* Clemency Plea; Lloyd, John M.; Wiechmann, Louis J.

## Surratt Boardinghouse
Located at 541 (currently 604) H Street, Washington, D.C. Booth (and others in his plot) met here on occasion. President

Johnson described the house as the nest where the egg (plot) was kept.

The house was deeded to Mary's husband, John H. Surratt, Sr., in 1853 as payment of a debt owed him. In October 1864, Mary Surratt decided to lease her inn and tavern in Surrattsville, Maryland (now Clinton, Maryland) to John M. Lloyd and move her family to the three-story brick house in Washington. The house could accommodate her family—son John and daughter Anna—leaving several rooms that she could rent, thereby relieving her financial burdens. Mary's daughter Anna and eighteen-year-old Honora Fitzpatrick shared a room. Louis Wiechmann, a close

friend of John Surratt, rented a room for thirty-five dollars a month. Ten-year-old Appolonia Dean, attending school in Washington, rented a room, and John T. Holohan, his wife, and two children were in two rooms on the second floor. Recently hired Susan Mahoney Jackson slept in the kitchen on the basement level. Mary Surratt had four paying tenants and, with the money from leasing the tavern to John Lloyd in Surrattsville, was able to manage her finances.

The house was located just a few blocks from Ford's Theatre on Tenth Street. When her son John became an agent of the Confederate state department working for Judah P. Benjamin, the tavern in Surrattsville and the boardinghouse in Washington became "safe houses" for Confederate agents moving between Richmond and various points in the North and Canada. Augustus Howell and Sarah Slater were two Confederate agents who stopped by the boardinghouse on more than one occasion.

On December 23, son John Surratt, serving as a Confederate courier and underground agent, was introduced to John Wilkes Booth by Dr. Samuel Mudd. Invited to Booth's room at the National Hotel, Booth enlisted Surratt into his conspiracy to capture Lincoln and take him to Richmond. Thereafter, Booth made several visits to the Surratt boardinghouse, where he met with Mary Surratt as well as John. Thus President Johnson said it was Mary Surratt who "kept the nest that hatched the egg" of Lincoln's assassination.

On Monday evening, April 17, Colonel Henry H. Wells, Washington provost marshal, sent Major Henry W. Smith and detectives William M. Wermerskirch, Eli Devoe, R. C. Morgan, and Charles Rosch to the boardinghouse with orders to arrest all of the occupants. While waiting for the people to gather their things, the detectives received a bonus: Lewis Powell showed up and was arrested along with the others.

The boardinghouse was put up for auction in November 1867 to satisfy Mary Surratt's creditors (the house and tavern in Surrattsville suffered the same fate in March 1869). In modern times it has passed through several hands as a Chinese grocery store and later as a restaurant. It stands today in private hands, looking basically as it did in 1865, with only minor changes, mostly in the interior of the building.

Sources: Elizabeth Steger Trindal, *Mary Surratt: An American Tragedy* (Greta, La.: Pelican, 1996); Edward Steers, Jr., *Blood on the Moon* (Lexington: University Press of Kentucky, 2001), 174–79.

*See also:* Surratt, Mary Elizabeth; Surratt Tavern

## *Surratt Courier*

Formerly known as the *Surratt Society Newsletter*. Newsletter of the Surratt Society, located in Clinton, Maryland. The newsletter is published monthly, twelve issues a year. It is an outlet for a great deal of the research that goes on by the numerous members of the society. It is rich in material that frequently does not find its way into the published literature. The first volume appeared in October 1976.

## Surratt House and Tavern

Located in Surrattsville, Maryland (now Clinton), in Prince George's County. John Wilkes Booth and David Herold stopped at the Surratt Tavern near midnight on April 14, 1865. They were in the early stages of their attempt to escape following Booth's murder of President Lincoln. Arousing John M. Lloyd, the tavern and inn keeper, Herold excitedly told Lloyd, "For God's sake, make haste and get those things." Without asking what things, Lloyd made his way up the stairs to a loft over the kitchen. He knew exactly what "those things" were: a pair of carbines left a few weeks earlier by John Surratt following an aborted capture attempt of Lincoln, and Booth's field glass, left earlier that same day by Mary Surratt.

During his interrogation by Union detectives, "From the way he spoke, he

Surratt House and Tavern

must have been apprised that I already knew what I was to give him." How did Herold know that Lloyd would understand his order? Only if Herold had been told beforehand that Lloyd had been informed about the guns and field glass that persons would be by to pick up. It was this thinking that put Mary Surratt in serious jeopardy.

The Surratt house and tavern had been constructed on 287 acres of land John Surratt had purchased in January 1852. The building would become a tavern, post office, and home to John and Mary Surratt and their three children. During the Civil War it would also be-

come a safe house for Confederate agents moving through Prince George's County. John Surratt, Jr., replaced his father as postmaster following his father's death in 1862. He would be removed from his post within a year for "disloyal acts."

In the fall of 1864, Mary Surratt, struggling to make ends meet, leased the tavern to John M. Lloyd and moved her family to the house at 541 H Street in Washington, D.C. Between the money from leasing the house and tavern to Lloyd and renting rooms to boarders in her Washington home, was Mary able to keep her husband's creditors at bay, at least for a while.

After Mary Surratt's execution on July 7, 1865, the house and tavern were eventually sold at auction in March 1869 to pay the outstanding debts Mary inherited from her husband. The facility became a private residence for the next hundred years, before it was donated to the Maryland National Capital Park and Planning Commission by its owners, Mr. and Mrs. B. K. Miller, Sr., of Clinton. Restored to its original condition, it was opened to the public in 1976. The Surratt House and Museum complex includes the James O. Hall Library and Research Center. The Surratt Society, a nonprofit volunteer organization, supports the facility.

Sources: Joan L. Chaconas and Thomas S. Gwynn, Jr., *25th Commemorative Booklet, 1964 to 1989* (Clinton, Md.: Surratt Society, 1989).

*See also:* Booth Escape Route

## Surratt Society
A worldwide, volunteer affiliate of the Surratt House Museum. The society is neutral on the guilt or innocence of Mary Surratt. Members conduct guided tours through the site, sponsor frequent bus tours over the John Wilkes Booth Escape Route, and provide other educational programs and events throughout the year. The society encourages continuing research in the field of nineteenth-century history and specifically the Lincoln assassination, through a monthly newsletter, the *Surratt Courier*, the publication of pertinent materials, and the James O. Hall Research Center. The group also serves as a fund-raising arm of the museum.

Sources: Submitted by Laurie Verge, Director of the Surratt House and Museum, Clinton, Md.

*See also: Surratt Courier*

## Surrattsville
Small village located approximately thirteen miles southeast of Washington, D.C., and site of the Surratt Tavern. Currently named Clinton, Maryland. Booth and Herold stopped here around midnight on the night of April 14, 1865, after Booth had shot Lincoln.

It was an early practice to name small communities after the postmaster. In 1854, John Harrison Surratt was named postmaster, hence the name Surrattsville. Following his death in 1862, his son, John Harrison Surratt, Jr., became postmaster. Andrew V. Robey replaced him in 1863 with the resulting change from Surrattsville to Robeystown. In 1878 the name was changed to Clinton. The origin of "Clinton" is unknown. In 1906 a high school was built in the community and named Surrattsville High School. The name remains to the present. Several area businesses use the name Surratts-ville as part of their designation.

Sources: Laurie Verge, "Why Clinton?," *Surratt Society News* 4, no. 6 (June 1979).

## Swan, Oswell (Oswald, Oscar) (1835–1890)

A free black who lived near Hughesville, approximately four miles southeast of Bryantown, Maryland. On Saturday, April 15, 1865, approximately two hours after leaving Dr. Samuel Mudd's house, John Wilkes Booth and David Herold came to the log cabin home of Oswell Swan. They were trying to find the home of William Burtles, a Confederate agent from whom Booth expected to receive help in his escape. Losing their way in the dark, they noticed a light and followed it to Swan's cabin. Swan gave them some food and whiskey. Booth offered to pay Swan two dollars if he would lead them to Burtles's house. Burtles lived less than two miles from Swan's farm. After further talk, Booth asked Swan if he knew the way to Samuel Cox's house, Rich Hill. He did. Booth offered him five dollars to take the two of them to Cox.

In traveling to Cox's house, the three men would have to cross the Zekiah Swamp, since Cox lived on the west side and Swan on the east. It took an expert guide familiar with the swamp. Booth upped the fee and gave Swan another five dollars. With Swan as their guide, the two fugitives reached Cox's place around midnight. Booth and Herold went inside while Swan remained outside. Later, Swan would tell the soldiers that Booth and Herold stayed inside the house four or five hours before they were taken to a pine thicket and hidden. Cox turned care for the two men over to another Confederate, Thomas Jones. Jones would provide food, drink, and newspapers to Booth and Herold while they hid out for five days before Jones could safely put them in a small skiff and send them out on the Potomac River, pointing them toward the Virginia shore.

Swan returned home with ten dollars in greenbacks in his pockets. Swan was taken into custody on April 27 and held in Old Capitol Prison until his release on May 17. He gave a statement giving most of the details of his time with Booth and Herold.

Sources: Statement of Oscar (Ausy) [Oswell] Swan. NARA, RG 153, M-599, reel 6, frames 227–29; William A. Tidwell, James O. Hall, and David W. Gaddy, *Come Retribution* (Jackson: University Press of Mississippi, 1988), 446–48.

*See also:* Cox, Samuel

## Swan, Mary

Former slave of Samuel Cox who remained with Cox as a free black. Picked up by the military in their sweep of Charles County, Maryland, in search of John Wilkes Booth and David Herold, Mary Swan told a story that contradicted Oswell Swan's story concerning Booth and Herold at the Cox home. Mary Swan said the two were never allowed inside the house and were turned away by Cox. "They did not come in the house, as he refused to let them in. I did not hear any more. If they came in I did not see them. Did not put on my clothes. I did not lay awake long. I heard Capt. Coxe [*sic*] shut the door on them. Nobody got them anything to eat or drink that I know of."

Sources: Statement of Mary Swan, NARA, RG 153, M-599, reel 6, frames 160–61; Statement of Mary Swan, NARA, RG 153, M-599, reel 6, frames 162–64.

*See also:* Swan, Oswell

## Taft, Dr. Charles Sabin (1835–1900)

Doctor who assisted Dr. Charles Leale in attending to Lincoln in the presidential box in Ford's Theatre, and later at the Petersen house. Taft, an army surgeon, was seated in the orchestra area below the box. Making his way to the stage area directly beneath the box, he announced that he was a doctor. Two men joined him onstage and quickly boosted Taft up so he could pull himself over the balustrade and into the box, where he found Leale already examining the president as he lay on the floor. Taft would later join several other doctors in the guest room on the second floor of the White House, where assistant army surgeons Joseph Janvier Woodward and Edward Curtis performed an autopsy on Lincoln's body.

The probe used to determine the path and location of the bullet in Lincoln's brain, along with the misshapen bullet and bone fragments from Lincoln's skull, was turned in to the War Department in an envelope bearing Secretary of War Edwin M. Stanton's signature by Dr. Taft: "Probe & Envelope containing bullet and bones taken from the brain of Abraham Lincoln by Dr. Stone April 15, 1865 in presence of Dr. Taft, Acting Asst Surgeon." These artifacts are in the collection of the National Museum of Health and Medicine, Washington, D.C.

Sources: Dr. Charles Taft, NARA, RG 153, M-599, reel 7, frames 664–66; Edward Steers, Jr., *Blood on the Moon* (Lexington: University Press of Kentucky, 2001), 121–22.

*See also:* Doctors; Leale, Dr. Charles Augustus

## Taltavul, Peter (1825–1881)

Proprietor of the Star Saloon, located immediately to the south side of Ford's Theatre. Booth ordered a drink from Taltavul before entering the theater and making his way to the presidential box. Taltavul was called as a prosecution witness at the conspiracy trial. He testified to Booth's coming into his saloon on the evening of April 14 and ordering whiskey and water. After drinking the whiskey and water, Booth placed the money on the bar and walked out. Taltavul claimed he heard screams coming from the theater approximately ten minutes later.

Contrary to popular accounts of Booth's interchange with Taltavul that evening, Booth did not say, "When I leave the stage I'll be the most famous man in America." That myth appears to have first appeared in *Prince of Players,* by Eleanor Ruggles, in 1953.

Sources: Statement of Peter Taltavul, NARA, RG 153, M-599, reel 6, frames 368–72; Poore, *Conspiracy Trial,* vol. 1, 179; Pitman, *Trial,* 72.

*See also:* Star Saloon

### Tanner, James (1844–1927)

Recorded witness interviews in the Petersen house the night of the assassination, taking down testimony in shorthand. Proficient in the art of phonography, a form of shorthand, James Tanner was pressed into service recording the statements of six eyewitnesses to the assassination.

At the age of eighteen, Tanner enlisted in Company C, 87th New York Volunteer Infantry. A year later the badly depleted regiment was consolidated with the 105th Pennsylvania Infantry. At the Second Battle of Bull Run (Second Manassas), he was severely wounded when an artillery shell shattered both of his legs below the knees. Following months of rehabilitation in which he learned to use his artificial limbs, Tanner attended the Ames Business College in Syracuse, New York, where he learned a form of shorthand.

In 1864, Tanner returned to Washington, D.C., and found employment in the Ordnance Bureau of the War Department. He moved into one of the rooms available in a boardinghouse on Tenth Street across from Ford's Theatre and next door to the Petersen house. On the evening of April 14, 1865, Tanner attended the performance of *Aladdin, or the Wonderful Lamp*, playing at Grover's National Theatre a few blocks

from Ford's Theatre. On learning of the assassination of President Lincoln, Tanner made his way back to his room. Near midnight, General C. C. Augur came out of the Petersen house calling out if anyone knew shorthand. Albert Daggett, fellow boarder with Tanner and a clerk in the State Department, told Augur his friend Tanner could take shorthand. Augur told Daggett to get Tanner and send him to the Petersen house.

Tanner later described the scene: "I found Secretary Stanton sitting on one side of the library [rear parlor that was used as a bedroom] and Chief Justice Cartter of the Supreme Court of the District at the end. They had started in to take what testimony they could regarding the assassination, having someone write it out in long hand. This had proved unsatisfactory. I took a seat opposite the Secretary and commenced to take down the testimony." A total of six individuals were questioned and Tanner took down their statements verbatim. The Union League of Philadelphia published facsimiles of the shorthand and English transcriptions in 1968.

In a letter written to a friend two days later, Tanner wrote, "In fifteen minutes I had testimony enough down to hang Wilkes Booth, the assassin, higher than ever Haman hung." By 1:30 A.M. the testimony was completed and Tanner began transcribing his notes into longhand, finishing just before 7:00 A.M. He went to the room where Lincoln lay dying and joined the deathwatch. At 7:22 A.M. Lincoln was pronounced dead and Reverend Phineas Gurley, Lincoln's pastor at the New York Avenue Presbyterian Church, was asked to offer a prayer. Tanner attempted to record Gurley's words, and Stanton's following Gurley's prayer, but later wrote that the point of his pencil broke, which prevented him from recording their remarks.

After the war Tanner returned to New York, where he began working his way up through various city, state, and federal jobs, including a brief stint as U.S. commissioner of pensions, in which position he was charged with "abuse of office and with liquidating the treasury's surplus." Following his resignation, Tanner became a pension attorney. In 1904, he was appointed register of wills for the District of Columbia. He died in 1904.

Sources: Maxwell Whiteman, ed., *While Lincoln Lay Dying* (Philadelphia: Union League of Philadelphia, 1968).

## Tattoo, *JWB*

Booth had inscribed his initials on the back of his hand with India ink when he was a young boy. The resulting tattoo was one element of proof that the body returned to Washington, D.C., was Booth's and not some surrogate, as claimed by some. Over the years there has been a good deal of controversy stirred up by the "Booth escaped" proponents, who maintain the body pulled from the burning tobacco barn was not John Wilkes Booth, but rather a surrogate who died in his place. Despite the considerable evidence that shows Booth died on the porch of Richard Garrett's farmhouse, the claim that he escaped to live on under various aliases persists. Among the forensic evidence that supports the conclusion that Booth died at the Garrett farm are the initials "JWB" that were on Booth's hand. The initials were located on the back of the left hand in the V formed by the thumb and index finger.

The most compelling evidence that such an identifying tattoo existed on Booth's hand can be found in the writings of his older sister Asia Booth Clarke. In 1874, nine years after Booth's death, she wrote a memoir about her brother. In describing her brother, Asia wrote: "He had the black hair and large hazel eyes of his mother. These were fringed heavily with long up-curling lashes, a noticeable peculiarity as rare as beautiful. He had perfectly shaped hands, and across the back of one he had clumsily marked, when a little boy, his initials in India ink."

These initials were known to everyone well acquainted with Booth and were cited by several in identifying the corpse the government claimed was Booth.

Marine Sergeant John M. Peddicord was on watch on the USS *Montauk* when the body from the Garrett farm was transferred to it. Several years later Peddicord would read the story that the body on board the *Montauk* was not that of J. Wilkes Booth, but of another man. Peddicord knew better, and realizing his special place in history, wrote an article about his experience of April 27, 1865 that was published in the *Roanoke Evening News*: "In the morning when [Sergeant Hartley] called me saying 'Come out here. I have something to show you.' I turned out on deck where he was along side a carpenter's bench on which lay the body of a man wrapped about in a soldier's blanket. My order from Hartley was 'Take charge of this body and allow no one to touch it without orders from Colonel Baker.' It was the body of the assassin, John Wilkes Booth, which had been brought up the river during the night by the detachment of troops who had captured him. At breakfast when I was relieved by Hartley while I was eating, we unwrapped the face and compared it with a photograph, and I also remember the letters in India ink on the back of his hand in pale straggling characters, 'J.W.B.,' as a boy would have done it."

The tattoo joins other pieces of physical evidence to support the conclusion that the body returned to Washington from the Garrett farm was Booth's and not some substitute.

Sources: Terry Alford, ed., *John Wilkes Booth: A Sister's Memoir by Asia Booth Clarke* (Jackson: University Press of Mississippi, 1996), 45; Edward Steers, Jr., *Blood on the Moon* (Lexington: University Press of Kentucky, 2001), 264–65.

*See also:* Autopsy, John Wilkes Booth

## Taylor, Joseph Walker

Joseph Walker Taylor, a major in the Confederate army, proposed one of the earliest plots to capture Lincoln and take him south to Richmond, Virginia. Taylor had impressive connections. He was the nephew of former president Zachary Taylor and a first cousin to Confederate major general Richard Taylor. More important, he was a first cousin to Sarah Knox Taylor, daughter of Zachary Taylor and the first wife of Confederate president Jefferson Davis. With these credentials, Taylor virtually had an open invitation to Jefferson Davis. Walker Taylor, as family and friends knew him, took advantage of his connections with Davis and sought a meeting with him in the summer of 1862.

Taylor had been stationed at Fort Donelson in western Tennessee in early 1862, serving on the staff of General Simon Bolivar Buckner. When Union general Ulysses S. Grant invested Fort Donelson, Buckner was forced to surrender the fort and its contents. Taylor, unwilling to surrender and spend his days in a Union prison camp, joined Nathan Bedford Forrest and his men and slipped out of the fort under cover of darkness and successfully made his way through Grant's lines to safety.

Taylor had been wounded in the cheek and neck and decided to convalesce in the Washington, D.C., home of Union brigadier general Joseph Taylor, brother of Zachary Taylor and uncle of Walker Taylor. The arrangement was not as strange as it may seem today, for the war divided many families north and south, and the people learned to accept all sorts of familial behavior. For example, Lincoln invited the widow of Confederate general Ben Hardin Helm, the widow being Mary Todd Lincoln's favorite sister, to stay with Mary in the White House following the death of her husband at Chickamauga.

During his convalescence, Taylor witnessed Lincoln's movements around Washington with little or no protection. Lincoln made several trips to his summer retreat at Soldiers' Home unescorted. Taylor realized Lincoln was extremely vulnerable at these unguarded times.

According to Jefferson Davis's aide de camp, Colonel William Preston Johnston, Walker Taylor left Washington and visited Davis in the Confederate White House, in Richmond, where he dined at breakfast with Davis and Johnston. Taylor proposed a scheme in which Taylor would take several handpicked Kentucky cavalrymen and make a raid of the Soldiers' Home and capture Lincoln. According to Johnston, Davis demurred, stating, "I suppose Lincoln is a man of courage . . . [H]e undoubtedly would resist being captured. . . . I could not stand the imputation of having consented to let Mr. Lincoln be assassinated."

Davis said no, but this was 1862, and by the spring and summer of 1864, things were looking very grim for Davis's Confederacy. In the spring of 1864, Davis authorized the establishment of a Confederate clandestine organization whose base was in Montreal, and funded them to the tune of $1 million in gold ($2.5 million in Federal greenbacks). This clandestine organization undertook several plots that can only be described as terrorist in nature. Authorized was the burning of major cities such as Boston, New York, Detroit, and Cincinnati; the poisoning of the New York water supply; and an attempt to spread germ warfare throughout the North. This latter plot included an attempt to infect Lincoln with the deadly disease of yellow fever. All of these plots failed either because the Confederate plan was leaked to the Union military or because the instigator of the plot got cold feet and fled back into Washington proper. Walker Taylor's proposal never went forward with Davis's blessing. What happened to the paper trail and persons involved in it? They may well decide it is time to come out in the open and tell their story.

Sources: Henry T. Louthan, "A Proposed Abduction of Lincoln," *Confederate Veteran*, June 1908, 157–58; Edward Steers, Jr., *His Name Is Still Mudd* (Gettysburg, Pa.: Thomas, 1997), 10–13.

### Taylor, Tom (1817–1880)

An English playwright whose most popular play, *Our American Cousin*, was playing as a benefit performance for actress Laura Keene at Ford's Theatre on the evening of April 14, 1865. President Lincoln wanted to take a break from his tiring duties and attend the performance. Written in the 1850s, the play was a comedic spoof set in mid-century England that centered on an American bumpkin from the backwoods and an eccentric, foppish British nobleman. Taylor's play was immensely popular and just the sort of humor the self-deprecating Lincoln enjoyed. Taylor wrote another play that figured in John Wilkes Booth's conspiracy. It was titled *Still Waters Run Deep* and was scheduled for a performance at Campbell Hospital, located on the outskirts of the District of Columbia. It was a performance meant to entertain the wounded soldiers confined there. Lincoln was scheduled to attend the performance set for March 17. But, like the time Lincoln altered his scheduled stop in Baltimore to avert a planned assassination at the time of his trip to Washington, Lincoln changed plans at the last minute and averted his own capture by Booth and his gang of conspirators.

Sources: James L. Swanson, *Manhunt: The 12-Day Chase for Lincoln's Killer* (New York: Harper Perennial, 2007), 12–13.

*See also: Our American Cousin*

## Telegraph

See: Heiss, William H.

## Tennallytown

A small community located in northwest Washington, D.C., transected by the Rockville Pike (Wisconsin Avenue) and Military Road, where a picket post was established regulating all traffic out of and into Georgetown, D.C.

On the morning of April 15, 1865, George Atzerodt had boarded a stagecoach in Georgetown, D.C., with the intention of taking it to the end of its line in Rockville, Maryland, approximately twenty miles northwest of Washington. All traffic out of Georgetown was halted at the military picket posts at the intersection of Military Road and the Rockville Pike in Tennallytown. Atzerodt left the stage and, making his way to head of the line, struck up a conversation with several of the soldiers standing picket. Using the money he had received only a few hours before from pawning his revolver, Atzerodt treated the soldiers to a round of hard cider. They included the sergeant of the guard, Lewis L. Chubb of the Thirteenth Michigan Light Artillery. At the head of the line was a farm wagon driven by Montgomery County, Maryland, farmer William Gaither. Atzerodt persuaded Gaither to let him ride along with him to Rockville. The pickets eventually cleared Gaither and his passenger, allowing them to pass through the last post out of Washington. Atzerodt had made his escape, at least from Washington, and was on his way to his cousin's farm near Germantown in Montgomery County, Maryland.

Chubb was court-martialed for allowing Atzerodt through the picket line, but was exonerated following his trial.

Sources: Edward Steers, Jr., *Blood on the Moon* (Lexington: University Press of Kentucky, 2001), 166–68.

*See also:* Chubb, Lewis L.

## Terry, William H.

A detective with the provost marshal's office in Washington under the command of Colonel Timothy Ingraham. Terry took charge of the items recovered from John Wilkes Booth's trunk in his room at the National Hotel. Among the items was a letter signed, "Sam." The letter was written to Booth by Samuel B. Arnold and became a primary exhibit used by the prosecution against Arnold and Michael O'Laughlen, who was mentioned in the letter. Terry was called as a witness by the prosecution at the conspiracy trial and asked to identify the letter and where it came from. The letter was then read into the record as Exhibit 43.

Sources: Testimony of William H. Terry in Poore, *Conspiracy Trial*, vol. 1, 419–21; Pitman, *Trial*, 41, 235.

*See also:* "Sam" Letter; Arnold, Samuel Bland

## Thomas, Daniel J.

A prosecution witness in their case against Dr. Samuel Mudd. Thomas testified that he had a conversation with Mudd sometime in March, a few weeks before the assassination, in which Mudd told him the president and his cabinet would be killed in six or seven weeks. Thomas was extensively cross-examined by Thomas Ewing and Frederick Stone, Mudd's defense attorneys. Thomas was unshaken during his cross-examination. The defense called Thomas's brother, Dr. John C. Thomas, who characterized his brother as suffering from nervous depression and having had "paralytic attacks" as a result. The object of the testimony was to discredit Daniel Thomas's claim that Dr. Mudd had said the president and his cabinet would be killed in six or seven weeks. Under cross-examination by the prosecution, Thomas said that he had no doubt that Mudd had said what his brother testified to, but that it was probably in jest.

Sources: Statement of Daniel J. Thomas, NARA, RG 153, M-599, reel 2, frames 1023–24; Testimony of Daniel J. Thomas, Poore, *Conspiracy Trial*, vol. 1, 435, vol. 3, 306; Pitman, *Trial*, 173, 174.

*See also*: Thomas, John C.

## Thomas, Electus (Eluctus)

One of the sixty-one slaves of Henry Lowe Mudd, Sr. Thomas was taken into custody to the Carroll Annex of Old Capitol Prison, where Colonel John A. Foster interviewed him on April 28. He stated that he lived with Dr. Mudd's father and that on the evening of Saturday, April 15, 1865, David Herold came by the road leading up to the house of Henry Lowe Mudd and asked Thomas where the road was to Allen's Fresh and the large swamp in the rear of it (Zekiah Swamp). Thomas said it was dark when the man (Herold) turned and left after Thomas oriented him by pointing out east and west. This testimony confirms, along with John Hardy's, that Booth and Herold left Dr. Mudd's house around 7:00 P.M. on Saturday and not between 4:00 and 5:00 P.M. as Mudd claimed. It appears that Booth and Herold became lost and wanted to find out the direction to William Burtles's house south of Bryantown. Once oriented in the proper direction, the two fugitives made their way to the cabin of Oswell Swan. After asking Swan the way to Burtles's house, Booth changed his mind and paid Swan to take them to the home of Samuel Cox.

Sources: Statement of Alexis [Electus] Thomas, NARA, RG 153, M-599, reel 6, frames 363–67; Statement of Eluctus [Electus] Thomas, NARA, RG 153, M-599, reel 6, frames 376–79.

## Thomas, John C.

Brother of prosecution witness Daniel J. Thomas (against Dr. Samuel Mudd). Daniel Thomas's testimony was damaging to Mudd. John Thomas was called as a rebuttal witness for the defense on behalf of Samuel Mudd. He stated that his brother suffered from nervous depression and had "paralytic attacks" that affected his judgment. Daniel Thomas stated to the military detectives investigating Dr. Mudd: "Mudd said the south would never be subjugated under Lincoln's administration because it was his opinion that the whole cabinet were abolitionists and they all would be killed within six or seven weeks from that day and also every union man in the state of Maryland. Said that the oath, which he'd taken in order to vote he did not consider worth a chew of tobacco. Mudd afterwards stated to Thomas that he had said what he had mainly to frighten him."

While he believed his brother had not lied about Dr. Mudd's statement, he believed Mudd had said it in jest.

Sources: Statement of John C. Thomas, NARA, RG 153, M-599, reel 3, frames 161–62; Testimony of John C. Thomas, Poore, *Conspiracy Trial*, vol. 2, 250–54; Pitman, *Trial*, 184; Daniel J. Thomas NARA, RG 153, M-599, reel 2, frames 1023–4; Poore, vol. 1, 435, vol. 3, 306; Pitman, 173, 174.

*See also:* Thomas, Daniel

## Thompson, Jacob (1810–1885)

U.S. congressman, U.S. secretary of interior from Mississippi who cast his lot with the Confederacy. Thompson was appointed by Confederate president Jefferson Davis to head the Confederate clandestine operations in Canada in 1864–1865. In the spring of 1864, Davis embarked on a bold plan using the sanctuary of Canada to disrupt the war effort throughout the North and to demoralize its citizens in an effort to defeat Lincoln in his bid for reelection in November 1864. Davis asked Thompson and Clement C. Clay of Alabama to serve as special commissioners in charge of the operations emanating from neutral Canada. To support the operation, Davis gave Thompson a draft for $1 million in gold along with a letter authorizing him "to carry out such instructions as you have received from me verbally," to further the interests of the Confederacy.

It was Thompson and Clay's charge to wreak as much havoc throughout the northern states as they could using a variety of resources. Among their various schemes was an attempt to liberate Confederate prisoners being held in northern prison camps, and interfering with the election in the fall of 1864 through the use of arson, bombings, and armed insurrection. Joining Thompson and Clay were several prominent men from the Confederacy as well as certain rogues.

Thompson attempted to support subversive groups in the North such as the Knights of The Golden Circle, the Sons of Liberty, and the Order of American Knights in their efforts to overthrow the local governments in several northern states and establish a pro-Confederate Northwest Territory. Thompson's

operation included efforts to free the Confederate prisoners held in the Union prison camp on Johnson's Island, in Lake Erie off Sandusky, Ohio; burn several northern cities, including New York, Boston, and Chicago; poison the Croton Reservoir, which supplied water to New York City; and cause epidemics of smallpox and yellow fever in certain cities. Virtually all of these operations failed to materialize, thus negating the hoped-for effect on northern morale and Lincoln's reelection bid. It seems certain that the failure of some of these operations was due to counterespionage efforts from within Thompson's organization. Thompson was relieved of his command in early 1865 and replaced by Edwin Grey Lee, who had no better success than Thompson during the final months of the war.

On April 14, 1865, Assistant Secretary of War Charles A. Dana had received a dispatch from the provost marshal of Portland, Maine, saying that Jacob Thompson would be arriving in Portland to board a Canadian steamer for Liverpool, England. Secretary of War Edwin M. Stanton had earlier told Dana to order Thompson's arrest, but on reflection told Dana to check with Lincoln and see what he wanted to do. Stanton remembered Lincoln's earlier remarks during the morning cabinet meeting on the 14th when asked what should be done with the various Confederate leaders. Lincoln had said it reminded him of a story: "There was an Irish soldier here last summer, who wanted something to drink stronger than water. He stopped at a drug shop where he spied a soda fountain. 'Give me plase a glass of soda water, and if yez can put in a few drops of whiskey unbeknown to anyone, I'll be obliged.' Now," Lincoln continued, "if Jake Thompson is permitted to go through Maine unbeknown to anyone, what's the harm?"

Fourteen hours later, as Lincoln lay dying, Stanton would abandon Lincoln's policy and issue orders to track down and arrest every member of the Confederate operation in Canada, especially Jacob Thompson. Stanton was convinced that Davis and his Canadian agents were behind Lincoln's murder. Stanton saw that Thompson was named as a co-conspirator of John Wilkes Booth as were Clement C. Clay and others in the Confederate operations in Canada. Thompson, however, fled Canada for England, where he remained until 1869. Returning to the United States, Thompson found his home and property in Mississippi devastated. He settled in Memphis, Tennessee, where he was living at the time of his death in 1885.

Sources: Richard N. Current, ed., *The Confederacy* (New York: Macmillan, 1993), 607–8; William A. Tidwell, *April '65: Confederate Covert Action in the American Civil War* (Kent, Ohio: Kent State University Press, 1995), 107–59.

*See also:* Canadian Operation

## Thompson, John C.

Son-in-law of Dr. William Queen, a Confederate sympathizer and agent in Charles County, Maryland. Booth was directed by Confederate agent Patrick C. Martin to contact Dr. Queen and his son-in-law. Martin gave Booth a letter of introduction to Drs. Queen and Mudd. Thompson was living at Dr. Queen's house in Charles County, Maryland, on the two occasions that John Wilkes Booth visited the county. He accompanied Booth to St. Mary's Church and introduced Booth to Dr. Samuel Mudd.

Booth first visited Charles County in November 1864, carrying a letter of introduction from Confederate agent Patrick C. Martin to Drs. Queen and Mudd. Booth returned to Charles County a month later in December. On both occasions Booth spent the night at Dr. Queen's and was taken to St. Mary's Church near Bryantown the following Sunday. There Thompson introduced Booth to Mudd. After meeting with Mudd following church services during his second visit, Booth returned to Mudd's house, where he spent the night. The following day, Monday, Mudd took

Booth to his neighbor George Gardiner, where Booth purchased the one-eyed horse used by Lewis Powell the night of the assassination. Mudd also accompanied Booth into Bryantown that Tuesday to the blacksmith shop of Peter Trotter, where Booth had his newly purchased horse fitted with four new shoes. Trotter told Osborn Oldroyd that he saw Booth and Mudd ride off together after he shod Booth's horse.

Thompson testified as a defense witness on behalf of Dr. Mudd at the conspiracy trial and revealed that Booth had carried a letter of introduction from "some one in Montreal of the name of Martin." The letter ties both Queen and Mudd to Martin. The letter would have no value unless Martin knew Mudd well enough to use the letter as an introduction for Booth.

Sources: Edward Steers, Jr., *Blood on the Moon* (Lexington: University Press of Kentucky, 2001), 121–22; Testimony of John C. Thompson, Poore, *Conspiracy Trial*, vol. 2, 268; Pitman, *Trial*, 178; Osborn H. Oldroyd, *The Assassination of Abraham Lincoln* (1901; reprint, Bowie, Md.: Heritage, 1990), 259.

*See also:* Martin, Patrick Charles

## Thompson, Kate
See: Slater, Sarah

## Thornton, James
Free black who operated the ferry between Port Conway and Port Royal on the Rappahannock River. Thornton carried Booth and Herold along with the three Confederate soldiers across the river early Monday afternoon on April 24. Willie Jett told detectives, "We crossed the river together. Herold sent the boy back with the wagon from there. Booth got on Ruggles' horse near the wharf, rode down to the boat and crossed the river sitting on the horse all the time. Ruggles carried his crutches."

Sources: Statement of Willie S. Jett, NARA, RG 153, M-599, reel 5, frames 86–99; Poore, *Conspiracy Trial*, vol. 1, 308; Pitman, *Trial*, 90.

*See also:* Jett, William Storcke "Willie"

## Tomkins, Charles H. (1830–1915)
Brevet colonel who served as one of the nine commissioners on the military tribunal. President Andrew Johnson appointed Tomkins as a replacement for Brevet Colonel Horace Porter, aide de camp on General Ulysses S. Grant's staff. Porter used his position with Grant to have him replaced on the tribunal. Tomkins, a dropout from West Point, began the war in the Second U.S. Cavalry and ended it as chief quartermaster, First Veterans Reserve Corps. He received a brevet brigadier general appointment

after the war for "faithful and meritorious services in the Quartermaster's Department during the war." He retired from the regular army in 1894 as a full colonel. He died in 1915 and is buried in Oak Hill Cemetery in Georgetown, D.C.

Tomkins was one of five commissioners who signed the clemency plea asking President Johnson to commute Mary Surratt's sentence from death to a life sentence.

Sources: Roger D. Hunt and Jack R. Brown, *Brevet Brigadier Generals in Blue* (Gaithersburg, Md.: Olde Soldier, 1990), 621.

*See also:* Military Tribunal

## "To whom it may concern" Letter

A letter written by John Wilkes Booth around November 1864 in an attempt to justify his actions against President Lincoln. During his last visit to his sister Asia's home in Philadelphia, Booth left a sealed packet containing two letters and money and papers with Asia, with instructions to mail the letters and give the money and papers to the indicated persons. The two letters were the "To whom it may concern" letter and a letter to Booth's mother.

In the letter Booth writes in rather dramatic prose about how Lincoln's policy, presumably referring to emancipation of the slaves, "is only preparing for their [blacks'] total annihilation." "This country," Booth writes, "was formed for the white not for the black man." There are several revealing passages in the letter; Booth writes that he "aided in the capture and execution of John Brown," and that he made "an income of more than Twenty thousand dollars a year" from his acting. He further writes, "My love (as things stand today) is for the South alone."

Booth writes that he has neither personal motive nor gain in his actions. In fact, he stands to lose a great deal, that is, his substantial income. It should be noted that Booth's last paid performance occurred in May 1864, leaving him without income over the past six months. He signs the letter, "A Confederate, ~~at present~~ doing duty upon his own responsibility."

When word of Booth's murder of Lincoln reached Asia and her husband, John Sleeper Clarke, the letter was turned over to U. S. marshal William Millward in Philadelphia. Millward gave the letter to the editor of the *Philadelphia Inquirer*, who published it on April 19. The letter disappeared; only the newspaper version survived. Searches throughout the records of the War Department came up empty. Some historians began to believe the letter was a hoax, and that Booth never wrote it as the paper claimed.

Then, 110 years after it was written, the letter was discovered by assassination historian James O. Hall among the papers of the Justice Department in the National Archives in Washington. People had searched the wrong records.

Sources: John Wilkes Booth, NARA, RG 153, M-599, reel 2, frames 616–18; John Rhodehamel and Louise Taper, *"Right or Wrong, God Judge Me"* (Urbana: University of Illinois Press, 1977), 124–34.

## Torpedo Bureau

The Torpedo Bureau was an agency created by Secretary of War George W. Randolph under the command of Brigadier General Gabriel J. Rains and approved by the Confederate congress in an act of October 1862. The bureau developed and placed various types of explosive mines both on land and at sea. By the very nature of its work the bureau was a secret service organization deploying agents to place explosive devices clandestinely to destroy both property and persons. The Confederate navy also had an agency developing mine warfare, called the Submarine Battery Service.

One of the Torpedo Bureau's employees, Thomas F. Harney, is believed to have headed an operation to mine part of the White House with explosives, killing President Lincoln and members of his cabinet in April 1865. The plot was aborted when members of the Eighth Illinois Cavalry captured Harney at Burke Station while Harney was on his way to cross the river and enter Washington.

Shortly after the fall of Richmond, William H. Snyder, a private in the Confederate army assigned to work in the Torpedo Bureau, sought an interview with Union colonel Edward Hastings Ripley on the day after Ripley's Ninth Vermont Volunteer Infantry occupied the city. Snyder alerted Ripley to a plot that placed "the head of the Yankee government . . . in great danger of violence." Snyder said that a party "had just been dispatched from the Torpedo Bureau on a secret mission . . . and he wanted to put Mr. Lincoln on his guard." The "party" coincides closely with Harney's deployment. When Harney was captured he was carrying various devices necessary to detonate explosives.

Sources: William A. Tidwell, James O. Hall, and David W. Gaddy, *Come Retribution* (Jackson: University Press of Mississippi, 1988), 155–68.

*See also:* Harney, Thomas F.; Navy Submarine Battery Service, Confederate; Snyder, William H.

## Townsend, George Alfred (1841–1914)

Noted journalist and novelist of the period. Townsend wrote extensively on the assassination at the time and years later. On the death of Dr. Samuel Mudd, Townsend interviewed one of Mudd's attorneys at the conspiracy trial, Frederick Stone. Townsend quoted Stone in Mudd's obituary:

> The court very nearly hanged Dr. Mudd. His prevarications were painful. He had given his whole case away by not trusting even his counsel or neighbors or kinfolks. It was a terrible thing to extricate him from the toils he had woven about himself. He had denied knowing Booth when he knew him well. He was undoubtedly accessory to the abduction plot, though he may have supposed it would never come to anything. He denied knowing Booth when he came to his house when that was preposterous. He had even been intimate with Booth.

This statement by one of Mudd's own attorneys is devastating to his claim, and that of others later on, that he was innocent of conspiring with Booth.

Townsend made a second important contribution to our understanding of Mudd and Booth's plot to capture Lincoln. In 1885, he interviewed Thomas Harbin, a former postmaster of Bryantown in Charles County, Maryland, who had also been a Confederate agent. Harbin told Townsend of a meeting arranged at the Bryantown Tavern on December 18, 1864. Harbin had been invited by Dr. Samuel Mudd so that Mudd could introduce Harbin to John Wilkes Booth. Townsend wrote in an article that appeared in the *Cincinnati Enquirer* on April 18, 1892:

> After church that day [December 18, 1864], Booth went into Bryantown a mile or two distant and in plain sight was introduced by Dr. Mudd at the village hotel [Bryantown Tavern] to Mr. Thomas Harbin who was the principal signal officer or [Confederate] spy in the lower Md. Counties. Harbin gave me all the particulars concerning Booth. He told me at the tavern that Sunday it was Dr. Mudd who introduced him to Booth who wanted some private conversations. Booth then outlined a scheme for seizing Abraham Lincoln and delivering him up in Virginia. Harbin was a cool man who had seen many liars and rogues go to and fro in that illegal border and he set down Booth as a crazy fellow, but at the same time said that he would give his cooperation.

Among Townsend's many publications is a popular pamphlet, *The Life, Crime, and Capture of John Wilkes Booth*.

Sources: Edward Steers, Jr., *Blood on the Moon* (Lexington: University Press of Kentucky,

2001), 78–80; Joseph G. E. Hopkins, ed., *Concise Dictionary of American Biography* (New York: Scribner's, 1964), 1076.

*See also:* Stone, Frederick; Harbin, Thomas Henry

## Townsend, Solomon

Captain in the First Delaware Cavalry, stationed at Monocacy Junction near Frederick, Maryland. Townsend received information from one of his sergeants, George Lindsley, that a "suspicious" man who spent Easter dinner at the home of Hezekiah Metz near Germantown, Maryland, spoke of the assassination as if he knew more than the newspapers reported. Townsend decided to send a troop of cavalry under Sergeant Zachariah W. Gemmill to Germantown to find the man and arrest him and anyone else who appeared suspicious. The troop, guided by army informer James W. Purdom, arrived at the home of Hartman Richter, where they found George Atzerodt asleep. They arrested Atzerodt and Richter, taking them back to Monocacy Junction, where they were questioned and then sent on to Washington by train via Relay, Maryland. Townsend did not share in the reward money offered for Atzerodt's capture.

Source: Statement of Solomon Townsend, NARA, M619, reel 455, frames 565–66; Statement of Z.W., NARA, RG 94, M-619, reel 456, frames 145–50.

*See also:* Gemmill, Zachariah W.

## Trap, Trappe

Variously identified as a "disreputable tavern" or "a house of entertainment" whose women occupants "attracted men," the Trap was owned and operated by Mrs. Carter, who had four daughters. The tavern was located approximately midway between Port Royal and Bowling Green, Virginia. After dropping John Wilkes Booth at the home of Richard Garrett a few miles south of Port Royal, Virginia, on Monday, April 24, the three Confederate soldiers and David Herold continued south toward Bowling Green. Reaching the Trap, the four men visited with the Carter ladies before continuing their journey. The following day, two of the soldiers, Ruggles and Bainbridge, along with Herold returned to the Trap before dropping Herold off at the Garrett home.

On Tuesday, April 25, the search party made up of Everton J. Conger, Luther B. Baker, and members of the 16th New York Cavalry stopped at the Trap and questioned the Carter women. They admitted that Confederate soldiers and a civilian man who fit Herold's description had visited the tavern on Monday and again on Tuesday, but there was no lame man among them. Puzzled at first, the search party decided to continue on to Bowling Green to get Willie Jett, relying on him to lead them to Booth. Their decision paid off. Jett was arrested at the Star Hotel and agreed to guide the soldiers to the Garrett farm, where Booth and Herold were hiding.

Sources: William A. Tidwell, James O. Hall, and David W. Gaddy, *Come Retribution* (Jackson: University Press of Mississippi, 1988), 468, 474; Edward Steers, Jr., *Blood on the Moon* (Lexington: University Press of Kentucky, 2001), 198–99.

*See also:* Booth Capture and Death

## Treasury Guard

Treasury Guard flags were borrowed by Harry Clay Ford and used to decorate the president's box the night of April 14, 1865. The Treasury Guards were a military unit made up primarily of employees of the U.S. Treasury Department for the purpose of helping to defend the District of Columbia. They were a regulation volunteer unit issued the appropriate flags by the quartermaster general. The Treasury Guards did not protect the president, nor did they have anything to do with protecting the treasury. The units comprising the Treasury Guards were issued uniforms and weapons and drilled much like other militia units. They were generally of poor quality, having little experience and no rigorous training.

The Treasury Guards were never called into active service nor drew a ration or military pay, and while they never fired a shot in battle, they occupy a special place in American history through their illustrious flags.

Sources: Joseph Edward Garrera, *The Lincoln Flag of the Pike County Historical Society: An Independent Analysis, Examination, and Presentation of the Evidence and History* (privately published, 1996); Susan P. Schoelwer, "The Connecticut Historical Society's Treasury Guard Flag: Silent Witness to Abraham Lincoln's Assassination" (Hartford, Conn.: Privately printed, 2001).

*See also:* Treasury Guard Flags

## Treasury Guard Flags

Most people know of only one flag that is the Treasury Guard's flag. It bears the distinction of having tripped Booth as he jumped from the box to the stage at Ford's Theatre after shooting President Lincoln. It is the blue regimental flag presently on display in the museum located in the basement of Ford's Theatre.

Treasury Guard flags were borrowed by Harry Clay Ford and used to decorate the president's box the night of April 14, 1865. The Treasury Guards were a mili-

tary unit made up primarily of employees of the U.S. Treasury Department for the purpose of helping to defend the District of Columbia. They were a regulation volunteer unit issued the appropriate flags by the quartermaster general. The Treasury Guards did not protect the president, nor did they have anything to do with protecting the treasury. The units comprising the Treasury Guards were issued uniforms and weapons and drilled much like other militia units. They were generally of poor quality, having little experience and no rigorous training.

The Treasury Guards were never called into active service nor drew a ration or military pay, and while they never fired a shot in battle, they occupy a special place in American history through their illustrious flags.

In all, there are six flags that are associated with the president's box on that fateful night in April 1865. Over a period of forty years, from 1900 to 1939, four

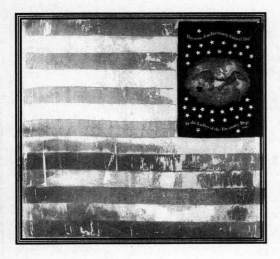

of the flags attributed to the Treasury Guards were on display in Washington, D.C., at one time or another. Three of the four flags were credited with having tripped Lincoln's assassin. The first of the four Treasury Guard flags is the blue regimental flag currently on display at Ford's. The second is the presentation flag currently on display at the Connecticut Historical Society. The third flag was on display in the Treasury building as late as 1939, and transferred to the National Park Service that same year, only to be discarded in 1969, having deteriorated beyond restoration. The fourth flag was transferred from the Treasury Department by Secretary of the Treasury Lyman Gage to Osborn Oldroyd and displayed in the Petersen House circa 1900 to 1932 (this flag may have come from the Treasury Department, but it cannot be classified as a Treasury Guard flag).

A fifth flag was loaned to Ford's property manager John Maddox by W. B. Blanchard of Washington, D.C. Blanchard, of the firm Blanchard & Mohren, Booksellers and Stationers, claimed he lent the flag to John Maddox. He said the flag was used to drape one of the balustrades, but was not the flag Booth caught his spur in. Maddox gave a statement to Judge Abram Olin on April 17, 1865, in which he stated he "went out to obtain a flag to be used that night." In a statement given in 1898, Blanchard told of lending the flag to Maddox and retrieving it after the assassination. According to Blanchard's statement, the other four flags used to decorate the box all came from the Treasury Department.

A sixth flag, made of wool bunting and measuring twelve feet, nine inches by eight feet, eight inches, is in the possession of the Pike County Historical Society in Milford, Pennsylvania. The flag descended in the family of Ford's stage manager, Thomas C. Gourley, through his daughter Jeannie Gourlay. This sixth flag may have been set aside somewhere in the box and later taken by Thomas Gourlay. Both Thomas and Jeannie were members of the cast the night of April 14, 1865. Jeannie Gourlay's only son, Vivian Paul Struthers, donated the flag to the Pike County Historical Society in 1954.

The four Treasury Guard flags, along with the flag borrowed by James Maddox from Blanchard and the flag on display in the Pike County Historical Society, constitute the six flags that are claimed to be associated with the president's box at Ford's Theatre on the night of Lincoln's assassination.

Of the six flags, only the blue regimental flag and the Connecticut Historical Society flag can be positively placed at the box. The placement of the remaining four flags is conjecture. It seems most probable that the Connecticut Historical Society flag and the Treasury Guard national flag were mounted upright on staffs on either side of the box, while the Blanchard flag and the Oldroyd flag may have been used to drape the balustrades.

Sources: Statement of Harry Clay Ford, NARA, RG 153, M-599, reel 5, frames 456–88; Poore, *Conspiracy Trial*, vol. 2, 548; Pitman, *Trial*, 99; Statement of John L. Maddox, NARA, RG 153, M-599, reel 5, frames 342–44; Joseph Edward Garrera, *The Lincoln Flag of the Pike County Historical Society: An Independent Analysis, Examination, and Presentation of the Evidence and History* (privately published, 1996); Susan P. Schoelwer, "The Connecticut Historical Society's Treasury Guard Flag: Silent Witness to Abraham Lincoln's Assassination" (Hartford, Conn.: Privately printed, 2001); Edward Steers, Jr., "A Newly Discovered Flag That Decorated the Presidential Box on the Night of April 14, 1865," *Surratt Courier* 26, no. 9 (September 2001), 3–6.

## Trial of the Conspirators

With John Wilkes Booth dead and John Surratt in hiding, the eight individuals were placed on trial before a military commission established by an executive order of President Andrew Johnson based on a legal opinion of Attorney General James Speed. The use of a military commission to try the accused was not without controversy, both at the time it occurred and throughout later years.

During the trial, a total of 366 witnesses gave testimony on a wide range of subjects. The number of witnesses was nearly evenly divided between the prosecution and the defense. Of the 366 witnesses, twenty-nine were black, all having been slaves at one time. These witnesses were identified in the trial record as "colored" to isolate their testimony from the white witnesses. In Maryland, as in many other states, "colored persons, free or slave" could not testify against a white person. Since the majority of "colored" witnesses resided in Maryland, testifying against white defendants was unusual if not unique to most of them. Of the twenty-nine black witnesses, eighteen testified for the prosecution and eleven testified for the defense.

The defendants were barred from testifying on their own behalf. This was consistent with the law in 1865. Defendants were prohibited from testifying on the grounds that they were incompetent witnesses, and to protect them from self-incrimination. At the time of the trial only the state of Maine allowed defendants to testify on their own behalf.

At one point George Atzerodt's attorney, William E. Doster, attempted to enter a statement (testimony) by his client by asking the official who recorded the statement while Atzerodt was imprisoned aboard the monitor USS *Saugus* to restate it in open court. Doster was challenged by Holt on the grounds that the statement should be excluded the same as a defendant, both being "incompetent."

The commission met for the first time on May 10 at 10:00 A.M. At this time not all of the defendants had been able to secure attorneys to represent them, a failing under the procedures of the military tribunal. President Johnson's executive order was read and the defendants were asked if they had any objection to any of the members of the commission. They did not. The defendants next heard the charges and specifications against them for the first time. Each of the defendants was charged with the crime of conspiracy to commit murder. The specification explained how each individual fit into the crime. While each of the accused had specifications tailored to their particular case, all were charged with "maliciously, unlawfully, and traitorously . . . conspiring . . . to kill and murder, . . . Abraham Lincoln, . . . Andrew Johnson, . . . William H. Seward, . . . and Ulysses S. Grant, . . . and assaulting, with intent to kill and murder, . . . William H. Seward, . . . and lying in wait with intent . . . to kill and murder the said Andrew Johnson, . . . and the said Ulysses S. Grant." (Although the term "traitorously" is used in the specification, the defendants were not charged with treason. Treason is a civil crime not triable by military tribunal.

Each pled "not guilty." The commission then adjourned to allow the defendants time to retain counsel and confer with their counsel on the charges and specifications. The defendants' counsel had to be approved by the commission as satisfactory to represent the accused.

On May 11, the commission met for a second time and approved counsel for Samuel Mudd and Mary Surratt. Frederick Stone and Major General Thomas Ewing, Jr., would represent Samuel Mudd. Frederick Aiken and John W. Clampitt would represent Mary Surratt. The remaining six defendants had not yet secured counsel and the commission adjourned until the following day, allowing them time to do so. Frederick Stone agreed to represent David Herold. Thomas Ewing would represent Samuel Arnold. William E. Doster would represent George Atzerodt while Walter S. Cox would represent Michael O'Laughlen. William Doster would also represent Lewis Powell while Thomas Ewing would take on Edman Spangler in addition to Samuel Mudd and Samuel Arnold. At this time Mary Surratt submitted Reverdy Johnson's name as co-counsel, along with those of John W. Clampitt and Frederick Aiken to represent her.

All the attorneys were approved without objection except for Reverdy Johnson. Commissioner Thomas Harris challenged Johnson's approval as counsel for Mary Surratt, questioning his fitness to appear before the tribunal. Johnson had opposed a law requiring qualified voters in Maryland to take a loyalty oath before they could vote. Johnson rightly challenged the requirement, declaring it unconstitutional. After some debate, the commission overruled Harris's objection and accepted Johnson as counsel for Mary Surratt.

By the third day, counsel for all the defendants were in place and ready to proceed. At this point Thomas Ewing and Reverdy Johnson rose to challenge the legal jurisdiction of the military tribunal.

The commission ruled on its own jurisdiction, denying the motion by Ewing and Johnson. Samuel Mudd then requested that he be tried separately from the others because his defense would be "greatly prejudiced by a joint trial." Mudd's request was denied. There was no legal reason to grant Mudd a separate trial. With this business concluded, the session was adjourned until the next day, when the actual trial would begin. The prosecution and the defense teams were complete, witnesses for the prosecution were in tow, and the government was ready to begin presenting its case.

Sources: Thomas R. Turner, *The Assassination of Abraham Lincoln* (Malabar, Fla.: Krieger, 1999); Thomas R. Turner, "The Military Trial," in Edward Steers, Jr., ed., *The Trial* (Lexington: University Press of Kentucky, 2003), xxi–xxviii.

*See also:* Military Tribunal

## Trial Papers
See: Investigation and Trial Papers Relating to the Assassination of Abraham Lincoln

## Tribunal, Military

See: Military Tribunal

## Trotter, Peter

Owned and operated a blacksmith shop in Bryantown, Maryland, near the Bryantown Tavern. Trotter was the blacksmith who shod the horse that Booth purchased from George Gardiner on December 19, 1864, with the help of Dr. Samuel Mudd. Trotter saw Booth and Dr. Mudd ride off together from his shop.

In 1901, Osborn H. Oldroyd interviewed Trotter during Oldroyd's walk over the Booth escape route. Trotter told how Booth brought him a horse that Booth had recently purchased (from George Gardiner) and asked him to shoe it. Booth had also purchased a new saddle and bridle for the horse from the store of Henry A. Turner, also in Bryantown. Booth's appearance at Trotter's blacksmith shop drew a crowd of people who were "charmed with his fascinating manner." According to Trotter, Samuel Mudd had accompanied Booth to Trotter's shop at the time, This occurred on Tuesday, December 20, 1864, during Booth's second visit to Charles County at the time Samuel Mudd arranged for Booth to meet the Confederate agent, Thomas Harbin at the Bryantown Tavern.

Sources: Osborn H. Oldroyd, *The Assassination of Abraham Lincoln* (1901; reprint, Bowie, Md.: Heritage, 1990), 259.

*See also:* Mudd, Dr. Samuel Alexander

## Tudor Hall

Maryland home of the Booth family. Junius Brutus Booth arranged to build a new house on the property he owned in Harford County, Maryland, near the town of Bel Air. The family had been living in a large two-story log home on the 137-acre farm. The new house, built in the Gothic style, was completed while the elder Booth was on tour in the west. He died November 30, 1852, on a Mississippi River steamboat near Louisville, Kentucky, while on his way home to the new house, which he never got to live in. The house was built along the lines of an English Tudor house that Booth had presumably seen plans for and liked.

Mary Ann Booth, Junius's wife, and three of her children still living at home—Rosalie, Asia, and John Wilkes—moved into the new home in 1852. Asia named the home Tudor Hall. The house passed through several owners over the next century and a half. It sold in 1999 at auction for $415,000. Placed on the auction again in 2006, it failed to reach the reserve price of $925,000. Harford County

Tudor Hall

representatives negotiated with the owners and purchased the home in 2006. It remains in outward appearance much as it did when completed in 1852.

Sources: Ella V. Mahoney, *Sketches of Tudor Hall and the Booth Family* (Bel Air, Md.: Privately printed, 1925).

### Tumblety, Francis J. (1833–1903)

Known as the "Indian Herb Doctor," Tumblety was arrested in St. Louis and placed in the Old Capitol Prison. At first Tumblety was confused with Dr. Luke P. Blackburn, the Confederate agent who devised the "yellow fever and smallpox plots," and was known as the "yellow fever fiend." The government also claimed that David Herold worked for Tumblety at one time, although there is no known evidence to support that claim. Tumblety was the classical nineteenth-century "quack" who made a living selling a variety of "potions." Tumblety was eventually released when it became obvious that he had no connection to the assassination.

In the mid-1880s, Tumblety traveled to England, where he was arrested as a suspect in the sensational "Jack the Ripper" cases. Tumblety posted bail and immediately left for France and soon after sailed to New York. John Littlechild, chief inspector for Scotland Yard, wrote that he believed Tumblety was "very likely" the prime suspect in the Ripper cases. Tumblety died in 1903 of heart disease.

Sources: Francis J. Tumblety, *Kidnapping of Dr. Tumblety by Order of the Secretary of War of the U.S. in 1866* (Cincinnati: Privately printed, 1866); Stewart Evans and Paul Gainey, *Jack the Ripper: First American Serial Killer* (New York: Kodansha International, 1995).

## Ulke, Julius

Photographed the deathbed shortly after President Lincoln was removed to the White House. Ulke was a Washington photographer who boarded at the Petersen house. He and his brother, Henry Ulke (1821–1910), had been in the Petersen house while Lincoln lay dying and helped carry hot water from the ground-floor kitchen to Willie Clark's room, where several doctors were caring for the president. Immediately after Lincoln's body was removed from the rear bedroom and everyone left, Julius Ulke set up his wet-plate camera and photographed one of the most haunting scenes in American history. The view shows the bed with its rumpled spread and blood-soaked pillow with bright sunlight streaming in the open front door of the house. The photograph was lost to history for nearly a century before its discovery in England. No photograph of the events surrounding Lincoln's assassination is as evocative as Ulke's picture.

Sources: Dorothy Meserve Kunhardt and Philip B. Kunhardt, Jr., *Twenty Days* (New York: Harper & Row, 1965), 83.

*See also:* Clark, William "Willie"

## Uniform Code of Military Justice

See General Order No. 100.

## Union Light Guard

Special unit formed to guard President Lincoln. Also known as the Seventh Independent Company of Ohio Volunteer Cavalry. Ohio governor David Todd had a special cavalry unit raised to guard Lincoln as he moved about the city, and to and from Soldiers' Home in northeast Washington. Beginning in the spring of 1864, the unit, known as the Union Light Guard, was camped near the White House on a particle of land known as the White Lot. The barracks were located directly south of the Treasury Department, opposite E Street. In keeping with his fatalistic nature, Lincoln disliked the guard, feeling it unnecessary and intrusive. It was during trips to Soldiers' Home, after failing to notify the guard he was leaving, that Lincoln was at greatest risk.

Sources: Robert W. McBride, *Lincoln's Body Guard: The Union Light Guard of Ohio* (Indianapolis: Edward J. Hecker, 1911).

## Urquhart, Dr. Charles (1794–1866)

A physician who was sent for to administer to Booth following his being shot by Boston Corbett. Urquhart lived in Port Royal, Virginia, on the Rappahannock River. Detective Everton J. Conger sent for Dr. Urquhart to come immediately to care for Booth after he was removed from the Garretts' tobacco barn and placed on the front porch of the Garrett house. Urquhart examined Booth and concluded that his wound was fatal. The bullet from Sergeant Boston Corbett's revolver had severed a part of Booth's spinal cord, passing through the fourth cervical vertebra. As a result, Booth became paralyzed from the neck down. His diaphragm continued to help supply oxygen to his lungs, but slowly failed, resulting in asphyxia. Urquhart returned home following Booth's death.

Sources: John K. Lattimer, *Kennedy and Lincoln: Medical and Ballistic Comparisons of Their Assassinations* (New York: Harcourt Brace Jovanovich, 1980), 69–70.

## Van Alen, James Henry (1819–1886)

On the morning of April 14, 1865, Lincoln received a timely letter from Brigadier General James H. Van Alen urging him to "guard his life and not expose it to assassination as he had by going to Richmond." On April 4, Lincoln, accompanied by his young son Tad and twelve sailors from the USS *Malvern,* walked through the streets of Richmond to the White House of the Confederacy, where he visited the office occupied by Jefferson Davis. Lincoln's actions that day were quite risky, exposing himself to being shot by a disgruntled Confederate. His bodyguard was inadequate to protect Lincoln should an armed group of Confederates have chosen to attack him. General Robert E. Lee was still in the field, and Davis was still in charge of the Confederate government. Fortunately, Lincoln's visit went without an incident, but the very act caused alarm among most people in the North.

Van Alen had served in the war during its first two years, achieving the rank of brigadier general. He died under mysterious circumstances when he either fell or jumped overboard from the Cunard liner *Umbria* while returning from a trip to Europe on July 22, 1886.

Van Alen had written to Lincoln on at least seven prior occasions and knew him well enough to invite him to stay at his home in New York. Lincoln responded to Van Alen's letter the same day writing, "My dear sir, I intend to adopt the advice of my friends and use due caution." As Lincoln knew, there was little he or anyone could do to stop a determined killer, especially if the killer was willing to risk his own life in taking Lincoln's.

Sources: Emerson Reck, *A. Lincoln: His Last 24 Hours* (Columbia, S.C.: University of South Carolina Press, 1987), 10–11; Roy P. Basler, ed., *The Collected Works of Abraham Lincoln* (New Brunswick, N.J.: Rutgers University Press, 1953), vol. 8, 413; Ezra J. Warner, *Generals in Blue* (Baton Rouge: Louisiana State University Press, 1964), 520–21.

## Van Ness Mansion

A Confederate safe house within the District of Columbia. Designed by Benjamin Latrobe, architect of the Navy Yard and south wing of the Capitol, the Van Ness mansion was one of the largest and most elegant private buildings in Washington. In 1865 it was the home of Thomas Green and his wife Anne Lomax Green, sister of Confederate general Lunsford Lindsay Lomax. It served as a safe house for Confederate agents in Washington. Both Green and his wife were arrested on April 18, 1865, as being implicated in Lincoln's assassination. Detectives found a letter to John H. Surratt among Green's papers raising suspicions that Green and Surratt were involved. Green denied knowing Surratt. Green was also suspected of being a mail drop for Confederate mail. They were held in Old Capitol Prison, but the government never charged the Greens and they were released on June 3.

Sources: Statement of Thomas Green, NARA, RG 153, M-599, reel 6, frames 515–40; William A. Tidwell, James O. Hall, and David W. Gaddy, *Come Retribution* (Jackson: University Press of Mississippi, 1988), 264.

## Van Tyne, Mary Ann

A witness for the prosecution in the case against Michael O'Laughlen. Mary Ann Van Tyne owned a boardinghouse located at 420 D Street in Washington, D.C., where both Samuel Arnold and Michael O'Laughlen stayed when in Washington. John Wilkes Booth visited them there on several occasions. She testified that Arnold told her they were in the "oil business" together. The prosecution was convinced the "oil business" was used by Booth as a code name for the assassination.

Sources: Statement of Mary Ann Van Tyne, NARA, RG 153, M-599, reel 6, frames 37–43; Poore, *Conspiracy Trial*, vol. 1, 139; Pitman, *Trial*, 222.

## Veader, Daniel H.

An eyewitness to the shooting in Ford's Theatre. Veader stated that he was seated in the third row of the orchestra. Veader's testimony differs from others in that he claimed there was no guard outside the box nor any person at all stationed there. Charles Forbes, the president's valet and messenger, was seated closest to the box and did stop Booth briefly. After a brief discussion, Forbes waved Booth into the box.

Sources: Timothy S. Good, *We Saw Lincoln Shot: One Hundred Eyewitness Accounts* (Jackson: University Press of Mississippi, 1995), 157.

## Verdi, Dr. Tullio Suzzaro (1829–1902)

Secretary of State William Seward's family physician. Seward was bedridden at the time of the assassination, having suffered serious injury in a carriage accident. At approximately 10:30 on the night of the assassination, Lewis Powell knocked on the door of Seward's house. He told Seward's servant, William Bell, that he had medicine sent by Seward's doctor, Tullio Verdi, with orders to deliver it directly to Seward. Powell's knowledge of Dr. Verdi and Seward's condition were, in all likelihood, learned when Powell reconnoitered the house on April 13 and again on the morning of the 14th. George Robinson, Seward's male nurse, told of Powell's visits in a statement given investigators on April 21: "A man came to the window of the dining room of Mr. Seward's house on the morning of the 13th and 14th of April and inquired each day of the health of the Secretary." Robinson identified the man as Lewis Powell. The statement is important because it shows that Booth was planning his murderous attacks at least as early as April 13.

Sources: Statement of George Foster Robinson, NARA, RG 153, M-599, reel 6, frames 94–96; Poore, *Conspiracy Trial*, vol. 1, 479, vol. 2, 3, 31; Pitman, *Trial*, 155, 156; Edward Steers, Jr., *Blood on the Moon* (Lexington: University Press of Kentucky, 2001), 126.

## Vicarious Liability

A legal principle that holds that any one person involved in a conspiracy can be held liable for the actions of another, even though the first person was not directly responsible for the ultimate actions of the other. This principle clearly applies to those conspirators who joined with John Wilkes Booth in his original plan to capture Lincoln. That plan resulted in Booth shooting Lincoln, thus rolling over the plot from capture to killing.

There are many examples of this principle in criminal cases. The best examples are the Charles Manson murders and the Timothy McVeigh bombing of the Federal building in Oklahoma City. The court held in Manson's conviction, that while he did not commit the murders and was even many miles away

when they occurred, he was responsible. By the same token, Terry Nichols, a partner with Timothy McVeigh, while more than a hundred miles from the scene of the explosion in Oklahoma City, was still held liable. Both Manson and Nichols were convicted under the vicarious liability concept.

Dr. Samuel Mudd and Mary E. Surratt had knowledge of a conspiracy to harm President Lincoln (capture him against his will and hold him hostage). The simple act of going to the authorities and revealing the conspiracy would have prevented his murder.

Sources: Robert R. Arreola, Angela R. Brown, Isabella Ord, and Norman Minnear, "Federal Criminal Conspiracy," *American Criminal Law Review* (Winter 1997), 617–44.

## Vincent, Thomas McCurdy (1832–1909)

A member of Secretary of War Edwin M. Stanton's staff. Vincent was in the Petersen house at the time of Lincoln's death. He later claimed he smoothed Lincoln's eyelids shut and placed a silver coin on each eye. The same claim was made by Maunsell B. Field, assistant secretary of the treasury, and by Colonel George V. Rutherford and Dr. Charles Leale. Each of the four men swore later that he was the one who performed the act. There is no evidence that Vincent or Rutherford were in the room when Lincoln died, although they were in the house at the time, presumably in the parlor, where Stanton held his investigation and directed operations in search for the suspected conspirators.

Sources: Edward Steers, Jr., *Blood on the Moon* (Lexington: University Press of Kentucky, 2001), 268–69.

## Von Steinacker, Henry

A witness at the conspiracy trial whose testimony implicated Confederate leaders involved in Booth's conspiracy to murder President Lincoln. Von Steinacker claimed he was a topographical engineer on the staff of Confederate major general Edward Johnson. Von Steinacker further claimed that while returning from leave to rejoin Johnson's division he met with three men, one of whom was John Wilkes Booth. Later, Von Steinacker claimed he saw the very same Booth meeting with officers of the Second Virginia Infantry, a part of the Stonewall Jackson Brigade, and that the meeting was about sending a detached group of men to Canada to aid in various attacks against northern cities in league with the Knights of the Golden Circle and Sons of Liberty. Among the various acts planned was the assassination of President Lincoln. He further testified that "detached service" was a term used for terrorist-type warfare.

According to the testimony of General Johnson, Von Steinacker was not a member of his staff, but was a private in the Second Virginia Infantry in the Stonewall Brigade.

Sources: Statement of Henry Von Steinacker, NARA, RG 153, M-599, reel 2, frames 462–65; Testimony of Henry Von Steinacker, Poore, *Conspiracy Trial*, vol. 1, 20; Pitman, *Trial*, 38; Testimony of Edward Johnson, Poore, *Conspiracy Trial*, vol. 2, 471–78; Pitman, *Trial*, 64.

*See also:* Johnson, Edward

## Wallace, James Watson

Alias used by Charles A. Dunham in Canada. See Dunham, Charles A.

## Wallace, Lew (1827–1905)

Member of the military tribunal. Major general, U.S. Volunteer Infantry. Wallace had served with distinction during the Civil War and is credited with holding off Confederate general Jubal Early and his army, who were intent on entering and sacking a poorly defended Washington in July 1864. Wallace set up a defensive position south of Frederick, Maryland, at the Monocacy River. His delay allowed time for the Union Sixth Army Corps to reach the outer defenses of Washington in time to repulse Early's attack. Early withdrew back to the Shenandoah Valley.

During the long hours and days of the trial, Wallace spent part of the time drawing credible sketches of the defendants and later painted a large picture of them gathered together in an allegorical setting. Wallace was one of four members of the tribunal who did not sign the clemency plea asking President Johnson to commute Mary Surratt's death sentence to life in prison. He later was appointed president of the military tribunal that tried Confederate captain Henry Wirz, in charge of the Confederate prison camp at Andersonville, Georgia. Following the war he took up writing fiction and in 1880 authored the famous novel *Ben-Hur*.

Sources: Robert Morsberger and Katharine Morsberger, *Lew Wallace* (New York: McGraw-Hill, 1980).

## Walter, Father Jacob Ambrose (1827–1894)

Roman Catholic priest who arrived early in the afternoon on July 6 and remained with Mary Surratt in her prison cell up to the hour of execution. At the

appointed hour, Mary Surratt was led from her room with Fathers Walter and Bernadine Wiget walking behind her up the steps and onto the scaffold platform. Walter and Wiget remained next to her as the sentence was read to each of the condemned.

Father Walter became part of a controversy involving Major General John F. Hartranft, the conspirators' jailer. Walter also visited Lewis Powell in his cell, and according to Walter, Powell told him that Mary Surratt "was innocent of the murder of the President." Powell went on to say that "as to the abduction of the President he did not know that she was connected with it, although he had fre-quent conversations with her, during his stay at her house." Judge Advocate General Joseph Holt, when he heard of Powell's statement, sent word to Hartranft to have Father Walter put the statement in writing and send it to him. Hartranft called Walter into his office and had him write out what Powell had told him.

Hartranft explained his own actions: "Believing that Judge Holt desired the best possible evidence as to [Powell's] sayings, I remarked to father Walter, that perhaps it would be better for me to add what [Powell] had said to me; to which he assented. I then made the endorsement, which I presume is in the possession of Judge Holt as nearly in the words of [Powell] as I could remember and added that I believed [Powell] had told the truth in this matter. In this, I did not by any means intend to express my own opinion of the guilt or innocence of Mrs. Surratt, but simply that I believed [Powell] had told the truth according to the best of his knowledge and belief."

Father Walter became a strong advocate for Mary Surratt's innocence and in his lectures and writings accused the government of executing an innocent woman. Walter heard Mary Surratt's last confession in her room and administered Communion to her. Walter attacked government witness Louis Wiechmann in his defense of Mary Surratt, accusing him of committing perjury during his testimony. Wiechmann countered by asking Walter why he hadn't made public Mary's confession in which she claimed complete innocence. Walter, Wiechmann said, could have done this with Mary Surratt's permission, which she surely would give. Walter never divulged the content of Mary's last confession.

Walter is buried in Washington's Mount Olivet Cemetery, not far from where Mary Surratt is buried.

Sources: Edward Steers, Jr., and Harold Holzer, eds., *The Lincoln Assassination Conspirators: Their Confinement and Execution, as Recorded in the Letterbook of John Frederick Hartranft* (Baton Rouge: Louisiana State University Press, 2009).

*See also*: Hartranft, John F.

## Warne, Kate

An undercover detective working for Allan Pinkerton. Warne, posing as president-elect Lincoln's sister, accompanied Lincoln on the train ride from Philadelphia to Baltimore and from Baltimore to Washington. Arriving in Baltimore at 3:00 A.M., Lincoln's coach was transferred to the Baltimore & Ohio Railroad line and continued on to Washington. The trip was part of Pinkerton's plan to have Lincoln pass through Baltimore nine hours ahead of schedule and thereby thwart a plot to assassinate Lincoln during his stopover in the city. Warne had worked undercover in Baltimore helping to expose the plot, and Pinkerton, recognizing her as one of his top agents, assigned her to accompany Lincoln on the final two legs of his inaugural journey.

Sources: Allan Pinkerton, *The Spy of the Rebellion* (Hartford, Conn., 1885), 45–103.

*See also:* Baltimore Plot

## Washington, Baptist

A former slave of the Mudd family and called as a defense witness for Dr. Samuel A. Mudd. Washington was called to refute the testimony of Mary Simms, another slave of Dr. Mudd, who told of Mudd's hiding Confederate soldiers in the woods near his house and providing food for them. She also testified to John Surratt being a frequent visitor to Dr. Mudd's house. Washington claimed Mary Simms had a reputation as a liar and was untrustworthy.

Sources: Testimony of Baptist Washington, Poore, *Conspiracy Trial*, vol. 2, 322; Pitman, *Trial*, 181.

*See also:* Simms, Mary

## Washington, Frank

A former slave of Mrs. Francis Mudd's brother, Jeremiah Dyer, called as a defense witness for Dr. Mudd. Washington worked for Samuel Mudd as his "plowman" in 1864–1865. He testified to being at the Mudd farm when Booth and Herold arrived early Saturday morning, April 15. He took care of their horses and stabled them in Mudd's stable. He was called by the defense to refute Mary Simms's testimony, stating he never saw any of the men (soldiers) camped at Dr. Mudd's or cared for by Mudd. As Baptist Washington, he told the court Mary Simms "was never known to tell the truth." Washington also testified that Mudd treated him "first-rate." This was in contrast to other witnesses' claims that Dr. Mudd whipped Mary Simms and shot one of his slaves, Elzee Eglent, in the leg for being "obstreperous."

Sources: Statement of Frank Washington, NARA, RG 153, M-599, reel 6, frames 485–87; Poore, *Conspiracy Trial*, vol. 2, 313, vol. 3, 283; Pitman, *Trial*, 181, 194; Statement of Frank Washington, NARA, RG 153, M-599, reel 6, frames 488–90; Poore, *Conspiracy Trial*, vol. 2, 313, vol. 3, 283; Pitman, *Trial*, 181, 194.

*See also:* Simms, Mary; Washington, Melvina

## Washington, Melvina

A witness for the prosecution in the case against Samuel Mudd. Washington was a former slave of Dr. Mudd. She supported Mary Simms's testimony, stating that she saw several men at Mudd's house; "some wore gray clothes and some little short jackets, with black buttons and a little peak on behind [shell jacket worn by the cavalry]." She testified that these men camped in the woods behind Mudd's house and that Dr. Mudd and Mary Simms "carried victuals to them." She also testified that on those occasions when these men were in the Mudd house or dining inside, two of Mudd's "boys" watched as lookouts, and when somebody was seen approaching the Mudd house, "these men rushed out from the table to the side door." On cross-examination by Thomas Ewing, Melvina Washington said the men would stay in the woods for up to a week, and that they were in Mudd's house on seven or eight occasions. The purpose of her testimony was to show that Mudd was a Confederate supporter.

Sources: Testimony of Melvina Washington, Poore, *Conspiracy Trial*, vol. 2, 160; Pitman, *Trial*, 171.

## Washington Arsenal

Site of the Old Federal Penitentiary cell block, the courtroom where the conspirators were tried, and the gallows where the four condemned conspirators were hanged on July 7, 1865.

Today, the site of the Washington Arsenal has been renamed Fort Lesley

Washington arsenal. Site of the hanging.

J. McNair. General McNair was highest-ranking officer killed during the Normandy invasion in June 1944. The arsenal is located on Greenleaf's Point at the foot of Fourth Street in southeast Washington. The post provides quarters and facilities for general and flag officers of the Department of Defense and is home to the National Defense University, Industrial College of the Armed Forces, and the Inter-American Defense College.

Part of the original arsenal building that housed Federal prisoners and was used as the courtroom in the trial of the Lincoln conspirators still stands. The building was converted into an apartment building for junior officers. It is located opposite the current Officers Club.

Back in 1791, Pierre L'Enfant, the designer of the Federal city, had designated a section of local land known as Greenleaf Point as a military base. The site was ideally situated on the southernmost tip of the city. Bounded by the Potomac River to the west and the Eastern Branch of the Potomac to the east, it was surrounded on three sides by water. The army developed the site as an arsenal in 1803. In 1831, a Federal penitentiary was built on the grounds, boasting of 160 cells in a building 120 feet in length and fifty feet in width. The cells, each measuring seven feet by three and a half feet with seven-foot ceilings, were arranged in four tiers. The upper tier was originally intended for female prisoners, but a separate addition was eventually added to the central cell block, providing cells for female prisoners.

It was in this addition that the Lincoln conspirators were held during their trial. As Major General Winfield Scott Hancock, commanding the Middle Military District, instructed, a door was cut into an adjoining room that had once served as the deputy warden's quarters. The arrangement allowed the prisoners to be moved from their cells directly into the adjoining courtroom without exposing them to onlookers.

At its peak, the prison complex was three hundred feet long and fifty feet wide, boasting cells for 220 prisoners. It was widely considered one of the best facilities in the country. No less vigilant an observer than Dorothea Dix, one of the era's most outspoken prison reformers, gave her approval to the facility, donating money to the prison library.

With the coming of the Civil War in 1861, however, the demands of the arsenal far outweighed the need for a Federal penitentiary, and President Lincoln ordered that it be turned over to the War Department to be used as additional space for the arsenal. The prisoners were transferred to the Federal penitentiary in Albany, New York. The old arsenal became a favorite place of Lincoln, and during the war he visited it often to observe the testing of new weapons. Less than a month before his death, on March 23, 1865, Lincoln set out from the arsenal docks aboard the *River Queen* to visit General Grant at City Point, Virginia. He returned to the arsenal aboard the riverboat on April 9. It would be his last trip outside of Washington.

Following their execution, the four executed conspirators were buried in the courtyard next to the scaffold, which stood just outside the building where the trial was held. Booth's body was buried earlier beneath the floor in the building where the warden's office was located. In 1867, the four bodies and that of Booth were exhumed and reburied in a large warehouse on the parade grounds. In 1869, President Andrew Johnson ordered that the remains of the five conspirators be turned over to the families.

Sources: Joan L. Chaconas, "Historic Fort McNair," *Lincolnian* 1, no. 3 (January–February 1983), 1–5; Michael J. Kauffman, "Fort Lesley J. McNair and the Lincoln Conspirators," *Lincoln Herald* 80, no. 4 (Winter 1978); Edward Steers, Jr., and Harold Holzer, eds., *The Lincoln Assassination Conspirators: Their Confinement and Execution, as Recorded in the Letterbook of John Frederick Hartranft* (Baton Rouge: Louisiana State University Press, 2009).

*See also:* Old Federal Penitentiary

## Washington Intelligencer
See *Washington National Intelligencer*

## Washington National Intelligencer
Washington newspaper. On April 14, 1865, Booth drafted a letter explaining his motive for his planned assassination of President Lincoln. He sealed the letter in an envelope addressed to the editor of the *Daily National Intelligencer.* Later in the day he met John Mathews, a fellow actor whom he had tried to enlist in his capture plot. Booth told Mathews he had to leave the city later that night and asked Mathews to deliver the letter unless he saw Mathews before ten o'clock that next morning. Mathews agreed, but on learning of Lincoln's assassination by Booth, panicked and burned the letter.

Sources: Statement of John Mathews, NARA, RG 153, M-599, reel 5, frames 302–14.

## Watson, John
Alias used by John H. Surratt, Jr.

## Watson, Roderick D.
A member of a prominent Charles County family who became involved in the Confederate underground. Watson made his way to New York City where he established a mail drop at 178 ½ Water Street. He was arrested in Baltimore and later in New York for disloyal practices, but eventually released on taking the oath of allegiance. Released on his oath, Watson returned to his clandestine activities. He sent a letter, dated March 19, 1865, to John Surratt asking him to come to New York on important business as soon as possible and to answer by telegram. Booth made several trips to New York, but there is no direct link between Watson and Booth. The letter to Surratt is the link suggesting a connection.

In his "lost confession," conspirator George A. Atzerodt speaks of a "party in N. York who would get the Prest. Certain." The plot involved mining the White House beneath the president's office with explosives and blowing up the president and members of his cabinet.

Sources: Letter from Roderick D. Watson to John Surratt, NARA, RG 153, M-599, reel 3, frame 114; William A. Tidwell, James O. Hall, and David W. Gaddy, *Come Retribution* (Jackson: University Press of Mississippi, 1988), 65, 415.

## Weaver, John Henry (1811–1877)
Baltimore undertaker hired by Edwin Booth to receive the body of John Wilkes Booth and arrange for proper

burial. On February 15, 1869, President Andrew Johnson, in response to a request by Edwin Booth, ordered Secretary of War Edwin M. Stanton to turn over the remains of Booth to the family. Weaver contracted with Washington undertakers Harvey & Marr to receive the body, and following identification, transport it to Baltimore, where Weaver would receive it. The body, in its new mahogany coffin provided by Weaver, was placed in a back room of his undertaking facility, where several friends and family members positively identified the remains as John Wilkes Booth. Weaver transferred the body to his personal vault in Green Mount Cemetery, where it remained until proper burial could take place.

Burial occurred on June 26, 1869, in the family plot. According to a report in the Baltimore *Sun*, between forty and fifty persons were in attendance. Weaver's record book shows he was paid eight dollars for his services.

Sources: George S. Bryan, *The Great American Myth* (New York: Carrick & Evans, 1940).

*See also:* Harvey & Marr

## Welles, Gideon

Secretary of the Navy appointed by Lincoln, Welles stayed on as Navy secretary under Andrew Johnson, serving overall

from 1861 to 1869. Lincoln affectionately called Welles his "Father Neptune."

The message that the president had been attacked and Secretary of State William H. Seward had been assassinated reached Welles just as he was preparing to retire for the night. Welles had gone up to his room and was in the process of undressing when a messenger arrived with the shocking news. Hurrying on foot the few blocks to Seward's house, Welles met Secretary of War Edwin M. Stanton, who had just arrived in a carriage. The two men rushed up the stairs and into the bedroom where Seward lay wrapped in bloody sheets. There seemed to be blood everywhere. The scene appeared more horrific than it actually was. Reassured that Seward would live, the two men next hurried to the house where the president had been taken. They arrived a few minutes past eleven o'clock.

The close atmosphere of the small room had become heavy with the odor of mustard balm and camphor. Welles began to feel light-headed and nauseous. He needed to escape the dreary room, even if only for a few moments. Shortly before dawn he slipped out the front door of the house and took a short walk. As he walked past the large groups of people gathered outside he was asked what news there was of the president. "Is there any hope, any at all?" Welles simply shook his head, too emotionally drained to speak. The crowds seemed overwhelmed with grief, especially the black mourners, who seemed to outnumber the white.

Returning to the house, Welles resumed his place near the president. It was a little past seven o'clock and Lincoln's breathing had slowed considerably. The deathwatch was drawing to an end. Sitting at the president's side was Assistant Army Surgeon Charles Leale, the doctor who had arrived first at the box in Ford's Theatre and had taken charge of the president.

At twenty-two minutes past seven o'clock the end came. Placing a finger against the president's neck, Surgeon General Joseph K. Barnes felt for some sign of a pulse. There was none. Carefully folding the president's arms across his breast, Barnes declared in a voice choked with emotion, "He is gone." A somber silence ensued as each person in the room seemed transfixed by the awful moment. It cannot be true. He cannot be gone. After what seemed to Welles to be several minutes, Stanton broke the silence by asking Lincoln's pastor, Reverend Dr. Phineas Gurley, if he would say a prayer. Gurley, minister of the New York Avenue Presbyterian Church, knelt by the bedside and waited as each man in the room sank to his knees. Gurley prayed for the nation, beseeching God to heal the wounds and restore a united country. He asked that God accept his humble servant Abraham Lincoln into His glorious Kingdom. When he finished the men rose to their feet with a fervent and spontaneous amen. Then Stanton, with tears streaming down his cheeks, uttered his immortal words, "Now he belongs to the angels," although some believe he said, "Now he belongs to the ages." A deeply religious man, it seems more likely that Stanton made the former statement.

Sources: Howard K. Beale, ed., *Diary of Gideon Welles* (New York: Norton, 1960), vol. 2, 283–86; Charles A. Leale, *Lincoln's Last Hours: Address Delivered before the Commandery of the State of New York Military Order of the Loyal Legion of the United States* (New York:

Privately printed,1909); Emerson Reck, *A. Lincoln: His Last 24 Hours* (Columbia, S.C.: University of South Carolina Press, 1987), 157; John G. Nicolay and John Hay, *Abraham Lincoln: A History,* 10 vols. (New York: Century, 1890), vol. 10, 302.

## Wells, Henry H. (1823–1900)

Colonel of the 26th Michigan Volunteer Infantry. Wells was serving as provost marshal for the defenses south of the Potomac at the time of the assassination. Wells had received several snippets of information from different sources that all had a common connector—the 541 H Street boardinghouse of Mary Surratt. He ordered his detectives to search the premises thoroughly and then arrest all of the occupants, whether they were suspects or not. The innocent would be sorted out later. Detectives showed up on the evening of April 17 and arrested all of the occupants and Lewis Powell who happened to stop by the house near midnight while the detectives were still there.

Lieutenant Alexander Lovett, a military detective serving on Wells's staff, was sent by Wells to Bryantown, Maryland, to aid Lieutenant David Dana and the 13th New York Cavalry, who had set up a headquarters there and were gathering information about Booth. In Bryantown, Lovett learned from Dana that two strangers had been to the home of Dr. Samuel Mudd on Saturday, April 15. Mudd lived five miles north of Bryantown. Lovett went to Mudd's house, where he interviewed Mudd and his wife. When Lovett finished questioning Mudd, he had a feeling something was not quite right. After listening to Mudd's account of the two visiting strangers, Lovett concluded that the injured man of the two was Booth. He took the information directly to Colonel Wells, his superior officer in Washington.

Wells went to Secretary of War Edwin M. Stanton and informed him that Booth was seen in the Bryantown area and that his leg was broken. Stanton ordered Wells to go to Bryantown and follow up on the information that he had received from Lovett. While Wells set up his office in Bryantown, Lovett returned to Mudd's house a second time and interviewed him and his wife. Dissatisfied with Dr. Mudd's "evasiveness and highly nervous demeanor," Lovett took him into Bryantown for further questioning by Colonel Wells. Wells interrogated Dr. Mudd extensively before allowing him to return home, cautioning him to return to Bryantown the next morning (Saturday).

When Mudd returned to Bryantown as ordered, Wells presented him with a statement that he had drafted from Mudd's answers the day before. He asked Dr. Mudd to read it carefully and, if he agreed with it, to sign and date it, which Mudd did. Wells, like Lovett, was suspicious of Mudd and felt he lied about not recognizing his visitor as Booth. On Monday, April 24, Wells, now convinced that Dr. Mudd was connected to Booth and his conspiracy, ordered Lovett to return to Mudd's house and arrest him.

Wells testified at the conspiracy trial as a major witness against Mudd, giving details of Lovett's and his interrogations of Mudd. Wells's testimony proved damaging to Mudd's claim of innocence.

Sources: Statement of Colonel Henry H. Wells, NARA, RG 153, M-599, reel 2, frames 73–80; Poore, *Conspiracy Trial*, vol. 1, 281, vol. 2, 45; Pitman, *Trial*, 158, 168; Statement of Henry H. Wells, NARA, RG 153, M-599, reel 7, frames 22–24.

## Wermerskirch, William M. (1832–1898)

A military detective on the staff of General C. C. Augur. On Monday, April 17, 1865, Wermerskirch and three other detectives from Augur's staff were sent to the Surratt boardinghouse at 541 H Street in Washington, D.C., with orders to arrest everyone in the house. While there, Lewis Powell showed up and was arrested along with the occupants. On Friday, April 21, Wermerskirch was charged with escorting George Atzerodt from the Baltimore & Ohio train depot near the U.S. Capitol to the monitor USS *Montauk*. Wermerskirch interrogated Atzerodt and learned the route he had taken, where he had stayed overnight on the 15th and 16th, and when he had gotten to the home of Hartman Richter in Germantown, Maryland. The night of April 15, Atzerodt stayed at Clopper's Mill in Montgomery County, Maryland, a few miles south of Germantown. The night of April 16 through April 20, Atzerodt stayed at the farm of his cousin Richter. Sergeant Zachariah Gemmill of the First Delaware Cavalry arrested him during the early morning hours of April 20 at the Richter home.

For his role in apprehending Powell, Wermerskirch received five hundred dollars of the reward money posted for Powell's arrest.

Sources: Statement of William M. Wermerskirch, NARA, RG 153, M-599, reel 3, frames 126–27; Poore, *Conspiracy Trial*, vol. 1, 33; Pitman, *Trial*, 123; Edward Steers, Jr., "George Atzerodt," in Edward Steers, Jr., ed., *The Trial* (Lexington: University Press of Kentucky, 2003), lxvi–lxxi.

*See also:* McDevitt, James A.

## Wharton, John W.

Wharton owned a store at Fort Monroe, Virginia, where Samuel Arnold worked as a clerk at the time of the assassination. Following Booth's failed capture plot at Campbell Hospital on March 17, 1865, Samuel Arnold returned to Baltimore frustrated with Booth and his antics. He began looking for work and was hired as a clerk in Wharton's store, reporting for work on April 2, 1865. At the time Lincoln was murdered, Arnold was working at the store oblivious to what Booth had done.

On Saturday, April 15, Maryland provost marshal James McPhail sent two of his detectives, Eaton Horner and Voltaire Randall, to Hookstown, a small community in northwest Baltimore, to arrest Arnold. Because Arnold served in the Confederate army he was required to register with McPhail's office in Baltimore. McPhail knew that Arnold and his friend Michael O'Laughlen were well acquainted with Booth. He sent his two detectives to Hookstown to bring Arnold in for questioning. The detectives discovered from Arnold's father that Arnold was employed in Wharton's store and headed to Fort Monroe, where they arrested Arnold and Wharton on Monday, April 17.

Wharton later became a witness for Arnold's defense, testifying to his employment and whereabouts from April 2 to his arrest on April 17.

Sources: Testimony of John W. Wharton, Poore, *Conspiracy Trial*, vol. 3, 340; Pitman, *Trial*, 241; Percy E. Martin, "Samuel Arnold and Michael O'Laughlen," in Edward Steers, Jr., ed., *The Trial* (Lexington: University Press of Kentucky, 2003), lxxxviii–xcvi.

*See also:* McPhail, James L.

## Wheeler, Rose (1830–1865)

Common-law wife of George A. Atzerodt. Wheeler, thirty-five years old, lived in Port Tobacco, Charles County, Maryland, with their two-year-old daughter. Wheeler, a widow, had four children, including Atzerodt's. Atzerodt had requested of Major General John F. Hartranft to see Wheeler, and Hartranft sent word for her to come the day before Atzerodt's execution.

Sources: Michael J. Kauffman, *American Brutus* (New York: Random House, 2004), 161–62.

*See also*: Atzerodt, George Andrew

## Whitehurst, Daniel W. (1807–1872)

Post surgeon at Fort Jefferson at the outbreak of the Civil War. Whitehurst resigned his position because of his wife's support for the Confederacy and moved to Key West, where he and his wife owned a home. In 1867, a yellow fever outbreak at Fort Jefferson in 1867 killed the post surgeon; Dr. Joseph Smith and Dr. Samuel Mudd took over in the absence of a trained medical doctor. Dr. Whitehurst agreed to return to the fort and serve as Mudd's assistant. The cause of yellow fever was not known and there was no treatment for the disease other than making the patients as comfortable as possible. Dr. Mudd summed up the medical situation when he wrote to his wife, "I could do more by a few consoling and inspiring words, than with all the medicine known to me." The epidemic ran its course, with the last case recorded on November 14, 1867.

Sources: Rodman Bethel, *A Slumbering Giant of the Past* (Hialeah, Fla.: W. L. Litho, 1979), 47–48.

## Wiechmann, Louis J. (1842–1902)

Wiechmann was the government's key witness in proving a conspiracy existed involving Mary Surratt, John Surratt, Samuel Mudd, and Lewis Powell. Wiechmann presented damaging testimony against Samuel Mudd and Mary Surratt in particular. Mudd's lawyers called several witnesses in an attempt to overcome the damage inflicted by Wiechmann's testimony. Sixty-six of the defense witnesses were mainly called to rebut his testimony.

Wiechmann had testified of a meeting between Mudd and Booth in which Mudd introduced John Surratt to Booth one afternoon in Washington. Wiechmann testified that he and Surratt were walking along Seventh Street in Washington when Mudd called out to Surratt from across the street. With Mudd was a man he introduced as John Wilkes Booth. The four men returned to Booth's room at the National Hotel, where "private conversations" were held between Mudd, Surratt, and Booth. Wiechmann placed the date of the meeting on January 15, 1865. It was Wiechmann's only mistake, and Mudd's attorneys attempted to discredit all of his testimony by focusing on the error.

While Mudd's attorneys had acknowledged that he had met Booth at St. Mary's Church near Bryantown in November 1864, they denied that a second meeting ever occurred in Washington on January 15 and produced several witnesses to prove that Mudd was at home during that time. Thus Ewing suggested that Wiechmann had perjured himself when he claimed a meeting took place of January 15. It was later shown, by Mudd's own admission, that Wiechmann was correct about a second meeting, but wrong about the date. The meeting, which Mudd admitted to several weeks later, took place on December 23, three weeks earlier than Wiechmann claimed. The commission, however, was not swayed by the defense's arguments and accepted Wiechmann's claim that a second meeting had occurred.

Wiechmann's testimony refuted Mudd's claim that he was not well acquainted with Booth. Unknown to the tribunal's commissioners at the time, but learned years later, was the fact that Mudd and Booth met a third time in Charles County, on December 18, five days before the meeting at Booth's hotel room in Washington. It was during this meeting that Mudd introduced yet another Confederate agent to Booth. The man was Thomas Harbin, an agent working for the Confederate Signal Service. Harbin agreed to join Booth's conspiracy to capture Lincoln.

Wiechmann's testimony was taken as evidence that Mudd had lied about his associations with Booth and had something to hide. It was sufficient to convince a majority of commissioners that Mudd was guilty, but not sufficient for them to vote the death penalty. Had they known what we know today, they would in all probability have sentenced Mudd to death.

Wiechmann was subject to attacks from Mary Surratt's supporters and those that had an ax to grind against the Federal government. He kept up a correspondence with several people who supported his position, and wrote a manuscript giving the details of his involvement with John and Mary Surratt. Wiechmann never published the manuscript, and it was not until 1975 that Floyd Risvold published it. The book, often ignored by mainstream historians, is nonetheless a valuable resource on the assassination.

Sources: Statement of Louis J. Wiechmann, NARA, RG 153, M-599, reel 7, frames 445–51; Poore, *Conspiracy Trial*, vol. 1, 69, 135, 369; Pitman, *Trial*, 113, 118, 120; Statement of Louis J. Wiechmann, NARA, RG 153, M-599, reel 6, frames 499–507; Poore, *Conspiracy Trial*, vol. 1, 69, 135, 369; Pitman, *Trial*, 113, 118, 120; Statement of Louis J. Wiechmann, NARA, RG 153, M-599, reel 3, frames 105–9; Poore, *Conspiracy Trial*, vol. 1, 69, 135, 369; Pitman, *Trial*, 113, 118, 120; Statement of Louis J. Wiechmann, NARA, RG 153, M-599, reel 3, frames 134–7, Poore, *Conspiracy Trial*, vol. 1, 69, 135, 369; Pitman, *Trial*, 113, 118, 120; Floyd E. Risvold, ed., *A True History of the Assassination of Abraham Lincoln and of the Conspiracy of 1865* (New York: Knopf, 1975).

*See also:* Mudd, Dr. Samuel Alexander; Surratt, Mary Elizabeth

## Wiget, Father Bernadine F. (1821–1883)

Priest who attended to Mary Surratt at the time of her execution. Wiget was president of Gonzaga College, located on F Street between Ninth and Tenth streets in Washington. He appeared as a character witness at the conspiracy trial on behalf of Mary Surratt. Wiget testified that he "knew her well" and that "everyone spoke very highly of her character as a lady and as a Christian." In fact, when Wiget was father superior at St. Thomas Manor School, he arranged for Mary Surratt's two sons, Isaac and John, to become students there.

In preparation for carrying out her death sentence, Mary Surratt was asked whom she wanted for spiritual comfort and she requested Father Jacob Walters and Father Bernadine Wiget. Walters and Wiget arrived early in the afternoon of July 6 and remained with Mary Surratt most of the time up to the hour of her execution. At the appointed time, the prisoners were conducted to the scaffold, with Mary Surratt appearing first, accompanied by her guard and Fathers Walters and Wiget. The two priests remained with her up to the moment of her execution.

Sources: Testimony of Bernadine F. Wiget, Poore, *Conspiracy Trial*, vol. 2, 174; Pitman, *Trial*, 135; Elizabeth Steger Trindal, *Mary Surratt: An American Tragedy* (Gretna, La.: Pelican, 1996).

*See also:* Surratt, Mary Elizabeth

## Williams, William S.

A military detective who worked for Washington, D.C., provost marshal

James O'Beirne. Williams was part of the early search for Booth and was present when Dr. Mudd was interviewed by Lieutenant Alexander Lovett at Mudd's house on April 18, and again on April 21. Williams told the court that he told Mrs. Mudd that they would have to search her house, and only then did she go and get the boot that her husband had removed from the man's broken leg. The boot had the name "J. Wilkes" written inside its top edge. Williams was at the bar of the Brawner Hotel in Port Tobacco in Charles County, Maryland, on Tuesday, April 18, when Thomas Jones came into the bar. Jones was caring for Booth and Herold, who were hiding in a pine thicket not far from Port Tobacco. After being introduced to Jones, Williams made the statement that he would give one hundred thousand dollars to the man who could provide information leading to the capture of Booth. Williams, years later, claimed he suspected Jones knew much more than he indicated and hoped to pry information from him. Jones, however, revealed nothing about Booth's whereabouts.

Sources: Testimony of William Williams, Poore, *Conspiracy Trial*, vol. 1, 294–301; Pitman, *Trial*, 88.

*See also:* Jones, Thomas Austin

## Wilmer, Lemuel Parson (1795–1869)

Episcopal minister whose parish was in Charles County, Maryland. He was an undercover informer for the Federal army during the war.

Wilmer's church, known as "Piney Church," was located due west of Dr. Samuel Mudd's house on the western side of the Zekiah Swamp. At the time of his interrogation, Mudd told the detectives that David Herold "inquired of me the nearest way to Mr. Wilmer's. I told them there were two ways; one was by the public road, leading by Beantown; the other led across the swamp directly across from me, by which they could save a mile, both are easterly." Mudd was suggesting that Booth and Herold headed west toward Wilmer's house when they left his place at sundown on Saturday, April 15. To the contrary, the two men headed east and then south, making a wide circle to the east of Bryantown, where Union soldiers were encamped. Detectives interviewing Mudd were convinced that Mudd told them the two visitors headed in the direction of Wilmer's to throw off the search party and thus allowing Booth and Herold more time to escape.

Sources: Statement of Dr. Samuel Alexander Mudd, NARA, RG 153, M-599, reel 5, frames 212–25.

## Wilson, Henry

Captain of the steamboat *John S. Ide*, which carried the search party to Belle Plain, Virginia, on Monday, April 24, and brought Booth's body back to the Navy Yard on Wednesday, April 26.

On April 24, Colonel Lafayette C. Baker received permission from Secretary of War Edwin M. Stanton to send a party of troopers into Virginia to search the area between the Potomac River and the Rappahannock River for John Wilkes Booth and David Herold. The *Ide* transported detectives Everton J. Conger and Luther B. Baker, along with army Lieutenant Edward P. Doherty and twenty-six members of the 16th New York Cavalry, from Washington to General Grant's former supply base at Belle Plain, Virginia, located on the Potomac River. Disembarking at Belle Plain, the search party made its way south to the Rappahannock River, then east along the river to Port Conway. Crossing the Rappahannock, the party eventually wound up at the farm of Richard Garrett, approximately five miles south of the river. Here they cornered Booth and Herold in Garrett's tobacco barn. After several hours of negotiation, the barn was set on fire and Booth was shot, ending the search.

Wilson had been ordered to remain at anchorage for two days before heading back to Washington. On April 26, Luther B. Baker transported Booth's body wrapped in an old army blanket back to Belle Plain, where it was taken on board the *John S. Ide* and carried back to the Washington Navy Yard, then placed on board the monitor *Montauk*, where an autopsy was performed.

Sources: Statement of Luther B. Baker, NARA, RG 94, M-619, reel 455, frames 665–86; Edward Steers, Jr., *Blood on the Moon* (Lexington: University Press of Kentucky, 2001), 196, 205–6.

## Withers, William (1836–1916)

Orchestra leader at Ford's Theater. Withers had written a special musical piece to be played during intermission. The intermission was delayed due to the president's arrival, interrupting the stage performance. Withers was backstage when Booth shot Lincoln, and received minor cuts from Booth as he rushed past Withers toward the rear door. Booth slashed Withers's coat, vest, and shirt, but only grazed the skin. Withers's special piece, titled "Honor to Our Soldiers," was not played until 125 years later, during a special performance.

Sources: Statement of William Withers, Jr., NARA, RG 153, M-599, reel 6, frames 468–71; Poore, *Conspiracy Trial*, vol. 1, 198, vol. 3, 10; Pitman, *Trial*, 79; Statement of William Withers, NARA, RG 153, M-599, reel 2, frames 564–66; Poore, *Conspiracy Trial*, vol. 1, 198; Pitman, *Trial*, 79, 104.

## W. L. Wall & Company

W. L. Wall appeared as a prosecution witness. His Washington auction firm had been hired by Confederate agent Godfrey Hyams to auction five trunks containing contaminated clothing in hopes of spreading contagion throughout the northern civilian population. Hyams worked under the direction of Dr. Luke P. Blackburn, a Confederate located in Montreal. Blackburn was a highly respected authority on yellow fever. In the spring of 1864, when a major yellow fever epidemic hit Bermuda, Blackburn went

to the island and offered his medical services. He collected the clothing and bedding of individuals who had died from the disease and shipped them to Nova Scotia in several large trunks. Believing yellow fever was a contagious disease, Blackburn ordered Hyams to have the clothing sold by auction and thereby distribute it throughout the civilian population. Hyams, using the alias "J. W. Harris," transported the trunks through Boston and Philadelphia to Washington, where he hired the firm of Wall & Company to auction their contents.

Sources: Statement of Godfrey J. Hyams, NARA, RG 153, M-599, reel 2, frames 1134–36; Poore, *Conspiracy Trial*, vol. 2, 409; Pitman, *Trial*, 54; Edward Steers, Jr., "Risking the Wrath of God," *North & South* 3, no. 7 (September 2000), 59–70.

*See also:* Blackburn, Dr. Luke P.; Hyams, Godfrey Joseph

## Wood, William Patrick (1820–1903)

Superintendent of Old Capitol Prison. Wood aided in both the search and interrogation of suspects in the assassination. Wood maintained a list of all those suspects placed under his guard at Old Capitol Prison. Of interest is the fact that of the prisoners being held there by Wood, six knowingly aided Booth and Herold in their attempted escape (Baden, Bryant,

Bainbridge, Cox, and Lucas), and five were called to testify at the conspiracy trial (James Ford, Clay Ford, Howell, Johnson, and Lloyd).

Wood took part in the initial phases of the search in Southern Maryland for Booth and Herold, but his effort stopped at the Potomac River. He was called as a witness on behalf of Mary Surratt, testifying that her brother J. Z. Jenkins was a loyal Union man. His testimony had no effect on the outcome of Mary Surratt's case.

Wood attempted to get part of the reward money offered for Booth and Herold's capture, but was unsuccessful. On July 1, 1865, Wood was appointed the first chief of the newly formed Secret Service in the Treasury Department. He served until 1869.

Sources: List of William P. Wood, NARA, RG 153, M-599, reel 3, frames 337–38; Statement of William P. Wood, NARA, RG 153, M-599, reel 7, frames 370–73.

## Woodland, Henry

Woodland was a former slave of Thomas Jones and stayed on working as a laborer for Jones after he was emancipated. Jones was chief signal agent in Maryland for the Confederate Signal Service. Jones entrusted Woodland with hiding the boat that Booth and Herold would use in crossing the Potomac River. Woodland lived with Jones in Jones's home, Huckleberry. Jones had been entrusted with the safekeeping of Booth and Herold as they hid in a pine thicket waiting for the first safe opportunity to cross the Potomac River to Virginia. Jones instructed Woodland to keep his skiff stowed among the high grass where a small creek emptied into the river. Each day, Woodland would take the skiff and go out on the river fishing. Returning each night, he would hide the skiff in the same spot in the grass.

On the night of April 20, 1865, Jones finally got the opportunity he had been waiting for. The area was clear of Union soldiers. Gathering up Booth and Herold, Jones made his way to his house, where he told the two men to wait outside. Jones went in and found Woodland seated at the table eating. Jones asked him if he had left the boat where he had been told, and Woodland said he had. The skiff was ready. Gathering up some food and drink, Jones left Woodland in his home while he led Booth and Herold down to the shoreline to where the boat was hidden. Woodland had done his job. Jones put the two men in the boat, handed Booth a small compass and candle, and told him to head for a particular point on the compass to reach the Virginia shore at Machodoc Creek.

Sources: Statement of Henry Woodlawn [Woodland], NARA, RG 153, M-599, reel 6, frames 450–53; Thomas Jones, *J. Wilkes Booth* (Chicago: Laird & Lee, 1893).

*See also:* Jones, Thomas Austin

## Woodward, Joseph Janvier (1833–1884)

Army surgeon who, with army surgeon Edward Curtis, performed the autopsy on Abraham Lincoln in the guest room of the White House. Lincoln's body was removed from the Petersen house in a plain pine coffin at approximately 11:00 A.M. on Saturday, April 15, and taken to the White House, where it was carried to the second-floor guest room and placed on two boards resting on trestles. Present were Surgeon General Joseph K. Barnes, Dr. Robert Stone (the family physician), army surgeons Charles Crane, Charles S. Taft, and William M. Notson, Assistant Quartermaster General Daniel Rucker, and Orville H. Browning.

Curtis later described the scene: "Dr. Woodward and I proceeded to open the head and remove the brain down to the track of the ball. The latter had entered a little to the left of the median line at the back of the head, had passed almost directly forwards through the center of the brain and lodged. Not finding it readily, we removed the entire brain, when, as I was lifting the latter from the cavity of the skull, suddenly the bullet dropped out through my fingers and fell, break-ing the solemn silence of the room with its clatter, into an empty basin that was standing beneath."

When the autopsy was completed, the body was embalmed and then dressed in the same black suit Lincoln had worn on his second inauguration. Woodward, along with General Barnes, performed an autopsy on Booth's body aboard the USS *Montauk* twelve days later.

Sources: Dorothy Meserve Kunhardt and Philip B. Kunhardt, Jr., *Twenty Days* (New York: Harper & Row, 1965), 94–95.

*See also:* Autopsy, Abraham Lincoln; Autopsy, John Wilkes Booth

## Wray, E. D.

Wray witnessed the shooting from his seat in the Dress Circle and later positively identified the assassin as John Wilkes Booth. He was one of three men who actually ran after Booth in an attempt to catch him after he dropped to the stage. In chasing after Booth, Wray picked up Booth's hat from the stage and turned it over to the Metropolitan Police Headquarters. He later wrote to Stanton requesting the hat be returned to him so that he might keep it as a "relic" of the murderer. "I was the 3rd person upon the stage and secured the murderers hat, which I placed at the . . . Metropolitan Police Head Quarters."

Sources: Statement of E. D. Wray, NARA, RG 153, M-599, reel 3, frames 1041–43; Statement of E. D. Wray, NARA, RG 153, M-599, reel 2, frames 865–66.

## Wylie, Andrew B. (1814–1905)

A justice of the Supreme Court of the District of Columbia. On the morning of July 7, Mary Surratt's attorneys, Frederick Aiken and John Clampitt, appeared before Judge Wylie and filed a petition seeking a writ of habeas corpus on behalf of Mary Surratt. In essence, they were asking Wylie to order Major General Winfield Scott Hancock to appear in civil court with Mary Surratt to explain why a military tribunal tried her. The petition based its request on the fact that she was a private citizen of the United States and not connected with the military in any way. Wylie issued the writ demanding a response at 10:00 A.M. before the Criminal Court of the District of Columbia.

Wylie approved the writ and instructed U.S. marshal David Gooding to serve the papers on Hancock, commander of the Middle Military District. Hancock had overall authority of the Washington Arsenal and prison. Ten o'clock came and went and Hancock failed to appear. At 11:30 A.M., General Hancock, accompanied by Attorney General James Speed, appeared before Wylie. Mary Surratt was nowhere in sight. Hancock responded to Wylie's writ, telling him that Mary Surratt was in his possession and would not be produced as ordered, "by virtue of an order of Andrew Johnson, President of the United States." Johnson responded to Wylie's writ with his own executive order:

> I, Andrew Johnson, President of the United States, do hereby declare that the writ of *habeas corpus* has been heretofore suspended in such cases as this, and I do hereby especially suspend this writ, and direct that you proceed to execute the order heretofore given upon the judgment of the military commission, and you will give this order in return to the writ.

Wylie was powerless to act and "yielded to the suspension of the writ of *habeas corpus* by the President of the United States." Mary Surratt and her condemned colleagues were executed a few minutes past one o'clock that afternoon.

Sources: Guy W. Moore, *The Case of Mary Surratt* (Norman: University of Oklahoma Press, 1954), 57–59; Edward Steers, Jr., ed., *The Trial* (Lexington: University Press of Kentucky, 2001), 250.

*See also*: Habeas Corpus

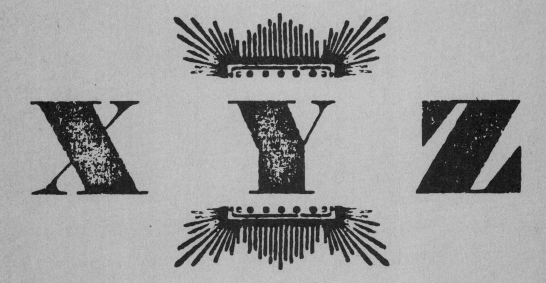

## Yellow Fever

Dr. Luke P. Blackburn, a Kentucky-born Confederate agent operating out of Montreal, attempted to introduce germ warfare by creating yellow fever epidemics in the North, exposing civilians to the clothing and bedding of people who died from the disease. The purpose was to demoralize the northern people, weakening their resolve and support of President Lincoln and bring about his defeat in the upcoming 1864 election. While people in the nineteenth century believed yellow fever was a contagious disease, spreading from one human being to another by physical contact, including contact with the clothing of infected persons, it was not contagious and could only be spread through the intervention of mosquitoes transmitting the virus through blood. Blackburn's diabolic plot failed, although a severe epidemic hit New Bern, North Carolina, leading Blackburn to believe he had limited success.

Yellow fever was among the most widely feared and violent diseases that ravaged the world in the nineteenth century. Historically, it may have first appeared in the Western Hemisphere among members of Columbus's second expedition to the Americas in 1495. It was first described as an epidemic in 1648 in Mexico, where it was believed to have been imported from western Africa on slave ships. During the seventeenth, eighteenth, and nineteenth centuries the disease was prevalent throughout the Caribbean.

Yellow fever was epidemic throughout the southern United States, especially along the Gulf Coast, where severe epidemics occurred at regular intervals. By 1900, as many as ninety epidemics had ravaged urban areas throughout the South. So severe was one epidemic in 1801 that it was believed to be a major factor in convincing Napoleon to sell the Louisiana Territory to the United States the following year.

The belief that the disease was infectious led Blackburn to undertake a plan designed to infect select populations in the northern states as well as Union troops stationed in the coastal towns of Norfolk, Virginia, and New Bern. Added to Blackburn's targets was Abraham Lincoln. While history has treated Blackburn's yellow fever plot against civilian populations and Abraham Lincoln with skepticism, it was not only real but also known at the highest levels of the Confederate government.

Included in Blackburn's diabolical plan was an attempt to infect President Lincoln and his family by sending him a black valise that contained several expensive dress shirts that Blackburn previously packed with the yellow fever clothing from dead victims. Blackburn believed that even if Lincoln did not choose to wear the shirts, their mere presence would infect him with the deadly disease. Afraid of the risk of delivering such a "gift" to the White House, Godfrey Hyams, the agent working with Blackburn, declined. The trunks were another matter, however, and Hyams would see to the distribution of their contents by way of auction.

Hyams carried out his assignment using the alias of "J. W. Harris," shipping five of the trunks through Boston to Washington, where he contracted with the auction house of W. L. Wall & Company to dispose of the infected clothing. Because Norfolk and New Bern were within the military lines of the Union army, Hyams had to contract the services of an army sutler to dispose of the infected clothing in those two cities.

Blackburn's motives, and those of his superiors, seem clear. Their ignorance of infectious disease in no way mitigates their guilt in attempting to unleash biological warfare against civilian populations. Indeed, they believed that Blackburn's trunks that had reached New Bern were responsible for the yellow fever epidemic that killed more than two thousand people in that coastal town. Blackburn's small valise of gift shirts designed to infect Lincoln with a deadly disease show that he was a target of the Confederate operation in Canada in the spring of 1864. Black flag warfare had come of age.

Sources: Edward Steers, Jr., "Risking the Wrath of God," *North & South* 3, no. 7 (September 2000), 59–70.

*See also:* Blackburn, Luke Pryor; Hyams, Godfrey Joseph

## Zekiah Swamp

One of the largest natural frontiers in the state of Maryland, the Zekiah Swamp is a twenty-mile-long body of marshy timberland and brush that runs in a north-south direction beginning five miles north of Bryantown near the home of Dr. Samuel Mudd, and ending near the village of Allen's Fresh at the mouth of the Wicomico River. The swamp was a favorite hunting area for the Algonquin Indians who inhabited the area before the white man arrived. The swamp's name is derived from the Algonquin-Fox word *sacaya*, meaning "dense thicket." It has had various spellings over the years including *Sacaya, Zachiah, Zachia,* and *Sakiah.*

Booth and Herold had to cross the Zekiah Swamp from east to west after leaving Samuel Mudd's house on the night of April 15, 1865, during their flight from Federal authorities. Passing to the east of Bryantown to avoid the Federal troops that recently set up their headquarters there, the two men made their way to the cabin of a free black by the name of Oswell Swan. Initially, Booth offered Swan five dollars to take them to the home of William Burtles, where they presumably would spend the rest of the night and the next day before continuing their escape. Booth suddenly changed his mind and asked Swan if he knew the way through the swamp to the home of Samuel Cox, telling him he would up his offer to ten dollars if Swan would take them to Cox. Swan told Booth he knew the way through the swamp and agreed to lead them to Cox's house. Swan skillfully piloted the two fugitives through the swamp to the home of Cox, where they arrived shortly after midnight.

Swan made a statement to investigating detectives detailing his interaction with Booth and Herold.

Sources: Statement of Oswell Swan, National Archives and Records Administration, M-599, reel 6, frames 227–29; Edward Steers, Jr., *Blood on the Moon* (Lexington: University Press of Kentucky, 2001), 149, 155–57.

### Zisgen, Joseph (1833–1914)

Joseph Zisgen was one of the twenty-six troopers of the 16th New York Cavalry who were present at the Garrett farm on April 26, 1865, when John Wilkes Booth was cornered and killed. Several years after his death, a soldier named Wilson D. Kenzie claimed that he and Zisgen were among the soldiers at the Garrett farm, and that the man killed there was not John Wilkes Booth. On March 31, 1922, fifty-seven years after Booth's death, Kenzie swore in an affidavit that he rode with the troopers as they closed in on Booth and Herold at the Garrett farm: "Joe Zisgen had discovered that it wasn't J. Wilkes Booth and they covered him up so no one could see his face. As I rode up Joe Zisgen called, 'Here, come here Sargent, this ain't J. Wilkes Booth at all.'"

Various records pertaining to Kenzie contradict most of what he claimed in regard to his service in April 1865, and the person killed at the Garrett farm not being John Wilkes Booth. It appears Kenzie learned the details of Booth's capture and death and used them to create a story sensationalizing the incident, with himself, and Zisgen, at the center.

Kenzie's service record shows that he was a good soldier who served his unit and his country well. His military exploits, however, are better documented than his extramilitary exploits in search of John Wilkes Booth. When Kenzie prepared his affidavit in 1922 he was seventy-eight years old and in the twilight of his life, an old soldier filled with memories of exciting times, some of which he may have shared vicariously through his old comrade, Joseph Zisgen.

Joseph Zisgen never left a statement or reminiscence on the subject. He never claimed the body at the Garrett farm was not that of John Wilkes Booth. It seems incredulous that he kept silent for so many years about such a startling obser-vation as the wrong man being captured at the Garrett farm.

Sources: Steven G. Miller, "Wilson D. Kenzie, the Linchpin of the Booth Escape Theories," in Laurie Verge, ed., *The Body in the Barn* (Clinton, Md.: Surratt Society, 1993).

*See also:* Allen, William C.

# ACKNOWLEDGMENTS

This work is the culmination of having spent thirty-five years studying and writing about Abraham Lincoln and his death. It could not have come about without the generous support and encouragement of several people who unselfishly shared their own research and knowledge with me over the years. First among these are James O. Hall (deceased) and William Hanchett, two of the finest scholars I have come to know. I thank them for their support. I wish to thank Laurie Verge and Joan Chaconas of the Surratt House Museum for always being willing to answer a call for help. My good friend Joseph Garrera, executive director of the Lehigh Valley Heritage Museum has been a constant source of encouragement to me and an able critic helping smooth the edges of my work. I also want to acknowledge my friend of many years Kieran McAuliffe whose unique *John Wilkes Booth Escape Map* makes a wonderful adjunct to this encyclopedia. In addition, Kieran discovered the previously unknown photographs of Patrick C. Martin and his associates in the Notman Archives (McCord Museum) in Canada, and graciously provided copies for this book. I want to thank Fred Hatch, editor and publisher of the *Journal of the Lincoln Assassination*. On learning of my manuscript Fred generously sent me copy of his own manuscript along similar lines. It was an act not often found among scholars competing in the same field. It proved a great help and I am grateful to him. I want to thank my good friend Adrian Hoare for sharing his research on George A. Atzerodt with me, as well as his research and the letters of William Reynolds. I also want to thank James E. Swanson for his foreword to this book. He has assumed a rightful place as one of the leading scholars in the assassination field, and I am grateful that he agreed to add his eloquent words to my effort. I want to thank the people at HarperCollins, Henry Ferris and Peter Hubbard, and their staff for the tremendous job they did in turning a collection of typed pages into a beautiful book. The contents are greatly enhanced by the final edit and design.

Last, but not least, I thank my wife, Pat, who, for most of our married life, has shared me with Abraham Lincoln and with history in general. Pat has been a steady source of comfort through all the ups and downs we both experienced along the rocky road of writing and publishing. She has smoothed the bumps and straightened the curves on numerous occasions.

# PHOTOGRAPHIC CREDITS

Acknowledgment is made to the following for the photographs and maps that appear in this book.

Author's collection: xiii, 8, 20, 36, 37, 49, 55, 57, 68, 81, 107, 126, 140, 142, 161, 214 (both), 225, 245, 260, 282, 286, 287, 289, 305, 309, 319, 329, 330, 336, 339, 346, 348, 403, 425, 444, 463, 476, 477, 478, 479, 480, 489, 495, 498, 501, 520, 522, 567, 574; City of Alexandria, Virginia: 221; Joan L. Chaconas: 413; Connecticut Historical Society: 547; Robert Cook: 103; Ford's Theatre Collection: 426 (both); Georgetown University: 240; Thomas Gull: 91; Kellie and Richard Gutman: 60; Blaine Houmes: 84, 235; Roger D. Hunt: 576; Kentucky Historical Association: 50; Illinois State Historical Society: 32, 226; Library of Congress: xxi, 11, 17, 137, 153, 171, 183 (right), 196, 216, 276, 285, 325, 342, 343, 371, 397, 401, 409, 411, 427, 429, 439, 493, 530, 537, 571; Lincoln Museum, Fort Wayne, Indiana: 10; Massachusetts Historical Society: 189; Kieran McAuliffe: 74 (map by), 75 (map by), 168, 259, 360, 386 (map by), 474, 497; Richard Dyer Mudd: 385; National Archives: 48, 125, 173, 362, 458; National Park Service: 176, 179, 217, 219, 546; Pennsylvania State Archives: 183 (left), 262, 270, 434, 457; Pike County (PA) Historical Society: 344; Gary R. Planck: 464; Floyd E. Risvold: 579; Richard Sloan: 104, 207, 247, 583; Surratt House Museum, James O. Hall Research Center: 23, 62, 63, 65, 128, 132, 135, 157, 158, 185, 200, 213, 236 (both), 240, 252, 265, 281, 278, 303, 310, 331, 372, 399, 465, 468, 505, 507, 510, 514, 517, 568; James L. Swanson: xvi; Thomas Thatcher: 156; Hallam Weber: 268; Robert Wick: 145